Table of Contents

Dedication

[The Author demonstrating the construction of a Set that he had designed]

Variety is the Spice of Life is dedicated to my late Father, Ted Loveday, whose unfortunate death in 1958 occurred when I was just 14 years of age. In those 14 years, often unrealised by me, he taught me a vast amount of knowledge about the Theatre and about Theatrical Scenery and how to design and build it; he taught me a considerable amount of knowledge about his Scenery-building firm of Brunskill and Loveday Limited and its constituent parts of John Brunskill Limited and of Loveday and Higson; he introduced me to the mechanics of many 'West End' and Provincial Theatres; and he introduced me to a vast number of his Theatrical friends and acquaintances. To say that he was the best of educators of 'Things Theatrical' would be an understatement.

Discussing a Set for the 1953 London Production of *Dangerous Curves* at London's Garrick Theatre - The Producer, Director, and Actor Terence de Marney; The Designer Guy Sheppard; The Scenic Artist Phil Harker; and, aged 73, my Father Ted Loveday.

All the photographs, letters, and other matter illustrated in Variety is the Spice of Life are , unless otherwise mentioned, owned by Ted Loveday other than all the Theatre Programme fronts which are owned by Brunskill and Loveday Limited (www.theatrical-scenery.info). Some of the information contained herein has been checked against Wikipedia otherwise the information comes from the memory of Ted Loveday and from the records of Brunskill and Loveday Limited.

ACT 1

Like every new arrival, I was clad only in my birthday suit when I popped out into this world. The date was 2 February 1944, an occasion not only recorded on my Birth Certificate but also stated in my 'Baby's "Progress Book' which adds that my arrival took place at 2.10pm in Shrublands Nursing Home in Croydon, a town now classed as being part of Greater London but then classed as being part of Surrey. My 'Baby's Progress Book' also tells me that I weighed exactly 8 Pounds when I arrived (a weight noticeably less than the 19 Stones that my bathroom scales currently 'shout at' me every time that I step onto them), that I first smiled one month later on 3 March 1944, that I first laughed two months after that on 6 May 1944 and that I was also baptised in May 1944 at Saint Peter's Church in South Croydon. It seems that I was slow to find much humour in the world around me - which was hardly surprising given that the Second World War was in progress and that Alois and Klara Hitler's maniacal son Adolf's disintegrating war machine was busy aiming bombs and rockets at Croydon's Airport, a subsidiary, during the War, to the Royal Air Force''s Kenley Airport but, before the War, London''s principal civil airport and, after the War until its closure in 1959, still a principal civil airport serving London and the Southeast of England.

In between getting used to fresh air after having been cooped-up in darkness for about 9 months and learning first how to smile and then how to laugh I was taken from Shrublands Nursing Home to a largish newly-built house named 'Highlands' by my Mother to remind her not only that she was Scottish through-and-through but also that her Father had been born in the Scottish Highlands in Murkle, a wee place just outside Thurso in the very north of mainland Scotland.

Otherwise known as 218 Pampisford Road, South Croydon, 'Highlands' was, I always felt, an attractive well-designed detached house and its demolition, along with other nearby houses of similar age, to make way for flats just 50 or so years after it was built caused me, in later years, much sadness. So, was it a 'happy 'house' during the 15½ years that I lived there? Well …

Highlands [*see photograph below*] was one of two end-houses in a row of 4 brick-built detached houses constructed by a Master Builder called Albert Soden whose building firm was based at 325 High Road in nearby Streatham. My Father, a Joiner and cabinetmaker, knew Soden well and had, before buying 'Highlands'", owned and lived in another Soden-built house at 8 Broadlands Avenue, Streatham, a house which my Father had named 'Yadevol', 'a name the mystery of which can be solved by holding the written word 'Yadevol' 'in front of a mirror [or writing it backwards, if more convenient !!].

On its first floor ''Highlands' had four Bedrooms, one of which my Father used as a Billiard Room-cum-Study; a largish Bathroom; and a separate Toilet : And on its mostly parquet-floored ground floor it had a Drawing-room; a Dining-room; a Morning/Breakfast-room; an 'Eaziwork' "fitted-Kitchen with a large walk-in Larder; a largish front-Entrance Lobby; a Cloakroom with W.C.; a Telephone-Room;

an 'outside' "W.C. situated in a small room just inside the backdoor; a Sunlounge sited adjacent to the rear of the Drawing-room; a self-contained garage sited under an L-shaped bedroom that was allocated to me; and, although not built until a few years after the house itself had been built, a one-storey extension half of which was a garage and the other half a Games-room for me. Outside, fronting the road and the road's then unadopted footpath, there was an attractive 'front' garden which was sheltered from the road by a red brick wall behind which were laurel bushes and lilac trees and a concrete D-shaped drive, bounded by rose bushes, running from one set of solid oak farmish-style entrance-gates to another such set of farmish-style entrance gates each set being sited within the red brick wall; and at the back of the house was a bowling green, alongside part of which was sited a large wooden well-equipped joiners'/carpenters' workshop. Beyond the bowling green was a triangular-shaped greenhouse surrounded by a very productive fruit and vegetable garden part of which accommodated a very solidly constructed, to my Father's design, wartime shelter with its own water and electricity supplies. Bounding the garden on its three non-house sides were solid wooden fences in which, in the fence opposite the house, was sited a gate giving access to a vehicle-sized lane beyond which was a public park.

So there we were, the three of us - my Mother, my Father, and I - living in a house, big enough for several people, with a garden the natural produce of which was, had we been vegetarians, probably sufficient to keep us more than fully fed.

My Mother, Helen Forrest Hamilton Shearer, was aged 34 when I was born. She was one of twelve children. Her Mother, a Gaelic-speaking Scot born Margaret Gold Forrest on 21 March 1872 in

Kilfinichen and Kilvicheon Parish in the then somewhat isolated island of Mull, had, on 4 November 1892 in Levenseat in mainland West Lothian, married Thomas John Davie, a Limestone Quarryman born in Levenseat on 13 April 1866. On 22 April 1894 Thomas and Margaret Davie had a Daughter, Mary Campbell, but two years later in 1896, as a result of an accident, Thomas Davie died causing, in the days when no State Aid nor private Pension Scheme whatsoever existed, Margaret to have to suffer much distress, desperation, and considerable hardship, circumstances made even worse by the fact that Margaret's own Father, William Gold Forrest, died on 12 March, aged 76, in the same year.

Enveloped in considerable poverty, on 30 April 1897 Margaret Davie [neé Forrest] married again, this time to Robert Sutherland Shearer, a Stone Quarryman from Murkle just outside Thurso in Caithness, who, desperately seeking work, had walked the 280 miles or so from Murkle to Badallan Cottage, a hamlet near Stane [*a Scots word meaning (in English) 'a place set with stones'*] 'in Cambusnethan, a village and parish, now part of Wishaw, near Shotts in Lanarkshire, where he found work in the harsh privately owned Coal Mines of nearby Shotts.

To-gether my Grandmother, Margaret, and my Grandfather, Robert, produced eleven children. Thus, along with Margaret's Daughter, Mary, by her first marriage, they were a family of two adults and twelve children, three of whom died as children, in one very small privately-owned Coal Company flatted dwellinghouse [more commonly known nowadays by the English description 'flat'], 'a damp and grossly insanitary [by to-day's so-called 'modern' standards] dwelling but a dwelling which, by the then standards of the area, was by no means unusual.

On 29 December 1911, in Glasgow, Margaret's by then 17-years old Daughter, Mary, married Andrew Angus, who had been born on 30 July 1891 at 41 Scott Street, Galashiels, a Mill town in the Scottish Borders. Andrew's Father, James, an Electrical Engineer, had, on 26 April 1889, married a lass, Wilhelmina Milne Noble, from Hawick, likewise a Mill town in the Scottish Borders; and, when Andrew was a child, James, his Wife, and their Son moved from Galashiels to Shotts where James found work as an Electrical Engineer in one of its coal mines. It was whilst living in Manse Road, Shotts that Andrew, working as a Coalminer, met Mary Davie who was then attempting to earn a living as a Domestic Servant.

To-gether Andrew and Mary had four children - Margaret, born on 27 November 1912; James, born on 1 June 1916; Wilhelmina, born on 8 October 1918; and Jane (known as 'Jean'"), born on 21 March 1926. The poverty in Shotts was such that much of the time, as was then the practice, the eldest of Andrew's and Mary's Children lived, and were brought up, as Brothers and Sisters to Mary's own 11 half-Brothers and half-Sisters.

Misfortune again struck my Grandmother, Margaret, and her Family for her second Husband, my Grandfather Robert, died, whilst still a young man, of a coal-mining-related illness forcing, once again, Margaret and her Family back into the clutches of extreme poverty : And at this point I turn to, and quote from, a letter written to me from Shotts in July 1979 by one of my Mother's Brothers, my Uncle Angus, by then a retired miner who, when aged 14, had, on leaving school, been 'forced' down the pits to spend much of his working life hewing coal for the benefit of others:

" We (as children) had a very unhappy home life. We lived then as a typical working-class family of that time, poverty-stricken, and

everybody had to [try to find] work, to sustain and keep yourself alive, what with strikes, no employment it was a terrible existence. This was the life your mother had to live through in her early life. As was the custom in those days, when girls left school they had to go to Glasgow or Edinburgh to work as domestics in some businessman's house. Your mother was no exception, she had to toe the line as well. She did not stick it for long as she had a yearning to be a nurse. The first hospital she worked in was in Paisley, next she worked in was Crichton Royal in Dumfries, then she worked in a hospital in Epsom in Surrey. Actually she had no home life at all ... she had a very troubled and unhappy home life as a girl, as we all had."

To many in Society, my Mother and her Family were ranked as being "the lowest of the low". [When an adult Uncle Angus had two children one of whom, Catriona, off her own bat, went to Edinburgh's Napier University where she achieved an Honours Degree in Journalism and thereafter joined the BBC in 2003 and subsequently became a principal Presenter of the BBC Television's national news programme *Reporting Scotland* !!]

In order to obtain in interview to be considered suitable to be offered work in a hospital it was necessary for my Mother to first obtain a written reference from someone, such as a Medical Doctor, of some 'standing' within the community which - given not only the extreme lowliness of my Mother's social existence but also the fact that in those days a Doctor was considered throughout much of Society of being on a level almost akin to that occupied by God - was almost an impossibility : But somehow my Mother managed to obtain one and, having obtained it, she proudly showed it to her Mother who, having read it, straightaway, in front of my Mother, deliberately tore it up into many pieces and, as the pieces fell to the floor, stated emphatically to my tear-enveloped Mother "They *don't* want the likes of *you*". Storming out my Mother then rushed back to the kindly Doctor who had given her the reference and who, on hearing what had happened, straightaway re-wrote the reference whilst advising my Mother not to show this one to her Mother but to instead go home, pack her bags, and go straight to Paisley, near Glasgow, whilst meantime he, the Doctor, would telephone the hospital and personally recommend that my Mother be offered employment. This my Mother did vowing, as she left Shotts, to never again return to Shotts whilst her Mother lived.

I know nothing of my Mother's time in Paisley : And so I move on to that greatest of all Scottish Psychiatric Teaching Hospitals, The Crichton in Dumfries, wherein on 15 April 1927, aged 17 years and just under 10 months, my Mother commenced her 60-hours per week employment as a Probationer 'Top Person's' Nurse at a wage of £44 a year, a sum which was contractually stated to be increased each year by £2 up to a maximum of £72 a year after 15 years' service.

Designed by William Burn, an Edinburgh Architect, the building of The Crichton Institution for Lunatics - as it publicly described itself on the one and only occasion, in June 1839, when it advertised for staff - commenced in 1835 and included, what were in those days, exceptional recreational facilities for both Staff and Patients, such facilities including badminton, tennis, bowling, golf, curling, dancing, theatre, cricket, association football, and billiards. But the origins of this substantial charitable institution, set in 30 or so acres of walled grounds about a mile from the centre of Dumfries, go back in time to the early 1800s to when a Dr James Crichton amassed a substantial financial fortune whilst working as an employee of the Honourable East India Company [a Company about which much more will be said later]. Having retired, after working as Physician to the Governor General of India, in 1809 James Crichton returned to his homeland of Dumfriesshire and upon his death in 1823 left a then huge sum of some £100,000 or so to be used for charitable purposes. Being of like mind his childless widow, Elizabeth, to whom James had been married for only 13 years, threw herself heart and soul into complying with her husband's wish and, overcoming attempts by her husband's family to declare his Will null and void, and against some strong local opposition, set about founding, what she intended would be, the best hospital in Europe for the humane treatment of the mentally ill. By the time that the 17-years old Helen Forrest Hamilton Shearer arrived there, via nearby Paisley, from her poverty-stricken upbringing in the depressing Lanarkshire coalmining town of Shotts The Crichton was indeed one of, if not the, finest Psychiatric Teaching Hospitals in Europe, a Teaching Hospital which went on in later years to fulfil a vision of James and Elizabeth Crichton that one day there would be a University in Dumfries for, although much changed, it not only became, in 1996, the Crichton Campus of the University of Glasgow but also, in the year 2000, became a multi-University Campus.

I am indebted to Morag Williams, Archivist of The Crichton Museum, for assistance given to me concerning my Mother's two and a half years at The Crichton. So what of the young escapee from Shotts ? Well, throughout her time at The Crichton she nursed in Department 1, "the 'top people's' section of the hospital where", Mrs Williams informed, "only the best nurses of correct demeanour, etc were placed" and where "therefore she would have been expected to sail through her training"". Clearly, despite the harshness and lowliness of her childhood upbringing, my Mother, by her seventeenth year, not only had offloaded/disguised many of her childhood attitudes but also had evolved a genuine commitment and dedication to psychiatric nursing. So, did she ever obtain that glorious wage of £72 a year after 15 years' service ? Well, no, for after two and a half years' of training and instruction at The Crichton in how to nurse and deal with psychiatric patients, training and instruction which included the perfecting of techniques in the restraining of violent patients, on 31 October 1929 she voluntarily left The Crichton, without, it seems, receiving a Completion Certificate, fled Scotland, and obtained employment, as a Psychiatric Nurse, in a hospital in the Epsom area in the South of England. The reason for her resigning and fleeing from Scotland appeared to be that she wished to get as far away as she, in those days, could from the harshness of Shotts and from the harsh attitude of her Mother. But was that the real reason for she did have an attitude of social climbing and two seemingly casual comments about the social status of some of those whom she nursed that she made to me when I was a teenager perhaps, although I certainly did not realise it at the time, indicated the real reason for her going the then long distance of nearly 600 miles from the Crichton Hospital in Dumfries to psychiatric hospitals in the Epsom area. Born and brought up in abject poverty and being trained in the Crichton to look after "top people" psychiatric patients she was seeking to move far away from Shotts to look after "the best" which, as she briefly mentioned to me, looking after the best is what she did : For, some 20 minutes or so from the centre of Epsom, the Royal Earlswood Hospital [subscribed to by Queen Victoria and Prince Albert, and otherwise known as the Earlswood Asylum for Idiots and the Earlswood Institution for Mental Defectives] was the 'dumping ground' for embarrassing members of the Aristocracy and of the UK's Royal Family including two daughters of the Bowes-Lyon Family, Nerissa (born in 1919) and Katherine (born in 1926), children of John Bowes-Lyons, one of the Brothers of HM The Queen Mother. Having been dumped in the Royal Earlswood Hospital the two sisters were never visited by any members of their Family which included their Aunt, The Queen Mother [who, as Wife of King George VI, became Queen of the UK in 1936], and their First Cousin, the Queen Mother's elder Daughter, the United Kingdom's HM Queen Elizabeth II. Their crime ? Learning difficulties. Seemingly, because their learning difficulties were a threat to the social standing of the Bowes-Lyon Family and thus of the UK's Royal Family, not only did Nerissa and Katherine have no visitors and even no clothes, even no underwear, to wear other than basic 'stock' garments provided by the Queen Victoria- and Prince Albert-originated Royal Earlswood Hospital itself but also no information about them was allowed to be circulated outside of the Hospital and those within the Hospital were not allowed to inform anyone about the patients, etc; and Burke's Peerage, the 'biblical dictionary' of UK Royalty and Aristocracy was deliberately given misinformation by the Bowes-Lyon Family which caused the two girls to be stated as being dead (In fact, Nerissa died in 1986 and Katherine died in 2014). Several other members of the Bowes-Lyon Family – Harriet (born 1887), Idonea (born 1912), Rosemary (born 1914), Ethelreda (born 1922) - were also confined to living their lives within the Royal Earlswood Hospital none of whom, like Nerissa and Katherine, ever, it seems, received even a birthday or Christmas card from the Royal Family, and yet HM The Queen Mother was the Patron of Mencap [the UK's Royal Society for Mentally Handicapped Children and Adults]!! So, perhaps it is understandable that my Mother remained, or had to remain, more or less silent about her years as a psychiatric nurse in the Epsom area ?

Except for an occasional comment that she made to me during the years of my childhood informing that she had enjoyed her life in Epsom my Mother gave me no information as to her routine life in

Epsom; and nor do I have information as to how and when she met my Father. So a gap in my knowledge exists until 24 February 1941 being the date, a Certified Copy of my Parents' Wedding Certificate informs me, when my Parents were married, my Father residing at 8 Broadlands Avenue, Streatham and being a 'Theatrical Contractor' and a Widower aged almost 61 and my Mother also residing at 8 Broadlands Avenue and being a 'Hospital Nurse' and a Spinster aged 31. Clearly they were, prior to their marriage, living to-gether.

My Father, Edwin [Ted] George Loveday, was born on 4 April 1880 at 26 Aylesford Street in London's Pimlico [a few doors away from where, in 26 St George's Square, Pimilico in 1912 Bram Stoker (born in 1847), a very close friend of my Father's Family, died in 1912]. My Father was the fifth of six children born to Charles Loveday and his Wife Jeanette Wood. Charles Loveday, a Piano Tuner by trade at the time of my Father's birth, was surrounded by things Theatrical. Henry Joseph Loveday, an older brother, was, for many years, Stage Manager to the famous Actor/Manager Sir Henry Irving at Irving's Royal Lyceum Theatre in London. Together Henry Loveday and Henry Irving shared the theatrical management services of Abraham Stoker, a Dublin-born former Law Student and former Civil Servant who joined Irving''s Company when aged 31 in 1878. Bram Stoker''s greatest claim to fame is as the Author of that most famous of all vampire horror stories, Dracula, published in 1897 : And, whilst it is claimed by some that it was the eeriness of the narrow streets and alleyways of the fine old Yorkshire seaside town of Whitby, the ruins of Whitby's St Hilda's Abbey, and the graveyard of Whitby''s Parish Church of St Mary that inspired Bram Stoker to write Dracula, much of the credit for Dracula must undoubtedly fall to Bram Stoker''s behind-stage working life within Irving's Royal Lyceum Theatre - For there could, for an Author of a horror vampire novel, have been no better influencing environment in which to write than the eeriness experienced by Bram Stoker as he sat in the cold, silent, darkened and dark wings in the offstage areas of Irving's Theatre whilst muted sandbagged-balanced ropes occasionally dangled and swayed in the Theatre's cross-stage drafts, whilst the silent blackened shadowy outlines of Theatrically-clad overly made-up and often Theatrically-distorted human bodies were occasionally projected by the beams of elementary electric lighting into the darkness of the offstage beyond, and whilst occasionally the near-entrancement of Irving's spell-bound Audience was broken by a cough, a sneeze, or even, occasionally, a muffled scream. The environment backstage within the Royal Lyceum Theatre - whilst the great Henry Irving and his fellow Actors and Actresses were stoically performing such haunting classics as King Lear (1892), Henry VIII (1893), Richard III (1896), Cymbeline (1896), and The Merchant of Venice (1897) - was ideal notwithstanding the fact that Irving's Theatre had, as Irving himself on his Programmes proudly boasted, lighting - crude and elementary by to-day's standards - "by Electricity, supplied by the Electricity Supply Corporation, Limited" [see below a copy of the front of each of the original Programmes for Irving's 1892 production of 'King Lear, his 1896 production of Richard III, his 1896 production of Cymbeline, and his 1897 production of The Merchant of Venice.]

My Father's great Grandfather was, in his day, a well-known Actor at The Theatre Royal in London's Covent Garden with the Kembles, a very prominent 19th century theatrical performing troupe and my Father's Grandfather was also an Actor but with the then famous Shakespearean Actor Edmond Kean. Several other family members went onto the Stage as Actors, Singers, and/or Dancers. Therefore, with the great Sir Henry Irving and my Father's Uncle Henry as close friends it was not to be unexpected that the young Edwin [Ted] Loveday would himself enter the Theatrical Profession. Indeed, given that almost the entirety of my Father's relatives since well before the commencement of the nineteenth century were in the Theatrical Profession it would have been very surprising had my Father not entered the Profession : And in 1899 - after having, in his early teens, been taught the crafts of Joinery and of Cabinet-making and having, in his later teens, experienced a thorough practical grounding in the on-stage skills of running, flying, and otherwise handling and moving scenery - the young Ted Loveday, aged 19, took the plunge and started his own Theatrical Scenery business, a business which was to become, on amalgamating with the rival firm of John Brunskill Limited in 1939, Brunskill and Loveday Limited, one of the most, if not *the* most respected of the United Kingdom's Theatrical Scenery builders of the 20th Century. But more of that later.

My Parents' marriage on 24 February 1941, followed by a Reception at The Comedy Restaurant in London's Panton Street, formally brought to-gether a Scot from Shotts with an appallingly impoverished background and an Englishman from London whose Theatrical background, though doubtless not that easy at times, was anything but appallingly impoverished. There was, of course, an age gap of 29 years causing, at the time of my birth, my Mother to be of an age approaching 35 and my Father to be almost 64. But, by all accounts from various sources, my Father - although burdened with suffering from pernicious anaemia [until the 1930s, an often fatal type of anaemia whose keeping at bay was the eating of chunks of raw liver every day] - was anything but a 63-years' old in attitude. Many a time, as I grew up, he would, even in his mid-to-late 70s, chase me on foot round the garden at Highlands, engage me in mock fights, challenge and compete with me in various energetic activities, and undertake most, if not all, of the activities that active fathers younger than half his age engage themselves in with their sons. Indeed, when alone with me his sense of humour was occasionally that of an older brother passing on to a younger sibling information that perhaps the younger sibling was not yet of an age to know. It was an attitude not shared by my Mother. "The Queen of Hearts, she made some farts ..." my Father poeticised to me one day until, having ended the word "farts", he was suddenly strongly reprimanded by my Mother thus causing me to never know, even to this day, the end of that fascinating little ditty. "Old Mother Hubbard went to the cupboard to get her young daughter a dress, and when she got there the cupboard was bare - and so was her daughter I guess" was another piece of entertaining poetry abruptly terminated my Mother thereby ever since causing me to wonder what else by way of 'education' I might have heard. I was very shocked, and could hardly believe it, when, shortly after his death when aged 78, I found out how old he actually was.

These days a hairbrush encounters increasingly less resistance as it passes across the top of my head from one side to the other, but in my early days I possessed an abundant crop of cascading blond curls : And one outing of note that, in my early months, I undertook - although I have no conscious memory whatsoever of it - was to nearby Carshalton Beeches where I was, by my Mother, entered into, and won, a local 'Beautiful Baby' contest. Apparently my success was very short-lived for, within seconds of the announcement of my being the most 'beautiful' "of all the babies present, complaints of 'cheating' "erupted on the basis that I was not a 'local'". Thus my title was, as happens to athletes found to have taken performance-enhancing drugs, taken away from me and awarded to another. Doubtless the experience was a great disappointment to my Mother, but I can not say that it has ever bothered me.

My earliest conscious memory is not of life at home but of the inside of a small Leathercraft Shop in Tenerife, a Spanish-owned Island sited in the Atlantic Ocean off the coast of Africa to where, on the banana boat-cum-cruise ship the SS [Sailing Ship] Alca, the three of us in October 1946, when I was aged 2 years and 8 months, had gone as part of a holiday cruise from the UK, a somewhat unusual activity in those days so shortly after the end of the Second World War. I remember that shop well : Within it was a fascinating glass-fronted counter stocked with all sorts of hand-crafted leather goods and behind which stood two people, husband and wife friends of my Father who, after many years in the Theatre, had retired to enjoy the remainder of their days in a climate that only rarely could be enjoyed in the UK.

The SS Alca [*see photographs below*] had been built in 1927, was owned by the Yeoward Line, and, operating out of the Mersey, its peacetime routine was to sail from Liverpool to Portugal thence to the Canary Islands and then, having en route collected a cargo of bananas - somewhat of a luxury commodity in those days - back to Liverpool.

When she left Liverpool on 16 October 1946 the Alca carried 92 fare-paying passengers, 57 of whom - including my Parents and I - stayed for the round trip, 8 of whom travelled only as far as the Portuguese Capital City of Lisbon, 11 of whom travelled only as far as Madeira, 6 of whom travelled only as far as Las Palmas, and 10 of whom travelled only as far as Teneriffe. From what I know, the Alca was a happy ship. Certainly my Father, if not also my Mother, enjoyed the experience for we sailed again on the Alca the following year when, being more emboldened than on the previous trip, one evening I, having been settled in my own exclusive cabin well in advance of the evening meal, had the temerity to press a button to summon a member of the Cabin Crew to my cabin so that I could order a plate of scrambled eggs, a request that was relayed to my Father for his consent or otherwise. Consent having been given, the plate of scrambled eggs duly arrived and young Master Edwin Loveday duly tucked in and thoroughly enjoyed himself, an attitude to food that remains with me to this day. On our second voyage the ship was under the command of Captain A Frith whose kind and courteous attention to his passengers [*see photograph below (the young Master Loveday sitting, with finger in mouth, on his Father's lap to the right of the photograph, my Father with cigarette in hand, whilst my Mother stands behind with her cigarette being held 'out of camera shot')*] helped to make this cruise a most enjoyable experience.

The SS Alca's life continued until she was broken up in 1955. But we never again went on a cruise either aboard the Alca or aboard any other ship. Instead most years our main holiday comprised of a journey by car - driven usually by my Father but occasionally, though rarely, by my Mother - through various countries of war-devastated non-Soviet bloc mainland Europe. Such journeys took us to Switzerland, South of France, Italy, Germany, etc [*see below photograph of my Mother and I at Lugano in 1948 and of me at Menton in 1949*].

The first school that I attended was St John's Preparatory, a private school for boys in Pampisford Road only a very short, at least for an adult, walking distance from Highlands. In its publicity St John's stated "Boys can be received into the School from the age of five". Given that I was just over 3½ years' old when I first attended, it seems that St John's either had a somewhat tolerant attitude to its intake age or that it needed the money !! [*The photograph that follows was taken in September 1948, shows me aged four years and seven months squatting [with my left leg stuck out] fourth on the left in the front row.*]

The school day went from 9.30 in the mornings to 4 o'clock in the afternoons but I only attended the morning sessions which ran from 9.30 to 12.30 in the afternoons; and for this my Parents paid the sum of 3½ guineas [£3.67½p] a term. I could have stayed for lunch, at a charge, to my Parents, of 1/- [5p] each time but, to my knowledge and recollection, I did so only once, on a day when my Parents attended a wedding somewhere. I enjoyed that lunch very much for, even to-day, I can still recall its delicious taste of mince and potatoes and of the rice pudding that followed. In fact I enjoyed it so much that the quantity that I ate caused me to fall so fast asleep that I was left where I was, lying almost flat out on the grassless ground underneath the spreading branches of a large tree, until my Parents arrived mid-afternoon to collect me.

St Johns was run by a splendid dedicated lady, Miss Ethel L. Polley, who made sure that I, although I only attended in the mornings, not only learned to read and write but also was very happy there. Amongst Miss Polley's former pupils at St John's had been Robert Dougal, subsequently a much admired and greatly respected BBC Television Newsreader and Presenter throughout many years now long past and who once publicly stated on BBC Television how happy he too had been at St John's under the guidance of Miss Polley and her Assistant Teachers.

But all good things, so it is said, come to an end; and my happiness at St John's, although the school catered for boys up until the age of 10, ended when I was transferred by my Parents to another private school, Cumnor House, sited just a few more yards/metres up the road from, and on the same side as, St John's, at 168 Pampisford Road. It was as if I had been deliberately extracted from something that I enjoyed in order to be placed into something that I hated, for I certainly hated Cumnor House and its, to my mind, bully of a Head Master, Mr Aird, a roundish bespectacled man whose working life seemed, to me at least, to be driven by a desire to put as much unhappiness, fear, and discomfort into the minds of his pupils as he could. [*He appears, bespectacled and with a pen sticking out of his front jacket pocket, second from the right in the middle row in the photograph below and, in my opinion, looking every bit like the frightening apparition that he appeared to be.*]

Perhaps because I had a hatred of Cumnor House School and its Head Master my mind is willing to only consciously recall very little of my life there. I do recall that its playing fields were about a mile [1.6 kilometre] or so's walk away and that, in crocodile-fashion, we boys regularly made our chaperoned way up Pampisford Road, then took a right turn into Edgehill Road, then along Edgehill Road to a high chain-link fence that surrounded the playing fields, and then through a gateway in the fence into the playing fields where we did an hour or so of sports before making the return journey back to Cumnor House. Whether or not the school actually owned the playing fields I do not know, but to us those playing fields were an integral part of, and an escape from the academic life of, Cumnor House.

Happily, but totally unexpectedly, one day in 1952, when I was aged 8, my having to suffer Mr Aird and his, in my experience, wretched school came to an end for, whilst being 'dragged' around by my Mother in Daniel Neal, a London Department Store, and School Outfitter, my Mother informed me that the clothes and other items that she was in the process of buying were for me to wear in another school, a Boarding School for boys, that I was soon to be sent away to in a place called Windsor.

I had no idea what a Boarding School was but my Mother ordered all sorts of clothes for me that day : This one, two of this, four of that, half-a-dozen of these, three of those, and so it went until it seemed that I had been measured umpteen times and that my Mother had purchased a large proportion of the shop's stock of boys' clothing. In those days not only did little boys such as I not ask questions but also persons such as my Mother did not take their purchases home - They had them delivered : And so we left Daniel Neal's Departmental Store empty handed and, on exiting the shop, met up with my Father who, in those days before such things as 'Yellow Lines' and 'Parking Meters' had been invented, was sitting outside waiting for us in his Pontiac car.

From Daniel Neal we went to London's West End where, after a meal, we went to see a Show, *Call Me Madam*, in London's Coliseum Theatre. Built for Oswald Stoll this Frank Matcham-designed Theatre had special memories for my Father for, when aged only 24, he had built the Scenery for its Opening Show in 1904.

Call Me Madam, with Music and Lyrics by Irving Berlin, had first been performed in the United States at The Imperial Theatre in New York in 1950 before being brought to London and presented by a good friend of my Father's, the Impresario and Band Leader Jack Hylton. It opened at The Coliseum in March 1952, with Scenery built by Brunskill and Loveday Limited. [*see below a copy of the Programme for the 1952 London production at London's Coliseum Theatre of 'Call Me Madam''*.] What the Show was about I, as an 8-years old, had no idea but, to me, its music was wonderful. Sadly *Call Me Madam's* American 'star' Ethel Merman did not appear in the London production and so I did not have the experience of personally hearing her superb powerful 'belter's' voice; but one of its Cast, as Senator Brockbank, was Arthur Lowe, an actor who, many years later, starred as Captain Mainwaring in BBC Television's hugely successful long-running *Dad's Army* production.

Back home in Croydon, some days after my bewildering Daniel Neal experience, I was given (i) a Tuck Box that my Father had himself made for me and upon which someone had, in bold black capital letters, neatly painted my forenames' initials and my surname and (ii) one of the large trunks that we, as a Family, had used on our SS Alca cruises and upon which also someone had, in bold black capital letters, neatly painted my forenames' initials and my surname. All the garments purchased at Daniel Neal plus other new items of clothing that my Mother had purchased elsewhere were neatly put into the trunk by my Mother after she had first, for identification purposes, sewn upon every item a Cash's label, a proprietary name of a manufactured small strip of white material into which had been machine-woven, in red, my forenames' initials and my surname.

As for the Boarding School in which, in September of that year, I was to be incarcerated I was given little information. So, my imagination had to kick in, and, having been told that the School occupied a Manor House in Windsor called Clewer Manor, my mind began to form a picture of what it might look like.

When it came time for me to go to school again, with my Father at the wheel, we drove to Windsor via the, then regarded as being in Surrey, town of Sutton where we stopped and parked just near some traffic-lights at a crossroads in the town centre. Leaving my Mother in the car, my Father and I got out of the car and went into a nearby Stationer's shop to buy a ruler, some pencils, some red ink and some blue ink, and various other items that the School had informed my Parents that I would need. Then back to the car and on to Hampton Court where my Father parked the car close to the main entrance to Hampton Court's famous Palace. The three of us got out and walked into The Palace's Grounds and alongside the River Thames, my Father explaining to me the history of The Palace, how England's King Henry VIII had 'stolen' it from his Chancellor, Cardinal Thomas Wolsey, and so on. To an 8-years' old it was exciting stuff; and, as we drove away after we had got back into the car, I looked out of the car's small back window at The Palace and said to myself that one day The Palace would be mine. Of course, it never has been and never will be, *but one can always dream* !!

The next stop that day was Runnymede where, unhindered by any of to-day's man-inserted 'Keep off the grass' obstacles, my Father pulled the car off the road and onto the grass where we parked up, got out of the car, and, for a while, my Father and I wandered alongside the River Thames where, as with Hampton Court Palace, my Father explained to me some of the history of this very famous historic place, the site where, in 1215, The Magna Carta Libertatum (Great Charter of Freedom), one of the most influential of all legal documents within Common Law jurisdictions, was signed.

Then it was back into the car, onto and through Old Windsor, and then into Windsor itself where we again stopped to get out of the car to, this time, admire the outside of Windsor's magnificent Castle, a castle founded in about 1080, my Father explained to me, by William Duke of Normandy known also as King William I, William the Conqueror, and, occasionally as, William the Bastard. As we walked we passed by Windsor's Theatre Royal Theatre outside of which my Father stopped to tell me of the occasion when he had sent Scenery to Windsor from his Works in Kennington. Nothing unusual in that except that the Scenery had made the somewhat, in those days, torturous journey from London to Windsor by means of a lorry pulling three trailers, each of the lorry and trailers being fully laden with Scenery. Having, from its outside, completed our admiring this largest of all inhabited castles, we then headed out of the centre of Windsor, me with feelings fluctuating between excitement and trepidation, towards the mysterious and intriguingly-sounding Clewer Manor. [As I boy I believed the story of the Scenery's journey in a lorry with three trailers from London to Windsor without any question, but as the years of my teenage years passed by I began first to doubt the truthfulness of the story and then, eventually, to reject it in favour of believing it to have been told to me in the manner that a Parent often tells, in order to entertain, believable but fictitious tales to children. Then, one day in the early 2000s, whilst at home watching a Television programme featuring true stories involving the Police and motoring incidents, I saw a Showman's laden vehicle pulling three laden trailers being stopped by Police as it trundled slowly along a British Motorway. Courteously a Woman Police Officer explained to the Showman that, despite his careful driving, what he was doing was unlawful; and equally courteously the Showman explained to the Officer and her male colleague that it was not. The Woman Officer then radioed for advice. Eventually she returned to the waiting Showman and, with a grin, informed him that he was in fact correct. So, I think that I owe my Father an apology !! (*However, given the Theatre Royal's smallish capacity the Scenery was probably not destined, at least in its entirety, for the Theatre Royal*)]

The routine of stopping at Sutton, Hampton Court Palace, and Runnymede was, with slight variations, the routine that was undertaken every time that we went to the Junior School at the start of a term. One of the slight variations was to go to Tagg's Island instead of Hampton Court Palace, the reason being was that the lease of Tagg's Island, an island situated in the River Thames not very far from Hampton Court Palace, had once been owned by a friend of my Father's - a Music Hall Artist, Theatrical Impresario, and out-and-out Showman by the name of Fred Karno whose once famous troupe, 'the Fred Karno Army', contained such as Charlie Chaplin and Stan Laurel. Tagg's Island thus held many memories for my Father. Born in 1866 Fred Karno, who early in his career had changed his surname from the somewhat mundane-sounding Fred Westcott to the audience-appealing Fred Karno, had, after he acquired the lease, spent a vast amount of money demolishing the hotel that was then sited on the island and building in its stead a lavish Casino, nicknamed the 'Karsino', designed by perhaps the greatest of all Theatre Architects, Frank Matcham, and intended by Karno to be the finest river hotel in all of Europe with the biggest and best of all casinos. With seating for over 800 people its Palm Court Ballroom was a superb domed dance hall whose Orchestra had as the Leader of its 'Riviera Band' a young Jack Hylton, a man who was to become not only a great international Band Leader but also one of the UK's greatest of Theatrical Impresarios. The Karsino's gambling facilities and many other attractions, including a plentiful supply of young Actresses and might-some-day-perhaps-be Actresses, caused it to be an instant magnet for Theatricals, for the 'Wealthy' of London Society, and for many Continentals who crossed the English Channel to enjoy what Karno had to offer on his sumptuous Tagg's Island including, before the days when a bridge connected the Island to the mainland, a short ferry ride in boats crewed by topless ladies. But the First World War caused the Karsino's decline and then, after the War, the eventual, and perhaps inevitable, bankruptcy of Karno himself. When we used to visit it in the 1950s it was but a sad shadow of its once former self. I well remember walking around the outside of the former Karsino to admire the many Houseboats that were moored-up around the Island; but I also remember Tagg's Island as a place where I received a severe verbal reprimand from someone unknown to me for attempting, in all innocence, to fish some splendid-looking very large goldfish out a pond sited in front of the steps that led up to the once famous Karsino's main entrance !!

But back to my first journey to Haileybury Junior School. We entered the grounds of Clewer Manor and drove down much of its longish driveway before, taking a right turn, we came face-to-face with the Manor House itself, a building that looked uncannily like what my mind had imagined it to be. My Father having parked his car close to the foot of the stone steps that led up to the main front doors, he and my Mother got out, and then, on instruction from my Mother, I got out. My Mother having made sure that my tie was straight, that my shoe laces were properly tied, and that I was thoroughly presentable, with my Father in front and my Mother holding my right hand firmly in her left hand, the three of us walked, in silence, up the steps. Thus for me life as a term-time resident of Haileybury and Imperial Service College at its Junior School at Clewer Manor, Windsor had begun. [Haileybury Junior School had been chosen as a result of a conversation that my Father had had with a Theatrical colleague of his, a good friend by the name of Tommy Robinson - a Scenery Builder and Props Maker who lived in Maidenhead and whose Son had been a Pupil at Haileybury Junior School. (I was, years later, told by my Mother that it had been intended that I would go to Dulwich College in South London but that, on his and my Mother's being shown around Dulwich College, my Father had formed the opinion that the heights and positions of the classrooms' windows were such that they caused the classrooms to be too dark and too miserable. As an adult I have driven past Dulwich College many times and am disinclined to believe her comment in favour of being of the Opinion that my Mother, in a desire to rid herself of my presence, probably said to my Father something like "Good Heavens, Ted, we can't send the boy to Dulwich. It's far too close to Croydon. Send him somewhere further away !!"." Having said that, I mention in 2007 I received an e-mail from an acquaintance in the Grand Order of Water

Rats who, at the time, was of an age slightly older than I who, in respect of his time as a Pupil at Dulwich College, commented to me that he could "remember virtually nothing about it" except "that it was a frightening place".)]

As my Parents and I arrived at the top of the stone steps one of the two large semi-glass-paned wooden doors opened, and out of the building stepped a smiling but, I thought at the time, austere-looking man who welcomed my Parents, greeted me briefly, and then ushered us into the building, across a large wooden-floored hallway, and thence into a room beyond where, after waiting for my Mother and Father to be seated, he pressed a bell-push before he himself sat down on the other side of a desk opposite to my Mother and Father whilst I stood nervously and silently behind them awaiting an instruction as to what I should do. Suddenly the door behind me through which we had entered opened.

"This is Matron," said the man, "She will show Edwin around the School."

Then, smiling directly at me, he said "Go with Matron. But first say 'good-bye' to your Parents."

He then stood up, stated "I'll leave you for a couple of minutes so that you can say your good-byes", and then, with Matron, he left the room.

"You'll enjoy yourself here," instructed, rather than said, my Mother who added "You'll make lots of new friends, and you can write to your Father and me and tell us how you are getting on".

My Father, perhaps being more sensitive to my feelings, offered the intended-to-be-reassuring comments "We're not very far away, and Mummy and I will come to see you in four weeks' time; and we can go out and explore Windsor and find somewhere nice where we can have tea to-gether".

It was all beyond my understanding. I had no idea of what was happening; and I suddenly felt very, very frightened as Matron, and the man returned. My Mother kissed me briefly; my Father stood up, kissed me, and gave me a reassuring hug. I took hold of a hand that Matron had held out for me; and, it being suggested by Matron that I say goodbye to my Parents, everyone, including me, seemed to say "Goodbye" to everyone else. The man held a door open for Matron as she said "Thank you, Head Master" :" And, leading me by the hand, Matron and I exited.

"We'll go first up to my Rooms where you can meet some of your new friends who also arrived here to-day," she said as she led me along a corridor to the bottom of a wooden spiral staircase. Up the creaking staircase this complete stranger and I went until we reached the floor above where, on leaving the staircase and turning to the right, we walked along a wooden corridor to a doorway on the righthand side. Matron opened the door and she and I went into the room where there sat, in silence and with expressions indicating almost nothing but fear, seven or eight other boys of similar age to myself.

"This is Edwin," said Matron, "and now that we are all here we can go for a little walk to have a look round the School. When we return we can have some tea and cakes."

So, with my already standing, the other boys got up, and we all exited the room, turned left, and in fearful and tearful silence followed Matron along the wooden corridor, past the spiral staircase, past a door on the left and a door on the right and then into a large bedroom with several metal-framed beds in it.

"This is a dormitory," said Matron who - with a white bonnet pinned on her head and a dark cape, held on by two red crossed straps, draped over her shoulders - went on to briefly explain "Dormitories are large bedrooms where lots of boys sleep".

We all crammed into the doorway to have a brief look at this wooden-floored carpetless uninviting austere-looking room. Then Matron announced "And now we'll go and have a look at some of the classrooms".

So, off we went back along the corridor to the creaking staircase, then down the creaking staircase to the floor below where we turned left into another corridor. With Matron still leading the way we boys gradually began to pluck-up the courage to ask each other's names, where we lived, and so on. Suddenly, on almost colliding with an aproned roundish man coming out of a room to our left, Matron stopped. "This is Dick," she said.

"Welcome to Haileybury Junior School, boys. You and I will be seeing a lot of each other while you're here," said Dick with a reassuring smile.

"Dick, looks after the boilers," explained Matron "In fact Dick looks after most of the School including the cleaning all your shoes until he manages to teach you gentlemen to clean and polish them yourselves."

"Want to have a look at the boilers, boys ?" Dick suddenly asked realising, I suspect, that this offer might extract us out of our doom and gloom.

"Oh, yes, please," was the eager response.

Dick crossed over to the other side of the corridor and opened a door thereby allowing a huge rush of hot air to escape out of the room beyond.

"Here, have a look, but don't go right in. Just stand at the top of the steps," Dick instructed.

So, with a smiling Matron stepping aside to let us all pass, we all went through the doorway and stood at the top of the steps and looked downwards with amazement at the two big fire-belching cylinders before us and at the huge heap of boiler fuel piled alongside them.

"Those boilers heat most of the School," Dick proudly exclaimed as, manoeuvring his way between us, he went down the steps to a door at the front of one of the large cylinders. Pulling a lever he opened the door wider to reveal in all its glory a tremendous bright red-yellowy glow. "That's one of the fires, gentleman, that heats the water that goes into these pipes," he said tapping some fat white-coated tubes, ""that go round the whole School and keeps it all nice and warm."

"All the School except the dormitories," Matron interjected.

"Yes, that's right. All the School except the dormitories. The dormitories have gas fires in them, as you'll find out to-night when you go to bed."

Facing us when we exited the Boiler Room was a long double row of wash-hand basins sited back-to-back. "Those," said Dick, pointing to the wash-hand basins," are where you wash yourselves when you come in from the rugger fields." "Mind you don't make a mess of my nice clean tiled floor," Dick jokingly warned us as he pointed to the floor tiles that surrounded the wash-hand basin supports.

Matron thanked Dick; and we all moved on, past dozens of empty hooks on wooden backing-battens sited on several walls, then down a couple of steps and into another, wider, corridor where, just before that corridor made a 90-degree turn to the left, Matron stopped, opened a door to our right and ushered us all in.

"These are the toilets," said Matron pointing to a row of half-doored wooden cubicles each with a toilet pan and high-positioned cistern in it, each toilet pan having neither a seat nor a lid but just a piece of curved mahogany wood fixed on top of each side.

On being asked by Matron "Does anyone want to use the toilet whilst we are here ?" we each made a dash into a cubicle to desperately relieve ourselves of the liquid within us that doubtless fear had caused to build-up over the last hour or so of our incarceration in this frightening but strangely exciting place whose architecture had, as we progressed through it, begun to change from old manorial to [then] new modernish.

Having each done what each of us desperately needed to do, on exiting the Toilet Block we all, following Matron, walked on until the corridor turned right at which point Matron, and thus we, stopped. To our left was a door which, Matron informed, led outside. Immediately ahead was another door : Having opened it, Matron announced "These are some of the Classrooms". Encouraging us to troop a metre or so into a seemingly endless room she then said. "But they are not the Classrooms that you will be using for your first year here. Follow me, and we'll go to *your* Classroom."

Now more emboldened and chattering amongst ourselves, we followed Matron out of the seemingly endless Classrooms, down a seemingly enormous length of, sloping downwards, corridor. Then we turned left past another staircase, and then turned right into an older-looking Classroom wherein stood a woman seemingly busy sorting things out.

"This is Mrs O'Connor," Matron announced; and then, turning to Mrs O'Connor, said "These gentleman are your new Students, Mrs O'Connor."

Mrs O'Connor stopped doing what she had been doing and came over to greet us. "Thank you, Matron," she said. Then turning to us she informed "I shall be your Teacher for your first year here and this Classroom will be *your* Classroom for that first year." "Have any of you been away to school before ?" she added with a voice of somewhat artificially-sounding tenderness. Not one of us said anything. After a pause, during which some of us evidenced noticeable sadness at having finally realised that we had reached the point of no return, Mrs O'Connor said "No matter. I'm sure that every one of you will like it here."

Then, with a "Thank you, Matron", Mrs O'Connor ended her brief first meeting with us; and, silent once again, we all, with Matron again leading the way, trooped out, went back up the corridor, back past the Toilet Block, then back past the empty hooks on their wooden backing-timbers, past the wash-hand basins and the Boiler Room, and back towards the bottom of the spiral stair. It was all rather frightening.

"So, that's the tour over," I, my misery returning, thought. But no, "Onto the Dining Room," Matron suddenly announced : And so onto the Dining Room we went where, upon Matron opening its door, we discovered, what seemed to us to be, a huge room full of long tables and long benches and with a few chairs at its far end - Tables, benches, and chairs where, each day, 120 boys and members of the Teaching Staff and sometimes Matron and her Assistant would sit to eat their breakfasts, luncheons, and teas.

As Matron was showing us where we would be sitting a man, with a white apron and bedecked with a large white hat, came to greet us. "This is Mr Webb, the Chef," Matron informed us. "He and Mrs Webb are very good cooks. In fact," said Matron with a genuine smile," they are *excellent* cooks". And with that statement of reassurance we left the Dining Room and headed towards a grand Staircase the first riser and tread of which were sited alongside the doors through which I had first entered the building, stairs which, in my fear and trepidation, I had not previously noticed.

"Now, boys, it's back to my Rooms. But first, as a treat - for no boys are usually allowed to use these stairs - we'll go this way," said Matron as she chaperoned us onto and up this far grander stairway to its first landing where, upon Matron's instruction, we all turned left then went only a short distance to the door to Matron's Rooms. Matron opened the door and then, standing aside, she ushered us all in to where a sumptuous selection of cakes and other goodies sat awaiting us. As we sat down, Matron, with a kindly reassuring smile, said "Don't worry, boys. I know how you feel. This is the start of my first term here also".

It would perhaps be amiss of me to describe my progress in life through the JS, as we boys respectfully and fondly called Haileybury's Junior School, without having first made reference to some of the other events that had occurred in my life prior to my entering the allegedly privileged world of the English Public School system.

Life at Highlands seemed, at least for me, to have a more-or-less fixed routine: Each weekday and some Saturdays my Father went to work; each Tuesday my Mother, with me in tow if I was not at school, would go into Croydon itself where, at 11am or thereabouts, she would meet with friends for 'coffee'; each Wednesday two Gardeners arrived to tend the garden and so forth; each Thursday a Maid arrived to help clean, in the morning, the inside of the house and its contents; and on Sundays, and on some Saturdays, some sort of hospitality for friends and business acquaintances – Actors, Designers, Producers, and so on - of my Father took place.

Apart from the Wednesday Gardeners and the Thursday Maid, in my very early years, my Mother seemingly not being too keen to involve herself in the rearing of a young child, there was also a live-in Nanny the first of whom was a young German woman. My Father had, before the Second World War, had many Jewish and other Theatrical friends and acquaintances in Germany and therefore, as soon as the War against Germany ended [just a few weeks after my birth] my Father tried to resume contact with some of those friends and acquaintances. Communications and life in general within Germany were, after the War, very basic and, for its People, often very harsh; but nonetheless a young Nanny, whose name I ceased to remember many years ago, was recommended by someone in Germany whom my Father had known before the War. However, we were never given much opportunity to find out whether or not she was a good Nanny for within less than a handful of weeks of her arrival at Highlands two men from the UK's Home Office arrived at the frontdoor, spoke with my Father, then entered the house, arrested the young woman, and took her away. We never saw her again for she was, apparently, a German spy and, despite the fact that the War with Germany had ended, was still spying for the then still very active

German NAZI Party. Our home had, the gentlemen from the Home Office informed my Father, been deliberately chosen - not, I hasten to add, by my Father's German friend - due to the fact that it was very close to Croydon Airport; and many Germans intended to still continue with the War.

My next, and only other Nanny, was from the Indian sub-continent, a fact which was another security risk in itself for, despite the fact that India was then a major portion of the British Empire and despite the fact that many Indians had fought loyally and superbly on Britain's side during the Second World War, there was considerable anti-British feeling throughout much of India [which then included also what are now known as Pakistan and Bangladesh] at the time. But the woman, whose name I also ceased to remember many years ago, was both excellent and thoroughly dedicated to my well-being. In fact she was so excellent and so dedicated to my well-being that I began not only to call her 'Mummy' but also to believe that she, not my Mother, was actually my Mother, a situation which ultimately caused my Mother to rid our household of this excellent woman's services in favour of my Mother herself, doubtless with considerable reluctance, assuming the role that she should have undertaken from the very moment that I was born, if not before. But I would have preferred that my Indian nanny had been permitted to continue for my Mother was not a very sympathetic Mother, doubtless an attitude that, sub-consciously if not consciously, she inherited from her own Mother. I was not only never allowed to play with, nor associate with, other children - not even with Alan Dixon, a boy roughly the same age as I who lived across the other side of Pampisford Road in a house directly opposite Highlands - but also only allowed to play with one toy at a time; and so if I tired of the toy with which I was playing I had to await a suitable occasion to surrender that toy to my Mother and ask/plead for it to be exchanged for another. The toy that I surrendered would, by my Mother, then usually be placed, well out of my reach, on the top of a splendid glass-doored, and very heavy, mahogany bookcase and another toy gotten down and, with obvious reluctance due to the inconvenience that I had caused, given to me to play with. There were not many toys either, thus causing the items that I could play with to be very limited, very repetitive, and often exceedingly boring. But this whole toy-control arrangement that my Mother persisted in operating, usually only during my Father's absences at work, eventually ceased when one day, when I was aged 7, I boldly, naïvely, and foolishly took it upon myself to climb onto and up to the top of the bookcase and myself effect a toy exchange. What I had not realised was that the higher that I climbed the more top-heavy and unstable the large bookcase and its contents became until eventually the whole lot - books, toys, and all - came crashing down on top of me. Had it not been for the fact that one of the doors swung open as the bookcase tumbled I would probably have been thoroughly crushed possibly to the extent of causing the termination of my existence. As it was a triangular-shaped piece of glass flew out of one of the glazed doors and penetrated itself deeply into my left leg just above my knee causing an ambulance to have to be summoned so that I could be taken to hospital. Not every house had a telephone but ours had : But No telephone-call was made to my Father who only found out what had happened when he returned from work that evening. He was both deeply distressed at what had happened to me and also incandescent with rage at my Mother whose actions in ensuring that I had little or nothing to play with had not been previously made known to him. He had, I know, considerable affection for the bookcase - which he had owned for many years, long before he had ever met my Mother - but nevertheless he, to ensure that never again could such an incident happen to me, that night smashed the bookcase into pieces, took all the wooden pieces down to near the end of the garden, and burnt the lot. It must have caused him considerable sadness.

Now realising how lonely and bored that I was at home whilst he was out at work my Father decided that henceforth he, insofar as it was possible, would take over the control of my daily life. Not only was he a Builder of Theatrical Scenery but also his firm made, to order, all sorts of other wooden items. One such item that his firm had made just prior to the incident with the bookcase was a large 'knee-hole' desk and, as fate [or 'Kismet' as I prefer to call it] would have it, the customer concerned had failed to collect it at the arranged time as he had, apparently, also done so previously. Thus my Father telephoned him and gave him an ultimatum: Either collect it by 2 o'clock the following afternoon else it would go to another 'interested party'. 2 o'clock came and went, and when at 10 minutes past 2 the gentleman concerned came to collect it he was told 'with regret' that it had been sold to the other 'interested party'. That night, a Friday, the Desk accompanied by a second-hand swivelling wooden office-chair, arrived at our home and was installed in an area within my L-shaped bedroom. Next day my Father and I went in his car the short distance to Croydon Airport where, with the assistance of some friends of his who managed the Airport, we loaded up with bundles of TWA [Trans-World Airlines] and Pan-Am [Pan-American World Airlines] leaflets which we took back home to my Desk. Then my Father produced, on loan to me, the portable Smiths-Corona typewriter that he himself used every week-day at work in his Office in Kennington; and he began to teach me how to type and, unknown to me at the time, how to be a businessman. Unfortunately the typewriter had to go back to work with him on the Monday, but every Friday night that typewriter was always returned to my Desk so that I, as the person 'in charge' of TWA and Pan-Am, could continue to learn how to run 'my empire'. Although I long ago ceased to use my Desk as a place from which to run a business, my Desk remains with me to this day; and I would defy anyone to remove it from my possession for, without doubt, that large wooden 'knee-hole' desk given to me by my Father when I was a little boy of seven years of age was a substantial determinant in my having been, for most of my life, an entrepreneur of some kind or other.

That Christmas also saw a radical change in my toy 'allocation' for my Father gave me the first of the toy electric trains that I also still possess - but no longer use. The 'Duchess of Atholl' 00-gauge Hornby railway engine and its control-box, 3-railed track, rolling stock, and many other items that he gave me that Christmas were put onto an 8ft x 4ft plywood board which was then placed on to the protected, by a specially made cover, top of my Father's billiards table thereby enabling me to enjoy much fun for many hours each week. But the arrival of that gift of the 'Duchess of Atholl' was not without incident. We were staying for Christmas that year at the Angles Hotel in Eastbourne. It was, unlike Eastbourne's Burlington Hotel where we had spent Christmas in 1951, a small 'family'-type Hotel owned by friends of my Father. I was, like most children of my era, a firm believer in Father Christmas; and, as such, I was determined that Christmas to at least try to see him if not to actually meet him. So I stayed up that Christmas Eve and, for much of the time after I had been 'sent to bed', stood behind my bedroom door awaiting Father Christmas's arrival. Eventually - after a long, long wait - the door slowly opened and first a hand then an arm came in. At that point my courage deserted me and, instead of standing my ground and actually seeing Father Christmas, I panicked, tried to slam the door shut, rushed back to my bed, and hid under the bed-covers. Father Christmas's language, as I rushed to the safety of my bed, was appalling, absolutely appalling : I could hardly believe it. Next morning - after I had awoken to find my splendid 00-gauge trainset at the foot of my bed - as my Mother, Father, and I went down to breakfast I noticed that my Father's right arm was bandaged. The coincidence has always puzzled me !!

Another Christmas period away from home, this time spent at the Pavilion Hotel in Bournemouth, also gave me cause to panic for the hotel, also owned by friends of my Father, suffered, whilst we were there, a serious fire on the day after Boxing Day. We, fortunately for us, were staying in the hotel's nearby annex which was not damaged by the fire. Needless to say, it was a sad occasion for many Christmas revellers staying within the main hotel building for some lost most, if not all, of the possessions that they had taken with them to Bournemouth. Whilst the hotel itself was being evacuated those of us in the annex were advised to remove ourselves onto a nearby grassed area sited more or less in front of the main building. By the time that my Parents and I got to the grassed area the main building was well alight with flames shooting high up into the air through a glazed ceiling area sited above the hotel's main staircase; and Firemen [there were no female Firefighters in those days] were in attendance all over the place. Once my panic had ceased excitement kicked in and I slowly ventured closer and closer to the main doors so that I could have a better view of what the inside of the main part of the burning building looked like. Suddenly I saw, highlighted by streaks of molten glass cascading downwards through the well of the main staircase, an elderly [Well, he seemed elderly to me then !!] dressing-gown-clad man groping his way up the main stairs from the hotel's not-yet-engulfed-in-fire foyer. He had got as far as the top tread of the first flight but before he could step onto a landing he was grabbed by a fireman, who had come up from behind him, and was gently led back down the stairs, through and out of the foyer, and placed, along with my Parents and many others, on the grassed area. Meanwhile I stayed where I was, as close to the entrance as I felt it safe to be, looking inside at the yet-to-be-hit-by-fire foyer and its area of main staircase. Then there, suddenly, was the elderly man back again on the staircase and this time travelling much more speedily up it as if in some desperation to get to something or somebody. Idiot that hindsight now tells me that I was, clad in my dressing-gown and pyjamas I rushed in after him and reached him at the same time as the same fireman again reached him. To-gether, as more and more streaks of hissing molten glass cascaded down through the stair-well, the fireman and I led him back down the stairs again and - as the three of us went through the lobby and with the fireman asking him time and again whether there was someone trapped upstairs, the hitherto silent and clearly almost totally bewildered man suddenly shouted "Let me go. Let me go. I want the toilet ! I want the toilet ! I want the toilet ! ""

We were in Bournemouth that Christmas because its Pavilion Theatre often staged Shows the Scenery for which was built by Brunskill and Loveday Limited, but whether or not my Parents had any special 'attachment' to Bournemouth I do not know. Eastbourne, however, did have a special meaning for my Father for not only was it in Eastbourne, during the Second World War when honeymooning abroad was almost an impossibility, that my Parents spent their honeymoon but also Eastbourne's Royal Hippodrome Theatre had, in 1883, been built for my Father's Uncle George Beaumont Loveday. Indeed, throughout my childhood we regularly visited not only Eastbourne and nearby Pevensey but also another favourite South Coast town of my Father's, Brighton [now, with Hove, a City] where most visits would be rounded off with seeing a Show, with Scenery having been built by Brunskill and Loveday Limited, at either The Theatre Royal, The Dolphin Theatre, The Dome Theatre, Her Majesty's Theatre, The Hippodrome Theatre, The Pier Theatre, or The Palace Pier Theatre. On arrival in Brighton the roads were such that one could, in those days, park almost anywhere, and more often than not my Parents chose to park along the seafront close to Volk's Electric Railway [originally longer than it is to-day, it was built in the 1880s by Magnus Volk and is reckoned to be the oldest electric railway in the world]. However, on one visit that the three of us made, in my Father's Pontiac car, to Brighton my Father chose to park his car near to the Indian-looking early 19th century Royal Pavilion [a publicly-owned former royal residence and seaside home of the then Prince Regent (subsequently King George IV) and of his successor William IV] on a road with a very curved camber. Usually good at parking, on this occasion, doubtless hampered by the fact that the Pontiac's rear window enabled only very limited visibility to be achieved, he experienced considerable difficulty reversing into his chosen parking space. Eventually, after much revving of the car's engine, he considered that he had more or less achieved his objective and, having switched off the engine, opened his door in order to step out to satisfy himself that he had satisfactorily parked the car. It was only when he began to step out that, on seeing that the ground below was further down than it should have been, did he realise that something was amiss : He had somehow managed - doubtless in part courtesy of the road's very curved camber - to park part of the rear end of his beloved Pontiac partly on top of part of the curved rear end of an already parked Volkswagen car.

A principal attraction, at least for me, insofar as Pevensey was concerned was its ruined Castle where, within its grounds in Pevensey

Bay, I could wander around pretending either that I was an arriving Norman Soldier fighting the English or that I was a native of Pevensey attempting to drive the Normans back from whence they had come. For my Parents, I suspect, the principal attraction was a nearby Hotel-cum-pub which, sited on a bend near to the Castle, offered enjoyable liquid refreshment. Hence we tended to go to Pevensey Bay only a couple of hours or so before setting out to return to Croydon and after we had spent an hour or so on the coastal shingle and in the sea off Pevensey itself. In the early days of our visiting Pevensey it was a small-to-medium-sized village somewhat isolated from nearby Eastbourne but as the years went by the size of the village increased whilst Eastbourne steadily expanded outwards towards it. Much of the village increase was due to the building of scores of bungalows sited, in the main, between the coastal shingle and the main road to Eastbourne. It occurred to my Father that were he to buy one of the newly-built bungalows we could have our own home in Pevensey to which we could go whenever it appealed to us. Chatting one Saturday with his old friend Arthur Dixon, the Manager of Croydon's Empire Theatre, he mentioned the idea and, in consequence, it was arranged that Arthur Dixon and his Daughter, Son-in-law, and their Daughter, would accompany us to Pevensey the next time that we went there. So, shortly thereafter, we all, my Parents and I in my Father's car and Arthur Dixon and his Family in his Son-in-law's car, travelled down to the South Coast for a day in Pevensey. I liked Arthur Dixon and got on well, very well with him and his Daughter but not, after that first joint visit to Pevensey, so well with Arthur's Son-in-law, Harold Norman. I was often left with Arthur's Grand-Daughter, Sandra, to play whilst the adults did whatever it was that they wanted to do. Sandra and I were almost the same age as each other but to say that we were 'good friends' would be a wee bit generous. So, on that day that we all first went to Pevensey, off Sandra and I went to the beach whilst my Parents, accompanied by Arthur and his Family, looked at some of the several nearby new bungalows that, via a site Office, were being offered as being for sale. Eventually Sandra and I returned to be informed that my Father and Mother had decided on the bungalow that they wished to buy. It already had a name - 'Brigadoon'. Whether my Mother had been influenced by the fact that 'Brigadoon' had a Scots 'ring' to it or whether my Father had been influenced by the fact that 'Brigadoon' was the name of a popular Musical Show [Some Scenery, including a waterfall (of which my Father was particularly proud), for which was built by Brunskill and Loveday] that, in 1949, had been staged at London's His Majesty's Theatre I do not know - But 'Brigadoon' it was. For some reason unknown to me my Father was, unusually, slow in getting under way with his intended purchase : Indeed, he never actually got under way with the purchase for, suddenly, Harold Norman announced that he had bought 'Brigadoon'. My Father was furious, absolutely furious; and, doubtless, had it not been for his long and close friendship with Arthur Dixon, thoughts of continuing the friendship would have ended there and then : But a deal was struck - We, provided that Harold and his Family were not using it, could use 'Brigadoon' whenever we wanted. However, we never did. Instead, often, when the Normans were staying at 'Brigadoon', we would visit Eastbourne and go on to Pevensey for an afternoon at 'Brigadoon' with the Normans and, after a meal cooked by Harold's Wife, thence, with the Normans, to the Hotel-cum-pub near the Castle at Pevensey where, Sandra and I not being of sufficient age to be allowed in, Sandra and I would remain outside amusing ourselves, often by annoying and irritating each other, whilst our Parents, as the hours passed by, consumed quantities of liquid refreshment within. Occasionally one of our Parents would come outside to, if we were in or near the car, give us a lemonade or orange squash and some packets of peanuts or 'Smiths Salted Crisps' or, if we were nowhere to be seen, go back in, with drinks and food still in hand, to inform the others "Oh, they must be playing in the Castle somewhere". Eventually, darkness having well and truly descended, we would all return to the cars, the Normans to return to their Scots'-sounding 'Brigadoon' and us to return - my Father, although steady on his feet and still able to drive without mishap, being, by to-day's standards, somewhat over the legal limit for driving a vehicle on the Public Highway - via the bendy, and at times somewhat boring, Eastbourne-to-London road to our Scots'-sounding 'Highlands'. Despite the 'arrangement' my Father never did forgive Harold Norman for, what my Father considered to be, the 'stunt' that he pulled : Thus it was somewhat surprising that a wee bit later my Father responded to a request from Harold and his Wife that he lend Harold some money.

Harold was a Second-hand Car Dealer and, as such, operated from, what had once been, the garden area in the front of his house in London Road, West Croydon. Business, apparently, was good, so good that he wanted to expand his forecourt by acquiring the next-door house and turning its front garden area into a car lot. The problem was that - whether or not because of his purchase of 'Brigadoon' I do not know - he did not have sufficient money to buy the house next door, convert it in the way in which he wished to convert it, and stock its front car lot with second-hand cars : And so my Father lent him £500, a Interest-free loan which, I suspect, came about because of my Father's many years' friendship with Harold's Father-in-law, Arthur Dixon. To-day a sum of £500 is, to most people, not much money : But in the 1950s £10 per week was a very good wage and therefore a sum of £500 was the equivalent of more than a year's worth of income for most people. So the loan was a very generous loan, and a loan which, possibly due to my Father's death in 1958, was never repaid.

Anyhow, back to when I was aged 7 and to some months after the arrival, courtesy of 'Father Christmas', of my trainset when a second garage was built at Highlands. The Builder was Roy Battershill who, with his mother, lived in a house across the road from us. He had, I believe, recently become self-employed and the job was given to him to assist him in establishing his business; and, other than one small - quickly rectified - teething problem which resulted in water coming into the garage at a point where its roof butted-up to the gable end of the house, he made a good job of it. Once that was sorted out, one half of the second garage was allocated by my Father to my trainset thereby enabling my Father's billiards table to revert to being used as a billiards table thus also enabling my Father to teach me how to play billiards, a game which I have ever since enjoyed but all-too-rarely, as the years have gone by, had the opportunity to play. My Father also provided me, within the garage, with a 'ping-pong' table, bats, and so on and ensured that most days my Mother's car, which occupied the other half of the garage, was driven out of the garage so that I could set up my 'ping-pong' table and play table tennis. Sadly, my Mother had no interest whatsoever in playing table-tennis and thus my opponent was usually two static closed garage doors whose challenging abilities were a bit … Well, 'wooden' to say the least. But I learnt how to play, and my skills, developed with the static assistance of the two doors, served me well a few years later when, aged 15, I won a tournament in Fort William in Inverness-shire and many years later when, working in the Insurance business in Dorking in Surrey and in the City of London, I would often play up to twenty games of table-tennis with colleagues during my lunch breaks.

Roy Battershill soon not only went on to achieve greater success in the Building Trade but also ceased living with his mother. A kindly woman, at least to me, Mrs Battershill was a neighbour whom my Mother did invite, occasionally, to Highlands : And on one of her visits 'across the road' to us she gave me a wonderful collection of very colourful silk cigarette flags, a sort of silk version of cigarette cards. Sadly, they have long since gone from my ownership but, as a child, I was very proud of them and, I confess, often … Well, boasted to others that I was the owner of such splendid items. Whether or not Mrs Battershill was a widow, was married, or what I do not know but she had a 'boyfriend' who lived not far away from Pampisford Road in a flat above, or alongside, the Red Deer Public House, a very noticeable building sited in South Croydon opposite the bottom end of St Augustine's Avenue. Shortly after she had given me the cigarette flags she invited my Mother and me to meet with her and her boyfriend in his flat; and thus to the flat we went. All went well for a half-hour or so until I expressed to Mrs Battershill my gratitude for her having given me the flags.

"What flags ?" asked the 'boyfriend'.

"These," I replied as I produced some of them from one of my pockets.

Suddenly the boyfriend's kind demeanour changed to an attitude of furious hostility as, turning to Mrs Battershill, he snapped "Those are the flags *I* gave *you* !!"."

Well, that was the end of that visit. We never saw him again. As to whether Mrs Battershill ever did … Well, we never met with her again either.

My Mother was not only not in the least bit interested in table-tennis but also she was not in the least bit interested in involving herself in any form of sport. She twice took me the few miles by car from Croydon to Streatham Ice Rink; and for many, many years thereafter she would occasionally make a point of reminding me of the 'sacrifices' that she had made in taking me to Streatham Ice Rink. She did however buy a second-hand 'clock golf' set which, without any notice whatsoever to my Father, she inserted firmly into the bowling green at the back of our house. She dug a hole roughly in the centre of the green and plonked an open-ended empty baked beans' tin can in it, and then she inserted twelve white-painted metal roman numerals, which formed the 'clock', in various positions into the grass and soil beneath. Her motive for buying the set and inserting it into the lawn were, I suspect, not to please me but to destroy one of my Father's greatest pastimes - enjoying the bowling green that he had so carefully laid out on the lawn which he and I regularly mowed, with great precision, in order to keep it in prime condition. What my Father said to my Mother when he arrived home that evening I can only guess at; but fortunately he had, on departing from his former home in Broadlands Avenue in Streatham, retained his membership of Streatham's Belmont Bowling Club to where, sometimes accompanied by me, he now regularly returned to enable him to continue to play his beloved game of lawn bowls. On one occasion he took me with him and, although I was not allowed onto any of the greens, I not only thoroughly enjoyed myself but also was well received by the many friends and acquaintances that my Father undoubtedly had at the Bowling Club : And I well remember the Club's canteen facility and the splendid fruit cake that was available that day. I also well remember - although I could not understand it at the time, for I had no idea that my Father was in his seventies - my

Father's embarrassment when, on greeting him within the Clubhouse, one of his acquaintances said of me "I take it, Ted, this is your Grandson then ?"

My Mother and Father slept in the same bedroom but in separate beds; and I well remember one day, when aged ten or eleven, entering their bedroom without first knocking on the door and waiting to be told by my Mother whether or not I was allowed to enter. My Mother's bed was nearest to the door and she, in her nightie, was in it. My Father was at the end of his bed undressing at the time and, having only just removed his shoes and trousers, was starting to unbutton his shirt. On seeing me enter my Mother, in a loudish voice, snapped at my Father "Ted, the boy !!". I well remember the incident only to that point. Why ? Well, for Mother to refer to me not as "Edwin" but as "the boy" seemed, to me, so impersonal and so unfeeling.

One of my other solitary pastimes was archery, a facility made available to me by a longbow made for me by my Father. Challenged by someone - not me - that he could not make a bow out of hardwood, he did exactly that - He made a bow out of hardwood [mahogany, I think]; and it was much used by me and lasted until it eventually broke some 26 years later. The arrows, made first by my Father and then by me, were made out of ordinary wooden dowelling to which, at one end, were affixed tips and, at the other end, nocks - both the tips and nocks having been purchased from a shop in central Croydon - and feathers that fell from some of the many birds that lived in nearby trees were glued onto the arrows at the nock ends to make the flights. My targets were usually sixpenny [2½p] coins placed on top of lengths of ¾ [19mm] inch x ¾ [19mm] inch pieces of rough sawn wood hammered, upright, into the ground. I became very experienced in shooting those coins off those ¾ inch x ¾ inch pieces of wood. But shooting sixpenny coins off bits of wood was somewhat boring at times; and so, with arrows of 36 inches [just under a metre] in length, I would often go into the public park that lay at the back of our house in order to see how high and how far I could fire my arrows. I knew nothing about the principle of trajectory - I just learnt through practice the best angle at which to fire my arrows in order to achieve the greatest length of flight. Such practice enabled me over time to become an archer of some skill which proved its worth on a least one occasion when local yobs [for want of a better word] took it upon themselves to adopt a practice of ridding our apple and pear trees of much of their delicious fruits. Their *modus operandi* was to gang to-gether, then each remove one shoe, then partly climb our high fence, hurl the removed shoes at the apple and pear trees in order to knock as many apples and pears as they could off the trees onto the ground, then climb over the fence, run into the garden and up to the fallen fruit, gather the fallen fruit and their shoes, rush back to and climb over the fence, put their shoes back on, and then run away with our fruit as fast as they could down the lane beyond the fence. Thoroughly fed-up with this constant thieving of his beloved fruit, my Father one day told me to lie in wait until the shoes had been thrown and then, as the miscreants began to climb over the fence, unleash a volley of arrows some several feet [300mm] over their heads. The results of the one and only occasion that I did this was not only that we lost no fruit whatsoever but also that we gained a selection of unpairable shoes. No miscreant or parent of any miscreant ever came seeking the recovery of even one shoe; and so I can only guess at the unpleasantness of what took place in the households of those who, on returning to their homes, had to explain why they only had one of the two shoes that each had left home with. Ah, happy days !!

Regular as clockwork, save on Bank Holidays, each and every weekday and each Saturday milk would be delivered to Highlands by the United Diaries whose horse-drawn milk float would be eagerly awaited by me for I was permitted to go out of Highlands onto Pampisford Road's then unmade-up grass-verged footpath and thence down the footpath a hundred yards or so to climb into the slow travelling milk-float whereupon I would be, seemingly unknown to my Mother, joined for a few minutes by Alan Dixon. To-gether we would sit there larking about whilst the horse plodded on its well-known and well-trodden path up Pampisford Road, unaided by the float's delivery man who was busy walking at speed here, there, and everywhere delivering bottles of milk, packets of butter, and other provisions to the houses on his route. More often than not the man's peaked cap would be deliberately left within the float so that I or Alan could don it and pretend that it was us, not he, who was the person in charge of the float and its horse. Eventually the one horse horsepower gave way to mechanised horsepower, a sad occasion for the Milkman to whom the horse had been a loyal friend and partner for many years, and doubtless a sad occasion for the Pampisford Road-programmed horse. It was a sad occasion for me too even though I was presented 'for keeps' with the cap which I had so often pretended was mine, a cap so covered internally with hair-grease that, upon my proudly returning to Highlands with my present, it was instantly taken away from me by my Mother and, with the comment "You don't want that *filthy* thing", placed in the dustbin never to be seen, nor worn, by me again.

An incident at Highlands which, unintentionally, perhaps enabled me to get my own back for having been deprived of my United Diaries' peaked hat involved not a hat but a pair of trousers which, to-gether with a shirt which I called Oscar. Whether I had gotten the name from hearing of the US Academy of Motion Picture, Arts, and Sciences' Awards, more well known as 'Oscars', awarded each year to honour achievements in the, principally United States', Film Industry I can not now recall, but one of the reasons that I created my Oscar was to make use of some inflated balloons left over from Christmas. First I, with my Father's co-operation, got a pair of my Father's old trousers and, having knotted the end of each trouser leg, stuffed inflated balloons down each leg. Then I safety-pinned an old shirt, with most of its front buttons done up, to the top of the trousers before proceeding to stuff inflated balloons down the shirt until both the trousers and the shirt were completely full of inflated balloons. Finally I buttoned the rest of the shirt buttons up; and that was Oscar. It was very lonely at times being an 'only child', and I have little doubt that, given that I was aged about eleven at the time, my principal reason for creating this unpredictable balloon-stuffed being was to give me some form of humanlike 'being' with whom/which to play. But one easily gets tired of such inanimate creations; and so, a day or so before I returned to School, I put Oscar inside an understairs' cupboard - and forgot all about him. Apparently, a day or so after I had returned to School, my Mother, on her own in the house whilst my Father was at work, went to the cupboard, opened its door … and, *bless him*, Oscar, arms and legs stretched out, leapt out at her terrifying the wits out of her. Had I been at home and not away at Boarding School when Oscar's 'assault and battery' upon my Mother took place I would doubtless have been punished in the way usually favoured by my Mother, namely by being sent, immediately, to bed to spend hours awaiting my Father's return from work so that he could administer the, 'ordered' by my Mother, "darn good thrashing" undertaken by means of the application, using a robust 3 inch[75mm]-wide leather belt-strap taken from a large cabin-trunk, of several 'strokes' upon my pyjama-clap backside. On one such occasion, when aged twelve, I had had enough of this usually, I felt, totally unjustified, and barbaric, treatment and so - as my Father, having raised his right arm high, commenced the belt-strap's downward stroke - I turned, grabbed the belt-strap, wrapped it round my right arm, pulled hard and wrenched it out of his grasp, and threatened to use it on him. He immediately stopped, put both his hands up in the air, and said "Okay. Enough's enough. It's not my idea. I only do it because you're Mother tells me to do it". The two of us then sat down on my bed and had a long, long chat after which never again did my Mother ever send me to bed other than for my normal bedtime of about 6pm [18:00 hours] which, in those days, was not an unusual time for most children to go to bed.

Along with his typewriter every Friday night my Father would often bring home a cardboard model which he would insert into a fully-functioning substantially scaled-down Theatre which he had made and given to me and which was permanently kept on a purpose-made stand in the Billiards Room. Each model was of a Theatrical Set [Scenery] that his firm was in the process of building or had just built; and he would use the scaled-down Theatre and the models to explain to me the technicalities and techniques of building, setting-up, moving, etc Scenery on stage. Over the years he and I would spend many happy hours to-gether analysing the Scenery for scores of real-life London Shows. Also, by means of the large workshop, or 'Shed' as we called it, that he had had built in the garden at Highlands my Father would explain and, by himself making joints and so forth, show me exactly how Scenery was built and how it was assembled and put to-gether. For me to feel that I was actually constructing *real* Theatrical Scenery was a wonderful experience, an experience that has served me well ever since.

Coupled with my Father's instruction as to how to run a business and his instruction as to how to design and build, etc., Scenery was the fact that from any early age I had, spasmodically, been appearing 'on stage'. The first such appearance was in April 1947 when I was aged 3, at London's Victoria Palace Theatre. The Cast was stuffed full of well-known Theatricals including 'the Forces sweetheart' Vera Lynn, Laurel and Hardy, Will Fyffe, and, to quote 'The Stage' newspaper, "a newcomer, Norman Wisdom, who took the house by storm with some of the funniest business possible". The occasion was a major Theatrical Charity event organised, under the umbrella title of *Rats Revel*, by the Theatrical Charity, the Grand Order of Water Rats, and its sister Theatrical Charity, the Grand Order of Lady Ratlings. I was there on stage representing the 'younger, younger generation of the Theatrical profession'. Sadly, I can remember absolutely nothing about the occasion, but 'The Stage' newspaper was, in its enthusiastic report on the occasion, kind enough to say of me that I already had "ideas about scenery".

The most enjoyable Stage appearance of my childhood that I can remember, and remember with considerable clarity, took place in 1952, when I was 8, at The Grand Theatre in Blackpool. The Show - first staged at The Connaught Theatre in Worthing in October 1951 and destined to go, after appearances in several 'Provincial' Theatres, into London's Hippodrome Theatre on 19 November 1952 - was *The Blue Lamp* starring Jack Warner, Gordon Harker, Bonar Colleano, and Susan Shaw, with Scenery built, needless to say, by my Father's firm, Brunskill and Loveday Limited. My Father knew Jack Warner, Gordon Harker, Bonar Colleano, and, to a lesser extent, also knew Susan Shaw.

I had arrived in the adjoining town of Lytham and St Anne's with my Parents for a holiday. We stayed in a Guest House in the front garden of which I would often play with three rubber quoits that I had brought with me. On one occasion one of the quoits unfortunately landed in the front garden of an adjoining house whose 'dragon-like' owner immediately seized it and, despite courteous and then stronger pleas from my Father, refused to hand it back. I was both annoyed and very upset by the woman's refusal to hand back my quoit to me; and thus, doubtless taking advantage of the opportunity presented to him by the fact that he had built the Scenery for *The Blue Lamp*, my Father suggested to me that, to cheer me up, we go to nearby Blackpool to have a look around the inside of one of its famous Theatres, The Grand. So off my Mother, Father, and I went; and it was whilst being shown around the Theatre's fascinating, at least to me, backstage area a few hours before 'curtain up' time that my Father asked me if I would like to go on stage and actually take part in the Show. I said "Yes", and very quickly - with the readily-given co-operation of Jack Warner, Gordon Harker, Bonar Colleano, and Susan Shaw - I found myself in an impromptu rehearsal; and that evening I was on stage.

The Blue Lamp, named after the blue lamps which symbolically hung, and still sometimes do hang, outside Britain's Police Stations, was originally, in 1949, a film, from a story by Ted [later Lord] Willis, which starred Jack Warner as Police Constable(*) [PC] George Dixon and Dirk Bogarde as a young villain, Tom Riley, and which concerned itself with the murder of PC Dixon by the young Tom Riley. Very successful as a film it was turned into a Stage play by Ted Willis. My humble part when the Show was being performed at The Grand in Blackpool was very simple: Part way through the Show the villain of the piece, now being played not by Dirk Bogarde but by Bonar Colleano, shoots and mortally wounds PC George Dixon, now being played not by Jack Warner (who was instead playing the part of Chief Inspector Cherry) but by Gordon Harker. As PC Dixon fell I arrived on stage and, on seeing the dastardly deed, stopped, opened my eyes wide in horror, and gasped. And that was it !! But, though very serious, it was fun, an experience heightened on the two other nights that I appeared in the Show for, before and after my miniscule appearance, in Susan Shaw's dressing-room, armed with a small gold-coloured, and genuine, gun loaned to her by her real-life boyfriend, Bonar Colleano, Susan (who, on stage, was playing the part of Diana Lewis, Riley's girl-friend) and I fired real bullets into a small target that hung in a wooden frame on the back of her dressing-room door. [Fortynine years later, in 2001, I wrote to The Grand Theatre asking if it would be possible for me to 'celebrate' my fiftieth anniversary of having appeared in The Blue Lamp by, in 1952, going once again backstage at The Grand. Sadly, times had changed since the days when, years earlier, going backstage was almost an automatic event for me for the reply that I received, though courteous, informed that - were I, as a member of the audience, to attend a performance of whatever Show was on stage at the time of my suggested visit - I might be able to go backstage if I asked when there and if the Cast was agreeable. Given the chances that my request might be declined, my Wife and I decided that it would not be worth the risk of travelling the 400 miles or so round trip from our home in Berwick-upon-Tweed to Blackpool and back only to be saddened by my request being rejected.] (*)There is some argument, based in part on the fact that at the top end of the Police 'hierarchy' exists the rank of 'Chief Constable', that PC, being the lowest rank in the Police 'hierarchy', stands not for 'Police Constable' but for 'Petty Constable'.]

In 1955 the Stage Show *The Blue Lamp* was 'taken over' by the BBC and became very well-known to millions of people as *Dixon of*

Dock Green, a series which ran on BBC Television for 21 years from 1955 to 1976. Of Jack Warner, Gordon Harker, Bonar Colleano, and Susan Shaw only Jack Warner transferred to the BBC's *Dixon of Dock Green* where he stayed throughout the entirety of the 21 years playing not the part of Chief Inspector Cherry that he had played in the Stage Show but starring, not as PC Dixon but, as Sergeant Dixon, the part originally played on Stage by Gordon Harker who, until his death, aged 81, in 1967 continued to play many 'character' parts in many Shows elsewhere. Jack Warner too survived for many years dying, aged 87, in 1981. The intertwining lives of Bonar Colleano and Susan Shaw were, however, far, far less fortunate for Bonar - a 'Star' of the era with great potential and whose many Stage performances included the part of Stanley Kowalski in Tennessee Williams's *A Streetcar named Desire* with Vivien Leigh at London's AldwychTheatre in 1949 [*see photograph below*] - was killed on 18 August 1958 whilst driving his car through Birkenhead when on his way back, with the Actor Michael Balfour as passenger, to a hotel after performing in *Will Success Spoil Rock Hunter ?* at Liverpool's New Shakespeare Theatre.

Aged only 34 and, at the time, a bankrupt with considerable debts, his death left his by now second Wife, Susan Shaw, whom he married in 1954 in London's Paddington Registry Office, so distraught that she could neither cope with bringing-up their very young Son, Mark, nor cope with Life itself. Mark was passed to, and brought up by, his Australian born Grandmother, the once famous Circus Contortionist Rubye Colleano [*see photographs below (1) , outside the garage at Highlands, (from left) my Mother, Bonar sitting in my Father's car, my Father, and I, and (2) Bonar's Mother Rubye Colleano*]

(1)   (2)

Susan, having degenerated into alcoholism, gave up acting in 1960 in favour of attempting bar work and office jobs, until, having been banned even from some of London's most notorious bars and clubs, she died, aged 49 in 1978, of cirrhosis of the liver. A very sad end to a once very attractive actress, an actress of great potential whose cremation in London's Golders Green Crematorium was ignored by almost everyone who had known her. Bonar's death was very deeply felt by my Father for Bonar [whose birth name was, like that of his Father, not Colleano but Sullivan had, as a child, in part been brought up by my Father. Born in the United States, Bonar from a very early age became part of his Parents' Circus Act; but his Parents realised that the nomadic lifestyle of Circus Entertainers would be likely to adversely affect Bonar's formal education. So, being very good friends with my Father, they arranged with my Father that, whenever possible, Bonar would stay with my Father. Thus my Father became a second 'father' to Bonar and Bonar a 'son' to my Father; and even though the Colleanos, when Bonar was in his early teens, bought a home in England their nomadic lifestyle continued.

Another of the Shows in which, in my childhood, I appeared - having been asked to do so in a manner akin to my appearance in *The Blue Lamp* - was *Noddy in Toyland* at London's Princes Theatre in 1955. For some reason unknown to me at the time and for many years thereafter, I did not enjoy it : The origin of my lack of enjoyment being only realised by me many years later when, whilst watching a television programme about the Show's originator, Enid Blyton, the authoress of many children's books including *The Famous Five* serious and the *Noddy* books, it was proclaimed that Enid Blyton, a former School Teacher, never liked children. I recall meeting her on stage at the Princes Theatre and, although she was kind and courteous to me, taking an instant - and, I confess, strong - dislike to her. I can only conclude therefore that the hostile 'vibes' that my senses received when I met her originated from her dislike of children.

Despite my disenchantment with *Noddy* 1955 had its non-Scenery 'entertaining' "moments for my Father one of which was entirely due to the Comedian and Water Rat Norman Wisdom. Founded, first as the 'Pals of the Water Rat', in the summer of 1889, nine years after my Father's birth, the Grand Order of Water Rats drifted into non-existence in the 1920s but, assisted by my Father, it was brought back to life by some of its stalwart Members in 1927 and was firmly supported until the day of his death by my Father who every year attended its principal fund-raising get-together activity, its Annual Ball. The 1955 Annual Ball was held in London's Dorchester Hotel, and that year's King Rat was the Comedian Tommy Trinder. My Father and Norman Wisdom were friends and, as the Night wore on, they, together with the Character Actor Cyril Smith [a Water Rat married to Anne Rendall, a Lady Ratling], wandered from table to table chatting with all and sundry, and, as they did so, drinks were aplenty. On their way home in the early hours of the next morning, with my Father driving, my Parents heard, to their puzzlement, the occasional 'jingle-jangle' of metal; and it was only as he undressed prior to going to bed that the mystery was solved - For out of his pockets cascaded several items of Dorchester Hotel cutlery which Norman, and perhaps Cyril Smith also, had secreted into the pockets of his dinner jacket.

Another 'entertaining' motoring experience suffered by my Father in 1955 occurred - whilst on his way back to Croydon from another drink-enjoying Water Rats' event in London [but this time without my Mother] - as my Father drove through Thornton Heath. In those days as one passed along the London Road through Thornton Heath one went alongside a pond laden with water the access into which was via a gently sloping cobbled cartway that had been put there for horses in days past. It was about 2 o'clock in the morning and there had been hardly a person to be seen throughout most of the journey : But as he approached the pond, sited across the road to his right, a woman suddenly appeared standing on the kerb to his left. Being a gentleman, my Father stopped the car and waved to the woman in a manner intended to encourage her to cross the road. She, in return and perhaps somewhat the worse for drink, bowed to my Father and, in so doing, waved to him in a manner intended to encourage him to drive on. My Father declined the kind offer and again waved to the woman that she should cross the road. However, she, in turn, declined his offer and instead again bowed to my Father and indicated that he should drive on. The stalemate was broken by the fact that each suddenly decided to accept the other's offer and in consequence my Father started driving his car forward and she started to step off the kerb and into the road in front of him. Taking evasive action, and doubtless with the drink somewhat dulling his ability to accurately judge exactly where he was and in which direction and at what speed he was travelling, my Father swerved the car to the right and in so doing avoided damaging the still-crossing-the-road woman. However, neither he nor his car was as fortunate for, with gathering speed, both shot down the sloping cobbled cartway and into the pond. As to the woman … Well, she disappeared into the night somewhere leaving my Father sitting semi-submerged, and by now wide awake, in his car suffering a badly cut bottom lip to mark where the car's steering wheel had, in the days before seat belts, impacted with my Father's face.

To say that the incident at the Thornton Heath pond was a 'one 'off' would be incorrect for nearby Mitcham also, in those days, had a pond laden with water the access into which was via a gently sloping cobbled cartway that had been put there for horses in days past. The circumstances of the Mitcham Pond incident are not clear in my mind, but the end result was the same, namely, my Father drove down the horse ramp into the Pond. The car's steering wheel seriously cut his lip.

Performing on stage, whilst somewhat of a novelty to me each time, was not my 'thing' whereas Scenery was and, indeed, remains very much 'my thing'; and so, when EA Sydney Beckwith, the Head Master of Haileybury's Junior School at Windsor, asked me in the year before I left the JS in 1957, if I would build a Proscenium Arch Stage within the School's then newly constructed gymnasium building I instantly said "Yes" even though I had neither any experience of building a Proscenium Arch Stage nor any real idea of how to actually go about it : But, as Beckwith doubtless well knew, my Father had a wealth of knowledge and experience of Proscenium Arch Stages : And so it was, of course, to him that I went for guidance. Thus one Sunday afternoon whilst on a 'day 'out' from the JS I was, whilst my Mother sat bored to tears nearby, given enthusiastic instruction on what to do and how to do it.

The White Hart at Sonning in Berkshire and its surrounding area was a lovely peaceful place to where we had gone on several previous occasions when my Parents had taken me out on a Sunday from school. Situated on one side of the River Thames The White Hart was 'counterbalanced' on the other side of The Thames by The French Fern Hotel. Between the two lay a bridge which gave easy access from the one to the other but, although I often went across the bridge and peered into the French Fern through some of its windows, I have never been inside The French Fern. But the walk over the bridge gave me the opportunity to look not only in each direction either side of the bridge at The Thames as it flowed quietly and calmly along its course and but also at a floating wooden pontoon/landing stage tethered to the riverbank alongside The White Hart, a pontoon/landing stage where on one hot sunny occasion, whilst attempting to, with a fishing-rod, catch fish, I fell asleep only to be awoken by the shouts of my Father as I, my fishless fishing-rod, and the now untethered floating pontoon/landing stage drifted slowly downstream. Some lads had, apparently, on seeing me fast asleep, deliberately untied the pontoon/landing stage doubtless in the hope not only that it would provide them with hilarious entertainment but also cause me to panic, dive fully clothed off the pontoon/landing stage, and desperately swim to the bank. But not only was the pontoon/landing stage not all that far from the bank but also the lads had left the pontoon/landing stage's ropes dangling not from the bank but from the pontoon/landing stage itself thereby enabling me to easily pull a rope 'on board' and then throw it as hard as I could onto the bank so that someone could pull me, my fishing rod, and the pontoon/landing stage back to the bank. I was thoroughly amused by the whole event, an attitude not, however, entirely shared by my Mother and Father.

One of the other entertaining memories that I have of The White Hart is of a caged parrot whose persistent conversation, even when its cage was covered thereby putting its mouthy occupant into darkness, was, to my Mother's horror and somewhat to my Father's amusement, liberally sprinkled with the phrase "F**k off", a phrase not previously known to me and certainly not explained to me by my Parents. Furthermore the word 'F**k' was, somewhat to my surprise, not contained within my school English dictionary thus causing its meaning to be completely denied to me until eventually one much-better-informed-than-I school colleague enlightened me as to its meaning; and even then, I now confess, I did not realise what it actually meant.

Another of the memories that I have of The White Hart at Sonning is of, when aged 9 or 10, cavorting down an adjacent steep hill on a homemade brakeless wooden scooter. When the rectangular wooden playpen, made by my Father, in which I, as a baby and very young child, had played had served its purpose my Father, as was often the practice in those days, did not throw it away but instead dismembered it in the belief that its parts might be of use in the future. Made of two 4-sided hinged beechwood frames, one at the top and one at the base, with several lengths of ½" [12½mm] hardwood dowelling running from top to bottom within each side, the dismembered playpen provided my Father several lengths of beech wood, umpteen lengths of dowelling, and some hinges. I had also, as a baby and very young child, had, likewise made for me by my Father, a truck in which, by means of using a piece of sash-cord as a sort of handle, I pulled all sorts of things around. When it was eventually dismembered it provided, for possible future use, a length of sash-cord, a piece of plywood which had been the truck's base, four lengths of timber which had been the truck's sides, and four metal rubber-tyred wheels and a screw for each wheel. Out of these various bits and pieces from my playpen and from my truck my Father, using also a substantial rectangular block of wood that he obtained from elsewhere, made me my wooden scooter. Towards the front of the block of wood he, as if making a tusk tenon joint, inserted a rectangular hole through the depth of the block. Then towards the end of one of the lengths of beech he drilled a hole of sufficient diameter to generously receive a piece of dowelling. Then from the outside of one side of the block of wood to the outside of the other side he drilled a hole of diameter to tightly receive a piece of dowelling thereby enabling, when the length of beech was inserted into the block's rectangular hole, a piece of dowelling to pass from the outside of one side of the block through the hole in the piece of beech and out through the other side of the block thus firmly securing the piece of beech thereby enabling it to act as the upright for a handle. Then, with me standing on the block of wood and positioning myself as if to operate my scooter, he determined the exact position in which it would be comfortable for me to hold a handle. Having marked the height he then cut off the surplus length of beech wood and then used some of that surplus to create a handle which he then, by means of glue and a fox-tail wedge joint, fixed onto the top of the upright. Then towards the front of the block he drilled a hole, of sufficient diameter to receive another piece of dowelling, through the block of wood and likewise did the same towards the back of the block of wood. Having inserted a piece of dowelling through each of the two holes he then, by means of inserting split pins through each of two holes drilled through each end of the protruding dowels, fixed the wheels onto the dowelling and then cut off the surplus dowelling : And, hey presto, I had a scooter which, by means of standing with one foot upon it and the other foot on the ground propelling it, enabled me to charge here, there, and everywhere upon the concrete driveway and footpaths at Highlands, steering being achieved by means of momentarily lifting the front wheels off the ground whilst at the same time pointing the thing in the new direction in which I wished it to go. But the steep hill at the side of The White Hart was something else for, the scooter having made its way to Sonning from Croydon in the boot of my Father's or my Mother's car, the hill enabled me, in those days when vehicular traffic upon such roads was somewhat of a rarity, to propel myself with ever-increasing speed from the top of the hill, down past The White Hart, and over the bridge to eventually come to a halt, with the assistance of my pushing foot now acting as a brake, outside The French Fern. Then back again, but walking this time, over the bridge and up the hill to start the venture all over again. All went well, very well, until the occasion when, my having just passed The White Hart and started the approach to go over the bridge, a car appeared coming over the bridge towards me its driver clearly intent on not stopping. Desperately, using my only means of braking, namely my foot against the surface of the road, I tried to stop but to no avail; and as the car, and its fist-waving-in-my-direction driver, continued past me I had no option but to leap off my scooter and crash headlong, my scooter still firmly held in one of my hands, into the weeds and other matter growing alongside the road. I was unhurt but shaken; and so my Father's reactions to this unfortunate incident were first to say "That's enough for to-day" and then to determine that next time, when we had returned to Sonning on another occasion, I went down the hill my scooter would have some form of brake fixed on it. Thus, when we next returned to Sonning and my scooter was produced from the boot of the car, it had upon its handle a wooden lever, with a spring attached, from which, via pulleys, two pieces of sash cord went one to a wooden block, with spring attached, sited in front of one rear wheel and the other to a wooden block, with spring attached, sited in front of the other rear wheel. Thus, having been ordered not to go so fast this time, the speeds of my next and subsequent journeys down the hill were superbly controlled by this simple piece of wooden mechanics. But by the time that I had been asked, in 1957, to build a Proscenium Arch stage my scooter had become a thing of the past.

My request of my Father as to how I, a 13-years old boy, should go about building a Proscenium Arch stage created much enthusiasm in him to teach me how to go about it and much enthusiasm in me to learn. I had, of course, warned him previously by means of a letter and thus he had come prepared not only with paper, pencils and a rubber but also with several models of Proscenium Arches : And so, whilst my Mother sat bored to tears by the occasion and with The White Hart's parrot every so often bellowing out his favourite phrase, the Teacher taught and the Student learnt : And the result, three or four weeks' later, was the construction - assisted by two school-friends allocated to me by the Head Master and encouraged by our Carpentry Master, Mr Smithers - of a purposely-designed, nominally by me but in reality by my Father, Proscenium Arch which, having been taken, section by section, into the gym from the School's well-equipped Carpentry Workshops, was, in part hung by ropes from iron trusses that supported the roof, erected and, using proper professional Theatre fittings such as cleats and plated rings kindly given by my enthusiastic Father, firmly positioned onto four rostra base units purchased for the occasion by the School.

When, some months later, I came to leave the School in favour of Haileybury's Senior School at Hertford Heath, Hertford my humble stage had done its job well and went on, I understand, to serve the School well for several years thereafter.

Despite my Mother's lack of enthusiasm for things Theatrical she did appear on television, the second time with me present in the Studio to watch her and her Lady Ratling friends each of whom, unlike my Mother, was a professional Performer. The Studio had been the historic Wood Green Empire Theatre, a theatre very well known to my Father as Brunskill and Loveday had built the scenery for well over 100 productions [*Merry Moments,* 1915 to *Seagulls over Sorrento,* 1954] staged there between its opening by its owner my Father's friend Sir Oswald Stoll, the Australian-born British theatre manager and the co-founder of the Stoll Moss Group theatre company. in 1912 until its conversion by Stoll Moss's Associated Television organisation into Britain's first commercial television studio in 1954. My Parents and I had already, earlier in the day, been to the Wood Green Empire to drop off my Mother so that she could join her Lady Ratling colleagues in order to rehearse the evening's Show. That evening, well in advance of the live transmission, my Father and I returned initially to join the invited Audience as they sat themselves down in the Theatre's Circle : But we soon found ourselves, doubtless because of my Father's 'standing' in the Theatre, invited to the Stalls where all the seating had been removed to accommodate the cameras and booms of this early Independent Television Studio. The year was 1957 and, except for the War years, television had been on the go in Britain since 1936; and so I suspect that this was by no means the first occasion that my Father had seen the inside of a Television Studio. Nevertheless, despite the sadness that he must have felt inside the former theatre which he knew so well, he seemed fascinated, but not as fascinated as I for, for this 13-years old on his first visit to a Television Studio, it was an absolute wonderland. In the area where once the Stalls had been there were Cameras here, Cameras there, a couple of wheeled trolleys with Microphones on long extending arms, large chunky cables lying all over the floor, and people, seemingly living an existence of organised chaos, everywhere. On the Stage people came and went doing this, doing that until eventually all seemed to come to order just before the House Tabs [curtains] closed isolating those on Stage and those Backstage from the now calming chaos in the Stalls and the quietening Audience in the Circle. As my Father and I stood alongside, what to me at the time seemed to be, an enormous contraption with a Camera and its operator at one end of it and two other men standing on a platform at the other end of it, with the House Lights still on a man came out in front of the Tabs and explained to all and sundry in front of the Tabs what was about to happen and what was intended to happen throughout the half-hour live black and white transmission that was soon to start. "Want to come up here with me ?" the Cameraman suddenly asked me.

"Yes," I replied.

"Up you come then. Be quick," he said as he gestured for me to get up behind him.

So, leaving my Father still standing alongside the, what I now know to be, Crane Camera, up I quickly climbed to be told by the Cameraman where to stand and to stay still and be quiet throughout the entire Show.

As the man who had come out in front of the Tabs finished walking down some steps in front of the Stage the House Lights dimmed almost to total darkness and, as they did so, the Cameraman, his Camera, and I suddenly went several feet [300mm] upwards away from the floor where, having stopped, we stayed for a minute or so. Then the Tabs opened and, midst the very bright Stage Lights, there on Stage, to a huge round of applause, was the Opening Chorus of The Grand Order of Lady Ratlings. What a wonderful time I had on that Camera. We went upwards, downwards, to the left, to the right, backwards, forwards, and finally, after the Tabs closed and the House Lights had come back on again, back down to the ground where, having climbed down and got off, I was reunited with my Father.

"Did you seen me ?" my Mother's voice suddenly asked.

"No. Why ? Have you been on ?" my Father replied.

Both he and I had been so engrossed in the activities of the Cameras and other items of Television paraphernalia that we had completely forgotten about her. It was a somewhat unpleasant drive back home to Croydon that night !!

My confidence in the building of the Junior School's Proscenium Arch stage was a far cry from the insecurity and lack of confidence that enveloped many an occasion in my early life at the JS for for many who are sent away to boarding school at the tender age of 8 or thereabouts the experiences of being torn from home and from life at home is traumatic and, for some, even barbaric. I suffered the former but fortunately, did not suffer the latter although I remember friends who did, some of whom throughout the entireties of their prep school boarding lives never really came to terms with it.

The first series of 'Letters home' that a lonely Newboy [as new arrivals were called] usually writes in such establishments - and in respect of which parents are warned by Head Teachers to expect and cautioned not to take too seriously - contain, as mine most certainly did, such tear-generating, in the writers and sometimes in the readers, phrases such as "I hate this place" and "Please, please, please, please, please come and take me home. Please". But, as one begins to make friends from within the seemingly vast ocean of unfamiliar faces amongst whom one is dramatically put, the fear gradually lessens and most, but not all, gradually find life to be a mix of seriousness, fear, mediocrity, and great fun. I certainly did.

My Mother, perhaps encouraged by her experiences aboard the 'banana boat' the SS Alca, always sent me to school each term armed with two or three large hands of green, very green bananas. Her theory was that as the weeks passed the bananas would ripen thereby enabling me to enjoy this, onetime very scarce, wondrous fruit in all its magnificence. The problems with my Mother's theory were that I, like most young boys, was none-too-keen to wait for a period of weeks whilst hands of bananas tried desperately to ripen, that I thus gave in to temptation and, as the weeks passed, ate them regardless of the fact that the skins were still green and their contents often hard if not very hard, and that I thus suffered many an upset stomach the excruciating pain of which I disguised by boldly announcing to all around me that my bananas were 'super'. However, I still remain very partial to bananas thus perhaps evidencing either that I am a slow learner or that I have a forgiving nature, at least where bananas are concerned !!

"Only common people from poor homes wear their pens and pencils in their outside top pocket" is a phrase that even to-day comes

to mind whenever I see someone with a pen, pencil, or even more in
the top outside pocket of his/her jacket or coat. Tables in the Dining
Hall at the JS were laid out in rows parallel to each other with the
Headmaster [known to us all as 'Becky'] and his Wife ['Mrs 'Becky'],
'accompanied by other teachers, sitting, overseeing us all, at one row
of tables at one, the top, end of the Dining Hall, Newboys sitting at
one, the bottom, row of tables at the other end of the Dining Hall, and
with the remainder of the boys sitting progressively, according to age
and length of time of incarceration within the School, at other tables
between the top row and the bottom row. In those far off days I was
very proud of the limited number of pens and pencils that I owned and
boldly displayed those with clips in the outside top pocket of my
jacket until on one occasion I heard the shrill voice of Mrs Beckwith
summoning me from my lowly position at the bottom end of the
Dining Hall to stand up and walk past the entirety of the 119 other
boys in order to "stand up straight" before her as she sat in her position
alongside her husband at the top table. Then I was made to further
suffer as she loudly announced to everyone present, and seemingly to
all the residents of Windsor as well, "Loveday, only poor people from
poor homes wear their pens and pencils in their outside top pocket.
Take them out *immediately*". Frightened, exceedingly humbled, and
very, very embarrassed I immediately started to do as I was told and
in so doing added to my fear and embarrassment first by dropping,
out of my hand, a couple of my pens onto the floor causing muffled
guffaws of tittering laughter to erupt throughout the entirety of the
Dining Hall and then, as I quickly bent down to pick them up, by
allowing the remainder of the pens and pencils to cascade downwards
all over the place on the floor. As the muffled guffawing tittering
laughter exploded into screams of delight the stern voice of Sydney
Beckwith loudly intervened with the one simple but very effective

commanding word "*SILENCE !!".* "I finished picking up my beloved, but now completely disgraced, collection of pens and pencils and, without a sound or even a muted chirp from anybody, turned and wobbled my way back to my seat at the lowly end of the Hall.

Part of 1954 Junior School photograph. Mr Beckwith and his Wife are in the middle. I am in the top row with pen shoved into my pullover. My Housemaster, DA Blundell is second from right of Mrs Beckwith, and Miss Shaw is next to DA Blundell. Mr O'Hara is next-but-one to Mr Beckwith. Matron is next-but-one to Mr O'Hara, and Mr Boardman is next-but-one to Matron. Altogether, a very happy school.

The Dining Hall generated many happy memories as well. For instance, Mr Webb, the Chef, ably assisted by his wife and visually assisted by his delightful and shapely teenage daughter, Carol, was always kind and considerate to us; and when the Webb Family left for pastures elsewhere there was much sadness felt by all of us. But Mr Webb's replacement as Chef by a Mr Edwards soon made us forget Mr and Mrs Webb if not also the attractive Carol, for the food served up by Mr Edwards was exquisite. Gone were the days of such as plain boiled potatoes : Instead piped creamed potatoes were the order of the day as were buttered carrots and other goodies. But Mr Edwards's reign, probably intended to be of a permanent nature, ceased after only one term. Whether or not his wondrous menus were of a nature that might possibly have bankrupted the JS I have no idea but back came the Webbs, and the delicious Carol !!

Mrs Higgins, a somewhat plump and seemingly, to us young boys at least, elderly 'kitchen lady' 'wot 'did' the washing-up [there were no machines 'wot did' the dishes in those days] and other kitchen chores was a lovely character, full of good humour and, as with the Webbs, kindness to us boys. I have never ever been keen to involve myself in washing dishes, but many a time my friend Henry Barnett and I voluntarily stood on a duckboard and assisted the struggling Mrs Higgins as she, helped by two very large white china-clay 'belfast' sinks, fought her way through the manual washing of mountain-sized piles of crockery and cutlery and of mammoth-sized pots and pans and so forth. But, I now confess, Henry and I, as much as we enjoyed the humour and company of this splendid woman, were not really as altruistic as any observer might have thought. No, in reality not only was helping Mrs Higgins an ideal way of gaining praise and admiration but also it was a very good way of getting out of having to sit through an hour or so's worth of reading, in silence, in lessons called Prep.

Henry Barnett and I were good friends both at the JS and later at Haileybury's Senior School. Jewish, during one term he invited me to spend a Saturday night and Sunday at his home in Regents Park in London. Driven there from Windsor by his Father, we entered the exclusive, and ostensibly very expensive, flat in which he and his Parents lived by means of a lift which rose directly from the main entrance foyer of the block in which the flat was sited to the very heart of the Barnett's flat itself. Henry and I spent much of our time within the flat playing with his electric train set. Having been lectured by my

Mother to "Do as you are told", "Do nothing which might cause offence", "Remember that they are Jewish and do not necessarily eat the same types of food as we do", "Be on your best behaviour", and so on, and so on, when it came to mealtimes at the Barnett's the last thing that I wanted to do was cause offence in any way : And so, having been presented by Mrs Barnett with a large slice of the first genuinely Jewish cheesecake that I had ever come across, I, despite its horrendously strong and off-putting cheese flavour, painfully tucked into it whilst at the same time mustering sufficient willpower to express delight and great enjoyment. "Another slice," asked Mrs Barnett, obviously pleased that I appeared to have thoroughly enjoyed the first slice. "Yes, please," I replied with theatrical enthusiasm : And, having eaten that second slice with the same theatrical expressions of delight and enjoyment, I was offered another and then, having eaten that, another, and then another. It was, for me, sheer and utter agony but, as my Mother had commanded me, I ensured that I did nothing that might cause my very kind Jewish hosts any offence. Thus I was surprised when, sometime later when back at school and attending some gathering to which all Parents had been invited, I overheard Mrs Barnett saying to my Mother "Edwin certainly seemed to enjoy himself. But, my God, *doesn't he eat !!".*" "So much for painful self-sacrifice," I thought.

Sadly, Henry, on one occasion, as a result of his Family's kind generosity to the JS's annual Guy Fawkes' Firework Display, unfortunately suffered a major embarrassment. His Family had personally bought and donated a large quantity of the biggest firework rockets that any of us had ever seen; and, well in advance of the occasion, Henry had gone out of his way to acquaint most of us with his Family's very generous gift. In those days 'Health and Safety' did not pervade Society to anything like the extent that it does nowadays.

No, in those days 'commonsense' ruled : And so the intended Firework Display had been positioned well beyond the reach of all of us boys; and, at the appointed time, it was, by selected members of the School's Staff, gotten under way. Rockets, not those gifted by Henry's Family, were set off, ignited Catherine Wheels spun, Bangers banged, and the whole thing, despite a slight drizzle throughout, went very well indeed. At least it did until the eagerly awaited Barnett family-funded climax came. Fizzle and phutt went the first monster rocket. Fizzle and phutt went the second monster rocket, and the third, and the fourth, and the fifth : And, as each drizzle-soaked monster rocket decided that fizzle and phutt was all that it was going do, expectation and excitement amongst us boys turned to laughter and ridicule and more and more laughter and more and more ridicule. Poor Henry !! Schoolboys can be the cruellest of people, even to their mates.

Just prior to going back to school at the start of one term my Father introduced me to two toys of his own era as a child, toys which he thought might be of 'entertainment value' for me at school. One of the toys consisted of a 3 inches [75mm] or so piece of ½ inch [12.5mm] wooden dowelling cut in half down the entirety of its length with the two halves being then bound to-gether by cotton thread with a another piece of cotton thread dangling from a hole drilled through the side of one of the halves of dowelling at a position just below the middle of its length. Apparently it was a type of toy much in use - and, so my Father said, much 'enjoyed' - during my Father's childhood. I was invited by my Father, as he firmly held his reproduction of his childhood toy upright in one of his hands whilst holding the dangling bit of cotton thread in his other hand, to place a finger on its top end to experience "a mild electric shock". Naïvely I did exactly as invited. Then my Father suddenly pulled the dangling bit of cotton thread and, out of the top end of the dowelling, shot the very sharp point of a sewing needle straight into my innocently-waiting finger. Electric shock, no. But a shock, hell yes, as the end of that damned needle was swiftly fired straight into my finger. "Yeeoow," I screamed. I took the 'toy' back to school but never did pluck up sufficient courage to inflict it on anyone despite the fact that it had, apparently, once been a much enjoyed piece of childhood entertainment !!

I did however enjoy the other 'toy' "given to me by my Father at the start of that term; and I did most certainly did use it when back at school, but only once for it was straightaway confiscated. What was it ? Well, it was a large roll of 1 inch [25mm] wide brown sticky paper on which, after it had been pushed up into a conical shape, one sat so that, as it was slowly forced by one's weight back into its original roll shape, it let out an excruciating sound akin to the sound of a person very loudly breaking wind for a continuous period of 10 seconds or so. Mrs Cousins, bless her, did not appear, publicly at least, to appreciate its humour. Hence its immediate confiscation only part way through its glorious sound-effect performance.

The financial cost to the United Kingdom of the Second World War had been enormous, an enormity aggravated by the fact that the UK owed considerable sums of moneys to the United States, debts which the US insisted that the UK must repay thus causing UK Citizens to have to suffer Food Rationing for many years subsequent to the ending of hostilities. One of the elements of Food Rationing still in existence in my early years at the JS was the rationing of sweets thereby causing us boys to only be allowed to have two 6d [2½ pence] bars of chocolate sweets each week. But my Father, with his usual Theatrical Scenery builder's ingenuity, had a way of overcoming that. As he had often to do for many Shows over many years, he carved out the insides of several books thereby leaving the two covers, the spine, ten or so complete pages at the start of the book, and nothing but the outside edges of all the other pages, each glued to its neighbours, with the final page glued to the back cover. Thus, when observed by any unknowing person, the book looked like a pucka book and when opened, provided that one did not try to open too many pages, also looked like a pucka book. So, just before the start of each term, I was given several largish volumes of these wonderful 'hidden box' devices each of which had been stuffed full of chocolate bars. Thus at least for the first few weeks of each term I could happily indulge myself with quantities of chocolate bars well beyond the quota allowed to me by Haileybury Junior School and Her Majesty's Government.

Haileybury Junior School has had its reasonable share of boys who subsequently became, in adult life, well-known personalities. One was the great car racing-driver Stirling Moss. Born in 1929, he had left the JS and become famous long before my arrival there : But one of our teachers, Miss Elizabeth Shaw, as Stirling Moss [subsequently, in the year 2000, to become Sir Stirling Moss] became more and more famous [he won many races in the 1950s including the British Grand Prix in both 1955 and 1957 before retiring after a crash at Goodwood in 1962 to become a Broadcaster and Journalist (although he returned to the race track in 1980 to race saloon cars)], would regale us boys with stories of what a 'pain-in-the-neck' he was throughout the years that she had taught him. The more his fame increased the greater the information of how bad he had behaved at school was told to us by Miss Shaw. Imagine my surprise therefore when, some years after I had left the JS, Miss Shaw appeared on a *This is Your Life* BBC Television Show which paid tribute to some of the good and to some of the great of the time. The occasion for this episode of the *This is Your Life* Show was a tribute to the achievements of Stirling Moss : And, lo and behold, there was Miss

Shaw, whose lack of enthusiasm for Stirling Moss whilst he had been at the JS had been made known to us with considerable relish, now praising the great man with such flattering phrases as "He was an excellent child when he was at school". "What a hypocrite !!" I thought.

Miss Sparrow was the School's Secretary 'bird'. 'An efficient youngish woman, we often saw her flitting here and there but we never really spoke with or personally encountered her. The same can not be said of the pipe-smoking stern and somewhat severe Mathematics Teacher, Mr O'Hara, whose cloak of sternness and severity would, in the last days of each term, suddenly disappear to reveal, as he read to us stories from the pen of the great Rudyard Kipling, a very kind and gentle side to his personality. O'Hara ['Buzzard' as we called him] was, without doubt, a man much committed to the well-being and good education of us all and totally committed to the well-being of Haileybury Junior School. Also, he was given to conscientiously maintaining, within the school grounds, various meteorological devices the readings on which he would faithfully each day both record and pass on to the Meteorological Office to assist in the forecasting of the Nation's weather. Buzzard, like many of the School's teaching and non-teaching employees, served the school and its many hundreds of passing-through pupils well, very well, for many, many years.

We boys were divided into four Houses - Athlone House, whose straight-ended tie was green; Dewar House, whose straight-ended tie was blue; Alexander House, whose straight-ended tie was red; and Goodhart House, whose straight-ended tie was yellowy-gold. I was in Athlone House whose Housemaster was DA Blundell. His principal nicknames were, needless-to-say, 'DAB' and 'Flatfish'. A teacher of

English, DAB not only taught me well but also, like all the Teachers, gave great encouragement to us all. Of course, he and I did not always see eye-to-eye : In fact, we often did not see eye-to-eye at all; and indeed on one occasion I was so incensed by him that, in my ignorance of my Father being then in his late 70s, I threatened that my Father would come to the School and beat him up. This bold challenge that I volunteered my Father for resulted in my Father being swiftly informed of the incident by the Headmaster and, at the Headmaster's request, attending the School to take part in my receiving a very severe telling-off by both the Headmaster and my Father !!

Of course there were some Teachers whose life-span at the JS was very short. One such character was a Mr Wilson. Whether or not his stay was intended to be short I do not know, but this man, with an often snifflely 'runny' nose, was on many occasion an item of ridicule for many of us. His greatest 'disgrace', insofar as we boys were concerned, came when one morning, having awoken and gotten out of bed, many of us looked out of our dormitory windows to see his underpants, vests, socks, and other garments dangling merrily on a high telephone line that ran from one school building across a yard to another school building. How anyone ever managed to get them there was beyond me, but get them there they did; and what hilarious entertainment, at least for us boys, they caused !!

Another teacher whose stay at the JS was relatively short was Mr Seckleman who was much respected by most, if not all, of us. I had, during one School Holiday, been on holiday at Lake Konstanz [Constance] in Germany and been fascinated by the German language. We were taught both Latin and French at the JS but not German but, having got to know that Mr Seckleman was a fluent German speaker, I, with hardly any persuasion needed, got him to agree to teach me some German. Sadly he left the JS shortly thereafter but I still remember, perhaps as a result of the high regard that I had for him, at least some of the German that he taught me : Indeed, my ability to count from 1 to 20 in German is still, even to-day, quicker than my ability to count from 1 to 20 in English. In those days, despite the facts that the Second World War had ended several years earlier and that we boys did not really know that much either about the War or about Germany and Germans, there existed, for us boys, a fascination about Germany and the Second World War. Indeed, on many an occasion during our 'break' times, as far as we were concerned the War was still on and the Germans were still 'the 'enemy' and therefore we would fight each other, some of us saying that we were British and some of us saying that we were Germans. To assist us in our limited knowledge of military equipment and of what British and German troops looked like not only did the School's wooden-panelled Library carry many large magnificently bound pictorial volumes dedicated to the First World War and to the Second World War but also many of us regularly read pictorial 1950s-published magazines, intended for boys such as us, featuring British soldiers knocking the hell out of German soldiers. But Mr Seckleman had something different : He had several books filled with genuine pictures of the horrors of the Second World War and in particular of the revoltingly barbaric horrors of German Concentration Camps. True, Concentration Camps had been invented by the British during the earlier South African Boer War, but their purpose and operation were far removed from the appalling gruesomeness and ill-treatment meted out by the Germans and their Allies within their Concentration Camps to the Jews, Gipsies, Russians, and others during the Second World War. The pictures of extreme and unbelievable cruelty within Mr Seckleman's books have made a lasting impression certainly upon me and doubtless upon many of my school chums who were fortunate to have been given access to them by Mr Seckleman, a man whose disgust at what had happened in the German Concentration Camps was very evident to us all.

The memories of other Teachers remain very much within my mind. Michael Francis Sandham [himself a former pupil of the Imperial Service College and its Junior School] taught me much both about the geography of, and the lifestyles within, the United Kingdom and also about the geography of the World as a whole and about the lifestyles of many of the World's peoples. But Mr Sandham also played a major part in one of my principal 'social' "activities, the running of the School's branch of the Peoples' Dispensary for Sick Animals [PDSA]. It was already in existence when I got involved with it, but shortly after I got roped in I became its Chairman and Michael Sandham its President; and it, until the very sad and very sudden ending of its Haileybury and Imperial Service College's Junior School's branch, played a major part in the latter days of my life at the JS. Every day we 120 boys each received - and had to drink, accompanied by having to eat a slice of bread and dripping or a slice of bread and Bovril - a 1/3rd pint[0.189 litre]-sized glass bottleful of milk. Each bottle was capped by a top made of silver tinfoil; and each top of silver tinfoil was, after the milk was drunk, collected by a gaggle of helpers, each helper having been enrolled, by means of filling-in and signing a registration form, as a PDSA 'Busy Bee'. In return for enrolling as a 'Busy Bee' each 'Busy Bee' was given, to proudly wear, a yellow badge with a picture of a bee boldly printed in black on it. When collected, each day the tops were taken to the double row of wash-hand basins sited near to Dick's boiler room. Once delivered there another band of enrolled 'Busy Bee' helpers would, with great dedication, thoroughly wash them before placing them into large circular wooden containers in which every day would also be placed any silver foil wrapper, from chocolate bars, and even from the cigarette packets discarded by those of our Teachers who smoked cigarettes, that could be obtained. I, as Chairman, organised the whole operation, including the issuing of forms and 'Busy Bee' badges, from an Office and a desk and chair situated in a damp brick-constructed shed, loaned to me by the School for the purpose, that was sited alongside a covered walkway that went from a main classroom building to the School's gymnasium. I think that, given that our operation was motivated solely by the raising of funds for genuine charitable purposes, most, if not all, of us were very committed and thoroughly enjoyed ourselves. We felt as if we were truly doing something positive and very worthwhile. But sadly our commitment seemed not to be appreciated by the Bromley Branch of the PDSA to which, during one School Holiday, my Father and I travelled, my Father having first telephoned the PDSA at Bromley to say that we would be coming, from Croydon, to deliver the four barrels of silver paper and silver foil that so many of us, including both teaching and non-teaching Staff, at the JS had dedicated ourselves to collecting. With my Father and I each carrying one of the barrels we, with me full of excitement, entered the 'hallowed' PDSA premises, my Father announcing to the woman behind the desk who we were and the purpose of our visit. After all these years I can, even now, still see that woman clearly as she, hardly looking towards us, dismissively said "Put them down there" whilst raising an arm to point to an empty area of the floor. "Pardon ?" said my Father somewhat disgusted at the almost totally unconcerned reception given to us. "Put them down there," repeated the woman. "But 120 boys have worked damned hard to collect all this silver paper and all that you can say is 'Put them down there' ," stated my now somewhat annoyed Father. "Well, thank you," added the woman. So, we put them down where instructed and then went out and returned with the other two barrels which we also put down : And that was it, for the woman spoke not another word - Not a word of acknowledgement, not a word of gratitude, nothing. My Father was furious, and I was so … Well, disappointed. We walked out, and I took off my, up until then, beloved 'Busy Bee' badge and threw it away. Normally my Father would have reprimanded me for such an action, but he said nothing, absolutely nothing. We went back into the car and drove back home. On returning to the JS at the start of the next term I had to suffer the embarrassment of telling Michael Sandham, our President who had done so much to encourage everyone within the School to take part, what had happened. He in turn, possibly to save me any further embarrassment, told the boys; and the whole undertaking was wound-up there and then. Many of us were not only very sad but also very annoyed at the lack of appreciation and lack of gratitude shewn by the PDSA's Bromley representative to my Father and me and thus to all those back at Haileybury Junior School who had, on behalf of the Peoples' Dispensary for Sick Animals, worked so dedicatedly to collect so much silver foil and silver paper. I can honestly say that even after the passing of over 50 years I still regard the dismissive attitude of that woman representative of the PDSA as being unforgivable.

Each year most UK Private Schools, if not most UK schools, have an annual photograph taken. I had to suffer them first at St John's School and then at Cumnor House School; and then, in 1952, the annual ritual, for me, commenced at Haileybury Junior School. However I have to say that, whereas over the intervening years I have occasionally glanced at those photographs with thoughts of "It's about time that I threw them away", I am now grateful to them for, as I look at them nowadays, they bring to the fore memories of people to whom, directly or indirectly, I owe much. For instance, looking, as I am now doing, at that July 1954 Haileybury Junior School photograph [see above] there, in the middle of the photograph, sits my old, now long deceased, Head Master, Sydney Beckwith; and to his right sits his Wife; and two persons to her right sits my old Housemaster, DA Blundell; and next to DAB sits Miss Shaw; and two persons to her right sits my old History teacher, Mr D Gillies-Reyburn; and four persons to his right sits Mr Seckleman. As I look two persons to Becky's left there sits the old Buzzard, Mr O'Hara; and two persons to his left sits Matron; and two persons to her left sits Mr Boardman; and six persons to his left sits Mr Sandham; and two persons to his left sits the School's very own Secretary 'bird', Miss Sparrow [Yes, that was her actual name !!]. The passing of the years have made each of these people now look ... Well, much younger and much less authoritarian than each ever did whilst I was at the JS : But, of course, the little boy who then sat whilst the 'school' photographer, hidden under a dark material cover attached to his camera, took his photograph is, and looks, to-day, as he types this story, now much older, and perhaps far more authoritarian, than he looked on that far-off day back in 1954.

It would be impossible for me to write this story had I, not a respect for, and an enjoyment of, History; and it is to Mr Gillies-Reyburn [himself a former pupil at the Imperial Service College and its Junior School] that I owe that respect for, and enjoyment of, History. For many years, as with many children, it was a subject which bored me stiff. So, why the change ? Well, one day we ten or so boys of his Class were all sitting each on a chair within two rows of chairs, each row sited alongside one side of a group of large tables that had been pushed to-gether to form one long table. At one end of the long table stood William Donald Gillies-Reyburn lecturing us on the 1746 Battle of Culloden, a vicious clash between - under the command of William Augustus, Duke of Cumberland ("Butcher" Cumberland) - those who supported King George II and the British Government (who won) and - under the command of Prince Charles Edward Stuart ("Bonnie Prince Charlie, the Young Pretender") - those who supported Bonnie Prince Charlie and the Jacobites (who lost). Suddenly, as if being taken over by the Battle itself, this largish solidly-built man let out a shrieking yell and, violently wielding an imaginary Highlander's claymore sword, in, what seemed to almost be, one effortless move he leapt from the floor onto the table and then, in a wonderful series of claymore-slashing strides, went between us from one end of the group of tables to the other end of the group of tables and then back again, and then, seemingly effortlessly again, jumped down back onto the floor. To this 12-years old sitting third down on the right from whence Gillies-Reyburn had made his shrieking claymore-wielding leap upon the table History, suddenly, had meaning, real live meaning. To Gillies-Reyburn I am also grateful for another piece of sustenance, this time of the liquid food variety. He was a fond drinker of chicory-enhanced coffee which he, or his Wife, used to purchase in powder form in small round containers. I had never heard of the stuff until one day, on seeing a couple of his discarded containers, I asked him about it and was informed that chicory, when ground, was often blended with coffee. We boys were strictly controlled insofar as our food and liquid intakes were concerned, but his suggestion was that next time he would leave a wee bit of chicory coffee in its container before discarding it and that he would discard it in a place where it would be accessible to me. This he did thereby enabling me, by means of adding a small quantity of cold water to the container's remaining contents and then applying heat under the can from some small pieces of wood that I managed to set alight, to taste it. I thoroughly enjoyed it; and the ritual of his leaving his discarded containers for my collection was repeated time and again. How he knew that I had the means to heat the cans I do not know except that I suspect that he knew of the cigarette-producing undertaking that I had once operated in the copse that was sited alongside the School's main driveway, an undertaking that caused me much enjoyment until the School's Staff, in their wisdom, decided to move in and close down the entire operation. Simply described, I had several boys collecting, for a fee, oak tree leaves and grass from within the copse. These they would deliver to me and a colleague, usually Henry Barnett or Roger James Crisfield [later to become a Doctor of Medicine and an Orthopaedic Surgeon], as we sat in a dugout that we had constructed approximately in the middle of the copse, a dugout that was accessed, and hidden, by means of a bush that was capable of being bent just sufficiently to allow a boy-sized person to squeeze by. Within the dugout we first shredded the oak leaves and then lay the shredded leaves and grass out to dry until the next day when we blended the leaves and grass to-gether before, armed with small hand-held Rizla cigarette-rolling machines and Rizla cigarette papers, we rolled the blended leaves and grass so that they became cigarettes, trimmed off the ends of the leaves and grass that projected from the ends of the rolled paper, our sometimes having also inserted a filter tip within one end of a cigarette paper before we rolled it, and then we passed the finished items on to some other boys who, taking a financial percentage for their efforts, sold them for us. Suddenly, though always half-suspected, a gaggle of Teachers arrived and, holding hands, walked through the entirety of the copse rounding up everyone involved in the enterprise, everyone that is except yours truly and my dugout colleague. I recall nothing more about that day except that, as we all sat at Supper that evening, Beckwith, having brought us all to silence, rose to make "a very important announcement". After a very long theatrical pause, a pause which certainly engendered a considerable fear of expulsion from School in me if not in many of us miscreants present at Supper that evening, he simply said that cigarette production had ceased and would not re-start. I could never understand why no punishment whatsoever was ever meted out - For use of the 'cane', that most feared of all punishments then in use within private schools, was a practice not entirely unfamiliar to Becky. Indeed, daily every time that we boys filed passed the School Office en route to the Dining Room for Breakfast, Luncheon, or Dinner we could not help but see, standing against the architrave to one side of the School's Office door, a cylindrical clay drainpipe tube almost stuffed full with a selection of the wretched things. Each had its own reputation : For it was said by those 'experts' who had suffered an application of four or six strokes upon the backside, by those pseudo 'experts' who knew someone who had suffered such an application, and even by those pseudo pseudo 'experts' who knew someone who knew someone who had suffered such an application [1] that the cane with no tape or no split was only mildly painful, [2] that the cane that was bound with two bands of tape at its bum-thrashing end was more painful; [3] that the cane that was bound only with one band of tape thereby leaving a substantially exposed bum-thrashing split end was bloody painful; and [4] that the cane that had no band of tape whatsoever on its well-split bum-thrashing end not only was bloody painful but also was so blood-extracting that any recipient of its applications could hardly sit down for a week. Rarely was a boy in fact ever caned for just the sight of those otherwise innocent pieces of wood mustered to-gether in their strategically-positioned cylindrical tube coupled with the knowledge that Beckwith did occasionally use the feared things was usually all

that was needed to keep us boys under, at least reasonable, control :
And I still count myself very lucky, very lucky indeed, that the
application of even one of them onto my backside never took place.
But I did know some boys who did experience receiving either "Six
of the best !!" or even just "Four of the best !!", and some of them
cried on and off for hours thereafter. Would I support the return of
caning [or, in Scotland, the tawse] into schools nowadays ? My
unhesitating answer, given that I believe that schools fail in their duty
to educate if they expel or exclude erring pupils, is "Yes, provided it
is applied only to those able to receive it and provided that it is applied
only very rarely and only as a last resort" : For, although I still cringe
at the thought of caning, my respect for the threat of caning as a
deterrent is considerable.

The neatly-moustachioed RJ Boardman I remember not only as a
man who set an example by always being, at least whenever we boys
saw him, smartly dressed but also as a man whom we boys rarely saw
without a flower set in a holder inserted in a button-hole in a blazer
or a jacket. He had, I believe, served in the Royal Air Force during
the Second World War and his attitude, at least to us boys, was always
akin to that of how many of us believed that the demeanour of an RAF
Officer should be. Always firm but fair with, and respectful of, us
boys he demanded of us politeness and a bearing in stature to match
his own.

A more elderly teacher whom I remember well was CF Simkins,
a resident at No.14 The Cloisters, Windsor Castle who, occasionally
if not more often, played the organ in the Castle's St George's Chapel,
a Royal Chapel of worship founded by King Edward III in 1338, re-
built by King Edward IV in 1475, substantially altered during the
reign of Queen Victoria, and famous to-day as being The Chapel of

the Most Noble Order of the Garter, an English Medieval Order of Chivalry within the gift, solely, of the British Monarch and which ranks above all other English and Welsh honours. Simpkins taught me Latin and Scripture. But I remember and respect him best of all for his enabling me to often, from when I became a seniorish pupil at the JS, assist him in his coaching and umpiring of cricket games for junior pupils within the School. I always enjoyed playing cricket, especially in the position of wicket-keeper; but ever since I can remember I have been burdened by hay-fever, a seemingly very rare affliction in those far-off days but nowadays - due, I believe, to the rapid introduction of so many chemicals into the food chain - so common that those who do not, in some way, suffer from it are becoming the rarities. So bad did I suffer from it that regularly, whilst keeping wicket, I would have to stop the bowler in his run-up, then take off my wicket-keeper's gloves, then take off [if I was wearing them] my inner gloves, then get my handkerchief out of a pocket within my white cricketing trousers, then wipe my eyes before going through the whole procedure in reverse prior to allowing the bowler to continue. It was, to say the least, embarrassing to me and, no doubt, highly annoying to everyone else. Indeed, I received little or no sympathy whatsoever from my peers who, boys being boys, treated me as if I was blubbering for no reason whatsoever and thus, at times, deserving of nothing but contempt. Hence my request of Mr Simkins to be allowed to assist him in his coaching and umpiring of those less senior than I. Simpkins was, at least to me and to those juniors for whose cricket he was responsible, a kindly man. Some years after I had left the JS and become a Pupil at the Senior School - and using, as an excuse, the enquiring as to the whereabouts of some Theatrical canvas that I had left at the JS - I wrote to him, and he, in his beautifully-crafted handwriting, not only replied to my humble letter-writing effort but also, within his letter, frankly confessed to me that Teachers, even in the Private Sector, sometimes find school life to be very boring . *If only I had known of that fact when at the JS* !!

Some of the unsung personalities of schools, whether the schools be in the Private Sector or in the Public/State Sector, are those characters who provide the ancillary education. I still remember very clearly two of those who provided such ancillary education at the JS. One was an ancient [Well, he seemed ancient to me at the time] teacher of 'the piano'. My Father - who, despite being the son of a Piano Tuner, could not play the piano - had bought me a secondhand baby grand piano so that I, hopefully, would learn to play it.

So, lessons were arranged [and doubtless paid for by my Father as an 'extra'] and at appointed times I would walk from the main School buildings, across a cricket field, through the long grass which bounded the field and in which we boys were occasionally 'fortunate' enough to find snakes with which to frighten each other, and out of the JS's ground immediately into the back garden of the ancient Piano Teacher's house, and thence into the old man's house where I would be seated on his piano stool and made to suffer his, what I considered to be, grumpy piano lessons. I still have my piano but regrettably I have never learnt to play it. The reasons for my non-playing capabilities are, I think, a combination of the old man's exceedingly boring and grumpy lessons and the fact that, whereas, as with most pianos, my piano has two foot pedals, his piano had three foot pedals thereby causing me, who could not cope even with two pedals, to be at a complete loss as to what to do with my feet. The other ancillary education provider whom I remember well was the large solid character who regularly came to the JS to teach Boxing. I have always enjoyed watching 'good' Boxing matches. To me, for instance,

Cassius Marcellus Clay/Muhammad Ali, a US born World Heavyweight Champion, was, and still remains, the greatest and most entertaining of many great heavyweight Boxers. But the, subsequent ending of his Boxing career - due to Parkinson's Syndrome [Parkinsonism] caused by the many impacts of very hard punches to his head - of Muhammad Ali illustrates what I, even as a child at the JS long before Ali ever became World Champion, have always feared about Boxing, namely the damage that can be inadvertently inflicted to the brain of one Boxer by another. I can not now recall the name of the gentle giant who came regularly to the JS to teach us boys how to box but I can recall his genuine understanding of my concern about his beloved sport. I always helped him out in any way that I could and he always encouraged me to do so but he never insisted that, other than to generally spar around, I take part in a serious Boxing match. I learned of his death, only a few years after I had left the JS, with much regret.

To believe from my reluctance to box that I was a meek and mild lad would be wrong, for, although I have never liked to box, I often enjoyed a fight and, even to-day, I will defend myself - and any other person who, in my opinion, genuinely deserves to receive what humble assistance I am able to give - with energy but not, if I can help it, with violence. As was perhaps evidenced immediately following the showing, at Haileybury Junior School, of an Errol Flynn film, had I been alive in the 17th century in the days when buccaneering was all the rage I might well have lived, at least until middle-age started to descend upon me, the lifestyle of a buccaneer. I can not now recall the title of the film but I remember well this famed Australian-born Actor as, on screen, he valiantly fought his way, cutlass in hand, through riggings and ropes to ward off invaders and defend his ship. Eagerly we boys had seated ourselves in the School's gym to watch the film and our eagerness was so well satisfied that when we afterwards returned to our classrooms most, if not every one of us, had, in our own minds, each become a swashbuckling Errol Flynn. Perhaps that dark exciting evening I went a wee bit too far for, having, in one of the classrooms that was linked to two others by width-of-room sliding doors that had been fully opened, jumped onto a table with my imaginary cutlass in hand, I launched myself towards the nearest dangling 'rope' intending to use it as a means to propel myself several feet through the air in order to engage in a fight with yet another Errol Flynn coming, unassisted by any form of rope, in the opposite direction towards me. The trouble was that my 'rope' was in reality the dangling flex of a pendant light-fitting which, upon my grabbing hold of it, released itself out of the ceiling-rose into which it had been attached and, accompanied by a very bright whitish/blue flash, in so doing threw the entire block of six classrooms into instant darkness. Suddenly every Errol Flynn, including yours truly, lost every element of swashbuckling courage and immediately ceased to be Errol Flynn as, in total darkness, panic overwhelmed each and everyone of us. I still count myself lucky not only that not one of my former Errol Flynn colleagues ever indicated in any way the former Errol Flynn responsible for the malfunction of the Classroom block's 20th century lighting system but also that the only punishment meted out was that the whole shipload of us was ordered to go immediately to bed thus causing us to that night avoid the otherwise nightly routine of having to say 'Prayers' just before departing for our dormitories. 'Prayers' was a nightly ritual which I usually not only took very seriously but also enjoyed. Our having been mustered together on the ground-floor of the Form Room block a Master would come, stand behind a Teacher's desk sited on a plinth, order that we all be silent, and then, after a pause to enable complete silence to be almost instantly achieved launch in to the first of three Christian Prayers. Those amongst us who were not Christians, namely the handful of our colleagues who were Jewish, had to attend and remain silent throughout but, their not being Christians, were required neither to bow their heads nor to recite, as we Christians were required to do, each of the three Prayers of which 'The Lord's Prayer' was always one. [Having, at the JS, eventually reached the age at which I was old enough to understand what I was saying when reciting 'The Lord's Prayer' I began to feel, and to this day still do feel, that that part which says "Forgive us our trespasses as we forgive those who trespass against us" should say "Forgive us our trespasses as we *should* forgive those who trespass against us".]

Yo-Yos - a trade name for small toys consisting of two wheels rigidly fixed to an axle around which a piece of string could be wound thereby enabling the Yo-Yo to be forcefully manoeuvred, whilst spinning furiously, backwards and forwards at some distance from the operatives to whose hands the strings are attached - were very much in vogue in those days. The normal length of a Yo-Yo string was about a metre but I was fortunate in that my Father had provided me with a considerable quantity of very strong waxed thread used by Theatrical Scenery makers for stitching lengths of canvas to-gether. By intertwining two lengths of this thread I was enabled to produce Yo-Yo 'strings' of several metres in length. However projecting a spinning Yo-Yo in the normal way using such a 'string' is impossible not only because of the limited space usually available to the operative but also because of the considerable force required by the operative to recover the spinning Yo-Yo back into his hand once the Yo-Yo had travelled to the string's maximum length. But leaning out of a first-floor window made the task possible; and what better 'fun' therefore than to lean out of a first-floor window and to project one's spinning Yo-Yo down towards some unfortunate boy who happened to be leaning out of a corresponding ground-floor window ? Needless to say, the supply of targets soon dried up as leaning out of ground-floor windows became a risk not worth taking; but the competitive projecting of very long-stringed Yo-Yos from first-floor windows continued for quite a while until eventually most, if not all, of us got fed up with Yo-Yoing and turned our attentions and energies to other things.

Roller-skating was another enjoyable pastime and one to which Becky gave us his full support for, throughout many a mid-morning half-hour [11am to 11.30am] break, we were given unrestricted use of the large tarmac area in front of the School's main entrance. Many boys were given roller-skates by their Parents but sadly my Mother, in her usual very restrictive and financially mean attitude towards me where toys and other enjoyable items were concerned, flatly refused to allow me to have a pair of my own skates. Thus I had to rely upon the generosity of others; but it was a generosity often provided and thus I was able to enjoy a considerable amount of roller-skating, although not as much as I could have done had I been provided with my own skates !!

To be fair to my Mother I must mention that she and my Father had given me a new bicycle for when I started my first term at the JS but that it disappeared within the first two weeks of my arrival and I never saw it again. I well remember the day that it was bought and, as I had not yet acquired sufficient skills to enable me to ride it, my Mother accompanying me as she and I - more I than she - pushed it up the long gradual incline from Croydon's town-centre to our home in Pampisford Road. About half way through the journey my Father suddenly arrived alongside us in his Pontiac car and, having offered me a gladly accepted lift for the remainder of the journey, manoeuvred my infuriated Mother into agreeing to herself push the bike the remainder of the way up the hill back home. Its loss at School only a very short while later caused me considerable sadness but, foolish though it now seems, I was too scared to say anything about the loss for nearly two weeks after I had realised that it had gone. When eventually I did pluck-up the courage to report its loss the School immediately undertook a large-scale hunt for it even to the extent of calling in the Police. But it was too late - the conclusion being, although no proof of any sufficiency was ever discovered, that builders working at the School had taken it. My Father was very sympathetic towards my plight but my Mother blamed me entirely for its loss, and it was some years before she relented and agreed to my being given another bicycle.

Haileybury Junior School had a grass tennis court and, very soon after my arrival at the JS, my Mother gave me a second-hand tennis racket with the instruction that I was to learn to play the game. The trouble was that my Mother, doubtless due to her own very impoverished upbringing, had a policy of giving me things that were too large for me, her theory being that I would "grow into" them. The frames of tennis rackets in those days were made entirely of wood and were thus, by comparison with to-day's tennis rackets, very heavy. Therefore, given my Mother's policy that I would "grow into" it, my tennis racket was, for an 8-years old boy, both very heavy and huge, so heavy and huge that I could barely lift it off the ground let alone hit a tennis ball with it. So, rather than become a laughing stock, I abandoned tennis completely.

Catapulting boys from one tree into another was an enjoyable activity. At least it was for a while. A group of us discovered, within the JS's grounds, a cluster of fir trees young enough and pliable enough to be bent sufficiently so that one of us could be loaded onto a bent-down tree and, on the tree being released, then projected several feet through the air into one or more of the other trees. This 'human cannonball' experience was thoroughly enjoyable until one day one of us, by the name of Barker I seem to recall, was unfortunate enough to impact himself incorrectly on landing in the target tree, so unfortunate that he broke one of his legs thereby causing not only it to have to be encased in Plaster of Paris for the rest of the term and beyond but us to have to abandon that fun activity !!

Professional Theatre is often a hard and vicious taskmaster, a destroyer of much happiness. Nevertheless many parents, usually mothers, goad their offspring into performing on stage, preferably, if possible, on Professional stage. I was privileged in that Professional Theatre had been all around me, and very much a part of my life, since the very second that I entered this world. But, always incomprehensible to me whenever it happened, just before the start of each term I was very firmly forbidden by my Mother to tell any of my peers about any of my Theatrical experiences. For most Mothers, to have had a son appear on stage at London's Victoria Palace Theatre with Laurel and Hardy, then the most successful comedy double-act both within the United Kingdom and the United States, would have been something to have been proud about - But seemingly not where my Mother was concerned. Her instruction to me was that it was never to be spoken of by me. I doubt very much that I had the courage to disobey my Mother's command whilst I was at the nearby day Preparatory Schools in Pampisford Road, but when at Haileybury Junior School temptation got the better of me and I did, at times, mention at least some of my Theatrical activities. Usually I was truthful, or more or less truthful, but on one occasion, perhaps encouraged by my hated piano lessons, I did quietly inform one of my friends, Stuart Kerner, that I had written a song which, at that time, was very, very popular. The song was 'Wonderful, Wonderful Copenhagen' [from the 1952 film 'Hans Christian Anderson' starring the American Actor Danny Kaye]. Stuart, trusting soul, believed me and, in all innocence, told others; and within a very short period of time it seemed that all the boys in the School had been told that I was the composer of this then hugely popular tune. Of course, not only was I the composer of absolutely nothing but also, despite my piano lessons, my ability to read, let alone write, music was just about nil. As I was very soon to find out as I desperately sought to withdraw the silly statement that I had made, starting an untruthful story is one thing, trying to stop it is something entirely different.

I also became short-sighted in another way - my eyesight. The National Health Service, which had been started in 1948 by Clement Attlee's post-War Labour Government, was in its infancy when I was at the JS and Eye Tests at the JS were unheard of. So, when I began to have trouble reading the words and diagrams, etc that my Teachers wrote on their blackboards, the well-intending response adopted by my Teachers was simple but, in reality, hardly successful and certainly not a solution to my problem. Teachers wrote things down on their large blackboards using white and coloured chalks; and so the blackboards, which were on wheeled wooden stands, would then be wheeled nearer to me each and every time that it was noticed that I seemed to be experiencing problems. I would then tightly fold the fingers of my left hand so as to create a small tubelike aperture through which, using one eye whilst keeping the other firmly closed, I would peer hard at whatever had been written or drawn. However, I was fighting a losing battle for my eyesight soon worsened considerably; and it was, after some months of this farcical technique of wheeling the blackboard towards me, the intervention of my Father, himself a wearer of spectacles, that came to my aid for he, not the School, realised that my eyesight might be in need of some 'proper' assistance. So, in the School Summer Holiday of 1956, when I was twelve, he and I trooped to an Optician [Batemans ?] in George Street, Croydon so that I could have my eyes tested. Lo and behold, the verdict was that I was myopic [short-sighted] and had need of spectacles. So, spectacles were prescribed and some time later my Father and I went back to the Optician's shop to collect them. But first, en route to the Optician's, my Father and I joined, as we did every year, a long snake-like queue of people, the queue ending in a wooden hut in Croydon's Park Lane, the hut being the place where one obtained licences for cars and so forth. Having collected a licence for each of my Mother's and my Father's cars we went on to the Optician's where I, or rather my Father, had had the choice of my having either publicly-funded National Health Service [NHS] frames or privately-purchased frames for my lenses. There were at the JS already a handful of wearers of spectacles some of whose frames were NHS frames. The choice of shapes of NHS frames was limited to one - round. It was thus a 'take it or leave it' situation insofar as NHS frames were concerned; and, to my mind, those who wore NHS frames, no matter how intelligent and/or how macho the wearers were, were made, by the frames, to look gormless, a sentiment widely held throughout the UK for many years and a sentiment which adversely effected many wearers of such specs. Thus the decision was that I was to have my lenses inserted not into NHS frames but into privately-purchased frames. So, proudly displaying my brand-new private frames on the bridge of my nose, I exited the Optician's shop and, with my Father alongside me, boldly walked onto the pavement with the intention of crossing over Croydon's busy George Street. What I had not realised was that it takes a while for one and one's eyes to adjust to spectacle lenses. In consequence of my ignorance I totally misjudged where the edge of the kerb was and ended up in a heap on the road !!

Back at School next term, with my new glasses, I found life much easier, much more enjoyable, and much more successful academically. One of my favourite spare-time activities was, using the new Raleigh bike which I had eventually been allowed to have, cycling not only within the attractive grounds of the JS but also from Clewer Manor into the midst of Windsor itself. The trips into Windsor were a privilege granted, I can not now recall why, by Beckwith only to four of us 'seniors' as we by then were : And it was a privilege much appreciated by each of the four of us not only because it enabled us to escape from the confines of the JS for a couple of hours one day each week but also because it made us feel that we were able to be trusted.

Cycling had its unpleasant moments, one of which was watching, as I rode very close by, one of my friends impale himself by one of his eyes, thereby losing the eye, on a hook of a coat rack sited near to one of the playing pitches. It was a horrifying occasion watching him, in effect, suspended by his eye from the hook. It is likely that to-day the School not only would have been prosecuted by the Health and Safety Executive and also sued by the unfortunate boy's Parents and, in consequence, been ordered to pay a fine and also compensation for what was, after all, something that was not the School's fault but also would have found itself being publicly pilloried not only by one if not more newspapers but also by 'do gooding' campaigners who 'latch' on to such unfortunate incidents and who often seem to be lacking in a willingness to appreciate and accept that a genuine accident is not really the fault of anyone.

Windsor not only is a very historic town but also is a very attractive town and I count myself very fortunate indeed to have been enabled to have had the freedom to cycle into it, wander around it, and enjoy it whilst being a Boarder within one of its schools. Immediately over the River Thames from Windsor is the equally historic and equally attractive, but altogether much quieter, town of Eton with its great English Public School, Eton College or, to give it its full title, The College of Our Lady of Eton by Windsor. The two towns are connected not only by a bridge which throughout my days at the JS was for both vehicular and pedestrian traffic but also by a rivalry in many things including - until the JS moved to Winfield Row, Bracknell in 1997 when it amalgamated with Lambrook School to form Lambrook-Haileybury School [Clewer Manor House and its Grounds were subsequently sold, the House being converted into flats and the Grounds having many houses built on them] - a rivalry between the two English Public Schools of Haileybury and Imperial Service College, as represented in Windsor by its Junior School, and of the much older Eton College, a rivalry which manifested itself one day in WH Smith & Sons' stationery shop in Windsor during a visit therein by my school chum, John Mitchell, and I. In those days Etonians, as the boys of Eton College are known, wore a somewhat old-fashioned and cumbersome attire which included a long-tailed jacket and a white bow tie beneath a winged shirt collar. They thus were easily, very easily, identifiable, perhaps a deliberate intention, and thus an easy target whereas we at Haileybury's Junior School wore no such out-of-the-ordinary garments save for our cap and its badge. As John and I browsed through the magazines and other items on the shelves of WH Smith in walked two Etonians and, on seeing us and realising the school that we attended, commenced to mutter very sarcastic comments aimed at John and me. We carried on browsing whilst pretending not to notice these two glaringly noticeable Etonian apparitions. Eventually they gave up trying to rattle us, turned, and headed towards the open doorway. Seeing our advantage John and I crept up behind them and, without saying a word to each other but clearly each knowing what the other had in mind, assisted the Etonians on their way out of the shop by each of us booting one of them up the backside sending him not only more speedily on his way but also straight across the pavement and, still upright, into the roadway itself. Doubtless too proud to indicate any weakness, each Etonian, on his unexpected arrival in the roadway, then turned left, walked back onto the pavement, and headed down the hill towards the bridge and thence back to Eton. John and I, bearing in mind a likelihood that we might soon have to suffer some form of revenge, then hastily existed WH Smith's, turned right, and headed, walking, having collected our bicycles from their parking positions outside the shop, as fast as we could up the hill in the direction away from Eton fortunate in the experience that the half-expected Etonian revenge never materialised.

The historic and picturesque town of Eton had within it not only its famous College but also such splendid eating places as 'The Cockpit', a building of noticeable age where, in years past, the often very profitable blood sport of cockfighting had taken place, a sport which, although still common in many countries, has been illegal in England and Wales since 1835 and in Scotland since 1895. Twice DA Blundell, my House Master and English Teacher, as a special 'treat' took me and three of my colleagues, as Senior Pupils who were soon to leave the JS, in his car to The Cockpit for Afternoon Tea. Whether he did it out of genuine enjoyment of our company or out of relief that he and the School were soon to get rid of the four of us I do not know : But what splendid Afternoon Teas they were - Lashings of delicious sticky buns, scones with 'mountains' of superb cream and heaps of strawberry jam, and excellent cakes; and all at his expense. Wonderful !!

FW Woolworth's shop in Windsor was always a weekly stopover whenever I cycled into Windsor. With Food Rationing now well and truly a thing of the Past the loose biscuits and 'pic-'n'-mix' sweets counters were always an attraction especially for their, as they seemed in those days to me to be, delicious coloured wafer finger-biscuits. In later years the taste of the same type of biscuit from Woolworth's seemed but a poor imitation of its former self. Perhaps the ingredients' formula had changed, or maybe my taste buds had 'matured'.

One shopping expedition into Windsor saw me boldly purchasing perfume for my Mother's birthday. Chanel No.5 was her favourite; and so Chanel No.5 was what I asked for. I was horrified, absolutely horrified, by the price that I was asked to pay, a price which not only all but entirely cleared out my finances but also brought home to me the reality of what it costs a woman - or her husband, partner, or whoever - for her to maintain a 'cut above the average' lifestyle. My Mother's birthday the following year saw me settling for, at a price that I *could* afford, a paperback copy of *Private's Progress,* a book by Alan Hackney which had been, in 1956, turned, by John and Roy Boulting, into a film starring Ian Carmichael, Richard Attenborough, and, amongst others, William Hartnell who subsequently became the first 'Dr Who'.

When my time at the Junior School was nearing its end I had to sit a Common Entrance Examination to determine whether or not I was a worthy subject to progress to my intended next destination, Haileybury and Imperial Service College's Senior School in Hertford Heath, Hertford. Unwisely I made the mistake of also assisting, whilst undertaking the exam, a friend to pass his Common Entrance Exam for his intended next destination [which was not Haileybury and Imperial Service College's Senior School in Hertford Heath, Hertford]. Bill, a farmer's son, was not only a good friend but he was also an excellent model maker who - armed with piles of wooden matchsticks obtained from Teachers who smoked and, obtained from us boys, piles of small cylindrical wooden sticks from confectionery lollipops and with an abundance of tubes of glue which he always seemed to have - could create wonderful models of almost anything. The risks of my helping Bill's Common Entrance Examination attempt were not only that, if found out, expulsion from the JS with dishonour might have resulted but also, unappreciated by me at the time, the possible/probable dilution of my own Common Entrance results and thus the lowering of my Class position on arrival at my new school. The former never happened but, as I found out when I duly arrived the next term at Haileybury Senior School, the latter most certainly did and was, I feel, a continuous academic disadvantage to me throughout my time at the Senior School. However, I passed my Common Entrance Examination which was my principal objective; and my reward from my Parents for my having passed was a gift of 10 x £1 Premium Bonds [A Prize Draw/Bond scheme introduced in 1957 by the UK Government], a small sum to-day but no means as small a sum in 1957. [Over fifty years have elapsed since I received those £10-worth of Premium Bonds and, apart from two small winnings each of £25, I am still awaiting the substantial financial return which, doubtless, that £10-worth of Premium Bonds was intended to bring. But I live in constant hope !!]

Before I left the JS and the friends whom I had made amongst the Staff, both academic and non-academic, and amongst the many boys whose intended moves elsewhere were not to be to Haileybury's

Senior School I was taken out one last time by my Parents. On previous occasions we had spent the hours to-gether often at and around the White Hart at Sonning but also at several other prestigious places near to Windsor, including some lovely hotels in and around the Ascot area. But on this occasion we went first to Old Windsor, then to Runnymede, and thence to a very pleasant hotel sited between Runnymede and Old Windsor where, as three of us sat quietly enjoying our afternoon tea, in walked Diana Dors and her retinue. Very attractive at the time, the former Miss Diana Fluck was then a very famous film actress widely known throughout the UK and elsewhere as a 'sex symbol' [*Good job, perhaps, that she changed her surname from 'Fluck' to 'Dors'* !!] and thus a very appealing character, even to 13-years' old boys. Encouraged by my Father, I went up to her and, mustering as much courage as I could, asked her for her autograph. Surrounded by, what can perhaps be described as being, a bunch of 'heavies' "Go away, little man" she contemptuously and dismissively responded. Hugely disappointed I returned to my Parents and, upon being informed of my complete and utter rejection by Miss Dors, my Father, an influential man within the Theatrical Profession at the time but clearly totally unknown to the former Miss Fluck, first cheered me up and then said to me of the great, and somewhat self-important, film star that she had not heard the last of that incident. I never did get her autograph, but many years later the Theatrical 'grapevine' did indicate to me that some occurence, never made known to me, in her career shortly thereafter had caused her to realise that perhaps her attitude that day had not been the wisest of attitudes for her to have adopted. Born in 1931 this very visually attractive 'sex symbol' of British films, who also became an accomplished Stage and Television Actress, subsequently became a somewhat larger-in-size and noticeably less visually attractive personality than when I had encountered her that day in 1957. She died in 1984 aged only 53.

My memories of Haileybury's Junior School include also those of my then friend Ben Symes who was one of those who never really seemed to come to terms with being at a boarding school for often, certainly in his first year or two, he could, like some others, be heard in bed some nights crying quietly to himself at the sadness of having been 'wrenched' from home. His Father was, I understand, a 'self-made man' whose business activities had enabled him to buy a very attractive, but small by comparison with his later purchase, home in 'up-market' Cookham Dene, near Maidenhead in Berkshire to which Ben invited me for lunch on several occasions, his Mother each time making the most delicious minces for the two of us to consume. From that home in Cookham Dene Ben and his Parents, and, I believe, a Brother and a Sister, moved to a much larger property. The move physically took place after I had left the JS but I was privileged to be shewn round the house and its estate just after his Father had bought it. The estate consisted of many acres within which it had its own brick-making factory. The house itself was, at least to this then 13-years old, enormous. When I saw it it was completely devoid of all furniture and all other objects except for a telephone. Ben and I, encouraged by the belief that somewhere within the house there was at least one ghost, had a tremendous time exploring this wondrous building until, that is, I picked up the telephone's receiver. "Hello, hello, hello," I, in a large otherwise empty room, shouted into the handset. Then Ben took over and likewise shouted "Hello, hello, hello" into the handset. Then it was my turn again to shout "Hello" into the handset. My having done so, suddenly a voice from within the handset shouted "Hello" back at me. I dropped the thing and the two of us, panic-stricken, ran like hell as fast and as far as we could from, what we momentarily took to be, the haunted telephone handset. Of course, hindsight tells me that the previous owner of this large, rambling, allegedly ghost-haunted house had never had the telephone disconnected and, in those days when telephone-calls from such establishments were routed via a local Operator, that therefore what Ben and I had heard was not a ghost but simply the local Operator taking revenge by shouting "Hello" back to us. But that final "Hello" darn near scared the s**t out of Ben Symes and me that day !! Sadly I never saw, nor heard from or of, Ben again after I left the JS.

I can not close this chapter on my life without mentioning a few other memories that remain prominent. The first is of bath times, happenings which took place twice every week and which saw us sitting entirely naked in, as baths, white china-clay 'Belfast'-type sinks whilst Matron or one of her Assistants poured hot soapy disinfected water onto our heads and then massaged it furiously into our scalps to ensure not only that our hair was thoroughly washed but also that any nit intent upon nesting there had second thoughts about doing so. The second is of the high chain-link fence that kept us and the neighbouring 'Berts' completely apart from each other - the word 'Bert' being, I have always assumed, short for 'Herbert' and the reason for the enforced separation being, I have also always assumed, a deliberate social divide because we were 'privileged' pupils at a 'private' School and they were 'ordinary' pupils from an 'ordinary' School. The third is of two very large beautifully hand-drawn and hand-painted books which, during an evening of a day out in Henley-on-Thames with my Parents, I had found dumped and abandoned in a tea-chest alongside a Book Shop. I took them back with me with the intention of keeping them. However, my Mother insisted that they were rubbish and ordered me to "throw them away" just before we entered the School's grounds. So, well in advance of the word 'fly-tipping' becoming a regular feature of the English Language, I hurled them into a ditch that bounded the outside of the School's wire fence which ran alongside Windsor's Imperial Road : And I am sure that many years later, whilst watching the *Antiques Road Show* on BBC Television, I saw the self-same two books being highly regarded and much praised for their contents. The fourth memory is of the pleasure of being allowed, in 1956, by Beckwith to, well after my peers had gone to bed, sit with him and his Wife in their private apartment to watch - on their very primitive, by to-day's standards, 'black and white' television - my Mother appearing in one of Independent Television's very early Variety Shows, the 1956 production of *The Lady Ratlings on Parade* staged by the band leader/impresario Jack Hylton, my Mother being a Member of the *The Grand Order of Lady Ratlings*.. [The Show, raising money for Charity, subsequently ran at London's Adelphi Theatre from 6 November to 24 November of that year, although, as far as I am aware, my Mother took no active part in that.] The fifth memory is of the utterly boring - and, it seemed to us boys, hugely lengthy - morning Church Services that, every Sunday, we were made to attend, having, regardless of weather, walked a mile or so there in crocodile fashion to the Church. Nearly every Sunday that we attended we were made not only to have to sit in silence, save for the singing of hymns and the reciting of, to most of us, meaningless Psalms, and suffer listening to, what to many of us was, an incomprehensible sermon but also to have to sit in silence and suffer listening to, what to every one of us was, a totally incomprehensible *nunc dimitis,*. It was as if the Church of England's local representatives were deliberately trying to teach us boys that the Church of England can be, and often is, excruciatingly boring. Not only that but we financially hard-up boys were each made to have to pay for the experience, for each Sunday a cloth collecting 'pocket' on a wooden handle would be passed around into which each of us was required to make a compulsory 'voluntary' donation of 6d [2½p], a trivial sum nowadays but a fortune to us pocket-money-dependent children of years gone bye. The sixth memory is of the occasions when the River Thames burst its banks in and around central Windsor and we boys were bussed into Windsor in order to, with great excitement, watch the local Fire Service in action 'mopping up', an activity which, in those days, seemed to be part and parcel of Life, it being accepted that if one built in a river's flood-plain it must only be expected that the river would, at times, seek to recover that which was rightly its. The seventh memory is of the first successful attempt - by the New Zealander, Edmund Hillary, and his Tibetan-born Sherpa, Tenzing Norgay - to reach the summit, on 29 May 1953, of Mount Everest. As with the excursions to watch the Fire Service 'mopping up' we were bussed into Windsor but this time to see a film of this, then, most impressive of events, an event which nowadays is almost a regular tourist undertaking. The eighth memory is also one of being bussed not into Windsor but in a *Windsorian* 'bus from the JS to far away, as it then seemed to us boys, London to see *The Royal Tournament,* a collection of Army, Navy, and Air Force events purposely formulated to excite and entertain the Public. Another memory is of a dumper-truck, sand, cement, and a host of other materials which came to-gether to create, in my last year at the JS, a much-talked of, and eagerly awaited, open-aired Swimming Pool. The fact that the principal users of the Pool, once the builders had completed their work, were not us boys but the School's Staff - whose sunbathing by the poolside that summer seemed to occupy, to our total exclusion, every non-academic daylight hour - seemed, at least to us boys and those of our Parents who had part-funded the thing, to be somewhat at odds with what we had been told was the reason for the Pool's having been built. The tenth memory is of a water-colour painting of a farmyard scene that I did and which was highly praised by our Art Teacher, Mrs Beckwith, for "its composition and perspective". I still retain the painting but am impressed neither by its composition nor by its perspective. The eleventh memory also features Mrs Beckwith. She had a wonderful collection of budgerigars [or was it canaries ?] which she kept in a purpose-built aviary and to which she dedicated many hours of careful attention each week. Sadly, someone, completely unknown to your's truly [Honest !!], unlocked and opened the aviary's double security doors and set the whole collection free to fly into the great wide-world beyond. The poor woman was distraught. The eleventh memory is of the day, in 1953, of the Coronation of Her Majesty Queen Elizabeth [the Second of England and First of Scotland], but that took place when I was not at school but at home on a half-term holiday. The twelfth memory is of the hot sunny day when a number of us boys went, with permission and by arrangement, strawberry-picking in Her Majesty the Queen's Windsor Castle Strawberry Gardens. How we got there I can not now recall, but there were twenty or more of us each of whom was commanded by one of the several accompanying [doubtless strawberry-loving] Teachers to only eat a maximum of a certain number of strawberries and warned that if we exceeded the maximum we might make ourselves if not violently ill certainly unable to eat our tea when we returned late that afternoon to School. The strawberries that we were to pick were to be brought by each picker to a van wherein were seated some more boys whose tasks were to sort and grade Her Majesty's delicious strawberries and then apportion them into quantities sufficient to enable them to be enjoyed on several occasions by each and every boy once we 'Strawberry

Pickers' had returned to School. I, being a School Prefect at the time, was placed, and left, in command of the 'sorters', 'graders', and 'apportioners' in the van and was given strict instructions to ensure that none of those in my charge, including myself, exceeded the limit stated. I endeavoured, at least at the start of the operation, to take my job very seriously and to faithfully adhere to my instructions All went well … at least for a while. My problem was that I have always enjoyed food, and I had a particular liking for good strawberries; and Her Majesty's strawberries were superb, so superb that I very soon, probably without realising it, exceeded my maximum and, as I am a great believer in leading by example, allowed everyone else within the van to soon exceeded their maximum. My liking for good strawberries continues to this day despite the fact that Her Majesty's strawberries caused me much pain and agony for hours on end after we had all arrived, strawberry-laden, back at School that evening. The last but no means least memory is of the formal sex education that we boys received whilst at the Junior School. The word 'none' would be sufficient to describe it save for the short, very short indeed, Talk given by Becky to all of us School Leavers a couple of days or so before we were about to depart at the end of our last term. The gaggle of we School Leavers were herded into a room close to the Dining Room where a serious-looking Becky greeted us and told us to sit down, be quiet, and listen carefully. Whereas these days formal Sex Education, and often sex itself, plays a major part in the lives of even very young children, in those days Sex was a subject about which most young children, many older children, and even many adults had neither any real knowledge nor any real information; and therefore for us 13-years old boys to be invited in for a Talk to be given by the Head Master on 'Sex' was somewhat akin to being invited in for a Talk to be given by the Head Master on the 'Creation of the Universe'.

'Most, if not all of us, had not a clue about Sex; and therefore when Becky, accompanied by basic illustrative charts, launched into a spiel about "The reproductive mechanism of the farmyard pig" we listened attentively; and when he had finished his Talk on "The reproductive mechanism of the farmyard pig" and we had subsequently left the room we went away believing - despite the fact that Becky had made no mention whatsoever of men and women 'having 'it off' with each other - that we were now very knowledge insofar as the subject of 'Sex' "was concerned. *Ah, happy memories* !!

[Queen Elizabeth's Coronation at Westminster Abbey was an expensive undertaking and so a Show, *Out of the Whirlwind,* was staged in the Abbey on 10 June 1953 to 3 July 1953 to help offset the costs. The Scenery was built by Brunskill and Loveday Limited. A copy of the front of the Programme appears under. Up until the latter part of the 1950s most Scenery was constructed manually using mainly, what nowadays might be deemed to be, old-fashioned hand tools. So, also under are copies of 2 photographs taken in the 1950s showing part of Brunskill and Loveday Limited's Newport Street, Lambeth works. Photograph (1) Shows 14 employees busy making Scenery in one of the Newport Street's Workshops and (2) shows Arthur 'Ginger' Oddy (whom I knew and whose Family kindly made the photographs available to me) with a measuring stick outside Brunskill and Loveday's Newport Street premises.]

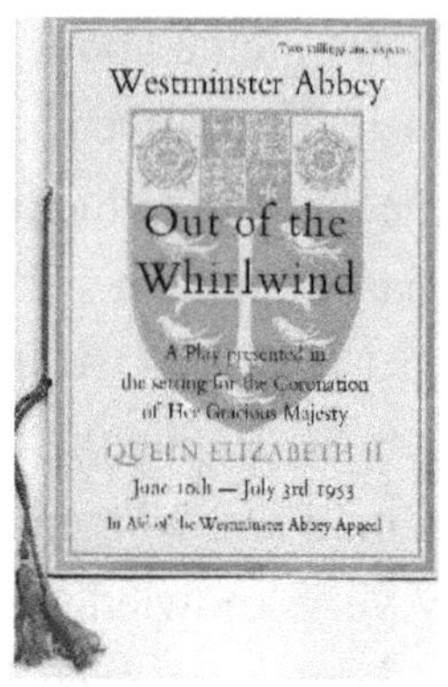

<table>
<tr><td align="center">(1)</td><td align="center">(2)</td></tr>
</table>

Soon after their marriage in 1941 my Mother twice fell pregnant by my Father and had an abortion on each occasion. Abortions were illegal then and are illegal now but since the introduction in 1967 of the Abortion Act mothers deemed to be medically at risk have been lawfully able to have their pregnancies terminated by suitably medically qualified persons. Such was not the case prior to the coming into force of the 1967 Act; and therefore there was then - as indeed still exists now but to a much lesser degree - a thriving, but very risky, trade in 'back 'street' abortions. There were also, as doubtless there still are, medically qualified persons who, for a payment, would, on a 'no questions asked' basis, undertake such a service. Thus - given that there were, in those days, no such things as 'the Pill' and that many 'Society' and other 'well to do' women often fell 'inconveniently' pregnant, either by their husbands or by persons whom their husbands might have been tempted to have seriously injured had they found out - it was not too difficult - especially if one was connected with, or had connections in, the Medical profession - to get an abortion regardless of whether or not the women were medically at risk had they not had an abortion. My Mother was certainly not medically at risk and she, having been a Nurse for many years, had many connections in the Medical Profession; and thus for her it was easy to arrange to have the job done by a medically qualified person. Also, my Father being 'in the Theatre' would have had access to such persons However, on the third occasion that my Mother fell pregnant my Father's insistence that my Mother give him at least one child won through : And so, for my Father, it was third time lucky, a feeling that was in no way reciprocated by my Mother.

My Father had been married before, in December 1902, when aged 22, to a Miss Julia Johanna Lee. The marriage had been a happy relationship but she died after 32 years of marriage in 1934. That marriage produced one child, John, born in 1905, who by the time of my arrival in 1944, had long since become an adult and left his Father's home. Much to his, and my, Father's considerable disappointment John did not want to have anything to do with his Father's business. Also, John married and the marriage produced a Son, Julian, although my Father was always of the belief that Julian was not John's Son.

John had, apparently, always been suspicious of my Mother's motives in marrying his Father and regarded his Father's marriage to my Mother as a threat to his inheritance. The threat, of course, was made even worse by my arrival into the Family mêlée that was now fast developing. Thus 1944 in 218 Pampisford Road, Croydon saw [1] my Father 'over the moon' not only at being married again, and to a woman more than 29 years younger than he, but also at my arrival, whilst at the same time, [2] my Father in increasing conflict with his firstborn Son, and [3] my Mother thoroughly irritated both by the fact that she had had to give birth to a child and by the fact of the existence of this annoying other character, John, with his Wife and their Son (my nephew) Julian.

Fortunately a child of the very tender age that I was at the time is, consciously at least, unaware of most that is going on roundabout; and therefore, consciously oblivious to the family-feuding battleground that was developing around, and because of, me, I spent much of my early days soaking scores of washable Terrytowel nappies, drinking loads of dried-but-mixed-with-water non-Mother-manufactured Ostermilk, and howling and sleeping.

Having, as best I could, managed for the first two years or so of my life to remain neutral in the enveloping conflict - despite the ejection from Highlands of my Half-Brother who was never, save for one brief moment in my fourteenth year, to be seen by me again - the first serious medical emergency that befell me occurred when I was about 3-years of age. It had nothing whatsoever to do with my Mother versus my Father : No, the cause of the emergency was entirely self-made. My Father employed two Gardeners on an 'every Wednesday' basis; and so, every Wednesday Mr Harding, the Gardener, and his Assistant, his Son Tony, would come to Highlands to, in the early days, sort out the barren mess at the rear of the house that was to become my Father's bowling green, with flower-beds alongside, and very productive vegetable- and fruit-growing areas beyond. They had use of a wheelbarrow which, as was the type of construction in those days, was of solid oak with a metal-banded oak wheel; and I had been provided by my Father with a scaled-down version of same [*See photograph under of me, Harding, Tony, and my wheelbarrow*] Whatever possessed me I do not know, but I, apparently, decided to emulate a weightlifter and in so doing sought to lift my wheelbarrow off the ground in order to raise it above my head. The result was a hernia !!

In those days 'Society' - which was noticeably divided into levels which included not only the so-called Upper Class but also the Middle Class, the in-between Lower Upper Class and Upper Middle Class, and the Lower Class - was still, despite the ending of the Second World War and the fact that widespread social changes were fast taking place, seeking to cling onto pre-War social habits; and thus Mr Harding was, in fact, never referred to as 'Mr' Harding - It was always simply 'Harding'.

Harding lived with his Wife and Son in a small first-floor flat within a former stables building sited further up Pampisford Road, near to St John's School, in the grounds of a house owned and operated by the charity, 'Dr Barnardos'. In fact Harding was the charity's gardener; and it was by arrangement with 'Dr Barnardos' that Harding and his Son, just a youngish teenager when he started his Wednesday job with us, that Harding was enabled to work for my Father on Wednesdays. Harding was, without doubt, an excellent gardener as indeed was his Son and pupil, Tony, whereas my Mother, sadly, was not anywhere near to being within their league for whereas she had ideas, principally involving colourful pansies, she had no real understanding of flowers. Every week after Harding and Tony had departed she could be found planting something somewhere and on arrival every Wednesday Harding and his Son would, regardless of the weather, look around, find the intruders, and remove them. Never a word was spoken on the matter either by my Mother to Harding or by Harding to my Mother. It was a 'ritual' that went on until the day that my Mother sold Highlands in 1959.

I have many happy memories of Harding, of Tony, and of Mrs Harding who often would come to Highlands in an evening to act as my baby-sitter whilst my Parents either went to a Theatre to see a Show or went to some other activity connected with my Father's work in the Theatrical profession. Indeed, I had such respect and admiration for Harding and his Son that I would often seek to involve myself in their gardening activities, happenings which were rarely discouraged. It was on such an occasion that my hernia emergency occurred. Many, many, many years later, I am still very sensitive in that area !!

Tony was a wonderful lad, almost, at times, like an older brother to me. His hobby, passion even, was making model aircraft which he fashioned not from kits but entirely from bits and pieces of wood many of which were given to him by my Father often in the form of kindling wood used to light coal fires, the most widespread form of heating in those days for, much of Britain being then awash with coalmines, coal was plentiful, as indeed it could be now if only attitudes to this God-provided fossil fuel would change. Harding and Tony themselves cut the kindling wood given to them by my Father for, on Wednesdays when it was wet and they were therefore unable to tend to our gardens, Harding and Tony would sit alongside a pile or two of wood supplied by me Father in the form of offcuts from timber used in his Scenery business and to-gether they would, sharpened axes in hand, happily chop away in our main garage turning lengths of 4" (100mm) x 1" (25mm) offcuts into splinters of kindling wood. Despite my enthusiasm to involve myself in this fascinating undertaking I was allowed only to stand at the doorway and gawk at what was going on.

My Parents' visits to the Theatre soon began to also involve me; and in consequence I was privileged not only to see many great West End [of London] and other Shows, not only to sit in many of the best seats in the Theatres to which we went, but also to meet many of the well-known, and not so well-known, actors, actresses, and other Theatrical personalities of the day for it was these people who were my Father's friends, an environment which, by the time of my arrival in 1944, he had enjoyed for over 60 years. At home in Highlands my Father would often entertain such people to drinks, to dinner, and to garden parties. We were assisted on such occasions by Hilda White, a Maid who not only loyally arrived at Highlands every Thursday to attend to whatever domestic situation my Mother required her to attend to but also would loyally arrive at Highlands on almost every occasion whenever she was asked to assist. A spinster in her 40s-50s she lived with her Mother in Newark Road near to the 'Bus Station in the Red Deer area of South Croydon and often talked in praise of her Sister and Brother-in-law, a Mr Frost, and their Daughter Merle. The Red Deer area of South Croydon straddled both sides of the Brighton

Road as it passed through South Croydon in the area of the Red Deer Public House. Besides many hundreds of terraced houses the area not only contained London Transport's local 'bus depot but was also, by means of several parades of shops, a thriving self-contained retail area where one could buy almost every daily item that one wanted. It was in one of these parades, almost opposite where St Augustine's Avenue, with its High Anglican Church, exited into the Brighton Road, that the Frosts lived and owned and operated a small Do-It-Yourself business that seemed to sell, not in packs of three or more but individually, every conceivable do-it-yourself woodwork and related item that one would ever need.

Every Thursday Hilda would walk from her home in Newark Road, cross over and walk alongside the Brighton Road, then turn into St Augustine's Avenue and walk up its hill until she came to where the Avenue forked, at which point she would take the left fork which took her to the parkland at the back of Highlands. Having walked through the park she would cross the small unmade-up roadway that divided the park from Highlands and then, via the gate in Highlands' boundary fence that had been purposely unlocked for her, would walk through our back garden and arrive, always punctually, at the house to begin her work. Often, in my latter years at Highlands when I was home from school, I would, unless forbidden by my Mother to do so, walk some, if not all of the way down St Augustine's Avenue, to meet her and to accompany this always cheerful and kindly personality the rest of her way on her journey to our home. The self-same pattern would be repeated whenever Hilda's presence was required at Highlands.

Those whom my Father entertained in the drawing-room, as my Mother insisted on calling it, at Highlands were many and included not only such Theatrical 'Greats' "as Jack Buchanan, Gladys Cooper, Noël Coward, Billy Butlin, Bud Flanagan [whose birth name was Reuben Weintrop] and his comedic 'double-act' colleagues who together performed for many years as the hugely popular *Crazy Gang*; the Band Leader and Impresario Jack Hylton, and the Ballet Dancer and co-founder of the London Festival Ballet (subsequently the English National Ballet) Sir Anton Dolin but also many slightly less publicly-known Theatricals such as the Actor/Producer/Directors John Clements and Robert Atkins [co-founder of London's Regent's Park Open Air Theatre], the Character Actor Cyril Smith (*see photograph under*), the Designers Guy Sheppard, Tony Holland, and Clifford Pember; the Theatre Critic Bill Bishop, the multi-talented Eric Maschwitz, and many Members of the Theatrical Charities, the Grand Order of Water Rats and the Grand Order of Lady Ratlings. In fact almost every facet of the Theatrical Profession was entertained at Highlands, including the Austrian-born Tenor, Richard Tauber. Of Jewish ancestry, Tauber, for whom the Hungarian Composer Franz Lehár often specifically wrote, was, in the 1930s, hounded by the NAZIs to such an extent that, when Germany annexed Austria in 1938, Tauber fled Austria, the Austrian Government withdrawing his Passport, and applied for British citizenship. One of the many Productions in which Tauber starred was the film 'The Lisbon Story' [which was subsequently staged (with Scenery, needless to say, built by Brunskill and Loveday Limited) - although Tauber did not take part - first at *The Imperial Theatre, Brighton* in 1943 before transferring, in 1943, to *The London Hippodrome* and then, in 1944, to London's *Stoll Theatre*]. Tauber's recording, from *The Lisbon Story*, of the song *'Pedro the Fisherman'* was hugely popular but, Tauber having caused some offence to my Mother during one of his visits to Highlands [perhaps, being somewhat of a 'Lady's Man', he slapped or pinched my Mother's backside or even passionately kissed her - I do not know], one day in 1958 when I was innocently whistling *'Pedro the Fisherman '* within earshot of my Mother she suddenly rushed over to me and ordered me in no uncertain terms to "Never ever whistle that song again !!"." Until after her death, I never, at least whilst she was anywhere around, ever did.

Often, in his day, called Britain's 'answer' to Fred Astaire [with whom he starred in the MGM film *The Band Wagon*], Jack Buchanan was superbly talented as a Dancer, Actor, Producer, Director, Theatre Manager, and all-round Theatrical. Born in 1890 in Helensburgh, a 'seaside' town situated on the north bank of the River Clyde a few miles north of Glasgow, he died, aged 67, in 1957 having starred in and staged many Shows for which my Father was often the builder of the Scenery. My fondest memory of him is of the courtesy and consideration that he showed to me personally, a youngster of some 9 or 10 years, when chatting to my Parents during the Interval of *As*

Long As They're Happy, a Show in which he was starring at London's *Garrick Theatre* and for which my Father had built the Scenery.

Dame Gladys Cooper - Actress, Singer, Theatre Manager, and the Mother-in-law of the Actor Robert Morley and Grandmother of the Broadcaster and Theatrical Raconteur Sheridan Morley - had first engaged the services of my Father to make Scenery for her back in the 1920s if not earlier. But alas my memories of the great Miss Gladys Cooper seem sadly to now be beyond my recall.

Of Bud Flanagan and his 'outrageous' *Crazy Gang* colleagues - the 'double-act' of Jimmy Nervo and Teddy Knox, the 'double-act' of Charlie Naughton and Jimmy Gold as well as 'Uncle Bud' himself - I recall best the time when they lined up at the front of Highlands in a competition to see which of them could hit a golf ball clean over the house. This frightening experience was made even more frightening by the fact that directly in front of them was a large leaded six piece window. I was, and still am, no Golfer but I venture to suggest that even the finest of professional Golfer's would consider the task of, standing some 5 or so metres in front of the house, lifting a golfball some 14 metres or so into the air in order to 'clear' the house and land the ball on the lawn on the other side to be an impossibility. But there they were, these five by-no-stretch-of-the-imagination youthful men, apparently determined, despite all protestations, to do so. They lined up, in a row, parallel to the house, practiced a few swings, each then put his ball on its wooden tee, and then … Whoosh, the clubs came down, the balls were hit, and … Well, virtually nothing happened save that the balls just sort of mildly flopped into the air before gently falling pathetically to a halt only half a metre or so in front of the tees from whence they had started their journeys. What none of us, now greatly relieved, observers had realised was that every ball was made entirely of cotton wool !! I should mention that the two other members of the *Crazy Gang*, Chesney Allen and Eddie Gray, were not present that day. Of Eddie Gray - or 'Monsewer' Eddie Gray as the theatrically moustachioed master-comedian and juggler, often described by other comics of the day as being 'the funniest man in the world', liked to be known - one story, true or otherwise, must, I feel, be related here: In the 1930s, when Policeman were regarded as being by no stretch of the imagination the most academic of people, Eddie Gray, having seen an approaching Policeman, went up to a nearby ordinary free-standing Royal Mail postbox and bent down and started shouting through its opening "It's okay. Don't worry. Here's a Policeman. Help'll soon be on the way." The Policeman came up to Eddie Gray and asked him what he was doing. Eddie Gray told him that a postman had come to collect the letters from the letterbox, had unlocked it and climbed inside to get the letters, that the door had slammed shut, that the postman was holding the keys, could not move his arms, and therefore could not pass the keys out through the opening so that someone could unlock the box and let him out. "You stay here and talk to him whilst I run back to the Sorting Office, tell them what's happened, and get someone to come with another key to let him out," said Eddie Gray to the Policeman. "Okay," said the obliging Policeman as Eddie Gray started to leave and run away in the direction of the Sorting Office. Having got round a nearby corner Eddie Gray stopped and looked back to hear the Policeman shouting through the opening in the letterbox "It's okay. He won't be long. He's gone to get someone to come to let you out". Having assured himself that the gag was working to perfection, off went a chuckling Eddie Gray, and left the, by now surrounded by onlookers, Policeman to it !!

In 1960 or 1961 my Mother, Auntie Lil, and I were sitting chatting. Auntie Lil, a lovely lady, was not really my Auntie but I had always called her that. She, like my Mother, was a Lady Ratling. In fact Auntie Lil had been the first Queen Ratling when the Grand Order of Lady Ratlings was founded back in 1929.

The three of us were talking about Commercial Television. "What Val did darn near killed Fred", I well remember Auntie Lil saying. Fred, Auntie Lil's Husband, was Fred Russell. Known as the 'Father 'of Variety' Fred Russell was totally committed to Variety Theatre, was a founder of the Variety Artists Federation, was largely responsible for the resurrection of the Water Rats in 1927, and was described by many as being the founder of modern ventriloquism : And Val was Val Parnell who as well as being Fred's Son was also Managing Director not only of Moss Empires and but also of Associated Television [ATV]. I knew Fred Russell but, to my recollection, I never knew his Son, Val. However, in early January 1959 I personally experienced some of Val Parnell's tactics.

My Father had died in October 1958. Still going to work every day, he was a fit man with a very active brain when, under somewhat suspicious circumstances, he died after having spent all of his 78 years involved in making Theatrical Scenery. In 1899, aged 19, he had started his own Scenery business [One of his first customers was Oswald Stoll for whom, when aged only 23, my Father built the first Scenery to go into Oswald Stoll's then brand new purpose built Frank Matcham-designed 3,000-seat London Coliseum Theatre] and in 1939 he amalgamated his successful business with Jack Brunskill's successful Scenery business to form Brunskill and Loveday Limited. At the time of my Father's death the Deputy Managing Director, under Val Parnell, of ATV was Lew Grade [Lord Grade] who, shortly after my Father's death, arranged to meet me at Brunskill and Loveday's Scenery Works in Newport Street, Lambeth. Jack Brunskill had no children, and I had been 'trained' by my Father not only to design and build scenery but also to run, at least his half of, Brunskill and Loveday Limited. I was not quite 15 when I had my, very courteous, Meeting with Lew, whom I had vaguely known for many years. Lew's intention was to get me to agree to the sale of Brunskill and Loveday to ATV so that ATV could use it to build its Film and Television Scenery. My Father, to whom I was very close, had throughout his entire life been passionate about Theatres and about Scenery and had no intention either of selling out or of abandoning Theatres : And neither had I any intention of selling out or of abandoning Theatres for I knew, for instance, how sad my Father had been when in 1953 the Empire Theatre in Croydon, under its Manager Arthur Dixon, had closed. The closing of Theatres had been going on for years and was increasing for, due in part to the transmission on BBC Television of HM the Queen's Coronation in 1953, television was on the ascendency. But the coming into existence of Commercial Television brought to the fore a ruthless streak insofar as some Theatre Impresarios were concerned, for Commercial Television was viewed as a potential goldmine : And I well remember not only how sad but also how bitter my Father had been when, in July 1957 after the final performance of *It's the Geography that counts*, London's great historic 1,000*plus*-seat St James's Theatre in London's King Street - then under the control of the American Impresario Gilbert Miller and the British Impresario Prince Littler who was also a Director of ATV - went dark, never to re-open, .

It required a lot of money to fund ATV; and the sites on which Theatres stood were often 'prime sites', and Moss Empires controlled a lot of prime sites. And who was running Moss Empires ? Why, Val

Parnell, Lew Grade, and Prince Littler - The very people whom hundreds, if not thousands, of Variety Artist(e)s looked-up to and relied upon for work and yet they were the very same people who were deliberately diverting moneys away from Theatres into Commercial Television for mass-entertainment productions such as *The Adventures of Robin Hood* and, later, *Danger Man* and *The Saint* and in the course of which were taking work and livelihoods away from Variety Artist(e)s .

Val Parnell and the other Impresarios did continue their interest in Variety Theatre so long as they felt that they could still make money out of it. Parnell, of course, is renowned for his ATV production [*Val Parnell's*] *Sunday Night at the London Palladium* which in its own way, with its weekly audience of many millions of viewers, took punters away from Theatres and thus assisted in the demise of Variety Theatres. And whilst all this was going on Val Parnell's public image, and his image within much of the Profession below the level of those who knew what was going on, continued to be that of a 'hard' "businessman but a businessman fully supportive of Variety Theatre and its Artist(e)s.

Needless-to-say, come what may Commercial Television was here to stay. One could not, neither did one want to, stop it : But the whole era was one of intrigue and manipulation by many who, some of us feel, could have and should have gone about things in a more sympathetic way and thus been much more considerate towards those in Variety Theatre whose livelihoods depended on what the likes of those who controlled ATV were doing.

Of the Band Leader and Impresario Jack Hylton, of the Actor/Producer/Director John Clements, of the Designers Guy Sheppard and Tony Holland, of the Lyricist, Novelist, Writer of musical plays and operettas, one-time Assistant Head of BBC Outside Broadcasting, one-time Head of BBC Variety, and one-time Editor of The Radio Times Eric Maschwitz, and of the Grand Order of Water Rats and the Grand Order of Lady Ratlings I write elsewhere. Of the Actor Cyril Smith I also write elsewhere; but first I mention one occasion when Cyril visited Highlands shortly after my Parents had moved there. A Fête, to take place in the public Park at the rear of Highlands, had been arranged by a Committee of Locals whose Chairperson, a woman of forceful personality, had persuaded a Theatrical of some note to agree, for a fee, to open the occasion. Unfortunately for her the Theatrical withdrew with only hours to spare. Disappointed, annoyed, but undaunted Madam Chairperson descended upon my Father, her having previously met my Mother and been acquainted by her that my Father was in the Theatrical Profession, and all but demanded of him that, with his 'connections', he supply a replacement. So my Father, with less than four hours in which to do as the woman had 'commanded', contacted Cyril who agreed to the request and got himself down to Highlands from London as quickly as he could. Shortly after his arrival my Mother, Father, and Cyril went, as quickly as they could, out of Highlands and into the Park beyond and arrived at Madam Chairperson's side with only a very few minutes to spare. My Father having hastily introduced Cyril to Madam Chairperson, explained to her who Cyril was, and informed her of the name of the Show in London's West End that Cyril was appearing in. Madam Chairperson then turned to face the assembled crowd, informed them that the Theatrical who had been billed to open the event had let them all down, and, turning to Cyril, began to introduce Cyril whose name she either had forgotten or never taken note of when informed of it by my Father. "Er ...," she said to Cyril, "what's your name ?" "Cyril Smith," replied Cyril who decided to give Madam Pomposity further assistance by adding that he was an Actor appearing in a Show then currently running in London's West End. "Well," she said in a forceful voice the loudness of which was such that everyone round about could hear her, "I suppose you'll do." Then she continued by saying to the assembled crowd "This is Cyril Smith. He's an Actor, and he's appearing in the West End somewhere." Aged 49 at the time Cyril, a veteran Performer, gave no noticeable evidence that he was somewhat shaken by the incident but he none-the-less never forgot it. Neither did he forget the fact that, despite a promise given to him by Madam Chairperson via my Father of a fee, no money whatsoever ever came his way save an Offer, which Cyril declined, made by my Father that he, my Father, would settle what Madam Chairperson had offered. My Mother and Father refused ever again to communicate with the woman for this was the second occasion that they had suffered her somewhat inappropriate attitude to her fellow beings. The first occasion was a visit undertaken by my Mother to the woman's home in response to a "Welcome to Pampisford Road" invitation to Afternoon Tea that my Mother had received from her. Present were only the woman, my Mother, and the woman's Maid; and, after the Tea, the woman showed my Mother around her well-tended garden. Having entered her Greenhouse and been shown its considerable stock of growing tomatoes my Mother was asked if she would like some tomatoes to take back home with her. Not only did Highlands have no tomatoes but also it was wartime and such items were in very short supply, and therefore my Mother readily accepted the offer. The woman then carefully weighed out 2lbs [0.907kgs] of tomatoes on a set of balances after which, having placed them into a paper bag, she passed them to my Mother with the demand "That'll be half-a-crown [12½p]" - a very small amount of money these days but a noticeable sum back in the early 1940s. So much for the "Welcome to Pampisford Road" !!

My Mother had a particular memory of her first meeting with the Actor/Producer/Director Robert Atkins. In 1932, together with the Director/Manager Sydney W Carroll, Robert Atkins founded The Open Air Theatre in London's Regent's Park where, over many years, he staged, and usually acted in, many Plays, with an emphasis on those written by Shakespeare. The Theatre being in the open air and Atkins, born in 1886, being of an era in which there had been no microphones his voice projection was both superb and very powerful. My Father built much of the Scenery for his productions, Scenery which Atkins re-cycled over and over again : And in the early days of my Mother's and Father's marriage my Father took my Mother for a stroll in Regent's Park and in so doing took her to The Open Air Theatre in order to introduce her to this fine Shakespearean Actor.

"Robert," said my Father to Atkins, "this is Helen, my new Bride."

Standing about two feet [600mm] directly in front of my Mother Atkins thrust his hand out to shake hands with my Mother and - seemingly forgetting that he was not performing on his Stage, with all the strength needed to project his powerful voice over the entirety of his [had there been one at the time] Audience - in full Shakespearean magnificence bellowed a two to three seconds' blast of "Hal…lo…wa". My Mother's instant response was to scream as loudly as she could, turn away from the deafening outburst, and, in a state of some terror, attempt to run away !!

From when I reached the age of nine or ten I was required to play my part in the hospitality that took place in Highlands. My job, which I thoroughly enjoyed, was to dispense drinks. Armed with a book entitled *Cocktails - How to mix them* by *Robert Vermeire* [*see under copy photograph of book's front*] I got quite good at dispensing cocktails and my dispensing of gins and tonics and of whiskies and other drinks became so much appreciated by their many recipients that my Father bought some *Dalex* Spirits measures thereby causing me to contain my spirits-dispensing generosity to much more financially-manageable levels. A smoker of both cigarettes and of Habana cigars and of La Tropical Jamaican cigars, he kept his cigars in a purpose-made [perhaps by himself] 2ft 6ins [750mm] (or thereabouts) high free-standing teak Humidor access to which was gained via a mirror-panelled door the key to which, wisely perhaps, I was never given. When aged 12 or thereabouts I was however given a cocktail cabinet-cum-bar and much pub material and many 'miniatures' hung on pegboards to go with it. For whatever reason, perhaps because my Father's Father's forename had been 'Charles', we called it 'Charlie's Bar'.

Such hospitality nearly always took place on a Sunday, being the only day in the week when many Theatricals could find at least some spare time away from their work within Theatres. But on one occasion, early in my childhood and well before I was capable of dispensing drinks, a Saturday had been chosen; and midway through the afternoon the frontdoor bell sounded. My Father opened the door and in front of him stood a wee Scotsman who, full of nerves, explained that he had come down to London from Scotland and had decided to take the opportunity to catch the train to East Croydon Station and from there find his way to where he knew that his favourite Sister now lived. The wee Scotsman was my Uncle Angus who, many years later, told me not only that as he got nearer to Highlands he became more and more frightened at the thought of meeting my Father, whom he had never met before, but also that he was amazed at the kindness shown to him by my Father. "Your Father," said a tearful Uncle Angus as he and I, fifty or thereby years later, talked of 'old times', " had a houseful of guests and yet he showed me in, a wee poor man frae Shotts and a complete stranger tae him, and he introduced me, yes, *he* introduced *me* tae *everyone* there and made me feel as welcome as welcome could be. And when I left *he* personally showed *me* oot and as he did sae he quietly said tae me 'Here, Angus, here's a Complimentary Ticket for you to go to the London Palladium to-night to see a Show. Just go to the Box Office, show them the ticket, tell them that you're my Brother-in-law, and you'll get one of the best seats in the house." "And did you ?" I asked him. "No," he said, as he wiped the tears from his face, "I went tae the Palladium but hadnae the courage tae go in. I just wandered up and down ootside the Theeter until the people eventually came oot, and then I made my way tae the railway station and caught the train back tae Glasgow." "How sad, how very, very sad," I thought.

Neighbours would occasionally be asked to one of the Theatrical 'get-togethers' at Highlands. To the left of our house was a vacant space but to the right lived Mr and Mrs Smith. He worked was, I believe, a Director of a pottery firm; and he and his wife had a small white dog called Chooky at whom Mrs Smith seemed almost every evening to take great delight in penetratingly shouting, as if for the entire population of South Croydon to hear, "Chook, Chook, Chook, Chook, Chooky. Chook, Chook, Chook, Chook, Chooky. Chook, Chook, Chook, Chook, Chooky". Had I been her beloved 'Chook, Chook, Chook, Chook, Chooky' I would have done my darndest to dig under the Smith's rear garden fence and get as far away from the wretched woman as I could : But, as far as I know, Chooky never did - Sucker !!

My Father and Mother kept, as a guard dog at Highlands, a large Airedale terrier the name of which I can not now recall. But I can recall the day that my Parents and I returned home to find not only that Highlands had been burgled but also that our so-called guard dog, having failed in its duty to protect the house and its contents, was, like many items that day, missing presumed, by my Father, as having been also stolen. Seven days or so later, whilst on his way to work, my Father saw the hound ambling its way, unaccompanied, down Brixton Hill. Having stopped and got out of his car and assured himself not only that it was our useless guard dog but also that it was, seemingly, being well fed by someone, he then made the decision to let it go on its way. Thus he and the dog parted never to see each other again. Twice after that my Father and I went to Kennard's, a large Department Store in central Croydon, to purchase a replacement dog from Kennard's, then famous, adjoining Arcade in which many Traders selling a variety of 'reasonably priced' commodities plied their trades. On each occasion my Father purchased a small white puppy intending to train it to become what the Airedale had never become, an efficient guard dog : But, within a week or so of having been purchased, each puppy was noticeably suffering ill-health and had to be 'put down' by a Vet. Nowadays, with much tighter legislative controls existing on those who retail animals, it is probable that neither dog would have been offered for sale on the ground either that it was too young or that it was, although seemingly fit, not well enough. But *caveat emptor* [buyer beware] was the legal policy in those days and thus liability fell not to the seller but to the buyer and therefore, if the dog was not of sufficient age to be sold or was ill when being sold … Well, tough - The buyer, not the seller, had to accept the consequences. So my Father, having been twice conned, never again sought to acquire another dog from Kennard's Arcade prefering instead to construct very solid wooden security shutters for every one of Highlands' accessible windows.

We did, however, buy a kitten from a Trader in the self-same Kennard's Arcade. It was a nice, fluffy, mainly black, little bundle - whom my Mother and I named 'Sally' - when it was bought but it speedily grew not only to a substantial size but, although most times Sally loyally kept within the confines of Highlands and its front and back gardens, also to become one of the most aggressive felines around. So aggressive did Sally become that our next door neighbour's fear that her beloved Chooky might suffer a mishap caused her to keep her beloved Chooky indoors most of the time thereby at least withdrawing from the neighbourhood the regular evening penetrating shout of "Chook, Chook, Chook, Chook, Chooky. Chook, Chook, Chook, Chook, Chooky. Chook, Chook, Chook, Chook, Chooky". Although the Second World War had by now been finished for some years there was a considerable amount of surplus War items on sale here, there, and everywhere; and one item that had caught my attention in a local Junk Shop was a battery-powered portable Army Signalling Lamp whose beam, courtesy of a splendid highly polished mirror, seemed to be able to be projected for miles. The lamp's two very large cylindrical batteries were, along with a Morse Code signalling devise, contained within a largish tin box which, by means of a webbing belt, could be carried on one's back. The box also housed the hand-held Lamp and its long cable which enabled the Lamp, when removed from the box, to be operated either by the person with the box or by a second person sited some distance from the box. I can not now remember whether the Signalling Lamp was given to me by my Parents as a Birthday present or as a Christmas present but I can remember that I spent many a dark late evening standing within the Billiard Room at Highlands concentrating, via a window that overlooked the back garden, the Lamp's splendid beam on Sally as our faithful, but increasingly annoyed, feline constantly sought to get out of the beam's way. Re-chargeable batteries did not exist in those days and it was only when there was no longer sufficient electricity within the batteries to power the Lamp that my pretence at trying to track enemy aircraft by using Sally as the target came to an end : But not before I had, in my then ignorance of things electrical, sought to by-pass the batteries by instead wiring the Lamp and its box of tricks directly into one of the house's, what was then, Direct Current [as against to-day's Alternating Current], 'Mains' Electricity unfused 15-amp round-pin power-points [as against to-day's fused 13-amp flat-pin power-points]. I have no doubt that Sally, in her way, had a darn good laugh at my expense for, on my switching on the power-point, there was an almighty bang from within the metal box, the projection of clear glass and mirrored glass in all directions, and a vast quantity of acrid smoke billowing out of what had, until the previous second, been the long cable that connected the Lamp to its box. Fortunately I was kneeling by the power-point at the time, else had I been touching the box, the cable that connected the box to the Lamp, or the Lamp itself ... Well, I dread to think of what physical injury I personally might have suffered. Sadly, some weeks later Sally, hitherto always very healthy, became ill to the extent that my Mother and I had little option but to take her to a Vet. Despite being aggressive, and despite having often been sorely tested by my beam-shining activities, Sally had always been a very faithful cat. My Mother and I, with increasing concern, sat in the Vet's Waiting Room for quite a while and had more or less concluded that … Well, that that was it. Thus we were very surprised indeed when the door to the Surgery was opened by the Vet not with an expression of concern but with a huge grin. Having announced that there was nothing seriously wrong with our cat he then asked my Mother "What did you say the cat's name is ?" "Sally," replied my Mother. "Well," said the grinning Vet," "you'd better change that 'cos he's the biggest tom cat that I've seem for quite a while". So, when we got back home 'Sally' became 'Sonny', although, having gotten used to responding to being called 'Sally', he would not answer to 'Sonny' and instead indicated his resistance to his new name by, instead of remaining within the bounds of Highlands, now roaming far and wide in order, no doubt, to fully realise his potential as a male cat, achievements evidenced by the regular arrival upon, what had been until my Mother destroyed it, my Father's bowling green of batches of kittens some of which, for short periods at least, we kept but the majority of which were taken by my Father to be disposed of.

Alan Dixon and his Parents lived directly across the road but I can not recall either of Alan's Parents ever coming to Highlands. In fact, I can not recall Alan's Parents at all. Perhaps they were never invited to Highlands thereby perhaps saving my Mother from being persuaded by them to allow me to go to their house. Next to the Dixons lived Marie and Harold Thompson. A pleasant couple with a married daughter who lived elsewhere but who could be seen regularly visiting her Mother, Marie was a Housewife who had a penchant for always doing her vacuuming around midnight and Harold was a Manager with Lloyds Bank in the City of London. On the far side of our nextdoor neighbours, the Smiths, lived a Dutch couple, Dr Blauuw and his Wife Mary. Another pleasant couple, Dr Blauuw was a Director of Unilever, the giant British-Dutch combine made up of the Dutch firm Naamloze Vennootschap Margarine Unie and the British firm Lever Brothers, and was often away in Holland or elsewhere in the world at large. Whether or not they had any children I do not know, but in his absences from home Mrs Blauuw lived by herself and would once a week or so 'pop in' to give me a small, usually hand-crafted by herself, present and to have a chat and a cup of tea with my Mother. Occasionally I would go to the Blauuw's house to play in her back garden, a garden in the middle of which was a pond with a delightful overhanging willow tree. When I was 10, much to Mrs Blauuw's sadness, for she loved her home in Croydon, she and Dr Blauuw sold their house in Croydon and moved back to Holland to a, then, state-of-the-art bungalow designed by Dr Blauuw. He was a kindly man, a comment also expressed by an elderly gentleman, Archie Alison, whom I met many years later in Berwick-upon-Tweed and who had worked as a Scientist at Unilever in London under Dr Blauuw. One of Archie's memories of Dr Blauuw was the reaction that Dr Blauuw expressed every time that Archie, or another of the team in which Archie worked, enthusiastically announced to Dr Blauuw some item of success that they thought had been achieved : With a smile the very approachable Doctor would encouragingly put an arm around the shoulders of the proud announcer of the success and say "Very goode, very goode. But vill it be of benefit to Unilever ?" It was only when, in 2003, I made enquiries of Dr Blaaw of Unilever's Corporate Archives in London and of the Royal

Netherlands Embassy in London that I realised that my one-time friendly neighbour of two doors away in Pampisford Road, Croydon had been an exceptional man who, as Ava Wieclawska of Unilever's Corporate Archives put it, had an "impressive career with Unilever". I reproduce below Ava Wieclawska's letter of 10 March 2003 and the letter of 26 March 2003 from Pammy Steegenga of the Royal Netherlands Embassy. Clearly, apart from his service with Unilever, he was also a significant figure in the military and in the civil reconstruction of Holland immediately the Germans were forced out of Nijmegen and back into Germany (*see the 1977 War film 'A Bridge Too Far'*).

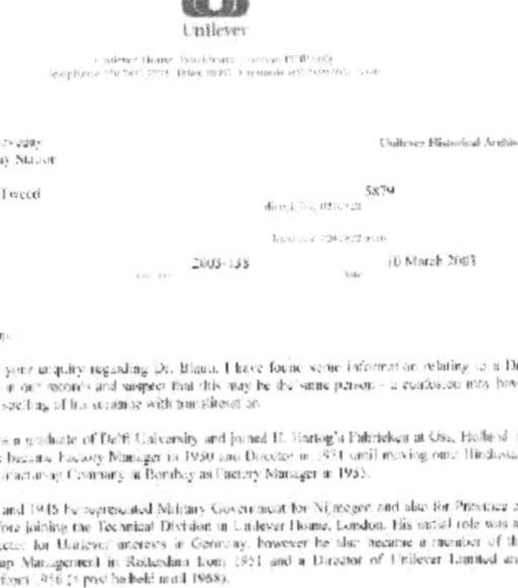

Dear Sir/Madam,

Thank you for your enquiry regarding Dr. Blauu. I have found some information relating to a Dr. A.F.H Blauuw in our records and suspect that this may be the same person – a confusion may have arisen over the spelling of his surname with transliteration.

Dr. Blauuw was a graduate of Delft University and joined H. Hartog's Fabrieken at Oss, Holland in 1926. There he became Factory Manager in 1930 and Director in 1931 until moving onto Hindustan Vanaspati Manufacturing Company in Bombay as Factory Manager in 1935.

Between 1944 and 1946 he represented Military Government for Nijmegen and also for Province of Gelderland before joining the Technical Division in Unilever House, London. His initial role was as Technical Director for Unilever interests in Germany, however he also became a member of the European Group Management in Rotterdam from 1951 and a Director of Unilever Limited and Unilever N.V. from 1956 (a post he held until 1968).

On 9th April 1962 he replaced a colleague as Head of the Techincal Division, where his time would be divided between London and Rotterdam. In addition, he was also responsible for the co-ordination of all Unilever's paper and packaging activities and interests from 1965, as Techinal Director of Packaging Services.

In 1966 he was awarded the Heinrich Nicolaus Gold Medal, in recognition of his services to the Bavarian Packing Industry and in 1967 he was appointed a Knight in the Order of the Netherlands Lion.

Finally on 13th May 1968, Dr. Blauuw retired from his impressive career with Unilever. He later died on 8th September 1978.

I am afraid we have no information concerning his wife but if you think I can be of help in any other matter then please don't hesitate to contact me.

Yours Sincerely
Ava Wieclawska
Archive Assitant
Corporate Archives

Dear Ms Sutherland-Loveday,

Further to your letter dated 18 March I am pleased to enclose information on the Order of the Lion of The Netherlands.

The Order of the Lion of The Netherlands was awarded to Dr AFH Blaauw as Member of the Board of Unilever NV by the Ministry of Agriculture and Fisheries, as decided by Royal decree of 16 February 1968, nr 1.

Dr AFH Blaauw has also received the Grand Cross of the Order of Orange Nassau by the then Ministry of War, as decided by Royal decree of 14 September 1946, nr 3.

One ritual, although I never regarded it as such, that occurred on many of the Sunday Theatrical 'get-togethers' that took place at Highlands would involve a visit by some of the guests up to my Father's Billiards Room sometimes to play billiards and/or snooker but always to look at my scaled-down Theatre into which I would place a model Set and explain to my 'audience' various technicalities that my Father had explained to me. Although I was not necessarily aware of it at the times, some, if not most, of my audiences to whom I was giving my explanations were either themselves the Designers, and Builders, of the models or the Directors or Impresarios of the Shows to which the models related or at least in some way connected with the Shows. One of those often present on such occasions was Stanley Earnshaw, who, on 28 May 1944, had attended my Christening by the Reverend EA Brown at St Peter's Church in South Croydon. Stanley Earnshaw was a Son of Arthur Thomas Earnshaw who had been the Electrician at London's *Duke of York's Theatre* until, aged 42 - to-gether with Phillip Sheridan, the 38- years old Electrician at London's *Strand Theatre* - he founded, in 1914, Strand Electric, the most successful of 20th century UK Theatre Lighting firms and the principal 'driver' of Stage and Television lighting technology throughout most of the 20th century. Arthur Earnshaw's

Theatrical relationship with my Father had been very close as was his Social relationship, for, to-gether with a whole cluster of other 'behind Stage' Theatricals, they had, in 1927, founded the Tableau Lodge, a Masonic Lodge consecrated on 18 February of that year and doubtless named, I suspect, in respect of a theatre's front-of-house curtains ('tabs'). From my early childhood I had known that my Father was a Founder Member of the Tableau Lodge, but I knew little more. I have a framed photograph that used to hang on one of the walls of the Billiards Room at Highlands and I also have a copy of the Tableau Lodge's Golden Jubilee Summons that, with a Letter of Invitation, had, out of courtesy to her being a Widow of a Founder Member, been sent to my Mother in 1977 : And so, in 2005, I decided to make further enquiries, and therefore wrote to the Writer of the Letter of Invitation at the address given on that Letter and enclosed a copy of the photograph with a request that, if possible, I be informed of who the characters in the photograph were. Given the many years that had passed since the 1977 Letter had been written, I only very slightly expected to receive - indeed I really did not expect to receive - a reply. However, on 4 November 2005 I received a telephone-call from a Lionel Devonish who informed me that he was the Lodge's current Secretary; that my letter had been passed by the current occupier of the house to which I had addressed my letter to the Daughter of the person to whom I had written, the current occupier having, purely by chance, known of the Daughter and of her whereabouts; that the Daughter, again purely by chance, knowing not only that Lionel was the current Secretary but also of Lionel's whereabouts, had managed to convey my letter on to him; but that he, Lionel, not knowing anyone in the photograph, had "inadvertently", so he said, overlooked it until, at the end of October 2005, he had received, 'out of the blue', a telephone-call from Jack Lovell, a nonagenarian who, although still a

Lodge Member, had not, due to his age and an inability to walk far, attended any Lodge Meeting for some considerable time. Jack had telephoned Lionel in a state of some distress for he had, over the previous month or so, had an increasingly strong feeling that someone was trying to get in touch with him and, thinking that it might be 'from the beyond' from one of his old Lodge cronies, eventually telephoned Lionel to find out if any Lodge Member had recently died. Lionel having informed Jack that no-one had died recently, the two of them chatted away and reminisced of times past. Then, just as the conversation was ending, Lionel said to Jack "By the way, Jack, someone has sent an old Lodge photo' asking to know the names of the people on it. I haven't a clue. Do you reckon you might know ?" "Send it to me," said Jack," and I'll have a look at it". Then Jack said to Lionel "What's the name of the guy who sent the photo ?" "Ted Loveday," replied Lionel. At that point Jack broke down and, after half a minute or so, then said to Lionel "Christ, I was the last person to speak with his Father before he drove home to his death. He was one of the kindest, nicest men who ever lived". Sadly, the Tableau Lodge no longer exists as a separate Lodge. [*See the photograph below of my Father's Founder's Medal.*]

Next day I telephoned Jack and had a long, at times very emotional, conversation with him; and on Monday 28 November 2005 my Wife, Margaret, and I, having attended a Water Rats' Ball in an hotel in London's Park Lane the night before, called at Jack's home in London where Jack and I, with my Wife an attentive but slightly bored listener, had a 3-hours chat about 'old times'. A former, much respected within the Theatrical profession, Maker of Theatrical Props, this still very mentally-alert nonagenarian was a mine of information and was able to tell me many things including the occupations of every Petitioner and Founder Member of the Tableau Lodge who were:

Albert Edward Wood	Master Carpenter at London's Royalty Theatre and Scenery Contractor
Arthur Thomas Earnshaw	Electrician at London's Duke of York's Theatre and co-founder of Strand Electric
Phillip Sheridan	Electrician at London's Strand Theatre and co-founder of Strand Electric
Wallace Cuthbert Saunders	Electrician at London's Kingsway Theatre
William Hollis Davies	Master Carpenter at London's Wyndham's Theatre and Scenery Contractor
Frederick C Hinton	Box Office Manager at London's Lyric Theatre
Francis Leonard Lyndhurst	Scenery Contractor
Harry D Marsh	Theatre Electrician

Lionel Walter Arter	Theatrical Contractor
John Frederick P Hill	Scenery Contractor
H Hunt	Theatre Electrician at London Daly's Theatre
Douglas Alexander Clark-Smith	Theatrical Producer
Robert Smith	Stage Manager at London's Palladium Theatre
Reginald Holt	Master Carpenter at London Aldwych Theatre and Scenery Contractor
Arthur W Stapley	Manager at the London Hippodrome Theatre
Charles John Cheesman	Scenery Contractor
John Crosbie-Frazer	Scenery Contractor
Frank Maurice-Wilson	Scenery Contractor
Edwin George Loveday	Scenery Contractor
John Brunskill	Scenery Contractor
H Flack	Scenery Builder
Albert Pennecost	Theatre Master Carpenter.

A true 'craft' Lodge with a bias, no doubt deliberately, in favour of Theatrical Scenery, this bunch of 'behind-the-scenes' Theatrical talent met regularly every fourth Friday in April, June, August, and October each year at The Comedy Restaurant, Oxenden Street, in London's Haymarket with Albert Edward Wood as the Lodge's first Master, William Hollis Davies as the Lodge's first Senior Warden, and Francis Leonard Lyndhurst as the Lodge's first Junior Warden. Nowadays perhaps a word to describe these characters and their Masonic Lodge might be 'cartel'" : But, whatever the founding purpose of their Lodge was, between them these Members of the Tableau Lodge not only were great friends socially but also in business, although often in competition with each other, they doubtless played a major part in the successful functioning of London's 'West End' Theatre throughout many years of the 20th Century.

Now back to my childhood outside of term-times: On Saturday mornings I could, after having got washed and dressed and having had breakfast, usually be found either sitting behind my desk 'banging away' at my Father's typewriter or perhaps being taken by my Father to one of his firm's two Scenery Works, one - my Father's old Loveday & Higson Works, the Cornwall Works - was in London's Kennington Green and the other - John and Jack Brunskill's old Works - was in Newport Street, Lambeth in London.

The freehold of the Cornwall Works had once been owned by the Duchy of Cornwall ['Kennington' originally meaning 'the king's town']. Very near to Surrey County Cricket Club's world-famous Oval Cricket Ground and to the equally famous Gas Holders which 'overlooked' the Ground [and which were often referred-to during cricket matches by Radio and Television Cricket Commentators in phrases such as "… and as he comes in to bowl from the Gas Works end …"], the Cornwall Works were sited in Montford Place adjacent to the Hayward Pickle Company's, sometimes somewhat pickle-pungent, 'Military Pickleworks'. Both my Father's Scenery Works and Hayward's Military Pickleworks suffered blast and fire damage during the Second World War when, on the night of 8 July 1944, one of Hitler's infamous pilotless winged V1 [Vergeltungswaffen 1] Flying Bombs landed, doubtless more or less intentionally, on one of the nearby Gas Holders, then owned by the South Metropolitan Gas Company, completely destroying not only much of the Gas Holders and their highly explosive contents but also eight nearby houses. [*The copy photograph under shows Montford Place with one of the Gas Holders at its Oval Cricket Ground end and, on the right of the picture, the (now demolished) Cornwall Works.*]

Pedestrian entry to the 'Cornwall Works' was either via two large wooden gates or via a wicket-gate sited in one of the large gates. I found going through the wicket-gate the more exciting, and so, if on Saturdays the large gates were shut, that was usually the way that my Father and I went in. Once in we walked across a yard and as we did so we passed, on our left, an open-sided shed where lengths of yet-to-be-sawn timber were stacked in order to be naturally seasoned [to bring them to a suitable condition for use]. At the far end of the yard, standing on their ends with their T-shaped handles resting against a high boundary wall, were two, no longer in use, hand-carts retained by my Father as reminders of the years when, in the early part of the 20th century, they had been used almost daily by Carters to trundle, by hand through London's mixture of decreasing horse-drawn traffic and increasing mechanically-propelled traffic, finished pieces of

Scenery from his Works to Scenic Artists elsewhere where the Scenery would be painted by skilled Scenic Artists before going on to Theatres or, without being painted, directly to Theatres in London where the Theatres' own skilled Scenic Artists would undertake the work, or to one of London's Railway Stations to be taken off the carts and put into specially converted Theatrical Scenery carriages - usually conversions of third-class passenger carriages - so that the Scenery could be taken from London directly to Theatres in such, then seemingly distant, places as Glasgow, Edinburgh, Liverpool, and Newcastle-upon-Tyne. Perhaps nowadays hard to imagine, but Scenery flats of 12ft [3.7M] in length, of 20ft [6.2M] in length, of 34ft [10.5M] in length if not even longer, staircases, all sorts of large and small pieces of Theatrical Scenery would be hand-pulled and hand-manoeuvred through the streets of London on hand-carts - What chaos they must have caused at times, especially when turning left or turning right, for they would have caused everything else to grind to a halt until the conclusions of the manoeuvres had been achieved !!

The Newport Street, Lambeth works were accessed not via a yard but straight from the street by means of large sliding doors in the side of the building itself thus enabling the passing public, both children and adults, to often peer inside to the point, occasionally, of actually wandering in to wonder at the illusions being created right there in front of them and to admire the skills and craftsmanship of, and to have brief conversations with, the talented makers of those illusions.

(*Newport Street works with the Railway Arches stores shown in the bottom left.*)

On the other side of the works in Newport Street were the main railway lines into Waterloo Station. Under the lines were large vaulted arches in which John Brunskill stored Scenery that he had made for D'Oyly Carte's Savoy Operas. [*See below copy of letter dated 20 June 1928 to Richard Collet at the Savoy Hotel.*]

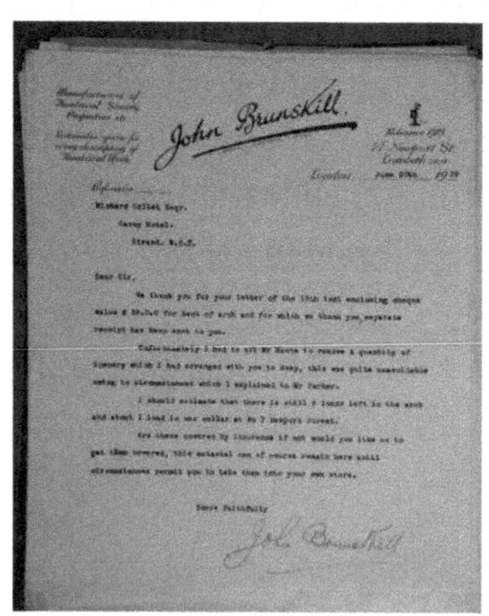

Apart from large belt-driven circular bench saws, large belt-driven bandsaws, belt-driven jigsaws, and belt-driven sanders, all tools used were hand tools. Following my Christening one of my Father's friends, a Timber Merchant, WC Ware and Sons Limited of nearby Kennington Lane, was kind enough, in anticipation that I would one day succeed my Father in his business, to give me a large belt-driven bandsaw only to have it returned to him by my Father with much thanks and with the comment "What do you want the lad to do with it ? Cut his bloody hands off ?"

Most, if not all, of the hand tools used in my Father's day were proudly owned and proudly maintained by each of the individuals who used them, most of the tools having had the imprint of the owner's name and/or initials stamped/burned firmly into them; and each tool was either carefully packed-up and taken home after the end of each working day or, if not taken home, placed in a position within the Works specially allocated to the tools and their owner. Thus a

Master Joiner, having spent several years at his trade, would be the proud owner, and conscientious maintainer, of at least one panel saw, one crosscut saw, one half-rip saw, one dovetail saw, one tenon saw, one bow saw, a pad saw, a file with which to sharpen his saws, and a setting tool with which to set the angles of the teeth of his saws. He would also be the proud owner, and conscientious maintainer, of at least one claw hammer, a pin hammer, a mallet, a carpenter's pincer, a gimlet, a brace and a set of bits for the brace, a hand drill and a set of bits for the hand drill, a try square, a sliding bevel, a scribing tool, a tape measure, a rule, a plumb line, a spirit level, a single-pin marking gauge, a double-pin mortice marking gauge, a nail set or other punch, a bradawl, a set of planes, a draw knife, a set of chisels and gouges, some screwdrivers, an oilstone and a slipstone with which to keep the blades of his planes and of his chisels sharp and his screwdrivers correctly ground, some files and rasps, a spokeshave, a knife, a sanding block, a candle with which to 'grease' the edges of the teeth of the saws to enable them to cut more smoothly, and an always-sharp joiner's/carpenter's pencil. Whereas these were the personal tools of his Trade and thus the proud personal possessions of the Master Joiner the business itself provided, for general use by the workforce, such joinery and carpentry items as dovetail templates, bench hooks, mitre blocks, saw horses, twisting boards, and shooting boards, clamps, bench grinders and wheeldressers, honing guides, large two-man and one-man cross cut saws, a counter-weighted mortice chiselling machines, glue pots and brushes, size tubs and brushes, and, of course, the woodworking benches and vices, the woodworking benches having been made by the workforce itself.

The Master Joiners and the Joiners yet to become Master Joiners at both the Cornwall Works and at Newport Street were assisted by Apprentices whose written contracts bound them to serve the firm for a period of years in return for which the Apprentices would be taught the full range of both carpentry and joinery skills sufficient to enable the Apprentices themselves to become fully proficient in the making of Theatrical Scenery which, in reality, meant that at the ends of their contracted periods of Apprenticeships the Apprentices, on becoming Joiners, but not yet Master Joiners, had learned almost everything that there was to learn first about carpentry and then about the more precise skills of joinery. But first Apprentices started not by using tools and actually assisting in the construction of Scenery but by making the tea at appointed break times; by regularly sweeping clean the floors and other surfaces onto which sawdust and wood shavings fell; by lighting, by means of the sawdust and wood shavings, and maintaining the several pot-stove fires that kept the insides of the buildings warm; by breaking the cakes of glue into small pieces before putting the broken pieces to soak in buckets of cold water to soften for a day before being placed into the inner containers of the gluepots; by thereafter keeping the gluepots topped-up and constantly ready for use when required by the Joiners; by ensuring that the sand and water buckets were always full and to hand in case a fire should ever occur; by, having first been taught how properly to do so, keeping sharp the various cutting tools used by the Joiners and Master Joiners.

Once the Apprentices had proven themselves to be competent and trustworthy at the tasks allotted to them the Joiners would instruct them in the types of timber used by the firm; would teach them the differences between, and characteristics of, hardwoods and softwoods and explain to them how to select timbers for the various jobs for which the timbers were intended to be used and explain to them the drying-out (seasoning) processes whereby the fluid contents within the timbers would be reduced to levels sufficient so as to prevent the finished timbers from warping and twisting; would introduce them to the many types of fixings - nails, screws, dogs, straps, trenails, dowels, glue, bolts, and so on - used in carpentry and joinery to enable timbers to be fastened to-gether. Only thereafter would the Apprentices actually work alongside the Joiners to learn the ways in which handtools should be held and used to make the many types of joints - housing, notching, rebating, mortise and tenoning, tusk tenoning, cogging, foxtail wedging, dowelling, scarfing, keying, halving, dovetailing, mitring, bridling, and so on - used to fix timbers to-gether. They would learn how to chamfer, to kerf, to make veneers, and to fix canvas onto flats and other items of scenery. They would also learn how to construct the various items - jacks, tip jacks, outriggers, braces, stiffeners, and so forth - affixed to items of Scenery to enable the Scenery to be moved, positioned, and stabilised on stage. They would be taught the techniques, and fittings, used in 'running' Scenery, in 'flying Scenery, in 'lashing' Scenery to-gether, and in all other techniques involved in the handling of Scenery. Once competent in all these aspects of the skills of the Theatrical Scenery Maker the Apprentices would be taught how to read the drawings prepared by the firm's draftsmen so that they could translate the drawings into manufactured items. Then, but constantly under the supervision of the Joiners and Master Joiners, they would be left to themselves construct basic Scenery items such as flats; and thereafter, having proven themselves competent in constructing such items, they would, but still under supervision, be left to construct more complicated items such as stairs and staircases. They would also be taught upholstery techniques to enable them to make chairs, beds, sofas, settees, and so on. Only when competent in all these skills would their apprenticeships be 'signed off' and they be entitled to be themselves called Joiners.

I, of course, was still a schoolboy and it would be some years before that part of my life ceased. But my Father took full advantage of his large wooden well-equipped joiners/carpenters workshop and store at Highlands to, over the years, also teach me much of that which his Apprentices were taught. Whilst I can not say that I loved every minute of his instructions I certainly enjoyed much of the times that he and I worked to-gether; and, looking back over the many years that have since elapsed, I am truthfully very grateful to him for the many skills and knowledge that he taught me. Many of the hand-skills in use in those days, and which he taught me, have nowadays been replaced by limited lifespan electrically powered, little if any skill needed, machines - such as drills, saws, planers - which, when they break down, are often wastefully thrown away to be replaced by other such electrically powered machines : And it is doubtful whether to-day any such type of craftsmen as existed when I used to visit my Father's Works now exist. If they do, they are rare characters indeed.

I remember vividly one Saturday visit that I made to my Father's Works in Kennington when my Mother actually deigned to accompany my Father and me. He was very proud of the fact that not only had his firm created, in wood and canvas, a functioning railway engine and tender complete with red-glowing firebox but also that the engine, when on stage to be seen by the audience to be involved in a dramatic crash, would be able to, simply by means of one out-of-sight Stagehand pulling on one single rope, fall off its rails onto its side. Having explained what was to happen, my Mother, taking her handbag with her, and I were invited into the engine's driving-cab by my Father who then disappeared out of sight to where, via a pulley mechanism, the end of the rope was hanging. "Ready ?" shouted my Father. "Yes," we replied. Suddenly the whole engine and its tender lurched up and over almost to one side; and my Mother, screaming, threw her handbag up into the air and far beyond where the engine was. I thoroughly enjoyed it : But clearly my Mother did not for, verbally, all hell let loose, and the rest of the week-end was sheer misery for both my Father and me !!

Sadly I have no photograph of that wonderful piece of Theatrical Scenery, but I do have a photograph of, what seems at first glance to be, one of the first of the famous London Transport Routemaster 'buses (It was not a Routemaster but a 'bus of the generation before) [*see below.*]. The Producers of the Show for which this piece of Scenery was created had intended to use an actual London Transport 'bus but the weight of a real 'bus was far too great for the stage to bear. Thus the piece of Scenery was made. Sitting on a boat truck (a castered wagon used to move Scenery), it was towed by a real London Transport 'bus from my Father'''s works through the streets of London to London's Coliseum Theatre; and, subsequently fully laden with a driver and passengers, it came into the view of the 1949 Royal Variety Show audience by means of a revolve (a turntable built into the stage). It was, in fact, in size only very slightly smaller than a genuine Routemaster but the size difference, certainly to the astonished audience, was not noticeable nor was the fact that its far [from the audience] side had been adapted to allow the actors and actresses, who played the parts of the driver and passengers, to climb into it. With the full co-operation throughout of London Transport, the red livery was genuine, the London Transport logo and the advertisements were genuine, the wheels and tyres were genuine, as were the lights and many other of its features. It was only when she went backstage after the show that Her Majesty Queen Elizabeth (the 'Queen Mother'), who had been in the audience, realised that it was not not a genuine 'bus but a piece of Scenery. When the Show's run ended the 'bus was bought by an Illusionist who used it for several years to astound many audiences by seemingly making a double-deck London Transport 'bus suddenly appear and disappear whenever he commanded it to do so. After several years of such magical use the 'bus was eventually broken-up and thus did finally disappear, save, that is, for this, and one other, photograph.

In the late 1940s/early 1950s it was felt by the UK Government and others that the people of the United Kingdom, having suffered much during the Second World War and having suffered much financial hardship throughout the years after the War, needed a celebration of some sorts to cheer them up : And so a 'Festival of Britain', to coincide with the centenary of the Great Exhibition of 1851, was thought of by the then Labour Government .

In London the Festival of Britain - intended to be a celebration of British, particularly English, history, culture, and science - was principally centred on the Battersea/South Bank area. In Battersea Park a 'Festival Pleasure Gardens' alongside the River Thames was created, the skylining feature of which was a 300ft [92M] self-supporting steel and aluminium cigar-shaped construction called the Skylon whilst in the adjoining area adjacent to Waterloo Bridge now known as *the* South Bank the Royal Festival Hall was constructed.

Below is a copy of a photograph of the auditorium and proscenium arch of Battersea Park's Festival Theatre. Designed by the Set Designer Guy Sheppard as part of the Labour Government's Festival of Britain Exhibition and part-built by Brunskill and Loveday, it opened in May 1951, had 368 seats, was fully equipped, and had 19 sets of Lines. Intended that it be in existence for many years, 5 months later, in October 1951, the newly elected Conservative Government ordered the closure, demolition, and removal of Battersea's Festival of Britain site including the Riverside Theatre.

I was privileged, although I did not appreciate it at the time, to be taken by my Father to a rehearsal of the first production staged by London's Festival Ballet Company at the Royal Festival Hall. Formed in 1950 - its name, the Festival Ballet Company, having been suggested by its principal female dancer, [Dame] Alicia Markova - and subsequently, in 1989, to become known as the English National Ballet, its base for the first years of its existence was London's Stoll Theatre. Under Anton Dolin as its Artistic Director and Julian Braunsweg as its Director General, it very soon achieved success both as a major ballet company and as a major touring ballet company; and by the time that it transferred to the Royal Festival Hall in 1952 it had become a *principal* ballet company.

My Father's firm had built the Scenery for all the Festival Ballet's performances at the Stoll Theatre and continued to do so when the Festival Ballet transferred to the Royal Festival Hall. Hindsight tells me that my Father's intention, in taking me to see the rehearsal at the Festival Hall, was that I should sit, learn, and gain an understanding of ballet. He had, I think, overlooked the facts that the concentration span of 8-years old boys is usually somewhat, if not very, limited and that the over 7 hours that I was required to sit substantially on my own in the stalls of a largely empty auditorium, with an occasional accompanied visit on-stage and backstage, was … Well, a very, very boring experience. True, I was constantly plied with ice-cream and, true, many people, including the foremost male British ballet dancer of his day, Anton Dolin [real name, Patrick Healey-Kay], came, several times, to chat to me. But, despite the many kindnesses shown to me throughout my enforced 7+ hours' stay within the Royal Festival Hall and despite the privileged uniqueness of the occasion, it was an experience which I would never wish upon any other 8-years old child, unless he/she has a passion for ballet. Fortunately, despite having eaten mountains of the stuff, my liking for ice-cream has never suffered but it was to be many, many, many years before I found myself able to easily watch ballet again.

An advantage of having a Father who was a principal builder of Scenery for many, many Shows, both in London and elsewhere, was the ability to see some of the best Shows around, many of which still stay in the mind even to-day. Another advantage was to be taken back-stage to meet with the performers and many of those backstage personalities without whose talents such Shows would not have been possible. There were, for instance, the Ice Shows, such as the 1955 productions of *Wildfire* and *Dick Whittngton on Ice* [*see Programme fronts under*], at the now no longer in existence Empress Hall in London's Earls Court. The multi-talented comedian, actor, ice-skater, and dancer Richard Hearne, who in 'private' life, was also a farmer in Kent, who starred in *Wildfire* was well-known to children as Mr Pastry; and Frankie Vaughan, another of the Show's stars, had already reached the heights of being a very successful singer, a position that he was to occupy for many years, his well-known and often imitated theme-song being "Give me the Moonlight". The Designer for both Shows was Guy Sheppard, the lighting for both Shows was by Stanley Earnshaw's Strand Electric Company, and the Props [Properties] for *Wildfire* were supplied by Jack Lovall, the gentleman whom I was to meet up with again many, many years later when he was a nonagenarian [see above].

Another great West End Show that I, as a boy, was fortunate to see, both as a member of the audience and then, after the Show, from backstage, was the Musical *Kismet*. Brought over from the United States and staged, also in 1955, by the Impresario/Band Leader Jack

Hylton in London's Stoll Theatre this tale of Arabian Nights in Baghdad starred Alfred Drake and Doretta Morrow, each of whom had also been the Show's Stars in the United States. Based, musically, on the rich exciting themes of the long-deceased Russian composer Alexander Borodin, with such songs as *Stranger in Paradise, And This is my Beloved,* and *The Olive Tree* this Musical is still, even to this day, an excitement-generator. The Scenery construction was shared between Jack Hylton's own Scenery Department and my Father's firm with Strand Electric being the Lighting provider. [*see Programme front below.*]

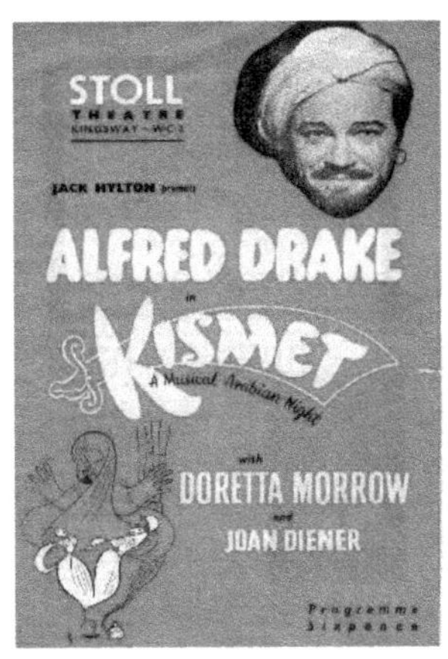

One Show of this era which I most certainly did not enjoy was the 1954 production of *Noddy in Toyland,* also at London's Stoll Theatre. In this I was, for two or three performances, a performer; and I hated it, absolutely hated it. With its Scenery built by my Father's firm, *Noddy in Toyland* was a Musical by Enid Blyton - the Writer of well over 600 books and the creator of many famous children's stories featuring such characters as *The Famous Five, The Secret Seven,* and, of course, *Noddy.* It was a very popular Show which, after its run at the Stoll, went on to be staged in London's Princes Theatre in 1955, then back to the Stoll in 1956, then to the Princes again in 1957, then to London's Victoria Palace Theatre in 1958, then back to the Princes Theatre in 1959. But, despite its huge success with children and, doubtless, also with adults, it generated within me a feeling of unease, a feeling that I could never understand until years later when, sitting looking at a television Show, I learned that this most famous of children's authoresses, whom I met on stage at the Stoll and who must have made a considerable sum of money as a result of her many children's books, never liked children. In fact, it was said, she actually hated children. I can only therefore conclude that my feeling of unease towards her Show must have originated when she spoke with me, for I possibly/probably sensed an aura of falsehood about her which caused me to dislike and distrust her.

One Author whom I did like was Anthony Buckeridge, who, like Enid Blyton, had been a school teacher and who, like Enid Blyton, was a well-known Writer of children's books. My meeting with him was, as far as I knew, purely by chance and had absolutely nothing to do with the Theatre. My Father, Mother, and I were on a touring holiday, in my Father's car, in Continental Europe and, on the occasion concerned, were staying, for one night, in a small boarding house in France. At the time I had a passion for reading *Jennings* books, many of which, if not all, were given to me as Birthday and Christmas presents, by our Gardener's Wife, Mrs Harding. One morning after breakfast, as I came down a flight of ordinary domestic stairs, I was avidly reading *Jennings' Little Hut* and thus completely oblivious to the fact that someone was coming up the stairs towards me. At approximately the midpoint of the flight of stairs the pipe-smoking man coming in the opposite direction collided with the book that I was, inconsiderately, reading. The narrowness of the stairway caused us both to have to stop. I apologised for what I had done : But, instead of being critical of my inconsiderate rudeness, he responded by asking me the title of the book. "*Jennings Little Hut*," I replied to which, to my utter amazement, he responded "I'm its Author, Anthony Buckeridge". What a courteous man he was. I was 'gob-smacked' by the fact that I had *actually met* and *actually spoken with* the Author of the famous *Jennings* books [and the, not quite so famous, *Rex Milligan* books]. Radio, not television, was the principal form of received home-entertainment at the time; and therefore, had I been aware that this former schoolteacher was also a very well-known Writer of many plays principally for BBC Radio's *Children's Hour* ... Well, the 'size of my head' would have known no bounds !! After my Parents and I left the boarding house to continue on our journey I never met him again, but I still retain my autographed volume of *Jennings Little Hut* [*see page under*]. Also, as the years have passed, given that Anthony Buckeridge was a Writer of Plays, I have occasionally wondered whether my Father and he had deliberately contrived my meeting with Buckeridge on that flight of stairs !!

To-day, with well over a billion bicycles worldwide and with well over 1.5 billion cars worldwide, it is hard to imagine that in 1880 the first chain-driven bicycle and the first gasoline-powered car had yet to be invented : And so when my Father was born in 1880 he entered a world whose attitude to transport was very, very different from what it is to-day. Nevertheless, my Father, when in his teens, not only was intrigued by the new *safety bicycles* but also, like many adept teenagers of his day, built, completely out of wood save for the chain, his own *safety bicycles*; and, as the 19th century gave way to the 20th century, he became a keen motorist and, just prior to the 1920s, was wealthy enough to buy himself a magnificent open-topped car. His intention, which he fulfilled, was to race it - in 'friendly' competitions with other Members of the Theatrical profession - round the world's first purpose-built racing circuit for cars at *Brooklands* in Surrey. His enthusiasm for motoring continued right up until his death, aged 78, in 1958 : And it was doubtless that enthusiasm for motoring which caused us as a Family, once I was old enough for it to be deemed safe for me to go, to cross to mainland Europe at least once nearly every year for a touring holiday.

Nowadays if one wishes to drive to, say, Paris, one simply has to drive, or go by train, under the English Channel/la Manche or drive to a ferryboat terminal such as Dover, then, armed with a ticket, drive onto a 'Roll-on/Roll-off' ferry, then drive off the ferry after it has arrived at a French port, and then, with or without the assistance of a map, drive along more-or-less excellent French roads until one reaches Paris - That simple. But in the 1950s a drive from the United Kingdom to Paris was very different. My Father was an early Member of the AA [Automobile Association (founded in 1905 to help motorists to avoid police speed traps)] and was one of the first policyholders of the AA-supported Motor Union Insurance Company. Thus from the AA he would obtain assistance insofar as route-planning was concerned and from the Motor Union Insurance Company he would, by negotiation, obtain Insurance cover for Continental motoring. Having negotiated a booking on, not a yet-to-be-invented 'Roll-on/Roll-off' ferry but, a 'Lift-on/Lift-off' ferry, having obtained all the other necessary documentation, and having managed to purchase some foreign currency, when the day of departure came my Father would, by means of bolting purpose-made wooden shutters onto the inside of each accessible [to thieves] window, secure our home. Then the three of us would get in the car and drive down to Dover's somewhat infant Car Ferry terminal where, after having completed the necessary paperwork and checks required at Dover, my Father would drive the car to a position alongside a waiting boat. Then we would get out of the car, my Father would then lock the car, empty it of most of its petrol, and hand the keys to one of the waiting stevedores, and we would stand back and watch. A crane would then lower a net in front of the car. Inside, and fixed to, the net were two substantial planks. The stevedore would then unlock the car, get into it, and drive it onto the two planks inside the net. Then he would get out, disconnect the car's battery, and lock the car whilst other stevedores secured the car to the planks. Then all the stevedores would stand well clear of the net, a signal would be given by one of the stevedores to the crane-driver, and the net, with our car inside it, would be hoisted up into the air well clear of the ground, then manoeuvred above the waiting vessel, and then lowered either onto the vessel's deck or into one of the vessel's holds where the net would be sufficiently lowered to enable the car to be entered and then hand-pushed out of the net to a suitable position where it would be tightly secured for the voyage across The Channel. Then the crane would lift the net and its boards out of the vessel to enable the process to be repeated for another vehicle. We would then walk up a gangplank into the vessel and settle down for the cross-Channel journey. On arrival at Calais the whole procedure would be repeated but in reverse thereby enabling us to recover our car so that we could continue on our way after first having purchased some petrol.

The first thing that one noticed when beginning to drive in France was, of course, the fact that "They drive on the other side of the road". The second thing that one noticed was that French road signage was substantially different from UK road signage. Experience overcame the former, and, given that my Father had had considerable pre-Second World War experience of driving in mainland Europe, "driving on the other side of the road" never seemed to trouble him. But road signage always did cause him a few problems, especially at round-abouts and with the French system where one must stop, even on main roads, to give priority to vehicles entering from side roads. To help UK motorists to overcome the differences between motoring in the UK and motoring in Continental Europe the AA provided a clear sticker with every known continental road sign and its meaning printed on it. The suggestion from the AA was that it should be stuck on the inside of the windscreen at a position easily visually accessible to the driver; but my Father's preference was to stick it onto a cardboard backing which he then suspended from the car's interior mirror. Each to his own, but I used to think, as I watched this dangling piece of vital information as it swung in all directions, that the AA's suggested method was better !!

On departing the Port at Calais the AA's route-planning assistance came immediately into its own. It consisted of a wad, or wads, of sheets of paper stapled to-gether. Each sheet would have (a) a route from somewhere to somewhere else stated and drawn on it and (b) a written commentary of what to look for as a means of assisting to negotiate from the somewhere to the somewhere else. Thus - with my Father driving, my Mother reading out aloud from the AA's splendid route-planner, and me sitting in the back - we would leave the Port to drive through War-devastated mainland Europe.

At this point I should perhaps mention that whereas both my Father and my Mother each held a Driving Licence neither had ever taken, let alone passed, a Driving Test. Driving (Competency) Tests were introduced in the UK in 1934 whereas my Father had started driving motor vehicles at the turn of the 19th/20th centuries, thus long before the introduction of the Tests. My Mother though did not start driving until the early 1940s. However, she also had never needed to take a Driving Test because they were suspended in the UK from 1939 until 1946 due to the Second World War. My Father loved driving and was a very experienced, and generally a very skilled, driver : But to my Mother driving was not something that one did because one wanted to but because either one had to or should, because of 'image', be seen to be able to do. So, when being driven through Europe I had one skilled Parent who thoroughly enjoyed driving and one unskilled Parent who disliked driving [and she was certainly not the best of navigators either !!].

Sadly I can not remember much of my first touring journey to Europe. I know that we went to Switzerland, to the South of France, and to Monte Carlo because I have photographs of me in Lugano, Menton, and Monte Carlo (*see photographs below*),

Menton

Lugano

Monte Carlo

However I can recall the second touring holiday : Undertaken in my Father's Pontiac car we went first to Paris, although 'simply' is not really the word to describe it for the bomb and other War damage in towns and villages around Calais were horrendous as indeed they were throughout much of mainland Europe. Many buildings, from the very large to the very small, were either substantially or completely destroyed as were many areas of most of the roads over which we travelled. It was very depressing even to someone such as I who had, throughout my childhood, seen the consequences of war damage and destruction in and around London, Croydon, and elsewhere in the South of England. Village after village in France was a mess, often a complete mess : And petrol was both difficult to obtain and, when obtained, very expensive, so expensive that my Father had, like others before they left the UK, been issued with vouchers which, upon presentation to the petrol pump attendant, would enable a discount on price to be obtained. Each drop of the petrol that was put into the car had to be strenuously and laboriously manually pumped by the 'petrol pump' attendant who also, because of the muck thrown up onto the car by the appalling road conditions, would thereafter do his or her best to clean the car's windscreen. Because of the Pontiac's heavy consumption of fuel the procedure of stopping for petrol, waiting whilst the petrol was manually pumped into the tank, and thereafter waiting whilst the attendant removed at least some of the filth from the windscreen became a frequent, initially entertaining but soon somewhat boring, feature of our holiday.

Once in Paris we stayed for some days and nights, the three of us in one bedroom, in an hotel on the Champs-Elysée, the windows of the bedroom overlooking the Champs-Elysée itself. Unlike a small hotel where we had stayed one night en route from Calais to Paris the hotel in Paris not only had running water but also had toilet facilities. It also had a, to me then, bewildering toilet-looking gadget the like of which I had never seen before. It was a bidet.

Despite France having suffered harshly during the War Paris was an organised contrast to much of that which we had seen elsewhere in France; and clearly my Father was no stranger to this wonderful City for, with little hesitation, he took my Mother and I to Parisienne tourist 'sights' here, there, and almost everywhere. Having been brought up in a culture of "Bed at 6 o'clock" I was not, sadly, a party to their night-time visits to my Father's Parisienne Theatrical haunts. In an attempt to relieve my boredom when having to stay in the hotel bedroom whilst my Parents went off to the *Moulin Rouge* and elsewhere I was given, in Paris, the largest Meccano set that I had ever seen. But the challenge of Meccano was not sufficient to overcome my boredom and, in a fit of pique at yet again being left on my own whilst my Parents went out to enjoy themselves, on the last night of my stay in Paris I gave in to temptation and stuffed as much of my Meccano set as I could down the hole within the bewildering toilet-looking gadget. I neither knew that that bewildering toilet-looking gadget was a bidet nor what a bidet was, and neither did I know that stuffing Meccano down a bidet would ... Well, (a) cause the hotel plumbing problems and (b) cause me to suffer a damned good hiding !!

We left the hotel next day; and journeyed from Paris on through War-devastated France down to Nice and thence to the Principality of Monaco and, within Monaco, to Monte Carlo, a place, like Paris, not unknown to my Father. After a day or so in Monte Carlo it was, sadly, back up to Calais and then across the Channel back to Dover and home to Croydon. So ended my second touring holiday, aged 7, in mainland Europe, my Father, aged 71, having driven every inch, save for the ferry crossings, of the way.

My second touring holiday through mainland Europe occurred a year later when, on this occasion, we went from Calais to Belgium thence to Holland, thence to Germany, and from Germany into Austria. Again, my Father, now 72 years of age, drove every inch of the way. It was an enjoyable but often depressing holiday for, again, we saw much War damage, much more than we had seen the year before. It was depressing, very depressing.

From Calais we drove this time, not to Paris but, up the coast through the war-devasted harbour town of Dunkirk - from where, in 1940, over 338,000 British, French, and other Allied troops had, often under very heavy German gunfire and bombing, been - using over 900 vessels of all sizes from large naval ships to very small privately owned sailing boats - evacuated to southern Britain. From Dunkirk we went on to the French/Belgium Customs' Border checkpoints and from there - having had our passports checked on the French side of the Border, having then passed through the checkpoints' 'no man's land' and then had our Passports checked on the Belgium side of the Border - we passed into Belgium and on to the equally war-devastated, and on this occasion very dismal and rain-soaked, seaside town of Ostend. Having toured round Ostend we turned inland and, passing destroyed or substantially destroyed building after destroyed or substantially destroyed building, we went, thoroughly depressed, on to Ghent where we stayed the night in an hotel [de Wilson ?] situated above a very noisy, and seemingly all-night, café down to which, not having managed to get much sleep, we went, next morning, for breakfast. It was 1952 and there were still 'mountains' of war-created rubble and scores of war-destroyed and war-damaged buildings all over the place. From Ghent we headed towards the Dutch coast and then, having had our passports checked again, passed out of Belgium, via the Belgium/Dutch Customs' Border checkpoints and their 'no man's land', into an equally war-devastated Holland. Each night we stayed in small hotels some of which were still partially, even substantially, bomb-damaged and/or bullet-ridden and most of which had neither proper running water facilities nor proper toilet facilities; and so, for our washing needs, we got used to being supplied with water in a jug that was positioned in a bowl on top of a dresser or some other flat surface and to being supplied with various sorts of portable commode-type facilities to cater for our toilet needs. One evening, as cloud-darkening, rain-soaked, wind-hurling skies seemed to be threatening to completely engulf us, we travelled, as fast as my Father could reasonably drive, across the great man-made Ziederzee dyke in considerable apprehension as the viciously windswept water on each side of us seemed to be indicating that any moment now it too would engulf us; and, boy, were we relieved when finally we cleared the dyke and reached solid land.

By the time that we crossed, this time, again having had our passports checked, via the Dutch/German Customs' Border checkpoints and their 'no man's land', into Germany I, certainly, and,

I think, my Parents also, had built up a considerably hostility towards the Germans and the damage that they had inflicted upon the French, the Belgians, and the Dutch.

Once in Germany we headed towards our holiday's principal destination, Lake Konstanz where we stayed for several days, by prior arrangement, with a German Farmer and his Wife in their farmhouse just a few hundred yards [metres] from the lapping waters of the Lake itself. To a 'townie' such as I was at the time, their farm with its chickens, ducks, geese, and cattle roaming, seemingly freely, around was idyllic; and the serene views across Lake Konstanz towards Switzerland and Liechtenstein were magical.

My Mother could not swim but my Father could and he decided that the calmness of Lake Konstanz [Bodensee] was the ideal place for me to learn to swim. He thus set about teaching me but, I confess, I was not a willing pupil, especially as I had, whenever he let go of me, no means of support whatsoever, not even such a thing as an inflatable armband. At the end of his second session of trying to teach me he expressed in no uncertain terms that he had had enough. That afternoon the three of us were supposed to be going somewhere to-gether but I, in a fit of pique, determined that I was not going to go. So, having given firm instructions to me that I was not to leave my room in the farmhouse, off they went whilst I stayed. But my conscience about not having learned to swim got the better of my ill-feeling and I became so upset by the fact that I had, in my refusal to learn to swim, annoyed my Father that I decided that, before he and my Mother returned, I must learn to swim. So, ignoring the emphatic "Stay in your room" instruction, I changed into my swimming trunks, went down to the lakeside and lay on my back on the slightly-slopping ground at the edge of the water. Gradually I pushed and manoeuvred myself, inch [25mm] by inch, into the water until, eventually and much to my pleasant surprise, I began to float. Having found that I was able to float I soon found that I was able, by thrashing around, to propel myself through the water; and, having found that I could propel myself through the water when on my back, I went back to the shore and eventually plucked-up the courage to repeat the whole process but this time lying on my stomach. When my Parents arrived back at the farmhouse I was there to greet them and, with great eagerness, to proudly announce that I could now swim. But, instead of receiving much expected and longed-for praise, all hell let loose and I was very severely reprimanded not only for disobeying the instruction to stay in my room but also for my actions in going down to Lake Konstanz and into the water without being accompanied by someone who could swim. Being now myself a parent I can easily understand my own Parents' hostility at my very dangerous stupidity but at the time ... Well, I could not see any real harm in what I had done !!

Another lesson that I learned was learned not only by me but also by my Parents for, as we sat with the Farmer and his Wife at dinner one evening, they sitting one side of a long wooden table and my Parents and I sitting opposite them on the other side of the table, the conversation turned to 'The War'. My Father had had German and Austrian Theatrical friends before the War some of whom had been Jewish and had, because of German inhumanity, not survived the War and therefore, even disregarding what we had seen so far on our journey, my Father's attitude towards Germany and Germans in general did not contain a great deal of sympathy. Indeed this was only 1952, just 8 years after a German V1 flying bomb had damned near destroyed his Kennington Works and much of his business. The conversation between my Parents and the Farmer and his Wife was always courteous; and I, mainly, just sat listening, observing, and doing what I was told. As our English-speaking hosts and my Parents, principally my Father, talked and discussed the War, I noticed the farmer's Wife's eyes becoming very watery; and then, as tears began to fall down her cheeks, she slowly, without saying a word and turning away from us, got up and went to a wooden dresser immediately behind where she and her Husband were sitting. Very quietly she opened a drawer, removed something from it, and then, equally quietly, she shut the drawer. Returning to the table, as she sat down, she reached across the table in front of her Husband to pass the object to my Father. It was a photograph showing two proud young uniformed German soldiers, or perhaps members of the Hitler Youth, standing side-by-side. The conversation between my Parents and the Farmer stopped, and then, having allowed my Father sufficient time to study the photograph, the tearful Farmer's Wife simply said "We too lost sons during the War". There was silence, absolute silence whilst my Father, for what seemed like an eternity, stared, deep in thought, at the photograph. Eventually the Farmer broke the eerie silence by quietly, but very emotionally, saying "We have no Family now. Just the two of us and that photograph" :" And, as tears began to roll down his face also, he, his voice very noticeably trembling, added "The War destroyed us as well". It was a lesson learned, and one which, had it been learned the previous evening, would doubtless have prevented the incident that had occurred earlier that day in Salem.

On 20 November 1947 the United Kingdom's then 21-years old Princess Elizabeth - Daughter of King George VI and subsequently, on the death of her Father in 1952, to become Queen Elizabeth - had married a Second Cousin-once-removed, the 26-years old Prince Philip, only Son of the then Prince Andrew of Greece who was the younger Brother of the then King Constantine of Greece. Prince

Philip's formal education had started in France, but when aged seven he was sent to Cheam Preparatory School in England until, when aged 12, in 1933 he was sent to the Kurt Hahn-founded and -run private boarding school, the Schule Schloss Salem, in the Castle, formerly the Abbey, at Salem where he stayed for less than a year before moving to attend school at Gordonstoun, a school, in Morayshire in Scotland, also founded and run by Kurt Hahn, Kurt Hahn having left Germany after having encountered anti-Jewish abuse by the increasingly powerful and influential NAZI [National Socialist (Nationalsozialismus)] Party of which Adolf Hitler had become the leader. [A major influence on Prince Philip, Kurt Mathias Robert Martin Hahn, who subsequently converted from Judaism to Christianity, also helped found the Outward Bound scheme and the Duke of Edinburgh's Award scheme.] So, given that 1952 was Queen Elizabeth's Coronation Year and that we were staying very close to Salem, we went to have a look, at least at the outside, of where Prince Philip had, albeit only for a short while, gone to school.

Whilst in Salem we went to a café to have something to eat and drink. In those days tourism, certainly as we know it to-day, hardly existed, and therefore the three of us were doubtless somewhat of a curiosity insofar as the café's several customers were concerned. My Father had been an acquaintance of the UK's Wartime Prime Minister, Winston Leonard Spencer Churchill [whose actress Daughter Sarah was also known to my Father, as was her first Husband, the Viennese-born entertainer Vic Oliver (Victor Oliver von Samek). [Winston Churchill despised Vic Oliver and when asked by Vic Oliver who was the Second World War personality whom Churchill most admired, Churchill unhesitatingly replied "Benito Mussolini". "Why Mussolini ?" asked Vic Oliver very surprised at the fact that his Father-in-law had named the hated (even by many of his fellow Italians) leader of one of the UK's Wartime enemies. "Because he shot his Son-in-law !!" was Churchill's instant reply.]

I can not now remember exactly what my Father was talking about in the café but I can remember that, after he had said on more than one occasion that Churchill had been a great Wartime leader, customers in the café started edging towards us. Eventually my Parents decided that we should quietly get up and leave the café. However 'quietly' leaving the café seemed not to be what the customers had in mind for, as the three of us got near to the door, it became very clear not only that the natives were none-too-friendly towards us but also that they intended to get hold of, if not my Mother and me, at least my Father. Being only 8 years of age and relatively fit I thought that it was fun but had I realised that my somewhat overweight Mother was in her mid-forties and that my Father was over seventy years of age I would, instead, have been very worried. However, once we had cleared the bounds of the café the gaggle of incensed Germans ceased the chase, doubtless contenting themselves with the knowledge that we had fled and that they had made their point !!

My Parents decided that next day we would drive into Austria at least as far as Innsbruck : And so next morning, with our friendly farmer-hosts giving us sandwiches and mementoes as they saw us off, we left the farmhouse and Lake Konstanz and headed towards the German/Austrian border. Our first priority was to get some very hard-to-find petrol, a commodity which my Father's heavy 2-door Pontiac car consumed a lot of. However, each garage-cum-petrol station that we came across had no petrol, at least not for us, and, as the already bad roads got narrower and their surfaces got increasingly worse, we were getting very worried. Eventually, with our car and its spare petrol cans completely out of petrol, my Father cruised the car off the, what nowadays might be described as being, dirt track onto a piece of spare ground to the left as the road itself swept upwards to the right. We were completely stranded. That was it, that was as far as we could go. Suddenly, within minutes, a car drew up and stopped behind ours, its German driver got out, and asked, in near perfect English, if we were in trouble. My Father explained that we had no petrol and had been unable to find anyone willing to sell us any. Without any hesitation the German told us that he would go and get some, that he would be away for about half-an-hour or so, and that we were not to worry : And so away he went. True enough, half-an-hour or so later he returned with several cans each full of petrol. He and my deeply grateful Father poured the very precious commodity into our car thereby enabling us to continue our journey towards Innsbruck : And the German gentleman ? He would not accept anything, nothing at all, except my Father's grateful thanks for what he had done for us.

As we approached and then entered the late Herr Adolf Hitler's homeland of Austria the weather was becoming increasingly cold, the skies were, although it was still daytime, becoming increasingly dark, the roads were becoming very, very dangerous in parts, and the Pontiac, being a wide car which often occupied much of the road's varying widths, seemed at times to be almost too wide for the road. Nevertheless my Father drove on determined to reach Innsbruck : And, after 150 miles [250 kilometres] or so, reach Innsbruck we did. To say that that journey had been a hair-raising adventure would be an understatement. Often my Father, as he drove higher up into Austria's Tyrolean Alps, had to rely on the car's headlights to see where he was going; and I, sitting on my own in the back, when looking out could often see little more than either almost near darkness or sheerlike drops. My Mother seemed rigid with fear. It was terrifying, moreso on the occasions, when meeting a vehicle coming in the opposite direction whose driver was disinclined to give way to us, when my Father had to reverse the car back to the nearest point where the road was wide enough to allow two vehicles to pass each other. When we reached Innsbruck my Mother and I were shattered. My Father, though, seemed to have enjoyed himself, although I suspect that much of his air of confidence was perhaps little more than veneer deep.

We booked in at an hotel and then, having unwound, went out for a bit of sightseeing and for a meal. For our meal we chose, what turned out to be, a beer-hall where we spent a couple of hours or so eating whilst surrounded by increasingly drunk stein-wielding lederhosen-clad Austrians (and Germans ?). Clearly, they were thoroughly enjoying themselves but seemed to have no time nor any consideration whatsoever for us. It was as though we Brits were still 'the enemy'. The somewhat hostile, to us, attitudes of seemingly all around us coupled with the flashing light from huge shafts of lightning followed by massive crashings of thunder going on outside caused us not only to leave earlier than we had intended but also to decide that next day we would head back out of Austria. We were, we felt, not welcome. So, next morning we started our journey back home to Croydon.

The following year our main holiday saw us heading back to Monte Carlo. By now my Father had changed his gas-guzzling Pontiac for a Vauxhall Velox car [LVB 317]. The reason for his choosing a Vauxhall was that the company that made Vauxhall cars, although taken over in 1925 by General Motors of America, had started life in 1857 as Alex Wilson and Company at the Vauxhall Iron Works in Vauxhall, London, an area of much sentimental meaning to my Father as Vauxhall was within the Lambeth/Kennington area. Trading as Vauxhall Iron Works the firm had built its first motorcar in Vauxhall in 1903 prior to moving to Luton in 1905 where the name changed shortly thereafter (1907) to Vauxhall Motors. However, it was not in my Father's new blue Vauxhall car but in my Mother's little maroon-coloured Morris Minor car [KLR 681] (*see photograph under showing KLR 681 outside 'Highlands'*) that the three of us, complete with suitcases and other bits and pieces, travelled to Monte Carlo and back.

Lack of petrol was again a principal problem, the one memorable experience being at the top of a substantial hill near to Saint Tropez just as we came within sight of the Mediterranean. We had been unable to get petrol for hours, not because of any reluctance to sell petrol to us but because of a sparsity of places that sold the stuff. Therefore we knew that the car was very low on petrol and perhaps might not make it up the landward side of the hill. But, with little or no option, and, somewhat unusually, with my Mother at the wheel whilst my Father kept making encouraging noises such as "Keep going, keep going, keep going !!", we kept going in the hope that, if we did not find a petrol supply, we would at least make it to the top of the, at times, seemingly endless hill thereby enabling the car to freewheel down the other side until we eventually did find a petrol supply. Make it to the top of the hill we did, but only just for a yard [metre] or so over the top and that was it - No more petrol either in the car or in its spare-petrol cans. But, instead of freewheeling, the car just came to a stop - The incline at that point was nowhere near sufficient enough to enable the car to freewheel of its own accord. So, out my by now 73-years old Father and I got, round to the back of the car we went, and, with my Father shouting instructions to my Mother to do this and to do that, he and I pushed and pushed and pushed until the car got up enough speed to go on its own. As the car started to trundle down the hill and gather speed it seemed as if either fate or my Mother intended that my Father and I were to be left waving, shouting, and running after it. However, some fifty of so yards [metres] later my Mother stopped the car. We caught up, my Mother got out, my Father and I got in, my Mother got into the front passenger seat, and, with my Father pushing the car by means of his right leg hanging out to enable his right foot to make contact with the ground, off we went until, freewheeling down the hill towards Saint Tropez, we eventually hit lucky and got petrol.

We stayed the night in Saint Tropez before, next day, travelling, via Cannes, on to Nice. With Nice as our base we explored and enjoyed not only Nice but also Cannes, Juan-les-Pins, Monaco, and Menton. Despite the impression that may have been given by our somewhat cramped means of very well made, and very reliable, British transport, and despite the financial restrictions placed upon UK travellers abroad by HM Government, money was, for my Father, by no means in short supply. There were no credit/debit cards in those days but nonetheless Monaco and its famous Casino in Monte Carlo were, certainly for my Father, a principal enjoyment; and they were an enjoyment shared by me for, whilst not a participant in its gambling activities, I was enabled, despite being only nine years of age, to accompany my Parents into the Casino [*see photograph below of me, with others, in front of the Casino*].

Our 1953 journey to Menton and back in my Mother's Morris Minor car had, despite the occasion when we ran out of petrol, generally been such a wonderful holiday that it was decided that the next year, for our main holiday, we would again go to mainland Europe in a Morris Minor. It was deemed, however, that KLR 681 should be replaced by a newer Morris Minor; and so KLR 681 was replaced by an almost identical car, NLH 960. Thus it was that in NLH 960, in 1954, we again set off for Continental Europe. This time our destination was Switzerland. No Monte Carlo Casino or, to my knowledge, any gambling this time but, with Interlaken as our base, a thoroughly enjoyable touring holiday in yet another thoroughly reliable British-made Morris Minor car.

In August 1955, when I was aged eleven, we, for that year, abandoned Continental Europe in favour of the British Crown Dependency Channel Island of Jersey. I had spent many hours looking at planes at Croydon Airport and had occasionally been privileged to be enabled to climb into the cockpits of, and pretend to fly, some of them : But going to Jersey was my first experience of actually flying in a plane, as indeed it was for my Mother. My Father had, however, before the War, made several trips by air to France and to Germany : And so, whilst flying to Jersey might not therefore have been a novelty for my Father, it certainly was an exciting novelty for me.

Setting off in my Father's Vauxhall car we left Highlands and, via nearby Purley, went onto the Brighton Road - not the Brighton Road of to-day nor the ones previous to that but the old Old Brighton Road, a road, by to-day's standards, somewhat akin to an idyllic leafy country lane. Meandering down the Brighton Road we went first to the entrance to the grounds of the, now closed since 1992, Cane Hill Mental Hospital in Coulsdon in Surrey where, wallowing in humorous nostalgia, my Father related an experience that he had had to suffer sometime in the 1930s: His firm had been contracted to erect a proscenium Stage somewhere within the large sprawling Victorian buildings that comprised this Psychiatric Hospital for the people of South London and the Southeast of England. Sometime after his men had arrived and gotten underway with the job he received a panic telephone-call from his Foreman, Arthur Pullinger, who asked him to come down to Cane Hill immediately for, when up high ladders erecting the various bits and pieces necessary to suspend the Stage's proscenium arch, his men were, despite attempts by the hospital's Staff to guard their safety, constantly having to put up with attempts by some of the inmates to grab the bottoms of the ladders, whilst the men were on them, and run away with the ladders causing the men to fall off. So bad had the situation got that my Father's men had 'downed tools' and were refusing to carry on with the job. So, my Father immediately left his Kennington Works and went down to Cane Hill to protest to the Management. On arrival he was directed to sit on a chair outside an Office. This he duly did; and within a few minutes a group of accompanied patients came by on their way to lunch. As they did so, one of those accompanying the patients ordered my Father off the chair to join the lunch party. My Father protested that he was not one of the patients; but his protests were not accepted, and he was made to join the patients on their way to lunch. It was only when within the Dining Hall and still vehemently protesting that he was not an inmate that it was eventually realised that he was indeed not an inmate. Never again did my Father's firm undertake any work for Cane Hill Mental Hospital !!

From outside Cane Hill Mental Asylum we went on through Merstham to Redhill. At Redhill we went alongside Redhill's Association Football Club, of which, for some reason entirely unknown to me, my Father was a supporter and to which, on two occasions [I declined to go again!!], he took me and required me to stand and, with him, shout the Redhill Supporters', somewhat boring [to me], chant of "Up the Hill, and down the other side". From Redhill my Father drove on down the Brighton Road to Gatwick Airport, a tiny place in those days compared to the sprawling size that the Airport is nowadays. Having parked the car in a soaking wet grassed area we walked across some concrete to, what appeared to be, the Airport's one and only non-aircraft hangar/maintenance building. Known as the "Beehive", this multi-purpose circularish building was connected by a subway to a mainline railway station thus enabling passengers and others to travel from London's Victoria Station to the airport's terminal building not only directly but also without having to suffer the vagaries that might otherwise have been hurled at them by Britain's often unpredictable climate.

Our conveyance from Gatwick to Jersey was, compared with to-day's massive jet planes, very small. Powered by four propeller engines it had room for only a few passengers. But it was exciting, especially when the hugely noisy engines started up, the propellers began to turn, and the plane began to move. Having made a turn to position itself for take-off the plane began to bounce its way down the runway and, after what seemed like an eternity, it then rose slowly into the air. "Yippee," I doubtless said to myself "we're flying. Wonderful !!"

We sat two abreast: My Father sitting alongside the center aisle with me sitting to his right and with a window to my right giving me a view both of the fields below and of the plane's starboard wing and of two of the plane's propellers,. My Mother sat in the seat immediately in front of my Father with a stranger sitting alongside her in front of me. It was fascinating looking down at the fields as they seemed to get smaller and smaller as, slowly, the plane climbed higher and higher before it eventually levelled off. Then soon the fields gave way to water and we began our journey over the English Channel.

Things started to go wrong when one of the engines on my side began to splutter, as was evidenced also by the erratic speed of its propeller. "Don't worry," said my reassuring Father to both my Mother and me, "the plane's got four engines. So, even if one packs up, the other three will get us there." After a while the spluttering engine ceased to splutter and its propeller ceased to turn,, but we nonetheless continued to fly on. Despite the fact that only three of the four engines were functioning everything did seem okay until, that was, the corresponding engine on the other wing decided to emulate its cousin on my wing. When it too conked out my Father reassuringly informed both my Mother and me that even with only two engines the plane was perfectly safe. But my Mother was, this time, noticeably not reassured even when, later on, the failed engine on my side suddenly spluttered back into action. After a while the other engine on my wing began to splutter as its propeller adopted an erratic speed similar to that that had been adopted earlier by its neighbour. Then, suddenly, it too stopped; and by now it was clear that even my Father was beginning to evidence alarm. But we made it to, and landed safely at, Jersey. However, our problems did not end there for my Mother - who, during the flight, had taken to very firmly, with both hands, gripping the top of the seat in front of her - was rigid with fear; and it took the combined efforts of my Father, myself, the stranger sitting next to my Mother, and several other people to wrench her hands free and to remove her, still in a very rigid condition, from her seat and eventually from the plane. A wearer, sometimes, of diamond rings, two of my Mother's rings, each on a different finger, were so badly distorted that they were embedded in her hand; and it was only some hours later that she had recovered sufficiently to enable the rings to be painlessly removed.

We stayed for our two weeks' holiday based in a very pleasant hotel in Jersey's Capital Saint Helier and - despite the fact that, unusually, we did not have the freedom of having our own car - in the main enjoyed Jersey and many of its attractions, such as the splendid Elizabeth Castle and even Jersey's very 'creepy' underground Hospital, a hospital constructed by the Germans, who occupied Jersey and the other Channel Islands during the War, using mainly, as slave labour, prisoners brought to Jersey from Eastern Europe, many of whom died whilst working and whose bodies, it was said, still lay buried deep within the concrete of the Hospital's walls.

The one incident that perhaps somewhat marred our holiday occurred in Saint Aubin's Bay. Where my Father was at the time I can not recall, but my Mother and I went down to the beach. As was my Mother's wont, not being a swimmer, she spent most of her time on the beach sitting in a deck-chair leaving me to build sand-castles, swim, and generally pither around occupying myself. So, with her sitting in her deck-chair, I decided to swim out to sea. Being by now a reasonable swimmer, I was not daunted by my self-appointed task and I was thus not aware of the panic that, after a while, I was causing. Apparently my Mother had fallen asleep and, on waking, could not see me anywhere. She thus 'threw a wobbly' causing several people, whilst she herself remained in her chair, to look for me. Suddenly a man shouted to my Mother that he could see me, and, having decided that I was in trouble and needed help, dived in to swim out and rescue me. I - as he was, unknown to me, swimming towards me - decided that I had had enough and should turn around and swim back to shore. Eventually, as I was swimming back to shore, I came across a man struggling, with cramp, in the water. Knowing next to nothing about life-saving techniques I nonetheless decided to 'rescue him'; and so I got hold of him and, with his struggling assistance, brought him back to shore with me. Nearing the waters' edge I was greeted by a round of applause for I had, apparently, saved the self-same man who had swum out to rescue me !!

For the next year's principal Holiday it was back to touring by car in mainland Europe again. Apart from having a holiday my Father had two other intentions: The first was for us to see our former neighbours, Dr and Mrs Blauuw, in their new home in Rijsbergen in Holland and the second was to meet up with Theatrical friends in Germany, friends whom he had last seen, and heard from, prior to the War. It was to be an interesting holiday !!

I have six principal memories of that vacation. The first is that - although the roads in France, Belgium, Holland, and Germany had improved over the years - there was still much Wartime devastation existing throughout mainland Europe. The second is of the kindness shown to us by the Dutch people as exemplified by a gentleman on a bicycle who, our being lost in Amsterdam, cycled ahead of us for over two miles to ensure that he got us on to the correct road that would take us to Germany. The third is of the wonderful reception given to us by Dr and Mrs Blauuw [*see photograph under of the Blauuw's purpose-built bungalow in Rijsbergen (I am standing in front of Dr Blauuw)*] and

of the splendid Dutch breakfasts that they gave us, the variety of tastes of which still remain with me to this day. The fourth is of the incident that occurred as we travelled through Germany on our way to fulfil my Father's intention of calling upon some of his pre-Wartime German friends. We had passed through the Dutch/German Border with no hassle and thence on through Hannover and elsewhere with no problem save for, in places, there still being a lack of running water with which to wash, etc.. It was only when, suddenly, we came across, on a wet miserable day, a lowering barrier that a problem occurred for, in the midst of 'peacetime' Germany, my Father had not expected his journey through Germany to be rudely interrupted. But rudely interrupted it was. Leaving my Mother sitting in the front passenger seat and me sitting in the back of the car my Father got out to find out exactly what the problem was. There he was, clearly getting more wet and more and more agitated, gesticulating with the two uniformed and armed, with holstered handguns and rifles slung over their shoulders, persons who, with their barrier now firmly down, were preventing us from going any further. Despite my Father producing passports and various other documents it seemed that he was fighting a losing battle, especially when one of the uniformed persons took his rifle off his shoulder and started pointing and prodding it towards my Father. Furious, my Father eventually gave up his protestations and returned to the car. We had, it seemed, reached the Soviet Union-controlled East Germany and no amount of UK paperwork, in order or not, would allow us out of West Germany and into East Germany. We thus had no alternative but to turn round and head back from whence we had come; and my Father never did make contact with his German friends of pre-Wartime days or indeed find out whether they were in fact even still alive. Beneath his fury there was much sadness. The fifth memory is of a splendid multi-piece glass crystal chandelier suspended from on high within the large foyer of a Dutch hotel during our return journey. We had stayed in the hotel the previous night and next morning a young member of the hotel's staff and I were throwing a beach-ball higher and higher to and from each other. Suddenly he threw the ball very high into the air, so high that it hit the ceiling at the point where the chandelier was clipped onto a ceiling-rose that suspended the chandelier from the ceiling. Horrified, the two of us stood there, absolutely motionless, as we watched this splendid glass and metal construction come crashing down to the tiled floor below to end its life in a mass of shattered pieces of glass all over the place. The sixth memory is of the incident that occurred with Her Majesty's Customs when we returned to Dover. When in Holland my Father's passion for cigars had tempted him to buy a few, quite a few, Dutch cigars which - although, many an Habana cigar smoker would doubtless say, are of inferior quality - are noticeably less expensive than Habana cigars and can be enjoyable. Thus Import Duty on 'luxury goods', including cigars, was payable when bringing such items back into the UK. My Father's purchase of Dutch cigars ran not to a small number but to a whole suitcaseful of the things; and so - on arriving back in Dover and being asked "Have you anything to declare ?", when his unfortunate answer was "No" and he was asked to open all our suitcases, lo and behold, there before HM Customs lay, for the whole wide world to see, his stash of Dutch cigars. Not only did the incident cost him a lot of money but also all his cigars were confiscated !!

Whether or not the 1956 holiday incidents caused my Father to perhaps feel that, at the age of 76, he was now getting a wee bit old for such challenges I have no idea but the next year's principal holiday saw us driving around, not mainland Europe again, but Wales. The first part of the holiday was a week based in the delightful castellated seaside town of Tenby in South Wales. Thence, for the second week, it was on, via Snowdonia and Ruthin, where my Father has friends who owned a public house business, to Llandudno in North Wales. We had been to both Tenby and Llandudno in 1954 where, in Tenby, we had spent a few days with two sets of friends, the Barratts and the Giffords, from Leicester and, in Llandudno, we had called at the, now long since gone, Pavilion Theatre to meet up with the Actress/Comedienne Beryl Reid. I remember the latter occasion very well. Conscious of the fact that I was a pupil at the Junior School of one of England's Public Schools my Mother ensured that, in order to meet this famous Theatrical personality, I must be smartly dressed in my school uniform with my shoes well polished, with my school cap set properly on my head, and with my school tie tied properly in its place. Woe betide me if anything were to be out of place !! The Pavilion Theatre was sited at the landward end of Llandudno's pier; and thus it was but a short walk from the promenade to Miss Reid's dressing-room. Whether or not the seagull concerned had deliberately 'sized me up' as I walked along the promenade before I got to the pier I do not know, but the wretched thing, as soon as I stepped onto the pier, 'bombed' me with as much sloppy ammunition as he or she could muster. My cap and school uniform were splattered with the stuff and, as far as my Mother was concerned, it was all my fault. All hell let loose. Despite my Father's comments that it was not my fault, I was hit hard by my Mother and told by her in no uncertain terms that I was an embarrassment to everybody. Miss Reid considered the incident to have been most unfortunate and quite funny and, doubtless out of sympathy for my plight, slipped me a note wishing me 'Good luck'. My Mother never did appear to forgive me "for the embarrassment that [I had] caused [her]" !! Fortunately, however, I remained blame free throughout the rest of our 1956 stay in Llandudno !!

The Summer Holiday of 1957 was, sadly, the last of our touring holidays for the years 1957 and 1958 were to see radical changes in our lives. For one thing I had, in July 1957 ceased to be a pupil at Haileybury's Junior School in Clewer Manor, Windsor in favour of, in September 1958, becoming a pupil of Haileybury's Senior School in Hertford Heath, Hertford.

Most, if not all, of us pupils at Haileybury and Imperial Service College's Junior School were totally unaware of the history of Haileybury [and of its Junior School], a history which, like the history of the Crichton Psychiatric Hospital in Dumfries [where my Mother had undertaken her training as a Psychiatric Nurse], owed much to the Honourable East India Company.

Founded by Royal Charter in 1600, under the title of The Governor and Company of Merchants of London, and granted rights by Queen Elizabeth I of England to trade with the East Indies, the East India Company was established by Merchant Adventurers to challenge principally the Dutch and their monopoly of the spice trade but also other such companies established by the French, the Portuguese, the Danes, the Spanish, the Austrians, the Swedes, and the Scots. Having, in 1609, built its own dockyard at Deptford in London the [English] East India Company soon had trading posts in Mombai [Bombay], Madras, and Calcutta and, from initially trading in spices, within well under one hundred years, operating out of its headquarters close to the River Thames at East India House in the City of London's Leadenhall Street, it became - assisted by its creation of its own very efficient navy, its own very efficient army, its own very efficient 'civil service', its own coin mint, and its own highly skilled medical staff - the monopoly trader in spices, tea, saltpetre, silks, cottons, and other very profitable commodities.

With the Company becoming increasingly powerful and in control of much of what we now call India, in 1784 an envious British Parliament, under the then First Lord of the Treasury [the Office nowadays known as 'Prime Minister'] William Pitt, established the Board of Trade, the intention being to transfer control of the Company's by now huge political, financial, naval and military activities from the Company to the Government. Half a century later, in 1834, Pitt's Government's early 'state control' tactic eventually caused the Company to have to cease trading for its own benefit in favour of acting as manager for the Government itself. Then, in 1858, its army was taken over by the Government and transferred to the Crown. Then, in the early 1860s, its Indian possessions were taken over by the Government and transferred to the Crown. Then finally, in 1874, the Company's existence was forced, by the Government's East India Stock Redemption Act, to come completely to an end. Thus State Control by politicians destroyed perhaps the greatest and most successful of all UK Private Enterprises. And what of the Honourable East India Company's splendid headquarters at East India House in the City of London's Leadenhall Street ? Well, at least Private Enterprise in the form of the Insurers Lloyds of London got that.

But in 1804, many years before it was forced to cease trading for its own benefit in favour of acting as manager for the Government, the then Directors of the then all-powerful East India Company, having decided to create an establishment for the education and training of the sons of its employees and for other youths intended to enter its administrative service, looked around for a suitable place upon which to build a College and chose, as its preferred site, a house and its lands at Hailey Bury on Hertford Heath near Hertford in southern England, their having looked also at, and rejected, other properties in the area including Hertford Castle, a castle once used by Henry VIII as a nursery for his children. On 23 October 1805, with a Surveyor instructed only the previous day, the Company's bid of £5,900 was accepted at auction. Thus the house and its lands at Hailey Bury came into the ownership of the Honourable East India Company : And then, not being content just to sit back and wait whilst a purpose-built College was created within its new acquisition, the Company immediately set about employing staff and admitting students into temporary College facilities in Hertford Castle. Having got the latter under way the Company then appointed an Architect and set about creating, including the bricks of its own making, its College at Hailey Bury even before the previous owners had fully vacated.

The land acquired by the Company consisted of 59 acres, a size deemed by the Company to be insufficient for the grandness intended; and so further land was acquired to enable a main entrance worthy of the intended College to be constructed, as were other lands over subsequent years. As its Architect the Directors chose the enthusiastic 27-years old Norwich-born William Wilkins, son of a Plasterer, whose drawings for the East India Company's new College, estimated to cost just under £51,000, were accepted by the Directors in 1806 and were translated, over a three-year period with the first stone being laid on 19 March 1806, into buildings containing the largest academic Quadrangle in Britain. Wilkins, a University friend of the 4th Earl of Rosebery, subsequently went on to design many buildings including not only Dalmeny House, the family home of the Roseberys situated overlooking the Firth of Forth near Scotland's Capital City of Edinburgh, but also the National Gallery in London's Trafalgar Square; the main building of University College London in London's Gower Street; the Shire Hall in Norwich; Downing College in Cambridge; parts of King's College, Cambridge and of Corpus Christi College, Cambridge. William Wilkins died, aged 60, in 1839, 33 years after his fellow Architect Henry Wilkes had, in 1806, added a splendid Grecian columnated façade to one side of his vast Quadrangle and 38 years before Haileybury's beacon-like Chapel was built.

As part of its desire to 'wind-up' the Honourable East India Company the Government, in 1855, passed an Act of Parliament requiring the Company to discontinue maintaining a College at, what was now known as, Haileybury, the Act decreeing that the College must close in January 1858, the College to become Crown property.

The Government's enforced closure of the College caused much suffering not least amongst the many businesses for whom Haileybury College had been a major, if not a principal, customer : And so, three years later, during which time it was temporarily used as barracks for troops returning from the Crimean War before being completely abandoned and then sold by the Government to speculators for £15,000, Mr Stephen Austin, a Hertford Printer, along with some other prominent local personalities, assisted by others with connections to the East India Company and its College, bought the, by now, 500-acre estate and its buildings for £18,000 and re-opened it, in 1862, as the English Public School, Haileybury College, a College incorporated by Royal Charter.

Most, if not all, of us pupils at Haileybury and Imperial Service College's Junior School were also totally unaware of the history of Haileybury's 'partner', the Imperial Service College. Founded in 1845 and originally known as Saint Mark's School and sited at the corner of Goswell Road and Clewer Lane in Windsor the number of its pupils soon caused the school to outgrow its original building; and so, in 1862, just as Haileybury College on Hertford Heath was re-opening, Saint Mark's transferred to, and re-opened at, new purpose-built buildings in Alma Road, Windsor. Financial Subscribers included Her Majesty Queen Victoria and her Husband, Prince Albert.

Initially a Day School, Saint Mark's commenced taking Boarders in 1870. They were accommodated in buildings constructed in Alma Road for the purpose. A Chapel was also built as were several other buildings that the fast-growing school found it necessary to have. Meanwhile, at the village of Westward Ho! in Devon, a row of houses had, in 1874, been converted into a school known as the United Services College. Its first Head Master transferred there from

Haileybury College with five of Haileybury College's senior pupils also making the transfer in order to assist Westward Ho! to get established. But in the closing years of the 19th century the United Services College in Westward Ho! encountered serious financial problems and in 1903 it ceased to function as a school and in 1906 its pupils, after temporary stays elsewhere, transferred to Saint Mark's in Windsor, Saint Mark's changing its name to the United Services College, St Mark's, Windsor. But in 1911 this school too ran into financial difficulties and the Imperial Services Trust was requested to assist.

The Imperial Services Trust was a Trust that existed to assist with the education of children of Army Officers; and it acceded to the request for help that it received from the United Services College, St Mark's, Windsor by taking over the College and re-naming it the Imperial Service College. The Trust's 'contacts' were such that, over the years, it was able to call upon the generosity of many wealthy benefactors whose donations of money and land enabled the ISC, as the School became colloquially known, to grow considerably. Also of considerable financial assistance was the fact that in the late 1920s the British Army's King Edward VII's Regiment of Horse disbanded and donated its substantial Endowment Fund, intended to assist the education of sons and descendants of its commissioned Officers, to the ISC. The Trust was also very fortunate in its appointment, in 1912, of Edward George Ambrose Beckwith as Head Master of its school for EGA Beckwith, the Father of EA Sydney Beckwith who was my Head Master when I was a pupil at the JS, was totally committed to the ISC. EGA Beckwith remained as Head Master until his death in 1935.

The expansion of the ISC was such that, in order to satisfy a demand for a separate Junior School, in 1920 the Trust purchased the estate of Edmund Baines Foster and converted the Clewer Manor part of the estate into the ISC's Junior School.

The Second World War, however, caused considerable financial distress to the Imperial Service Trust to the extent that the Trust felt it necessary to seek the amalgamation of its school in Windsor in order to enable its educational activities to survive : And so, in 1942, after making an approach to Haileybury College on Hertford Heath, a not dissimilar undertaking given Haileybury's military connections, the Imperial Service College and the Trust's funds - including a bequest made by Rudyard Kipling, a former pupil of the old United Services College at Westward Ho! in Devon, to the Imperial Service Trust of his manuscript of *Stalky & Co* - amalgamated with Haileybury College to form Haileybury and Imperial Service College. [Haileybury and Imperial Service College is regarded as being one of England's 'great' public schools, a public school being a misnomer for in England a public school is an up-market fee-paying independent school whose pupils tend to be those from wealthy families whereas in Scotland a public school means just that, a non-fee-paying school which is genuinely open to all and sundry.]

Thus in 1942 128 boys and some of the ISC's teaching Staff moved from Windsor to Hertford Heath, but the Junior School at Clewer Manor remained - under the, by now, Head Mastership of Edward George Ambrose Beckwith's Son EA Sydney Beckwith - to be known as Haileybury and Imperial Service College's Junior School. The facts that the first Head Master of the old United Services College at Westward Ho! in Devon had been a Housemaster at Haileybury and that five pupils of Haileybury College had been amongst the first pupils at Westward Ho! doubtless assisted the amalgamation of the Imperial Service College with Haileybury College.

Thus it was with that connection of military and educational history that the English Public School of Haileybury and Imperial Service College at Hertford Heath greeted me, an insignificant New Boy, upon my arrival from its Junior School in Windsor in September 1957.

On arrival at Haileybury's Senior School in Hertford Heath the semi-idyllic life that we boys had enjoyed at Haileybury's Junior School was instantly, at least for me and for most of my JS colleagues whom I have met during the years since, replaced by a far different, and much less friendly, lifestyle. For one thing, the buildings and the grounds of the Senior School were each far bigger than that which we had experienced in Clewer Manor and were thus very intimidating as was the number of totally unfamiliar faces that surrounded us : For the number of boys, 500 or so, at the Senior School far exceeded the number of boys, 120 or so, at the Junior School as, of course, did the number of full-time, all male, Teaching Staff each of whom regularly wore, doubtless in order to convey authority, his academic black gown if not also a mortar-board [a square-topped black cap]. The one gown-and-mortar-board-wearing exception was the one formally-unqualified Teacher, Edward James Miller.

Boys at the Senior School were divided into 11 'Houses': Allenby [named after Field-Marshall Viscount Allenby, a Student at Haileybury College from 1875 to 1878], Bartle-Frere [named after the Right honourable Sir Henry Bartle Frere, Governor of Bombay from 1862 to 1867], Batten [named after the Reverend Joseph Batten, the second Head Master of Haileybury when owned by the East India

Company], Colvin [named after John Colvin, a Student of Haileybury when owned by the East India Company and Lieutenant-Governor of India's North-West Provinces from 1854 to 1857], Edmonstone [named after Sir George Edmonstone, a Student of Haileybury when owned by the East India Company and Lieutenant-Governor of India's North-West Provinces from 1858 to 1862], Hailey [named after the hamlet from which Haileybury derived at name], Kipling [named after John Rudyard Kipling, a Student of the United Services College from 1878 to 1882], Lawrence [named after both (1) the Right Honourable Lord John Lawrence, a Student of Haileybury when owned by the East India Company and Viceroy and Governor-General of India from 1864 to 1868 and (2) his Brother, Sir Henry Lawrence, Commander-in-Chief of India from 1856 to 1857], Melvill [named after the Reverend Henry Melvill, the last Head Master of Haileybury when owned by the East India Company], Thomason [named after James Thomason, a Student of Haileybury when owned by the East India Company and Lieutenant-Governor of India's North-West Provinces from 1845 to 1853], and Travelling [named after Sir Charles Trevelyan, a Student of Haileybury when owned by the East India Company and Governor of Madras from 1859 to 1860]. Although the Honourable East India Company had long since ceased to exist and although India had received its independence from United Kingdom rule back in 1947, everyday life within Haileybury and Imperial Service College when I entered through the portals of its Senior School in 1957 was still heavily influenced by the East India Company and its rule over the Indian sub-continent still in existence; and, as I passed through my life therein, it often seemed to me that we Students were being educated in a style befitting those who, on leaving Haileybury, were to be rulers of others.

Prior to the end of my last term at the JS I had been asked which House at the Senior School I would like to be a member of. Unless a Father or a Brother had been a pupil at the Senior School, other than that which we had gleaned from rumours and from very limited bits of information that somehow filtered down from Haileybury in Hertford Heath to us in Windsor, none of us at the JS had any real idea whatsoever about any of the Houses at the Senior School. But, based on the little information that I had, I made my assessment and stated my choice. I can not now remember the House that I chose but it was certainly not the House that I was allocated to, Lawrence.

As with my having to visit, with my Mother, the School Outfitters, Daniel Neal's, prior to my going to Haileybury Junior School so with my having to visit, with my Mother, the School Outfitters prior to my going to Haileybury Senior School. The then, but now no longer, prestigious Department Store firm of Frederick Gorringe near Buckingham Palace in London was the Senior School's appointed Outfitters [with, also, a branch sited within the School itself]; and the routine adopted by my Mother and me was more-or-less the same as that adopted when we had gone to Daniel Neal's - This one, two of this, four of that, half-a-dozen of these, a dozen of those, and so it went until it seemed that I had been measured umpteen times and that my Mother had purchased a large proportion of the shop's stock of boys' clothing. One very noticeable difference was the style of shirts that had to be bought. Each shirt had a very long front and a very long back but no fixed collar, only a rim which had a hole at the back and two holes in the front. But each shirt was also accompanied by at least one completely independent collar which had a hole at its middle and a hole at each of its ends. I thus had to be taught by the 'Gentleman's' Sales Assistant how to wear these shirts: One, before putting a shirt on, first put a collar stud through the hole at the back of the rim. Then one took a collar and positioned it so that the stud also went through the collar's middle hole. Then one took another, longer, collar stud and positioned its hinged front piece so that it lay at a right-angle to the backpiece of that stud. Then one placed that longer collar stud through one of the front holes. Then one put the shirt on and buttoned-up the front buttons. Then one pushed the longer collar stud through the other hole thus causing the stud to hold the top of the two sides of the shirt to-gether. Then one brought the collar round from the back of one's neck and fixed it firmly to the shirt by means of pushing the front stud through each of the collar's other two holes and then operating the stud's hinged front piece so that it was positioned parallel with its back piece thereby locking the collar into position. Having mastered that laborious technique I was then taught by the self-same 'Gentleman's' Sales Assistant how to include the application of a necktie [tie] within the procedure, which one 'simply' did by inserting the tie into the collar immediately after one had secured the collar onto the shirt's back stud and thereafter bringing the tie round the neck contemporaneously with bringing the collar round the neck prior to fixing the collar to the front stud. It was all very, very *'Dickensian'* !!

One item of clothing that, because she considered the price to be extortionate, my Mother did not buy for me, but which she should have bought for me, at Gorringe's was the 'regulation' 2-piece School herringbone-pattern suit. Instead, she bought a similar garment elsewhere and, true to her theory that I would 'grow into it', it was of such a size not only that it was intended to last me the entirety of my intended five years at Haileybury Senior School but also that it had a surplus of several inches on each of its jacket's sleeves and several inches on each of its trousers' legs causing my Mother to have first to 'take it in' and regularly thereafter to 'let it out'. I was very fortunate indeed that throughout my time at the Senior School, despite the fact that visually it was clearly evident that my suit did not comply with what was stipulated, not once was my suit nor I ever challenged.

Unfortunately on the September day in 1957 an hour or so prior to my departure for Haileybury Senior School an incident occurred which has adversely effected me ever since. Filled with a mixture of 25% eagerness and 75% fear, in the process of getting dressed I sat on the end of my bed and put on my right sock. Having put on my right sock I then twisted slightly to my left to put on my left sock and, as I twisted, I bent downwards and forwards and then felt a violent very sharp pain at the base of my spine and down the entirety of my left leg. After several seconds I managed, in considerable, but slowly decreasing, pain, to put on my left sock but then found that I was unable to stand up. So I sat there until the pain had subsided sufficiently to enable me to stand up. But I found that, on standing up, I was unable to stand up straight. So, in a contorted hunched position, I stood more or less motionless for, what seemed like, an eternity until the pain had subsided sufficiently to enable me to fully straighten. With my back still painful and aching at the base of my spine and with my left leg suffering 'shooting' pains I somehow managed to finish getting dressed and make my way downstairs to my Mother, the former professional and much-experienced nurse, who, on hearing of my suffering, expressed no sympathy whatsoever. Her concern that we would be late were I not to hurry up was, it seemed, of far greater importance to her. So, with the pains and aches slowly going away, I completed the rest of my chores, such as helping to load my trunk and other items into my Father's car : And thereafter the three of us left Highlands bound for the mysterious, to me, Haileybury and Imperial Service College at Hertford Heath, near Hertford.

A Pipe Smoker whose presence could often be smelt in advance of his arrival, Edward Fisher Williams, MBE - seemingly a bachelor, a former Officer in British Intelligence during the Second World War [and one of whose favourite phrases during my time at the Senior School, whenever he was about to challenge me concerning an alleged misdeed that he had been informed of, was "My spies inform me, Loveday, that you … "], and the man destined to be my House Master for the next 4 years or so - greeted us in his 'Rooms' and, his having assured my Parents that "Edwin will enjoy himself here", my Parents then bade me farewell and departed leaving me in his charge. True enough, he was the person in overall charge of Lawrence House but, as I was soon to find out, the people who, insofar as us New Boys were concerned, actually ran our lives within Lawrence House were the House Prefects, a small group of 17-years old and 18-years old boys within Lawrence who were in the latter days of their journey through Haileybury Senior School. 'Bullies' would not be an inaccurate word to describe some of them.

There were 48 boys in Lawrence House and we all slept each in his own bed sited within two equal rows of beds, one bed facing another, each row sited on one side of a very long wood-floored non-carpeted dormitory, each of us boys being separated from the other boys in the same row by a wood partition of about a yard/metre in height, with New Boys at one end of the dormitory, House Prefects at the other end, and the rest, in a progressive order, in between. Within our wood partitioned confine we each had a somewhat ancient iron-framed bed with a, usually very comfortable, horse-hair mattress; an equally somewhat ancient grey-painted 3-drawer nest of drawers; a smallish cork mat on the floor; a row of hooks screwed into wooden panelling on a wall, the hooks having a ledge above from which hung a curtain the existence of which allegedly turned the edifice into a sort of wardrobe; and, below the 'wardrobe', running the length of each side of the dormitory, was a very large, usually always very cold, iron 'heating' pipe. Compared with the outside world, our bedroom accommodation was so basic it was almost verging on the primitive.

With the half-dozen or so of us nervous and bewildered New Boys within our cubicles in the bottom end of the 'junior half' of the dormitory [dorm] a House Prefect's voice from the top of the 'senior end' would often be heard shouting "Fag" thereby causing us New Boys to have to instantly cease doing whatever it was that we were doing in order to respond immediately to the command by walking [We were not allowed to run in the dorm] as fast as we could to whomsoever it was who had shouted the dreaded word. The last boy to arrive would be the one burdened with whatever it was that the Prefect wanted done. To have not complied was not an option for there was only one alternative, namely to have to suffer several applications of a viciously-wielded cane upon one's backside. It was this barbaric ritual of fagging that first brought home to me the disadvantage of having to suffer, the often 'hell-like' agony of, a 'bad back' for whatever it was that was troubling my back caused me to be usually the last to arrive and thus to be the victim of whatever it was that the Prefect wanted done. Fortunately though the cane was never applied.

September was the start of the 'Winter Term', a Term which, sports-wise, was devoted to rugby, a game that I had thoroughly enjoyed during my time at the Junior School and in which I had been proud to be part of the Junior School's School Team. But the game of rugby, although taken seriously at the JS, was almost a religion at the Senior School; and woe-betide anyone who dropped a pass or who made any other mistake whilst playing rugby at the Senior School for

- whereas at the JS mistakes, although criticised at the time and perhaps for several hours thereafter, were soon forgotten - at the Senior School the maker of a mistake on the rugger field, especially in a match, was often reminded of it throughout the remainder of the Term. [*James McConnell* in his book *English Public Schools* defines the rugby culture existing at Haileybury in those days when he says "Haileybury had the reputation of being a tough school and indeed its Rugby XV were a hard bunch to meet"]. Every week-day afternoon other than on Wednesdays we played rugby and on every occasion my back caused me, despite my having played the game for five years before I arrived at the Senior School, to make many mistakes : And so, what with my back causing me to have to suffer the many fagging tasks given to me by Prefects and to have to suffer the criticism of errors made on the rugby field, I eventually plucked up sufficient courage to seek medical advice.

A former pupil of Haileybury between 1925 and 1929, Surgeon Captain Peter de Bec Turtle, OBE (Officer, Order of the British Empire), VRD (Royal Navy Volunteer Reserve Officer's Decoration), OStJ (Officer, Most Venerable Order of the Hospital of Saint John of Jerusalem), RNR (Royal Naval Reserve), MRCS (Member, Royal College of Surgeons), LRCP (Licentiate, Royal College of Physicians), DPH (Diploma in Public Health), MRCGP (Member, Royal College of General Practitioners), FRSH (Fellow, Royal Society for the Promotion of Health), FRCGP (Fellow, Royal College of General Practitioners), and Honorary Surgeon to Her Majesty The Queen, etc - a short, roundish, soccerball-on-legs-shaped, and, in my opinion as one of his patients who never seemed to receive much, if any, sympathy from him, an arrogant and self-important man - was the School's Resident Medical Officer. I therefore one day went, in trepidation, to the School's own medical facility, the San

[Sanatorium], made an appointment and subsequently attended the 'great man' in his large imposing, and intimidating, Consulting Room and explained that I was suffering agonising pains in my back and 'shooting' pains in my left leg, was often unable to fully straighten up, and in consequence was finding rugger and other things very difficult. I well-remember his instant, very short diagnosis: "It's 'nerves', boy, 'nerves' ". So, with no alternative available to me, I did as I was told and went away and tried to carry on as best I could. But matters got worse, and so I made another appointment, and yet again attended on this somewhat god-like character and received this, again well-remembered, diagnostic response "I've told you before, Loveday, it's 'nerves'. You're a New Boy here and you're nervous. That's all that's the matter with you". I attended on him in his Surgery on one more occasion and, although I have no recollection of what he said on that occasion, his response caused me to write a pleading letter to my Father who, very soon thereafter, arrived at the School, took me home to Croydon, and then took me to Croydon General Hospital where the diagnosis was that I was suffering from a slipped disc. To-day, many years later, I still suffer, sometimes very painfully, from disc problems, a suffering which, I am sure, I would not have had to endure all these years had Surgeon Captain de Bec Turtle properly diagnosed my slipped disc problem. Needless to say, the 'great' Dr Turtle and I did meet in a Doctor/Patient relationship on other occasions during my time at the Senior School. Sometimes 'mass injections', in order to counter some infliction or other that was 'going round', would have to be given to all us pupils. On such occasions the boys from each House would attend Dr Turtle's Consulting Room where we would all line up; each take our jacket off; then roll up a sleeve of our shirt; and then wait until, using the same syringe over and over again, suddenly Turtle would thrust a fluid-laden needle into our arm and then, after having injected the fluid, withdraw the needle; and then one of the School's Nursing Sisters would wipe off any oozing blood before telling us to roll our sleeve down and put our jacket back on. One day rumour had it that there was "Ball-bag rot going round"; and, sure enough, all us 500 or so boys were, House by House, ordered up to Turtle's large Consulting Room. In its turn each House-load lined up, but this time there was no syringe and no needle. Instead we were ordered to drop our trousers and pants, open our legs slightly, and lift up our 'vital parts'. This we did; and thus each of us stood there with our trousers and pants down, with our legs slightly open, and holding our 'vital parts' until Turtle - armed with the type of washing-up mop that Henry Barnett and I used to use at the Junior School when assisting Mrs Higgins to do the washing-up - and Sister, holding a white enamelled bucket three-quarters filled with a red solution, arrived in front of us. Then Turtle dunked the mop into the bucket and, with a short sharp swing, whacked the head of the mop between our legs right onto [if he was accurate enough !] the underside of our, now upwards facing, 'vital parts'. Then, having said "You can pull your trousers up", on Turtle went to his next attempt at target practice !!

On one occasion when I went to see Dr Turtle the 'consultation' finished almost before it had begun. In I went. "How are we to-day ?" he asked. "Well, er ... " I started. "If you're well there's no point in coming to see me then, is there ?" Then he shouted "NEXT," to the next awaiting boy : And that was it, Consultation over !!

Fortunately the talents of Dr Turtle, OBE, VRD, OStJ, RNR, MRCS, LRCP, DPH, MRCGP, FRSH, FRCGP, and Honorary Surgeon to Her Majesty The Queen, etc., did not include dentistry. 7. Before I went to the Senior School my teeth had always been attended to by a Mr Boetius, a Dentist in Addiscombe sited on the bounds of Croydon. I liked Mr Boetious and never had any qualms about visiting him in his largish house in Addiscombe Road, although I did not like the smell of his Surgery and detested the smell, and taste, of the strong piece of rubber that he occasionally required me to bite on within my mouth.

Haileybury Senior School was, to me and, I suspect, most if not all my fellow pupils, the place where in years past the Honourable East India Company educated and trained its future military personnel. I had no idea, until many years later, that that was not the case for, in thinking back to my days of being treated by Mr Boetius in his dentist's chair in Addiscombe I came across information that not only did his house once belong to the East India Company but also that much of the area of Addiscombe including his house was a Military Academy belonging to the East India Company and known as the East India Company's Military Seminary. Founded in 1809 the Military Seminary was intended to train boys to serve as Officers in the East India Company's private army in India and, following the Indian Mutiny in 1857, it was closed by the Government and demolished in 1861 the Government determining that, as the Government already owned both the Royal Military Academy at Woolwich and the Royal Military College at Sandhurst, the East India Company's Military Seminary at Addiscombe was surplus to requirements. So, the East India Company's buildings situated in Hertford Heath had been used to train its Administrators and in the East India Company's buildings situated in Addiscombe had been used to train its Officer Soldiers : And whereas the buildings of the East India Company in Hertford Heath still exist, insofar as the East India Company's Addiscombe site is concerned only 3 smallish houses remain, the rest of the site being evidenced/commemorated by

5 subsequently developed parallel roads - Outram (named in respect of *General Outram*), Havelock (named in respect of *General Havelock*), Elgin (named in respect of *General Elgin*), Clyde (named in respect of *Field Marshal Clyde*), and Canning (named in respect of *Governor-General Canning*) - running off Lower Addiscombe Road.

Whilst at the Junior School, possibly due to a combination of being very young and thus having 'baby' teeth and of Mr Boetious's careful attention to the well-being of my teeth, I never had any cause for dental treatment : But at the Senior School an event did cause me to require dental treatment. I was drinking out of a glass bottle. Passing by, Andy Fairclough, a good friend of mine who subsequently became a Doctor of Medicine, jokingly pushed the bottle causing it to smash the back of one of my two front teeth and leave a nerve partially exposed and the front of the tooth uneven and with a very sharp corner. I thus eventually, due to a combination of pain caused by the exposed nerve and of inconvenience caused by the tooth's sharp corner, went to the San where I saw Sister who made arrangements for me to see the School Dentist in Hertford. A few days later I sat in the Hertford Dentist's chair whilst the man prodded about examining the broken tooth. Then he declared that the nerve would sort itself out but that the two front teeth needed grinding down until they were level otherwise I would have problems eating and even speaking. A Boetious he most certainly was not for straightaway, without any anaesthetic of any kind whatsoever, he set to and, with a small abrasive grinding-wheel, slowly ground down my two front teeth until, to his satisfaction, the entirety of one was level with the entirety of the other. The pain shooting through my unanaesthetised nerve was indescribable.

I had the misfortune to have to suffer the man and his style of dental treatment on one other occasion. My teeth seem to work in tandem with each other. In other words, if a tooth on one side of my mouth needs attending to the corresponding tooth on the other side of my mouth will need attending to; and on this occasion I thus had two teeth which each, in my Opinion, needed a filling. In those days, however, extracting teeth rather than filling them seemed to be the preferred treatment meted out by School Dentists. I thus sat in the man's chair whilst, this time with local anaesthetic, he pulled out two of my top teeth, one on the left and the other on the right. After the extractions I felt that there was something stuck in my gum immediately above where one of the teeth had been. But the man would not agree. Shortly thereafter a little bulge appeared and, as the weeks passed, the lump became a noticeable inconvenience to me : And so back I went. But he would not agree that something was stuck in my gum. Many years later, long after I had left Haileybury, a piece of tooth, or bone, fell out of my gum, and the lump instantly disappeared !!

When I had arrived, aged 8, at Haileybury Junior School back in 1952 the size of Clewer Manor and its surrounding land was such that it seemed huge. As the years went by, and as I grew taller, the size of the place seemed to decrease accordingly : But the size of the Senior School and the expanse of its grounds completely dwarfed its junior relative in Windsor. On my arrival at Haileybury Senior School I found it to be intimidatingly large, doubtless a deliberate intention of those of the Honourable East India Company who, back in 1806, had instructed William Wilkins to design its original buildings and its very large Quadrangle, a Quadrangle which, when it rained, could seem to be a very austere and uninviting place [*see following photograph of*

In fact 'intimidation' seemed to be a core feature of Haileybury's culture, a culture enforced by four levels of caning. The Head Master, Christopher Patrick Crawford Smith in my time, rarely used the cane. House Masters were known to use the cane but not very often. House Prefects used the cane usually occasionally but sometimes often, as was the practice of School Prefects. Whereas the means of application adopted by The Master, as the Head Master was known, and by House Masters could perhaps be described as being 'considerate' the means of application by some House Prefects and by some School Prefects could well be described by the word 'barbaric' for they would position a boy over the end of a table, then cause him to pull down his trousers whilst they walked two yards [metres] or so away from him before turning round, raising the cane to shoulder height if not higher, and then - after running at the unfortunate victim as he shut his eyes and gripped the table in full knowledge of what was about to happen to him - bringing the cane down as hard, it seemed, as they could on the underpants-clad backside of the by now terrified unfortunate. I, fortunately, never experienced this barbaric performance but I certainly knew some who had to suffer four or six 'of the best' wielded upon them in such a fashion. By the time that I arrived at the Senior School caning was 'on the way out' : But it was said that sometime in the 1930s the School's food was so bad that all the boys refused to eat it and in consequence The Master of the day caned every boy. He stood, apparently, in the middle of the Quadrangle and had each boy file past him, bend over as he did so, at which point in time the boy received four 'of the best'. It was said that the experience damned near totally exhausted the Head Master who nevertheless was determined to, and did, complete the punishment.

However, in my time at the Senior School 'Dates' ['Lines' being the equivalent in many Boarding schools elsewhere] not caning increasingly became the preferred method of punishment. A very large piece of paper with, listed upon it, a very large quantity of achievements, and the dates of those achievements, by well-known foreign and/or British born individuals and by not so well-known, if not totally unknown to such as I, individuals was made available to the miscreant who would be ordered to write the list out 'twice', '5 times', '10 times', '15' times, or even '20 times' dependent upon the perceived level of his wrongdoing. But not only did the miscreant have to write the list out he also had to write it out neatly, very neatly, on paper specially printed with lines upon it to ensure that the letters, such as 'd' and 'p', that he wrote were positioned correctly. It was, as doubtless was intended, a boring, time-consuming punishment and one of which I did have experience.

Having spent five years at Haileybury Junior School I had made many friends by the time that I left to 'go up' to the Senior School. Some of those friends went to schools other than the Senior School but others went to Haileybury Senior, some at the same time as I did, some before I did, and some after I did. Thus when I arrived at the Senior School I expected to continue the friendships that I had made at the Junior School. I also expected that Haileybury's Junior School would be respected by those at the Senior School. My illusions were shattered almost from the very minute of my arrival at Haileybury Senior for I found not only that, due to the influx over the years of boys from many other schools besides the Junior School, the Junior School was held in anything but high regard but also that Haileybury's House system and Haileybury's persistence on respect at all times for 'seniority' initially destroyed friendships made at the Junior School.

A good friend of mine at the Junior School had been Graham Barber whose Father ran a Trading business in Casablanca in Morocco. When at the JS I had been keen on stamp collecting and over the years Graham, whose Father wrote to him regularly from Casablanca, had given me many envelopes with Moroccan stamps on them. So, on seeing Graham shortly after I arrived at the Senior School, I went over to chat with him. But Graham had 'gone up' to the Senior School two terms before I; and so for me to start a conversation with him was a 'no-no'. He, though, could, as he was my 'senior', start a conversation with me : But that was frowned on not only because I was a New Boy, and thus just about the 'lowest of the low', but also because I was in Lawrence House whereas Graham was not in Lawrence House but in another House, Kipling. Another good friend at the JS had been James Mark Saxby. A member of the then famous Saxby's Pork Pie Family of Northamptonshire - although he was more closely related to the Leather processing branch of the Family - his arrival back at the JS at the start of each term armed with a very welcome stock of the Family's pork pies had always been appreciated, as indeed was his almost constant jovial company. But he had arrived at the Senior School a term ahead of me and was thus now, as with Graham Barber, my 'senior' and therefore could not be spoken to by me unless he spoke to me first. Furthermore, his House was Hailey not Lawrence and thus the two of us were therefore not encouraged to speak with each other anyway. It was, to my mind, an isolating and very socially-destructive system.

As with Haileybury Junior School, the Senior School also employed, within its non-teaching Staff, characters, often not very well educated themselves, whose commitment and encouragement play, although unknown and thus unappreciated at the time, a major part in one's education. One such character was John Mannion, Lawrence's House 'Servant', a man employed both to keep the dormitory and other parts of the buildings of Lawrence House clean and to serve us Laurentians, as we boys in Lawrence House were known, at table in the Dining Hall, a vast dome-covered building internally bedecked with oil-painted, sometimes austere, portraits of Honourable East India Company and Haileybury and Imperial Service College individuals of prominence in years past.

John - a roundish, bouncy, jovial man to whom we boys could express our fears and concerns in the knowledge that we would be listened to with sympathy - was a very loyal friend to us boys. His background was, however, anything but what one would expect of a person employed within one of England's great Public Schools. Born and brought up, I believe, in the Manchester area, his early adult years, excluding his time in the Army during the Second World War, had seen a close involvement with Manchester's criminal fraternity, an involvement which he was determined to end on meeting Mary, who was to become, shortly before his arrival at Haileybury, his Wife. On taking up the menial job offered to him by the College John was given, as part of his employment the tenancy of one of the College's tied cottages sited on part of the College's estate in nearby Hailey Lane. Every day he would, certainly at our breakfast-times and lunchtimes if not at our evening mealtimes also, wait on us at table ensuring that each and every one of us got not only his fair portion of the food available but also, if possible, got any extra food which might be asked for. Between breakfast and lunchtime John could usually be found cheerfully working away cleaning the dormitory and the several back-to-back wash-hand basins, the two baths, and four showers sited in a room which adjoined the dorm. It was unusual for John to be found by any of us in a mood that was not cheerful and happy; but on one occasion in my early days as a pupil at the Senior School I found him in the dormitory not only sad but also very concerned, concerned because he had received a telephone bill which he could not pay, a situation with which, in his determination to now 'go straight' and to never again break the Law, he could not cope. The debt was £11, a noticeable sum in those days given that it was doubtless somewhat more than his weekly wage.; and he broke into tears when he told me. Many of my decisions are taken 'on instinct' and, to other people, seem to defy logic; and so, out of the Term's £1-per-week pocket-money given to me by my Parents and despite the fact that it was almost all the money that I had at the time, I lent him £11 thereby enabling him to pay his telephone bill. Whether or not his wife Mary ever knew about that telephone bill and about the distress that John suffered as a result of it I do not know. But I do know that not only did John faithfully adhere to his promise to repay me but also he and I remained loyal friends until the day that, many years after I had left Haileybury, he died.

Mention of the several back-to-back wash-hand basins, the two baths, and four showers sited off the dorm reminds me of several things. Firstly, whereas bath times at the Junior School had each of us sitting in small 'Belfast'-type china clay sinks at least at the Senior School we had proper baths into which to put ourselves. Hot water, however, seemed to be, by the College, likened to gold dust for only twice each week were we each allowed to have a bath; and even then hot water was so severely rationed that a rota system was operated. After a shallow level of water had been run into the bath the first 'fortunate' would climb in, wash himself, and then, within ten minutes, be required to climb out to make way for the next 'not quite so fortunate' who would likewise, having climbed in, wash himself, and then, within ten minutes of his entry into the bath, climb out to make way for the next 'even less fortunate' who, having entered and washed himself, would then climb out within his allotted ten minutes so that some of the by now filthy scum-concoction known, still, by the name of water could be run out of the plug hole to enable fresh hot water to be run in to replace it. Then the procedure would continue until the sixth boy had had his bath. Then, upon the sixth boy's departure, the entirety of the scum-laden mixture would be run out via the plug hole, a Prefect's cloth-holding hand would hastily be run around the inside of the bath as an illustration of intent to clean the bath, the Prefect would then put the plug back into its hole, and the bath would be re-filled with clean hot water; and another six boys would take their turns at 'having a bath'. The fact that there were two baths not only enabled twentyfour boys to be processed through the bathing system in just over two hours but also caused an element of competitiveness to exist between those using one bath and those using the other bath. Secondly, whereas we 48 boys were only allowed to partake of a bath twice in every week there was little restriction upon the number of times each week for taking a shower. These, however, had hardly ever experienced hot water let alone dispensed it; and so - when being used, say, to remove considerable quantities of mud applied to the body during a game of rugger - their abilities to make one properly clean were, moreso given that the pressure of boys wanting to use them gave one only a half-minute or so in which to use them, somewhat suspect. Thirdly, Lawrence House had only one toilet, the theory being that it would only be required for use at night-time for during the day all boys were required to use the 'White City' - a somewhat ancient and very draughty, and often very cold, large semi-circular complex of urinals and water-closets [WCs] sited, for use by all boys at Haileybury, adjacent to Lawrence House and Edmonstone, the House which occupied the ground floor beneath Lawrence. This monstrosity of light and heavy relief for us boys was demolished shortly before my time at Haileybury came to an end and in its stead were constructed proper shower and toilet facilities within each House thereby also bringing to an end the primitive bathing system endured by so many for so long. However, true to form, at least in Lawrence House, the number of new showers and new toilets that were installed seemed somewhat insufficient for the number of boys whose use they were intended for. Furthermore, the quality of construction seemed … Well, some of us thought that more money should have been spent on them !!

Every year the College put on a Show to which parents and friends were invited; and in my first year that Show was the light opera *The Mikado* by the Parodist and Librettist *William Schwenck Gilbert* and the Composer *Sir Arthur Seymour Sullivan*. I had absolutely nothing whatsoever to do with either the performing of it nor the staging of it but nonetheless I, like many boys, responded to the College's 'command-like' request to invite parents and friends; and so both my Mother and my Father, along with myself, sat on wooden benches in 'Big School' as members of the Audience.

Big School abutted, at right angles, the building that contained Lawrence House's Dormitory. It served both as a large educational area in which we pupils were made to sit in silence to study and to take formal exams and - because it had a splendid, by the standards of the day, proscenium-arched Stage area - as a place in which theatrical entertainments often took take place. It also contained EF William's Study and his private Rooms. My Father, then aged 77 when sitting that night as a member of the Audience, had spent a lifetime within the top levels of professional Theatre, and often in his later years had the habit, when attending a Show [whether it be in London's 'West End' or elsewhere], of 'nodding off' and, occasionally, snoring, sometimes somewhat loudly. Surrounded by fellow pupils, my being a New Boy, and knowing of my Father's habit of 'nodding off' and sometimes snoring, I grew increasingly concerned that my Father would 'nod off' and snore thereby causing me much embarrassment. But no, he stayed alert and thoroughly absorbed throughout and, after the applause died down at the conclusion of the performance, said to me as we stood up to leave our seats "That was one of the *finest* performances I have ever seen". Maybe he was kidding me, but he had certainly enjoyed the Show; and his considerable compliment from one so experienced in Professional Theatre made me appreciate that the achievements of truly dedicated [to their audiences] amateurs can sometimes be as good as, if not better than, the achievements of many professionals.

I remember well the large 'heating' pipe that ran behind each of the beds within Lawrence House's dormitory being 'on' only once during my stay at the Senior School, and that was on an occasion when the School was 'open' to visitors. At all other times this piece of plumbing was always cold thereby contributing to the general climatic coldness that usually existed in the dormitory. Not allowed hot-water bottles, we were expected to adhere to Haileybury's so-called military background and thus to be 'brave' and 'tough' and to therefore cope regardless of how cold the dorm was. I, in the latter part of my first year, decided that - notwithstanding the School's Spartan and, doubtless, money-saving policy - if I could not have a hot-water bottle, I would devise something that would at least keep my feet warm : And so I acquired two large cylindrical, what in those days were called, bell batteries the terminals of each I wired to-gether with bare wire and then wrapped the surplus bare wire from each battery around the toes of a foot. The idea worked a treat but my rudimentary knowledge, at that time, of things electrical caused me not to realise that within a short time each battery would run 'flat'. Thus, after two nights of bell battery-heated feet, I was again without any warm feet.

Going to sleep at nights in the dormitory was often a problem, especially in the summer. Counting sheep did not seem to work; and so to some degree I managed to overcome the problem by playing a tune in my head using the panes within the two sash windows in one of the dormitory's opposing window frames in which, starting at the top left hand pane, to count out the music.

I also remember well my introduction to cooking. I had not realised that, whereas at the Junior School all meals had been provided by the School, at the Senior School one would be required oneself to undertake at least the provision, if not also the cooking, of some food, food which was required to be purchased at the School's own Tuck Shop [or 'Grubber' as it was known to all boys other than those who were in Lawrence House], a private sub-contracted undertaking whose retail prices seemed - despite the fact that in those days retail prices of food were, in the main, HM Government controlled - unsympathetic to us boys. My first request of my Parents for when they undertook their first visit to me, was to supply me with a kettle, a milkpan, and a large and a small saucepan. Thus, on that first visit, the three of us went to FW Woolworth & Company's shop in Hertford where the necessary purchases were made; and until then I survived, when having to provide for myself, on toast, toast with cold baked beans, toast and jam, and anything else involving toast that I, with my very limited resources, could create. Armed with my kettle and pans I was now able to not only make some tea, with milk that the College did provide, but also to try my hand at being a chef; and for my first attempt at trying to be a chef I chose onion soup. Faithfully following the instructions stated upon the packet that I had purchased for the occasion I cut open the packet and slowly chucked its contents into the specified amount of water which lay slowly heating in my milkpan as it sat upon a gas ring. Then I stirred and stirred and stirred : But, unlike the image of creamy soup illustrated on the packet, the content of my pan refused to convert itself into soup preferring instead to remain as water and hundreds, if not thousands, of bits and pieces of onion and other matter. Perhaps the fault lay in the fact that the pressure put upon me by others wishing to use the gas ring caused time to be very much against me or perhaps the fault lay in the fact that I really had little idea of what I was doing and thus did not apply any finesse to my actions : But, whatever the reason for the non-co-operation of the contents of my packet of onion soup, I was forced to remove my pan of concoction from the gas ring and, using a tin mug and spoon that I had brought to School with me at the start of Term, drink and crunch my way through onion-tasting water and a variety of multi-tasting solid lumps and pieces of this, that, and the other whilst at the same time announcing to anybody who cared to listen that it was "Delicious". Sadly my kettle lasted only until about the middle of my third term at Haileybury Senior School. Having one day filled and put it upon a gas ring in full flow I left the room to attend to something in a nearby sink. Some minutes later a voice shouted "Your kettle's boiling" to which I shouted "Thanks" back but went on doing whatever it was I was doing. Then the voice again, this time somewhat louder and more emphatic, shouted "Your kettle's *boiling*". I again shouted "Thanks" back and again I went on doing whatever it was that I was doing. Eventually, rather than shout again, the voice arrived alongside me and said "I think you'd better come and have a look at your kettle". So I left whatever it was that I was doing and returned to my kettle which had indeed boiled - For there it was, now only a molten piece of aluminium with a severely distorted handle still attached at both ends to it, sliding slowly down, in a sort of circular glob, the side of the, still in full flow, gas ring. "Why didn't someone turn the gas off ?" I asked. "You put it on, you turn it off," was the, typical Haileybury-type, reply that I received. Over 60 years later and, although they are hardly used nowadays, I still have my old Woolworth's pans.

A piece of basic electrics that, in my own time and totally untutored, I experimented with within my first year at Haileybury Senior School was a primitive type of radio receiver, a crystal set. Public radio broadcasts had first commenced in the United States in the 1920s having evolved from a transmission made in 1878 by David Hughes. Guglielmo Marconi, who is often erroneously credited with the invention of radio, built, on the Isle of Wight in England in 1897, the world's radio transmission station; and the first radio programme was broadcast, from Brant Rock in Massachusetts in the United States, on Christmas Eve in 1906 its signals being picked-up by ships at sea. With radio transmissions becoming established in both the United States and the United Kingdom, with Station 8MK in Detroit having, in 1920, transmitted news programmes in the United States, and with, in 1922, Marconi broadcasting entertainment programmes from Chelmsford in England, it had been realised by early United States and United Kingdom manufacturers of radio receivers that forming a Company to transmit regular programmes to the public of the United Kingdom would enable them to sell a much greater number of radio receivers than they would otherwise sell. Thus they set in motion the founding of the British Broadcasting Company and, in their search for a General Manager for their proposed new Company, they put an advertisement in the United Kingdom's *Morning Post* newspaper, an advertisement which was read in London by an out-of-work 33-years old dour, seemingly deeply religious, Scotsman from Stonehaven in Kincardineshire who had little, if any, idea what radio broadcasting was about and who, despite the fact that the advertisement said that only qualified persons need apply, wrote a letter in response applying for the job. Receiving only deathly silence from the 'founding Fathers' of the British Broadcasting Company, the 33-years old increasingly desperate job-seeker got despaired of the infant British Broadcasting Company and instead got himself a political job assisting Sir William Bull, the Conservative Member of Parliament for Hammersmith, a job which enabled him to meet many prominent politicians of the day, such as Austen Chamberlain, Lord Birkenhead, and the great, but somewhat out of favour at the time, Lloyd George. However on 7 December 1922 the dour Scotsman from Stonehaven in Aberdeenshire, who still knew next-to-nothing about radio broadcasting, received a letter from Sir William Noble of the British Broadcasting Company. The letter was an invitation to an interview; and the day after the interview he was offered the job of being the newly formed British Broadcasting Company's first General Manager. Thus on the 30 December 1922 John Charles Walsham

Reith - with a staff of four, including himself - commenced his employment with the BBC. In 1927 the BBC ceased being a private Company, was granted a Royal Charter, and became the British Broadcasting Corporation with John Reith becoming its first Director-General, a position he held until 1938, having overseen both the establishment of BBC radio services throughout the United Kingdom and the establishment, in 1936, of BBC television services, albeit then restricted to 2 hours per day transmissions from Alexandra Palace, an entertainment and sports complex in London.

But at Haileybury and Imperial Service College, although by the time of my arrival there in 1957 the British Broadcasting Corporation had been transmitting radio programmes for thirty years, not only were we boys not encouraged to listen to the radio but also we often ran the threat of punishment for so doing, especially at night-times when we were supposed to be in bed asleep. The Senior School was assisted in its harsh attitude by the fact that the BBC's radio transmissions were in the main, insofar as many of its younger listeners were concerned, boring, if not totally boring. It was thus to the much more musically 'with it' Radio Stations that those of us with some form of radio receiver tended to tune : And the 'with it' Radio Station of the day was Radio Luxembourg, a commercially sponsored undertaking the signal reception of which was often so variable that it was chaotic. Thus the problems that faced characters such as I who wished to receive at least half-decent entertainment whilst in bed and supposedly asleep were [1] how to secrete a radio into the bed without the risk of its bulkiness being noticed - for in those days conventional radio receivers were huge compared to the sizes that they are to-day, and [2] how to devise an aerial of sufficient size to enable signals to be received - for in those days many conventional radios required aerials of many yards/metres in length. The answer ? A 'crystal set' using the bed's metal bed-base and its springs as the aerial.

A crystal set is a very simple radio wave-receiving device consisting of a coil of copper wire, a crystal detector, an earphone or two, and an aerial : But after a while the novelty of listening, through earphones, to crackling radio signals wowing backwards and forwards through the airspace wears off and one's enthusiasm, certainly my enthusiasm, for crystal set radio-receiving technology - despite the entertaining anchoring and disc-jockeying of Radio Luxembourg personalities such as, the subsequently disgraced, Jimmy Saville and the fascinating gambling advertisements whose wording was such as to extol us listeners, for instance, to contact an address in "Keynsham, Bristol. That's" said the voice of the Advertiser, Horace Batchelor, "spelt 'K - E - Y - N - S - H - A - M', Bristol." - soon passed. It simply was not worth the hassle.

Having to be in bed by, and with 'lights out' at, 9.15pm [21:15] we boys in the Junior End of the dormitory were not allowed to speak from 9.15pm until after a bell within the dormitory rang to wake us up at 7am [07:00] the next morning. Thus, if one did not have a radio to listen to and if one could not get to sleep, there was little alternative but to devise some means of trying to pass the time until one did eventually fall asleep. I often tried to relieve the boredom by looking at the six panes of glass in each of the two sliding sashes in the casement window opposite my bed; then thinking of a number or a tune; and then seeing how many times, starting at the top right pane of glass, would be needed to count the number or hum, to myself, the tune before the last digit of the number or last note of the tune would arrive at the bottom right pane of glass. Totally boring : But it usually, eventually, managed to send me to sleep.

For many children birthdays are usually something special, but for most of us who happened to have our birthdays during term-time whilst at Haileybury Senior they were more or less just another day : And so, when my fourteenth birthday occurred on 2 February 1958, it was, save for receiving a present and a couple of cards from my Parents and a present and a card from Aunt Ginger, just another day. I can not now remember what my Parents gave me but I can remember what Aunt Ginger gave me for this kind lady - who was in fact no relation whatsoever but the Wife of a friend of my Father's who was one of the Merchants who sold Timber to my Father's business - always gave me the same thing on every one of my birthdays, namely an excellent Dundee Cake contained within a round tin which one opened by first applying a tin-opener, supplied fixed to the underside of the tin, over a small strip of metal that projected slightly from the side of the tin and then turning the tin-opener round and round so as to unwind onto the tin-opener a strip of metal from the entirety of the circumference of the tin thereby dividing the tin into a top piece and a bottom piece thus enabling access to the succulent cake to be achieved.

Most people, myself included, keep their birthday cards only for a limited time and then they throw them away. But my Father's card that year was somewhat different from the usual run-of-the-mill type of card.; and so I kept, and still keep, it. The card was unusual for those days in that, on its front, it featured, under the words 'come clean', a man in a dressing-gown carrying a tablet of soap. Nothing unusual in that perhaps except that the tablet of soap was, and still remains, a genuine tablet of Lux Toilet Soap. It was slightly for that reason that I kept the card but it is what is said inside that card which has, at least for me, to-day a greater meaning for printed inside the card are the words 'I know it's your Birthday' under which my Father wrote "so with it goes my best wishes & love XXXXX from big Edwin" [*see following photograph of the card's front*].

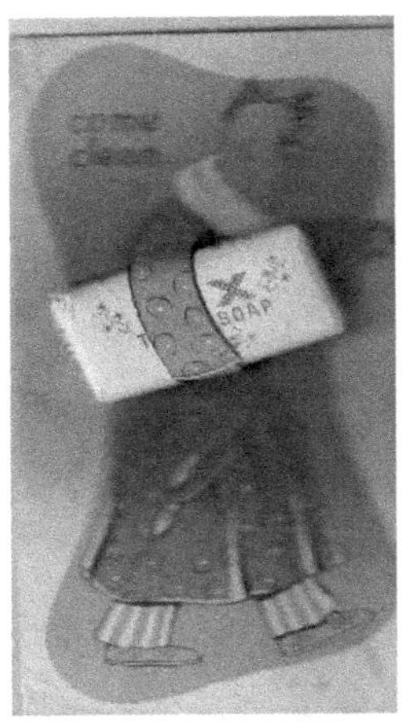

That year's Summer Holiday saw us again off in my Father's Vauxhall car. This time it was to be for a week in a hotel in Bude in Cornwall and thence on to the Chy-an-Albany Hotel in Saint Ives in Cornwall for a week. On the way we stopped off first in the historic town of Bath in Somerset where, after having looked around its famous 2,000-years old Roman hot-water spring mineral baths, we had something to eat in Bath's elegant 1795-built Pump Room. What we ordered and what we got were not entirely the same and, after having eaten, upon querying why we had been charged for things that we had been served but not ordered and not eaten, my Father was informed that, despite the fact that we had neither ordered the items concerned nor eaten them, we must pay for them. When my Father stated that he had no intention of paying for them the Cashier loudly replied "Well, even though you didn't order them or eat them you've got to pay for them 'cos you breathed over them" to which I suddenly, without any hesitation whatsoever, even more loudly exclaimed "Well, your waitress also breathed on them when she brought them to us. So why doesn't she pay for them ?" A noticeably annoyed Cashier then decided, very reluctantly, that we need not pay for them after all.

From Bath it was on to look around Lynmouth in Devon where, in August 1952, over 30 people had died and over 100 buildings had been destroyed due in part to vast quantities of water cascading down through the town from Exmoor which had become water-saturated due to very heavy rains and in part because the River Lyn, as it passed through Lynmouth, had been narrowed to enable commercial premises to be built on its flood plain thereby restricting the river's natural flow.

From Lynmouth, and its higher-sited 'sister' town of Lynton, it was on to Bude which I remember principally for two reasons. The first was its tremendous surfing waves. I neither had a surfing board nor could I surf but I loved swimming out a distance to meet the big powerful waves as they began to crash their way in towards the beach. Round and round inside the waves I would go, time and again being bounced off the sea-bed, as the awesome power of the waves swept me quickly back to the water's edge. The second was of seeing a van parked in the dunes near to where my Mother and I were. I looked at this vehicle as its occupants offloaded their surfing boards and the other gear that they had inside it. It was clearly being used not only for carting surfing gear around but also, given that it had bedding and other 'domestic' items in it, as the surfers' living quarters. Nowadays camper-vans and motorhomes are, if not commonplace certainly, very popular but in those days they were a rarity. In fact I had never seen one; and it occurred to me that perhaps my Father might be interested in buying some vans, converting them into living accommodation, and selling them. With great enthusiasm I made my thoughts known to my Mother who promptly scotched the idea by emphatically stating "Don't be so stupid". "

My School Summer Holidays lasted about eight weeks and sometime during the latter part of my School Summer Holiday that year in 1958, after we had returned from Cornwall, my Father called me to his desk in the Billiard Room at Highlands where he informed me that he wished to tell me how his business was run "in case" he said "something ever happens to me". By that time his instructions to me over the years of how to design, build, fly, run, etc., Theatrical Scenery, and of the many Shows to which he had taken me, had taught me much about Scenery and much about the mechanics of Theatres : And, of course, I already knew how to sit behind a desk typing and pretending to run a business, and doubtless my time running the PDSA Busy Bees at Haileybury Junior School had given me further insight into how to run a business. But in reality I knew very little about running a 'real' business. So, with his puzzling statement "in case something ever happens to me" a bewilderment to me, he and I, in the total absence of my disinterested Mother, spent several hours in each of three consecutive days talking in depth about the ways in which Brunskill and Loveday Limited - a firm which, I now know, was one of the most, if not the most, successful of the United Kingdom's 20th century Theatrical Scenery building firms - worked. In those three days he taught me how to estimate for materials, how to issue quotations, how to order materials, how to keep accounts, how to write 'proper' business letters, and many other things necessary for the successful functioning of a business. But he never explained to me his puzzling statement "in case something ever happens to me" although he did mention on several occasions that my Mother had "no interest in the business whatsoever". Aged, by now, 78 his instructions on how to run Brunskill and Loveday Limited were interspersed with stories of some of the, by then humorous, happenings that had occurred over the years. The time, for instance, when John Reith, the 'founding' Director-General of the BBC, had approached him in 1935 and said "We've got this thing called Television. Are you interested in building all the Scenery for it ?" My Father informed Reith, a man now known to have been not as interested in television as he really should have been, that he would have to think about it; and three days later he telephoned Reith. "No," said my Father, a man with over 40 years of experience within the top spheres of the Theatrical profession "we're not interested. There's no future in Television." Winston Churchill telephoned him one day in the early months of Churchill becoming Prime Minister during the Second World War. "I want you to build coffins," boomed Churchill at my somewhat startled Father. As with Reith, my Father said that he would think about it. "No, we won't build coffins," said my Father when he telephoned Churchill back, "We've always built to entertain the Public. I refuse to bury them !!" "In that case," Churchill immediately replied, "you've lost your Timber Licence." Without a Timber Licence my Father's firm could not, of course, build Scenery. But still he refused to build coffins. It must have been a very worrying time for him and for his fellow Managing Director, Jack Brunskill. However, within a short time later Churchill telephoned again. "You can keep your Timber Licence," said the Great Man, "but on one condition." "What's that ?" asked my Father. "You build dummy towns and villages so that we can plonk them in the middle of nowhere and fool the Enemy," replied Churchill. "Done !" said my Father. So Brunskill and Loveday Limited, along with other Scenery Builders both within the Theatre and within the Film world, set about building all sorts of wood and canvas constructions intended to fool the Germans into thinking that they were real houses, real factories, real tanks, real airplanes, and a whole host of other real things.

Despite the fact that I now had a considerable knowledge of how to actually run a very successful Theatrical Scenery business I had to go back to School that September with the same instructions from my Mother that I had always received, namely that I was never to mention my professional Theatrical connections and activities. A slight relief from the harshness that one endured at Haileybury in one's early years was the fact that I was commencing my second year at the place and was thus no longer either a New Boy or expected to have to endure fagging. But little else had changed save for the fact that I had by now made new friends both from within Lawrence House and within the Classes that I had to attend. The fact that my Parents were due to travel to arrive at Haileybury just before 1pm on Saturday 18 October 1958 to take me out for a few hours was at least something for me to look forward to. Indeed my Father had always seemed to get as much enjoyment out of those visits, both at the Senior School and the Junior School, as I did. Thus I was most certainly not expecting the drastic change in my life that occurred at about 10:30 on Thursday 16 October 1958.

There were no mobile 'phones in those days, just land lines : And the main Formroom Block within the School - in those days often called, as it was and still is entitled to be, a 'College' - was sited opposite Lawrence House's dormitory and Williams's Study directly across the Wilkins-designed very large Quadrangle. Such was the distance across the Quad that it would take someone some time to travel on foot from one side of it to the other side of it, a fact undoubtedly known to Williams when, in his Study that morning, he received a telephone-call from my Mother. She informed him of the reason for her telephone-call and requested to speak with me. I was in the Formroom Block; and thus a 'runner' was found by Williams and dispatched to the Formroom Block to summon me to the telephone. By the time that the boy arrived, had spoken with the Teacher whose lesson I was attending, and my being informed that I was needed back in Williams's Study some several minutes had passed; and by the time that I arrived at Williams's Study yet more minutes had passed. It was therefore some ten minutes or thereabouts before I arrived at Williams's Study.

Upon my arrival in Williams's presence, wondering why I had been summoned I said to him "Yes, Sir ?" He, covering the telephone's mouthpiece, replied "Your Mother is on the telephone. Your Father has been taken ill." I walked up to the telephone, Williams handed the receiver to me, and I asked my Mother "How is he ?" My Mother replied "Pardon ?" So I asked again "How is he ?" "But he's dead," said my Mother clearly very surprised at my question as to my Father's health. Williams, it seems, not only had been told by my Mother that my Father had died the previous night, not only had kept my Mother waiting on the telephone whilst I was summoned to speak with her, but also seemingly had not, despite his having been an Intelligence Officer in the British Army, the courage to tell me of my Father's death. The best that he could bring himself to do was to say not that my Father had died but that my Father was ill. It was to be many years before I forgave him.

I was given little time to absorb the reality of the situation. Instead it was arranged that I should go straightaway to Lawrence House's Dormitory, change into my best clothes, and then walk the short distance from the College to the Green Line 'bus stop on Hertford Heath to catch the number 715 'bus that would take me to London where, outside the BBC's Broadcasting House in Portland Place, at the 'top' end of London's Regent Street I would be met by Hilda, our part-time Maid at Highlands, who would accompany me on another Green Line 'bus that would take the two of us to the bottom of Saint Augustine's Avenue in South Croydon from where we would, via Saint Augustine's Avenue, walk up to Highlands.

I spent two weeks at home in Highlands during which time, on 20 October, the Croydon Coroner, JW Bennett, determined, after a Post Mortem had taken place, that my Father had committed suicide by means of poisoning, via his car's exhaust fumes, by means of Carbon Monoxide. I, however, was deeply suspicious of the verdict principally for four reasons.

The first reason for my suspicion was my Father's intended visit [as an entry in his diary for that year evidences (*see following copy photograph*)]

to me at Haileybury on Saturday 18 October. I had a very close relationship with my Father and there is no way, except for the intervention of something beyond his control, that he would have broken an undertaking to me, certainly not an undertaking as important to me, and to him, as a visit to me at Haileybury. For him to have written in his somewhat sparsely entered diary for that year, under its heading of 'Sat 18 October', "visit Edwin about 12 to 12.30 Haileybury. Herts" meant exactly that, namely that regardless of anything else, save for the intervention of something outwith his control, he <u>would</u> visit me at Haileybury on Saturday 18 October 1958.

The second reason for my suspicion was the 3-day very detailed 'Course' of business management instruction on how to run Brunskill and Loveday Limited that he insisted on giving me. I had no idea at the time of how old my Father was but I was only fourteen years of age, and yet here I was being given detailed instructions on how to run his business "in case" he said on several occasions during those 3 days "something ever happens to me". It seemed an odd, a very odd thing for him to say : And he offered me, and would give me, no explanation of what he meant.

The third reason for my suspicion was that his health was good - apart from pernicious anaemia, which was kept under control by monthly 'liver' 'injections; his business was successful; he was highly respected and had many friends and acquaintances, within the Theatrical profession; and he had no 'money worries' : But there not only existed 'friction' between him and my Mother but also existed within my Mother a very noticeable disinterest in my Father's business.

The fourth reason for my suspicion was my Mother's description of the events that had taken place on the Wednesday night. To me they did not 'add up'. My Mother was a Member of the Theatrical

Charity, the Grand Order of Lady Ratlings, which met, for 'Lodge' Meetings, in London's West End every other Wednesday afternoon. After the Meetings my Mother was in the habit of spending an hour or so socialising with other Lady Ratlings before she went home. Although she had her own car, because she did not like driving she would travel home via the Green Line 'bus service which would bring her to a 'bus stop in the Red Deer area of South Croydon where my Father would be waiting, in a car, for her. My Father would then drive her home from the 'bus stop. On arriving home my Mother would go into the house whilst my Father first opened the garage and then put the car away in it. Simple as that, and a routine that had been adopted on many occasions. But according to my Mother, my Mother arrived at the 'bus stop that Wednesday night and my Father was not there. She waited an hour in the pouring rain and then - despite the facts that it was pouring with rain, was windy, and was becoming increasingly dark; despite the fact that, although mobile 'phones and other such means of telecommunications did not then exist, she could, via one of at least two nearby public telephone-boxes, have telephoned home [CRO 7932] to attempt to speak with my Father; and, despite the fact that, had she telephoned my Father and been unable to speak with him, she could had got a taxi to take her home - chose, in by now almost complete darkness except for the light from street lighting and nearby houses, to walk home via Saint Augustine's Avenue, thence in near total, if not total, darkness through the park at the back of our house, thence through the back gateway at the end of the garden at Highlands, and then down through our back garden to the house itself where, upon seeing a light in my Father's car's garage, she went into the garage where, upon having opened the garage's side access door, she nearly choked on carbon monoxide fumes before she found my Father, with a travel rug tightly bound round his legs, sitting, dead, upon the back passenger seat of his car, its engine still running and belching out carbon monoxide fumes. A very plausible story until one takes into consideration certain facts that doubtless were not made known to the Coroner, namely [1] my Mother did not like waiting around for long, and she certainly would not have stood in the pouring rain at a 'bus stop for an hour; [2] my Mother was not a great walker and certainly would have opted for a taxi rather than choose to walk the, what was to her at least, long distance from the Red Deer to Highlands; [3] my Mother was frightened, to the extent at times of being terrified, of the dark and certainly would not have chosen to walk in the wind, rain, and darkness through the many large trees that existed in the park at the back of Highlands; [4] with certain exceptions, the back gate in the fence at the end of the garden at Highlands was always kept locked by means of a lock, which was accessed by the insertion of a key from either side of the gate, the lock being 'backed up' by two bolts each sited on the house side of the gate. The key to the lock was a large key that was always kept within the house. Thus anyone wishing to unlock the gate when the bolts were closed, which they always were unless the gate was in use, would have to be on the house side of the gate thus causing someone on the park side of the gate to have to climb over either the six feet [circa 2 Metres] high gate itself or one of its six feet [circa 2 Metres] high adjoining fences, an undertaking which my noticeably non-athletic and somewhat portly Mother would doubtless have found impossible to achieve. No, my Mother's explanation of events that night of Wednesday 15 October 1958 did not, and could not, add up. But then I was not at the Coroner's Inquest !!

One ironic incident that occurred in the August prior to my Father's death on 15 October is perhaps worth a mention if only for the lesson which it taught me. When a child my Father had attended the North Brixton Sunday School - and throughout his life he cherished a book presented to him, when aged eight, by the Reverend Canon Hussey as 'A Prize for *Good Conduct and Regular Attendance*" whilst a pupil in the Sunday School's Seventh Class. As the years passed he and his 'best friend' at Sunday School, a lad of about the same age as my Father, remained close friends and when, in the 1934 or 1935, my Father, then in his 50s, bought an acre or so of land just off the then London-Eastbourne Road at a position approximately midway between London and Eastbourne his longtime good friend asked my Father if he could buy the back part of it in order to build himself a bungalow. My Father loved Eating Apples, particularly Cox's Orange Pippins which he regarded as being the finest of all apples - And even in later years when dentures had replaced many of his upper and lower teeth he would take a Cox's Orange Pippin; polish it on a clean handkerchief or on his trousers; shake it to hear the reassuring sound of its pips rattling around inside it; smell it to enjoy the unique Cox's aroma; and then, having removed his dentures and with the apple in his left hand and a knife in his right hand, cut digestible-sized pieces off the apple; and then, chomping away by means of only his gums, savour and enjoy, one by one, each piece as it passed on its journey through his mouth. His reason for buying the acre or so of land was thus to grow Cox's Orange Pippin apples, nothing more nothing less. However, the size of the land was too much for what he needed, and he thus agreed his longtime chum's request : And so the conveyance of the rear half to his friend was duly undertaken. Access to the rear half, once the bungalow had been built, was to be solely by means of a pedestrian right of way through the Apple Orchard, a means of access which, as the bungalow was in the process of being built, was, his chum decided, not enough for he now wanted not only pedestrian access to his bungalow but also vehicular access to his bungalow, something which could only be achieved by my Father's sacrificing some of his Orchard. This was unacceptable to my Father for it would have seriously interfered with his grand scheme of growing Cox's Apples : And so the two good friends of over forty years standing rowed and fell out; and not only was the bungalow never completed but also the Apple Orchard was a failure. Both portions of the land were subsequently sold and neither chum ever again spoke to the other until, two months' before his death in the August of 1958, my Father received a telephone-call from his former very good friend's wife. She and her husband were now, and had for some years been, living in retirement on England's South Coast in Hythe in Kent; her husband was dying and had, his Doctor had told them, not very long to live; and he was insistent that, before his death, he should 'make it up' with his old Sunday School chum. Unable to muster the strength to travel the 80 miles [130 kilometres] or so to London he had asked his wife to ask my Father if he, my Father, would possibly travel down to Hythe so that the two of them could meet up again. So, with my Father driving, the three of us went down to Hythe so that these two 78-years old one-time great friends could at long last 'bury the hatchet'. It was a very sad but happy day as the two old cronies talked themselves through the 70 or more years that had passed since they had first met each other in the North Brixton Sunday School of long ago. Throughout the return journey to Croydon I, somewhat unusually, sat in the front of the car alongside my Father whilst my Mother, mainly in silence, sat in the back. There were not many other cars on the road that night; and as my Father drove through the darkness, occasionally chatting but often in silence, I could glimpse, courtesy of the headlights of oncoming cars, tears in his eyes some of which gently ran down his face to be caught in a handkerchief which, being the gentleman that he was, he brought to his face seemingly to stifle the somewhat theatrical coughs that he made now and then, coughs which doubtless were intended to mask the fact that he was crying. Many thoughts of years past must have gone through his mind that night on the journey back to Highlands. Occasionally he repeated to me criticisms of himself and of his old childhood best friend for their having been so damn foolish as to have retained such animosity towards each other over something which, in contrast to their friendship, had hardly any, if any, worth whatsoever. He was clearly very cut up at the stupidity of it all and cautioned me to never ever let anything interfere with genuine friendship. The outcome of the visit to Hythe ? His old chum recovered his health and went on to live for another couple of years or so. My Father ? Well, he died two months' later !!

After my Father's cremation and shortly before the expiry of my two weeks at home my Mother informed me that the School had telephoned her and suggested that I had been home for long enough and should return to Haileybury otherwise my education might suffer. So, with Hilda accompanying me on a Green Line 'bus from Croydon, I made my way to a 'bus stop outside the BBC's Broadcasting House and waited for the number 715 Green Line 'bus to take me back to Hertford Heath. James Harold Wilson - the UK's Prime Minister on four occasions in the 1960s and 1970s - used to seem to take pleasure in telling the story of how, as a young boy, he one day had stood outside the Prime Minister's residence at No.10 Downing Street in London and vowed to himself that one day he would be its occupant. On the day, a very lonely day, that I stood waiting for the 'bus outside the BBC's substantial Broadcasting House building I looked at Broadcasting House, and looked at it, and looked at it and, as people passed in and out of its parade of entrance doors, I said to myself that one day I would undertake work for the BBC within Broadcasting

House. As with Harold Wilson's commitment to himself my commitment to myself was also achieved for some years later I did enjoy many happy times both working for and playing rugby for the BBC. I never, however, worked within Broadcasting House but did work within other BBC premises.

Meantime my return to Haileybury was not greeted with any form of counselling whatsoever. Indeed, apart from some sympathy given to me by some those of about my age who were in Lawrence House and by some those who sat within the lessons that I had to attend, it was as if the death of my Father had never happened. One did not cry at places such as Haileybury in those days. One did not even indicate unhappiness. One just put up with it and did as one was told. Even expected sympathy from 'Men of the Cloth' who served as part of the Teaching Staff seemed not to care, assuming that they had been at least told by someone, that one's Father had died and that one was thus very distressed. "Stiff upper lip and all that" was seemingly what mattered.

The House Prefects did, however, make an exception for me. They hit upon the idea that I should be punished for having been away from College for two weeks and ordered me to clean two metal dustbins "until they shine". So, with no option but to comply, I thus - with the assistance of a large 'Belfast'-type china-clay sink, some running water, and a scrubbing brush - set about cleaning the insides of two metal dustbins whilst, giggling around me, boys were encouraged to occasionally throw rubbish and so on into the dustbins so as to prolong my punishment for having been away. The attitude shown to me by some of the Teaching Staff was not all that sympathetic either. The Ordinary Level ['O' Level] General Certificate of Education Examinations [which were the secondary-level academic qualifications in existence in England, Wales, and Northern Ireland from 1951 until about 1986] were in the pipeline and I had opted to study, principally, Physics, Mathematics [Maths], and Chemistry. At one point in my journey through Haileybury Senior School Gerald Lionel Daltry tried to teach me Chemistry and when it came to our studying 'the poisonous effects of carbon monoxide' I encountered emotional problems and eventually had to tell him that I was experiencing difficulty coping with the subject. He asked me why, and I explained to him that my Father had recently died of carbon monoxide poisoning. I shall remember until my very last moment upon this earth exactly what it was that he said in his reply to my telling him that I could not cope: "You will just *have* to cope, won't you, Loveday !" Years later, as an Old Haileyburian who occasionally, like all Old Haileyburians, received invitations to attend some Old Boy gathering I received from the self-same, now long-retired, GL Daltry invitations to attend Old Boy 'bun fights' in the North-West of England where GL Daltry lived. Needless to say I have just ignored them for to have done otherwise might have caused me to give in to the temptation to tell him exactly what I think of the callous way in which he responded to what was, in effect, the cry for help that he received from me.

Haileybury Senior School did have some splendid Teachers for whom I had, and still retain, considerable respect. My Maths Teacher for a while was Edward James Miller. Formally unqualified and surrounded by a Teaching Staff many of whom were substantially formally qualified, he was an excellent teacher. Herr Müller as he was called, probably in part because he arrived at Haileybury in 1943 whilst the Second World War was in full rage and in part because he had a slight speech impediment which, on occasions, made him sound as if he was a German. I had always been quite good at Maths and indeed, in response to verbal questions, was often told, firmly but humorously, by him to "Shut up" so that others could have a chance. He was strict, amusing, and entertaining; and the respect and rapport between him, as our Teacher, and us, as his pupils, was such that we learned much from him. "You big stiff" was an occasional, somewhat suggestive, phrase used by Herr Muller in his class when telling us off.

About mid-way through my time at the Senior School I was asked by Herr Müller, doubtless because he knew of my Theatrical background, to help him stage 'The Agony of Agamemnon', a play concerning the ancient Greek hero Agamemnon. He chose to stage it not upon one of the School's two formal stages, 'Big School' and the 'Bradby', but outside in a colonnaded area which adjoined the School's Dining Hall. At the time my House Master, EF Williams, and I were not on very good terms - indeed we were enjoying an increasingly hostile relationship - and, upon seeing me hanging drapes [curtains] from the stone entablature that topped the columns, demanded to know what I was doing. I truthfully informed him that I was helping Mr Miller stage 'The Agony of Agamemnon'. "Oh, no you are not," he said before ordering me down and, once I had completed my descent to ground level, informing me that I was banned from any more stage work throughout the rest of the term. I thus had no option but to find Herr Müller and inform my Producer/Director that I could no longer assist him to mount his production. Having replied "We shall see about that" and told me to stay where I was, I was left somewhat in limbo until his return a short time later when he informed me that I should now return to doing what I had been doing and that my House Master was now no longer raising any objection to my assisting Herr Müller in his staging of 'The Agony of Agamemnon'.

Needless to say, relations between myself and Williams were certainly not improved by the incident !!

Later on, at about the midpoint of my progress through Haileybury Senior, I was taught Maths by another splendid teacher, Brian Peter Warmoll. BP, as we tended to call him when he was out of earshot, was charged with educating my colleagues and me, each of us having passed the ordinary Maths 'O' Level Exam, to a standard sufficient to enable us to pass the 'O' Level Examination in Additional Maths. On the days that we had Maths the Maths lessons were the first of the morning's lessons and my problem - caused by my now devoting quite a lot of my spare time to the School's Theatrical activities to the extent that, with Williams's reluctant agreement, I was often not getting to bed until after midnight - was that I often nodded-off, sometimes very soundly. Eventually my nodding-off became such a ritual that BP gave up on me, one day stating that the chances of my passing the Additional Maths Exam were just about nil and that, if I did pass it, he would take me to his home for tea - an honour indeed !! Spurred on by BP's challenge, and out of respect for him and thus not wishing to let him down, I passed the Exam - but I never got my tea. He lived with his Mother and it seemed that he had, being firmly of the opinion that I would not pass the Exam, never sought her agreement to the idea. BP's kindness and commitment to us Students manifested itself in other ways such as his generosity in purchasing, entirely out of his own moneys, a 'bus by which to transport from Haileybury to the River Lea and back those Students who were interested in rowing. Purchased by BP in the days long before any form of compulsory road worthiness test had come into being, it was a single-deck coach which, when he acquired it, was not in the best of conditions. I was not one of those who was interested in rowing but, when Warmoll asked me to assist him to get his 'bus into a better condition, I, out of gratitude to him for his tolerance of my sleepy behaviour in his class, readily agreed. Thus the two of us set to work, his having cautioned me that he thought that the hinges of the driver's door were a little bit suspect. So, it was to the driver's door that I first went. Putting my foot into a purpose-built recess just under the bottom of the door's frame, I reached up and grabbed the door's handle intending to pull myself up whilst at the same time opening the door thereby enabling me to swing into the cab. But my intention was thwarted when the entirety of the door divorced itself from its two hinges and, with my still holding the handle, crashed down onto the ground with my arriving hard down on top of it. Clearly the vehicle was in a much worse condition that its eager buyer had realised. But the two of us, assisted shortly thereafter by other volunteers, soldiered on thereby eventually enabling the College's rowers to have a means of transport of which they, and its owner, could be proud.

Another teacher whom I liked and respected was Edward Sumner Etheridge. We called him, not to his face of course, 'Loopy' Etheridge. Why, I do not know for he was a kind, usually mild man and anything but a crazed man. Indeed at times he could be somewhat crafty; and so perhaps 'Loopy' is a mis-spelling for 'Lupy' from the word 'Lupine' meaning 'Like a wolf'. He taught me Scripture, as indeed, did at times Christopher Patrick Crawford Smith, the School's Head Master, known to all and sundry as 'The Master'. I vividly recall the day when Etheridge was calmly explaining to us the history and activities of the Salvation Army. A somewhat mischievous colleague of mine, Robert Boyd Bowman, doubtless intending to liven things up a bit and having therefore been occasionally asking niggling questions, suddenly stuck his arm up in the air whilst saying "Sir, Sir, Sir". "Yes, what is it, Bowman ?" asked the increasingly exasperated mild Mr Etheridge. "Sir," repeated Bowman, ""Aren't they the people who give you cups of tea ?" At this point the deeply religious Etheridge, whom none of us had ever heard even utter the mildest of swear words, suddenly snapped. "BOWMAN," he shouted across the room at the startled miscreant," you're always thinking about your BLOODY BELLY !" Mrs Etheridge, a person somewhat larger than her husband, was an equally kind soul. Whether she ever went shooting with a shotgun or whatever I do not know but occasionally, as we boys lay in bed trying to get to sleep, the sound of not-too-distant shotgun or rifle fire would occasionally be heard, and it would not be unusual for some wag within our dormitory to be heard saying of Mr and Mrs Etheridge "She's got him this time !""

Christopher Patrick Crawford Smith, The Master at Haileybury Senior School from 1948 until 1963, had arrived at the Senior School having come from being Warden [Head Master] of Trinity College, Glenalmond, an 'upmarket' boys' boarding school in Perth and Kinross in Scotland, a land in which the words 'Public school' mean not, as in England, an exclusive, and often very expensive, school but a publicly-funded school akin to that which, in England, is known as a 'State school'. There were about 550 boys at Haileybury at any one time and incredibly, like many a Head Teacher within the Private Sector, 'the Beak' as we called him, knew not only the forenames and surnames of each and every pupil but also quite a bit about the background of each and every pupil. Despite all the administrative and other burdens put upon such a man charged with overseeing the smooth academic functioning of such an establishment whose full-time teaching Staff alone numbered over 30 he regularly taught in Class : And as a Teacher he sometimes taught me English and he sometimes taught me Scripture; and at all times whilst teaching he was a very knowledgeable, calm, firm but fair teacher for whom I, for one, felt it a duty to behave 'properly' and learn when in his Class.

But all that took place in the future. What of the end of my first term without my Father ? Well, on the appointed day my Mother arrived in her Morris Minor car to collect me and take me home to Croydon. Most boys went home from Haileybury by train. In fact so many Haileyburians went home by train at the end of each term that it was a major logistical undertaking which involved [1] much earlier risings than usual, [2] much earlier breakfasts than usual, [3] two multi-'bus departures to Hertford Railway Station, and [4] the 'hanging about', seemingly for hours, by those of us not travelling by train whilst we awaited the arrival of those coming to Haileybury to collect us - and my Mother was always the last, or very nearly the last, to arrive.

My Mother and I stayed at home that Christmas : And it was a lonely, very lonely and very boring, at least for me, Christmas made worse by the fact that my bedroom was sited immediately above the garage in which my Father had died. Gone was the fun of previous holidays, gone were the visits to Shows that we had always undertaken, and gone were the visits made by Theatricals to our house. Instead it had been arranged that after Christmas was over I was to travel to Brunskill and Loveday's works in Newport Street, Lambeth in London to meet with Lew Grade who wished, I was told, to buy Brunskill and Loveday Limited and wanted my agreement.

I had known Lew [Louis] Winogradsky and his Brother Bernie [Boris] Winogradsky ever since I could remember. Born in the Ukraine on Christmas Day 1906 Louis Winogradsky, his quite 'well off' Father and his Mother, and his Brother fled Russia in 1912 to escape the persecution of Jews that was rife within Russia and its Empire of which the Ukraine formed a part. They settled in London's East End, Winogradsky Senior taking on several jobs before becoming a Presser in the Rag Trade. Having arrived in England speaking only Russian and some Yiddish, Louis, with a photographic memory and an excellent ability to read English, was soon speaking near perfect English. A third Brother, Leslie, was born and later on a Sister, Rita, was born. Being good at sums Louis became first an Accountant and then, after the introduction from the United States of the Charleston dance, took up dancing and shortly thereafter became the Charleston Champion of Great Britain. Dropping the name Winogradsky in favour of Louis Grad, he then went on to become Charleston Champion of the World. A second name change finally turned Louis Winogradsky into Lew Grade, a man who was to become one of the most 'powerful' and influential men - along with his Brother Boris, who changed his name from Boris Winogradsky to Bernard Belfont - within British Theatre, British Films, and British Commercial Television.

Shortly after the start of 1959 my Mother thus drove me to the Newport Street Works where Jack Brunskill and Lew Grade and two others were standing just outside the large Scenery Doors which opened giving substantial access from the street into that part of the works where Scenery was flown, waiting for us. We then all went into the building where we were joined shortly after by my late Father's business Accountant, a man by the name of Gillespie whom I hardly knew, and my late Father's business Lawyer, Stanley Jarrett of London's Shaftesbury Avenue, whom I can not recall ever having met before.

After a short while, leaving Jack Brunskill and my Mother, Lew, the others and I went into the Office that Jack and my late Father had shared. We all sat down, Lew and his 'team' sitting on one side of, what seemed to me to be, a huge desk and I and my 'team' sitting opposite them on the other side of the desk.

Lew, well known to be one of the greatest 'deal makers' within the Theatrical Profession, expressed considerable sympathy for my loss, was very polite, and very courteous. I was aged fourteen, this was my first ever business Meeting, and I was, to put it simply, absolutely terrified.

How long the Meeting lasted I can not now recall : But I can recall that neither Lew's 'team' nor my 'team' said hardly anything at all. It was purely a discussion between the vastly experienced Lew and the totally inexperienced me; and it concentrated on the simple, but to me, totally unacceptable fact that Lew wanted me to agree to his acquiring my Father's interest in Brunskill and Loveday Limited. I had a good idea that Brunskill and Loveday Limited was a very successful business but, although I had learned a great amount of information about Brunskill and Loveday from my Father, I had no great knowledge of the depth of its success : But nevertheless I did know that my Father had been determined that I should succeed him; and I for my part was determined that I would succeed him. I thus refused point-blank to give in to Lew Grade : And I well remember a smiling Lew Grade, at the end of our Meeting, getting up and, whilst thrusting out a hand for me to shake, saying simply "Well, done. You win". Smoking was not only commonplace but also very much in fashion in those days; and Lew was renowned for smoking large, usually Monte Cristo, habana cigars. They were, so to speak, his trade mark. But, oddly enough, I can not recall whether or not he even smoked one cigar in my presence that day. Neither can I recall what happened after Lew and I got up and shook hands except that I can remember momentarily pausing at the open roll-top desk used by my Father and collecting from it a small card that my Father had, with laughter, shown to me when I last visited the Newport Street Works with him. The card, which I still retain, was issued to Employers by the Government during the Second World War. It read:

It has come to the Management's attention that employees' dying on the job have been neglecting to fall down.

This practice must cease as it is almost impossible to distinguish between death and the natural movement of some employees.

Any employee found dead in an upright position will be dropped from the pay-roll.

M.P. L/3576

A few days later my Mother, in her Morris Minor car, drove me, my large trunk filled with clothes, my tuckbox filled with odds and ends, and various other items back to Haileybury for the start of the Spring Term : And, as we parted, I received the usual firm instruction not to mention my Theatrical activities to anyone, an instruction that was still totally beyond my understanding but one which, because my Mother was my Mother, I nevertheless tried to respect, but not totally for it is not easy to always not give in to temptation. Therefore, when the opportunity arose to build scenery for productions upon the School's 'Big School' Stage, I had let it be known that I knew quite a bit about Theatrical Scenery, how it was built, how it was moved around on stage, and so on. Thus my active involvement in the behind-scenes activities of most, if not all, productions at Haileybury commenced usually with me, in practice if not in name, as Stage Manager, a position of responsibility which also found me often in charge of the projecting of films that the School occasionally showed in Big School. Although more often than not happy and 'at home' with most things Theatrical, film is a medium which I respect but is a medium which is nowhere near as 'natural' for me; and therefore, whereas I find such things as scene changes in a stage show to be instinctive and cause me little or no trepidation, the seamless changing of an expiring film reel for its replacement follow-on always filled me with dread. Thus I was often tempted to burden an assistant with this challenging task so that, if anything went wrong, I could at least share the blame with someone else.

Looking back to-day at the equipment that we used on stage in Big School, and elsewhere wherever we staged a Production within Haileybury, brings forth within me the occasional chuckle of nostalgia. For instance, whereas to-day most Stage Lighting is an art form in itself which requires the use of precision-made equipment, our principal lighting was constructed out of 4lb [1.8Kgs] cube-shaped metal tins of a type once used by Grocers from which to sell loose biscuits. Having removed, and cast aside, the tin's top we would polish the silver-coloured inner surfaces of the tin until we achieved the maximum shine. Then we would drill a hole, of sufficient size to take a lamp-holder, in the middle of the tin's base. Then we would affix a handmade holding bracket to the outer side of each of two of the tin's sides. Then we would, by means of the holding brackets, secure the tin onto a lighting-bar or some other means of suspension or, if to be used as a footlight, onto the floor. Then we would insert a lamp of the required wattage, and finally we would connect the lamp-holder to some form of lighting control system. If a coloured light projection was required we would affix a piece of celluloid of required colour over the entirety of the front of the tin thereby enabling the lamp to project its light through the celluloid thereby enabling the colour to be projected. Likewise, if some form of pattern was required to be projected, a cut-out of the pattern would be affixed over the entirety of the front of the tin. In both such circumstances holes would have to be drilled through the four sides of the tin so as to both release excess heat created by the lamp and prevent the celluloid from melting or the cut-out - if made from cardboard, hardboard, or wood - from catching fire. Crude by to-day's standards, but in those days challenging, inexpensive, and, more often than not, very successful. Follow-spots and other such lights whereby beams of light could be projected over long distances required the addition of mirrors set into the base of the tin, a means of construction which was often not-too-successful thus causing either professional such lights to be hired-in or, if the budget allowed, purchased or such lighting techniques not to be used thereby requiring the production format to have to be adjusted so as to be coped with entirely by the good old 4lb biscuit tin lighting system.

In the short period of my being at Haileybury Senior School prior to my Father's death my Parents and I had, when they had visited me at Haileybury, taken to going, for luncheon, to *The White Hart Hotel* in Hertford and in consequence we soon got to know the Proprietors, Claude and Vi Watson. Following my Father's death my Mother continued the practice and, on the first such occasion, noticing my Father's absence Claude enquired as to my Father's whereabouts to be, of course, informed by my Mother that he had died. Claude and Vi's response was instant: We were, that afternoon, to be their guests at their home in Ware Road a short distance from Hertford's town centre.

Claude, his Wife, and their two Children [a Son and a Daughter] made us wondrously welcome. To-gether we all went, in their car, on trips to nearby, what nowadays would be called, tourist attractions, the furthest of which was the BBC's fascinating Radio Transmitter

Station at Brookman's Park where we watched, as part of the visitor 'tour' provided by the BBC, hundreds, if not thousands, of gallons of cooling water cascading over massive pieces of electrical equipment which, without the cooling water, would have over-heated and expired within no time at all. Back at the Watson's house, whilst Vi made tea or my Mother and Vi were chatting, Claude and I and his Son would go downstairs to play with a train set that this former Engineer had constructed within the semi-basement of their split-level house. The Watsons were, at least to this then somewhat bewildered boy, pure kindness itself.

At the end of that Spring Term my Mother, late as usual, collected me from Haileybury and drove me back to a now very lonely and, without my Father, psychologically very empty Highlands. I was thus very keen to, as soon as I could, pay a visit either to Brunskill and Loveday's Kennington Works or to Brunskill and Loveday's Lambeth Works, if not to both, and to, in my humble way, take over, albeit only until I next returned to School, from where my Father had left off. I envisaged wandering around, as I had often done in the past, watching, with excitement and a very keen interest, pieces of Scenery all over the place each piece being at a different point of construction. I looked forward to the sweet smells that ooze from newly sawn timbers, to the smell given off by melting and bubbling horse glue, and to the many other experiences that had always been conscious and subconscious parts of my visits, including the kind greetings from 'the men' that had always been given to me, the "G'nor's Son". Nothing however had prepared me for the shattering blow that my Mother dismissively, and, in my opinion, cruelly, announced to me when I enquired of her as to "When are we going to the Works ?" "Brunskill and Loveday's been sold" was all that she said or would say. The next shattering blow came very shortly thereafter when she announced that she intended to sell Highlands.

By way of house-hunting we went first to have a look, by appointment, at a 'mock Tudor' house a couple of miles or so from Highlands. It was a pleasant enough house, if somewhat small compared with Highlands. But, sited more or less diagonally opposite a chocolate factory where George Payne & Company made its famous 'Payne's Poppets', the place reeked of chocolate, a constant aroma which was at first interesting and enticing but which, as we lingered within the near empty house, soon became somewhat overpowering. So that house was a 'no-no'. We looked at one or two other properties, each of no interest, and then, on a Sunday a few days later whilst casually visually house-hunting from the comfort of my Mother's car, and in territory which was totally unfamiliar to us, we found ourselves alongside a small parade of shops in Putney Bridge Road, Putney in Southwest London opposite a pleasant riverside park, Wandsworth Park. Stopping the car my Mother 'ordered' me to go into a Newsagents and ask if they knew of any property for sale nearby. At first the answer from the Assistant in the shop to whom I spoke was "No", but then another Assistant said "Hang on. There's a block of flats down by the River that's being renovated. They've got an Office which is open on Sundays. How about looking at them ?" So, having received instructions as to how to get there, I went back to the car, and off we went to have a look. Sure enough there was this large group of blocks of flats, Kenilworth Court, in Lower Richmond Road, Putney undergoing major upgrading works. A large board affixed to the outside of one of the blocks of flats stated that the Selling Agent was Norman Hishfield, that the works were being undertaken by a Scots Company, Doran Construction of Perth, that the Selling Agent's had a Sales Office within Kenilworth Court, and that that Sales Office was open seven days a week. Anything to do with Scotland, except Shotts and her own Mother, attracted my Mother; and so, having parked the car in Lower Richmond Road near to the main entrance to Kenilworth Court, to the Selling Agent's Sales Office we went.

We were greeted by a Mr and Mrs Collingwood, a pleasant husband and wife couple, also Scots, who had been sent down to Putney from Perth by Doran Construction to, in effect, oversee the conversion of a substantial number of empty flats within Kenilworth Court, the original construction of which had, in stages, occurred in the first years of the 1900s. Substantially built, attractively designed, with well laid-out gardens within the Court area itself, and with the flats at the front of Kenilworth Court overlooking the River Thames Kenilworth Court did indeed look interesting as did the 'package' then being offered by Doran Construction to those who purchased. In return for the Purchase Price one acquired a flat on a 99-years' lease; one could, within the limitation of the electricity power supply available, have the flat completely re-wired with whatever circuitry layout one wanted and using the, then, new 'flat pin' 13-amp ring mains alternating current [AC] system; one could have the kitchen fitted to whatever layout one wanted; one could choose, from a nominated supplier in nearby Surbiton, a fireplace of one's own liking for installation; one could have alterations, such as the installation through a dividing wall of a serving-hatch, undertaken; and one could have the entire flat painted in whatever colour or colours one wished and papered with, within reason, whatever wallpapers and ceiling-papers one wished. Having been impressed both by the Collingwoods and their tea-pouring hospitality and by what was being offered by Doran Construction we left Kenilworth Court my Mother having arranged to return another day so that we could have a look inside some of the flats that were on offer.

My Mother and I had immediately liked Kenilworth Court, its layout, and its very-near-the-river position but I had no desire whatsoever to leave Highlands. In fact my attitude was very simple: My Father had been taken away from me; my Father's Business had been taken away from me; and I was darned if I could see any reason why my Home should now also be taken away from me. So eventually my Mother and I, after much unpleasantness and a good deal of shouting at each other, struck a deal - She would buy a flat of my choosing in Kenilworth Court, then sell Highlands, and live within the flat for the rest of her life, having ensured that on her death the lease of the flat would pass, at no financial cost, immediately to me. It was on that understanding that we thus, a day or so later, returned to Kenilworth Court so that I could select a flat.

All the flats that we looked at were spacious and had pleasant views either of Kenilworth Court's own attractive Court or of the River Thames. Nearly every flat had a landing sited outside its front door, the landing being shared by other flats; and nearly every landing was accessed both by stairs and by a lift. An exception was the block that was numbered 26 to 30 which had, save for two small basement flats, only one flat per landing. A disadvantage was that it, unlike the other blocks, lacked a lift. But the block numbered 26 to 30 was more 'private' than the others. The block was sited at the corner of Lower Richmond Road and Waterman Street and the flat in that block that we looked at was No.28. On its Lower Richmond Road side No.28 had two large rooms each of which looked out over Lower Richmond Road to (a) to the right, a small petrol station, owned by a firm called 'Blue Star', then beyond to Putney Pier and the River Thames at a position where the annual University Boat Race between Oxford and Cambridge Universities starts and (b) to the left, the Star and Garter Public House with the Star and Garter Mansions, a block of flats, above it; and on its Waterman Street side it had one large room, a medium-sized room, a kitchen, and, beyond but through the kitchen, a small room each of which looked out over Waterman Street to a terrace of attractive little houses. The flat also had a bathroom, one medium-sized entrance hall which gave access to the two rooms on the Lower Richmond Road side, and a 33ft [10M] corridor which went from the entrance hall past two of the rooms and the kitchen to the bathroom. Outside the bathroom, sited from floor to ceiling, was a very hot 3"[75mm]- diameter iron pipe through which ran a constant flow of very hot water which enabled every flat to be provided - by means of two very large coal-fired boilers sited within what had once been a basement flat within another block within Kenilworth Court - with a constant supply of hot, very hot, washing and bathing water - But not central-heating which, in those days, was a rarity save in such buildings as schools. The flat was a second floor flat, and it appealed to me immediately in part because of its size and layout and in part because of its splendid views of Putney Pier, of the River Thames, of nearby Putney Bridge, and of the constant flow of pleasure and commercial craft, such as Tugs and their many freight-carrying Barges that then existed on the Thames. So that was the flat that I chose, and that was the flat which my Mother, for just over £4,000, thus committed herself to buying. [*See the following photograph which shows the view of Putney Pier from the Lounge of 28 Kenilworth Court.*]

Our having decided that the larger of the front [Lower Richmond Road] rooms would be a lounge, that the other front room would be my Mother's bedroom, that the larger of the side [Waterman Street] rooms would be my bedroom, that the smaller of the side rooms would be a dining-room, and that the small room beyond the kitchen would house, amongst other things, my desk, the work to rewire the flat, redecorate the flat, and to, in effect, convert it to our requirements got underway once my Mother had signed the Contract to buy the flat.

My Mother used as her Conveyancing Lawyer not my late Father's business Solicitor but his longtime friend and non-business Solicitor, Arthur Sidney Coldham of Chingford, a town then described as being in Essex but now described as being just another part of London. The price that she paid was approximately 60% of the price that she received for selling Highlands, a house which she put on the market on a Monday and for which she verbally accepted an Offer the next day thus indicating either that she had inadvertently asked too little for it or that she intended to sell Highlands as quickly as she could regardless, or almost regardless, of what she could have got for it. Perhaps, if she had acted inadvertently, she consoled herself with the fact that she sold Highlands for about 300% more that what my Father had paid for it - But then, of course, my Father had not only added a large second Garage and a Sun-lounge but also created both a very attractive front garden and a very functional back garden with an excellent lawn and a very productive fruit and vegetable area.

Much of the contents of Highlands - including my Father's superb mirror-fronted cigar humidor and his billiards table, and my table-tennis table - were, without reference to me, disposed of by an Auction House in central Croydon. But, thankfully, my piano and my fully-functioning model Theatre were retained and went with us to Kenilworth Court where the piano went into the lounge and, there being no room for it within the Flat itself, my model Theatre went, with the kind co-operation and permission of the Management of Kenilworth Court, free of any charge into a large unused cupboard sited immediately beneath the floor of the Main Entrance to 26 to 30 Kenilworth Court. But life in 28 Kenilworth Court compared with life in Highlands was somewhat cramped. I still had my trainset and its board but nowhere to put it; and so the board sat, with the trainset's track firmly fixed to it, on one of its sides sited between a bed in my bedroom and one of my bedroom's walls. In the early days of our being at Kenilworth Court I occasionally got the trainset and its board out and put them onto one of the two beds that were in my bedroom; but the instability of the thing due to the bounciness of the bed made the whole exercise useless causing my trainset and its board to become a permanently unused feature sited on one of its sides between the bed and the wall thus causing it to be, in effect, denied to me.

As was her Right my Mother, via the Auction House in Croydon, disposed of many personal items belonging to my Father and of many items, such as furniture, which my Father had contributed to his marriage to my Mother but she retained all of my Father's hand-tools which he had kept at Highlands. She hardly knew, if in fact she knew at all, how to use any of them except the screwdrivers and hammers but nonetheless she carefully retained them, wrapped them neatly into bundles, and, with instructions to me that I was not to touch them "because they belong to me not you", placed some of the bundles high up in a built-in kitchen cupboard and the rest high up in a built-into-the-wall cupboard in my bedroom, a cupboard one shelf of which I was permitted by my Mother to use as a sort of 'do-it-yourself' area for making and repairing things. I still have, and have over the years since my Mother's death used, the tools, some of which are now over 100 years old, and all of which had contributed to the manual construction of 'Scenery built by Loveday & Higson', Scenery that went into many a Theatre in London's 'West End'. Given that she had disposed of many of my Father's items, her retention of those tools defied logic; and it was because of her retention of those tools that I began to feel that, although now gone - with his ashes well and truly scattered on land within The South London Crematorium, the influence of my Father seemed to be still very much in existence. It is a feeling that I still retain to-day and which has motivated and influenced me many times during my Life.

I was fortunate that in those days Kenilworth Court had locked 'Bike Sheds' one of which was, in return for a small rent paid by my Mother, allocated to me thus enabling me to safely and securely store my Sturmey-Archer-geared Raleigh bicycle. The Shed had no electricity, but that was soon overcome by means of my rigging a primitive lighting system consisting of several torch bulbs wired, via a switch from my train set, to a series of batteries. One inconvenience, however, which my Mother straightaway imposed upon me was her denial to me of a key to the flat thus causing me to have to seek and obtain permission each and every time that I wanted to leave the flat.

It was to be a means of control applied upon me almost until the day, twenty years later, that she died. Thus whenever I wished to use my bike I had first to obtain her permission to leave the flat and arrange with her the time at which I would arrive back so that I could be let back into the flat.

Putney - with its many Boat Houses sited on the Embankment alongside the River Thames, with the fascinating movements of many types of both pleasure and commercial crafts upon the River, with the passing along Lower Richmond Road of Young and Company's horse-drawn dray wagons as, assisted by the dray wagon's Driver, they regularly instinctively plodded their eye-blinkered way from Young's Wandsworth Brewery and back in order to deliver beer to, among other of Young & Co's Public Houses, the Duke's Head, a Public House sited out of sight from the Flat just a few yards [metres] along Lower Richmond Road from the Star and Garter - was, in those days, a super place in which to live; and during one of my early excursions I discovered that not far away in one of the side streets off Putney High Street there was a Youth Club. As I cycled past it one day not only did it seem to me an interesting hive of activity but also I noticed that some of the youths were playing table-tennis, a game which, despite my having had no human opponent against whom to play, I had enjoyed whilst living in Croydon. So, upon my return to the Flat, given my enthusiasm for table-tennis and my desire to get to know other youths, I told my Mother what I had seen only to receive the comment that I was to "Stay away from that place" because, she said, "People who go to places like that are 'common' ". So that was the end of that idea. However, one idea that she did not object to, or was unwilling to object to, was the suggestion from one of her Lady Ratling colleagues, the Actress Claire Ruane, that I take part in a Television Advertisement that was to be made in Putney for the firm of J. Sainsbury Limited [nowadays, as the Public Company of J Sainsbury plc, a major UK Supermarket, property, and banking undertaking but then, as the incorporated Private Company of J. Sainsbury Limited, principally an 'over the counter' retail Grocery-cum-Provisions Merchant business with shops in and around London including one in Putney High Street]. It was, Claire Ruane suggested in a telephone-call to my Mother and me, to Sainsbury's Putney High Street branch that, if I wanted to, I should go the next morning as she would be there as part of the Cast that was making the Advertising Film for Sainsbury's to be shown on ITV and I could, if I wished, take part : And so, next morning, up to Sainsbury's in Putney High Street I went where I found Claire, other Actresses and Actors, and a Film and Production Crew milling around the open entrance of Sainsbury's shop which was, that day, closed to the Public. Other than Claire I did not know another soul and really had little or no idea who or what anyone was. However I was quickly introduced to the Film's Director who, I suspect had no idea who or what I was or why I was there; but, on Claire's telling him that I would be taking part, I soon found myself involved with the proceedings. In those days retail prices charged by the Grocery trade within the UK were strictly controlled, a fact of life adhered to by most, but not all, retail traders until the 1960s Government of Prime Minister Harold Macmillan brought into force its 1964 Abolition of Resale Price Maintenance Act, an Act which caused, over subsequent years, the demise of many, many thousands of small- and medium-sized UK retail businesses. The firm of J. Sainsbury Limited was one of those retailers which, until the abolition of resale price maintenance, adhered to the prices which retailers were, through Trade publications such as Shaw's List, told that they had to charge. Thus the price that Sainsbury's charged for, say, New Zealand-produced Anchor butter was exactly the same price that was charged for Anchor butter by 'corner shop' retailers, retailers on Council Estates [Housing Schemes in Scotland], 'village' shops, and so on throughout the UK. Thus, with very few exceptions, regardless from whichever shop the Anchor butter was purchased the retail price for it was always the same. So, in its drive to expand its business, Sainsbury's adopted an attitude of implying to the public that their Anchor butter, although the same and the same price as Anchor butter elsewhere, was superior because their Anchor butter was sold, as were all of Sainsbury's Provisions, over marble slabs. Therefore wherever there was a Sainbury's Shop many a Shopper, including my Mother, shopped at Sainbury's because they were of the belief that, because of the marble slabs [that were a feature of every Sainsbury shop], one got a better product when one shopped at Sainsbury's. The Advertisement being filmed that day thus centred around a Customer purchasing a product sold to her by a Sainsbury's Shop Assistant handing the product to her first on and then over the top of one of Sainsbury's marble slabs. Dressed smartly, in the manner that Sainsbury's sought to portray its Customers, up Putney High Street towards the door of Sainbury's the Actress playing the part of the Customer went. As she made an elegant quarter turn to her left a young man who happened to be passing opened the door and held it open for her to pass through into the Shop. Then, once in the Shop she made straight for the marble-slabbed Provisions' counter where, on and over the marble slab, the 'purchase' of whatever it was that she was supposed to be purchasing took place. Then she turned round and - displaying, directly to one of the cameras that were being used, satisfaction with her purchase - towards the door she went. The whole thing was rehearsed a few times until the Director felt that every movement, every nuance, every action conveyed exactly what Sainsbury's wished, via the medium of an Advertisement on

Independent Television, to convey to the General Public. So, this time it was 'it'. The Actress playing the Customer took up, a wee bit down Putney High Street from Sainsbury's door, her starting position; the Actors and Actresses, including Claire Ruane, within the Shop who were playing the Parts of Shop Assistants and Customers, took up their starting positions; the 'Extras' playing the Parts of the General Public walking up and down Putney High Street took up their starting positions; the Director, his Camera Crews, Lighting Crew, and Sound Crew took up their positions; and I, as the young man who happened to be passing, took up my position. Then we all swung into action. From the second that the Actress playing the Customer set off timing was essential, especially for me as I had to arrive at the door at exactly the moment that, the Customer having made her quarter turn, it was evident that she intended to enter the Shop. My timing had not been too good in some of the earlier rehearsals but I had got it down to perfection in the last one and so I was hoping, and praying, that it would be perfect this time also. The second that the Customer set off I set off and walked a pace or so up the High Street passing very close to the Shop and, as I drew alongside the Shop door's hinges, I stretched my left arm fully so that my left hand could get hold of the door's handle thereby enabling me to apply sufficient strength to open the door to allow the Customer unrestricted access into the Shop. Fortunately all went well - at least with that shot - and my services, for which I was never paid anything, were no longer needed. I thus hung around until the Director was completely satisfied with everything; and then I went home eager to see the Advertisement, and myself, when eventually it was shown on television. In the early days of Independent Television the Advertisements shown on television were a mixture of Advertisements for the products of large, often international, businesses and of Advertisements for the services obtainable from small- and medium-sized local firms. Thus watching Advertisements was an entertainment in itself - Some were good, some were very good, some were not so good, and some were … Well, not good at all; and even to-day some, such as the one that featured two pigeons, are well remembered: "My feet are killing me," said one of the pigeons as he/she plodded, in agony, around London's Trafalgar Square. "Darn't worry, luv. We've got them *cheep* Evening Returns on the Underground," the other replied. Then there was one for Esso 'Blue' Paraffin, an often used heating fuel in those days, which featured a cartoon-type character describing himself not as the 'Esso Blue Dealer' but as the 'Esso Do Blealer'. Eventually my eagerly-awaited Sainsbury's Advert came on screen and in it there was I - at least, there, with the Advert commencing with the Customer wealthily sweeping into the Shop, were part of the fingers of my left hand, and just part of the fingers of my left hand. Well, at least making the Advert had been both an experience and fun !!

Besides going to her fortnightly Wednesday Lady Ratlings' Lodge Meetings, other than to go shopping, or 'window shopping', up Putney High Street and in Department Stores such as Swan & Edgar's (closed in 1982) in London's Piccadilly Circus, Arding and Hobbs in Clapham Junction, and occasionally to Bentalls in Kingston upon Thames and, every Thursday morning, to 'go for coffee' in Zeeta's at the top of Putney High Street, my Mother hardly went anywhere. We never went to any of London's many Museums, Art Galleries, or, indeed, Theatres. Instead my Mother spent much of her time either cleaning the already very clean Flat or standing by the kitchen sink puffing away at the inevitable Kensitas cigarettes whilst looking out of the window at the, often very limited, activity beyond or, as an alternative to cleaning and looking out of the kitchen window, watching television.

The occasional trip to Bentalls in Kingston upon Thames happened in part because Bentalls was an excellent Department Store; in part because after visiting Bentalls we would, before going home, usually go round Kingston's excellent open-air Market; and in part because, having lived in a flat in Kingston when working as a Psychiatric Nurse in Epsom, Kingston apparently held good memories for her. My first memory of Kingston was, when aged about nine, of going, with my Parents, to a Wedding in Kingston. Of his five siblings my Father had two Brothers - Herbert Fredrick [Born in 1874] and Charles Edward [Born in 1876] - and three Sisters - Getrude Lydia Jeannette [Born in 1875], Jeanette Louise [Born in 1877], and Ethel Lily [Born in 1884]. Theatrical records held by Brunskill and Loveday Limited indicate that Jeannette Louise, like my Father, followed Uncle Henry Loveday and others into the Theatrical Profession for in 1890, aged only 12, she appeared as a Dancer in Aida, Les Huguenots, Roberto il Diavolo, La Gioconda, and Orfeo at London's Covent Garden Theatre, in 1892 as a Dancer in La Favorita and in Dick Whittington at London's, now long since gone, Olympic Theatre, and in 1893 as a Wood Pigeon in Cinderella at London's Lyceum Theatre. Doubtless her Uncle Henry Loveday, Stage Manager at the Henry Irving's Lyceum Theatre, was a help to her, as indeed he doubtless was to my Father in his early years, but, clearly, to have performed in such Theatres at such young ages, my Aunt Nettie, as she was referred to by my Father to me, was a talented Theatrical : And this perhaps explains why it was that, of the siblings, both she and my Father kept in close contact with each other until my Father's death in 1958, Aunt Nettie dying three and a half years later, aged 84, in 1962. In 1895, when aged 18, she had married 25-years old Kennington-born John [Jack] Chalmers Brown. In 1917, Brunskill and Loveday's files inform, my Father was in partnership with Jack, as Brown and Loveday, in the building, along with John Brunskill's firm, of Scenery for *Arlette,* a Show staged between 6 September and 22 December that year at London's Shaftesbury Theatre having first, commencing on 28 August that year, had its pre-London staging at The Prince's Theatre in Manchester [see below - copies from the Show's Programme and copies of the Show's Sets on stage at The Shaftesbury]. By the time that *Arlette* went on stage at The Prince's Theatre Jack and Nettie Brown's union had produced seven children, the first having been born in 1898 and the last in 1917. No other record can be found within Brunskill and Loveday's files of my Uncle Jack and my Father co-operating on any other Show.

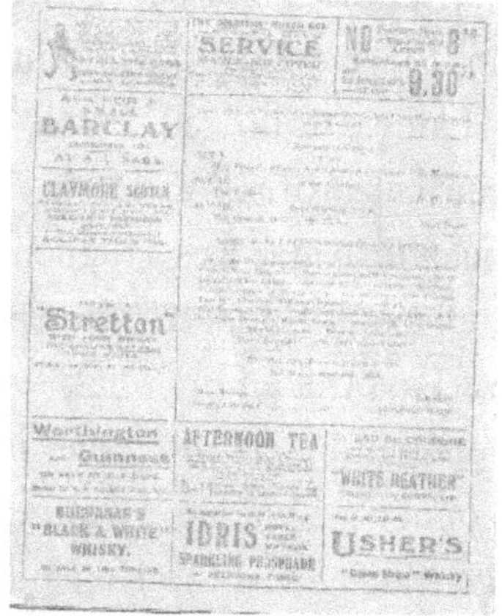

ARLETTE. SHAFTESBURY THEATRE. 1917

ARLETTE. SHAFTESBURY THEATRE. 1917

At the time of his marriage Jack had been a Foreman Painter, then he became a Prison Warder in the United Kingdom's then, in those days, far off Colony of Hong Kong before, having returned to England, becoming a Builder. It thus seems that the two of them may have co-operated, as Scenery Builders, on just the one Show - At the request, one wonders, of his Wife Nettie whom, to my knowledge, I met only once - that day in Kingston when, aged about nine, I went to a Wedding. Sadly I can not remember her. Indeed I can not remember the Wedding. However, for me it was an exciting day. A Cousin, a Brother of the Bridegroom, had built himself an open-top, red coloured, 2-door sports car and kindly offered me a ride in it. So, with me sitting in the passenger seat, off we went from the Church to the Reception. On getting into the car I had found the seats to be a bit of a problem for, it seemed to me, either that he had put them in the wrong positions - the driver's where the passenger's should have been and the passenger's where the driver's should have been - or that he had not anchored them properly to the floor. Whatever he had done, I found myself constantly sliding onto the passenger door and, his not being the slowest of driver's, the drive through Kingston was for me, whilst exciting, somewhat of a challenging experience. Eventually, as he drove through the Town Centre's Market, the inevitable happened - My door flew open causing me to be thrown out onto the ground between the feet of some customers milling around a Greengrocer's stall. Within a matter of seconds my Cousin stopped the car, put it into reverse, and, with the car sounding as if it was breaking wind, came back to collect me. But the damage had been done - My nice smart, especially for the Wedding, suit was filthy causing me, on arrival at the Reception, to - despite profuse apologies from the car's manufacturer and my Father's insistence that it was an accident and thus not my fault - receive from my Mother not only the entire blame for the incident but also, out of sight of everyone else, a, fortunately using only her hand, 'walloping' on my trouser-clad backside.

My Mother's trips for 'coffee at Zeeta's' every Thursday in Putney was a continuation of a ritual that she had undertaken every Thursday when in Croydon. In Putney she went by herself to meet, at Zeeta's, with Lady Ratling friends [such as Norman Wisdom's second Wife, Freda, and my Mother's very good friend the Variety Performer Harry Tate Junior's Wife, Hallie] : But in Croydon I, when on holiday from School, had always to accompany her and be totally bored whilst for an hour or so she chatted away with two or three Lady Ratling friends with whom she met to have coffee. "Never speak unless spoken to" was the order of the day insofar as I was concerned during those coffee mornings in Croydon and, although her Lady Ratling friends would regularly attempt to involve me in conversation, it was clear that my presence, insofar as my Mother was concerned, was to be disregarded if at all possible.

In our early days at Kenilworth Court the view, from behind net curtains, out of the kitchen, diningroom, and my bedroom windows was of a row of neat little terraced houses, and their occupants, on the other side of Waterman Street. Now long gone, these little houses, their well-tended window boxes, their well swept steps were very attractive and indeed were a genuine pleasure to look at; and it was with considerable sadness that we watched the removal of their occupants, the demolition of the houses, and the replacement of those attractive little houses by Council-owned flats. 'Progress' the Council called it : But whatever it was called by the Council the demolition of the terraced houses and their replacement by flats was certainly the end of what clearly had been a happy little community of very neighbourly terraced house dwellers. Not that the change in any way altered my Mother's ritual of standing by the kitchen sink puffing away at her cigarettes, a ritual that she maintained almost until the end of her life twenty years after she and I first arrived at Kenilworth Court.

Swan & Edgar's, a Department Store sited in London's Piccadilly Circus at the corner of Regent Street, was a particular favourite shopping 'haunt' of my Mother's for there she would often find, serving as Shop Assistants behind counters, some of her Lady Ratling cronies. Known as 'resting' within the Theatrical Profession, such jobs - sometimes liked, sometimes tolerated, sometimes strongly disliked, sometimes hated - filled-in gaps between periods of employment within the Theatre, periods which, due to the fickleness and uncertainties of the Theatrical Profession, might last just a handful of days or, with luck, a fistful of months. Thus it was not unusual for my Mother, accompanied sometimes by me, to spend an hour or so chatting away with Shop Assistants who, when on stage, were well-known Actresses, Singers, Dancers, or whatever. Clapham Junction was a place where we went to get 'bargains', not that we needed some of the items that my Mother bought. We would park the car somewhere in the region of Clapham's, then very popular, Street Market, then walk through the Market to Arding and Hobbs, a wonderful, but slightly 'downmarket' compared with Swan & Edgar's, Department Store the quality and prices of whose bedding, curtain materials, and many other items were excellent. Then back through the Market, buying fruit and veg and other items as we went, we would go; and then to the car and back home to Putney.

When we lived in Putney, most of our Christmases and New Year's Eves were spent somewhat boringly in the flat - Just the two of us. The first Christmas Eve had us going up Putney High Street in search of a electric washing-machine, a somewhat rare item in those days and one which we had no need of when in Croydon as much of our washing, and ironing, was undertaken by a Laundry Service and those items, such as socks, which were not dealt with by the Laundry Service were easily dealt with by hand, by my Mother, within the kitchen at Highlands. But in Putney, for whatever reason, my Mother found herself having to do the lot; and washing large items such as sheets required, she felt, some assistance. Hence her decision to buy a washing-machine. My Mother found what she thought she needed - a 'top-loader' made by Hoover - but was uncertain; and so we returned to the flat so that she could 'think about it'. With the items to be washed piling up, with little spare space in the flat to accommodate them, and with the Christmas/New Year Holiday period, during which all the shops would be shut, almost upon us there was an urgent need to buy something : And so the decision to buy was made and I was sent, armed with the purchase money [33 x £1-notes I recall], back to the shop to effect the purchase. Delivery to the flat was included within the price, and all went well until I informed the Assistant that my Mother wanted the washing-machine that evening. "Impossible," I was told. "Your Mother will have to wait until we reopen after the Christmas/New Year Holiday period". Trading in London's East End taught me many things one of which was, in those days when Credit Cards and other such pieces of 'Plastic' had never been heard of, the power/influence of money : And so, on having my request that the machine be delivered that evening rejected, I drew the wad of £1-notes out of a pocket inside my jacket, quickly fanned it in front of the Assistant, and, as I began to put it back into the pocket, simply said "Pity. My Mother won't want this machine then". It was delivered to the flat that evening !!

Late the following Christmas Eve I was sent up Putney High Street by my Mother to purchase a light-fitting that she had seen in British Home Stores [BHS]. BHS's Putney Store's downstairs Lighting Department was a veritable Aladdin's Cave of light-fittings; and, indeed, BHS was well known for it. However, by the time that I arrived that night the whole Store was in almost total darkness. Somewhat disappointed, as I turned to go back to the flat I half-heartedly pushed one of the entrance doors and, lo and behold, it opened. So I went in and, once in, noticed a light shining up the stairs that led down to the Lighting Department. Then I heard the sound of voices coming from the area of where the light was coming from. So over to, and down, the stairs I went; and there, assembled in a far corner, were, with glasses and bottles in hands, the Staff seemingly having a Christmas drink.

"Excuse me," I said as I started walking from the foot of the stairs towards them.

"Who the hell are you ?" said a startled voice.

"I've come to buy a light-fitting," I replied.

"You've what ?" shouted another, amazed, voice.

"I've come to buy a light-fitting," I repeated.

"How the hell did you get in here ?" asked a suit-clad bloke as he walked briskly towards me as if to grab hold of me.

"Through the main doors," I replied in as innocent a voice as I could muster.

"Bloody hell," said another suit-clad bloke as he quickly rushed passed me as he headed towards the stairs, "have we forgotten to lock the bloody doors ?"

Yes, they had. Never mind, I got the light-fitting !!

My Mother being a Scot, she and I, as Scot's custom would have it, each New Year's Eve - save on one occasion when we were in London's Piccadilly Circus - always had, as Midnight struck, a drink of sherry to ensure that we never went thirsty throughout the coming year; a mince pie to ensure that we never went hungry throughout the coming year; and beside us, regardless of the fact that the flat had no functioning coal fires, a lump of coal to ensure that we never went without warmth throughout the coming year. On the New Year's Eve that we ventured to Piccadilly Circus the festivities were somewhat miniscule by to-day's standards. With the, then usually unprotected save for wooden shuttering put up to safeguard it at New Year, Statue of Eros, the Ancient Greek God of Love and Sex, standing proudly in the centre of Piccadilly Circus, with the brightly lit advertising hoardings illuminating everything round about, and with vehicles continuing to go around Eros as if it were just a normal evening in London, as the clock turned half-past eleven increasing numbers of pedestrians - some sober, some on their way to being drunk, and some well and truly drunk - began to arrive causing scrummages to form on the pavements and utter chaos amongst the traffic on the roads. Then, with two or three minutes to go before Midnight, the amount of traffic suddenly decreased to almost nothing. Then, half a minute or so before Midnight, silence descended upon most of the crowd as nearly everyone sought to listen for the start of the sound of the Midnight chiming of 'Big Ben', the famous bell in the Clock Tower of the nearby Houses of Parliament. Having not yet drunk any alcohol, my

Mother and I manoeuvred ourselves to the edge of the pavement opposite Eros and Shaftesbury Avenue beyond. In front of us stood a sort of line of bottle-wielding Irish-sounding 'gentlemen' clearly somewhat the worse for drink. By now all vehicular traffic seemed to have entirely deserted Piccadilly Circus. Then, as 'Big Ben' began to strike Midnight, suddenly, as everyone began to loudly welcome the New Year into being, from Leicester Square a solitary red London Transport 'bus came into view and, as the, fortunately empty of passengers, 'bus passed from right to left in front of the bottle-wielding Irish-sounding gentlemen, up went their arms as if having been choreographed; and every single one of their bottles went crashing either through a window of the 'bus or hard against the 'bus only to bounce off it and head back more or less in the direction from whence it had come.

The Grand Order of Water Rats' and Grand Order of Lady Ratlings' Annual River Trip from Westminster Pier to Hampton Court was an occasion which, when living in Putney, my Mother rarely missed : And I well remember one such trip or, to be more precise, the occasion of our arrival at the Pier at Hampton Court [or, to be accurate, at East Molesey]. My Mother and I had spent the latter part of the journey sitting on deck chatting with a Lady Ratling by the name of Marianne Lincoln, a friend of many years, whose husband was a Water Rat by the name of Nat Jackley, a man then aged about 50. Nat - a noticeably very thin man with a 'rubber neck' the gyratory movements of which were an entertainment in themselves, came from a well-known Theatrical Family and was by then very well known as a Performer both on stage and in films. Marianne was not only Nat's Wife but also at times his Stage Partner, his Manager, and his Script Writer. Although fond, if not very fond, of each other, their relationship was sometimes somewhat 'strained' to say the least.

Throughout the Trip the boat's bar was, for most Water Rats and Lady Ratlings, the most popular place and, whilst Marianne stayed sitting at a table on deck being plied with drinks, Nat spent much of his time below deck entertaining himself, and being entertained, with liberal supplies of alcoholic refreshment. As the boat neared the Pier's pontoon most on the boat, including Nat and many of those below deck, assembled on deck, in various stages of mental awareness, alongside the open area of the side of the boat which would receive the gangway to allow everyone to exit the boat onto the Pier's pontoon. My Mother, Marianne, and I stayed seated at our table which was sited on the other side of the boat, Marianne, with full glass in hand, facing the hordes as they eagerly waited to get off the boat. Suddenly a somewhat panic-stricken cry went out informing that someone had, instead of waiting for the boat to complete its manoeuvre of coming against the Pier's pontoon, tried to jump the distance of a couple of yards [metres] or so from the boat onto the pontoon, had completely missed the pontoon, and fallen into the water between the boat and the Pier's pontoon. "Nat's fallen into the River," someone shouted to Marianne. "So what ?" Marianne shouted back as she threw her glass and its content over her shoulder into the River behind her. "I've finished with him anyway !!" The boat was stopped; Nat was fished out and put back on board, none-the-worse for his premature departure from the boat; the boat's manoeuvring against the pontoon was safety completed; and, the gangway having been run onto the boat and properly secured, we all departed for an hour or so on dry land before returning to the boat for the return trip to Westminster.

After my Father's death my Mother seemed never to want to involve herself in a 'relationship' again. Thus my Father's death had caused my Mother to be without a Partner when going to the Balls,

Dinners, Luncheons, and the like that the Water Rats and Lady Ratlings regularly involved themselves in; and this solitude she found, like many widows find, to be most awkward and somewhat embarrassing. My having left Haileybury thus caused me to become, insofar as Water Rats' and Lady Ratlings' Annual Balls were concerned, her Partner. Having been brought up in the 'world' of Water Rats and Lady Ratlings I knew of their superb Annual Balls but had never, until the October of 1962, been able to attend one. Thus for me the Lady Ratlings' Annual Ball in October 1962 was a very exciting occasion not only because it was the first time that I had worn a Dinner Suit but also because it was the first time that I had gotten to see and meet in one place with so many well-known Theatrical personalities - many of whom, often anonymously, did so much for Charitable Causes. Unfortunately not only do I no longer seem to have the Ball Brochure for the 1962 Lady Ratlings' Annual Ball but also I can no longer recall in which of London's Park Lane hotels the event was held : But I can well recall, not only because I still have the Ball Brochure [*see copy of the following front cover*]

but also from memory, the fact that the 1963 Lady Ratling's Annual Ball was held at London's then only Hilton Hotel, a towering property of twentyeight floors in Park Lane overlooking Hyde Park. Queen Ratling that year was Marie Jackley; the Guest of Honour was Violet Carson, a splendid Actress and an excellent Pianist, and a charming lady who was then starring in ITV's long-running weekly Show 'Coronation Street' as Ena Sharples; and one of the other many 'celebrity' Guests was Wilfrid Bramble, the 'Star', with Harry H Corbett, of the weekly BBC Television Show 'Steptoe and Son', a Show which, as a person employed within the BBC Props Department, I knew reasonably well. That 1963 Occasion is, to me, also memorable for a couple of other things: The fact that I was completely astounded by the 'huge' and, I would argue, extortionate price that I had to pay to buy my Mother a simple single glassful of plain orange squash and the fact that, as the first course of the Dinner was being eaten, small flakes of new ceiling plaster cascaded down upon some of us, including my Mother and me. I also recall that my Dinner Suit, when I tried it on a week or so before the Ball to see if it was still okay, had noticeably 'shrunk'; and the only persons, in my opinion, who could be to blame were the firm of Dry Cleaners in Putney High Street from whom I had just received it back after having taken it there to have it cleaned and pressed. So, annoyed, to the Cleaners I went. I was adamant that they had given me the wrong Suit and they were equally adamant that they had not. My having produced my Cleaner's Ticket and with the 'discussion' between us seemingly getting nowhere, an Assistant, without a word and very much to my surprise, first unstitched a small area in the jacket and then unstitched a small area in the trousers. Then the Staff evidenced to me a hidden number inserted by them within each of the jacket and the trousers. Pointing out to me that the number in the jacket and the number in the trousers were identical to the number on my Cleaner's Ticket the Assistant then politely said "May we suggest to Sir that perhaps Sir is a little larger than he was last year ?" I slunk back to 28 Kenilworth Court a defeated man; and arrangements had to be made with a Tailor to quickly undertake the necessary work to my Dinner Suit to enable it to accommodate the now larger me.

Between the 1962 and 1963 Lady Ratlings' Annual Balls was the November 1962 Water Rats' Ball, a somewhat bigger occasion that took place in The Great Room of The Grosvenor House Hotel in London's Park Lane. [The Grosvenor House Hotel was opened in the 1920s having been built on the site of the London home of the Dukes of Westminster, whose family name is Grosvenor. In the 1930s, despite its being an hotel, it staged several Stage Shows for which my Father's then firm, Loveday & Higson, built the Scenery.] The Comedian Ben Warriss - whom, with his Mother Mary, I had known ever since I could remember - was that year's King Rat [*see, the following front of the 1962 Ball Brochure*];

Rupert Davis, the 'Star' of BBC Television's 'Maigret' (a French fictional detective series based on books written by Georges Simenon), was Guest of Honour; and the Guests included many of the great Theatricals of the era. Billy Butlin and Fred Pontin, both of Holiday Camp fame, were regular Guests at Water Rats' Balls for many years. Each was always a generous donator to Charity and at every Water Rats' Ball at which the two were present each would always be as competitive with the other as they were in business : And it was at the 1962 Water Rats' Ball that I commenced smoking Habana cigars, an enjoyment that remained with me for over 50 years. One of those present was a shortly-to-become Water Rat by the name of Harvey Riscoe, the son of Water Rat Johnnie Riscoe, a Theatrical Agent and keen Golfer, and his Lady Ratling Wife Vi Riscoe. Harvey Riscoe- who married Sandra Butlin, one of Bill Butlin's two daughters - and I were chatting as we stood in front of a row of trestle-tables each of which was covered by an overhanging sheet on which were piled the prizes for a tombola raffle. Amongst the prizes were some boxes of Habana cigars. I, as a child, had often seen my Father, and some of his Theatrical friends and acquaintances, both male and female, smoking Habana and Jamaican cigars; and I had thoroughly enjoyed the aromas of these vegetable products, but I had never smoked even a part of one. Suddenly Harvey bent down and, having reached beneath one of the overhanging sheets, pulled out from beneath one of the tables a small number of cigars. Handing me a cigar-cutter and turning away from the table he said "Here, try one of these". So, I cut off the capped end of the cigar, stuck the now uncapped end in my mouth, and, with Harvey holding one lighted match after another to the cigar's other end, did as I had seen my Father often do: rolled the cigar round to enable the flame to evenly light it. Then, as Harvey lit himself a cigar, I slowly drew on the cigar in a manner which I hoped evidenced that the smoking of Habana cigars was a way of life for me. That smoking of my first Habana cigar was, without doubt, a challenge for its strength was far greater than I had expected. So, to the late Harvey Riscoe (he died in 2009) I, if not my Bank balance, am indebted.

King Rat for the next year's Water Rats' Annual Ball was another longtime acquaintance, the Comedian Ted Ray [*see, the following front of the 1964 Ball Brochure*]

whose Wife, Sybil, was a Lady Ratling. One 'penguin suit' 'personality' whom I certainly did not expect to see that night in 1964 came, handshaking-arm outstretched and with an enormous grin, towards me as if a ghost from nowhere : It was Dick - that splendid boiler-room and multi-skilled character whom I had last seen the day when I had left Haileybury Junior School back in 1957. At the JS to me and to everyone else he was always 'Dick'. We never needed to know his surname and so we never bothered to find out what it was.

Thus to see him coming towards me at a prestigious Water Rats' Ball in The Great Room of London's Grosvenor House Hotel was the last thing that I expected. I certainly knew the two people walking beside him - an Actor Water Rat Len Howe and his Lady Ratling Actress Wife, Audrey Maye. I had known them for years, but what on earth was my friend of years now past, who had given me and many other young boys so much kindness and encouragement and so many reassurances when we needed them, doing with them ? Apparently there had, for some years, been a plot afoot between my Mother, my Father, Len Howe, and Audrey Maye not to tell me that Dick was in fact Len Howe's Brother. But what a shock. What a shock !! Showbusiness is a great leveller of Class. Harry Seltzer, a good friend of mine for over 60 years until his death in September 2004 in Brinsworth House, the Entertainment Artists' Benevolent Funds' Home in Twickenham, had, in August 1909, been born in extreme poverty in [Kingston upon] Hull in Yorkshire and as a child rarely had any shoes. So he used to scrounge around until he found two worn-out shoes, preferably a right one and a left one, which, having ripped off the remains of their disintegrated soles, he would, by means of laces or bits of laces that he had also found, tie onto his feet and, pretending that the shoes were proper shoes with soles, in his bare feet play and walk around the streets in them until either it was time to return to his poverty-stricken home or else his feet had become so painful that he could neither play any more nor walk any further : And yet, through sheer hard determination, as a child he became an excellent [shoe wearing] Tap-dancer and Ventriloquist, made his first professional Stage appearance, as a child Performer, in The Alexandra Theatre in Hull's Charlotte Street, spent many years on stage, became a friend/acquaintance of Prince Philip, and in 1969 became the Water Rats' King Rat. [See under copy of front of 1969 Water Rats Ball brochure.]

One of those present in 1964 was the great comedian and superb Magician, Water Rat Tommy Cooper [although anyone seeing his Stage Act who did not know that he was, in reality, one of Britain's finest Magicians, would hardly believe him to be a Magician at all]. I remember Tommy with much fondness. His Wife, Gwen, was, like my Mother, a Lady Ratling; and one Wednesday evening Tommy and I were sitting on adjacent barstools in a Public House near to where the Lady Ratlings were having their fortnightly Lodge Meeting -

Tommy waiting for Gwen and I waiting for my Mother. Tommy was sitting with his left arm on the bar and I was sitting with my right arm on the bar and, as we chatted, a friend or acquaintance of Tommy's came in and, from a distance, greeted him. As Tommy turned towards the guy Tommy's left elbow caught my glass of cider emptying its contents all over the place. The word 'upset' is hardly sufficient to describe Tommy's reaction. One could not have found a more genuine and apologetic man. The premature death, when aged 63, in 1984 of this 6ft 3ins [1.91M] comedic genius whilst performing on stage in London's Her Majesty's Theatre was a great loss to Variety Theatre.

Despite the harshness and severity of her grossly impoverished childhood, my Mother supported the Conservative Party - a situation very much at odds with the Left Wing politics of her Parents and Brothers and Sisters most, if not all, of whom despised Conservatives for it had been Conservatives who had - prior to the nationalisation, under Clement Attlee's Labour Government, of the Coal Mines in 1947 - been the owners of the Lanarkshire Coal Mines which had inflicted, and maintained, the impoverishment upon so many families who lived within the areas of the Lanarkshire Coalfields. Although she voted Conservative my Mother was not an 'active' Supporter; and perhaps her background, unknown to me at the time, explains why it was that I suffered no hindrance nor criticism from her when I decided to join the Putney Liberal Association. I knew little about Politics at the time other than that there appeared to be, in England, a choice of three principal political Parties - One on the 'Right' which was called either 'Conservative' or 'Tory'; One on the 'Left' which was called either 'Labour' or 'Socialist'; and one seemingly in the 'Middle' which was called … Well, just 'Liberal'. Insofar as Politics is concerned I am at heart a simple person and as such am of the opinion that often the best path to choose in order to best suit most people, and thus

Democracy, is the 'Middle' path. It was thus on that simplistic basis that I chose to join, what I at the time believed to be, the 'Middle' Party in English politics. However the one and only Meeting of the Putney Liberal Association that I ever attended soon put paid to that idea. I can not now recall either the Agenda of that Meeting or the names of anyone, other than I, who was present but I do know that I found the Meeting to be somewhat 'Left Wing', intolerant of the opinions of those with whom the majority at the Meeting did not agree, and, I felt, childish, very childish. I never attended another Meeting of the Putney Liberal Association.

An excursion on my bike one day took me up Putney Hill, through Putney Vale, and almost to the Robin Hood roundabout at the start of the very busy, even in those days, Kingston By-pass where I found, to the left of the main road from Putney just before it entered the Robin Hood Roundabout on the A3, an Archery Club. But, as with the Youth Club, I was not allowed by my Mother to involve myself with that either. But I was never restricted in where I cycled; and thus cycling into Central London became a regular, and often very exciting, activity. An incident that occurred at Hyde Park Corner on the day that I decided to cycle from Putney to Oxford Street and back will always remain very clear within my mind. Granted, the volume of traffic in London in those days was not as great as it is nowadays but nonetheless the volume - with cars, taxis, 'buses, lorries, and all manner of vehicles seemingly coming and going in all directions - was considerable. But, using common-sense, one learned to respect other road users and to cope : And so, having come into Hyde Park Corner from Victoria, then successfully negotiated my way round Hyde Park Corner and passed some substantial road works at the commencement of Park Lane, I was somewhat bewildered when two Policeman, standing diagonally opposite me on a footpath on the other side of Park Lane, beckoned me towards them. As I cycled nearer and nearer to them their beckoning seemed to get more and more urgent causing me to cycle faster and faster. On reaching them one of the Policeman pointed up Park Lane in the direction of Marble Arch. "Look," he said, " You don't want to cycle straight into that lot do you ?" I looked, and there, heading at considerable speeds towards where I would have been had not the two Policeman decided to 'rescue' me, was a vast mass of all shapes and sizes of vehicles. Unknown to me as I commenced my journey up Park Lane had been the facts that Park Lane was in the process of being substantially widened so as to convert it into a dual-carriageway; that I had inadvertently passed a sign prohibiting all types of vehicular traffic, including cyclists, from entering Park Lane from the Hyde Park end; that towards the Marble Arch end of Park Lane the flow of all traffic travelling down Park Lane from the Marble Arch end was controlled by traffic-lights; and that, once released by the traffic-lights, vehicles travelling down towards Hyde Park Corner were often driven at speeds of which the word 'maniacal' would not be too harsh a description. Had it not been for those two Policeman, I would not have stood a chance !!

I had encountered Police, but this time somewhat 'over the top', 'efficiency' on one previous occasion, whilst in Croydon in the years when I was a pupil of Haileybury Junior School. Out cycling one day on the outskirts of Croydon I had discovered a £1-Note [last issued in England in 1981] lying in a gutter alongside the road on which I was cycling. A Pound being not an insignificant sum in those days when one could buy over 20 loaves of bread for a £1, and my having been taught always to be honest, I picked up the Note and cycled with it well over a mile to Croydon Police Station where I handed it to the Desk Officer who then asked me to give a Statement during the course of which I was asked to give an exact description of the gutter in which I had found the Note. To me a gutter was a gutter was a gutter, and thus I was unable to give a precise description. As a result of my failure to give this 'vital' piece of descriptive evidence a Constable was detailed to accompany me back to where I had found the Note in order that a precise written description of the gutter could be made. With the Officer walking beside me and with me pushing my bike I went back to the exact spot when I had found the wretched thing. The Officer wrote his description of the gutter in his notepad, and the two of us then walked back to the Police Station so that my Statement could be completed. Having signed my completed Statement I was informed that if no-one claimed the Note within a month ownership and possession of it would pass to me. By the time that my School Holiday had finished and I had gone back to School I had more or less forgotten the incident but my Mother soon revived my memory when next she visited me at Haileybury. "Don't you ever send the Police round to my home again," she emphatically stated to me after we had gotten into the car. Apparently a week or so after the expiry of the one month since I had made my Statement two Police Officers had, to her considerable embarrassment, arrived at Highlands and knocked loudly on its the front door. Intending only to hand the note to me the Officers had, in my Mother's opinion, given the impression to any neighbour who might have seen their arrival or heard their knocking upon the door that a crime possibly undertaken by my Mother had been committed. It seems that perhaps a "What will the neighbours think ?" attitude was of more importance to my Mother than the giving of praise to me for my honestly !!

My Mother's totally unsympathetic attitude towards me over the £1-note caused me to panic on two subsequent cycling occasions. The first occurred close to West Croydon Railway Station when I was cycling along a road racing a train travelling on a track alongside the road. The train had just left the Station and was building-up speed. As the train gathered speed I foolishly changed gear whilst peddling furiously. The result was that the gears suddenly jammed causing me to be somersaulted over the handle-bars and to land, whilst being knocked unconscious, on the road. An ambulance was summoned, and I woke up just as I was being lifted off the road in order to be put into the ambulance. I panicked, struggled, and pleaded with the ambulance crew to take me home rather than to hospital. Eventually they agreed and, having put me and my bike into the ambulance, took me home. An explanation was given by the ambulance crew to my Mother, who thanked them for everything that they had done. However, I received no sympathy but was instead, by way of punishment, sent straightaway to bed. The second incident occurred at a road junction in South Croydon where the Sanderstead Road forks off from the Brighton Road. In those days many clothes were hand-made; and my fly-buttoned trousers, having been made by my Mother, were no exception. As I cycled, standing up, as fast as I could along the Brighton Road heading towards Purley a much faster moving taxi went alongside me on my right-hand side and then started to cross immediately in front of me so as to go into the Sanderstead Road. I had no option but to turn my bike slightly towards the left so as to, hopefully, avoid the taxi colliding with my bike : But as the taxi's rear bumper passed alongside me it caught the bottom of my right trouser leg and ripped my right trouser leg clean off leaving me, as the taxi carried on without stopping, with my left trouser leg still attached to my trousers and my right trouser leg lying on the Brighton Road. Just after I and my bike had fallen in a heap on the ground I noticed that across the other side of the Brighton Road was a Butcher's Shop sited in a small parade of shops. So, having picked myself and my bike up off the road, I gathered up my torn-off trouser leg, walked across the road and into the Butcher's Shop, whereupon, with a mixture of concern and humour, one of the Staff helped me tie on my trouser leg with several pieces of string. I thus discontinued my journey to Purley and instead cycled and walked back home to Highlands. Needless to say, the person at fault for damaging my hand-crafted trousers that had taken "many hours to make" was deemed not to be the taxi-driver but me !!

Generally speaking, I enjoyed cycling and did a lot of it. Often, when living in Croydon, I would cycle miles either just for the sake of it in order to pass the time or to undertake some form of self-imposed mission such as fishing for minnows in a pond or collecting eggs directly out of birds' nests. Fishing for minnows was a relatively simple undertaking: Armed with a couple of jam jars around the necks of which I had tied some string, I would cycle to my selected pond, then, with my bike parked nearby, lie on my stomach on the edge of the pond and suspend the jars into the water until I eventually managed to obtain sufficient water and fish in them, then I would, having suspended the content-filled jars from my bike's handle-bar, very carefully cycle back home and, over a period of a couple of days or so, enjoy watching the fish swim around in the jars until eventually they died for, apart from any feeding matter that happened to be in the pond-water that I had brought home, buying fish food for my unfortunate captives was something that I was never, by my Mother, permitted to do. But then in those days the care and well-being of creatures such as fish hardly entered the thinking of most people. Hunting for birds' eggs - another 'sport' for which the care and well-being of the creatures concerned hardly ever, if ever, entered the thinking of most people - was somewhat of a more challenging undertaking for it involved, usually, the climbing of trees, some quite large, in order to access the nests: To ensure that I spent a reasonable time away from home [and from my Mother] I would deliberately target an area of trees some miles away from Highlands. On arrival, having parked my bike, I would watch the birds for a while in order to ascertain exactly where their nests were, then I would select some of the nests and thereafter climb up to them to remove some of the eggs that I found in them. Then, to ensure that I broke as few of the eggs as was possible, I would, with the eggs stuffed in my pockets, carefully climb down the trees and, on returning to my bike, place the eggs into my bike's saddle-bag, a container that I made out of wood and canvas and which I painted black so that, at least to the casual observer, it resembled a 'proper' saddle-bag. Having repeated this ritual several times in order to get as many eggs into my saddle-bag as was possible, I would then cycle back home and proudly add my new collection to those which I had previously obtained on other such excursions. The facts that, when I was raiding the nests, life existed within at least some of the eggs and that I was doubtless turning happy parent birds into very sad parent birds neither crossed my mind nor was ever made known to me by anybody, including the many adults who passed by and watched me as I undertook my egg collecting - For egg collecting was commonplace in those days whereas to-day it is, rightly so in my Opinion, considered by Society to be cruel. Perhaps it might have been of some interest to those birds whose nests I robbed to know that on one occasion, my having observed from their actions that flying seemed to be not all that difficult, I decided to myself attempt to see if I could at least, to some degree, float in air if not actually fly. During the Second World War my Father was a volunteer Warden with the ARP [Air Raid Precautions] - an organisation with over a million unpaid part-time volunteer Wardens whose duties included distributing gas masks, ensuring that blackout

Regulations were complied with, and attempting to extinguish fires caused by German incendiary bombs - and as such he had been issued with a Stirrup Pump [a single-person hand-operated pump with several feet of hose] with which to pump water from buckets onto fires, an armband embellished with the initials 'ARP', a tin hat, and a large waterproof cape. After the War he, as many did, retained the Stirrup Pump, armband, tin hat, and cape. I often found the Stirrup Pump to be a good 'toy' with which to play : And in my desire to, at least partly, emulate the birds whose nests I had robbed, it seemed to my that, if I was going to launch myself from a height, I should first do so having taken the precaution of being accompanied by some form of parachute - and what better item to use than my Father's large waterproof, now no longer used, cape. So, having tied bits of rope to the cape so as to create a crude parachute, I climbed, with my parachute up onto a large wooden coal 'hole' that butted Highlands' garden Shed, and from there I climbed up onto the Shed's roof where, after having clambered up to the roof's apex, I sat down and tied my parachute onto myself. Then I stood up and, having eventually mustered sufficient courage, from a height of some 12 feet [3.6 Metres] or thereabouts launched myself forwards off the roof in order to land, within a very short period of time, on the grass that lay the other side of a brick-bounded footpath sited adjacent to the Shed. All had gone well, so very well that, having picked myself up off the grass, I straightaway, with my parachute still attached, went back to the coal 'hole', again climbed up onto the Shed's roof, again clambered up to the roof's apex, and this time, having no need to tie my parachute on, immediately stood up in order to again launch myself forwards off the roof. Given that birds do not have parachutes, "This time," I thought, "do it without the parachute and see how you get on". So, having discarded the parachute, I again launched myself forwards off the roof and landed more or less on the self-same spot where I had previously landed. The most noticeable difference this time was that the landing was such that the word 'excruciating' is the only word that I can think of to describe the pain that my right foot and lower right leg felt as the grass and I met each other. Realising that I would receive no sympathy whatsoever from my Mother for my self-inflicted suffering I just put up with the agony until it eventually wore off : But it taught me two things - One, my Father's wartime cape, despite the crudity and primitiveness of it, had, as a parachute, at least been of some assistance and, two, flying was both out of the question and never to again be attempted.

Bird eggs and minnow collecting ceased when we left Croydon. But Putney had other forms of interesting events.

One 'stunt' that my Mother tried to pull in the early days of our living in Putney was to take me, privately, to a Psychiatrist in the Maida Vale/St John's Wood area of London in order to have him examine me and declare me to be a Schizophrenic [A person suffering from a psychiatric disorder which can cause delusions and an inability to distinguish between reality and non-reality]. So to the Psychiatrist we went, my Mother making it known, and evidencing, to him that she had been, at The Crichton in Dumfries and in Epsom, highly trained in Psychiatric Nursing, was thus well experienced both as a result of her time at The Crichton and subsequently at Mental Hospitals in the Epsom area, and therefore indicated that she knew a Schizophrenic when she saw one. The Psychiatrist however, having put me through various tests, firmly declared me to be not a Schizophrenic but to be of 'sound mind', intelligent, and a very healthy person, a declaration not at all well received by my Mother. I can only guess that my Mother's motive was to rid herself of me, but after we returned to Putney she never ever pursued that idea again.

Life during term-time at Haileybury Senior School trundled on. At the age of fourteen one was required to 'volunteer' to join the Combined Cadet Force [CCF], a military activity which was usually taken very seriously, at least every Wednesday afternoon when the CCF, in effect, took over life within the College. The CCF was divided into three Sections - Army, Navy, and Air Force - and its overall operation centred around the College's Armoury and the Navy Section's Parade Ground. Reasonably secure - although not secure enough when raided by the Irish Republican Army [the IRA] some years after I had left Haileybury - the former was where hundreds of rifles and other weaponry and vast quantities of, mainly blank, ammunition were stored and where two former, but still very active, Army Sergeants, CSMI [Company Sergeant Major Instructor] WA Lawrence and CSMI JG McCrory BEM [British Empire Medal], were based and the latter was a pucca, but small, Parade Ground used principally by the CCF's Navy Section, although we all, regardless of which Section we were in, used it on occasions. Most of the, all Male in those days, Teaching Staff had, due mainly to the Second World War, served in the Armed Forces and some, like my own House Master, had achieved high, or reasonably high, rank. Thus there was no shortage of genuine military knowledge and skills within Haileybury's Teaching Staff and therefore at any one time the CCF's Commanding Officer, a member of the Teaching Staff, was always a person of allegedly proven military skill. Also, many of Haileybury's former pupils and of the Imperial Service College's former pupils had undertaken careers within the Armed Forces, some achieving high rank. Therefore the military culture within Haileybury was very strong. Thus, when, aged fourteen, it came my time to 'volunteer' and

I passed on to my House Master [a former Officer in Military Intelligence who, when in command of Haileybury's CCF from 1950 to 1954, had been promoted to the rank of Lieutenant Colonel] my Mother's comments that she did not like guns and would rather that I did not carry a rifle, I received no sympathy whatsoever but instead the simple, but fear-generating, reply "Fine, Loveday. Then you'll carry a Bren Gun instead !!"

Each year there were two principal foci insofar as the College's CCF activities were concerned: A day on Manoeuvres on Hatfield Heath and an Annual General Inspection by some senior, if not very senior, Member of Her Majesty's Armed Forces to whom Haileybury and Imperial Service College had contributed, and continued to contribute, many such characters. Despite my House Master's instruction that I would carry a Bren Gun instead of a rifle, Wednesday afternoons often found me presenting arms, sloping arms, shouldering arms, and so on with, thankfully, with a rifle not a Bren Gun. But I did on occasions have to carry a Bren Gun instead of a rifle. One such occasion each year was the annual trip for Manoeuvres on an often very muddy Hatfield Heath where - ably assisted by a 're-loader' allocated to assist me by carrying a spare, but completely devoid of ammunition, magazine for my Bren Gun - I would, in true military style, walk and run 'cautiously' around seeking out 'the enemy' [played by other Haileyburians likewise brought to Hatfield Heath for the occasion]; jump down into ditches to avoid non-existent bullets from blanks fired by 'the enemy' at my colleague and me; climb up out of the ditches once we had deemed that 'the enemy' had given up on us in favour of seeking out some other suckers elsewhere; crawl, often in mud, along on my stomach - holding my Bren in both hands in front of me to protect it from getting muck and mud into its barrel - when seeking to go from point A to point B at times when we thought that to do otherwise might put us within the sights of 'the enemy'; roll over and over - again holding my Bren in both hands in front of me to protect it from getting muck and mud into its barrel - some times just for the fun of it, other times because that was what was required of us because that was what we had been taught to do in certain situations; and so on. Carrying a Bren Gun, despite its weight disadvantage of nearly 23lbs [10.4kg] when compared with a Lee-Enfield rifle's weight of only 8lb 11oz [4kg], gave one a feeling of superiority over those armed only with a .303 rifle, for a Bren Gun - initially developed in the 1930s in Czechoslovakia [as the then united two Countries of the Czech Republic and Slovakia were, until 1993, known] it was much used by the United Kingdom and other Allied Forces throughout the Second World War and remained in use by UK Forces up until and beyond the Falklands War in 1982 - not only was a much more efficient weapon, with a firing rate of about 500 x .303 bullets per minute compared with a Lee-Enfield's firing rate of about 25 x .303 bullets per minute, but also it held within its magazine far more bullets than the five bullets that a .303 held within its magazine. For me, and doubtless for my 're-loading' colleague, the downside of this superbly-crafted light machine-gun was that, whereas those with Lee-Enfield .303 Rifles actually had five, albeit blank, bullets within their magazines that they could actually fire, I and my colleague were allowed not even blanks. Instead, whenever I pulled, or pretended to pull, the trigger of my Bren Gun, I would shout to my colleague who would then furiously activate a football-supporter's type of rattle thereby creating a sound vaguely similar to the sound of bullets being fired. Oh, what fun !!

With Haileybury's background being substantially that of the East India Company it was inevitable that somewhere there would have to be a proper Army-like Assault Course, although, oddly enough, such did not exist until the boys of my era built it. Thus, as part of our CCF activities, several of us were ordered to set to and build, to proper military specifications, solid high walls of wooden tree-trunks lashed to-gether with rope which, once completed, had to be run at and climbed over; water-filled ditches which had to be swung over by means of suspended ropes; mud areas which had to be crawled through; pivoted, in the manner of seesaws, half tree-trunks which had to be walked along; and so on. The building of the Assault Course was a challenge for us as was, deliberately, its use by everyone else in the CCF once we had completed it. But it was fun to build. Something else that was fun was the firing at targets using .22 rifles both within the College's own Indoor Rifle Range and within its much longer Outdoor Firing Range. Unfortunately I was not the most accurate of shots, my not realising until almost at the end of my time at Haileybury that, although seemingly right-handed, it was more suiting for me to use a rifle in the manner of a left-handed person, a practice which I had naturally adopted at home in Croydon when using a bow and arrow but which I was not in any way encouraged to adopt when using a rifle at Haileybury - For to be either left-handed or ambidextrous was, it was then considered by many teachers throughout the UK, an indication either of a clumsy personality or of a criminal personality.

The Assault Course proved itself to be a very good means of training for those, of whom they were many, intending to go, once they had finished their time at Haileybury, into the Armed Forces; as indeed did the Outdoor Firing Range which also proved itself to be a very dangerous place for the unwary or unthinking. On one occasion we who were constructing the Assault Course were witness to three unauthorised characters, deep in conversation and oblivious to where they were, slowly wandering across the lines of fire just before several rounds of lethal live .22 shots were about to be released. I dread to know what would have happened had not the Officer-in-Charge of the Firing Range had his wits about him and instantly ordered the targets not to be elevated thereby causing rifles not to be fired thereby causing the three oblivious conversationalists not to be shot.

The Army Section - of which I, like many, was a humble cannon-fodder member throughout the entirety of my 'voluntary' service within the CCF - was comprised of Companies which were composed of Platoons which were composed of Sections. The structure of command-issuing was very simple: The lowest of the low - of which I was a proud member of increasing experience as the years went by - were looked down upon by Lance-Corporals who, in turn, were looked down upon by Corporals who, in turn, were looked down upon by Sergeants who, in turn, were looked down upon by Company Sergeant-Majors [CSMs] who in turn were looked down upon by Lieutenants. I took the CCF reasonably seriously but never felt able to take it too seriously due to the fact that, in my opinion, had the thing been for real, the courage levels of many who - as Lance-Corporals, Corporals, Sergeants, CSMs, and Lieutenants - went round giving Orders to those over whom they had, for whatever reason, been promoted had probably somewhat less than the courage levels of many who were at the receiving ends of their, sometimes ludicrous, Orders. There were, of course, exceptions : indeed, some of my colleagues went on, after leaving Haileybury, to achieve considerable success, and high Ranks, if not very high Ranks, within Her Majesty's Armed Forces. Although we were usually drilled by Non-Commissioned Officers [NCOs] of our own amateur kind the task was occasionally undertaken by genuine Members of the Armed Forces, one of whom was Company Sergeant-Major Lewis, a real-life Royal Marine Drill Sergeant. I twice encountered this splendid personality, for whom I had much respect, whose voice command-projection was everything to be expected of a man entrusted by Her Majesty to install instinctive reaction in her fighting Troops. Having gotten us toy Soldiers to line up in file on the Naval Section's Parade Ground at the commencement of his afternoon's training session he would, with the deepest of voices, then slowly and very forcefully shout "Platoon. Platoon", and then pause for a second or two before, with the shrillest of voices, suddenly, with all his might, scream "Shun !!" Instinctively - and, as if hit unexpectedly by a very fast-moving bolt from a crossbow - we would immediately come to a rigid attention, the straightness of our bodies equal to that of any real soldier. The man was a sheer delight. Always the Professional, he also had a superb sense of humour which at times he put to use to encourage within us a desire to turn the tables on him so that he, in turn, could turn the tables back on us. Having, one day, had us marching up the Parade Ground, then 'about turning', then marching part of the way back down the Parade Ground, then 'left wheeling', then 'left wheeling' again before marching us part way back up the Parade Ground, he suddenly ordered us to "Squad, Halt !" So, "Halt" we did except, that is, for myself and one other. Deliberately the two of us kept on marching, our intention being to find out what CSM Lewis would do next. Suddenly, using the high-pitched level of his magnificent commanding voice, he screamed "Hey, you. Is your Muvvers in the Follies ?" Given my Theatrical background and the fact that the 'Follies' - especially those of Florenz Ziegfeld [a very well-known 20th century American Producer of lavish Shows including Show Boat on New York's Broadway and his Parisienne Follies Bergère-inspired Ziegfeld Follies] - were sectors within the Theatrical Profession, I shouted back "Yes, Sergeant Major !!" to which CSM Lewis immediately responded by shouting "Well, Sunshine, you can tell your Muvver that her bleedin' Son ain't in the Follies, he's in the Army; an' if 'er Son and 'is Mate don't 'About Turn' and come back this very instant 'er Son and 'is Mate ain't never gunner folla 'er into the Follies !!" So, the two of us immediately 'About Turned', marched smartly back towards a slightly grinning CSM Lewis, 'About Turned' again, and re-filed ourselves into the rest of our, by now also grinning, Squad. Had I ever become a genuine Soldier and found myself serving alongside CSM Lewis I would have entrusted that man with my life.

Many of the College's Staff, both Teaching and non-Teaching, not only had fought in the Second World War but also had retained souvenirs from the Second World War. John Mannion, Lawrence House's loyal Servant, was one such person and, whereas many Wartime souvenir gatherers had returned to the UK with such as a German helmet or a German bayonet, John had returned with a fully-functioning leather-holstered German Officer's automatic pistol complete with built-in rodding and cleaning kit and several rounds of ammunition each round having an impressed NAZI swastika upon its base. For whatever reason John decided to gift the holstered pistol to me, but not its ammunition of which I had no knowledge at the time. Whatever became of it I do not know for I soon sold it on to one of my peers - whose journey through Life-beyond-Haileybury saw him eventually becoming a very senior, and much decorated, Member of Her Majesty's Armed Forces - for a, much more useful to me at the time, Wolf Cub electric drill and a £5 note. Had I not done so I might have subsequently been presented with a dilemma for some time after I had rid myself of the pistol, whilst using the outside toilet at John's tied-cottage home, I discovered, lying at the bottom of the toilet pan, several rounds of the pistol's ammunition. It had been John's intention to also rid himself of those rounds of ammunition but by means not of giving them away but of flushing them down the toilet in order that no-one would find them. Unaware, I suspect, that the weight of them would not take them up and over the toilet's built-in U-bend he was, needless to say, not successful.

Of the College's military Annual General Inspections, I remember, for three reasons, my third one in particular. Turnout each year had to be immaculate. Those of us in the Army Section had each to, using an electric iron which in those days one lawfully plugged into the 'bayonet' socket of a pendant light-fitting, press his uniform; clean, using khaki-coloured blanco, his webbed belt; polish, to a sparklingly high standard, the brassware on his belt and polish his cap badge; and clean his boots. The cleaning of boots was the most competitive of the undertakings and the one that was the most time-consuming and demanded the most skill: A chunk or two of black shoe polish would be put into the bowl of a large spoon; the bowl of the spoon would then be placed over a flame, probably of a candle; when the polish had melted, it would be poured over that part of the pair of boots that required the greatest shine, namely the toe-caps; then the spoon would be turned over so that the very hot underside of the bowl of the spoon could be applied onto the polish so as to evenly rub, insofar as was possible, the cooling, but still very hot, polish into the leather of the toe-caps; then, once the polish had cooled, a cloth would be furiously, in bursts, applied onto the polish whilst, between bursts, spit was also applied onto the polish thereby ensuring, over a period of time, that the boots were 'spit and polished' to a standard of shine sufficiently high not only to impress the Inspecting Officer but also to outdo the boot-polisher's competitors. After my second Annual General Inspection it had occurred to me that the application onto the toe-caps of my boots of some of the content of a small can of black gloss paint would not only be likely to achieve the same end-result but also save me a lot of time and inconvenience. Thus a few days before my third Annual General Inspection I applied some black gloss paint onto each of the toe-caps of my boots. The result, once the paint had dried, was that the toe-caps of my boots had as good a shine as any boots that I had seen at any previous Annual General Inspection. Indeed, having been buffed-up a wee bit, they shone to such an extent that a good friend at the time, Simon [Sid] Lofts, was almost mesmerised by them and asked me how I had managed to achieve such a splendid result with seemingly little effort. So I told him; and he then asked me if he could have some of my gloss paint so that he could paint the toe-caps of his boots. Next day, Sid having painted the toe-caps of his boots the night before, we all assembled near to where the Inspection, on Haileybury's principal rugger pitch in front of where Haileybury's superb Chapel and Terrace are sited, was to take place. Then, in orderly fashion, we were all marched out and assembled Platoon by Platoon, Company by Company to enable the great man, once we humble mortals were all in position, to eventually undertake his Inspection; and, whilst he did so, we had to stand there, 'to attention' and facing only to our front, for what seemed like an eternity, each of us one arm's length from his neighbour. One of my colleagues, standing to attention some three or four places to my right, was feeling none-too-well. Sid Lofts, meantime, was standing 'to attention' one arm's length to my left. I, fortunately, although short-sighted, have a wide angle of vision and am thus able to see further to my left and right than many others can see to their lefts and rights. I was thus able to watch, with increasing concern, my none-too-well colleague swaying slightly forwards, slightly to the left, slightly to the right, and slightly backwards as he desperately tried to keep himself from dropping his rifle and falling down. As was the wont of Inspecting Officers, the Inspecting Officer, accompanied by the senior Officer from amongst us boys and by his own Adjutant, took his time. Every so often he would stop immediately to the front of some unfortunate to straighten, even if it was already straightened, the unfortunate's tie or to pass a comment or to adjust a belt or straighten the angle of a rifle. The effect was to cause many of us, as we awaited our turn to be looked at, to tremble internally in anticipation that we would be one of those selected for some implied misdemeanour. As the Inspecting Officer arrived in front of my none-too-well colleague he doubtless noticed, if he had not already done so, that my none-too-well colleague was none-too-well. "Are we alright ?" he bawled out. "Yes, Sir," came the semi-shouted reply. "Are we sure ?" the Inspecting Officer then shrieked out. "Yes, Sir," came the second but not-so-loudly-shouted reply. "Good !" exclaimed the Inspecting Officer as he moved off down the line. The very moment that he, the senior Officer from amongst us boys and the Inspecting Officer's own Adjutant had passed my not-so-well colleague dropped his rifle onto the ground and crashed, oblivious to all that was going on around him, straight down to where, only a second or two before, the legs of the inspecting Gilbert and Sullivan trio had been standing. With not a word having been expressed as to the well-being or otherwise of my, by now, not-at-all-well and only partially conscious colleague, the trio passed in front of me then on until the Inspecting Officer found himself eye-to-eye with Sid Lofts. Straightening, if only for the purpose of impressing others, Sid Lofts' tie the Inspecting Officer then looked down towards the ground to see, at the base of Sid Lofts' legs, two piles of foot-shaped gravel out of which grass seemed to be growing in all directions. Not a word was said as the Inspecting Officer, the clearly very annoyed and embarrassed senior Officer from amongst us boys, and the Inspecting Officer's own, clearly very amused, Adjutant moved on !!

Another 'fond' memory that I have of my friend Sid Lofts was the day that he and I, with several others, went on a 5-mile run. Haileybury, like many if not most private schools, was a great believer - rightly so, in my opinion - in the theory that a healthy and fit body assists the mind not only to be healthy and fit but also to be active. Thus during the Winter/Christmas and Spring Terms, on weekdays other than on Wednesdays, when we were not playing rugger one of the enforced 'options' was to go 'on a run'. I was always a moderately fast 'sprint' runner but, because of the fact that I suffer from hay-fever, long-distance running has always caused me problems insofar as breathing is concerned. However, the fact that one suffered from breathing problems was, at Haileybury, for most of us not an acceptable reason for not going on long distance runs. Thus, on this particular day, when, accompanied by Sid Lofts, I had got about half way round the 5-mile run I was struggling and had had enough. So had Sid. So the two of us decided to take a short-cut back to College through a field. It was quite a large, upwards-sloping field with a haystack sited within it about three-quarters of the way between where we were, alongside a hedge and an adjoining wire fence, and where we intended to exit the field at its top. Scattered here and there throughout the field, but mainly in its bottom half near to the hedge and its adjoining wire fence, were, what to us 'townies' seemed to be, some harmless cows chewing away at the grass. We reckoned that we could, via a gap in the hedge, climb over the wire fence and then walk up the field past the haystack and then out over, what looked to us like, a similar wire fence on the far side of the field. So, without any trouble, over the fence we went and started our walk towards the haystack. Within seconds the animals had stopped chewing and were now both looking at us and starting to walk towards us; and so we increased our speed a wee bit. Then the animals started coming, from various directions, more quickly towards us; and so we increased our speed a wee bit more. Then the animals increased their speeds; and it was then that the two of us noticed that the 'cows' did not have any udders, appendages which even we 'townies' knew that cows should have. Suddenly realising that the 'cows' were not cows but bullocks if not bulls, Sid and I started to run like hell up the field towards the haystack. As we ran we realised that the distance from the haystack to where we intended to exit the field was much further than we had thought. So, having rushed past the left-hand side of the haystack, we took temporary shelter around the far side of the haystack whilst we recovered our breaths before we made the next mad dash towards the far wire fence and out of the field. Sid, who had reached the far side of the haystack just before I did, tapped me on the shoulder and suggested that I look round to see what he could see. There, looking sternly at us from the other end of the far side of the haystack, was the biggest bull that I had ever seen. I can not remember running from the haystack to the wire fence but I can remember that when, in desperation to get out of the field, we reached the wire fence we discovered that it was made of barbed wire and that, unlike its friendly cousin at the end of the field, it was not too keen to assist us in climbing over it !! How we made it to and over the fence I do not know, but made it we did - Much, I suspect, to the disappointment of the bull who by now was close, very close indeed, behind us.

Most times I enjoyed sprinting but found, for some reason beyond my understanding, that I sprinted best when not involved in competitive races [save when on the rugger field when chasing, or being chased by, a member of the opposing team]. Thus, whilst at Haileybury I tended to be more a spectator than a competitor; and it was as the latter that I, with many others, witnessed a most unfortunate incident. In those days sports such as discus-throwing were undertaken without any protective netting, barriers, or whatever; and on this occasion a lad was 'powering-up' in the process of throwing the discus. Already he had brought the discus back twice and had therefore created a lot of pressure sufficient to, when he next 'powered-up', turn 360-degrees and release the discus with tremendous force : But - just before he, with his discus-holding arm fully stretched, commenced his 360-degree turn - the discus slipped backwards out of his hand and, spinning furiously, headed not, as it should have done, a considerable distance in front of him but, at tremendous speed, straight towards the crowd of spectators standing some distance behind him. Everyone, including me, scattered as quickly as we could out of the way of the very fast moving projectile, everyone except an unfortunate wheelchair-bound lad who, on seeing the discus heading straight towards him, did his very best to manoeuvre himself and his wheelchair out of the way. Sadly, however, he did not make it in time and the discus, as it travelled on its unstoppable way, sliced through his neck. Fortunately the injury was none-too-severe.

One physically harmless sport, if one can call a card game a 'sport', that I was next-to-hopeless at was Whist, something in which, towards the very end of Term, Williams involved some of the senior members of his House. Many of my peers had had ample practice in card-playing during Holiday times. Due to my Mother's lack of interest in card-playing - other than the academically totally unchallenging games of 'Snap' and 'Happy Families' [Mr Plod the Policeman, Mrs Brick the Builder's Wife, Master Chops the Butcher's Son, Miss Sawdust the Carpenter's Daughter, etc] - I had had no such experience; and thus, when invited/ordered by Williams to take part, I went into the foray greener than green. However, I soon realised that Williams had made a mistake, for he offered two prizes - £1, which was a noticeable amount of money in those days, for the Winner and a largish bar of chocolate for the 'unfortunate' loser. Knowing that I had no hope whatsoever of winning this incomprehensible, to me, game I thus set out to be the 'unfortunate' loser : And not only did I manage to become the 'unfortunate' loser but also, with a pang of sympathy for those who had tried so hard and yet in the end had achieved absolutely nothing, I thoroughly enjoyed my block of chocolate. Indeed, I enjoyed it so much that I managed to manoeuvre myself into being invited/ordered to join the next end-of-Term's session of Whist; and, would you believe, achieved the same dismal result, and was presented with a similar block of delicious chocolate, yet again ? *And to think that Williams had been in Military Intelligence* !!

My experience of cattle on the day when Sid Lofts and I encountered the bull was not the only experience that I had, whilst at Haileybury, of avoiding the intentions of a charging bull. Harding, our Gardener at Highlands, had two elderly [Well, on those days they seemed elderly to me] Sisters who lived in nearby Hoddesdon. Within the first year of my arrival at Haileybury Senior the two siblings, of whom I had never previously known, wrote to me, doubtless at Harding's suggestion, inviting me, one Saturday afternoon, to their home for tea. Having obtained the necessary 'Exit Pass' from my House Master, EF Williams and having changed into my 'Sunday' suit, smartened my tie, etc., I set out to walk the 2 miles [3.3 kilometres] or so from the College to their home in Hoddesdon. Acquainted with the fact that my journey would be shorter were I to, about midway to Hoddesdon, leave the main road in favour of a footpath, I eventually left the main Hertford Heath to Hoddesdon Road and continued along the suggested footpath. Bounded on the left-hand side by a denseness of trees, bushes, and shrubs beyond which was a field with grazing cattle in it and bounded on the right-hand side by a three-strand galvanised wire fence, the footpath eventually narrowed to a width of just a single track on which two persons could pass only with a modicum of difficulty. Eventually, in the distance, coming slowly towards me along the footpath was, what I took to be, one of the grazing cattle which had wandered out of the field. I carried on going forwards, as did my opposite number. Clearly, however, there was not sufficient room on the footpath to enable the two of us to pass each other : And so I began to lob stones and sticks towards it causing it to stop its forward progress towards me in favour, after a pause, of going backwards at a speed roughly equal to my speed going forwards. It seemed happy with the arrangement despite occasionally either being surprised when banging into some obstacle alongside it or stopping altogether as if to rest for a few seconds. After a fair distance of going backwards it decided to have a much longer rest than usual causing me to have to cease my journey meantime. I have never liked being late for appointments, and my appointment with the Misses Harding was no exception. Thus, as the seconds of non-activity, save for my lobbing stones and sticks, multiplied I began to get concerned. Eventually the beast resumed its backwards journey; and all seemed well again until, suddenly, it stopped, then bowed its head whilst, at the same time, several times 'grinding' its two front hooves hard down against the ground. At this point I realised that, insofar as I was concerned, all was not well, a realisation enhanced when suddenly, with a speed seemingly coming out of nowhere, it charged fast, very fast in my direction. Turning left and seeking to attempt to fight my way through the trees, bushes, and shrubs seemed not to be an option for me as did - given the weight and increasing speed of my footpath adversary - turning round and running like hell back along the footpath. So, there was nothing for it but to, notwithstanding my 'Sunday' suit, seek to hastily force my way through the three-strand galvanised wire fence in the hope that I could somehow get through it and out onto the other side before the, what I by now had realised was, bull impacted with me. Fear somehow gives humble mortals a speed and a strength which otherwise they appear not to possess; and I can only conclude that that was the cause of my arriving on the other side of the fence at the same time at which the, by now well and truly charging, bull arrived at the very same spot where I would otherwise have been.

HG Roberts - Now there is a name that sticks in the memory. By the time that I arrived at the Senior School in 1957 Hugh Goronwy Roberts had been on the Teaching Staff for 25 years and was to remain on the Teaching Staff until his death, as a result of a car accident, in 1964. Mind you, several of his colleagues had, by the time of my arrival, been on the Teaching Staff for longer than 25 years. For instance, Edgar Charles Matthews had been there for 35 years, William Alexander Carnegie Nurden for 30 years, Francis Robert Thompson for 29 years having also been a Pupil at Haileybury, and Frederick James Seabrook for 26 years having also been a Pupil at Haileybury. Longevity insofar as life as a Member of Staff, teaching or otherwise, at Haileybury was concerned was nothing unusual. Subsequent to sitting 'O' Levels - of which I passed Latin, French, English Literature, English Language, History, Geography, Physics-with-Chemistry, Maths, Advanced Maths, and Scripture - one was 'streamed' into one of Classics, Languages, or Science. I have, and still retain, a very wide range of subjects' interests but, because I felt that it would be the most appropriate for me on leaving School and going into the Theatrical Profession as a Maker and Designer of Theatrical Scenery, I chose Science. Within Science I had the option either of Physics, Maths, and Chemistry or of Physics, Maths, and

Biology. Although I had, probably because of my Father's death having been caused by carbon monoxide poisoning, neither a liking for nor an interest in Chemistry I chose it in preference to Biology because the thought of spread-eagling and pinning down some unfortunate, although deceased, animal and cutting it open and into pieces with a scalpel had even less appeal to me. Had it been possible, I would have dropped Chemistry in favour of learning German in part because I had enjoyed learning the little amount of German that I had learned, courtesy of Mr Seckleman, whilst at the Junior School and in part because I felt, given that German technology played a major part in worldwide engineering achievements, that, for anyone studying Physics, German would be a worthwhile language, and an advantage, to know. But dropping Chemistry in favour of learning German was not a possibility, due in part to the fact that my House Master was also Head of Languages and would not even begin to listen to my suggestion when I raised it with him. Thus I concentrated on learning Physics and Maths and on tolerating, insofar as I could, Chemistry. It was then that HG Roberts - who had a Son as a Pupil at Haileybury whilst I was there - entered the scene, for he was one of my Physics Teachers. But my memory of him is principally not as Physics Teacher but of the day that my friend Ian Michael Donald Linton Weston asked me to explain, to anyone who asked, the reason for his not being at School that day. Ian's Father, Major General GPL Weston, was the Commanding Officer of the Army Air Corps at its base in Middle Wallop, which is sited between Andover and Salisbury. Ian's Father had been requested/required to attend on the Queen at Buckingham Palace and had taken Ian with him. My Physics Lesson was a double Lesson which started at 5pm and finished at 7pm, just before the commencement of Supper. Shortly after the Lesson had gotten underway Roberts asked where Weston was. I responded by putting up my arm. "Yes, Loveday ?" asked Roberts, a man not known to be blessed with a great deal of humour. "Buckingham Palace, Sir," I replied. "I'll ask again," said Roberts. "Where is Weston ?" Up went my arm again. "Yes, Loveday ?" said a noticeably annoyed HG Roberts. "Buckingham Palace, Sir," I again replied, this time surrounded by muted sniggering. "I'll ask one more time. *Where is Weston* ?" he said slowly, emphatically, and in a voice indicating much annoyance. Up went my arm again. "Yes, Loveday ?" an exasperated voice snapped back. "Buckingham Palace, Sir," I replied for the third time. "OUT !! " he shouted instantly whilst pointing to his Classroom door. Thus 'out' I went to stand in silence for the rest of the two-hours' Lesson in a cold corridor outside the door to his Classroom hoping, perhaps beyond hope, that Roberts might at sometime come out and, if not apologise to me at least, talk to me. But I was still standing in that cold corridor when the bell rang to inform that the Lesson had finished and that it was now time for everyone to make a dash from the Science Block some quarter of a mile or thereabouts to the Dining Hall in time for Supper; and I was still standing there when, everyone else having long since gone, eventually Roberts came out and dismissed me from my 'punishment' with the comment that he hoped that I now regretted my rudeness to him and with the instructions that I should now go back into the Classroom to collect my books and that thereafter I should go as quickly as possible, but without running, to the Dining Hall in the hope that I might arrive in time to be let in so that I could at least have some Supper. So, into his Classroom I went and, having collected my books, then dashed, half walking half running, to the Dining Hall where I found that I was locked out, not allowed in, and thus been denied my Supper !! Incidentally, Ian Weston, after his time at Haileybury ended, subsequently joined the Army rising to the Rank of Lieutenant Colonel before retiring into 'civvy street' and becoming Bursar of an Educational Trust.

Douglas John 'Killer' Cook, a former Lieutenant Colonel in the British Army in India and Burma during the Second World War, was another of Haileybury's Teaching Staff of whom I have a strong memory. He never taught me but his reputation of being a caning enthusiast who lacked humour was widespread. Sundays were days when, in the mornings, we were required to attend Chapel after which we were encouraged to quietly study. On the particular Sunday morning concerned I had gone from my place of study to make an enquiry of one of my colleagues who was, with others, studying quietly in the School's main Form Room Block. I found him in 'Killer' Cook's Form Room. The man himself was not there and was not expected either to be there or to come there that morning : And so, knowing that no other Teacher was likely to be neither within the Form Room Block nor anywhere near it, I borrowed Cook's gown and mortar-board from their hook behind his Classroom door, put them on, and, in a spirit of joviality, went from one Class Room to another 'commanding' all and sundry to "Work hard, Boy, or else ...". On returning to 'Killer' Cook's Classroom I opened its door, rushed in, and had just started issuing to those sitting down my 'command' of "Work hard, Boy, or else ..." when I saw 'Killer' Cook standing quietly and motionless behind his desk on its plinth. He looked at me with a frightening stare but said not one word as I, very, very sheepishly, took off his gown and mortar-board and hung them back upon their hook, and then, desperately wishing that I had never entered his Classroom let alone borrowed his gown and mortar-board, slunk out of his Classroom ensuring that, very quietly, I shut his door behind me. For days thereafter I anticipated some dreadful wrath of vengeance descending on me. But it never did. Eventually it seemed to me that perhaps the fearsome 'Killer' Cook was in reality not so fearsome after all and that, on his telling the story to his Teacher colleagues, my actions that Sunday morning had evoked considerable laughter.

Engaged by the School on a casual basis, Sergeant Cox of the Police's then Hertford Constabulary arrived one term during the latter part of my time at the Senior School to teach Unarmed Combat to a selected few of us. The afternoon training sessions took place in the School's Gymnasium one day each week over a period of several weeks. We all took it very seriously and were taught defensive techniques some of which to-day would certainly not be acceptable to Society. For instance, we were taught that to immobilise a drunken person lunging at us with a knife we should turn as he lunged and, whilst turning, lock his knife-holding arm in one of our arms and then, as he continued to propel himself forward, run with him, his knife-holding arm now firmly locked in one of our arms, towards the nearest wall whilst gouging two fingers one each into either one of his eyes or one of his nostrils before ramming his head hard against the wall thereby knocking him unconscious. Needless to say, on such techniques we only trained, each of us with a partner, in slow motion and we neither actually gouged an eye nor rammed a head. We were also trained to cope with an attack by a vicious dog of a size such as an Alsatian by grabbing the two front legs of the dog as it almost landed upon us and then, in a continuous movement, pulling the legs wide apart so as to split the dog down the middle thereby killing the dog. We never had any real dogs upon which to practice the theory, and to date I have, thankfully, never experienced a situation wherein I have ever had to put my training to the test. Throughout, our training was totally defensive, never offensive, and to that end we were taught to instinctively react quickly, very quickly. Our training often required us to walk up and down the Gym whilst others - some hostile to us, some not hostile to us - walked in a variety of directions around us so that eventually we were able to subconsciously differentiate between the hostiles and the non-hostiles and react accordingly. The effectiveness of that training in subconsciously reacting has never left me, has resulted in my being hostile on some occasions when being innocently 'attacked' by Doctors and other Members of the Medical Profession attempting to give me injections and other intrusive medical treatments, such as 'stitches', that are undertaken without general anaesthetic, and has given me an appreciation of why it is that some Members of the Armed Forces, even long after they have left the Armed Forces, react instantaneously and sometimes violently, very violently, when presented with an intrusion into their 'air space' of even a mild threat of attack upon their persons. My subconscious having been trained, by Sergeant Cox, to react automatically when confronted with certain situations I have, over the years, sometimes been saddened when reading of some of the Sentences meted out by Judges, Sheriffs [in Scotland], Magistrates, and others to those who have, through no fault of their conscious selves, done injury to third parties.

Anthony Leonard Casimir - who had been a Brigade Bandmaster with the Royal Scots Fusiliers prior to his 18-years' stint at Haileybury - was a Member of the Teaching Staff who, although he never taught me, gained my respect. He taught Music, a subject often regarded by many boys at Haileybury - including, I regretfully confess, me - as being somewhat 'cissy'; and he was, by all accounts, an excellent Teacher. I would occasionally encounter him usually either in the School's Bradby Hall, a building which overlooked Haileybury's splendid Terrace and which contained several Music Rooms and a small proscenium-arched stage which at times required my presence, or just walking somewhere from one part of the College to another. He could so easily have just passed by and, save for acknowledging the obligatory indication of respect that we boys were expected to express whenever we passed a Teacher, completely ignored me : But he never did for he would, regardless of what he was doing or where he was going, nearly always stop, usually briefly but sometimes for several minutes, to have a chat. Such simple kindnesses cost nothing and were often very much appreciated, especially after the death of my Father.

Robert Bruce Holgate Butler was the man who, as Head of Art at Haileybury from 1957 to 1985, had to suffer the burden of trying to get me interested in undertaking water-colour painting. He failed for, although I had, and still have, considerable respect, and often much admiration, for many water-colourists and their medium, I lack the patience that that art-form demands. I am also partially colour-blind, an inconvenience for which, over the years, I have developed, and have had to develop, some counter-techniques but an inconvenience which, in RBH Butler's Art Classes, added to my lack of enthusiasm for the dedication and preciseness that he required of his Students insofar as water-colouring was concerned. Nevertheless he and I got on well for outwith his formal Classes we occasionally worked to-gether on the Big School Stage, I responsible for the designing, and occasionally co-designing with RBH Butler, and building of much, if not all, of the Scenery and he responsible for its painting. A 'sore point', but never made known by me, occurred in the annual Winter/Christmas Term productions staged on the Big School Stage by the Teaching and non-Teaching Staff. Intended, principally, to entertain the boys at the expense of those by whom they had been taught, and called 'Pastimes', everything, save for my Stage Design and Stage Management activities and for the Scenery shifting and electrical works undertaken by my Crew of hand-picked boys, was undertaken by adults; and it was thus the practice that all principal credits, including those of Stage Manager and Designer, were given to adults. Thus it was RBH Butler to whom the credit for Stage Management and Design were given. But, what the heck, Pastimes were, at least for me, fun not only in respect of the productions themselves but also in respect of the provision of the tea and sandwiches that were required for evening rehearsals, a responsibility which, for some reason which I now forget, fell entirely to me. Sometime during the day I would attempt to ascertain the numbers who would be attending that night's rehearsal, then I would multiply it by a multiple of 2, 2½, or 3, and then I would put my requisition in to the Head of Catering in the College's Kitchens at the rear of the Dining Hall. That evening I and a colleague would call at the rear doors of the Kitchens to collect a 4-wheeled truck onto which had been placed, in long metal trays, rows of all the various types of sandwiches, wrapped in greaseproof paper to keep them moist, that I had ordered; a large tea urn or two, dependent upon the quantity that I had ordered, of tea; milk and sugar, and, within reason, whatever sliced slab-cake, also wrapped in greaseproof paper, that I had requested; and crockery and spoons more than sufficient for the amount of food and tea that I had ordered. My colleague and I would then, by means of its large steering handle, pull the truck out of the Kitchens onto the roadway which bounded the rear of the Kitchens, and which had a gentle incline down towards the back of the Big School Stage, and then, swinging the handle round by 180-degrees, the two of us would, having pushed all the truck's contents as far back in the truck as we could, jump into the front of the truck whilst at the same time pushing the truck so that it began to go, under its own heavily laden momentum, down the roadway passed the end of the

Kipling, Batten, Melville block of Houses and on to a side door sited within Big School near to the Stage. Later that night, the rehearsal having finished, everyone having eaten and had their cups of tea, everything having been packed up, the House Tabs [Curtains] having been drawn closed, all Stage and Auditorium lights having been killed [turned off], and everyone other than I having gone, I would, by myself, pull the truck back to an arranged position at the rear of the Kitchens where I would leave it but having first removed all the surplus food - of which there was usually a considerable quantity - save for a token gesture which I would leave to indicate to the morning's incoming Kitchen Staff that not everything had been eaten. Sometime next day I would, having retained some of the cake and sandwiches for myself and the three colleagues within Lawrence House with whom I was by then sharing a Study, go round the Study Block and elsewhere gifting [for free !!] to eagerly awaiting recipients, the remainder of the cake and sandwiches.

The four of us Laurentians had our Study on the first floor of the two storey Study Block building. Within our Study we were, as we had been before we reached the age at which we were granted use of a Study, expected not only to study but also to cook some of our own, somewhat very basic meals. The facilities provided to us for cooking were exactly that which had been previously provided to us - basic gas rings. Sited outside our Study in a corridor which gave access to several other studies, the number of gas rings provided for all of us fell well below the number that should have been provided to enable each of us to cook without being hassled by others also wanting to use the gas rings. Thus, for instance, the basic foodstuff common to all, namely bread intended to be toasted, was, given the very limited time available to us, barely put on to the primitive gauge-covered piece of metal, called a Toaster, placed upon a gas ring before it had to be speedily turned over and then removed to accommodate the next piece of bread awaiting to be toasted by someone uttering comments such as "Come on. Hurry up. I haven't got all day, y'know".

When studying within formal Study Periods within our Studies we were not allowed to have a radio or a record-player on : We were expected to study in silence, a practice with which I did not entirely agree because I felt, and still do feel, that 'mood' music assists one to study. So I bought myself a second-hand chair into the back of which I inserted a hidden speaker which was wired, via a switch inserted into the underside of one of its arms, to a radio sited beneath the chair's base. Thus I was able to study seemingly in silence but in reality with 'mood' music quietly encouraging me to study perhaps harder and more intensely than I otherwise would have done. Study Inspections by Teaching Staff were a regular feature of life. Undertaken without any notice and, usually, during times when the Studies were unoccupied, they were intended to discover not only untidiness but also those things which Haileybury 'frowned' on. Standing dispensing drinks behind my bar at Highlands I had acquired a liking for Harvey's Bristol Cream Sherry, for Sandeman's Port, and for cider; and thus, when my Mother asked me what I would like for my seventeenth birthday, I replied that I would like some cider. I had anticipated that, with luck, she might give me a bottle of cider but, instead, just prior to the beginning of the Spring Term of 1961 she gave me, much to my surprise, a smallish wooden cask filled with the stuff which I managed to just get inside my tuck box the lid of which was unable to be fully closed thereby causing me to have to put a rope around the tuck box to hold its lid down. My Father had been of an era in which letters, certainly those of importance and/or of confidentiality, were sealed by means of dropping molten sealing-wax onto the envelope's flap thereby ensuring that the envelope could only be opened if the sealing-wax was broken. Thus anyone looking at the back of such an envelope would instantly know whether or not it had been tampered with. Following my Father's death I had retained several sticks of his sealing-wax and therefore, having been instructed by my Mother that the barrel of cider was not to be opened until my Birthday on 2nd February, I applied sealing-wax onto the knots of the rope that bound my tuck-box; and faithfully adhered to my Mother's instruction.

When the 2nd February arrived I broke the seals, undid the rope, removed the barrel, and tapped it by hammering into the barrel the wooden tap that accompanied it so that I and my Study colleagues could enjoy some, but not too much at any one time, of the barrel's contents. When we had finished our drink or two I put the barrel back into my tuck box and re-tied and re-sealed the rope. Sealing the rope with sealing-wax thus not only acted as a deterrent to any boy who might have been inclined to have a drink without my permission but also enabled me to detect any attempt by anyone to enter my tuck box.

We boys were not allowed to have locks on our Study doors which caused the Studies to be somewhat exposed to prying persons intending to, for whatever reason, visit them; and much of the time during each week-day our Study, like the other Studies, was unoccupied. However all went well until one day I returned to our Study and noticed not only that the seals had been broken and the rope disturbed but also that the tuck box was slightly out of the place in which I had deliberately positioned it. I undid the rope but it seemed that the barrel itself had not been disturbed which at first indicated to me that some boy had, out of curiosity, had a look inside but then had lacked the courage to proceed further. However, word soon reached me that there had been a Study Inspection by one or more of the

Teachers. Needless-to-say, given that the consumption of alcohol was not only forbidden but was possibly punishable by expulsion from Haileybury, I was very concerned. I thus removed the tuck box and its content from my Study. One of the many things taught to me by my Father insofar as Theatre is concerned is that Audiences look forward, look downward, look sidewards, but rarely move their heads much to look upward. Given that I was, in effect, in charge of the College's Big School Stage I therefore took my barrel and its content to the one place where I knew that it could not only be placed in complete darkness but also be positioned so high up that it was likely to be completely out of sight of anyone looking for it. Thus, having carried my tuck box and its barrel onto Big School Stage, I lowered one of the ropes by which we flew [raised and lowered] Scenery, undid the rope that bound the tuck box, took the barrel out of the tuck box, tied about half of the tuckbox's rope round the barrel, tied the Stage's flying rope onto the barrel's rope, hoisted the barrel so high up into the Stage's very dark scenery flying area that even I could hardly see it, then returned my tuck box to its position in my Study, stuffed it so full of books that its lid could not shut properly, and tied the remainder of the rope around it.

Next evening, as my three colleagues and I sat 'innocently' waiting for our Study to be, in effect, raided, in came, completely unannounced, two Teachers. "Study Inspection," announced one of them as we sat there seemingly completely unaware of their intended action. Having been told to stay in our chairs, we watched as the two of them, their target undoubtedly being my barrel and its contents, started looking at shelves, then under and behind books, looking in cupboards and behind their contents, then looking in one of my colleagues' tuck box before they arrived at my rope-bound tuck box. Despite the fact that my name was boldly and visibly painted on it one of the Teachers asked "Who's is this ?" "Mine, Sir," I replied. "Untie it and then sit back down," I was told. So, I got up out of my chair, went over to my tuck box and untied it, and then went back to my chair and, as instructed, sat down. The two teachers then hovered over my tuck box before one of them lent forward, flipped its lid open, and revealed books, books, and yet more books. What a couple of idiots they looked as we four desperately fought within ourselves to stop ourselves from sniggering with amusement.

Next day I was summoned to see Williams, my House Master, who demanded to know what I had done with the barrel. My attitude was simple: Without any evidence there was no case for me to answer. Thus he and I struck a deal - I would surrender the barrel and its contents, it would then be confiscated and it and its contents be returned to me at the end of Term, and nothing more would be said or done about it. We shook hands on our deal, I surrendered the barrel, Williams confiscated it and it was returned to me at the end of Term, and nothing else ever happened. Whether or not Williams ever suspected that I had hidden it somewhere on or within the Big School Stage I never knew for he never asked but when the barrel was returned to me the day before the end of Term its contents had, 'mysteriously', been greatly reduced from the amount of cider that had been there when I handed it over to Williams for, whereas the barrel was about half-full when it was confiscated, on its return to me the barrel had less than a pints'-worth or so remaining in it; and therefore it seemed that Justice had been served, for all parties to the incident had doubtless benefited by it !! But there was one, minor, casualty: Christopher Ivor Davenport-Jones. Subsequently, after leaving Haileybury, to become, I believe, a Doctor of Medicine, Dave Jones - I and others having found the remainder of the cider far too strong to drink - boldly volunteered to finish off what was left. He did so with much flourish and great gusto only to suffer head-aches and an upset stomach for some hours thereafter !!

Of Big School I have many memories one of which involved my former good friend at the Junior School, Mark Saxby, and a Master who never taught me, John Alexander Bentley. Having been a Pupil at Haileybury from 1931 to 1936, Bentley - or 'Major' Bentley as he was sometimes called despite the fact that his actual Rank outside of his promotion to Major within Haileybury's CCF was as that of Captain in the Royal Artillery in Burma during the Second World War - had joined Haileybury's Teaching Staff in 1946 and had earned himself something of a fearsome reputation. His wont, as was the wont of some others of his colleagues - when taking Prep in Big School was to occasionally leave his desk and chair, sited upon the Stage, and progress down steps built into the sides of the front of the Stage so that he could wander up and down amongst us boys as we sat there in silence doing our work. We sat on hard wooden benches working at long wooden desks which could accommodate up to seven or eight of us but which usually accommodated just four or five of us. The wooden desks and their benches were positioned in rows, three desks and their seats to a row with wide aisles separating one desk and its benches from another desk and its benches thereby enabling the likes of Bentley to wander from the Stage down one aisle with the centre row of desks and benches to his right and an 'outside' row of desks and benches to his left, then behind the boys sitting at their benches in the row furthest from the Stage, and then back down the other aisle to the Stage with the centre row of desks and benches still on his right but with the other 'outer' row of desks and benches now on his left. His usual procedure was, on arriving back at the Stage, to turn around reverse the process until, arriving back at the Stage again, he would re-mount the steps and return to his desk and chair. A man who seemed always to be wearing his gown and its flowing 'sleeves', Bentley, whilst undertaking this regular excursion, always adopted the unpleasant, and at times painful to some of us boys sitting at the end of the rows nearest to the aisles, of swinging his gown 'sleeves' in a circular motion thereby causing some of those whom he passed to have to suffer being painfully hit by a swinging 'sleeve'. Mark Saxby, sitting several rows in front of me, was one such sufferer of Bentley's unpleasant tactic. Saxby suffered a 'swipe' as Bentley walked passed on his first journey up an aisle from the Stage and he suffered another such 'swipe' on Bentley's return journey back down the aisle to the Stage. Clearly Saxby had been hurt by the first swipe and clearly he was hurt by the second 'swipe'. But - instead of, as most if not all of us usually did, just sitting there and silently suffering Bentley's painful infliction - Saxby, by now a boy of solid structure, on the second occasion suddenly rose up to his full height and boldly and firmly stated to 'Major' Bentley "If you hit me again, Sir, I'll knock you into the middle of next year !!" None of us dared to cheer, but Saxby had clearly made known, at least to this product of Haileybury in the 1930s, that the physical imparting of Haileybury's 'control through fear' culture was not acceptable to those of us at Haileybury in the early 1960s.

Another means of control, but academic not physical, was the 'Fortnightly Report' whereby not only was one's academic progress reported on, subject by subject, by each of one's Form Teachers every two weeks but also one was required, individually, to meet with one's House Master every fortnight to have the Reports read out and one's academic progress analysed. On one of the occasions on my journey through Haileybury Senior School when I was doing none-too-badly insofar as my academic progress was concerned I had been first in my Class in each of Latin and French for two fortnights but in the third fortnight I had, whilst still coming top in French, dropped to second or third place in Latin. This to my House Master, Williams, was unacceptable; and thus I was ordered by Williams to undertake several hours of 'extra Latin' throughout the next fortnight to bring me "back up to the standard expected and required of [me]" :" And so, for the next fortnight, I had to forego several hours of my somewhat precious spare time in order to be burdened with yet more Latin. I was so peeved by this, what I considered to be, unjust 'punishment' that I determined to go to the College's Bookroom - manned by Harold Pamphilon, a kindly character, and good friend to us boys, whose loyalty to Haileybury, as one of its 'servants' [a description originating from the days of the East India Company], lasted from when he joined Haileybury's non-teaching Staff in 1918 until his retirement from Haileybury in the 1960s - and purchase a Latin Dictionary in the belief that reliance upon same would give me a distinct advantage over most, if not all, of my peers within my Class. What I had not bargained for was that my use of my excellent Latin Dictionary would give me an advantage also over my Teacher of Latin, for it turned out that I was able to use words of Latin beyond the knowledge of my Latin Teacher causing him to confiscate my Dictionary to save him from the embarrassment of being regularly 'publicly' confronted by me with Latin words of which he was totally ignorant. [Until then I had not realised that Teachers, in order not only to be successful but also to impress those whom they teach, need only stay one step ahead of those to whom they are imparting their, often limited, knowledge.]

Happening before one reached the age at which one experienced 'Study Life' at Haileybury, were, for boys who had been baptised into Membership of a Christian Church, Confirmation and, for every boy, the taking of General Certificate of Education 'O' Level Examinations. Confirmation - the rite by which baptised Christian persons are admitted into full fellowship of their Church - was undertaken not because those being confirmed 'felt' within themselves that they should be confirmed but because the conveyor-belt/sausage-machine system by which Students were expected to progress through Haileybury required it. For as long as I can remember I have always had a profound belief in, and respect for, a Being much greater than us humble mortals but, again for as long as I can remember, I have never had a respect for categorising, allocating, and grouping people into 'Religions' for, if only for one reason, 'Religions' have throughout many countries for many centuries been the cause of many, often very vicious and very devastating, wars; and I certainly do not believe that, just because they have reached a certain age in their lives, boys who have been baptised into Membership of a Christian Church should be made to be confirmed. Thus I again found myself in conflict with my House Master, Edward Fisher Williams, who demanded to know of me as to why it was that I was, unlike every other baptised boy, refusing to be confirmed. My answer was simple: "Sir, I do not feel within myself that I should be confirmed but, if I ever do feel within myself that I should be confirmed, I will be confirmed". This was unacceptable to him and his continuing to insist that I should do as everyone else did and be confirmed evoked from me the comment that each boy at Haileybury whom I knew who had been confirmed seemed to be of the same character after confirmation as he had been before confirmation : But that comment only made the increasingly embattled relationship between Williams and me that little bit worse. It seemed to me that the only thing that I missed out on by not having been confirmed was the regular sip of 'Holy Water' undertaken at the Communion Services in Chapel attended by those who had been confirmed. However I did one day chance to overcome that deprivation when asked by one of Haileybury's Teaching Staff

Chaplains to assist him in storing the bottles of 'Holy Water' in a recess behind the College's Chapel's splendid organ - a voluntary assistance generously rewarded, although unknown to the Chaplain, by a slurp or two of the not-so-weak-in-alcohol stuff, each bottle of which was clearly marked on its label as being "Vino Sacro from Exeter" !!

Generally speaking the College's Chaplains, each of whom also both taught formal lessons and assisted in many other of the College's activities, were kindly people. On my arrival at the Senior School in 1957 the Chaplains were the Reverend Donald George Stanley Upton, known to all as 'Rev Up', and the Reverend Richard Frederick Thomas, 'Rev T'. Rev Up left Haileybury in 1958 [but returned in 1985 to finally retire from Haileybury in 1986] and his position was immediately filled by the Reverend Philip Richard Llewelyn Morgan who left the Senior School in 1973 to take up the position of Head Master of the Junior School, a position which he held from 1974 until 1987.

My taking of my 'O' Levels, needless to say, had its own sagas. For instance, those of us, and that was nearly everyone, who took French 'O' Level had to undertake, in a semi-darkened somewhat damp room akin to an imitation hovel, an oral part of the Examination. Each Student was politely 'invited' into the room and made to stand in front of a desk behind which were seated two Examiners who then launched into 'Conversational French' as it was called. Having launched into, and dealt with, the usual introductory comments and phrases such as "Bonjour" and "Comment t'allez vous" the 'meat' of the exercise was then entered into. The problem that I and other Examinees found was that, although most of us had been learning French for several years, including some three years or so before we had arrived at the Senior School, we had not actually been taught how to speak French as the French speak French. No, we had been taught to speak French by means of the careful and *correct* construction of sentences. A noun *must* go here; a verb *must* go there; an adverb *must* go somewhere else; an adjective *must* go yet somewhere else; and so on. Thus, when called upon to speak French not only did we omit to gesture, grunt, and groan as most Frenchmen do when speaking to each other but also the words did not flow as they would in normal conversation of one French person to another. Instead there was a rigidity of posture and many a pause within our speaking whilst we mentally debated within ourselves as to the correct order in which we should be placing the words that we were about to utter. Thus what eventually came out of our mouths was not Conversational French akin to that which would be spoken by an ordinary 'day to day' French person but French akin to that which would be spoken by an academic French person striving to ensure that he was speaking grammatically perfect French. Never mind, I passed but not before, at the end of my far from perfect spiel [*German* !!], one of the Examiners had, with a grin, said to me "You know, Loveday., that's the best bit of Cockney French that I've ever heard".

The one 'O' Level Examination that I took and was expected to pass but did not pass was Woodwork. All my life I had been involved, courtesy of my Father, in Joinery and Carpentry in one way or another both practical and theoretical. It was a natural part of my background; and I had been fortunate at the Junior School to have had a good Woodwork Teacher and at the Senior School to have also had an excellent Woodwork Teacher, SH Devereux. I spent many hours in the large, well-fitted, and well-equipped [for those days] Woodwork Shop at the Senior School and, because of the confidence that he had in my ability, Devereux often left me to instruct some of the pupils whilst he instructed others. We worked at times almost as a partnership. Indeed, on the occasion when it was decided that the Woodwork Shop should have some form of mechanically-powered saw it was I who, with Devereux's agreement, decided upon the type and make of saw that we should have. Thus when he learned that I had failed the 'O' Level Exam he at first found it hard, almost impossible, to believe. The cause of my failure lay, I have always believed, in the way in which the written part of the Examination was conducted. I was its only Examinee, and therefore my taking of the Exam had to be scheduled into the taking by others of an Exam in which I was not involved. Thus I and all the others arrived in Big School, they to take their 2-hours Exam in whatever the subject was that they were taking their Exam in and I to take the written part of my Woodwork Exam. Everyone else's Exam Papers were issued, silence was observed, the command to take the Papers out of their envelopes was given, and the Examination was gotten under way. At least, everyone else's Exam was gotten under way : My Papers had not yet arrived. I sat there for nearly an hour before my Examination Papers arrived, and I got under way as quickly as I could. Just over an hour later the command "Stop writing" was given; and everyone except I stopped. "That includes you, Loveday," a voice boomed out. I protested that I had another hour to go; but my protest was swept aside, and so I too had to stop writing. Thus I was only allowed just over one hour to undertake a 2-hours' Exam. Devereux, on my behalf, subsequently protested but in vain. Thus I failed - or, in my opinion, was deliberately manoeuvred to fail - my Woodwork 'O' Level Examination, an incident in respect of which I was relieved that my Father was no longer alive. However, despite my failure in what, for me, should have been the most successful of my 'O' Levels, the College did ask me to design and build, in oak, a self-supporting double-sided newspaper reading stand for use in the College's Reading Room, a request with which I complied with considerable enthusiasm and for which I designed and constructed an item of furniture which, I subsequently observed, stood the test of time, and suffered many boys leaning heavily against it for many years long after I had left Haileybury.

The Summer of 1959, the year after my Father had died, saw my Mother and I travelling by train from London via Glasgow to Fort William. It was still the 'age of steam'; and en route to Glasgow the chuff-puff engine and its coal-tender that were pulling the coaches in which we were travelling stopped just before a track cross-over somewhere not far south of Crewe to allow a slow-moving goods train to cross from a track on one side of our main line to a track on the other side. As it trundled across the main line the goods train apparently broke down causing us to be stranded for some hours until eventually the goods train was enabled to continue its journey. We therefore arrived in Glasgow some hours behind schedule thus causing us to miss our train, leaving from another Glasgow station, to Fort William. The delay in Glasgow was aggravated by the fact that my Mother had written to one of her Sisters, my Aunt Ina, requesting that she travel from her home in Wishaw, some 20 miles or thereby from Glasgow, to meet us and have a cup of tea and so on. Aunt Ina had replied to my Mother, her Sister, stating that she was meeting someone else for tea that day and therefore could not meet us. My Mother was furious, a fury that remained with her for many years. I can only guess at the origin of Aunt Ina's refusal to meet with my Mother and suspect that it goes back to the time, early in 1952 when I was eight, that my Mother and I had travelled to Wishaw to stay with Aunt Ina, her Husband John, and their Son Hugh ('Wee Hughie' as he was then called) so that my Mother could attempt to patch-up her appallingly bad relationship with her own, and Aunt Ina's, Mother. Whatever Aunt Ina's reason, given our train's lengthy delay in arriving in Glasgow, her decision not to meet us at least saved her from having to wait, doubtless increasingly bored to tears, for hours on a cold draughty platform of one of Glasgow's then collection of Main Line railway stations.

My not-much-above-the-poverty-level Aunt Ina, Uncle John, and Cousin Hugh lived in an upstairs flat [or 'flatted dwellinghouse' to give its then Scots description] within a 2-storey dwellinghouse which was part of a Housing Scheme [or 'Housing Estate' as it would have been called had it been in England] owned by the local Council in Newmains in Wishaw, Lanarkshire. Immediately behind the flat at the end of its short garden sat a, what seemed to me to be, mountain of coal but which was in fact a bing [very large mound of coal waste] on, and in, which the locals roundabout scavenged for any bits of decent coal that they could find for their fires. Many of the area's folk were unemployed. Uncle John was fortunate in that he had a job of driving and operating the local Co-Operative Store's articulated mobile shop; and it was, apart from when I was amusing myself climbing up and down the fabulous - at least to me a "*toonie frae the sooth of Angland* " - bing, with Uncle John in his articulated mobile shop that I spent much of my time when in Wishaw. He was a kind man who did his best to entertain and amuse me, although his patience on one occasion must have been sorely tested for just prior to getting out of his cab in order to go into his articulated trailer to serve his customers, he gave me a large bottle of orange and a glass. To me, a bottle of orange needed first to be shaken, then have its stopper removed, then some of its contents poured into a glass, and then have water added to the contents in the glass. Within his cab Uncle John did keep a bottle of water; and so, in his absence, I set about the routine of shaking the bottle, etc. Having furiously shaken the bottle I then removed its stopper only to experience a considerable amount of the bottle's contents suddenly squirting out at great speed all over the place thoroughly soaking Uncle John's seat and much of the rest of his cab as well. I had never come across *fizzy* orange before !!

On that occasion my Mother and I stayed in Wishaw for several days during which, one evening, everyone except I went out leaving me safely 'tucked up' in bed and with several toys and a pile of Penguin chocolate biscuits sufficient in quantity to keep me happy for several hours. Suddenly, a half hour or so after they had departed, the foot end of the bed, without any warning whatsoever, shot upwards towards the ceiling causing the whole bed to end up inside a large cupboard with me now lying upside down surrounded by my pile of Penguin biscuits which, within a short period of time, commenced to melt and cover my face, pillows, and much else around my head in chocolate. I had neither heard of nor seen a sprung wardrobe-bed before; and there I now lay, entirely on my own within the flat, upside down inside this thing until, what seemed like, many hours later everyone returned and I was rescued. It was to be many, many years before I would face eating another Penguin biscuit !!

The visit that they had made that evening had been, I was to learn many years later from my Uncle Angus, to my Mother's and Aunt Ina's Mother, my Grandmother. She lived with Uncle Angus and his Wife, my Aunt Kate : But my Mother's attempt that night to patch-up her appallingly bad relationship with her Mother was anything but successful. Indeed it was so bad that Uncle Angus and Aunt Kate had to, in effect, tear the two screaming women apart from each other and to thereafter - with Aunt Ina, Uncle John, and my Cousin Hugh - witness my Mother furiously departing Uncle Angus's, Aunt Kate's, and my Granny's flat vowing in no uncertain terms never to return to Scotland again. So, as we travelled from London en route to Fort William in 1959 my Mother and I left Glasgow without my Mother's having seen the person who once had been her favourite Sister, Aunt Ina, a woman who doubtless had found it hard to forgive my Mother for the incident that had occurred in her brother Angus's home some five years earlier.

Our two weeks' stay in Fort William was very enjoyable. We stayed a wee walking distance out of the town centre at the Highland Hotel. With its superb panoramic views over Loch Linnhe, the Highland Hotel was the ideal base from which to walk down into the town or up into the hills that surround Britain's highest mountain, Ben Nevis. On one of my walks, on a Sunday, I passed two top-hatted, dark coated men, each of whom was making notes with a notepad and pencil, standing outside a small kirk [church] greeting each person as he or she went in. I was not unused to seeing people entering a church but I had never before seen men in top hats and dark clothes, each with a notepad and a pencil in his hands, standing outside making notes as people went in. So, after I returned to the hotel I went looking for Hamish, the barman. For a while I was unsuccessful for I had not realised that, because it was a Sunday, alcohol was not able to be served, at least not in that area of Scotland. However I did eventually find him odd-jobbing round the back of the hotel. The two 'mysterious' men, Hamish told me, were the kirk's Elders [Officials] and they were writing down the names of those who were attending the kirk so that, later that day, they could call upon those who had not attended to seek explanations for their non-attendances.

A visitor can not do justice to Fort William without at least visiting, at least the base of, Ben Nevis. But I was destined to do more than that for I was fortunate, or at least so I thought, in that not only were two men, one of whom was a Welsh Methodist Minister, who were staying at the hotel intending to actually walk-cum-climb up to the mountain's summit but also they invited me to join them. Armed with some sandwiches and flasks of hot tea prepared for us by the hotel and with a couple of lengths of rope that one of the two men had acquired from somewhere, and having announced that we would be back at the hotel by seven o'clock that evening, we drove to a small car-parking area close to the mountain itself. It was a pleasant enough day; and the visibility seemed to us to be more than good enough as, leaving the car and clad in clothes well suited for a half-day or so strolling in coldish sunshine, we three totally inexperienced, but very confident, characters - a Welshman, an Englishman, and a half-Scots/half-English youth - set out to accomplish our great challenge. It was easy going, very easy going at first; and, as we chatted merrily to each other, I for one wondered why it was that there were only us three humans around. After a while, as we got noticeably higher up the mountain and as we found it more and more necessary to try to actually climb rather than walk, we were accompanied, more or less at the same distance from us all the time, by some sheep who seemingly preferred to look down on us from on high rather than walk in front of us or behind us or even below us. As the temperature slowly got progressively colder we slowly got progressively colder, and our attempts at climbing became increasingly necessary as we journeyed on whilst all the time being, in effect, shadowed by the sheep. Eventually, as the by now disintegrating footpaths seemed more often than not to be replaced by obstacles such as boulders and crumbling mountainside, walking often had to be more or less abandoned in favour of ... Well, perhaps the word 'scrambling' is more accurate than the word' climbing'. Still, the sheep, keeping their distance above us, stayed with us and by now had adopted expressions which plainly informed that they were often saying to each other "Just look at that trio of idiots". With our lengths of rope proving to be little better than useless, especially as not one of us had any real idea as to how to tie knots let alone use the ropes properly, on and on we went, as did our accompanying sheep who by now had taken to, every so often, cascading tirades of small stones down onto us as if to tell us to turn around and get off their mountain. But we persevered until - sometime, we reckoned, well beyond half way - the Welsh Minister suddenly sat down and, very loudly, exclaimed "I can't go any further up this bloody mountain". As if the hills round about wished to emphasise his sinful expression, the words "bloody mountain" time and time again echoed all around us until, eventually, the sound ceased as if to emphasise to us the loneliness of our predicament.

After a period of some minutes, by which time a mist had appeared both above us and below us, the Minister agreed that - as we were by now probably not all that far from the summit and as he did not wish to have to, upon his return to the hotel, admit to his Wife that he had failed in his quest to conquer the mountain - we should soldier on : And thus soldier on we did. As we plodded, scratched, and scrambled on our feet were becoming sore, our clothes were becoming wet, and our accompanying sheep had given up cascading tirades of small stones down onto us in favour of cascading quantities of much larger, sometimes very large, stones down onto us as if they were now determined to engage us in some kind of territorial warfare. But eventually, and despite the sheep, we reached the mist-shrouded summit whereupon we found, as if put there deliberately to offer a sarcastic greeting to us, bits and pieces of what seemed to be an Austin Seven car !!

With our footwear in various stages of disintegration and with our clothes by now thoroughly saturated, descending the mist-shrouded mountain, still constantly accompanied by our flock of critical sheep, proved to be as difficult as, if not at times more difficult than, going up it : And upon our cold, wet, and very hungry arrival back at the car park we found ourselves to be the centre of a minor scare, for it was by now well past the seven o'clock that we had said that we would be back at the hotel by and our absence had caused the Wives of each of my colleagues, and even my Mother, to very seriously wonder if some tragedy had not befallen us. Hindsight tells me that, if my analysis of the thinking of those sheep was correct, not only were the sheep right in regarding us as a trio of idiots but also they were right in attempting to dissuade us from our foolish venture by hurling stones down on us - For we were unskilled, unprepared, and totally inexperienced, and thus should never have undertaken the venture.

The stay in Fort William did, however, have its lighter sides. I entered and won a table-tennis tournament and still retain the not very expensive paperback book of incomprehensible, at least to a non-Gaelic speaker such as I, Gaelic songs with which I was presented. Also, one of those staying at the Highland Hotel was an elderlyish wheelchair-bound lady whom I occasionally assisted as she journeyed down the hill from the Highland Hotel into the town-centre of Fort William and back. She was a lovely chatty lady and I enjoyed the experience ... Well I did enjoy it until the fourth occasion when I was momentarily distracted and, forgetting what I was doing, let go of the two handles by which I was holding onto the chair. Thus gravity took over. Faster and faster down the hill went the elderlyish lady in her chair with me running after them. In those days there was not much vehicular traffic around and thus I, the wheelchair, and its occupant were on the road and not on the pavement. Suddenly, as the speed-gathering wheelchair and its occupant were venturing across over a main road, I stumbled at which point in time what seemed like the only car in Fort William, travelling from right to left across the road in which we were travelling, intervened between me and the wheelchair, narrowly missing the wheelchair as it did so. I recovered and continued on after the now somewhat distant wheelchair which suddenly swung to its left causing it to ram up against a kerbstone and come to an abrupt halt. Two or three seconds later both I and the driver of the car arrived at the wheelchair where, to my considerable relief, we found its elderlyish occupant sitting and, in fits of laughter, exclaiming that she had not enjoyed herself as much for years !! What a wonderful woman she was !!

The table in the hotel that my Mother and I sat at at mealtimes accommodated four people. The other two were a Miss Christabel Silcox and a Miss Marjorie Reed, both from Southhall in West London. They had each recently retired and the period of their stay was contemporaneous with ours. Thus there was much mealtime conversation between the four of us; and it was only some time after that I found out that one had been a Headmistress and the other her Deputy. [They had very thoughtfully insisted that the information be withheld from me because they did not wish to spoil my holiday !!] I have always, in the main, 'enjoyed' my food and had at the time a particular liking for sausages; and the two sausages served to each diner in the Dining Room each morning were excellent. Indeed, no-one could have had a justifiable reason to complain at the amount, let alone the quality, of food supplied at breakfast each morning by the hotel. Their eating capacities being not as great as mine, at one breakfast early in our stay the two ladies asked me if I would like one of each of their sausages. My answer was, needless to say, an unhesitating "Yes" :" And so each passed one of their sausages to me.

Unbeknown to me, thereafter the two ladies let it be known to the other breakfast eaters that I liked sausages; and so began a ritual whereby each morning at breakfast all 'surplus' sausages were passed from table to table until they arrived at our table and were passed to me. The quantity of all these extra sausages was such that it was considerably in excess of what I could eat, and so each day I retained those that I could not eat at breakfast so that I could munch away on sausages whenever I felt peckish during the rest of the day. I was not, however, the only hotel guest with a passion for food for the Welsh Methodist Minister was not averse to collecting 'surplus' food but his food collecting took place not within the hotel but within a very popular restaurant in the centre of Fort William. High Teas, a Scottish meal consisting of an amalgam of 'tea-time' and an 'evening meal' were, in those days, very popular throughout Scotland, and indeed were often the main meal of the day for many a Scots household. Fraser's Restaurant - owned, I believe, by the local Co-Operative Society - offered two types of High Tea, each on an 'eat as much as you like' basis. For 2/6d [12½p] one had an ordinary High Tea but for 7/6d [37½p] one had a Salmon High Tea. It was the latter which was very popular with the Minister for in return for his 7/6d [37½p] he and his Family could have as much food, including as much salmon, as they wanted. Therefore he and his Family went to Fraser's nearly every afternoon and, armed with a stock of paper bags, sat in the restaurant and ate as much as they could and also took away with them as much food as their paper bags would hold. Looking around this very popular [need one ask why ?] restaurant, it was noticeable that it was a procedure not unique to the Minister and his Family. Whether or not his ultimate Employer agreed with what he and his Family were doing I do not know, but neither I nor my Mother agreed with it - But then, of course, I had my daily supply of surplus sausages to rely upon !!

Our fortnight's holiday in Fort William and the several coach trips to nearby historic battle sites and other places of interest that we went on whilst there were very enjoyable and, like most holidays, seemed to end all-too-soon, as did the entirety of my Summer Holiday away from Haileybury Senior School into whose welcoming arms at the start of the Winter Term I returned with the usual lack of enthusiasm that had now become the norm at the start of any of my terms at the Senior School.

As Autumn days gave way to dark nights, shorter days, and increasing coldness of Winters the, many would say magnificent, buildings of Haileybury College always seemed to me to become increasingly depressing, moreso whenever it rained for rain running down buildings often causes the stone of those buildings to look depressingly dark. Despite Hertford Heath's nearness to London Haileybury in those days seemed very remote from the outside world, a remoteness the feeling of which was encouraged by what was called 'Lock-up', a time every evening at around 6 - 6:30 when all main gates, some with barbed wire on their tops, and other gates were closed and locked thereby containing all of us boys within confined bounds out of which, unless we had formal permission, we were not, usually, able to venture.

One occasion, entirely unintended, that I did venture outside of Lock-up without any permission whatsoever resulted from a game of football that several of us were, using a tennis ball, playing in a first-floor room which overlooked the gravel on Haileybury's Terrace. The room was Lawrence House's 'Junior Common Room', a room in which we Laurentians of around fifteen years of age socialised, made toast on gas ring burners, each studied at a specifically allocated desk unit, and generally used as our base. It was thus in this room that one night, with me as a goal-keeper, several of us were playing our game of football. Doubtless carried away by enthusiasm and a determination to prevent a goal from being scored, and being much more athletic then than I am now, I dived into the path of the ball. I must have momentarily forgotten that I was in a first-floor room and not on some grass pitch somewhere, for my dive took me straight through the open lower sash of a window causing me to cascade down onto the gravel below. I sat there with blood spurting out of my, seemingly badly, lacerated left wrist whilst I waited for, hopefully medical, attention to arrive. After some time, his having found someone who had a key to enable him to exit Lock-up by means of a wicket-gate in one of Lock-ups large gates, a Master arrived, quickly surveyed my injury by means of the limited light available to him via the window through which I had just come, told me to apply pressure to my wounds to stem the flows of blood, and then ordered me to stay where I was whilst he contacted the Sanatorium for help. After what seemed like an eternity a sedan chair, with one boy holding the front ends of its two supporting poles and another boy holding the rear ends of its two supporting poles, arrived whereon the chair was lowered to the ground and I was told to get up and get into it so that I could be transported to the San. So into it I got, each of the two boys grabbed his ends of the two poles, and away I was transported towards the San. It could not have been easy for them in part because the San was a fair distance from where I had been sitting; in part because the sedan chair had, because of Lock up, to be taken on the roadway that went around the perimeter of most of the College's main buildings; in part because the sedan chair itself was heavy; and in part because I was no lightweight. Eventually the lad at the back announced that he had had enough and put his ends of the poles down. So I, jokingly, got out and volunteered to take over from him !! Then it was decided that, as we were not all that far from the San, I should travel the rest of the way on foot. Thus the sedan chair was abandoned and the three of us walked the rest of the way to the San. Fortunately Dr Turtle was not available that night, and so my injuries were attended to by one of the College's two qualified Nursing Staff in whom I had complete trust. Being of a disposition disinclined to favour 'stitches' I asked if the wounds could be dealt with by some other means; and thus, after having removed grit and other matter from the wounds and sterilised the entire area, Sister [as each Nurse was called] carefully and sympathetically, and very successfully, closed the wounds by means of sticking plaster. I left the San that night with the instruction that I must return next morning to see the Doctor. This I did. He, without interfering with the sticking plaster, pronounced that treatment had been undertaken satisfactorily and that I must return at some later date to have the sticking plaster changed. This I did and, apart from still having two scars above my left wrist, the wounds have never troubled me.

Graham Clive Foster, a year older than I and thus my senior and thereby only able to be spoken to by me if he spoke to me first, a talented and athletic Laurentian, was a person who caused me both grief and pleasure. Grief in that he seemed to take pleasure in deliberately annoying me and pleasure because it was he who, despite the aggro that he gave me, invited me to become an Editor of the House Magazine, also called 'Laurentian'. I well remember one night just after I had progressed from being a Member of the Junior End of the Dormitory to being a Member of the Senior End of the Dormitory. It was well past 'lights out' and thus, apart from the House Prefects who were entitled to stay up later than anyone else, each and everyone of us was supposed either to be sleeping or trying to get to sleep. But Graham, having gone to bed, decided that, assisted by two others, he would get back out of bed and cart me, in my metal framed bed, up and down the Dorm. So, up my bed, with me in it, was lifted and carried at increasing speed down the wooden floored Dorm to the far end of its Junior End. Then, turning round, Graham and the others carted me back up the Junior End into the Senior End then up through the Senior End to its far end and then back again through the Senior End into the Junior End towards its far end. Then someone, listening for our House Master, mildly shouted "Williams". My bed and I were very hastily returned from whence it had started its journey, Graham and his fellow miscreants rushed back into their beds and lay there pretending to be asleep, and I lay within my by now dishevelled bed likewise pretending to be asleep. The door at the far end of the Junior End of the Dormitory opened and in, without either saying a word or turning on any of the lights, walked Williams. With the soles of his shoes squeaking as they impacted the Dormitory's well-maintained, by John Mannion, varnished floor Williams walked slowly up the middle of the Junior End towards the Senior End. He probably did not but it seemed as if he knew what he was looking for. As he got nearer and nearer to my dishevelled bed I waited for, what I thought would be, the inevitable pointing at my bed and saying "Loveday. What's this ?" But, as he got to within a couple of yards [Metres] of my bed, the only sound that I heard was from the bed itself as suddenly the whole structure, with me in it, collapsed and crashed down onto the bare wooden floor below, the bed's wired and sprung metal frame still partly fixed on one of its sides to the metal 'headboard' end whilst the metal 'footboard', by now completely divorced from the rest of the bed, slid across the floor towards where Williams had suddenly stopped. After a terrifying, at least for me, pause of silence Williams, without saying a word, turned, walked slowly back into and through the Junior End of the Dormitory and out through the doorway from whence he had come to return to his own nearby bedroom to, so John Mannion at the end of that Term told me, release a fit of almost uncontrollable laughter at the clown-like piece of entertainment that he had just witnessed.

Most Houses at Haileybury had, at one time or another, their own House Magazines which, save for the professional printing and guillotining [cutting to size] outside of Haileybury of the covers, were produced entirely in-House and issued and sold at the end of each Term. Over the years some undertakings had ceased to exist - mainly because production costs, including the professional printing and guillotining of the covers, far exceeded sales' incomes due, substantially, to an unwillingness by would-be purchasers to pay money for, what they considered to be, a not very worthwhile content. But Lawrence, and a less-than-handful of other Houses, still maintained the tradition.

The first edition of Lawrence's House magazine, The Laurentian, was published in December 1953 under the editorship of Anthony Warren Davies and carried within it a message from one of Lawrence House's most famous Old Boys, the Right Honourable Clement Richard Attlee, KG [Knight of the Garter], OM [Order of Merit], CH [Companion of Honour], PC [Privy Councillor], the First Earl Attlee and Viscount Prestwood of Walthamstow, Deputy Prime Minister to Winston Churchill during the Second World War and Labour Prime Minister from 1945 to 1951, who had attended Haileybury from 1896 to 1901 subsequently, before becoming a professional Politician, becoming a Barrister in 1906, a Lecturer at the London School of Economics in 1912, and a Major in the First World War. [*The letter, dated 13 October 1953 by which Attlee conveyed his message for publication is hereafter reproduced.*]

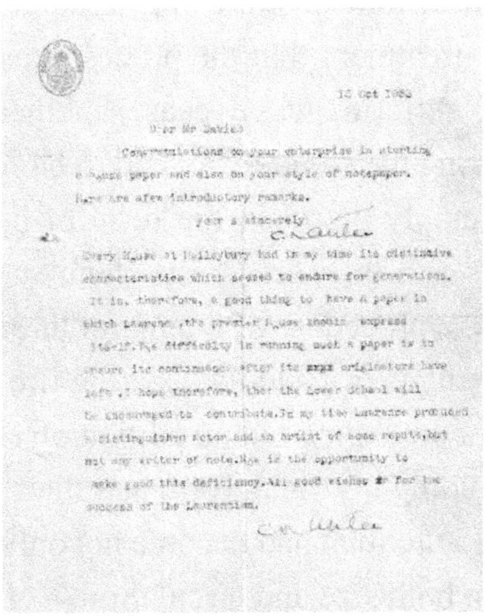

With EF Williams as Editor-in-Chief, Graham Foster became The Laurentian's Editor in the Spring Term of 1960 and invited Michael Anthony Freedman and, perhaps because I had a typewriter and could type, me to join him, as Co-Editors, in the Winter Term of that year. Despite then being a failing publication of decreasing content and circulation, and of no interest outside of Lawrence House and of little interest within Lawrence House, the workload to produce it was noticeable. Labour intensive, its content had to be typed onto - or, if doing graphics, cut out of - waxed stencils which were then run through a manually fed and operated duplicator. The clogging of my typewriter by the constant pounding of its letters and numerals into the wax of the stencils was a regular, and very frustrating, occurrence my remedy for which was to often apply a small wire brush onto the letters and numerals so as to remove the wax. A result of this process was the distortion of the typewriters many metal arms which often caused the arms to jam to-gether and me to have to frequently halt the entire process in order to unjam and straighten the bent arms. I soon realised that my somewhat ageing portable typewriter, which was the one that my Father used to lend to me in Croydon, was suffering badly as a result of the ill-treatment that the process was causing it to have to suffer. Thus, if its suffering was to cease, another, less harsh, means of frequently removing the stencil wax had to be found. An answer, I discovered, was to apply petrol in the form of lighter fuel onto the letters and numbers and then set fire to them so as to burn off the offending wax. Thus a procedure of typing for three-quarters of a hour or so and then applying petrol and then setting fire was adopted : And by that means I went on to type out an edition of The Laurentian each Term until and including my final Term as Editor in December 1961 by which time The Laurentian had become not only profitable but also somewhat greater in both size and circulation. Not that the making of a profit seemed to please its Editor-in-Chief for, when Graham Foster stood down as its principal Editor and I took over the job, with Mike Freedman as my co-Editor, in the Spring Term of 1961, I was asked by Williams what I intended to do with the magazine. "Make a profit," I told him

"That's what every Editor has said. So, just how are *you* going to achieve it ?" he replied with a sort of sneering contempt.

"By enlarging its content and putting the price up," I replied.

"Hmmm, I see, "he said as he turned away and pulled on his pipe, the disbelief in his voice being such that not only was it very noticeable but also it caused me to say to myself "Right, I'll show him !!" :" And show him I did for when I eventually ceased to be the Laurentian's Editor not only was this modest little publication making a profit but also its circulation had extended to a couple of handfuls or more boys who were not Laurentians. Mike Freedman stood down and was replaced by Tim Nicholson as my co-Editor and, with Tim's agreement, I started to create, what I intended to be, a columned newspaper format to be included within the magazine. I soon discovered not only that cutting out the heading and sub-heading in a wax stencil was a bit of a laborious chore but also that typing in columns was a greater challenge than I had at first thought that it would be. However, I persisted and eventually proudly presented my would-be front page to my Editor-in-Chief for his consideration. My objectives insofar as this section of the Laurentian was concerned were that its content should reflect news events of the day, that it should do so in a humorous way tinged with sarcasm, and that, above all, it should be entertaining. Looking at it now it seems pathetic, but such was not the analysis in the early 1960s.

Williams took it away to read it and came back to me the following day. "I can not allow you to print this, Loveday."

"Why not, Sir," I asked in bewilderment.

"Well, just read the first article," he replied firmly as he passed the thing back to me.

"To you, Sir ?" I asked.

"Yes, to me, Sir," he snapped.

So I read out the first article: " 'TOILET ROLLS UP 1d [0.42p]. It was announced yesterday morning that there would be an increase of 1d on all leading makes of Roll owing to a pay increase asked for by the National Union of Toilet Paper onto Little Cardboard Formers Winders. Asked if the NUOTPOLCFW would get their rise soon, a spokesman said "Not in my lifetime they won't'. " I finished and waited to be criticised, although for what reason I did not know.

"Well, Loveday ?" he asked.

"Well, … er … what, Sir ?" I replied.

" 'Toilet Rolls', Loveday. 'Toilet Rolls'. I can not allow you to use the word 'Toilet' in the House Magazine. It is just not acceptable," was the response. I was gobsmacked, and instantly abandoned that idea. It just was not worth the hassle. [*The 'offending' article - TOILET ROLLS UP 1d - is hereafter reproduced.*]

My Mother, in her manoeuvrings against my Father, had, in obtaining the verdict of Suicide that she had wanted, it seems overlooked one thing, namely that in England and Wales in 1958 Suicide was deemed to be a Crime, the Common Law Crime of 'Self-Murder'. Only when the Suicide Act of 1961 [Section 1 of which states "The rule of law whereby it is a crime for a person to commit suicide is hereby abrogated"] came into force was Suicide in England and Wales deemed to be no longer an Offence. Thus having, in the eyes of the State, committed a Crime my Father was required by the State to pay a Penalty, the Penalty being the forfeiture of his 'estate'. In other words, everything that my Father owned, including his money, was, in effect, confiscated by the State leaving my Mother with only that which she herself owned which, as far as I understand, was the house, or a half-share of the house, in Croydon, shares in Brunskill and Loveday Limited that my Father had gifted to her, her own personal items, and anything else in which the State did not express an interest. Insofar as my School Fees were concerned these, fortunately, had already been accounted for prior to my Father's death; and thus I was enabled to continue my education at Haileybury. Thus, financially, at Haileybury I was very hard- up, a somewhat discriminating and embarrassing disadvantage at times especially when some of those around me evidenced, directly or otherwise, wealth if not considerable wealth. One very noticeable, at least to me, discriminating feature was the fact that, whereas others seemed sufficiently funded to be enabled by their Parents to consume several tubes of toothpaste each 12-week term, I was burdened by my Mother with having to try to survive on only one tube of toothpaste; and only if I was able to prove to my House Master that, despite having faithfully complied with my Mother's requirement of me, I was, say in the seventh week of my 12-week Term, in genuine need of a second tube would the necessary chitty be written enabling me to purchase, with the cost being charged to my Mother, a second tube. I therefore, in order to attempt to disguise my lack of financial wherewithal, endeavoured to create some form of income.

Repairing broken spectacle frames for a small fee was one undertaking that I hit upon. I had had to occasionally repair my own specs, and so why should I not, for a small fee, repair other peoples' specs ? Business turned out to be quite good for - armed with a soldering-iron that, using Kensitas cigarettes' gift vouchers, had been given to me by my Mother as a Christmas present and assisted by a very small quantity of small panel pin nails that I collected from my woodworking activities - I soon found that there was a demand for my services not only from some of the boys but also from some of the Staff, both Teaching and non-Teaching. But the financial return was insufficient to be all that noticeable. Thus I involved myself in the hiring of bandages to such as those who had incurred a scrape or two on the rugby field and elsewhere. The prices that I charged - 2d per time or 1d if the bandage was returned washed - were, I and my customers felt, very reasonable, but, although I made a profit, I doubt whether the overall income was a great, if any, multiple relative to my having had to purchase the bandages in the first place. One disaster was my purchase, during one Christmas Holiday period, from *Boots the Chemist* in Putney High Street of a dozen small bottles of *Regesan Chilblain Liniment* made by *The Boots Pure Drugs Company*. I knew nothing whatsoever about chilblains save that they had something to do with feet. So, my theory was simple: To many of us, despite its being situated in the South of England, Haileybury often seemed, physically if not also psychologically, a very cold place with consequent coldness often being felt in feet; and therefore, if only to create an 'in the mind' cure, the application onto cold feet of a solution which had at least something to do with being beneficial to cold feet seemed a good idea. But no-one, absolutely no-one, wanted the stuff, and therefore, at the end of the Spring Term in which I had tried to sell it, I was left with all my bottles of chilblain liniment : And I still had them on my return to College at the start of the Summer Term. As luck would have it however, part way through the Summer Term various areas of Lawrence House were plagued by ants and, come what may, nothing seemed to discourage them. Boldly printed on my bottles of *Regesan Chilblain Liniment* were the words 'Poison - For external use only'. "What the heck," I thought, "why not try it out on the ants ?" Whether by chemical reaction or by drowning I do not know, but *Regesan's Chilblain Liniment* proved so successful in annihilating my test batch of ants that, other than my 'test' bottle [which I still have], I soon sold my entire stock of otherwise useless chilblain liniment.

Save when taken out by Parents to a meal at the nearby College Arms, a sort of public house-cum-hotel, we boys in Haileybury rarely mixed with the villagers who lived immediately outside the College in Hertford Heath. It was as if some kind of physical but invisible social barrier existed between us and them. But the barrier did come down on one occasion when some of us were invited to a fête on the Green in Hertford Heath. As I wandered around this somewhat socially challenging occasion I noticed, piled high on a table, masses of very large scrumptious-looking apples for sale at '12 for 1d [0.42p]"; and so I bought a quantity of them and, after returning to College, set to and sold them all at 1d [0.42p] each thereby making a substantial profit. I also made, temporarily at least, a substantial number of enemies, for I had forgotten that, unlike eating apples, cooking apples can cause very painful upset stomachs - And my cooking apples certainly did not let me down in that respect.

The only regular money-maker that I involved myself in that actually made me a decent profit was the hiring of bicycles. I, like many boys, kept a bike at Haileybury which I housed in one of several secure sheds that were sited alongside Haileybury's main drive that goes from the College's Main Gates, sited on the Hertford-Hoddesdon Road, to the College's Main Entrance-cum-Main Formroom Block. At the beginning of each term there were often bikes in the Bike Sheds that had been left by those who had left Haileybury at the end of the previous term and were now OHs [Old Haileyburians]. Some bikes had been deliberately left to await collection at a later date, some had been left in error, and some had been deliberately abandoned : And therefore only when the College was certain that a bike was no longer wanted would the College arrange, by auction, its disposal. The usual selling price for an abandoned bike was in the region of 10/- [50p].

I thoroughly enjoyed cycling, but taking my Raleigh bike to and from Haileybury in my Mother's Morris Minor car was hardly possible, and the inconveniences and costs that would have been incurred in having it transported to Haileybury and back by rail were unacceptable. Therefore my initial reasons for buying one of Haileybury's auction bikes were simply that I felt that I needed a bike at Haileybury as well as a bike at home and that this was the best way of obtaining one. Thus for 50p I got myself an abandoned Hercules bike and proceeded to thoroughly enjoy it whenever I could throughout the rest of my time at the Senior School. Shortly after I got my Hercules bike I found myself receiving requests to borrow it; and thus it occurred to me that if I had more bikes I could rent them out. With only one bike auction per term I therefore had to wait until the next term before I could take the plunge and buy more bikes. But buy more bikes I did : Two in fact, and it proved such a worthwhile venture that the following term I bought two more. But then 'Authority' decided that I now owned more than my fair share of bikes, and so my bike-hiring enterprise was limited to four, plus my original Hercules which I kept for my own use. However there is a downside in any such operation, the downside being 'maintenance and repairs' for often a hired-out bike would be returned needing this done to it and needing that done to it in order to rectify the damage that it had suffered during the hire.

But it was my good friend John Mannion, the Lawrence House Servant, who came up with the money-spinner that took me into the real world of Trading. "Nylon stockings," said John. "That's where the money is."

I was sixteen and, when at home, living at the flat in Putney; and John's suggestion was that I should, on Sundays during my school holidays, sell nylon stockings in London's famous Petticoat Lane Street Market. I had no idea where Petticoat Lane was, knew nothing about Street Markets, knew even less about nylon stockings, and had no idea whatsoever how to go about buying nylon stockings let alone selling them. "But that," said John "doesn't matter 'cos when you get down London's East End you'll soon learn".

Petticoat Lane's Sunday Street Market in London's then somewhat poverty-stricken East End occupied, principally, three streets: Middlesex Street, formally known as Petticoat Lane; Wentworth Street, and Goulston Street. So, early one Sunday morning, having obtained the agreement of my Mother, I travelled by London Underground ['Tube'] from Putney Tube Station to, I think it was, Aldgate East Tube Station and from there walked to The Regent Warehouse Company in New Goulston Street, just off Goulston Street, The Regent Warehouse Company having been recommended to me by John. By the time that I arrived the whole area was bustling with, mainly Jewish, Traders setting up stalls, with Traders pushing and pulling 'barras', and with Traders carrying this, that, and the other. It was fascinating, and I was very nervous.

John had recommended The Regent Warehouse Company to me because, he said, they were Wholesalers and would sell me "One of this, one of that, one of whatever might sell" and that way I could buy a selection of sizes, colours, and what-have-you; find a pitch [*an area of ground in a street market*] in nearby Goulston Street; plonk the stuff, in their boxes, on the ground; and try my luck. So, utterly clueless, in through the doorway of The Regent Warehouse Company I went. "Name ?" demanded a miserable-sounding Jewish voice from a man sitting perched on a highish stool at a wooden tally-desk to the left just inside the doorway. "Loveday," I stated, and 'Loveday' he wrote down at the top of a feint-ruled piece of paper. In front of me, to the right of me, and to the left of me from floor to ceiling in The Regent Warehouse Company's not very big premises were banks of rows and rows of, seemingly D-I-Y-made, wooden slatted shelves packed high with smooth-feeling cardboard boxes full of cellophane-packaged nylon stockings. I was not totally 'green' for John had given me a crash course on 'deniers' [the unit of weight for nylon stockings] and had told me that "the best seller at the moment is Diamond mesh" :" And so, starting with the shelves immediately to my right and being constantly watched by the Jewish gentleman sitting at his tally desk, I commenced my journey round the inside of The Regent Warehouse Company collecting, as I thought fit to do so, one pair of stockings out of a box here, one pair of stockings out of a box there, a pair from a box over there, a pair from a box down there, a pair from a box up there, and so on until I was so laden with packets of nylon stockings so slippery that I could hardly stop them from falling all over the place. With my cash firmly within an inside pocket of my jacket I arrived, the mountain of cellophane packaged nylon stockings wobbling on my hands, back at the tally desk to be greeted by a harsh, semi-shouting voice firmly stating "Ma boy, I'm a Wholesaler not a Retailer. OUT !! " With that he grabbed my mountain of stockings, cascaded them all onto his tally desk, and waved an arm at me its hand pointing emphatically to the doorway. That was my first encounter with The Regent Warehouse Company causing me thus to return to

Putney not only having not made one penny by way of sales but also being noticeably financially out of pocket as a result of having to pay a return fare on the Tube. Not a very worthwhile experience !!

When I returned to Haileybury at the start of the next term one of the first questions asked of me by John was "How did you get on ?". I told him exactly what had happened and that - as a result of his instruction that I take "One of this, one of that, one of whatever might sell" I had been thrown out of The Regent Warehouse Company. "You idiot," he said, "When he asked your name you should have called yourself something Jewish not 'Loveday'." So, on a Sunday some weeks later, during the next School Holiday I returned to The Regent Warehouse Company and repeated the ritual that I had gone through on my first visit but this time there were three differences: The first was that, when asked my name, I replied 'Goldberg'; the second was that, on returning to the tally desk, I paid for the mountain of cellophane wrapped packets of nylon stockings that I had selected; and the third was that I then went out into New Goulston Street thence into Goulston Street with my mountain of stockings, plonked them on the ground, and attempted to sell them. However, not only was trade non-existent but also I soon found myself suddenly being accosted by a complete stranger who asked me if I had paid to occupy the piece of tarmac onto which I had plonked my wares. It was then that I found out that one had to pay not only to buy the goods that one hoped to sell but also for the use of the insignificant piece of road on which one hoped to sell them. The matter was however soon resolved and, having paid the Market Superintendent the money that he demanded for my use of the tarmac, I continued to try to sell my wares.

Alongside me was a Trader with a 'barra' with pots, pans, and all sorts of shiny new things on it. He was doing a roaring trade.

Eventually we got chatting; I with my undoubted 'Upper Class' English Public School accent and he with his darn-to-earth no-nonsense, but very sympathetic, Jewish Market Trader's 'lilt'. Nowadays much is bought on credit but in those days most, if not everything, was bought for cash. "Ma boy," my wise neighbour slowly said to me," a man has only so much to spend. If he only has 10/- [50p], you can not sell him something for 10/6d [52½p]. Cut your prices, ma Son. Cut your prices." So, cut my prices I did, and I began to sell my stockings to the extent that I all but sold out. I was a very happy lad that day as I returned home.

Next Sunday and for a couple of other Sundays that holiday it was back into the Tube to London's East End, then to The Regent Warehouse Company, to its nylon stockings-laden wooden shelving, and to the man behind his old wooden sloped-top tally desk. Clearly he must have realised that I did not really know much about what I was doing, that I did not know my 'market', for on my second visit, as I started going round his shelves, he climbed off his stool and, having come over to me, quietly said "Next time you come don't try to sell 'em vot *you* think they vont. Find out what *they* vont, then sell it to them". So that Sunday was less of a selling exercise and more of a learning curve to find out exactly what it was that the punters wanted so that the following Sunday I could go back to The Regent Warehouse Company and its tally desk-sitting owner, Mr Jacobs, to buy not what I thought might sell but what that I more or less knew *would* sell.

Mr and Mrs Jacobs were lovely people; and over that holiday and the Christmas holiday that followed my next Term back at Haileybury - not, of course, that, strictly speaking, Mr and Mrs Jacobs, being Jewish, celebrated Christmas - and the Easter holiday after the next

Term - not, of course, that Mr and Mrs Jacobs celebrated Easter either - I had many a chat with this kindly couple as I journeyed round their homemade shelving selecting my goodies for the day. I got to know a little about them, about their Daughter - their one and only child, I think - who, with her Husband, had emigrated to Australia. "Oh, so far, so very far avay," Mrs J would occasionally say with sadness tingeing her voice as she spoke. Whether or not the Jacobs ever sussed that 'Mr Goldberg' was neither 'Mr Goldberg' nor Jewish I do not know but I suspect that they must have done so for - despite the fact that my talking with them and with those Jewish Traders who traded near to my pitch caused me to subconsciously bring Jewish inflexions into my manner of talking - with my then ignorance [save for very small items of knowledge that I had learned from Jewish schoolfriends such as Henry Barnett, Stuart and Edward Kerner, and Neil Vyner] of Judaism, its customs, and so on it would probably have been very easy indeed for them to realise that I was in fact a fraud insofar as 'Mr Goldberg' was concerned. Nevertheless, each Sunday morning when I arrived through their doorway the tally desk-sitting Mr Jacob would look up, smile, and noddingly slowly say "Good morning, Mr Goldberg. Good morning". Sadly, one rarely meets their kind nowadays.

My stocking-selling was not restricted to Petticoat Lane for my return to College each time was always accompanied by an ordered stock of stockings for John to sell on to a network on non-Teaching Staff that he evolved. The Sunday before the start of a Term at Haileybury, having by now gotten to know and trust my fellow Traders and also confident that they trusted me, I would leave my pitch in the very capable hands of one of them whilst I nipped to a nearby red public General Post Office-owned Telephone Box to make a telephone-call to John Mannion to find out what brands, types, and so on of stockings he wanted me to take back with me to Haileybury. With my being in the East End of London and John being in Hertford Heath the call had to go via a Telephone Operator who, on one occasion, as John started giving me his Order, interrupted to say "Ooo. I'll 'ave some ov' 'em". "Get off the line," John and I shouted at her : But she stayed on the line until eventually we discontinued the call just to get rid of her. A few minutes later I tried again only to be greeted by the same chirpy cheeky voice saying "Coo-ee. Yes, it's me again". Given that she was probably the only Telephone Operator on duty insofar as that 'phone Box was concerned John and I decided that we had no option but to tolerate her; and thus she stayed with us throughout the entirety of the call and, with her Cockney voice and bubbling Cockney humour, caused so much hilarity that the three of us were in fits of laughter for much of the time.

My Petticoat Lane activities, simple and insignificant though they were, doubtless taught me a lot about the ins and outs of trading and possibly also about Joe Public; and I was always somewhat sad when the day's trading came to an end and I had to pack-up, say my good-byes to my fellow Traders, and travel back home to Putney for, whilst the flat and its Thameside situation were excellent, for much of the time life was dull, boring, and often, insofar as the relationship between my Mother and me was concerned, strained and occasionally very strained, aggravated undoubtedly by the fact that one day my fully-functioning model Theatre disappeared from its below-stairs cupboard and was never seen by me again. "You'll never use it. So I've had it removed" was the only explanation that my Mother ever gave to me. To say that I was disappointed would be an understatement.

Needless to say, my Mother had her own friends from the days before she met my Father. Lynne Ryan, a fellow former Psychiatric Nurse from my Mother's nursing days in the Epsom area, and her husband Chris had had a Public House, the Surrey Yeoman Arms, in Dorking. From there they moved to The Plough Public House in Smallfield near Horley in Surrey. My Mother, Father, and I had gone to The Plough on several occasions prior to my Father's death and my Mother continued to make the occasional visit after his death. The Ryans were a nice 'homely' couple well suited, I thought, to the 'log fireside' atmosphere that permeated The Plough. Following my Father's death it was on a cold, overcast, and uninviting Winter's day that we next visited them. In fact the weather was foul, but nonetheless, and despite the fact that my Mother's driving skills left much to be desired, onwards we went and, as we approached that part of the London-Brighton Road where we had to start looking out for the sign that indicated that we had to turn left onto the minor country road that would lead us to the somewhat, in those days, isolated Pub, snow began to fall - But my Mother was very fond of Lynne and Chris and nothing was going to stop her from visiting them.

We stayed three hours or more by which time darkness had fallen as indeed had a considerable quantity of snow. A sufferer of 'night blindness' my Mother was none-too-keen to try to drive back home to Putney; but Lynn and Chris had little or no facility within their small country Pub to put us up for the night, and so my Mother had no option but to rise to the challenge and take us home. As we left the Pub's car park it was difficult to know exactly where the surface of the road was : But, increasingly enveloped in falling snow, we slowly, very slowly journeyed on in the direction of the London-Brighton Road. Eventually we caught up with a van going even slower than we were. We could not overtake it and, courtesy of our car's headlights shining through the window in each of the van's two rear doors, we could see that lashed with ropes partway up the inside of the van, behind the driver, was a long rectangular wooden box. So, just like a funeral cortège, there the two slow-moving vehicles were each groping its way through the near blinding snow. Suddenly the knot of the rope that was holding-up the end of the box that was nearest to us slipped allowing the rope to slacken and its end of the box to drop down a wee bit, then a bit more, and then another bit more. The volume of falling snow caused my Mother and me to be able to see nothing else but the back of the van and its slowly moving content. It was eerie, very, very eerie. Then, as the lid of the box began to open, a head, sliding in our direction, began to appear followed shortly after, as the van slowly bumped its way along the snow-obliterated road, by a pair of shoulders. Then the top of a man's chest came into view as the wooden box slowly disgorged its human content. Eventually we reached the London-Brighton Road at which point the van, its driver, and the van's human cargo turned left towards Crawley and we turned right towards London. Thankfully we never saw that van again.

Whereas life in Highlands had seen much entertaining during my Father's lifetime life in Putney saw, save on a handful or so of occasions, no entertaining whatsoever. After my Father's death we never went to see another West End Show nor any other Show. It was as if, other than her personal connections with the Grand Order of Lady Ratlings, my Mother had determined that all Theatrical connections were to be completely discontinued. The atmosphere in the flat - doubtless not helped by my occasionally reminding my Mother that, in my Opinion, she had deliberately killed my Father - was at times appalling. However, regardless of my Opinion as to the cause of my late Father's death, my Mother was still my Mother and as such a close bond did exist. Thus, when the two of us went, in 1960, by train on a Summer Holiday to Alassio in Northern Italy we determined, and did, enjoy ourselves. At breakfast each morning in our hotel in Alassio we were accosted at our table by a man, Senior Secundo Pedrozzini [the 'second son of Pedrozinni'], who, it seemed, either fancied my Mother or considered her, a tourist, to be 'easy pickings'. As far as I am aware he was to find himself to be out of luck on both counts; but nonetheless he was both entertaining and interesting as indeed were the strolling tenors, such as Alexandro Gatti, who, uninhibited, wandered through the streets and squares of Alassio evidencing excellent singing voices and delighting hundreds of people as they did so. [Had such occurred in Britain the Singers, had they persisted, would doubtless have found themselves facing the threat of a Charge such as 'Breach of the Peace' !!] A day-trip by 'bus into France and thence to Monaco and its Casino in Monte Carlo relived old memories; at least it did until I was challenged on the steps of the Casino as to my age by a mountain of a very smartly dressed man. "Sixteen," I said. "Too young," he replied. Having been inside the Casino when with my Father and never been challenged I was … Well, annoyed. Without a word, he lifted me up by my lapels, took me down the steps, and deposited me almost in a nearby flowerbed. I got the message but nonetheless turned towards the Casino and, looking straight at it, shook my fist and vowed that one day I would return and get my own back on Monte Carlo Casino. [I have since returned but have never sought to even attempt to fulfil my vow !!]

Christmastimes at Putney seemed … Well, with just the two of us, somewhat lonely. We had decorations - loads of streamers that had been brought from Highlands - but the hostility, even though subconscious for much of the time, between my Mother and me coupled with the gap of 34½ years in our ages did not engender a great social atmosphere. My Christmas presents - those which did not consist of nuts, apples, oranges, or some other form of fruit, often stuffed into socks - had a tendency to have been acquired courtesy of the cigarette manufacturing firm of J Wix whose Kensitas cigarettes my Mother - perhaps because J Wix operated a coupon trading scheme via its Kensitas brands - smoked many thousands each year thereby causing her, accompanied by me, to, in the run-up to Christmas, travel to J Wix's Kensitas Coupon Showroom in London's Holborn where, having previously (a) selected, from a catalogue, the items that we wished to acquire and (b) elastic-banded the bundled-together piles of coupons that would be required, we would exchange the coupons for the presents that I myself had selected. Mind you, I should not, perhaps, complain too much for my Kensitas-acquired Black and Decker Drills, Drill Stand, Circular Saw attachments, Soldering Iron, and many other items, items which I may well never have been given without the assistance of J Wix, served me well over many years.

One visitor who did occasionally come to the Flat was the Actor, Cyril Smith. A friend of my Father's for many years, Water Rat 'Uncle' Cyril was one of those Actors who, through having decided never to quite become a 'Star', was nearly always in work usually on the Stage [famously as the hen-pecked ferret-keeping husband Henry Hornett in the 1955 to 1958 production of *Sailor Beware !*, a Show which ran to 1,230 performances at London's *Strand* Theatre] but also in Films and in Television [in such as, as Merlin, ITV's 1956-57 series *The Adventures of Sir Lancelot* and, as Arthur Wormold, in the BBC's 1960s series *Hugh and I*]. The reason that the friendship continued after my Father's death was, I suspect, that his Wife, Anne Rendall, was a Lady Ratling and, as such, a good friend of my Mother. Often my Mother and I would go to their flat in 34 Carlisle Mansions, Carlisle Place, Victoria, in London for some sort of Water Rats/Lady

Ratlings 'Get To-gether'. I suspect that Cyril's reason for visiting 28 Kenilworth Court was that I had a tape-recorder into which, whenever he visited us, he would speak his 'lines' for whatever Show it was that he was soon to take part in and then play the 'lines' back to himself several times over until he had mastered them. Tape-recorders were somewhat of a rarity in those days, and I had acquired mine purely by chance: My Mother and I had gone to visit Phanti Ludlow, a Lady Ratling whose ostensibly very wealthy, sometimes chauffeur-driven, Husband, Ronnie - a Water Rat and Magician known professionally as *N'Gai* - had died evidencing not wealth but, like his Stage act, only an illusion, an illusion of wealth to the extent that Phanti's sudden decline in lifestyle caused her eventually to reside in the Lady Ratling's Residential Home at 13 South Side, Streatham Common in South London, a house generously gifted, as was his wont, to the Lady Ratlings by Sir Billy Butlin [another friend of my Father's (*see below a copy of a photograph showing Sir Billy standing next to my fur-clad Mother with my Father, cigarette in hand, standing next to my Mother*)],

the founder of the famous 'Butlin's Holiday Camp' business. Phanti, who 'liked a drink', at the time of our visit to her that day, lived in Sheen Court, a block of flats in East Sheen; and, as she always did and despite her totally unexpected downward change in financial circumstances, she entertained us well - plying my Mother with gin and me with Scrumpy due, apparently, to her having been unable to "find any cider" for me - and, in the course of the visit, she gifted Ronnie's, very large by to-day's standards, tape-recorder to me because, she said, she had "no idea, Edwin dear, how to work the wretched thing".

Most of the leasehold flats within Kenilworth Court were privately and independently owned, but the Management Company did retain ownership of a few flats which the Company rented out. One such 'retained' flat was one of the two Basement flats within the block of which No. 28 formed a part and another was the top flat within the same block. Mr and Mrs William [Bill] Remy lived in the Basement flat. He was, as far as I knew, English and an excellent Painter and Art Restorer in Chelsea whose talents were such that he decided one day to test his skills by making a pair of 'antique' candlesticks and attempting to sell them via one of London's principal Auction Houses, a test which he successfully completed thereby giving him much pleasure in having proved that even some of the Country's finest experts were not as knowledgeable as they would have others believe. Mrs Remy was French and a principal Fashion Buyer for the 'up market' Department Store of Harvey Nichols in London's Knightsbridge, then and for many, many years thereafter, so it was said [but not true], Harvey Nichols's only Store. Bill Remy and his Wife most times when at home kept themselves very much to themselves but nevertheless, whenever I called on them or met them in the streets, were always very courteous, kind, and friendly. The elderlyish couple, Mr and Mrs Waller, who rented the top flat likewise kept themselves to themselves and they too were nevertheless very courteous, kind, and friendly. Always oozing politeness and old fashioned mannerisms, Mr Waller was rarely seen without his being dapperly dressed in a dinner jacket, striped 'City' trousers, white shirt, and a black bow tie whereas Mrs Waller used always to give the impression that she was either about to depart to undertake a day's cleaning-work somewhere or had just returned from having done a day's cleaning-work somewhere. None of the wooden floors within their flat, which was identical in layout and size to No.28 save that its ceilings were lower and partly coombed, had no carpets but instead all were uncovered except for lengths of linoleum [the 'poor man's carpet'] here, there, and everywhere. Whether or not he was, or had ever been, a moneyed Gentleman I do not know but he certainly gave the impression of having been one at sometime. By the time that I knew them, despite Mr Waller's smart and dapper attire, circumstances were such that I doubt whether they in fact had 'two pennies to rub to-gether'. Nevertheless, prior to the start of each of my early Terms at Haileybury Senior School after we had moved to Putney, Mr Waller would ring the front-door bell of No.28; on the door being opened to him, he apologised for inconveniencing us; and then invited me to go upstairs with him where, within their flat, Mrs Waller would present me with an enormous tray of the most delicious of homemade Bread Pudding for me to take back to School with me. "Throw it away. You don't know where it's been," would be my Mother's reaction when I arrived back down at No.28. : But "Throw it away" I never did for each and every one of the slices of Bread Puddings that the Wallers so kindly made for me was far, far too tasty for that. Sadly, upon my return from College at the end of one Term, the Wallers no longer lived in Kenilworth Court. The phrase "Non-payment of Rent" and the word "Eviction" came to mind.

The Management Company at Kenilworth Court was responsible for managing not only the flats that it rented out but also, amongst other things, the maintenance of the external fabric of, and lifts etc within, the various blocks of flats which to-gether comprise Kenilworth Court. It obtained its non-rental income for such purposes by means of Services Charges levied on all the flats. Major R. Harvey Wright, a former Royal Artillery Officer, had been appointed by the Company to be its Manager and thus he was the man in charge of the day-to-day functioning of the Management Company; and he operated from a below-ground-floor Office situated in one of the blocks of flats. Mathematics seemed not to be Major Wright's forté whereas I was quite good at the subject, and, in consequence, one day in 1960 he asked me if, when on holiday from School, I would assist him, on a free-of-any-charge basis, in doing the Company's day-to-day Accounts. I liked Major Wright, his humour, and his cheerfulness, and so, on a handshake, I agreed and very soon found out that his understanding of my assisting him was such that it fell to me to do most of the day-to-day Trading Accounts - Service Charges, Maintenance Bills, that kind of thing. By now most, if not all, of the flats within Kenilworth Court that had been offered for sale by Norman Hirschfield had been bought and therefore the Management Company was receiving Service Charge income from in excess of 150 flats and thus my free-of-any-charge services to Major Wright and the Management Company were somewhat time-consuming. He was aware that I enjoyed constructing things out of wood and that there was no suitable space within No.28 to enable me to do so and that I thus had need of workshop space and, also, that I was making a wood-and-canvas canoe at Haileybury and that I would therefore need somewhere, if possible, within Kenilworth Court to house it. So, again on a handshake, he, on behalf of the Management Company, and I struck a bargain: I could have use, free of any charge, of a derelict basement half-flat as a workshop and use, free of any charge, of a largish empty space under the entrance to one of the blocks of flats in which to house my canoe.

The facility given to me to house my canoe was an absolute godsend for otherwise I would, once I had got it to Putney from Hertford Heath, have had nowhere to put it other than either to seek some form of home for it from the likes of Chas Newnes, an acquaintance who was the owner of one of the nearby famous Thameside Boat Building businesses [and who provided several of the Launches to be seen on The Thames each year accompanying the University Boat Race 'fought' between Oxford University (the 'Dark Blues') and Cambridge University (the 'Light Blues') as they raced each other from Putney Pier to Mortlake], or inside 28 Kenilworth Court, something which, given the canoe's non-collapsible length, my Mother would never have considered let alone allowed. So, upon its delivery by van to Kenilworth Court after it had arrived at London's Liverpool Street Station following the end of the Term in which I had constructed it, I trundled it - by means of a couple of bicycle wheels that I had constructed, at Haileybury, into a sort of trailer - down into its new, easily accessible, home from where, several times each week during the School Holidays, I would, on its wheels, take it to, usually, the slipway nearest to Putney Bridge from whence I would, whilst often being deliberately stared at by people on the Putney Pier side of Putney Bridge, launch it and, having tied its wheels firmly to its stern, then paddle either up The Thames towards Teddington and back or, more often, down The Thames towards Tower Bridge and back.

Encouraged by SH Devereux, our Woodwork Teacher, several boys at Haileybury each made himself a canoe, and one lad even made himself, almost entirely out of sheets of marine plywood, a small sailing dingy. To make my canoe I had first, in Haileybury's

Carpentry Workshops, to, using a hand-held Bow Saw, cut, out of marine plywood, several shaped frames of decreasing size and then remove as much surplus wood from them as I could so as to hollow them out not only to make them as light as was possible but also to enable, towards the canoe's bows, my feet to be placed as far forward as was possible and storage facilities to be available within the canoe's stern. Then I constructed a central keel-piece, running from the bow to the stern. Then I added a shaped solid piece of marine plywood to each of the bow and stern and fixed the keel-piece to them. Then, on each side, I added several lengths of strips of marine plywood each terminating in tapered fashion at the bow and stern. Then I added more strips of marine plywood in order to give me a solid base on which to sit. Then, to complete the canoe's carcass work, I built a cockpit the sides of which rose several inches above the 'body' of the canoe so as to prevent water from spilling into the canoe when in use. The next major undertaking was to clad the whole thing in waxed canvas, a procedure which required the waxed canvas first to be heated so that it would expand, then to be placed over the entire canoe and - by means of some filthy black tar-like waterproof 'gunge' and several galvanised clout nails - fixed in place at the bow, stern, and - the canvas having been suitably cut - around the cockpit. Once assembled the canoe's canvas then shrunk tightly around the canoe's carcasswork thereby creating a very tight fit. In order to achieve the heating-up of the canvas the canvas was, on a very hot dry day, taken outside and placed on tressles on the, previously meticulously swept, ground and - with the carcasswork of the canoe having been placed, upright, more or less in the middle of the canvas - left sufficiently long enough to enable the Sun to do the job. Once it was deemed that Sun's heat had achieved all that it was capable of achieving I then set to and fixed the canvas on to the carcasswork. I then fixed a brass strip over the outside of the canvas at both the bow and the stern and then removed all the surplus canvas - If I personally was carrying any surplus weight at the start of that exercise I had most certainly lost it by the time that I had finished. Next day, with the canoe now back in the Workshops, the finishing timbers around and within the cockpit had to be constructed and then fixed in place. Then the thing was painted, in two coats of white waterproof paint on the topside and in two coats of blue waterproof paint on the belowside, save for the cockpit timbers to which several coats of marine varnish were applied. Once I had finished painting and varnishing it I added a flag on its bow for 'good measure' and a nameplate displaying the name 'Sutherland' on each side of the cockpit. Hitherto I had no idea whether or not the thing was in fact watertight, an essential part of the construction if one, as I did, intended to use it in such as the fast-flowing and often very challenging River Thames. So, prior to its delivery to Putney, to the College's large open-air Swimming Pool it went for a, thankfully very successful, thorough test.

Nowadays Society has enveloped itself in a, sometimes over-zealous, Health and Safety culture : But such was not the case in the 1960s; and so, armed only with a red [not that the colour mattered] plastic football shoved tight into the bow and another red plastic football shoved tight into the stern, and with no thought whatsoever insofar as wet-suits and lifejackets were concerned, I spent many happy, and usually very challenging, hours paddling my way from Putney Bridge up and down various lengths of The Thames. Tugs, sometimes towing as many as three two-abreast sets of Barges, would regularly pass me by creating, in their wakes, dozens of waves the sizes of which would often cause the side and/or bow of my canoe to regularly disappear beneath the surface of the water only to surface two or so seconds later leaving bloated dead rats to slide, sometimes assisted on their ways by flicks from my paddles, back into the filthy water from whence they had come, the timbers around the canoe's cockpit preventing the wretched things from landing on my lap. Driftwood, of which there was a constant supply, in all shapes and sizes was another challenge as were the huge man-made water intakes, sited within the River, which supplied Fulham and Battersea Power Stations with, for cooling purposes, thousands of gallons of water every minute. Indeed those intakes, which were not only themselves clearly visible to all persons within the River but also clearly marked with large signs advising extreme caution, I found to be particularly challenging for, as they sucked in their many thousands of gallons within a sort of whirlpool scenario, it was, for me, exciting to find out exactly how far in I could safety go before beginning to feel that, if I went any further, my canoe and I too might be sucked in. Needless-to-say, my canoe and I never were sucked in; but greater wisdom gained over the years that have since passed has made me realise that only a semi-idiot would do such a thing !!

The Thames from Teddington Lock, where it becomes non-tidal, to its mouth was - in part because London was then still a 'working' commercial Port; in part because much commercial traffic, including Tugs and their Barges, still plied up and down it; in part because of the considerable pleasure and sporting traffic that also used it; in part because of the strengths and rise-and-fall distances of its tides; and in part because of the flotsam and jetsam, filth, and vermin that it contained - a very challenging river which caused much time to be consumed by those attempting to travel along it in a craft as small as a one-person canoe; and the furthest that I ever managed to get from Putney was Tower Bridge, a distance that I managed to achieve only once. But, regardless of the fact that in reality I never actually got very far in it, my simple hand-made canoe provided me with a vast amount of enjoyment, an enjoyment which, one day, came to a devastating end, not in The River but in the 'boathouse' that Kenilworth Court's Management Company had so kindly made available to me. Inevitably within a group of blocks of privately-owned flats such as Kenilworth Court flats are bought and sold which causes 'old faces' to go and 'new faces' to come. One such 'new face' was another boy from another English Public School. There is often not only much rivalry between English Public Schools but also much snobbishness and arrogance amongst their products. Having been brought up in the Theatrical Profession wherein there is a constant intermix of persons from all cultures and all social backgrounds it is the character of the person and his/her abilities and achievements which are paramount to me not his/her cultural or social background : And thus, when asked by the Management Company if I minded sharing the 'boathouse', I had no objection to someone else also putting his canoe in the 'boathouse' the size of which was more than sufficient to amply accommodate both. So, into the 'boathouse' this other canoe went; and, when I next went to get my canoe, I found that my canoe had been removed from its place and dumped upside down, with its wheeled trailer upside down on top of it, and that, in its place, was a brand new factory-built expensive-looking canoe festooned with a notice on it stating "Keep Off". I had never met its owner, and knew little about him other than the name of the Public School at which he was/had been a Pupil, but I got the distinct impression that his attitude, despite his being a new arrival within Kenilworth Court, was that he was 'superior' to all others. However, I manoeuvred my canoe past his ostentatious object, turned it back onto its wheels, and took it down to The River. On my return later that day I parked it, as neatly as I could, in the 'boathouse' alongside his in such a way so as to ensure that his was in no way obstructed. On my return next day I found his canoe gone and mine, as before, unceremoniously dumped upside down at the back of the 'boathouse' with its wheels this time lying several feet away from it. I was not amused, but, on finding him in the 'boathouse' when I came back later after having been canoeing I attempted to introduce myself, to ask him what the problem was, and to see if we could not reach an amicable arrangement suitable to us both. His arrogance was almost beyond belief for he informed me that, as his Public School was 'superior' to mine, he [who was about the same age as I] was thus 'superior' to me and therefore, moreso as my canoe was undoubtedly 'home-made', his canoe should have precedence over mine and that my canoe should stay in the place at the back of the 'boathouse' allocated to it by him. Each of us was disadvantaged by the fact that the height of the ceiling of the 'boathouse' from its floor was considerably less than our heights causing neither of us to be able to stand up - Perhaps, under the circumstances, an advantage else a fight might well have ensued. He then left leaving me to park my canoe as best I could : But, upon my return a couple of days later, there was my canoe back again at the rear of the 'boathouse' with its wheels unceremoniously dumped several feet away from it. I was livid : But what I had not realised until I took it down to the strand alongside the slipway to the River and went to launch it was that it now had three small holes in its bow which rendered it useless until repaired. So I took it back to the 'boathouse' and, by means of some waxed canvas and a very generous application of some of the filthy black tar-like waterproof 'gunge', a tube of which I had retained from when I had made the canoe, I repaired it and continued to use it on The Thames until, with the hostility being shown to me by my 'boathouse' colleague continuing, I found it one day to have in one side of its bow a gash the size of which was beyond my ability to repair. Lying alongside his canoe, as it often was, was a long pole with a marlinespike fixed to one end of it. However, not having witnessed the damage being done I could only but assume that it was his marlinespike that had been the implement used to effect the damage. I complained to the Management Company who subsequently spoke with him and, in consequence, I never saw him, his canoe, or his marlinespike again; but neither did I ever use my canoe again, although it remained within the 'boathouse' until I eventually left Kenilworth Court in order to reside elsewhere. [*See under, Photograph of my canoe with a fellow Lawrence House Member, subsequently to become Lieutenant Colonel, Tim Nicholson, sitting in it.*]

Alastair Laird, one of Doctor Laird's children, was another Kenilworth Court resident unfortunate enough to encounter a teenage bully living within Kenilworth Court : But, whereas the teenage bully whom I encountered reserved his bullying talent for attacking possessions, Alastair, a smallish and somewhat timid lad at the time, was unfortunate enough to suffer a teenage bully who reserved his bullying talent for, like many a teenage bully, attacking boys smaller than he. Waterman Street, the road that ran alongside Kenilworth Court from Lower Richmond Road down to the Bricklayer's Arms public house and, in those days, beyond until it met up with Felsham

Road, was in the process of being re-tarred when Alastair's bully struck. Alastair was standing on his own watching hot tar being applied to the road's surface when, suddenly from behind and with no warning whatsoever, his bully pushed him causing him to fall forwards into the, fortunately by now, cooling tar. Although Alastair suffered no serious injury both he and his clothes had tar stuck on them. I was with Doctor and Mrs Laird in their flat when Alastair tearfully came in initially causing both his Father and his Mother considerable distress as he blurted out his story to them. Doctor Laird, a much respected Doctor both within Kenilworth Court and within the East End of London Hospital in which he worked, immediately, assisted by his former Nurse Wife, swung into, what seemed to me to be, an instinctive medical reaction. There was nothing that I could do, and thus I left. I had never before spoken with Alastair's assailant but I not only knew of him but also knew where he lived - in the flat immediately below No.28. So I half-expected to meet him as I returned home : But, instead of going straight home, I decided to first go and have a look at where the incident had happened. Lo and behold, there the bully was still in Waterman Street. Although he was a somewhat solid-looking lad, and doubtless intimidating-looking to those smaller than he, I was an inch or so taller than he; and so, without any intent to myself apply any physical violence, I went up to him, rose to my full height, and asked him how he would like it if someone bigger than he was to do to him what he had done to Alastair. Without a word he turned and, with me following him in complete silence, quickly walked along Waterman Street to Lower Richmond Road and thence into the Main Entrance to the block of flats where Nos. 27 and 28 are sited. Then, still in silence, up the stairs the two of us went, he to No.27 and me to No.28. A short while later there was, despite the fact that our frontdoor had a very effective bell on it, a series of loud bangs on our front door. Having been told by my Mother to "See who that is", I went to the front door and opened it. In, without any invitation whatsoever, came Alastair's assailant's Father, a man as solid-looking as, if not more solid-looking than, his Son to, in an intimidating bellowing voice, inform me that, unless I came up with a good excuse, he was intending to go to the Police to report me for having assaulted ['battered', to use the, I believe, correct legal word] his Son. I had never touched the lad, but that, apparently, was not the story that the Son had told his Father - and the Father took some convincing to finally accept the reality of what had actually happened. Indeed, for much of the conversation - a conversation that took place within earshot of my Mother who remained throughout elsewhere within the flat - it seemed as if the Father's impression of his Son was that he was a 'little angel' who would never dream of applying violence on someone else; and it was only when I eventually got him to appreciate that Doctor Laird was possibly, if not probably, going to go to the Police to report what my neighbour's beloved Son had done to Alastair that the trespasser within 28 Kenilworth Court finally ceased his intimidatingly verbal assault on me and withdrew out of our flat intending, he said, to speak with Doctor Laird. I returned to Haileybury a few days' later having seen neither the Son nor the Father again; and upon my return, twelve weeks later, to Kenilworth Court for the start of the next School Holiday I was pleasantly surprised to find that our neighbours in the flat below, who had not resided there for long, had gone. Doctor Laird never did go to the Police preferring instead, I understand, to be of the opinion that, the Father and he having discussed the Son's actions, it was better that the Son learn the error of his ways by being punished by the Father rather than by being punished by the Criminal Law and thus be tainted by incurring a Criminal Record, albeit a very minor one. I can not say that I disagree with Doctor Laird's decision although I wonder whether, given the Father's undoubted bullying attitude of hostility towards me, the Son's attitude ever really changed. In fact, having met the Father I felt sorry for the Son !!

By the latter part of 1961 my time at Haileybury - which should have run on until the end of the Summer Term of 1962 and thus seen me not only achieving 'A' Levels but also participating in the College's 1862-1962 Centenary Celebrations - was coming to an end for not only had I gotten fed up with the place but also events were to cause me to hand in my resignation.

Haileybury had always been proud of its association with the Honourable East India Company, and thus the build-up to Haileybury's own Centenary within the purpose-built East India Company's College was undertaken by most, including me, with much enthusiasm. For my part, with other boys cutting blocks of wood and mounting them for me onto the face-plates of three woodworking lathes, I churned out in excess of a hundred bowls and ashtrays - each intended for sale on Saturday 23 June 1962, the principal day of the Celebrations - made in a variety of woods including my favourite wood [for its graining but certainly not for its somewhat unpleasant smell whilst being worked], namely Rosewood. I also designed and built a side-stall to be erected on the grass of the College's Quadrangle whereby people could, during the Centenary Celebrations, test their skills at releasing metal bombs onto targets, a contraption which consisted of a revolving metal bicycle wheel operated by means of a geared-down main's electricity-operated motor and a low voltage electromagnet, which held the bombs, fixed onto the wheel, the magnet releasing the bombs whenever the low voltage current was switched off. I was also, for the first time in my life at the Senior School, to actually act in a Show - Gilbert and Sullivan's *Yeomen of the Guard* on Haileybury's Big School Stage - rather than design and build the Scenery for it. However, things did not go to plan for the termination of my time at Haileybury ended much sooner than I or anyone else had intended for, unbeknown to me, and thus 'behind my back', one of the School's Teachers had, in the Christmas Term of 1961, written to Brunskill and Loveday Limited to ask for canvas for Scenery which, he stated in his letter, I had said he could have at a considerably reduced price. On receiving the letter an unamused Jack Brunskill, my late Father's fellow joint Managing Director, telephoned my Mother demanding an explanation. In turn, my Mother telephoned me demanding to know what I thought I was doing in "upsetting Jack Brunskill like that". I was furious and demanded of the Teacher concerned - Lieutenant Colonel Edward Hugh Frere Sawbridge OBE [Officer, Order of the British Empire], himself a former pupil at Haileybury from 1945 to 1951 - [1] an explanation for what, 'behind my back', he had done, [2] an apology to me, and [3] a written apology to Jack Brunskill. EHF Sawbridge, a man much respected within Haileybury, refused all of my demands. I therefore informed my House Master, with whom I had had a 'ding-dong' relationship throughout much of my time at the Senior School, that I was neither prepared to tolerate this incident nor, unless Sawbridge complied with at least my demand that he apologise to Jack Brunskill, prepared to continue at Haileybury and that I would thus resign at the end of that Term. For whatever reason(s) it was I, not Sawbridge, who was made out to be the 'villain of the piece'; and thus I wrote out and handed to Williams my 'Notice to Quit'. Williams then telephoned my Mother who, a day or two later, travelled to Haileybury in order that she and Williams could attempt to talk me out of resigning. I had not realised not only that I was now passed the age at which it was a legal requirement that I must attend a school but also that neither the School nor my Mother could insist that I remain at Haileybury. Thus my resignation was accepted and I left Haileybury at the end of the Christmas Term of 1961.

The issue of 'canvas on the cheap' did not end there however for, in April of 1962, still feeling very bitter I wrote to Sawbridge and in no uncertain terms told him exactly what I thought of his having gone 'behind my back'. He never replied. Instead he took my letter to the Master, CPC Smith, who, on hearing Sawbridge's explanation but in the absence of seeking any comment from me, wrote to me stating that unless I apologised to Sawbridge I was never to visit Haileybury again. I reconsidered the strength of the content of the letter that I had written to Sawbridge and in early May telephoned Smith to apologise for the way in which I had worded my letter but not for its content. I likewise wrote a second letter to Sawbridge : But there was no way that I was going to withdraw my criticisms of what had occurred. Thus I remained banned from ever visiting Haileybury again.

In those days, during the Summer Holidays, a team from Haileybury College played an annual Cricket Match against a team from Cheltenham College, another one of England's 'great' Public Schools for (in those days) boys and a school of similar age to Haileybury College and with, like Haileybury, close connections to the Military and to India. The venue for the annual joust between the two Colleges was Lord's Cricket Ground, the famous 'Home of Cricket' in London's Saint John's Wood : And, as Lord's was in no way within the bounds, or control, of Haileybury, in the August of 1962 I went there both to watch the Match and to meet up with some of those with whom I had shared my years at Haileybury College in Hertford. I confess that I can remember absolutely nothing of the game for, insofar as I was concerned, it paled into insignificance compared with one event that took place: I was merrily chatting away with a group of boys with whom I had been at school and with John Mannion, Lawrence House's loyal Servant. Suddenly John spied CPC Smith, the Master of Haileybury College, heading at speed towards us. Knowing of the situation existing between Smith and me as a result of EHF Sawbridge's request of Jack Brunskill to be supplied with canvas 'on the cheap', as soon as John said "Christ, here comes Smith" everyone scattered leaving me entirely on my own. Within seconds there, alongside me to my right, was Smith. Almost breathless, and totally contrary to what I had expected, he blurted out "My dear Loveday. I was hoping to meet you here. I am so sorry, for I have only just learned the truth". I had always liked Smith and was glad that he had the courage to meet with me face-to-face. I wrote to him some days later to express my gratitude to him for, what was undoubtedly, a very genuine apology for the events that had occurred and to clarify the fact that the 'ban' imposed upon me whereby I was never again to visit Haileybury had been removed. Some days later, after he had returned from a holiday in Scotland, I received a written response from him expressing an apology; but neither I nor Jack Brunskill ever received any communication from EHF Sawbridge. *Perhaps it got lost in the Post* !!

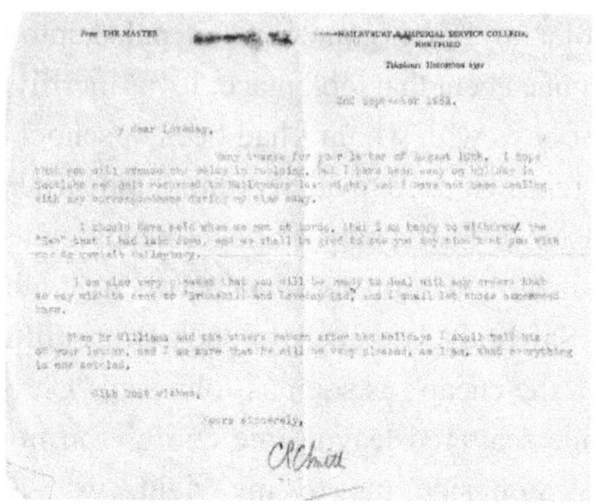

[*My dear Loveday*

Many thanks for your letter of August 10th. I hope that you will excuse the delay in replying, but I have been away on holiday in Scotland and only returned to Haileybury last night, and I have not been dealing with any correspondence during my time away.

I should have said when we met at Lords , that I am happy to withdraw the "Ban" that I had laid down, and we shall be glad to see you any time that you wish now to revisit Haileybury.

I am also very pleased that you will be ready to deal with any orders that we may wish to send to "Brunskill and Loveday Ltd", and I shall let those concerned know.

When Mr Williams and the others return after the holidays I shall tell him of your letter, and I am sure that he will be very pleased, as I am, that everything is now settled.

With best wishes, yours sincerely, CPC Smith]

Shortly after that surprising mid-afternoon incident that day at Lord's John Mannion and I, at John's suggestion, decided to leave the

'Home of Cricket' and visit a few pubs. No-one had heard of the 'Breathalyser' in those days and thus our 'pub crawl' took in several pubs, the last of which was in Hounslow, West London. Almost straightaway, as we entered the pub, John recognised an old friend of his and, as the two met, they hugged each other like long-lost brothers. Suddenly, after they had released each other and John had introduced me to him, John said to him "Show him your legs". Immediately the guy, full of pride, pulled up his two trouser legs to expose a line of scars down the lower half of each leg. "How odd," I thought.

"Now tell him how you got those scars," John said to him.

"John was sent to get me. I wouldn't go. So he shot me," said John's grinning friend.

Apparently John, in his days in Manchester, had been involved in Gangland activities; and one of his 'jobs' was as a 'Go Getter' instructed to fetch those whom his Gang's Leader wished brought to him. The guy in the pub was one such unfortunate but he, on receiving John's instruction to go with him, had refused to obey the 'command'. Thus John shot him and then took him, and his then useless legs, to where it was that he had been told to take him. And the gun ? Yes, it was the self-same gun that John had 'kindly' gifted to me during my days as a Student at Haileybury !!

I have always been very grateful to Haileybury Senior School for the breadth of academic education that it gave me but I have always remained very critical of the often 'harsh' manner in which we boys were treated. Of course to-day Haileybury is a very different school from the, to quote James McConnell in his book *English Public Schools*, "tough school" that it most certainly was during my time there. Influenced heavily by the enveloping traditions of the East

India Company and by the attitude of that Company's College when at Haileybury of, in effect, breaking boys' characters in order to mould boys into what the College believed was required of those destined, on leaving Haileybury, to rule others, Haileybury in my day, certainly in my case, seemed to have little or no regard for the boys' own personalities, seemed to have little or no regard, in my case, for the fact that since the day of my birth my Father had, as had been stated to Haileybury by my Father, expended much time and energy educating me in both theoretical and practical business skills of a type required within his sphere of the Theatrical Profession and that I thus had a character that had been deliberately substantially moulded by my Father before I ever set foot within Haileybury's College on Hertford Heath; and seemed to give little or no thought to the possibility that my Father's very sudden death not only might have considerably effected me emotionally but also might have caused me to need sympathy if not also some in-depth form of counselling to assist me to come to terms with it. The rigidity of the system that then existed at Haileybury was doubtless not assisted by the fact that both the Master, CPC Smith, and my House Master, EF Williams, were seemingly staunch bachelors whose dealings with children, for that is what we Students were throughout much of our times at Haileybury, lacked the 'fatherly' type of rapport and understanding that, in many situations, was often needed. John Mannion, the Lawrence House Servant, once asked Williams why it was that Williams's own bedroom was as basic and as austere as that provided within our Dormitory, to which Williams responded that his bedroom was, with minor exceptions, deliberately kept basic and austere to enable him to try to experience for himself the conditions in which we boys had to exist. Had there been a Mrs Williams Williams's attitude to us boys would, I feel, have been noticeably more sympathetic and understanding : But, certainly in my time, there was no Mrs Williams and, to my knowledge, never had been and nor was there, as far as I know, even a 'girl friend'; and thus when it came to be my turn to be promoted to House Prefect there was no-one to point out to him the injustice of his deliberately by-passing my promotion which he did, to not only my embarrassment but also the embarrassment of my peers who were promoted, for well over a year. Personally, I found his attitude in deliberately by-passing me not only very embarrassing but also excessively petty and childish; and when it came to his having to strike a bargain with me whereby he had little option but to promote me I just felt sorry for the guy. My promotion to House Prefect came about just before the start of my last two weeks at Haileybury when, for a reason which I can not now remember, the boys of the Junior End of the Dormitory refused to co-operate with some instruction or other given to them by one or more of the House Prefects. The event turned into a stalemate that no-one, not even Williams, seemed able, regardless of whatever punishments were threatened, to overcome. Doubtless some form of entrenched principle was involved. Eventually word came to me that Williams would like to see me. So I went and met him in his nearby Study; and he asked me if I would help resolve the situation - a request that he must have found difficult to make. All the House Prefects were personal friends of mine and, as Editor of the by then popular House Magazine, I was reasonably highly regarded throughout the rest of the House; and therefore most Laurentians would at least give me the courtesy of listening to what I had to say. From my earliest days at the Senior School I had always hated the fagging system which, although it undoubtedly was by then on its way out, was the system which influenced the way in which House Prefects would communicate, not with but, to the Junior End of the House. For my part I respected people as individuals and preferred to listen to what they had to say rather than adopt the attitude of preferring to only listen to what was required of them to say. So my response to Williams was that I would, on his agreeing to at last promote me to my long-overdue position of House Prefect, go listen to what the Junior End had to say, discuss their grievance(s) with them, and, if possible, talk with them until an acceptable solution was reached. It took me, I remember, under half-an-hour to resolve the issue; and, if only for the last two weeks of my last Term at Haileybury Senior School, I at long last was a House Prefect.

Contrary to my having been very happy throughout most of my time at Haileybury's Junior School in Windsor I had had more than enough of Haileybury's Senior School in Hertford Heath and was thus very pleased to leave it. But what to do ? Brunskill and Loveday Limited had, in 1959, been deliberately manoeuvred away from me (a) by my Mother, who wanted me to go into her Profession and become a medical Doctor, and (b) by Jack Brunskill, who wanted to rid himself of his connection with my Father and who, I believe, would never have ever become a Builder of Theatrical Scenery had not his own Father given him little or no option. However, entering the Medical Profession was a non-starter with me and I was thus not prepared to even consider her idea. Thus my Mother and I had, some time before I left Haileybury, reached a compromise solution: I would become an Electrical Engineer.

Probably because of my interest, almost from the day of my birth, in Theatrical Scenery Construction I had always been interested in Physics and Maths, each of which is an element in the design and construction of Theatrical Scenery; and thus becoming an Engineer, given my Mother's in-depth hostility to my going into The Theatre, did seem a reasonable option until, that is, I paid a visit to Trafford

Park in Manchester. Whilst at Haileybury I had been written to and provisionally accepted by Metropolitan-Vickers/Associated Electrical Industries [AEI] to undertake, at their expense, a 3-year Manchester University/AEI 'Sandwich Course' whereby Manchester University would educate me in the theories of Engineering and Metro-Vic/AEI would provide the practical Engineering experience. The condition was that I had to stay an employee of Metro-Vic/AEI for a certain number of years. Suitably kitted out, including a sort of Tyrolean-type hat with a feather stuck in its band that had been purchased for me by my Mother specially for the occasion, I travelled by train from Hertford to Manchester for a 3-day 'get to know us' event at Metro-Vic in Trafford Park. When I arrived at my allocated digs I found that I had two companions, each from another English Public School. Our digs were in a terraced house in Greyhound Lane, Manchester, our accommodation and board paid for by Metro-Vic. My evening meal, my having travelled nearly 200 miles that day from Hertford to Manchester and thus being 'starving', consisted in its entirety of [1] a 6d [2½d] tin's-worth, the smallest size available, of Baked Beans dumped on two slices of buttered toast and [2] some tea to drink. Next morning the fare was identical save for the fact that two more slices of buttered toast and some marmalade were added. That evening it was back to the 6d-worth of baked beans on two slices of toast, and so on throughout my stay there The mattress on my bed was stuffed full with horsehair or straw and was therefore very supporting and thus very comfortable; but the weather was atrocious for it rained throughout the entirety of my stay in Manchester thus causing the mattress to have a slight damp feel about it. Other than the other two Metro-Vic intendees I encountered only one other person in that depressing terraced house, the woman who owned it and served us with our, what can best be described as being, samples of food and who, on the day of our departure, had the cheek to come up to us as we departed and demand an extra 6d from each of us. "Why ?" we asked. "Rent increase," she replied. "Nothing to do with us. Talk to Metro-Vic," we told her. "Can't," she told us. "I've agreed a rent with them but I want 6d more from each of you. So, you'll have to pay it, won't you ?" Like idiots we each left having first parted with 6d to this greedy, miserly woman whose imprint upon me was such that even to-day whenever I think of Manchester I think of her and her wretched little backstreet terraced house and her bloody awful 6d tins of baked beans !!

The hospitality given to us by Metro-Vic was, however, a complete contrast to the stinginess evidenced by the woman in Greyhound Lane. We went each day to a different part of the Trafford Park Works and so on; and each day, shortly after our arrival, we were given biscuits and cupfulls of coffee. At Lunchtime we were plied with generous helpings of very tasty food, and mid-afternoon we were given cakes and more cupfulls of coffee. I was very impressed not only by Metro-Vic's hospitality but also by the scale of its engineering operation that was going on in its Trafford Park Works. Principally Metro-Vic was making huge turbines for export in sheds that were so large that, looking through the doorway at one end of one of them, I was hardly able to see the other end. Certainly the University/AEI 'Sandwich Course' deal that Metro-Vic was offering me was very attractive but I felt that it was not for me; and so, during a Meeting with the Director of Personnel, I stated that I did not think that I could work for Metro-Vic. My stated, and truthful, reason was that I found the operation to be too big, too impersonal for me. I suspect however that our dismal digs, and the constant rain of Manchester throughout my stay there, also had a slight influence on my decision.

Early in the new year of 1962 the telephone in 28 Kenilworth Court rang. I was not allowed to answer the 'phone. Thus it fell to my Mother, who had imposed the restriction upon me, to do so. But the call was for me. The man at the other end was Eric Maschwitz. What he said to my Mother I do not know, but I was very soon, and with noticeable annoyance, summoned to the 'phone by my Mother who, once I had taken over the handset, immediately departed to another room in the flat.

Worthy of a large book in itself, Albert Eric Maschwitz OBE [Officer of the Most Excellent Order of the British Empire] - a longtime friend of my Father and a person known to me for much of my childhood - was one of the most talented, and influential, of UK Theatricals of the 20th century. Actor; Writer of Musicals, Operettas, Plays, and Books; Broadcaster; Lyricist; Editor of the BBC's *Radio Times* magazine; *US* Academy Award (the 'Oscars') nominee; Member of the UK's Secret Intelligence Service and of the Special Operations Executive during the Second World War [during which he attained the rank of Lieutenant Colonel] he was Head of Television Light Entertainment at the BBC when he telephoned me in January 1962. His purpose in making that telephone-call was to say to me "I want you to join the BBC". When I told him that my Mother would not agree he replied "Don't take any notice of what your Mother says. Write to me here at the BBC's Television Centre". So I wrote to him at the BBC's Television Centre, and a few days later he replied. [*see copy letter under*].

BBC Television Centre London W 12

25th January 1962

Dear Mr. Loveday,

Thank you for your letter of 23rd January. Of course I remember your father very well: he was one of my mainstays during my chequered career in the theatre and a dear friend into the bargain. I sympathise with your desire to get into television, it is a fascinating business. On the other hand, there is nothing I can do to help you beyond passing your letter with a recommendation to our Appointments Officer at Broadcasting House, whose department is the only "way in". This I am doing today in the hope that something successful may result.

Yours sincerely,

(Eric Maschwitz)

E.S. Loveday Esq.,
28 Kenilworth Court,
Lower Richmond Road,
Putney, London.

Dear Mr Loveday

Thank you for your letter of 23 January. Of course I remember your father very well : he was one of my mainstays during my chequered career in the theatre and a dear friend into the bargain. I sympathise with your desire to get into television, it is a fascinating business. On the other hand, there is nothing I can do to help you beyond passing your letter with a recommendation to our Appointments Officer at Broadcasting House, whose department is the only "way in". This I am doing today in the hope that something successful may result.

Yours sincerely

A short time afterwards I received formal documentation and an Application Form from the BBC's Appointments Department. I filled in the Form and returned it to the Appointments Department; and heard nothing more, not a word, not even a postcard of acknowledgement. As the weeks went by I came to the conclusions either that Maschwitz had changed his mind or that my humble Application had, in consequence of my having sent it to the Appointments Department and not to Maschwitz himself, found its way into a file the spine of which was marked with something like the word 'Rubbish' upon it or that my Mother had made contact with Maschwitz and made it abundantly clear to him that under no circumstances would I be joining the BBC. [A favourite story, at least to me, of Maschwitz concerned the Operetta *Goodnight Vienna* which, with the Composer George Posford, Maschwitz had written in the 1930s for the BBC's Radio service. The day after it was broadcast the film Producer/Director Herbert Wilcox bought the film Rights and, in 1932, turned it into a very successful film starring Anna Neagle (Wilcox's Wife) and Jack Buchanan. In 1946 a Stage version of *Goodnight Vienna* went on tour within the UK. Having attended a 'white tie' dinner Maschwitz was, one night, in the process of being chauffeur-driven home when he passed Lewisham Theatre in South London. On seeing that his Show, *Goodnight Vienna,* was in the process of being performed there he had his Chauffeur stop the car. Having entered the Theatre's foyer Maschwitz found it to be empty save for a man who was busy sweeping the floor.

"How's the Show doing, my man ?" asked an eager Maschwitz.

"Well, guv'na, itshlike thish," said the man as he stopped sweeping and lent on the top of his broom's handle to speak to the, unknown to him, great Eric Maschwitz, "*Goodnight Viennaaar's* going danne in Lewsham 'bout as well as *Goodnight Lewsham* would go danne in Viennaaar".

A somewhat disappointed, if not annoyed, Maschwitz - perhaps best remembered to-day for his lyrics to the song '*A Nightingale sang in Berkeley Square*' - turned, went out the Theatre and back to his car and told his Chauffeur to drive on.]

Shortly after Maschwitz's telephone-call to me my Mother - still, despite her very obvious very strong dislike for the Theatrical Profession, an active Member of the Grand Order of Lady Ratlings and a consistent attender of that Order's fortnightly Wednesday afternoon's Lodge Meetings - was given a message to pass on to me by Mrs Ann [Curly] Flanagan. The message had come from her Husband, Bud Flanagan (whose voice can be heard singing *Who do you think you are kidding Mr Hitler ?* at the start of each episode of the BBC TV series *Dad's Army*). Put simply, the message asked me to be Stage Manager and Scenery Builder for the Grand Order of Water Rats [GOWR] and the Grand Order of Lady Ratlings [GOLR]. Both Orders being Charities it was, needless to say, understood that no money, other than in respect of any expenses that I incurred, would enter the equation. But money has, despite any impression that I may have given over the years, never been a principal motivation with me; and, insofar as these two great Theatrical Charity organisations were concerned, just the honour of being asked was sufficient reward in itself. Therefore, despite the fact that my Mother enveloped Bud's message within such comments as "You need to find yourself a proper job, one which will pay you a decent wage not one that'll give you nothing in return", I send word back to Bud via my Mother and Curly that I would be delighted to become the GOWR's and GOLR's Stage Manager and Scenery Builder : And so I set to and helped organise and run various charitable activities that the GOWR and GOLR involved themselves in. The most memorable, for me, was a Show that the GOWR and GOLR jointly staged in Saint John's Hospital in Clapham in South London in April 1962. Featuring several Water Rats - including Bud; Ben Warriss, a famous Performer at the time and who that year was the GOWR's 'King Rat', the principal and most honourable Office within the Order; and Cyril Smith, a 'leading' Actor in many a West End Show over a period of many years - and several Lady Ratlings including Joy Ganjou, who, as Juanita, undertook [but not at Saint John's] the most terrifying of very fast-moving sequences as part of an Adagio Act [a spectacular stage dancing Act wherein a female performer would often, sometimes at frightening speed and spinning, be 'thrown' from one or more male dancers to other male dancers] of 'The Ganjou Brothers and Juanita' in such Shows as the 1945 *Aladdin* Pantomime at London's Cambridge Theatre and the 1955 production of *Paris by Night* at London's Prince of Wales's Theatre; Joan Hurley, a much relied-upon and very popular Actress; and the Actress/Singer/Comedienne Sunny Rogers, who often, and for many years, 'supported' Artists such as the Comedian Frankie Howerd. Not only did I have the honour and immense pleasure of being the Charities' Stage Manager and the Builder of all the Scenery and Props that were required but also I was, insofar as the Show at Saint John's was concerned, privileged to accompany Bud as he, several hours before the Show, went round some of the Wards, in the company of the Hospital's Matron, chatting to and with as many patients, some of whom were very ill indeed, as he was able to do within the time available to him. Very famous at the time and renown for his considerable comedic humour, Bud would go from patient to patient his intention being to bring as much humour as he could to each and every one of them; and, as he passed from one patient on to the next, I followed giving out presents of chocolates and cigarettes [which, in those days, were not known, at less publicly, for being harmful !!]. Some of those with whom we spoke were almost at death's door and, in order to see the Show, had to be wheeled into the Hospital's Theatre within their beds. About two-thirds of our way through one of the wards Bud, having spoken and joked with one, seemingly very happy, lad and then been very quietly informed by Matron that the lad was only fourteen years of age and had but only a few days to live, stopped and, after I had given the lad a box of chocolates and wished him well, Bud - who, although one of the UK's greatest comedians at the time, was certainly no soft-centred character - beckoned me over to him and, with tears in his eyes, said "You know, it's unbelievable. I'm here to cheer these guys up and yet there's this fourteen years' old lad, who knows that he'll be dead within two or three days' time, and he's a bloody sight more cheerful than I am. It's cracking me up".

'Maigret' by the French Author, Georges Simenon, was a hugely popular detective series on BBC Television at the time, and our Show at Saint John's was centred around a sketch, featuring Joan Hurley, based on 'Maigret'. I made the Scenery - including a canvas Backcloth and a substantial scene-change Gauze, and the Props for the Show - in the kitchen of the flat in 28 Kenilworth Court in the knowledge that the only transport available to me to cart the stuff from Putney to Clapham was my Mother's Morris Minor car. Thus everything had to be designed so that it could fold to fit in its entirety onto the back seat and boot of that Morris Minor car. Thus multiple hinging was involved so that much of it could be folded in concertina-like fashion. My Mother, in her usual fashion, gave me no help save to lend me, without any instruction, her manually-operated 1930s' Frister & Rossmann sewing-machine and to absent herself completely from what I was doing. Thus when it came to having to sew the Gauze I found myself at first completely bewildered insofar as operating her sewing-machine was concerned. However, I eventually mastered it to such an extent that, with the sewing-machine sitting upon the kitchen table, I was able to rapidly feed the Gauze through it. Things were going splendidly until I began to smell burning. Fortunately the Gauze contained a built-in fire-retardant otherwise disaster would have struck not only the Gauze but possibly also the flat itself for, as I fed the stitched Gauze out of the sewing-machine, I was, unrealised by me, pushing it in the direction of a child's 'safety' fire that, years earlier, had been purchased to keep me warm when I had been a baby in Highlands. Eventually several yards [metres] of the stuff had piled themselves on top of the fire causing the Gauze to have little option to, despite the fire-retardant, begin to smolder. A dousing with water from one of the kitchen taps soon solved the problem - save for the leftover acrid smell which, for reasons known only to my Mother, was never remarked upon.

There was, in the Show at Saint John's, music to be played and songs to be sung, and so, to do justice to the occasion, I wanted some good quality 'live' Musicians : And who better to ask but the then legendary Band Leader and Impresario Jack Hylton, and who better to act as intermediary for my request but one of Jack's friends, Bud Flanagan. So, on my behalf, Bud asked Jack if he would lend me some Musicians from London's Victoria Palace Theatre. Jack's response was an immediate "Yes" but, ever the Showman and self-promoter, he added "but only if he [*me*] bills them as 'A three-piece Orchestra from the Victoria Palace by kind permission of Jack Hylton' ". So, 'A three-piece Orchestra from the Victoria Palace by kind permission of Jack Hylton' it was, not that I had ever before heard of a three-piece Orchestra.

The Audience consisted mainly of Patients, many of whom had been wheeled in in their beds, the Patients' attendants and Patients' relatives, and friends of Patients but also included members of the Public many of whom came to give financial support to Saint John's Hospital. All-in-all it was a packed house well before I, as Stage Manager, pulled the ropes that operated the travelling draw-curtains the opening of which got the Show under way. Singers sang, comedians and comediennes cracked jokes and made people laugh, and Joan Hurley gave a show-stopping performance as the French Detective Maigret. Time just flew by; and then suddenly there the Cast was taking its end-of-Show bow. Without any warning to me whatsoever my presence on stage was demanded by Ben Warriss in order that he and Bud could present me with a Five Year Diary within which every Performer had signed his/her name. As I stood there, overwhelmed by the presentation so kindly given to me, it began to occur not only to me but also to others that, my being also the operator of the curtains the closing of which would end the Show, the Show could not end until, somehow, I managed to exit myself from front of stage to where I could operate the curtains. So, doubtless looking somewhat like a stumbling fool, I progressed backwards and sideways until I eventually was sufficiently out of sight to enable me to grab the ropes that closed the curtains. Phhheww !!

Sitting in the Audience that night was a diminutive guy, a Water Rat called Georgie Wood, who, as 'Wee Georgie Wood', had for over 30 years famously, and very successfully, appeared on stage with the Music Hall Comedienne Dolly Harmer in a double-act she playing his mother to his playing her son. Apart from being a much-admired Performer Georgie Wood, born George Bamlett in Jarrow in 1895, was also a regular writer of articles for, and contributor to, The Stage newspaper; and it was principally as a writer for The Stage that he was there in the Audience that night : And in his column in The Stage that featured that Show at Saint John's Hospital Georgie Wood kindly and very flatteringly said of my assistance that the Water Rats and Lady Ratlings had been delighted with the help given by "Edwin Loveday, son of the late, well-liked, Ted, of the famous scenery firm of Loveday and Higson". I was puzzled by the fact that he had referred not to 'Brunskill and Loveday Limited' but to one of its forerunners, 'Loveday and Higson', a firm that had ceased twenty-three years' previously back in 1939 when 'Loveday and Higson' had amalgamated with 'John Brunskill Limited' to form 'Brunskill and Loveday Limited'. So when next I met him I asked him why he had stated 'Loveday and Higson' and not 'Brunskill and Loveday'. Expecting him to say that he had made an error, I was very surprised when he told me that he had done it deliberately because, he said, he, like others such as Bud Flanagan, resented the fact that Jack Brunskill and my Mother had deliberately denied to my Father the ability of my Father's Son [*me*] to continue what my Father, and John Brunskill [Jack's Father], had created.

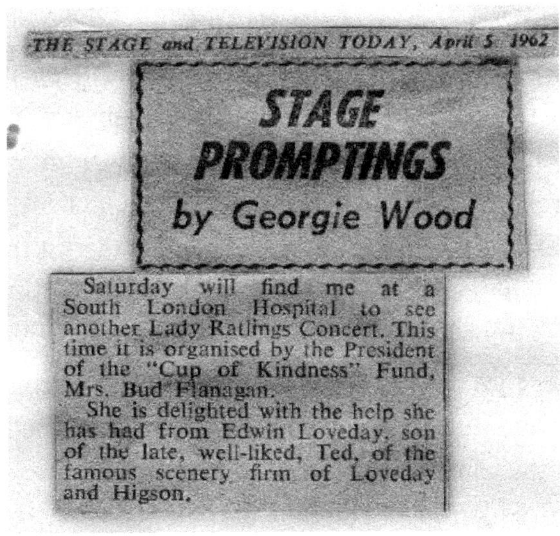

Personalities such as Georgie Wood OBE - who had been King [Water] Rat in 1936 - and Bud Flanagan OBE - who had been King [Water] Rat in 1945, 1946, and 1951 - were certainly no 'second raters' insofar as the Theatrical Profession was concerned. Indeed, each was a very influential personality within the Theatrical Profession; and Georgie Wood's comment to me that day, along with Bud's desire that I should be the Water Rats' and Lady Ratlings' Stage Manager, caused me not only to begin to seriously realise that there was much more to the achievements of Brunskill and Loveday Limited and its predecessor firms than I knew of but also that those achievements, along with the achievements of other such 'Back Stage' businesses within the Theatrical Profession, perhaps deserved to be as well recorded within the history of British Theatre as the achievements of many 'Stars' of the Stage who, without that which those 'Back Stage' businesses had achieved, might never have become 'Stars'. Georgie Wood's comment to me that day is thus one of the motivations for this book.

Shortly after the Show at Saint John's I received that which I had almost given-up on, a letter from the Appointments Department of the BBC. It informed me that my Application had been provisionally accepted and that I should now attend an Interview at the BBC's Television Centre in Wood Lane, Shepherd's Bush in West London. So, at the nominated time on the nominated day outside a nominated room I sat, alone, awaiting to be summoned inside for my Interview. Other than within the Reception of the recently-constructed Television Centre - a complex which, even in those days, was an overawing place for anyone who had not previously been there - I had met no-body; and thus, when the door was opened, I had expected to meet at least the familiar face of Eric Maschwitz. But no, the door was opened by a man totally unknown to me who politely greeted me and then ushered me into a windowless room which, save for a desk either side of which was a single chair, was almost empty. As he sat down on the chair furthest from the door he indicated to me to sit on the other chair. Then, having introduced himself with the words "My name's Mo(u)lson", he launched into the Interview. All that I can remember about him besides the name of 'Mo(u)lson' that he stated to me was that he had a withered hand. [Many years later, in 2006, Tony Dent, a friend of mine who worked for 30 years or so within the BBC's Personnel Department before leaving the BBC in the 1990s, asked me who had interviewed me when I had applied to join the BBC. I, needless to say, told Tony that the person's name was "Mo(u)lson", and his reply was that he had never heard of him. My conclusion to thus puzzling mystery, given also that I was, as far as I am aware, Mo(u)lson's only Interviewee and that the Room in which the Interview took place was almost devoid of everything, is that perhaps the Interview was a 'set-up' by Maschwitz. Maschwitz died in 1969 and I never asked him, and it is therefore likely that I shall never know. However, I was, subsequent to that Interview, offered a 6-month temporary Contract, commencing that May, within BBC Television's Properties [Props] Department.]

When the letter from the BBC announcing the Offer of employment arrived at 28 Kenilworth Court I was, needless to say, very pleased and immediately replied accepting the Offer. Most Parents in such a situation would be pleased. However, such was not the case insofar as my Mother was concerned. Her reaction was to vow never to watch BBC Television again, a vow which, as far as I know, she adhered to for the rest of her life except that she made two exceptions: One was in respect of BBC Television's very long running *Dixon of Dock Green'* series and the other was in respect of the BBC's *'Doctor Findlay's Casebook'* series. The 'Star' of *'Dixon'* was Jack

Warner, whom my Mother knew and whose two Sisters, Elsie and Doris Waters, were friends of my Mother and Father : And, when a Nurse, my Mother had been, and still was, an avid reader of anything written by the Scottish Novelist, Dr Archibald Joseph Cronin, the author of the '*Doctor Findlay's Casebook*' books on which the BBC series were based.

Armed with a tin sandwich-box in which were two rounds of jam sandwiches made for me by my Mother ["You like jam. So I've made you jam sandwiches", a routine adopted by my Mother on nearly every one of my working days despite the fact, as I made known to her on many occasions, within an hour or so of my departure from Kenilworth Court the jam had made its way through the bread so that there was more jam on the outside of the bread than there was on the inside thereby causing each sandwich to become a soggy fruity mess. At least the sandwiches were always wrapped in greaseproof paper thereby preventing the jam from escaping any further !!] I travelled from Putney Bridge to Shepherd's Bush on a number 220 London Transport 'bus and excitedly arrived at Television Centre for my first morning of being an employee of BBC Television. I had with me an instruction from the BBC that, on arrival at Television Centre, I was to proceed to a Mr Sutton's Office within the Properties [Props] Department. Having enquired at Reception as to where the Props Department was, and clutching my sandwiches-containing tin box, I, in compliance with the directions given to me at Reception, found my way to a large area in which Scenery of all shapes and sizes was being built and then to another large area in which nothing particular seemed to be happening. Having passed through those two areas I then passed through a doorway to some stairs. Having gone up the stairs I found myself in the Props Department only to discover that Mr Sutton occupied not an Office as such but an area within a room that was stuffed full of Props. After very shyly introducing myself to someone I was then introduced to Mr Sutton and thereafter taken to a row of chairs and told by Mr Sutton that there were to be eleven persons starting work that morning, ten of whom were to remain upstairs within the Props Department itself and one of whom was to work downstairs within an area called 'Movement Control'. As yet, Mr Sutton informed me, he had not been told which of the eleven of us was to be a 'Movement Controller'. So, we eleven all sat there that morning until almost eleven o'clock when Bob Sutton came across to us and announced that it was I who was to go downstairs to be a Movement Controller. So, back to the stairs and down them I went, then across the area, where nothing particular seemed to be happening, to a set of double-doors beyond which, Bob Sutton had told me, was Movement Control.

Before I had left the flat that 1962 morning my Mother had given me firm instructions amongst which were "Always act politely", "Don't forget to mention that you've been to Public School", and "Always speak 'properly' so that they know that you've been to Public School". Thus, when I arrived at the double-doors I knocked 'politely' upon them, and received no response whatsoever. So I knocked politely again and still received no response. Thus I again knocked politely and again I received no response. Then suddenly I heard a loud voice from a white apron-clad man passing behind me telling me to "Open the bloody thing and just walk in". So, "open the 'bloody thing" and walk in is what I did; and there to my right, sitting at two desks pushed to-gether, was one man with two others standing behind him. I stopped just inside the door and, loudishly, said "Er, my name's Edwin Sutherland Loveday".

"Can't hear you," the voice of one of those standing boomed back.

"My name's Edwin Sutherland Loveday," I, more loudly, repeated.

"So what ?" replied the booming voice.

"Mr Sutton's sent me here," I responded.

"Ah," said one of the men standing behind the person sitting at the desks, "you're the guy whose starting this morning, are you?"

"Yes," I replied.

"Well, come over here and we'll introduce ourselves to you and tell you what the job's all about," he said.

So, over to the desks I went.

"I'm Ken Monk," said the man sitting at the desks, "and I'm in charge of this .. er .. operation". "This," he continued as he introduced me to the other two," is Tom Metcalfe and this is Mac MacAulay".

"What did you say your name is ?" asked Tom Metcalfe.

"Edwin Sutherland Loveday," I replied.

"Edwin !" he said. "Edwin ! Christ, you must have a better name than that. We can't bloody call you 'Edwin' "

When I had been at Haileybury Senior School, immediately following my Father's death but not realising the manoeuvrings that were going on against me insofar as Brunskill and Loveday Limited was concerned, I had decided that I would be wrong of me to, within the Theatrical Profession, 'trade' on my Father's name and that I should therefore create an 'identity' of my own. Despite my Father's first name being 'Edwin' he was always known as 'Ted Loveday' and thus I determined to remain 'Edwin'. But 'Edwin Loveday' was still similar to 'Ted Loveday' and so I had introduced, without a hyphen, my second name of 'Sutherland' into my surname. I had, whilst at Haileybury, explained my decision to CPC Smith, the Master, who informed me that I was legally entitled to do what I wished to do and that, if that was what I wished, I would henceforth be known as 'Edwin Sutherland Loveday' not as 'Edwin S Loveday'. But my arrival in Movement Control that morning seemed to blow that intention, at least insofar as BBC Television was concerned, completely out the window for, Tom Metcalf's having bluntly told me that 'Edwin' was not on, I immediately informed Tom and the others to call me 'Ted'; and then, when Tom went on to make further, one might say, not very polite comments about 'Sutherland Loveday', I immediately dropped the 'Sutherland' and became, as my Father before me had been, 'Ted Loveday'.

Whilst Tom and Mac went about their work Ken Monk explained to me what Movement Control was all about. "We're responsible," he informed me, "for the movement of all BBC Television Props, including Hired Props, throughout the London Area.

"Here in Television Centre are thousands of Props that belong to the Corporation [as the BBC is referred to within the BBC] that are used in the Centre [as Television Centre is known within the BBC], in Lime Grove [the BBC's then Lime Grove Studios], in Alexandra Palace, in Ealing Film Studios, in all sorts of places in London.

"The Grove [as the Lime Grove Studios were more often than not called within the BBC], initially at least, temporarily houses the Props that the Corporation hires in," he went on.

"Stuff that's hired in, we bring into the Grove, check 'em out, then move 'em around to wherever they're wanted: Here in the Centre, Ealing, some Rehearsal Hall or Drill Hall somewhere. You name it.

"Them cages over there," he said, pointing to several large wheeled cages stuffed with all sorts of items," are there ready to go into the Studios here in the Centre. It's not actually our job in Movement Control to move them in and out of the Studios. That's up to them upstairs," he said indicating towards Bob Sutton's 'Office'. "But we do help. In fact, we all muck-in together here.

"Them over there," he said pointing to some smallish yellow-coloured vehicles," is 'Teddy Trucks'. You, being a 'Ted', should be alright with them," he said with a smile. "Props and us use 'em for towing those cages and so on around. Otherwise you'd kill your bloody self trying to move some of 'em cages without the Teddy Trucks.

Ken, very polite and quietly spoken most of the time, was an entertainment in himself as he explained to me some of the ins and outs of being a Movement Controller.

"Now then," he said as he went on with his explanations, "we've got a 7-tonner going down to Ealing 'cos we've got '*Carmen*' in one of the Studios down there and they need some stuff for it. So, you go with Mac here in the van down to Ealing and you'll soon get the hang of it. But first park your tin can in that row of metal cupboards. There's a free one, that's yours. Then, with Mac, find Norman Bushell, and off the three of you go down to Ealing."

"The tin can's got my sandwiches in it," I said.

"I thought so," he said, "but you won't be needing them 'cos when you get to Ealing, whilst they're offloading the stuff for 'Carmen' you'll probably go into the Canteen for half-hour or so. Mac'll show you."

So, with my tin can safely stowed in the tall upright metal cupboard allocated to me, off Mac and I went to find Norman and his 7-ton van. My first day as a BBC Employee had really started.

Mac and I sat in the front passenger seat as Norman Bushell expertly drove his partly laden van out of the rear gates of Television Centre and into the adjoining road, then into Wood Lane, then down to and round the one-way system of Shepherd's Bush Green, and thence on to Ealing and into its world-famous, by then BBC-owned, Film Studios. Once in the Film Studios' complex Norman parked his van outside the large open doors of one of the Studios, climbed out, and, whilst others came to offload the van, the three of us walked over to the Canteen to enjoy not only some of its offerings but also the company of several, some well-known, Actors and Actresses. Everybody, it seemed, was, regardless of who or what they were, a friend of everybody : And this was work ? Wonderful !!

Our session at the Canteen over, Norman, Mac, and I wandered back to the van and, it having been decided that we had plenty of time to spare before we had to start the journey back to Television Centre, we went into, via a small side door, the Film Studio where 'Carmen' was being recorded. Over the years prior to my joining BBC Television I had seen the insides, and backstages, of many a Theatre but I had never been inside a Film Studio before; and thus for me it was a completely new, and very exciting, experience. Not unlike a Television Studio, a Film Studio often had at least two very large, very heavy, and well soundproofed doors by which large pieces of

Scenery and other items could be taken in and taken out of the Studio. Of necessity, these soundproofed doors were usually kept shut whilst filming was being undertaken thereby preventing outside noise and air from coming in thus causing the air within the Studio not only to become stale but also - in part because of the very large amount of heat given off by the often considerable quantity of necessary lighting used within the Studio - to become hotter and hotter and hotter. To some extent some of the increasing temperature within the 'Carmen' Studio was offset by means of large extractor fans and internal ducting equipment built into the Studio . But even with the large fans and ducting equipment, the temperature within the 'Carmen' Studio slowly got hotter and hotter and hotter. Perhaps this would have been okay had it not been for the fact that that particular day what were being filmed were horses, with their costumed riders, going round and round within a Set designed to resemble a genuine Spanish Bullring. "Never work with animals" is an old Theatrical maxim, for, with exceptions, animals rarely do what is required of them. Thus time and again everything had to stop so that the animals and their riders could be re-positioned in the hope that 'this time' everything would go according to plan. Unlike humans, horses have a habit of doing their businesses whenever the urge takes them regardless of where they happen to be, which, in itself, was, on this my first experience within a Film Studio, an often repeated occurrence. Thus many a time the filming had to stop, and the whole undertaking re-started, simply because the delivery by a horse of its business had been, unacceptably, caught on film : And whenever dollops of horse business landed on the sawdust-strewn Studio floor someone, armed with a shovel and stiff broom, would have to rush in to remove it to join its fellow dollops sited in a nearby increasingly large heap. Therefore as the Studio got hotter and hotter so the stench of horse manure got stronger and stronger. But those making 'Carmen' had schedules and financial budgets that had to be adhered to; and so the start-stop-start-stop-start filming had to roll on and on, and the very large, very heavy, and well soundproofed doors had to remain shut. We three were fortunate in that we had to return to Television Centre and thus we could and, unlike everyone else in that Studio that afternoon, did leave that increasingly manure-smelling hothouse well before the Director decided that he had got his 'shots' and that the large heavy doors could be opened to allow fresh air in and the stench out.

Other visits to Ealing were equally fascinating. For instance, one Studio had built within its floor a small swimming-pool known as a 'tank' used to film such scenes as men drowning and, using models, warships engaged in battles.

Dixon of Dock Green, the BBC's 'spin-off' TV series from the 1951/52 Stage Show *The Blue Lamp* was also, in part, filmed in Ealing Film Studios. The bulk of the Series was undertaken within Television Studios, but at the beginning and at the end of each episode Sergeant Dixon, played by my Father's old friend Jack Warner, would have a little 'chat' to the Public : And it was these little 'chats' which were filmed at Ealing and subsequently 'slotted' into the pertinent episodes when transmitted. The Set was always the same, a small flight of steps leading to the entrance to 'Dock Green' Police Station atop of which was sited a blue lamp. Six or so "Evenin' all" introductions were shot, one after the other with a pause of some minutes between each, one per episode. Out from the doorway would come Sergeant Dixon to deliver his "Evenin' all" speech to, what would be, the viewing Public. Then, the Director having satisfied himself that Jack had delivered his speech to perfection, back Jack would go only to come out again some minutes later to deliver another

"Evenin' all" speech for the next episode. Then back again and out again until all six or so "Evenin' all" speeches had been satisfactorily undertaken and recorded. Then, after a rest and something to eat, Jack would return to his position on the Set in order to go through the whole ritual again but this time to record six or so closing speeches each of which would be slotted in to end its pertinent episode. The whole thing within Ealing was undertaken on a sausage-machine basis and was so professionally undertaken and edited that I doubt whether any member of the viewing Public ever realised that each introduction and each closing speech had been recorded entirely separately from the rest of the transmissions.

We returned from Ealing Studios first via a café on Ealing Common, where we each had a cup of tea and a slice of something, and then sometimes via a firm called 'Greenery of Hampton' from which the Corporation hired all sorts of real but no longer growing vegetation, such as trees and bushes, so that they could be used to 'furnish' a set within a Studio to help fool the viewing public into believing that what they were viewing was real growing vegetation : And at the end of the hire, unless the stuff was in a state of total collapse, we in Movement Control had the responsibility of returning the hire by taking the stuff all the way back to 'Greenery of Hampton'. Methinks that 'Greenery of Hampton' must have done well out of the BBC !!

One had to be a quick learner in Movement Control as each of us four was an equal in responsibility and so on except that Ken, because he was in charge, was a wee bit more equal than us other three. Our day in Movement Control would always start at the two wooden desks. Thereafter one of us - usually Ken, a man somewhat older than each of the other three of us - would stay manning the desks and its two telephones whilst the other three of us would be delegated, or would delegate ourselves, elsewhere. Often the first port of call for at least two of us would be to Lime Grove Studios to return Hired Props, to collect Hired Props, or to undertake a mixture of both return and collection. Whatever the task(s), the first 'real' task at The Grove, after our Driver had very carefully reversed his van down a narrow steep slope which went from the public highway to under the building, was to go and enjoy a good wholesome breakfast within The Grove's, usually well occupied by other BBC employees, Canteen - For, it was said by some of us, only when 'fired up' with a good BBC breakfast could work really get under way !!

Hired arms, and occasionally ammunition, were items which sometimes came into Lime Grove. After I had been at Movement Control for a few weeks I was asked by my three colleagues if I would like the 'honour' of being appointed the Movement Controller in charge of, and responsible for, Arms and Ammunition; and, naïve that I was, I said that I would. The Corporation shortly thereafter hired in several somewhat ancient, but still functioning - albeit crudely - Arab rifles for use in a Programme being made in Television Centre. I, as the Movement Controller now in charge of Arms and Ammunition, was informed when they had arrived in Lime Grove and been installed in the Grove's secure room used for such purposes. I thus set about arranging for their collection from the Grove and transportation the short distance to Television Centre. I had also that day to arrange for a clock that had been repaired to be collected from Camerer Cuss, a shop on Shepherd's Bush Green, and delivered to the Centre. The combination of the two was a simple task but one which demanded concentration on security because of the temptation given by the Arab rifles - for Shepherd's Bush and its environs had a reputation of being one of those areas in London that housed many a member of the criminal fraternity. Thus I instructed that the van was to go from Television Centre directly to Shepherd's Bush Green where it was to go around the one-way system of Shepherd's Bush Green until it reached Camera Cuss. Taking with it its driver and five other men, instead of the usual two other men, the van was to stop immediately outside Camera Cuss, whose staff were to be advised of its arrival, whereon two of the men sitting alongside the driver in the front of the van would alight, collect the clock, take the clock to the rear of the rear, drop down the van's tailgate, and then, assisted by the other three men who were to be in the rear of the van, secure the clock in the back of van before getting back into the front of the van. The van, with its clock onboard, was then to drive around the rest of the one-way system of Shepherd's Bush Green in order to turn off to go directly to Lime Grove. At Lime Grove the van was to reverse down the slope into the Props area beneath the building whereupon the secure room was to be opened and the rifles transferred immediately and directly into the van which, with all its crew on board, would then come directly back to me at Television Centre where the rifles would be counted off and checked into a secure unit. Easy !!

So, its driver and the other five men having had everything explained to them in some detail, the van set off to go the short distance to Shepherd's Bush Green whereupon the van entered the one-way system. However, having done the journey to Lime Grove on scores of occasions, the van's driver continued round the one-way system and 'automatically' turned off to go to the Grove. Shortly after making the turn the driver realised his mistake and consulted with his two colleagues in the cab as to what to do. The decision, based, apparently, on the fact that there were an extra three men on board, was taken to carry on to the Grove, collect the rifles, and then go to Camera Cuss to collect the clock. All went well at the Grove, and they therefore trundled on to Camera Cuss where the driver stopped the vehicle and stayed in his cab whilst his two front-seat colleagues got out to go into Camera Cuss where the Staff were expecting them. However, instead of going straight into Camera Cuss the two went to the back of the van and, in the knowledge that the rifles should be safe because there were three men guarding them, lowered the tailgate and thereafter went into Camera Cuss. Due to a hitch within Camera Cuss there was a delay causing the, by now somewhat bored, three men in the back of the van to be tempted out of the van to find out what was happening. When the five men returned, two of them carrying the clock, to the van they discovered not one rifle left inside the van. The whole lot had gone, completely gone, and not one of the many scores people passing by on Shepherd's Bush Green had, apparently, seen a thing !! It was when the Police telephoned me at Television Centre that I began to realise why it was that my three, much more experienced and wiser than I, colleagues in Movement Control had so kindly appointed me as the Movement Controller in charge of Arms and Ammunition !!

Another unfortunate incident involving a lorry under the 'command' of Movement Control also fell to me to have to suffer. The vehicles belonging to the Corporation that we in Movement Control used had to be obtained from a pool of Corporation vehicles. Usually we used the same 7-tonners but occasionally we operated in conjunction with 'Scenery' in which event we used larger, articulated lorries. Either, as was more usual, 'Scenery' obtained the artic from the Corporation's pool and made space in the lorry for our stuff or we obtained the artic and made space in it for 'Scenery' to put their stuff in. On this occasion we had obtained the artic; and, once its loading had been completed by both us and 'Scenery', off it and its Driver and two other persons went to Television Theatre, formerly The

Shepherd's Bush Empire Variety Theatre. The run - out of Television Centre, into and down Wood Lane, turn left into the traffic-laden one-way system on Shepherd's Bush Green, and then three-quarters of the way round the one-way system to the 'Theatre' - took only a few minutes and was a fairly regular run. Sitting by myself at the desks in Movement Control some three-quarters of an hour or so after the artic had left the Centre I received a telephone-call from the Police. "Are you in charge of a wagon that's trying to reverse into your Theatre ?" I was asked.

"Yes," I replied.

"Well, your Driver's holding up all the traffic in London," the firm, not-too-happy voice at the other end of the 'phone went on. "Kindly do something about it … *Now !!* "

I was puzzled for the Driver that day was well experienced in taking loads from Television Centre to Television Theatre where, having pulled over to the far side of the road outside the Theatre, he would put the vehicle into reverse and, with the guiding assistance of his colleagues, negotiate the vehicle in an arc backwards across the road and pavement in front of The Theatre so as to enter and drive up the short narrow private roadway to the Theatre's Scenery doorway through which the contents of the artic's trailer could be offloaded. In those days there were no separate Heavy Goods Vehicle Licences; and so anyone legally entitled to drive a 7-ton wagon was also legally entitled to drive the much larger articulated wagons. What I had not realised, because no one had told me, was that the Driver had never driven an artic before and had little or no real idea of the difference between the techniques required in reversing (a) a fixed-body vehicle and (b) a two-part vehicle consisting of a driving/tractor unit and a separate, save for its pivotal connection, trailer unit. Apparently he tried and tried on several occasions but on each occasion had gone in every direction other than the correct one. Traffic fed into the one-way system at Shepherd's Bush from several major roads, including one which originates from London's Oxford Street [which in those days was open to all sorts of traffic flowing in both directions] and beyond. Thus the entirety of West London's road system as far back as the Bayswater Road - if not to Marble Arch, Oxford Street, the Edgware Road, and Park Lane - was being adversely effected as our increasingly panic-stricken Driver made desperate attempts to achieve his aim of getting his vehicle up to the Empire's Scenery doorway. Suddenly, apparently, he 'flipped' and just sat there, rigid, within his cab in which, for some reason known only to himself, he had locked himself in. At times like these, especially when the flow of traffic in West London is grinding to a halt, exceptional skills are required : And I certainly did not have them. The best that I could do was contact the Office within the Corporation which dealt with Movement Control's requests for vehicles, explain the situation, and pass the buck. So, pass the buck I did; and a replacement driver, with spare key, was hastily dispatched to resolve the problem.

I can not now recall where my Movement Controller colleague Tom Metcalf lived - locally in Shepherd's Bush, I think - but my immediate boss Ken Monk lived close to Denham Film Studios and Mac MacAulay lived across London in Tottenham. I had the pleasure and enjoyment of one day being invited, with others, by Ken to his home for a most enjoyable meal and I likewise had the pleasure and enjoyment of eating a meal with Mac and his Wife in their home in Tottenham, although the pleasure and enjoyment were somewhat diminished by an incident that occurred on the way there. A keen and very experienced motorcyclist, Mac travelled to and from work across London everyday on his motorbike; and that therefore was the means of transport offered to me for my journey with him to Tottenham from Television Centre and then from Tottenham to the flat in Putney. Although I had spent many, many hours riding pedal bikes, I had never ridden on a motorbike before. Mac's response was that it was easy and that all I had to do was sit on the seat behind him, hold on to him, and lean as he leant. So, off from Television Centre at the end of the working day and through London's rush-hour we went. I soon discovered that it was not as easy as he made out, but nevertheless we crossed London and reached Tottenham. With less than a quarter of a mile to go, and with London's rush-hour traffic seemingly all around us, he and his bike took a very sharp left-hand turn almost doubling back on whence we had come. He took the turn okay as did the bike, but I fell off and found myself sitting, surrounded by cars seemingly passing by in all directions, painfully upon the road's hard tarmac surface. Amidst several shouts of "Are you alright mate ?" and a couple of rounds of applause, I got up, climbed back on the bike, and on we went to Mac's house and his waiting Wife who, with Mac, entertained me to a splendid meal. However, I withdrew my acceptance of his kind offer to take me home to Putney and instead chose to use the London Underground.

One of Movement Control's regular trips insofar as hired Props was concerned was to The Old Times Furnishing Company - a well-known, within the Theatrical Profession, hirer of Props to anyone and any organisation that wanted to hire Props. I had known of it by name for some years but since my move to Putney I had known it by sight also for not only was it situated in Lower Richmond Road not far from Kenilworth Court but also it was, during weekdays and Saturdays mornings, such a hive of activity that anyone passing by could not help but notice the vehicular activity going on outside it for - with no single Yellow Lines, double Yellow Lines, Parking Meters or other form of so-called traffic management in existence in those days - parking outside and nearby was no problem. Two or three times each week we in Movement Control would despatch a lorry, its Driver, and a Crew to, via Lime Grove, OTP [Old Times, Putney] to return previously hired items and collect more hired items. If we did not have much to return and collect it would be a simple matter of parking the lorry as near as was possible, without causing obstruction, to OTP's vehicular entrance and just walking to and fro to return items and collect the items that had already been assembled for us : But if a considerable amount of Props was involved our Driver would, as soon as space was free, reverse our vehicle through the vehicular entrance and into the yard beyond so that the offloading and loading could be undertaken. OTP had, within its then modernish several-floored building, thousands of Props not only of all shapes and sizes but also of almost every kind imaginable. The Highway Authority's adjoining pavement was, during OTP's working hours, used by OTP as a kind of overspill area which often caused much interest amongst passers-by and, moreso, amongst local children who often seemed to be genuinely very fascinated by the place moreso whenever a vehicle with the name and/or logo of a television programming or film making undertaking on it drew up. "Can I 'elp, Mister ?" some of the children would ask as we carried something or other out of the van and into OTP or vice versa.. With the BBC at the time making and transmitting such Programmes as *Dr Who ?*, *Z Cars*, and *Top of the Pops* there were always the inevitable enquiries of us such as "Is that for *Dr Who ?* ?"; and the likely response of course being "Yes" even if the item or items concerned were going nowhere near *Dr Who ?* !!

An old school friend from my days at Haileybury Senior School, Tony Temple, somehow found out my telephone number and extension at Television Centre and, one Friday afternoon, telephoned me to invite me to luncheon at his, and his Parents', home near Stanstead (When I edited the Laurentian Tony was my Sports Reporter). Knowing that Tony's Father was an eminent Barrister [as, indeed, both Tony and his Brother, Victor, subsequently became], I dressed smartly for the occasion and, having, with her permission, borrowed my Mother's Austin A40 car, I drove from Putney towards Stanstead. Realising, as I neared Tony's home, that I was somewhat early, I decided to pull the car off the road in order to rest up a while so that I would arrive at Tony's home more or less at the stated time. Thus, seeing a flattish grassy area to my left, I pulled the car off the road only to have its nearside front go down into a slightly water-filled deepish ditch the existence of which had been completely hidden by the long grass. It was a Sunday which, in those days, was a day when most people either went to church or stayed at home; and therefore, with nobody around and with nothing for it but to try to physically lift the front of the car out of the ditch, I got out of the car, stepped down into the ditch, got hold of the front of the car, and, slowly, very slowly managed to lift and manoeuvre the car so as to get its front nearside wheel back onto a hard surface. Thereafter, having returned to the car - my feet and shoes soaking wet and mud ridden, my trousers looking a sorry messy sight, and my hands and lower arms covered here and there with dirt and oil - I continued my journey on to Tony's Parents' house : And a most attractive serene house it was.

I rang the front door bell and waited. I rang it again and waited. I rang it again and this time I heard, in the distance, the sound of shoes coming in my direction. The door was opened and a pleasant, Canadian-sounding voice enquired "Yes ?"

"My name's Edwin Loveday, and I've come for lunch," I replied in my best English Public School accent.

"But you were expected yesterday," said Tony's Mother.

"To-day," I responded.

"No, yesterday," she emphatically replied before going on to say "I don't think that we have anything other than cornflakes that we can offer you."

I could not believe it for not only had I not driven all the way from Putney just for a bowl of cornflakes but also this was a household whose head was one of the most eminent lawyers in the land whose earnings must therefore surely be more than sufficient to enable much more than just cornflakes to be offered. However, I was invited in, made very welcome, enabled to clean myself up, and in fact entertained to much more than just cornflakes. After the meal I was invited by Tony's Father to plant a newly-purchased tree within their splendid garden; and I left that evening a very contented person having agreed with Tony that, if ever I got married, he would be my Best Man. I also stated that I would arrange that at my Wedding Reception my Mother-in-law, whoever she might be, would ensure that he got more than just a bowl of cornflakes offered to him !!

My qualification to obtain the Driver's Licence that enabled me to drive to Tony Temple's had not been achieved without a noticeable series of experiences. I had first driven a car during the last months of my Father's life. He had adopted a policy of, on Friday nights during my School Holidays, parking his car in front of its garage when he arrived home. Then he would open the garage doors and I would, with him sitting by my side telling me what to do and when to do it, drive the car into the garage and park it. But, after his death, I had to wait until I was of the legal age for driving a car before I would again get behind a steering-wheel; and by that time my brain had all but forgotten my humble experiences as a driver of my Father's car into its garage. Thus, in the first School Holiday after I had reached the age of 17, it was off to the British School of Motoring [BSM] in Putney for twelve 1-hour lessons.

The first lesson was taken up with my being introduced to driving and then, in a BSM dual-controlled car, lurching around the roads and streets of Putney. The second lesson was much more adventurous. Over Putney Bridge we went. Then along Fulham Palace Road to the Kings Road in Fulham. Then along into the Kings Road in Chelsea. Then through Sloane Square where, a short distance off of Sloane Square, we did a three-point turn so that we could head back from whence we had come. By now London's 'rush-hour' was beginning to loom and the volume of traffic was thus noticeably increasing. Given that my Mother at the time still had her Morris Minor car and that it would therefore be that vehicle in which I would take my Driving Test, the BSM Instructor and I were in a Morris Minor owned by the BSM, the only noticeable practical difference between the two vehicles being that the BSM's Morris Minor had a dual set of foot controls whereas my Mother's only had the conventional single set of foot controls. Insofar as the public highway is concerned Sloane Square is in fact a sort of elongated roundabout; and where we re-entered Sloane Square there were two lanes of traffic the contents of each wishing to move as fast as possible into and round the roundabout. As we travelled into Sloane Square the Morris Minor was in the nearside lane and, needless to say, as we reached the head of our queue of traffic as it entered the roundabout, I, like most learners do in the early stages of their careers as learners, unintentionally stalled the car. This enabled a whole phalanx of vehicles in the outside lane to pass by and enter the roundabout whilst causing all behind me in my lane to have to wait whilst I sat there fumbling in my attempts to get my vehicle going again. Then, suddenly, all was well, and slowly I engaged first gear and very slowly off we started to crawl. Then, lo and behold, a long articulated flat-truck lorry came alongside me and, without stopping, charged into the flow of traffic that was going round the roundabout. As the artic's cab swung to the left I panicked and slammed on the Morris Minor's brakes. Then, immediately to my right, I noticed the rear wheels of the artic's trailer passing alongside me and the trailer's flat-truck body beginning to pass over the front of the curved bonnet of the Morris Minor. The only comment that issued from my Instructor, as the two of us sat there wondering what was going to happen next, was "If you can get out of this you can get out of anything !!" Well, I did get out of it. I do not know how, but I did.

Following my twelfth lesson I went, with my Mother in her Morris Minor, to the Test Centre in Wimbledon and failed my Test. The reasons given were; [1] Failing to pay proper attention at a junction, [2] Failing to use my vehicle's internal mirror often enough, and [3] Failing to give enough hand-signals. I had three further lessons with the BSM and undertook a considerable amount of driving within my Mother's Morris Minor with my Mother sitting alongside me as my accompanying qualified driver. However, given that she was neither enthusiastic about driving nor good at driving, perhaps being accompanied by my Mother instead of by someone else was not the best of ideas - But it was her car, and I thus had no choice.

I took my second Test at Wimbledon after a lapse of over twelve weeks, the lapse being due to my having had to return to School. Again I failed and for the same three reasons as on the previous occasion. This time I was made aware of which junction within Wimbledon I had failed to pay proper attention to. It was the junction on the Broadway opposite the Station where a Pedestrian 'Zebra' Crossing was sited. Thus one had the options, when entering the main road, of [1] stopping before the Pedestrian Crossing, in which case one did not have a sufficient enough view of traffic flowing along the main road, [2] stopping on the Crossing, which was illegal, or [3] driving over the Crossing, thus causing one's vehicle to project out into the main road. The Crossing is now no longer; but I never did, even after having gained many years' experience as a qualified Driver, solve the riddle of which, if any, of the options to choose.

I decided that I would take my next Test not in Wimbledon but in Twickenham. Having thus gotten rid of the problem of failing to pay proper attention at a junction I was left with having to solve the problems of failing to use my vehicle's internal mirror often enough and failing to give enough hand-signals. To my mind I had always made considerable use of my vehicle's interior mirror, but I realised after my second failure that, whereas I have a wide range of vision and can easily look into my mirror without moving my head, the Examiner would not be aware of my using the mirror unless I made it obvious to him/her that I was. So I determined to emphasise my use of the mirror by means of making large ostentatious moves of my head. Nowadays formal hand-signals as then defined within the Highway Code are almost a long forgotten art form, which is regrettable as hand-signals are useful both in certain everyday driving occurrences and on rare occasions when the vehicle's own indications, for whatever reason, are not working. But in those days hand-signals were compulsory and I had to accept that, although I thought that I was giving enough hand-signals, two Test results had stated that I was not. So I determined that I must upgrade the frequency at which I gave hand-signals.

As my Mother and I parted at the entrance to the Test Centre I went in leaving her to go to a nearby café for a cup of coffee. As before on my Tests I did what I was told to do but this time I made large ostentatious moves of my head every time that I looked into the mirror and I made hand-signals on every occasion that I found an excuse to make hand-signals. I was determined to pass *this* Test - I had to. When we got back to the Test Centre the Examiner told me to switch off the engine, which I did. Then he sat back, drew a deep breath in through his nose, and then exhaled loudly out of his mouth. "Oh, God. Here we go again," I thought. "I've failed again." After what seemed to be a very, very long pause he said "Mr Sutherland Loveday. I have a good mind to fail you". My heart sank.

"Why ?" I asked in bewilderment.

"You've given a hand-signal for every *bloody* thing you've done," he replied and then, with a grin, added. "But you've passed". What a relief !!

After the necessary paperwork was completed I went to the café where I proudly, and with much relief, told my Mother that I had passed the Test. "About ten minutes ago … I know," she said, "I choked on my coffee about ten minutes ago and it went all over the place. What a mess it made." From the café, my Mother's Morris Minor now without its front and back 'L' [Learner Driver] plates tied onto it and with me driving, we returned to Putney; and thereafter whenever I have driven I have always done so with a comment in mind made several times to me by my Father in the days when I used to park his car in its garage "Always think of everyone else on the road as being an idiot".

In the February of 1962, after I had been asked by Eric Maschwitz to join BBC Television but before I had received any communication back from the BBC's Appointments Department in response to my Job Application, my Mother suggested to me, in hopeful anticipation that I would pass my third Driving Test, that we go on a two-week driving holiday, my Mother and I to share the driving, down to Gibraltar and back, a total distance of 3,000 miles [4700 kilometres] or thereabouts; and a journey which to-day could take less than 48 hours to complete : But such was not the situation in 1962 when, at the beginning of March, and assisted by sheets of typed-out route directions and information helpfully provided, collated, and bound to-gether in bundles for us by the AA [Automobile Association], and with my Mother having told me only hours before we left Putney that Doctor Laird had advised her not to drive, we departed for Gibraltar. [Doctor Laird, a Scotsman, was not my Mother's Doctor but a near neighbour in Kenilworth Court. Much respected within the East London hospital in which he worked, Doctor Laird was highly thought-of generally. Married to a Welsh woman who, prior to marrying Doctor Laird, had been a nurse, he and his Wife had three Children each of whom was of a similar age to myself.] I was in fact relieved by my Mother's decision not to drive because she was certainly not a good driver, a fact that had made itself very apparent when one day when I was sixteen years of age we went for a drive in the car to Chessington Zoo [now part of Chessington World of Adventures]. Nearing the Zoo she drove the car into a roundabout intending to drive three-quarters of the way round it before exiting out of it. Going completely round the roundabout first once then twice was amusing. Going round it a third time was a wee bit embarrassing.

Going round it a fourth time was a bit unnerving. It became very unnerving when, as we began the fifth journey round the roundabout, she stated that she did not like roundabouts and, as she did not know the road, could not pluck up the courage to make a left turn to get out of this one. Eventually she did manoeuvre the car out of the roundabout and we did arrive at Chessington Zoo : But God only knows what would have happened had she been tasked with having to 'drive the wrong way round' a roundabout in Continental Europe, something which, when previously driving abroad, she doubtless had, although I was unaware of it, always left to my Father.

My Mother, shortly after I had passed my Test, sold her beloved Morris Minor and bought, in its stead, a brand new Austin A40 car, 896 XPK. In general cars nowadays are very reliable, roads throughout much of mainland Europe are more often than not very good if not sometimes excellent, breakdown assistance is usually readily available anywhere within a short period of time, petrol and diesel are usually frequently to hand, each country on the journey is nowadays a democracy within the European Union, and most people throughout Europe speak, or at least understand, English. But such were not the situations in 1962 when in general cars were unreliable and prone to breaking down, roads were often bad if not appallingly bad by to-day's standards and sometimes even almost non-existent, breakdown assistance outside of the UK was often almost unheard of, petrol and diesel could be hunted for for hours before being found, Spain was under the harsh dictatorship of Generalísimo Francisco Paulino Hermenegildo Teódulo Franco and Portugal under the harsh dictatorial Prime Ministership of Dr António de Oliveira Salazar, the two Dictators causing many citizens of each country to often live in considerable fear; and rarely outside of northern France could a citizen be easily found who could speak English let alone understand it.

Having crossed the English Channel and thereafter arrived in and passed through Calais we drove most days sometimes spending our nights in small hotels, sometimes spending our nights being put up in private homes, sometimes spending our nights trying to sleep in our very cramped little A40 car, and sometimes spending our nights, or chunks of them, just driving from one destination to another. As we had only a fortnight to get to Gibraltar and back to London we had little opportunity to park up and walk round towns and other places of interest : But - with main roads then not by-passing but passing through city and town centres, with the numbers of vehicles on the roads being then far less than the numbers that are on the roads to-day, with the entireties of city and town centres being easily accessible to vehicles, and with there being almost no restrictions on where and for how long one could park one's car - we managed to see and enjoy, at least the outsides of, many more buildings than would be the case to-day. As we went - via Rouen, Le Mans, Tours, Poitiers, Bordeaux, and Bayonne - south through France, my Mother adamantly doing no driving whatsoever "because Doctor Laird told me that I mustn't", the conditions of the roads got steadily worse as did the hospitality, although never at any time hostile, of the French. But when we exited the Basque area of France and then entered the Basque area of Spain the contrast in attitudes towards us was very noticeable and we found the Basque people of San Sebastian and surrounding areas within Spain to be wonderfully friendly, very welcoming, and very hospitable towards us. Relying, as we did throughout the entirety of our 2-week journey, on the route directions and information provided to us by the AA, having passed through Bilbao and Santander we arrived one dark night at around 8pm in the midst of a medium-sized village which seemed to have only one building with a light on. By now we had realised that Spain, or at least some parts of it, was under curfew; and so to that building we went in the hope of finding someone able to speak some English who could point us in the direction of a hotel, or at least somewhere with beds, where we could stay the night. We opened the door to the building to find, to our considerable surprise, what seemed like the entire population inside not only watching television but watching an episode of the US series 'Bonanza' which, at the time, was a very popular television programme back home in the UK. The trouble was that - whilst we easily recognised Hoss, Ben Cartwright, and all the other Bonanza characters - the whole thing had been dubbed in Spanish and we had not a clue what they were talking about. Not that that mattered for within seconds we were surrounded by the room's occupants curious as to who we were and, once they had worked out that we were travellers from the UK, eagerly wanting to assist us : And we were certainly in luck that night for not only was this the village's Inn but also it had, although very basic, comfortable bedrooms in which we could stay the night. Nobody spoke English but that did not stop them from, without being asked, bringing each of us drinks and, in long crispy roll-type unbuttered loaves, the biggest and juiciest steaks that I had ever seen. They were superb as was the cheerful hospitality given to us, complete strangers, that night. We left next morning very impressed indeed; and, having subsequently journeyed on and stopped in Coruña and many other places besides, we arrived, just after 9pm next night at the Spanish-Portuguese Border. Although it was late and everything, bar the Spanish and Portuguese Customs posts, in complete darkness, we were in good time, or so we thought, because, the AA's information told us, the Portuguese Customs post, like its Spanish counterpart, did not close until 10pm. After being processed through the Spanish Customs we drove out into No Man's Land and, having crossed No Man's Land, arrived at the Portuguese Customs post only to find it, although lit up, completely closed and uninhabited - For, whereas the Spanish Customs post stayed manned and open until 10pm, those manning the Portuguese Customs post had decided to leave their post at 9pm causing my Mother and me to be stranded within No Man's Land. Thus we had no options but either to stay in No Man's Land until the Portuguese Customs post opened in the morning or to go back to the Spanish Customs post and ask to be allowed back into Spain. Feeling slightly annoyed that the Officers at the Spanish Customs post had not warned us that we could not enter Portugal because Portugal had, in effect, closed at 9pm, we nevertheless opted to return to the Spanish Customs post and ask to be allowed back into Spain. With expressions of amused self-satisfaction that Government Officials seem sometimes to have, the Spanish Customs Officers allowed us back into Spain; and, having gotten back into Spain and with my now feeling wide awake, we drove twenty miles or so back up the road from whence we had come until eventually I pulled the car off the road so that we could first have something to eat and then find a couple of convenient places in which to undertake necessary functions before returning to our little car to sleep. Sometime around 2am, the two of us by now having been asleep only for a little while, I was suddenly and violently awoken by a rifle, that had been thrust through my open window, being prodded against me. There, outside the car, were two members of Generalísimo Franco's Police demanding, first in Spanish and then, with difficulty, in broken English, to know what we were doing and why we were there at a time well past curfew. With my Mother and I filled with the belief that we were about to be, perhaps, shot and that this therefore might be the end for both of us, I eventually managed to explain what had happened and why we were there. The whole incident, fortunately, ended with a laugh and the two Policemen giving us, by means mainly of gesticulating arms, their best wishes for a safe journey. So, eventually, we fell asleep again, but as soon as the Spanish Customs post re-opened we were there, re-processed, and, regardless of whether or not the Portuguese Customs post had yet opened that day, back in No Man's Land and very eager to get out of it and into Portugal.

Once across No Man's Land we found, to our relief, the Portuguese Customs post to be now open for business; and so, having been processed by its Customs Officials, it was into Portugal and on towards the city of Porto. Throughout our journey through Spain and whilst journeying from the Spanish/Portuguese Border towards Porto three things about the roads were very noticeable: The first was that they were often, by UK standards, very bad and sometimes almost non-existent; the second was that every now and then there were mounds of small stones sited on each side of them; and the third was that every so often a man could be seen either on the road itself or alongside the road either sweeping it or else putting a shovel into or pulling a shovel out of it. Our having passed through Porto the same three happenings continued: The roads were often very bad or almost non-existent, mounds of stones were now and then to be seen, as was a man either with a broom or a shovel. The conditions of the roads were self-explanatory but the mounds of stones and the men with their brooms and shovels remained a mystery until it was some time later explained to me that to each mile or so of road there was allocated a man whose responsibility it was to maintain his allocated length of road so as to keep the road passable, principally for animal-drawn traffic but also for mechanically-drawn traffic, and that the mounds of stones were regularly deposited to assist these men to do their jobs of filling in what we would probably call potholes.

Throughout our journey through Portugal we found every Portuguese person whom we encountered to be very polite, very courteous, and very pleasant - Nothing was too much trouble. In one particular, high-positioned and very windy, town we parked up intending to find somewhere to eat. The strength of the wind was almost beyond belief and, our having struggled against it to get out of the car, we found ourselves suddenly surrounded by men with ropes each rope tied at one end to a ring or other form of anchor-point fixed in the ground. Indicating to us what they were doing, they threw ropes over the car and secured the loose ends to other anchor-points thereby battening down our car in order to prevent it from being blown about. We offered monetary tips to these kindly souls but each and every one of them refused, as they did when the reverse process was undertaken when, after we had returned from our meal, we came to drive away. Wonderful people !!

As when in Spain we either stayed the night in various types of whatever accommodation we could find or we stayed the night in the car or I just kept on driving. But in Portugal we also made use of small Government-owned hotels one of which, when nearing the Capital city of Lisbon, we tried to find but could not. As we would have done had we been in the UK, we sought assistance from the Police and in so doing obtained the willing assistance of a Policeman sitting, seemingly very bored, at a desk in a somewhat small and boringly bare Police Office. Relieved, I think, to see someone, he explained to us not only the directions that we needed to get us to the hotel but also took it upon himself to telephone the hotel's Manager to inform him of our impending arrival so that rooms could be made ready for us.

As with Spain, Portugal, or at least parts of it, were under curfew; and our arrival at the Police Station had occurred noticeably after the start of curfew. Thus when we eventually got to the hotel we had neither passed anyone since we had left the Police Office nor was there anyone to be seen in the streets around the hotel. It was eerie, and when we arrived at the hotel the hotel's Manager was terrified, absolutely terrified for, whereas in the UK the Police were relatively harmless, in Portugal, unknown to us until we it had been subsequently explained to us by the English-speaking Manager, a telephone-call from the Police could engender, as it certainly had on this occasion, considerable fear in the recipient. After twenty minutes or so, his having met us and realised that we were two genuine travellers from the UK, the Manager, who by now had gotten a room and a meal ready for each of my Mother and me, relaxed and the experience of the terrifying telephone-call became something for him to smile, probably with relief, about.

Next morning, after a splendid breakfast, I went out to our A40 car to, as was the recommended practice in those days, change the wheels around so as to even the wear on each tyre. Just after I started one of the hotel's Waiters, unable to speak any English whatsoever, indicated to me that he would like to assist me; and so the two of us undertook and completed the task. I was very grateful to him and offered a tip, but he emphatically refused and, as he did so, drew away from me causing me to puzzle at his reaction to my genuine attempt to express my gratitude to him for the assistance that he had so kindly given to me. Chatting with the Manager just before my Mother and I departed to continue our journey on to Lisbon I mentioned the kind help given to me by his Waiter and the fact that his Waiter had not only refused my tip but also had seemed offended by my attempt to give him the tip. "But, Sir," said the Manager, "it was an honour for him to be allowed by you to even touch your car". I left that hotel with, and still retain, a feeling of considerable sadness for the way that these kind people were treated by their Prime Minister, Dr Salazar, and his Government.

Lisbon, with its superb but sometimes crumbling architecture, was a city well worth seeing but its poverty, often in evidence in the narrow streets through which we walked during the day that we stayed there, was yet more evidence of how 'held back' the ordinary Portuguese were by their dictatorial Government. Cheerful souls - stringing out their washing on lines that ran high across the streets from one building to another or sitting in doorways talking across the streets to each other or padding about from one building to another in shoes many of which should have been replaced many months before - were evident all over the place, but it seemed to me often to be a cheerfulness that disguised deep unhappiness and discontent.

Moving on from Lisbon we went on alongside the Atlantic Ocean down to the Mediterranean coast and thence through the Portuguse-Spanish Border back into Spain and, heading towards Seville, into a heat that, despite its being March, was almost unbearable. With the roads still being, in places, appalling, but by now being without any men to ensure at least some degree of road-worthiness, we took a left-hand forked turning which, a few miles later, I felt that we should perhaps not have taken. We thus looked out for someone from whom we could seek some guidance. But for miles and miles, as we drove on, we saw absolutely no-one, no-one at all until eventually, in the distance across a parched cropless field, I saw a man just standing there seemingly doing absolutely nothing whatsover. With there being little difference between the surface of the so-called road on which we were driving and the surface of the parched field in which he was standing, I turned the car off the road and drove it across the field to him. " Do … you … speak … English ?" I slowly asked him in the belief that, like nearly everyone else whom we had met, he would neither speak English nor understand it.

"Christ, I bloody ought to," he promptly replied "I cum frumpt Manchester."

Yes, we were on the correct road, this solitary British walking-holidaymaker told us : And so, after chatting with him for a while, we journeyed on, and on, and on until eventually we reached the outskirts of Seville.

The road by now was better than those which we had earlier driven on, and it was lined on both sides with citrus fruit-bearing trees. At one point to my left was a man reaching up to pick some fruit off one of the trees. On the other side of the road, some distance towards Seville from the intending fruit-picker, was a Policeman, his rifle slung over his shoulder. Seeing the man reaching up intending to pick the fruit, the rifle was quickly removed, aim was taken, and a shot fired over the man's head causing the man to, very quickly, cease doing what he was doing and run away. The Policeman put his rifle back on his shoulder and, perhaps having seen us UK citizens in our little car heading towards him, walked away from the man as if the incident had never taken place. I was horrified.

We stayed in the wonderful city of Seville for a couple of days during which time we sat in Seville's Bull Ring in some very well-positioned seats which enabled us to clearly see most of what went on within the Ring. I had, prior to leaving Putney, bought a second-hand Bell & Howell Sportster IV ciné-camera and with this I, a complete amateur, took three reels-worth of film of the various fights that took place that day. Sadly however, when I returned to the UK and had the films developed, it was discovered that the camera was not functioning correctly and the bull fights that I had filmed could, and still can, only be seen with considerable difficulty. Whilst in Seville we were, one evening, taken on a private visit deep into the vaults of a substantial silk warehouse the magnificent colourfulness of whose vast contents was almost beyond belief. The silks were superb, absolutely superb. Sadly not only were the prices well beyond the limited budget that we, as travellers going outside the UK, were allowed by the UK Government to have but also we had not the capacity within the limited space available to us in our little car to cope with any of these splendid, simply splendid, fabrics.

We left Seville considerably impressed by the City and journeyed on towards the famous Sherry-producing town of Jerez de la Frontera, where we had a wee taste or more of the famous product, and thence from Jerez we went to Algeciras and then onwards to our destination, the British fortress of Gibraltar. Despite the 'hidden' wealth of Spain so clearly evidenced in Seville, much of the roads over which we had to travel prior to reaching Gibraltar continued to be little better than appalling as were the life-conditions of the citizens whom we saw. At one point in our journey through southern Spain we came across an extended family living in extreme poverty in a large cave, the cave being the only place that they could find that provided them with both shelter from the southern Spanish heat and drinking water in an area whose rivers were completely devoid of water.

Between Algeciras and Gibraltar I again felt that we might have made a wrong turning; and therefore, in the sweltering heat, I stopped the car and got out to ask a soldier, who appeared to be on guard duty outside a Spanish army camp, whether or not the road that we were travelling on would take us to Gibraltar. Despite the very high temperature there he was, on his own, standing to attention, facing the Mediterranean, his feet some several inches up inside his overlong thick army trousers, his rifle in the 'slope arms' position and being held by a hand some six inches [150mm] or so inside an overlong sleeve of his thick army jacket. Had it not been reality I would have taken him as being some idiotic character from a silent film. I hardly spoke a word of Spanish and he seemed to be able to speak not one word of English, but he was clearly relieved to find himself engaged in something other than just standing, in isolation, to attention with nothing else to do but hold his rifle in place and stare out into a vast emptiness beyond. I soon discovered, however, that the name 'Gibraltar', when pronounced correctly in English, meant absolutely nothing to him, and so I pronounced it in various different ways. But the negative result was the same each time. So I showed him a map not only with 'Gibraltar' clearly marked on it but also with the Spanish/Gibraltar Border, along with the outline of southern Spain, clearly marked on it. But, despite his obvious willingness to assist, he seemed totally clueless even as to where he himself actually was. Gibraltar, it seemed, to him just did not exist. So, having expressed my thanks to him as best I could, I went back to the car; and we continued on our journey towards, hopefully, Gibraltar. Indeed, it was not all that long after that we actually saw Gibraltar, and it was not all that long after that that we arrived at the Spanish Customs post on the Spanish/Gibraltar Border. Thinking back to the poor unfortunate uniformed Spanish Soldier whom we had just met I could not help but conclude that Generalísimo Francisco Paulino Hermenegildo Teódulo Franco was not too keen on teaching map-reading skills to his army's cannon-fodder, especially those positioned near to the British fortress of Gibraltar.

Although it was noticeable that our desire to go to Gibraltar was not greeted with enthusiasm we got through the Spanish Customs with no trouble and, having crossed No Man's Land, easily passed through the British Gibraltarian Customs and into Gibraltar itself. Then, what a contrast ... Not only had we spent the last few days driving over miles and miles and miles of some of Continental Europe's most shambolic roads, not only had we driven miles and miles and miles seeing hardly anybody whomsoever but also we had only just encountered the most comedic of military uniformed personalities that I had ever seen; and yet here we now were on some of the finest tar-macadamed surfaces one could drive on, with scores smartly dressed and clearly relaxed people passing us by in all directions, and with the smartest dressed of British Policemen on traffic control. It was an incredible, and hugely welcome, sight.

The penultimate evening before we had left the UK we had had dinner with the person, Dorothy Kay, who then now owned and occupied the house in Pampisford Road, Croydon that Dr Blauuw and his Wife had owned and occupied prior to their departure to their purpose-built house in their Dutch homeland. A fascinating personality, Dorothy Kay insisted that when in Gibraltar my Mother and I must call upon a good friend of hers, a Commander in Her Majesty's Royal Navy who was stationed in Gibraltar. She would, she said, make contact with him within the next day or so to let him know that we were coming; and before we left her home that night she wrote and gave us a note to hand to him by way of introduction. So, during the morning following the day of our arrival in Gibraltar we called at his Quarters to meet with him and enjoy his generous liquid hospitality. En route from where we were staying we had called in at Gibraltar's Rock Hotel to make a luncheon reservation. My Mother's favourite drink was gin, usually, but not always, drunk by her as 'gin and it' [gin and Italian vermouth]. However the Commander's generous hospitality was, for my Mother, gin not 'gin and it'. The Term before the Term that I left Haileybury Senior School a Laurentian colleague and friend of mine, Tim Nicholson, who subsequently went on to become a Lieutenant Colonel in the British Army before retiring to work in the City of London, announced to me that he intended to 'sign up' in the Army for nine years; and so, in the general chit-chat between the Naval Commander and my Mother and me, I mentioned this and added that I thought that 'signing up' for nine years was too long a time to commit oneself. That, it turned out, was somewhat of a foolish comment for suddenly the Commander's joviality turned, though not for long, to seriousness for his emphatic response was "I have signed on for *life* !!"

My Mother and I left the Commander's company in order to adhere to the time that we had booked for our luncheon at the Rock Hotel, then one of Gibraltar's most prestigious of eating establishments and a complete contrast to most of the eating establishments that we had visited during the previous week. As we walked from the Commander's Quarters to the Hotel my Mother, a person who was by no means a novice insofar as the drinking of gin was concerned, expressed a comment that she was beginning to feel none too well; and as we neared the steps to the Hotel's main entrance she began to drift slightly from side to side until, on arrival at the entrance itself, she collapsed in an unceremonious heap on the ground. Having, with assistance, picked her up, I managed to partly drag her and partly to get her, supported by me, to walk into the dining-room and then to the table that had been reserved for us. Having sat her down, I then found that, in order to keep her from flopping her head onto the then empty plate set before her, I had no choice but to sit alongside her instead of at the place laid for me opposite her. Doubtless the Staff, and probably some of the other diners within the room, had realised that she was drunk - a state in which I had never seen her before - but no-one made mention of it, certainly not to me as I struggled to eat my meal and to, at the same time, cope with my Mother as she drifted in and out of consciousness whilst somehow managing to eat her meal. Fortunately the food, as we progressed through it, seemed to decrease the drunkenness to the extent that, when we got round to our drinking our coffees at the end of the meal, she seemed to have substantially recovered. For me the whole episode was not only very embarrassing but also very puzzling because I had seen her drink more gin on previous occasions and she had never ever gotten to this stage. It was only when someone later that day explained to us that the Commander had doubtless plied my Mother not with the type of gin that is normally drunk in the UK but with Dutch Naval gin - a drink, apparently, considerably stronger than UK gin - that the puzzle was solved.

We had not realised that, in those days, the public highway went round only part of the Rock of Gibraltar; and so that night, despite the fact that it was darkish, we decided to drive round the entire Rock. After a few minutes we found ourselves being politely and courteously halted by a uniformed British Policeman and his descending barrier. The barrier having been fully lowered to its horizontal position he then came over to us and explained that his barrier was as far as we were allowed to go. Then, suddenly and completely to our surprise, he asked "Would you like a cup of tea?" So, we parked the car and went with him into his cabin sited alongside his barrier. Chatting merrily away as he made the tea he told us, on a "don't tell anyone" basis, that not only was much of the Rock hollow but also that, whereas its outside noticeably bristled with radio listening and receiving devices which formed part of the UK's defence systems, its hidden inside consisted of miles of tunnels substantially stuffed full of arms and ammunition and other Military gear just in case, for instance, the Spaniards, in pursuance of Spain's constant claim to ownership of the Rock, ever tried to invade Gibraltar [somewhat of an impudence, I have always thought, given that Spain occupies, on the other side of the Straight of Gibraltar, several areas of land including a somewhat larger chunk of land which it calls Ceuta which, had it not been for Spain's persistent ownership of same, would otherwise belong to Morocco]. As we drank our tea he chattily informed us that Military observers strategically positioned on the Rock had in fact alerted him to our presence well in advance of our arrival at his barrier. One other surprise was that affixed to the shoulders of the jacket of our host's Police uniform was his Police identity - 'PC 49'. In the late 1940s/early 1950s a very successful BBC Radio Series had been *The Adventures of PC 49'*, a series emulated in the *Eagle* Comic throughout much of the 1950s, the *Eagle* being a weekly Comic eagerly read by schoolboys such as I and my colleagues at Haileybury Junior School in Windsor. Thus 'PC 49' had, in the 1950s, been a major part of the lives of boys such as I; and now, blow me, here I was, on a very large hollow rock sited at the mouth of the Mediterranean, actually chatting and drinking tea with a real life, and very courteous, PC 49. "Pity that it was not still the 1950s and that I was not still at the JS," I thought, "otherwise I could have gone back to school and proudly announced that I had *actually met PC 49.*"

Next day, after having seen, and fed, some of Gibraltar's famous Barbary Apes - it being said that Gibraltar would cease to be British if ever the Apes left the Rock, we left the 3-miles [4.83 kilometres] long British Fortress and Crown Colony of Gibraltar and drove back into Spain and on up Spain's east coast heading, via Málaga, for the magnificent Moorish City of Granada and its famed ancient Palace and Fortress of The Alhambra - a name hitherto, for me, synonymous with Theatres such as The Alhambra in London's Leicester Square and The Alhambra in Glasgow - where we met, and after a night's stay within a building within, or very close to, the Palace, subsequently had breakfast with John Freeman, Journalist and a Labour Member of Parliament, who went on to become, amongst other things, a contributor to such programmes as BBC Television's *Panorama,* Britain's High Commissioner in India, Britain's Ambassador to the United States, and Chairman of London Weekend Television [LWT], and who was, when we met him, the Editor of *The New Statesman*, a weekly UK 'left wing' magazine. Thereafter, in our faithful little A40 car, it was on - via Almeria, Alicante, and many other places - to the great Spanish City of Valencia. We arrived there next day after having spent, doubtless to compensate for the high costs incurred in Gibraltar and perhaps, although I do not know, in Granada also, a night within a couple of very, very basic but very clean and tidy rooms provided to us within a small, almost village-like, town by a charming elderly, but totally non-English-speaking, woman who clearly went out of her way to do her very best to make our stay enjoyable, which it was.

Valencia I remember principally because, having spent several hours wandering around eating, drinking, and happily looking at some of its many very attractive buildings, we then realised that we could not remember where we had parked the car and in consequence spent over two, somewhat unhappy and increasingly unpleasant, hours desperately looking for it for not only was it our only means of transport but also it had everything that we needed, including most of our Travellers' Cheques and money, within it. Eventually, and with huge relief, we found it - untouched and exactly where we had left it. But had our loss of our car taught us a lesson ? No.

It had been our intention to drive inland from Valencia to Spain's Capital City of Madrid but a chance conversation in a café caused us to learn that we had miscounted the days of our holiday that we so far expended and that we were thus running one day behind schedule. Therefore the 220 miles [354kilometres] to Madrid and the 384 miles [618 kilometres] from Madrid to our next intended principal destination of Barcelona had to be abandoned in favour of going directly from Valencia to Barcelona. causing us considerable regret in that we never got to see Spain's Capital City. So, from Valencia we travelled on, via Tarragano and many other places, to Barcelona where, it shames me to confess, we, because we had learned nothing from our loss of our car in Valencia, again lost the car in circumstances identical to those that we had imposed upon ourselves in Valencia. But, as with Valencia, we eventually found it - untouched and exactly where we had left it. But the two experiences, the one in Valencia and the other in Barcelona, taught me to never again leave a vehicle in an unfamiliar environment without having first written down on a piece of paper exactly where I had left it.

Scheduled by the fact that we had a return crossing from France across the English Channel to Dover booked, having 'lost' a day we now began to feel under some pressure to speed up a bit and thus to head for the Spanish-French Border as quickly as possible. However, that idea soon evaporated when we arrived, just a few miles [kilometres] up the road from Barcelona, at the attractive sleepy Spanish seaside village of Calella. We needed, sometime that evening or night, either to park up and sleep in the car for the night or to find a house or hotel in which to stay for the night; and, with the

Mediterranean lapping gently at its shore, Calella was just too tempting a place not to stay. Thus, with a "What the heck" attitude, we booked in for not one but two nights at the Hotel Mediterrani. Such, of course, meant that, having changed all the tyres around for the second time on our holiday, on leaving Calella, having spent hours lazing on its beach, we were now running two days behind schedule : And so it was "foot down hard" and to the Spanish-French Border as fast as was possible. As a newly-qualified driver I was, despite the still poor and sometimes dangerous, and occasionally very dangerous, qualities of the roads that then existed, thoroughly enjoying myself - even though I was doing all the driving. As we left Spain and re-entered France I could not help but reflect not only upon the many kindnesses which had been shown to us by both the Spanish people and the Portuguese people but also, with sadness, upon the repressive way in which the ordinary peoples of both Nations were being treated by their respective Governments and Dictators, Generalissimo Franco and Dr Salazar.

Once back in France we headed north to and through Perpignan. We had hoped to have been able to divert through the Pyrenees to the tiny state of Andorra but the fact that we were now two days behind schedule caused us to have to leave that visit "for another time". Onwards we went until eventually we decided to pull in at a restaurant somewhere for a meal and perhaps, hopefully, find somewhere to stay for the night. Finding what we thought was the ideal place for both we pulled in at quite a well lit, and somewhat British-looking, hotel over to our right.

France's then President, General Charles de Gaulle, a man once hugely popular with most French people, certainly those who lived north of that area of France known in the Second World War as *Vichy*

France, as a result of his leadership of the Free French during the Second World War but who had fallen out of favour with many Frenchmen as a result of his decision to give to Algeria - a north African Nation ruled and controlled by France since the French invaded it in 1830 and considered by France to be a part of France - the independence from France that so many Algerians, often using considerable violence, were seeking. The analysis of General de Gaulle's Aide, Geoffroy de Courcel, as to how General de Gaulle felt towards Algeria was that the General did not want to surrender Algeria but believed that, because France's struggle with Algeria was draining France economically, France had no option but to surrender Algeria to the Algerians. To many French people their wartime hero had thus become a traitor : And it was within this atmosphere, although completely unknown to us, that my Mother and I entered that hotel that night.

We were the hotel's only guests and, as such, great attention was lavished upon us by our French host and his French Wife. A wartime Member of Britain's Royal Air Force [RAF], our host entertainingly regaled us with his enthusiasm for Britain, for the RAF, for the many friends he had made in the RAF and in Britain, and for Britain's wartime leader, Winston Churchill. He was a charming man, and when we told him of my Father's acquaintance with Churchill his enthusiasm for the man seemed to extend to the point of almost knowing no bounds. As we ended the meal his almost constant presence was replaced by that of his equally charming Wife with whom my Mother then made arrangements that we would stay the night. Sometime later, my Mother and I having retired from the dinner table to sit and enjoy coffees and drinks in front of a homely log fire, our host, now dressed from head to toe in, what can perhaps be described as being, combat gear, returned and, very, very politely, tendered his apologies to us saying that he must now leave us because, he quite openly stated, General de Gaulle was passing nearby that night and he and his colleagues intended to blow him up. My Mother and I were horrified. A little while after he had gone we tendered our apologies to his Wife and said that, because we were running behind schedule, we had decided that we could not stay after all : And, as soon as we could we hastily left the hotel, got back into our car, and drove on.

By now it was well past midnight, and the problem of finding somewhere to purchase petrol befell us. Thus our first concern, once we were well clear of the former RAF man's hotel, was to find a petrol station. We drove on and on until, eventually, on the left-hand side of the road, shining like a beacon in the otherwise pitch darkness, we saw the lights of a petrol station. "Thank God for that," I thought as we turned off the road into the petrol station's forecourt. Having drawn up alongside the pumps we waited for someone, as was the practice in those days, to come out to serve us. Fortunately, we thought, we would not have to wait for long for we could see, sitting in a small cabin, illuminated by a single electric light dangling down from its ceiling, a man seemingly fast asleep. So I sounded the horn to wake him. I sounded the horn again, and then again. But he remained where he was : And so I got out of the car and went over to the cabin to wake him up. He was facing me as I walked up to the cabin and tapped on the window. Even that did not wake him; and so I went round to the glass-panelled door at the side of the cabin with the intention of going in to physically shake him to wake him up. It was when I got to the door that I saw the reason why he had not come to serve us. Stuck in his back was a knife, and down the back of his clothes was a streak of blood. I rushed back to the car and, as I opened my door, said to my Mother "He's got a knife in his back. He's dead

!!" My Mother never did like the dark, and so, with her almost screaming "Let's get out of here. Let's get out of here", I got into the car, re-started its engine, and off we went as fast as our little car would take us. To say that we were both very concerned would not be an over-exaggeration. As to whether or not our friendly ex-RAF host had anything to do with it … Well, I do not know : I can only guess.

Our journey back up through France took us to Paris where at last our faithful little Austin A40 car let us down for, as - guided by an arm-waving, whistle-blowing, baton-wielding, traffic-controlling Gendarme standing on a plinth - we entered a roundabout, the car's engine cut out causing the car to glide to a standstill in the middle of traffic that was seemingly coming and going in all directions. With much embarrassment, and with hardly any mechanical knowledge as to what to do, I sat there trying, again and again via the car's ignition key, to re-start the car. Just as I got out of the car suddenly there the Gendarme was standing alongside the car's bonnet. "Help," I naively thought, "had arrived." But no, Monsieur le Gendarme stood there, still blowing his whistle, and still wielding his baton but now wielding it in a circular motion in such a way that every time its circular motion caused it to reach the bottom of every downward stroke it thumped against the top of the car's bonnet. Gesticulating furiously at me with his non-baton-wielding hand he was clearly ordering me to remove myself, my Mother, and my British car from his roundabout. But there was absolutely nothing that I could do, a situation which neither pleased him nor engendered in him any sympathy for my predicament whatsoever. To my relief a passing motorist stopped alongside us, got out of his car, and said something to the blue-uniformed 'circus act' who then stopped his performance and returned to his plinth. Unable to speak a word of English, our rescuer indicated to me to open the car's bonnet. Then, once the bonnet was opened, he wiggled and pulled at a cable that was sited near to the engine, and then indicated to me to try again to start the engine. This I did, the engine 'fired', and, having expressed my sincere gratitude to him in what little French I could muster [*despite having studied French at Haileybury and received an 'O' Level for my efforts* !!], off we went as fast as we could away from the wretched Gendarme and his roundabout.

After having toured round central Paris, and despite our unpleasant experience of its Police Force's 'circus act', we enjoyed, from our once again faithful little car, the many tourist sights that we were able to see that Saturday afternoon. Then we headed out of Paris towards Calais intending to find a small or smallish hotel in which to stay the night. Eventually we arrived at what seemed the ideal place for there, in the centre of a 'sleepy' little town that was almost a complete visual contrast to Paris was a large building proudly displaying, amongst other words, the word 'Hôtel' above the very large double doors which clearly formed its main entrance. Having parked the car, I climbed the stone slab steps up to the doors but found them to seem to be jammed if not locked. So, whilst several elderly men sat on the steps looking in my direction and puffing away at their pipes, I banged hard on one of the doors. Having received no response, I banged again. Still no response. So I banged again. Still no response. So I banged again. Then one of the elderly men took his pipe out of his mouth, tapped it on an adjacent stone wall, slowly rose up from his group of chattering and grinning colleagues and, taking his time and himself with a large grin, walked up the steps to where I was standing. "Monsieur," he said slowly," Zee 'Hôtel de Ville' is zee … er … Town Hall et le Town Hall ees … er … not … ees not … er .. open on zee Saturdays !!" "Well, so much for 'O'Level French," I said to myself. Mais c'est la vie, n'est pas ?

With the elderly Frenchman's broken English and my appalling conversational French I managed to find out where there was an hotel; and so off my Mother and I went to the real thing. Very modest and basic, and with render falling off its outside walls, the hotel was nonetheless very comfortable and, as we were its only guests, the attention paid to us was very good as indeed was the food : And, after a good night's rest, it was off next day for the remainder of the journey to Calais where we arrived that night amidst some of the foulest weather that we had encountered since we had left home. As we drove round Calais looking for a hotel in which to spend our last night in France the rain was vicious and incessant, the wind was horrendously strong, and the night was cold and dark, very, very dark. Indeed, the weather that night made Calais look as if it was competing to be the most inhospitable town in France. It was dreadful. Contrary to my expectations, Calais did not abound with hotels or, if it did, we certainly did not find them. However, we eventually found a newish-looking house with an illuminated sign in its window which simply said, in English, "Vacancies". It was not exactly what we were looking for but by now we had an "Ah, well ..." attitude; and so I parked the car and, having fought against the wind to open our doors, out of the car we got and up to the house's frontdoor we went. Having rung the bell we waited, and waited, and waited until eventually the door was opened by an apparition wearing a pair of tartan slippers and clad in a nightie with a dressing-gown over it.

Our having explained that we wanted a couple of rooms for the night, the 'apparition', in the most wonderful of enchantingly French accents but speaking absolutely perfect English, instantly invited us in "out of the wind and rain" and, pointing to a beautifully furnished room, said "Take your coats off, sit yourselves down, and I'll make us a cup of tea".

In her mid-eighties, this splendid character had apparently been married to a wealthy Englishman, a City of London Banker, and had, for more than thirty years, lived in some splendour in London's St James's where she had enjoyed a lifestyle that most can only dream of. The house that we travellers had stumbled upon that night had been built after the Second World War on the site of where her beautiful Family home had previously stood. After the War she, accompanied by her husband, had returned to Calais for a visit to discover only rubble and ruin where once splendour had stood. Overcome with emotion caused by the suffering endured by her beloved home in Calais she and her husband had returned to their home in St James's full of hatred for what the Germans had done. It was only after her husband had died and she had returned to Calais to supervise the building of her former home's much more modest replacement did she learn that the destroyers of her home had not been the Germans but the RAF on a bombing mission !!

"So, how did you feel when you found out that it was the RAF not the Germans who had destroyed your home ?" I asked her.

"Of course, I forgave them instantly, for what else could those lovely boys have done ?" she replied with a smile.

A complete anglophile, and clearly very well educated, she had insisted that the builders of her new house use, insofar as was possible, only things that had been made in Britain "For the French," she said, despite the fact that she was French "make only rubbish, only rubbish". Every hinge in the house was British made, every door-handle was British made, the cooker was British made, the kettle was British made, the beds were British made, even the tiles on the roofs and the cast-iron gutterings and downpipes were, apparently, all British made.

"And when you come back again to Calais," this wonderful, full of life octogenarian insisted, "you must bring me rolls and rolls of British-made toilet paper".

"Why ?" asked my Mother.

"I ask all my British guests to bring me British-made toilet paper when they return because I can not buy British-made toilet paper here in Calais, and French-made toilet paper is crap - And you can not remove crap with crap," she replied her voice loudening as she emphasised the latter part of her sentence.

My Mother and I had intended not to stay up too late that night as we had a ferry to catch next morning and then, once across the English Channel and through UK Customs, a drive up the A2 trunk road from Dover back home to Putney in Southwest London. But characters such as this wonderful French lady are not only fascinating they are almost unique; and therefore it was well past midnight before we got to our beds. Next morning the most splendid of English, not French, breakfasts had been laid out for us to ensure that we were "well fed" for our journey. It was thus, after breakfast, that, with much regret, we had no option but to leave the company of this most entertaining, charming, courteous, and, for her age, most energetic of people. One could only but guess at how this still elegant lady must have looked in her heyday in London's St James's.

We arrived in the Ferry departure area an hour or so before our pre-booked departure time, our fortnight's, very educational, adventure on Mainland Europe nearly, but not quite, over. The volume of cross-Channel traffic now bears little comparison with the volume then when cars awaiting to go on to the Ferry had to form, principally, a single queue, each side of which was bounded by a kerb thus preventing, unless one wished to risk damaging one's car, one from queue-jumping or from turning one's car out of the queue. Not wishing to miss the Ferry, we had arrived ahead of anyone else and therefore our little car was at the head of the queue. With time to spare, we decided first to get out and 'stretch our legs' and then to walk a little way towards the town centre to have a look around. Unfortunately we walked a wee bit further than we had intended, and on our return we found a host of car occupants prevented from driving on to the Ferry because our car, the lead car in the queue, was preventing every other car from boarding. But all turned out okay; and all the cars got on to the Ferry in sufficient time to allow it to head off to Dover at its appointed Departure Time.

On arrival at Dover I drove the car off the Ferry and into Her Majesty's Custom's shed where we waited and waited and waited. Whilst in Gibraltar I had bought a Sanyo 'Transcontinental' radio of a type then something of a novelty in the UK and of a type doubtless that would attract Custom's Duty were I asked to declare it. The puzzling thing was that there appeared to be no Customs Officer around; and so, after a while, I asked a nearby AA [Automobile Association] Patrolman what we should do. Should we get back in the car and drive on or what ? "Well," said the AA man, "they'll be around here somewhere looking at you and at how you are behaving. So, if I were you, given that you've been standing here for a while, I would get back in your car and drive on. If they think that you've acted suspiciously they'll stop you." So, my Mother and I got back into the car, drove on, went out of the shed, and headed through and out of Dover on the A2 Trunk Road towards London only to be stopped, not by Customs nor by the Police but, by a lorry driver kindly shouting at me "Oi ! We drive on the left here in Britain, y'know !!"." I was very grateful to him for, my having, since passing my Driving Test, driven many more miles on the "wrong side" of the road, I had clean forgotten that in the UK we are, at times, somewhat different from the rest of Europe.

The rest of the journey back to Kenilworth Court was completely uneventful; and, sadly, once back in Putney I had - after having offloaded and parked the car within its allocated space, No.49, in Kenilworth Court's own car-parking area - to surrender the car back to my Mother who, now that we were back home, re-assumed her usual attitude of tight control over my activities a control that denied to me the ability even to possess a key to the front door of No.28. If I wished to leave the flat I had to ask and either agree a time when she would let me back in or make an arrangement whereby I could borrow a key provided that both I and it returned to the flat within a stated period. Even when working for the BBC I was not given possession of a key to the flat but was dependent upon her letting me back into the flat following my return from work each day.

When my Mother had been pregnant with me she met a woman whose pregnancy, her first pregnancy, had reached about the same stage as hers. Ruby Weeks was her name, and my Mother and she struck up a friendship which continued for many years. One Sunday in 1963, by which time Ruby Weeks and her husband now had two children and were living in Eastbourne, my Mother and I, with me driving, went down to Eastbourne via Brighton to see them. We deliberately went via Brighton in order to see, in Brighton, an elderly Jewish friend of my Father, an ex-NAZI Concentration Camp internee, now somewhat ill and living in a Jewish Guest House which he himself owned. I am uncertain, due to the passing of time, as to whether we went by arrangement or just on the off-chance. Nevertheless, on arrival my Mother got out of the car and went up a concrete path to the Guest House's closed front door. She knocked on the door but received no response. She knocked again, and again she received no response. She knocked a third time, and yet again she received no response. She therefore turned and, as she walked back down the concrete path towards the car, a top floor window was opened and a person learnt out. "Hold on, hold on," he shouted. "I'm coming down". So my Mother returned to the front door and waited. Eventually it was opened by the man who had shouted down to her. A while later my Mother, clearly somewhat shocked, returned to the car and got back in. "He's in there," she said of the person whom she had intended seeing, "but the knock on the door has terrified him so much that he has hidden himself away and will not come out." The Jewish gentleman concerned having been a victim of NAZI ill-treatment during the Second World War, a knock on a door, despite the passing of nearly twenty years since the ending of the War, to him meant perhaps the arrival of Death itself.

We travelled on to Eastbourne where, my now being a smoker of Habana cigars who had just smoked the last cigar that I had with me, I drove first to the Cavendish Hotel which, being considered at the time by many to be Eastbourne's premier hotel, we felt would have a stock of cigars thereby enabling me to purchase a couple or so. I boldly, as if a residing Guest of the place, went in and up to Reception.

"Do you have Habana cigars ?" I asked.

"Yes, Sir," came the reply.

"May I purchase some ?" I continued.

"Are you a Guest, Sir ?"

"Yes," I replied.

"Then the Head Waiter will be with you soon, Sir," the Receptionist said.

A minute or so later a very smartly dressed man pushing a cigar humidor on a trolley arrived.

" Are you the Gentleman, Sir, who requires cigars ?" he asked.

"Yes," I replied.

"Are you a Guest here, Sir ?" he enquired.

"Yes," I again replied.

He then opened the humidor and enabled me to select my intended purchases.

After an horrendous price was quoted to me I was then asked by the person whom I took to be the Head Waiter whether I wished to have the amount added to my bill or whether I wished to pay "now".

Having, in fact, no choice I opted for the latter, was directed to Reception, paid over my money, and, with my newly-purchased sticks of Cuban tobacco leaves, returned to the car whereupon we drove on to the Meads area of Eastbourne to see Ruby Weeks and her family.

Her elder child, a boy, had been a 'blue baby' [a baby born with a serious heart defect] and thus much sadness and concern had surrounded not only his birth but also much of his early years. His parents were very devoted to him and, in consequence, had adopted a policy of, if possible, giving him everything that he had asked for. His particular interest in his latter teens seemed to be photography, and therefore after my Mother and I had arrived and been greeted by Ruby Weeks and her son we were introduced to an impressive display of cameras and related equipment owned by the now somewhat very healthy-looking lad. It was explained to us that, because of his illness, there was no pressure upon the son to find work and that therefore he had no job at that time but instead spent much of his time indulging himself in his hobby of photography. The lad, mountainously praised by his mother, then went out leaving me to listen whilst my Mother and Ruby Weeks chatted away. Eventually the front door opened and in, from work, came the other child, a daughter. She looked, I felt, somewhat sad; and, having been briefly introduced to us, she was ordered by her mother to go to her bedroom and stay there. "She's a waitress in one of the hotels," said her mother : And that was all that she said about her. Clearly much was lavished on the son and little was lavished on the daughter, an attitude to Life which I felt to be disadvantageous in the long run to the son and his parents and grossly unfair to the sister. After a while Mr Weeks, about whom little had been said by Mrs Weeks as she and my Mother chatted away, returned from work. His arrival back home could first be heard by the sound of a key being placed into a lock in the front door and then the sound of the frontdoor opening and closing. "Ah, there's Mr Weeks," Mrs Weeks informed us. A quarter of a minute or so later the eagerly-awaited Mr Weeks entered the room; and there before me stood the same smartly dressed man who, only an hour or so earlier at the Cavendish Hotel, had asked of me "Are you a Guest here, Sir ?" I had been rumbled : But what a nice man he was, and not only could he not care less whether or not I was a Guest at the Cavendish but also, he told me, he had known all along, as indeed had the Receptionist, that I was not a Guest !! We stayed a while longer, had a meal, and then left; and as I drove back to Putney that night I determined that if ever I had children I would ensure that insofar as was possible each would be regarded by me as being the equal of the other.

Although my Mother kept a firm control on most things that I did or wanted to do she did occasionally, very occasionally, permit me to use her Austin A40 car in return for my checking its oil, cleaning it, and so on. One Christmastime, with the snow lying on the ground, we were concerned that, as it had not been used for a while, it might not start. I therefore went into the Courtyard at Kenilworth Court where, on the then Car Parking Space No.49, the car was parked and tried, unsuccessfully, to start it. So, its having refused to start, I then released the handbrake, put the car in neutral, pushed it back a wee bit so that I could turn it and face it towards the Court Yard's Main Entrance. My objective was that, having turned it, I would put it into gear, pull the manual choke out, turn the ignition on, and, by myself, try to 'bump start' it. After slipping and sliding around a wee bit I managed to get it facing the Main Entrance. Then I put it in gear, pulled the manual choke out, turned the ignition on, and, via the open driver's door began to push it whilst at the same time holding on to its steering-wheel with the dual intention of steering the car and pulling myself quickly in in order to apply the brake and disengaged the clutch should, in the unlikely event, the car actually start. However not only did the unlikely event actually happen but also, as the car slowly propelled itself towards the Main Entrance, I slipped and fell causing me to let go of the steering-wheel and thus of the car. Lying on the snow-covered ground was not an option for beyond the Main Entrance was Lower Richmond Road and beyond Lower Richmond Road was the solid wall of a Café sited at the corner of Lower Richmond Road and the Embankment. Up I got and in great haste pursued my Mother's driverless car which, by the time that I managed to catch up with it and get in and apply the brake and disengage the clutch, had managed to self-propel itself about three-quarters of the way across an otherwise, fortunately, trafficless Lower Richmond Road. What a close shave that one was !!

My Mother's A40 car caused me to develop a fondness, which I still retain, for driving; and during one excursion to Norwich in Norfolk to see Mike Norgate, a friend of mine from Haileybury Senior School, I encountered my first experience of running out of, or almost running out of, petrol. London to Norwich was, via the A11 in the then pre-M11 Motorway days, 114 miles [184 km] or thereabouts. The road was good but, through Thetford Forest at night, at times somewhat frightening. The weather that afternoon when I left Putney was quite good and by the time, some two and a half hours or so later, I came to an 'A Fine City Norwich' sign which informed me that I was at last in the outskirts of Norwich. Snow had obliterated much of the land round about. Mike lived not in Norwich but 5 miles or thereby away in Taverham : And as I attempted to find my way there the weather got worse and worse, a situation aggravated by the fact that all life seemed to have disappeared, all life that is until a rabbit shot out seemingly from nowhere and went in front of my car causing the car's driver's side front wheel to, with an echoing 'crunch' sound, run over it. I stopped the car and got out but was unable to do anything other than watch, with sadness, the unfortunate creature's last few twitching dying seconds. Having got back into the car I drove on until, eventually, I saw, through the by now fast-falling snow, a Public House to my right. Feeling completely lost I stopped the car and went in to ask directions and, very much to my surprise, discovered from the Landlord that I was within a very short distance of where Mike and his Parents lived. I was a complete stranger to this man yet, as I turned to leave his Pub, he suddenly asked me if I would like "a pint of something to drink". Having downed his hospitality I offered to buy him a drink in return. "No. You be on your way now," was his kind, and very much appreciated, response. I was very impressed.

Knowing that the A40 car needed petrol to get me back to London and being determined to get back to London I left Mike that night at about 11.30pm intending to go into Norwich to get sufficient petrol to enable me to get me back to London. When I arrived in Norwich it seemed, until at ten minutes past midnight when I came across one solitary Policeman, as if the whole City had closed down for the night. "Where can I get some petrol ?" I asked him.

"Where be you going ?" he responded in a wonderful Norfolk accent.

"London," I told him.

"London ... Well, now, let me see," he said slowly and thoughtfully, "the nearest petrol station at this time o'night be .... London."

"London ?" I said with disbelief.

"Yes, London," he replied.

"You won't get any petrol in Norwich this time o'night All garages be closed this time o'night," he depressingly declared.

So it was back to Mike Norgate's to, if possible, scrounge at least some petrol. Fortunately his father was able to give me some but certainly not enough to get me back to London. Anyhow, grateful for what he had been able to give me, off I set on my journey back to London. On and on I drove - through the haunting Thetford Forest and through, at one point, a 'mountain' of snow the height and formation of which had caused almost a tunnel to form over the road

- until eventually, with the car's petrol indicator informing me that the petrol tank was almost empty, as I neared Cambridge I saw, in the distance, an illuminated sign announcing "Marshall's Garage". So I thought "Aim for that sign and park up until the Garage opens up". Wonder of wonders, not only was there sufficient petrol in the tank to allow me to just reach Marshall's Garage but also the Norwich policeman was wrong - For Marshall's Garage, sited approximately half way between Norwich and London, was, despite the early hour, open and I was thus able to fill the tank and continue my journey home to Putney. What a relief that was !! Moral of the story ? Always carry spare petrol - A lesson which, I confess, I did not really learn until some years later.

At times life within 28 Kenilworth Court was, for me at least, somewhat stifling and certainly a contrast to my life within the BBC where, as a Movement Controller within its Television Props' Department I had many varied, and often very interesting, tasks to do, one of which - on the morning of the historic day of 10 July 1962 when the first communications satellite, Telstar, began receiving and publicly transmitting signals on the day after it was launched - was to accompany my crew in its van to Phillips the Map Makers in London's Fleet Street to collect a large rotating globe of the world hired by the Corporation to be used, live, in the studio to indicate the orbital path being taken by Telstar. The London traffic gave our van and its Driver no end of problems causing us to arrive at Phillips somewhat later than intended, a major hindrance given that we were working to a very tight live Programme transmission schedule. We were not helped by the fact that Fleet Street was a very busy road the width of which was not that great especially when partially obstructed by our parked 7-ton[ne] van when being loaded-up : And we were also not helped by the fact that the globe itself was not only large but also had stuck upon it representations of countries and continents each made of plaster-like material thus making the thing a very fragile object to manhandle through and out of Phillips' shop, across a pedestrian-crowded pavement, up the slope of a van's tailgate, and then into the back of the van itself. Arriving back at Television Centre the van was driven as near as possible to the Programme's Studio which, unusually, was not one of the then 4 functioning principal Studios [2, 3, 4, and 5] existing in those days but one of the 'Continuity Studios', such being very small Studios used mainly for such transmissions as one person sitting on a chair behind a desk talking straight to camera, for one person sitting in an armchair interviewing another person sitting in an armchair with perhaps just a table between them, or for a person making an announcement 'off camera' in the event of a delay in, or breakdown of, a programme. As such Continuity Studios neither had purpose-built large doors to enable large items to be taken in and out nor much space to comfortably accommodate more than two, maybe three, participants and a couple of technical people, including a cameraman. A Continuity Studio was therefore not designed, not intended, to accommodate six or so persons manhandling a very large fragile globe into it, then manhandling the globe around its inside so that it could then be manually lifted onto a motorised hook to enable the globe to slowly revolve whilst the Show's Presenter, sitting in his chair sited between the revolving globe and a desk, could talk to camera and use the revolving globe as a means of explaining what it was that he was talking about. Furthermore, the situation of the Studio itself - positioned midway between two floors and accessed either directly by a staircase of just sufficient size to accommodate the globe or indirectly by a lift of just sufficient size to accommodate the globe but which went only either to the floor below the Studio or the floor above the Studio - did not help our desperate attempts to get the wretched, and seemingly increasingly heavy, thing positioned on its motorised hook in sufficient time to enable us to vacate the Studio well before the Studio's red Transmission Light came on. Eight of us, having got the globe out of the lorry and to a position on the floor just in front of the ground-floor doors to the lift, stood waiting for the lift to arrive and its doors to open. It seemed ages before the 'ding' was heard and the doors opened. But, when we lifted the globe up and started to carry it into the lift we realised that the lift could not accommodate both us and our burden; and so the decision was made that we had no option but to abandon the lift idea and instead physically carry the thing up the stairs to the Studio. So, with six of the eight of us taking hold as best we could without damaging the delicate plaster-like material representations of countries and continents, we lifted up our burden and proceeded, one tread and riser at a time, to climb the stairs, the other two of us steadying the thing and preventing it from rolling out of our grips and cascading back down the stairs.

As we reached the Studio doors, our backs and arms now feeling increasingly painful, we were greeted by panic-stricken technicians telling us to "Hurry up. Hurry up. Hurry up" - As if we could do anything about it !! With Transmission Time preventing us from being able to stop and rest for a few seconds once we were in the Studio, we continued without a desperately needed break to carry the thing passed the camera, passed the Presenter's desk, then passed the Presenter's chair until we reached a position immediately below the globe's suspended motorised hook. It was then that we discovered that we had neither sufficient energy left to lift the wretched thing the required 3 feet [900mm] or so off the floor so that it could be fitted onto its hook nor sufficient time before transmission to enable us to do so. So, with the agitated Presenter by now established on his seat and positioning himself correctly in front of the camera, four of us made a very hasty exit out of the Studio leaving the other four of us to huddle as close as we could to-gether behind the globe praying that we would remain out of the camera's sight, and thus out of the sight of viewers, for the entirety of the half-hour live transmission and that each of us would remain sufficiently motionless so that the globe would neither been seen by millions of viewers to move nor to start to roll across the Studio and thus be seen by millions of viewers damaging the Presenter's chair and perhaps flattening the Presenter. What a relief it was when suddenly, after just over half an hour of sheer agony, a voice informed us and the Programme's nervous, but very professional Presenter, that the Transmission had ended and that we could all now relax !!

I one day had to send a van and a Props Department crew to nearby Acton to collect a piano that the Corporation had hired for a Show. A simple job, or so I thought until I received a telephone-call asking me to come to Acton as soon as possible to sort out a problem that had arisen - The lads could not get the piano out of the flat. The BBC had its own pool of taxis to which we Movement Controllers had access if we genuinely needed them; and so into a taxi I got and down to Acton I went. I was greeted outside the basement flat which housed the piano by three Props Department colleagues who informed me that since they had telephoned me they had learned from the attractive and somewhat seductive woman whose flat it was that the Producer of the Show for which the piano had been hired had stated that it had been agreed that those who came to collect the piano would, if necessary, remove any wall that obstructed the piano's removal. My friends had explained to the woman that demolishing and removing walls was not their job : But she was adamant that the demolition and removal of the wall, if necessary to get the piano out of her flat, was part of the hire contract entered into by her and the BBC - She even had a copy of the contract to prove it. Stymied, I and my colleagues chatted with her, each of us feeling that there was something odd about this hire; and as we chatted we discovered that the Show's Producer was her boyfriend, that she wanted the wall demolished and removed, and that her boyfriend had arranged the hire with the intention that the BBC [and thus the TV Licence Fee payers] would be the mug who would do the job, free of charge, for her. With mumblings, murmurings, and polite utterances such as "No, Love, we ain't going to do the job" and "You'd better get proper tradesmen in and pay them if that's what you and your boyfriend want" we all departed leaving her piano considerably out of position in the exactly the same place that it was when I had arrived on the scene.

Chiswick is an area of London not far from Television Centre and it was from a firm called 'Chiswick Aquaria' that the Corporation often hired live animals, fish, etc for its Shows. Thus I or one of my Movement Controller colleagues would regularly have to send a van or taxi to Chiswick Aquaria and back for a goldfish or two or for a snake or whatever. But the Corporation did retain its own stock of hired aquarium fish for its weekday nightly very popular topical 'To-night' Programme, a Show, 'anchored' by Cliff Michelmore, whose group of seemingly intrepid Reporting Journalists - such as Fyffe Roberston, Alan Whicker, Geoffrey Johnson-Smith - would 'feed in' reports from all over the UK and from the world in general - often major achievements in those days but which to-day are taken more or less for granted. Sitting in his chair behind his desk and with a multi-gallon aquarium as a major feature behind him acting as if it were a moving backcloth, Cliff Michelmore would introduce the Show, guide the viewers into and out of various reporting items, and then, with his regular closing phrase of "And the next 'To-night' will be tomorrow night", close the Show, all the while, whilst he was in camera shot, with fish gently swimming in the multi-gallons of water behind him. Each night, sometime after the Show had finished and after everyone had left the Studio and the Studio been put into darkness, a Cleaner would arrive, switch on sufficient lighting within the Studio for his/her needs, then mount a mechanised floor-sweeping and cleaning machine, and proceed to drive around the Studio sweeping and cleaning the floor. It happened every night until one night, whilst passing between Michelmore's chair and the multi-galloned tank with its many fish swimming within it, the cleaner inadvertently misjudged the width and direction of the sweeping and cleaning machine and, instead of passing between chair and tank, drove the machine into the tank causing a 'mountainous' discharge of water and fish to cascade all over the Studio floor. Until then the 'To-night' Programme's fish and their tank had had nothing to do with us in Movement Control; but next day there we were sending a taxi to Chiswick Aquaria to collect a hired small glass bowl full of water and a couple of goldfish to be put on Michelmore's desk for that evening's production of 'To-night'.

One BBC hire that I felt was financially well 'over the top' was undertaken to satisfy a requirement on a London-made Programme which featured the then famous "Coals from Newcastle" saying. Because the Show's Producer, Director, or Designer had insisted on using only genuine coal from the Newcastle upon Tyne area in the Northeast of England the Corporation actually paid to hire, not buy, a bag of coal from a supplier in Newcastle and to have Movement Control send a van 280 miles [440 kilometres] or so up to Newcastle to collect it and bring it down to London where it was, only for a minute or so, used on the Show. Then, next day or the day after, because the bag of coal had been hired not bought, the bag of coal was returned to the supplier in Newcastle. *We in Movement Control just did as we were told* !!

Despite the vehicles that were available to us internally within the BBC there was always the need, due to demand created by the large volume of Props being moved around London by the BBC, to engage the services of outside Contractors of whom we had a list the names upon which were, more often than not, the names of former BBC employees who had left the BBC's employment with the intention of contracting to the BBC because, they felt, they could make more money out of the BBC that way than by working directly for it as employees. The Government's Ministry of Transport Test, the MOT, had yet to come fully into existence and thus, whilst the BBC kept its own vehicles in good condition, there was no serious requirement put upon many Contractors other than that vehicles should be in a 'roadworthy condition'. The relationship between Movement Control and the Props Department in general and the Contractors was very good and therefore, with Contractors often being either single-person units or father and son outfits, if a Contractor required some personnel to assist Movement Control and/or Props in general would provide it. The condition of some of the Contractors' vehicles - often purchased second-, third-, fourth-, or fifth-hand - was, by to-day's standards, so bad that breakdowns were a regular feature as were the chaotic delays which they caused in the streets of London and back at Television Centre and Lime Grove. The worst delay that I can remember happened to the nicest of the, for want of a better word, rogues with whom the BBC contracted. Always smiling and always very willing to oblige, he had the most enormous of pantechnicon-vans the length of which was so long that it had developed a noticeable sag midway along its length. I had ridden in it on several occasions and was aware of the fact that it sometimes needed the assistance of one of the passengers in the cab to enable the vehicle's always smiling, and usually always talking, Irish owner/driver to change gear, a sometimes very embarrassing experience if stuck, say, in the middle of a traffic-lights' controlled junction and the vehicle's gearbox was not in a co-operative mood. On this occasion we had set off from Television Centre intending to make several stops in various arranged places throughout London in order to collect hired, and sometimes very valuable, goods at each stop. The one stop that we had not anticipated fortunately occurred not in the middle of a traffic-lights controlled junction but in a somewhat unusually quiet road. One moment this enormous, by now almost fully laden, van was lurching along on its way to Lime Grove to offload its hired goodies; and the next moment there it was, having ground to an unexpected and very sudden halt, the weight of its valuable cargo having defeated its by now all but clapped-out chassis. Two vehicles had to be summoned from the Corporation's own fleet of lorries so that, by now in the middle of London's 'rush hour', the contents of this now almost deceased monster could be transferred, item by item, into them and taken to their destination at Lime Grove.

Collapsing vehicles were not, however, the speciality of those with whom the BBC contracted for the BBC itself displayed one such of its own vehicles to anyone and everyone who had occasion to enter Television Centre via its front entrance. The day that I had arrived for my interview with Mo(u)lson I had noticed a rather sad-looking vehicle parked in front of where Studio 1 was subsequently built. There it lay throughout the entirety of my time as a Movement Controller, its middle sagging so much that it almost met the ground beneath it. Enquiries that I made informed me that this particular beast belonged to the BBC's Outside Broadcast Unit who had ladened it so heavily that it had broken its back whilst out on location and had had to be dragged all the way back to Television Centre to be offloaded of its very valuable technical equipment and had been left thereafter to suffer in silence in the position in which I, and many hundreds if not thousands of others, had seen it.

It was difficult at times to determine whether the Corporation encouraged or discouraged financial waste. I had to, one day, accompany a delivery of furniture to the BBC's Television Theatre in Shepherd's Bush. Formerly the Shepherd's Bush Empire Theatre, the 'Theatre' was used for all sorts of audience-participation Productions. We had various items of furniture on board including three completely different suites of three-seat settees each with two armchairs. My Props List informed me that they were all for the one Production, a Play. I knew the Play, and it thus puzzled me as to why, in a Play that normally required only one settee and two armchairs, the Play's Designer, Producer, or Director required three settees and six armchairs. I had occasion to go back to the Theatre later in the day and, with time to spare, sat in the Auditorium to watch what was going on. I watched as the Designer concerned stood first here upon the Stage, then there upon the Stage, and then here in the Auditorium, then there in the Auditorium. Then, having had one settee and its two chairs set in position on the Stage she ordered their removal and replacement by the second settee and its two chairs. Then she again went through the ritual of positioning herself in various places before ordering the removal of the second suite, its replacement by the third suite, and again went through the ritual of positioning herself in various places. Then she ordered the removal of the second suite and its replacement by the first suite and, having again gone through her positioning ritual, declared that that settee and its two chairs was the suite that she wanted. She then obtained her Director's agreement with her choice and declared that the other two suites be removed entirely from the Stage. Some time later I queried this, to me, puzzling activity with Stephen Bundy, a Senior Designer with BBC Television and told him that I considered his colleague's activities to have been somewhat wasteful not only of money but of valuable time. He agreed but explained to me that it was an acceptable practice because, if ever the Corporation's money became 'tight' causing Production budgets to have to be cut, the discontinuation of such budgeted-for activities would be undertaken without any adverse noticeable effect being perceived by the viewing Public. At about the same time a colleague within the Props Department decided to help himself to a few dozen very small waste offcuts of wood from the Scenery Department that had been placed down a chute into a skip the contents of which were to be removed for incineration. Suddenly the heavy hand of BBC bureaucracy descended upon him and he was ordered to attend upon a senior Member of the Corporation's Staff to explain his actions, actions which, he was informed in no uncertain terms, amounted to theft. He explained that he and his family's home was heated by coal fires and that he had a genuine need of kindling wood and that he could not understand why wood intended to be incinerated could not be taken by him, and others, for such a purpose. But the heavy hand of BBC bureaucracy would not yield, and he was informed that, if he ever again removed even one piece of wood offcut from the skips, his employment with the Corporation would be instantly terminated.

Shortly after I joined BBC Television I was required to join a Trades Union, the National Association of Theatrical and Kine Employees [NATKE]. So, as I had no choice, I joined and each week thus had to pay a subscription to a Union with which I had no particular sympathy and which seemed to be of little, if any, benefit to me or to my fellow Members. Indeed, many who worked within the physical areas of Television Centre in which I worked seemed to have the same or a similar attitude as I as was evidenced one afternoon when one of NATKE's Shop Stewards, just an hour or so before the end of the working day, came round not only to tell us that there was to be a Union Meeting that evening at 6.30pm but also to, not request but, order us to attend. I had no after-work commitments at the time but nonetheless such short notice was, to say the least, very inconvenient. Many of my colleagues were married, some with children, or had commitments which more or less demanded that they leave work at the end of the working day. But the Union Official, a somewhat short little man by the name of, I think, Sid, would have none of it : To him the Union and its Meeting were all important. So, armed with a book in which to register the names of those who said that they could not or would not attend in order that the non-attender would subsequently receive some form of Union sanction, he went up to a, particularly large, Scene Shifter and demanded of him that he must attend the Union's Meeting at 6.30pm that night. Greeted by a very dismissive and roaring "What ?", the all-powerful little Union man again demanded the Scene Shifter's attendance at the Union Meeting that night. Without another word the Scene Shifter thrust his right hand under the Union man's chin; and, using that right hand, raised the guy a foot [300mm] or so off the ground; then kicked a wooden box over the concrete floor in the direction of a nearby wall; then, with the struggling and unable to speak Union man still firmly gripped in his right hand, went over to the wall; stepped up on to the box; held the Union man as high up the wall as he could; and then dropped him onto the concrete floor and, wiping his hands as if to remove the remains of some unpleasant substance from them, said "What was that about a Union Meeting ?". Thereafter, at the end of the working day, we each went our different way as usual, and that night's Union Meeting was never heard of again. I like to think that maybe the Union man's experience that evening made him realise that his Union existed not for the benefit of him and his fellow Office-bearers but for the benefit of the likes of that Scene Shifter.

Unfortunately all did not go well in one instance that involved a colleague-friend and a Union. I can not now recall his name but he applied for and, after an interview, was offered a junior management job at Elstree Film Studios. Having handed in his notice he left the BBC's employ and turned up at Elstree at the appointed hour on the appointed day. Having been warmly greeted by his new management colleagues he was, later in the day, approached by a Union Representative. "Card," said the Representative without, apparently, having introduced himself.

"Pardon ?" said my former, now engaged as Elstree Management, colleague.

"Union Card," came the reply. "I'm the Union Representative".

"But I don't need a Card. I'm Management," said my former colleague.

"I don't care what you are. You still need a Card," was the blunt dictatorial response.

Fumbling in his pockets my former colleague, by complete chance, found his NATKE Union Card and proffered it to the man.

"Wrong Union," said the Union man : And that was it. My former colleague did not manage to even complete his first day at Elstree.

One of my colleagues who worked upstairs in Props was a pipe-smoking avuncular character by the name of Bob Street. Although he had, so I was told, problems at home, he always seemed to be a kindly soul. I, like most BBC Employees, had joined the BBC Club; and therefore when Bob, a Member of the BBC Club's Rugby Section, got to know that I had spent many years playing Rugby Union Football and asked me if I would join the Rugger Section, or Rugby Club as it was more commonly known, I, despite the fact that I had left Haileybury hating the game, told him that I would. By now the Rugby Season had started and, Bob having explained to me where the BBC Sports Ground was and that a game was to be played there the coming Saturday, I agreed to turn up for a game. So, with no car available to me at the time and with the BBC's Sports Ground being too distant for an 'easy' cycle ride, when the Saturday came I walked, taking with me my rugby kit that I had still retained from my days at Haileybury, the short distance from Kenilworth Court up Putney High Street to Putney Railway Station from where a train took me to Motspur Park. Still full of loathing for the game of Rugger I alighted from the train at Motspur Park and began to walk along the platform to the exit. Part way along the platform I stopped and asked myself "What the hell am I doing here ?". I then exited the platform and crossed over to the other platform firmly intending to abandon the idea of playing rugger for the BBC and to instead return to Putney. But, as I stood there waiting for a train to take me back to Putney, I kept thinking to myself "I can't let Bob down. I can not let Bob down". So, eventually, with the sound of an approaching train travelling in the direction of Putney getting nearer and nearer, I exited that platform, left the Station, and, with absolutely no enthusiasm whatsoever, started the 1/2Mile [0.8kilometre] or so walk from the Station to the BBC's Motspur Park Sports Ground. Having walked some distance down the road and passed, on my right, a large sign indicating another Sports Ground I then saw, to my left, a wooden-gated entrance proclaimed on an adjacent board to be the BBC's Sports Ground. "Well, this is it," I nervously thought as I passed through the open vehicular gateway and started to walk down the flowerbed-lined roadway towards the, what looked to be, main door of the Club House. Once inside I found myself in a largish but, save for some rows of team photographs hanging on a wall, empty wooden-floored Sports Hall. Straight ahead was a door which appeared to open out onto a Sports Field. Clearly that was not the way to the Changing Rooms; and so that left me with a choice of four other doors. The one immediately to my left seemed worth trying, but that turned out to lead to the largest bath, save for the Roman baths in Bath in Somerset, that I had ever seen. So I tried the opposite door to my right, but that led into, what seemed like, kitchens. So then I tried the furthest door to my right, but that led to, what seemed like, a largish lounge area. Finally, with no options now left to me I went to the one remaining door where, lo and behold, upon opening it I saw tables, chairs, and a shuttered Bar close to which was a wooden staircase with sounds of human voices coming from the top of it. Thus, by now feeling extremely nervous, to and up the staircase I went, opened the door at the top, and, passing through the corner of a Billiard/Snooker Room, exited through another doorway where I found the source of the sounds of human voices - Blokes in various stages of undress getting ready to play rugby; and there amongst them, and much to my relief, was Bob Street and another colleague from BBC Props Department, Alan Mansey.

That unenthusiastic walk that day along the road to the BBC's Sports Ground in Motspur Park, undertaken not because I wanted to undertake it but purely because I had felt unable to let a colleague down, was the start of 9 very happy and thoroughly enjoyable Seasons of playing Rugby for the BBC. Whether we won or not that day I can not now recall, but I can recall that my new-found Rugby colleagues, who came from all levels and spheres, crafts and trades within the

BBC, greeted me with considerable courtesy and friendship. I was made very welcome and went out to play feeling as if I were part of a team; and when I returned to work the following Monday I felt much more a part of the BBC than I had previously felt. Not having had a BBC Rugby 'top' when I had arrived at Motspur on the Saturday, and nobody having been able to find a spare one for me to play in, I had had to take to the field wearing my old Lawrence House 'top' from my days at Haileybury; and so a priority for me was to buy a 'top'. On the Saturday Bob had mentioned to me that a colleague in Props, Mike Preece - who had, the previous Season, played a few games for the Corporation but had given up - had a second-hand 'top' to sell. I knew Mike and got on well with him but the thought of a second-hand 'top', even one that had only been used a few times, did not appeal to me. But I told Mike that I would look at it, and a couple of days later he brought it into work with him. Despite the fact that Mike had several times charged around the rugby field in it it looked brand new; and, made by the Team's 'outfitters', Lillywhites, its quality was superb. So, Mike and I struck a deal, and I bought it for 10/- [50p]; and, despite considerable usage over many years by me on the 'Rugby Field' [and later on occasions by my Wife as a dress], it still remains a garment of excellent quality and, in my humble opinion, puts to shame many Rugby Football and Association Football 'tops' produced nowadays.

Moving Props around, moving them in and out of vans and into and out of Studios, etc., stirs up dust and, with my hay-fever, dust was a major problem for me. Furthermore, having been brought up in the Theatre side of the Theatrical Profession, Theatre was a greater attraction to me than Television, although I found the latter to be a fascinating medium in which to work; and I am truly grateful for having been enabled to have been a Movement Controller. But in the

October of 1962 I left the BBC formally and began working in London's Old Vic Theatre on the south side of the River Thames in Waterloo. Not only had I hoped that my move away from the BBC would at last cause my Mother to discontinue her, insofar as I was concerned, anti-BBC attitude but also I thought that by now she would, at least have begun to, have accepted that my future lay within my late Father's business, namely that of Scenery building. But I was wrong, very wrong.

However, before I left the Corporation's permanent employ it seemed that the Almighty had decided that HM Customs & Excise should have its revenge on me for my, in effect, having, upon my return from my trip down to Gibraltar and back, smuggled a Sanyo 'Transcontinental' radio into the UK. It was a warm sunny Sunday afternoon. I was the only Movement Controller on duty and as such was in charge of the movement of an articulated vehicle destined to go from Television Centre to Alexandra Palace and back. This was my second such occasion, the only differences from the first being that I had been one of two Movement Controllers on duty that Sunday and, leaving my colleague at Television Centre, had travelled with the vehicle to AP [Alexandra Palace] and back whereas this time I had to stay put in TVC [Television Centre]. Not that I particularly wanted to again travel to AP for my first, and only, visit there had enabled me to see most of what there was that was interesting, at least to me, within the vast building insofar as BBC Television was concerned for, whereas once - from the inauguration of BBC Television in November 1936 until the 1950s when TVC, save for experimental colour transmissions undertaken in the mid-1950s, took over - AP had been the centre of the BBC's television service, by now the BBC used that part of Alexandra Palace that it occupied for little more than as a base for BBC Television News, anchored [presented] by Richard

Baker, and as a pigeon infested space in which to store some items of scenery. The artic[ulated vehicle] concerned was a vehicle used regularly by the Scenery Department not by Props and whenever used by Scenery alone was allocated to Scenery and thus did not fall within the ambit of our Movement Control Section. However, for some reason unknown to me, whenever both Scenery and Props jointly used it it did fall within the ambit of our Movement Control regardless of which Department had the larger load; and on a 'run' to Alexandra Palace, given that our load would consist perhaps of only a couple of chairs and maybe a table and one or two other bits and pieces, it was inevitably Scenery whose load occupied most of the vehicle. Therefore the driver would park his vehicle's tractor and trailer unit close to the Television Centre's Design Block's main Scenery doors and thus some distance, but not all that far, from the two desks within Movement Control that we Movement Controllers worked from. Being a Sunday there was, in comparison with Mondays to and including Fridays, hardly anyone in Television Centre; and so I, foolishly, being somewhat bored, left my desks, and my Sanyo 'Transcontinental' radio which was standing on one of the desks blurting out music, and went from Movement Control out into the adjoining service roadway to have a look at the Scenery as it was being loaded into the artic. I made a point of not going too far so that I could both hear my 'phones should one or both of them ring and hear my radio. Quite a few pieces of Scenery, to be taken to Alexandra Palace, were loaded into the vehicle and, when that loading was complete, someone from the Props Department then loaded a few Props into the vehicle. When everything had been put in I, as the person responsible for the load, then, with one of the lads from Scenery, checked the load to ensure that it was secure. Then I turned to the waiting Driver, confirmed that everything was okay, and watched him and two lads from Scenery climb into the vehicle's cab. It was only when the vehicle began to pull away that I realised that I could no longer hear my radio. I thus rushed back to my two desks only to find that my beloved Sanyo 'Transcontinental' radio had gone. The position that I had stood in when watching the vehicle being loaded had given me a very good view not only of the Scenery 'dock' but also of much of the areas around it. Therefore I had been able to see everyone who could possibly have had access to Movement Control during the period when I was away from my desks and, given that there was hardly anyone around that sunny Sunday afternoon, there was only one person - who had once, that afternoon, passed to and fro in and from the direction of where drapes, gauzes, and backcloths were hung near to the double doors through which, on my first day in Television Centre, I had first entered Movement Control - who could possibly have accessed my radio; and he was a senior member of the Scenery Department. I informed the Corporation's Security Department who, having, they subsequently said, made enquiries, came up with a negative response. Given the history of the radio I could anticipate only disadvantage to myself were I to report the matter to the Police. Hence my conclusion that, although they did not know it, HM Customs got its revenge on me after all !!

I suppose that had I, whilst an employee of BBC Television, 'pulled' one of the many Theatrical 'strings' that were available to me, I could have, on leaving the BBC, gotten myself a job within some form of Theatre Management somewhere, probably within London's 'West End' if I had wanted it : But I felt that, if I was to build and perhaps also design Scenery, I should know exactly what it was like to actually physically handle Scenery on stage for, put simply, I did not have, and still do not have, much regard for those who are, more or less, only theoretically qualified. During my time as a Movement

Controller I was, outside of the BBC, approached and temptingly offered the job of Assistant Stage Manager [ASM] at Richmond upon Thames's Richmond Theatre [originally known as The Richmond Theatre and Opera House, then, amongst other names, The Richmond Hippodrome]. I thus went to Richmond upon Thames to have a look at this fine old Victorian Theatre - designed by perhaps the greatest of all UK Theatre Architects, Frank Matcham - and was certainly impressed by it. However, it was London's famous historic Old Vic Theatre in Waterloo that appealed to me; and thus I deliberately chose to be employed at The Old Vic as a 'Scene Shifter', otherwise known as a 'Stagehand'. I would not have missed the experience for the World, but, my God, did we have to work hard, very hard !! However, some time before I left the Corporation's full-time employment I found myself in conversation with Stephen Bundy, a conversation which, hindsight leads me to believe, was possibly/probably manoeuvred into being by the self-same Eric Maschwitz who had caused me to work for the BBC in the first place.

Stephen Bundy, whom I knew of but had, to my recollection, never met before, had, years earlier, been, I understand, a Scenic Artist and Designer with Alick Johnstone, one of the two principal firms of Scenic Artists in the London area throughout much of the first half of the 20th century [The other firm being The Harkers (founded in the latter part of the 19th century by Joseph Harker, a man considered to be one of, if not, the finest of all Scenic Artists, the firm being continued after Joe Harker senior's death by two of his sons, Joe junior and Phil at the helm, another son being the Actor Gordon Harker)]. Stephen, who had known my Father, joined BBC Television in its very early days, if not the start, of its Television Service and as such was one of the 'founding Fathers', at Alexandra Palace, of Television Design within the UK. His wealth of knowledge of Scenic

Design for the Theatre and of Scenic Design for Television was thus of the highest level. On that day that he and I met near to his Office in the Design 'block' in Television Centre his approach was simple: "You're Ted Loveday's Son, aren't you ?". After I had told him that I was we chatted about this, that, and the other before he informed me that in the September of that year he would be running, in conjunction with the BBC, a 'Night Class' Course on Scenery/Set Design at the Hammersmith College of Art and Building, a somewhat, to my mind, depressing edifice sited diagonally opposite the BBC's Lime Grove Studios; and he made the suggestion that I might like to enrol. It was an idea that appealed to me although, when I mentioned it to my Mother, not to my Mother whose response was "I don't know why you want to waste your time with that type of thing. Every Designer who've I've ever known never had any money nor ever would." - A blatant untruth, for some of the many Designers whom I had had the good fortune to meet, some in their splendid homes, prior to my Father's death were not only very successful but also certainly not lacking in wealth. Thus, after another 'casual' encounter with Stephen in which he encouraged me to enrol for his Course, I agreed to his suggestion : And one darkish wet September evening I therefore went to the College and joined the snake of human enrollers as they slowly progressed their way up a staircase to the room in which to pay their money and sign to enrol on whatever Course(s) on offer that they wished to enrol.

There were about fifteen or so people on Stephen's Design Course on the Tuesday evening when it got under way; and his first actions - after having greeted us all, given us an outline of what would be happening over the next few weeks, and made sure that we had each been provided with, or brought, the necessary drawing equipment - were to direct our attention to a list of a dozen or so Theatrical Scenery terms and expressions that he had written on a couple of blackboards and to ask us to write down, on sheets of quarto-sized paper provided to us, what, if we knew, the terms and expressions meant. The terms and expressions - such as 'Strike' [to remove Scenery, Properties, and/or Lights], 'Border' [a drape or other material hung, usually, horizontally above a stage with the intention, usually, of masking the tops of other pieces of Scenery], 'Stiffening' [a horizontal, sometimes vertical, means of holding adjoining pieces of Scenery in position relative to each other]; 'Boat Truck' [a castered wagon on which units of Scenery or other items are moved around on and/or off stage], 'Line Set' [three or more lines running through the same pulley block in order to evenly lift or lower a batten from which Scenery or Lights are suspended], 'Profile' [the shaped edging of a, usually framed, piece of Scenery], 'Tripping' [a method of raising and/or flying Scenery from its base, and other positions, as well as from its top], 'Sunday knot' [a knot in a separate piece of rope used for holding two or more Scenery-flying lines to-gether so that the lines can be operated as a single line]; etc - were each known to me [my Father, I suspect, would have looked down on me with considerable disappointment, if not horror, had they not been]; and thus it was with a sort of swollen-headed pride that I soon finished writing down what each term and expression meant. But my fellow Students were clearly not familiar with most of the terms and expressions. Thus Stephen, noticeably in his element and in masterful fashion, took considerable delight in explaining, at length and in detail, exactly what each and every term and expression meant. My fellow Students, both male and female, were clearly very interested and engrossed in what he had to say to the extent that suddenly, even for me, the two-hour Session had come to an end. The next Tuesday evening most, if not all, of us were back again to continue our enjoyment of Stephen's Design Course. Again he had written a list of terms and expressions on his blackboards and again he asked us to, if possible, write down what they meant. As with the previous week, I knew them all and was thus able to soon complete my answers, but, as before, my colleagues were clearly not familiar with most of them. Thus Stephen explained in detail what each meant, and again the two-hour Session seemed, at least to me, to be over in no time. The previous Tuesday, like everyone else, I had, at the end of the Session, tidied up, bade Stephen "goodnight", and left : But this time, as I went to leave, Stephen asked me to stay back and "have a word" with him. "Look," he said after everyone else had left, "there's little point in your continuing with this Course. Why don't you do some designwork for the Corporation ?"

"I don't have a drawing-board," I said.

"Have you got a kitchen table at home ?" he asked.

"Yes," I replied.

"Is it square or rectangular with straight sides and a flat top ?" he asked.

"Yes," I told him.

"Then, you've got a drawing board," he said. "Now," he went on, as he passed a sheet of paper to me on which he had already made some notes "what I'd like you to do is first copy this onto a piece of paper".

I had a Secretary's Notepad with me and thus quickly, and somewhat roughly, wrote down on one side of one of its sheets what Stephen had neatly written down on his piece of paper. [*A copy of my sheet of paper follows.*]

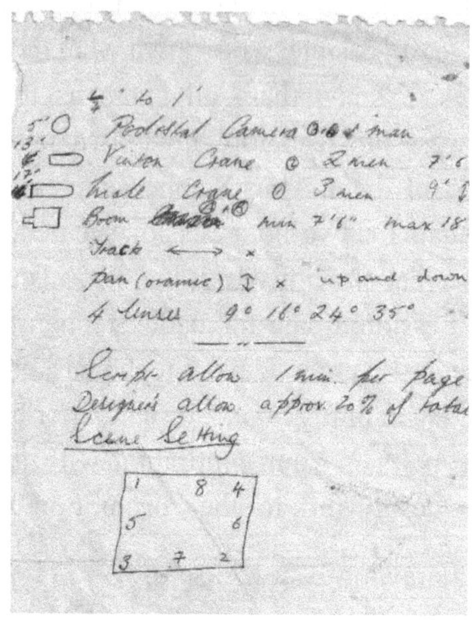

At the top, written as ¼" to 1', is the Scale to which one then worked when designing Scenery for Television. Underneath are the symbols, lengths, and number of [in those days male] operatives relevant to the principal types of Cameras [Pedestal, Vinten, and Mole] then in use within BBC Television. Beneath those are the symbol and retracted minimum and extended maximum dimensions of the Boom Microphone units then in use. Beneath those are the arrowed symbols then used to indicate the tracking and panoramic movements of Cameras and Boom Microphones; and beneath those are the angles, in degrees, of each of the four static lenses [9, 16, 24, 35] which then fronted each of the Cameras. Beneath those are notes stating the amount of time that Designers, and others, were then usually expected to allow relative to a Show's Script; and beneath those is a diagram indicating where - in order to avoid, if possible, the entanglement of, often many, cables running to and from Cameras

469

and Booms, Sets should be positioned in a Studio (The first Set, in the order of usage, being indicated as 1, the second as 2, and so on).] As I scribbled Stephen produced [1] half a dozen or so transparent large sheets of paper on which were printed 'BBC Television' and, on a ¼" grid format, the layout, and other features, of one of the Studios at Television Centre and [2] several large sheets of white drawing paper all of which, when I had finished scribbling, he passed to me with the comment "Next time I see you, at, say, about 9pm in my Office in a month's time, I want you to have drawn - both as a Floor Plan on these stock printed Studio layouts and in Elevation on these pieces of drawing paper - a non-ceilinged standard Box Set, a Set based on the Musical 'The King and I', a Set for a Choirboy singing 'O for the Wings of a Dove', and a Set for 'Music for You' [a popular monthly music Show transmitted by BBC Television in the 1950s featuring Eric Robinson and his Orchestra."

As I turned to leave the room he added "Oh, I forgot … Standard Television Scenery usually has a height of only ten feet."

"Why only ten feet ?" I asked.

"Because that's the maximum height that the lifts at Alexandra Palace could easily take !!" he replied.

Fortunately I had driven to Hammersmith College that night in my Mother's A40 car and thus had no problem in taking my surprise bundle back home to Putney; and as I did so I was somewhat overwhelmed by the trust that Stephen appeared to have in my humble design abilities, increasingly nervous about the task to which I had committed myself, and increasingly excited by the fact that it seemed that I was about to embark upon a career as a Designer within BBC

Television - an excitement no way shared or encouraged by my Mother !!

Hitherto I had been used, when designing Theatre Scenery, to using, principally, a Scale of ½" to a foot but transferring to the BBC's Television requirement of ¼" to a foot presented no problem. What did present a problem, over and above my Mother's hostility to the whole idea [though she did permit me to use her kitchen table], was ensuring that I got everything correct. The standard Box Set [a three-sided Set of the type regularly in use in Theatres throughout the land to portray such as room interiors] presented little or no problem but a Set based on 'The King and I' was altogether another matter for the Stage Show - which, starring Herbert Lom as the King, had been staged at London's Drury Lane Theatre from October 1953 to January 1956 - was very well known and the Film, released in 1956 and starring Yul Brynner as the King, was so well known that it seemed that everybody, even those who had never seen either the Show or the Film, knew most of the music from it and much of the Scenes in it. Thus I found trying to create, out of my own mind, a Set based on 'The King and I' to be hugely daunting. But salvation came in the form of the sleeve from the Long Playing [LP] Record of the music from the film, a sleeve which - adopting a policy used by many Designers - I cribbed and suitably adapted so as to indicate that it was, at least to a considerable extent, nearly all my own work.

I had decided to leave the Choirboy singing Felix Mendelssohn's 'O for the Wings of a Dove' until last because, I naïvely thought, that one would be the easiest of the four. Thus my third effort was 'Music for You' which I decided would consist of a very low podium for the Orchestra's Conductor to stand on, a selection of rostra units of various heights for the Orchestra to be sited on, and one large suspended drape [cloth] backing the lot. It was only when I got under way with the Choirboy singing 'O for the Wings of a Dove' that I realised that it was nowhere near as easy as I had thought that it would be. Indeed, it turned out to be the hardest of the four. For inspiration I went first to London's Saint Paul's Cathedral where I sat in various seats and stood in various places both within and outwith Sir Christopher Wren's masterpiece, but inspiration entirely eluded me on every attempt that I made. I thence went to Westminster Abbey where again I tried and tried to be inspired, but again inspiration entirely eluded me on every attempt. "Maybe," I thought, "I was trying to create something that was altogether too grand" :" And so, on another day, I went the few yards [metres] from 28 Kenilworth Court along Lower Richmond Road to Saint Mary's Church at the Bridge end of Putney High Street. But, again, it was hopeless. By now my four week's were fast running out, and I was in a state of semi-panic. Then suddenly - as I walked, in the daytime and with no particular thoughts in mind, from Putney's Embankment over the small bridge onto Putney's famous, and [as was well known locally] often used on dark nights by cigarette-lighting homosexuals seeking business, River Towpath - inspiration hit me : No grand Cathedral or part thereof, no Abbey or part thereof, no Church or part thereof - just a Choirboy dressed in white standing, on his own, in front of nothing whatsoever but a black drape [curtain]. It was as simple as that.

At Television Centre two Walkways, each sited over a roadway which serviced the Studios, linked the Scenery Block - the oldest part of Television Centre, its having commenced building Scenery for the BBC's Lime Grove Studios [formerly the Gaumont-British Film Studios] back in 1954 - with the main building. Both the Props Department and the Design Department, as well as the Scenery Department itself, were housed within the Scenery Block, and at that time Stephen Bundy occupied an Office sited immediately adjacent to where the Walkway nearest to Television Centre's Main Entrance abutted the Scenery Block. I had occasionally walked past his door but never, until that day four weeks after I had last spoken with him in the Hammersmith College of Art and Building, been inside. To say that, as I stood there with my rolls of drawings and knocked on his door, I was nervous would be an understatement. On his invitation to "Come in" I, fumbling as I sought to ensure that my drawings would not be damaged, opened the door and went in to be greeted by his usual courteous self; and, a few seconds later, I began to offload my offerings and display them before him. For what seemed like an eternity he perused, seemingly with considerable interest, each and every one of them. Then, with a smile, he simply said "Well done" and passed to me, as a gift, four white flat cardboard cut-outs, each scaled at ¼" to a foot, that he had made - one for each of the Pedestal, Vinten, and Mole Cameras and the fourth for the Boom Mike that I had drawn four weeks' earlier on my piece of paper in my Secretary's Notepad. Then he guided my right hand so that I would place the cut-outs, in turn, on each of my four Floor Plan drawings and, as we moved the cut-outs around, explained to me, with the assistance also of some of his own, already drawn for existing Shows, Floor Plans which featured the outlines of cut-outs in various positions on them, how Cameras and Booms must be illustrated on Floor Plans in positions so as to ensure not only that cabling running across Studio floors must not be interfered with but also that such cabling, and other items on Studio floors such as carpets, must not be 'bumped' by Cameras else either, if a Camera is transmitting at the time, the 'bumping' would violently effect the stability of any picture that was being transmitted or, regardless of whether or not a Camera is transmitting, the 'bumping' might adversely effect the electronic and/or mechanical functioning of the Camera. Suddenly it was almost midnight and this most fascinating instruction had to come to an end, for each of us had a home to go to. As we went to leave the building by a back staircase we went into another room so that Stephen could show and explain to me what it was that Design Assistants - the people who, for the benefit of those who construct the Scenery - draw in greater detail the drawings produced by Designers. Although deserted when we called, the room was clearly, during the daytime, used by several people for, on Drawing Boards and elsewhere, there was an abundance of Drawings and Models of Sets; and on the walls were sheets of drawings one with nothing but doors drawn on it, one with nothing but door frames drawn on it, one with nothing but windows drawn on it, one with nothing but window frames drawn on it, one with nothing but sections of staircases drawn on it, and so on. "These," said Stephen, "are 'stock' items". As I looked he explained to me that, for instance, the sheet with nothing but doors on it illustrated all the various types of doors, each with its own reference number, held in stock by the BBC so that all that the Designer and/or Assistant had to do was, rather than detail a required door on drawings, outline a door on the drawing and state the stock number of the door to be used. Hitherto I had experienced a world wherein more or less each door, etc been drawn in detail by a Designer or an Assistant for my Father's firm to construct specially for the Show for which the door, etc was required; and therefore the conveyor-belt type of system operated by the BBC wherein, insofar as was possible, only doors already held in stock by the BBC were used was something of a novelty. It was clearly a system that, when used, made Life a wee bit easier. However, sadly the ending of my time as a paid employee of BBC Television and my decision to work at the Old Vic caused me, after he and I parted that night at Television Centre, not to see Stephen again for quite a while.

The Old Vic was, when I joined its Staff shortly after I left BBC Television in 1962, staging 3 Plays, each on a '2-days' on' basis - Ibsen's *Peer Gynt*, Shakespeare's *The Merchant of Venice,* and Ben Jonson's *The Alchemist* with, after some weeks, *The Merchant of Venice* being replaced by Shakespeare's *Othello*. Every day, including Sundays, of every week I left the Flat, walked up Putney High Street to Putney's Main Line Railway Station, caught the train to Waterloo, arrived at Waterloo Station, left Waterloo Station, then crossed Waterloo Road to arrive at The Old Vic at about 8.30 am. Each night, other than Sundays, at some time around midnight I would reverse the process arriving, zombielike, back at the Flat at around 1am next day. Sometimes, as the train neared Putney, I was so fast asleep that I would not wake up until the train was at least two Stations down the line passed Putney. I would then have to get out of the train, cross over to the platform which catered for the London-bound trains, and catch the next train back to Putney having, occasionally, on arrival back at Putney to explain to an employee of British Rail [the joint Railway/Train operator in those days] why it was that I had just got off a train that was heading in the opposite direction from where my ticket informed that I was supposed to have come from. Sundays were the exceptions to getting back to Putney at 1am next day, for on Sundays we finished at The Vic at around 1pm thereby enabling me to get back home sometime during the afternoons. To my mind The Old Vic's schedule, caused by the '2-days' on' cycle of staging 3 Shows a week and the facts that each Show had a lot of both Scenery and Props, was ridiculous; and it is certainly a schedule which I would rarely recommend for it was, at least for us full-time Stagehands who did not live close to The Vic, shatteringly exhausting. But I had to accept it for I had known before I signed-on at The Vic what its routine was.

Stagehands in Theatres such as the 'Vic' were made up, principally, of two groups of people: The first being a permanent 'core' group of full-time Staff and the second being regular part-timers, such as Taxi-drivers wanting a regular something-to-do to earn money during their 'quiet' taxi-driving periods, who came into the Theatre not only in the lead-in time before a Show to undertake the extra work involved in actually 'operating' the Show whilst it was being performed but also for some of the Scene-shifting Rehearsal times. Because, during a performance, a Show has to run like clockwork both the core group and the regular part-timers had to function as one team and thus all, not just full-timers, were not only skilled in their craft as Stagehands but also, at least work-wise, trusting of each other so as to be able to rely unhesitatingly on each other to do and inter-change each others jobs. Thus joint rehearsals in both setting-up and striking scenery was essential for both groups. Therefore "I'll come in if I can" was not an attitude that could be tolerated in a part-timer who, although only a part-timer, was as essential to any Production as was the permanent core group of Stagehands. Trust and camaraderie were the keys.

With the '2-days' on' cycle that The Vic was operating the first of each two days included not only an evening performance, and also a matinée if the first day was a Wednesday or a Saturday, but also a combination of setting up the Scenery and dressing the set(s) with whatever Props had to go on it(them), tolerating Actors and Actresses - some of whom were very enthusiastic and very co-operative, some of whom had 'seen it all before' and just did what they were told when they were told, and some of whom were so full of their own importance that they were a bl**dy irritation at times - as they were put through rehearsals by the Director, and having to cope with the forays onto the Stage of the Lighting Designer or an Assistant so that the angles or shadings of lights could be tweaked in order to better light the Set and/or an Actor or Actress. Suddenly lunchtime would arrive at which time and after which time, unless there was a matinée performance to be coped with, there was suddenly nothing to do until an hour or thereby before the evening Show. For me it was impractical if not impracticable to even try to go to Putney and back to the Vic in the time available : So, the choice was either to hang around within the Theatre or go walkabout somewhere or both. The decision was usually to go walkabout somewhere; and that often meant first a walk over Waterloo Bridge to go to Yates' Wine Lodge in The Strand to enjoy a glass or more of Port. Thereafter I would stroll round other parts of nearby London - Trafalgar Square, Covent Garden, Shaftesbury Avenue, etc - just to pass the time until I was required back at The Vic. Not far from The Vic was a Street Market, and so, occasionally, I would wander down there more often than not just to have a look at the goodies on offer and to have a listen to the wonderful patter that many Street Traders entranced many a punter with. Occasionally I would go down the Market with the intention of buying something; and on one occasion one excellent purchase that I made was a pair of workshoes. Up until working at the Vic I had relied on ordinary shoes, but the pressures on the feet caused by Scene shifting, especially on a raked (sloping) stage, was too much of a challenge for normal footwear and thus to the Market where I knew that I was likely to be able to purchase a good hardy pair of shoes for the job : And what a purchase it turned out to be. The cost was 10/- [50p] , and the shoes were so well made that not only did they give me considerable comfort whilst working at The Vic but also they lasted for years and years without hardly any visible evidence of wear upon their soles and heels. In fact I only got rid of them because I eventually grew sick and tired of the sight of them.

Life at The Vic was often a complete contrast to life at the BBC where, my time at The Vic made me realise, we had been spoilt, very spoilt. Whereas, for instance, we had often dined in quarter- or semi-luxury in, say, Television Centre, the eating facilities at The Vic were very basic, doubtless caused by the fact that space within Theatres, especially older Theatres, was often very, very limited. Thus, whereas at the BBC my BBC colleagues and I had sat at tables in purpose-built, and often very noisy, dining-rooms, at The Vic I and my colleagues there often sat in silence or semi-silence under the stage eating our food, and surrounded by Props and much clutter besides, whilst Actors and Actresses thumped around on the stage above us. I have always had a liking for fish and chips and, on one occasion at The Vic, took advantage of a nearby 'Chippie' to buy some fish and chips which, during a performance of The Merchant of Venice, I took below stage to eat. Within minutes the Front-of-House [FOH] Manager appeared and quietly but very firmly asked "Who the hell's eating fish and chips ?" In charge of most things that went on in the Auditorium and elsewhere in the building in front of the stage the FOH Manager had, apparently, been inundated with complaints from Members of the Audience concerning the smell of fish and chips permeating throughout the entirety of the Auditorium. "Remind 'em it's The Merchant of Venice they've come to see an' tell 'em they're bloody lucky we ain't charging for the smells of Venice we're givin' 'em," one of my colleagues humorously but unsuccessfully told the FOH Manager. But to no avail, for I was ordered to go outside the Theatre to finish my fish and chips and enlightened in no uncertain terms that the eating of fish and chips in a Theatre is strictly forbidden.

Not that I and my fish and chips were the only challenge that the FOH Manager had to cope with from those with whom he did not normally come into contact. One of the great Character Actors at the Old Vic whilst I was there was Wilfrid Lawson who appeared as the Button Moulder in Peer Gynt. A superb Actor with a wonderful trembling voice which he could project to perfection throughout the entirety of the Auditorium without any need whatsoever of any artificial assistance such as a microphone. An 'old hand' with many years experience, he was, when on stage, usually a joy to watch and to listen to. But Peer Gynt is a play with many Acts and many Scenes and Wilfrid did not make his, eagerly awaited by the Audience, entrance until Scene Seven of Act Five. Like many Theatres the Old Vic had a Public House as a neighbour. Given that there is, for Actors and Actresses, often not much to do within Theatres when not actually on stage, such places are well used by performers : And Wilfrid was no exception for more often than not he would be found frequenting the Public House whilst awaiting his turn to be told by a 'runner' first that he had "Ten minutes, Mr Lawson" and then, five minutes later, "Five minutes, Mr Lawson" before his entrance on stage. On the particular night concerned Wilfrid, clad as usual in his Button Moulder's costume, had spent much time sitting on a bar stool downing a few glassfuls of liquid refreshment; and so, having arrived off-stage after having received his 5-Minute Call, he was not quite as steady on his feet as he perhaps should have been.

The superb Australian-born Actor, Leo McKern - whose most famous 'part' was probably that of Horace Rumpole in *Rumpole of the Bailey*, a seven-series television production, first transmitted in 1975, written by the lawyer John Mortimer QC [Queen's Counsel] - played the part of Peer Gynt and as such he opened Scene Seven having positioned himself on stage in semi-darkness in front of the House Curtains [Tabs] just after the Auditorium lights had been dimmed.

With Wilfred - carrying, in his right hand, a long-handled casting-ladle and, in his left hand, a bag of tools - standing immediately behind the closed Tabs at the point where the two curtains which form the Tabs met, McKern as Peer Gynt, informed, in three-quarter darkness, the Audience that he had lots of corpses to bury and then shouted for a gravedigger. This being Wilfrid's entrance cue, the Tabs were manually opened, by two Stagehands each of whom stood behind one of the curtains, to a distance sufficient only to enable Wilfrid to pass from behind the Tabs out in front of the Tabs which then were closed whilst Wilfrid walked slowly forwards onto a small Apron Stage temporarily positioned immediately in front of, and thrusting from, downstage-centre so as to form an extension to the main Stage. To highlight the Button Moulder, and thus Wilfrid, the beams from two Spotlights, one of which was positioned within the right-hand side of the Auditorium and the other within the left-hand side of the Auditorium, were focused upon the Apron Stage thus causing Peer Gynt to be momentarily put into almost complete darkness thereby causing Wilfrid to be the only person in view.

True to the script, Wilfrid, having walked as far as he could go without falling off the Apron, first having placed one foot firmly down and then the other foot firmly down, positioned himself on the Apron Stage. Then, much more heavily than usual, he banged the base of the casting-ladle's long handle down hard upon the Apron Stage noticeably using the casting-ladle and its long staff as a means by which to steady himself. Then he lowered his left arm down so as to place his bag of tools on the Stage but, instead of lowering his arm fully down, he allowed the bag to drop, with a loud clatter, some six inches or so onto the Stage. Then he slowly raised his left arm and pointed his left hand towards the Audience who, as always, was silent whilst eagerly awaiting to hear this great Character Actor speak : And speak he eventually did. But instead of saying, as he should have done, "Well met, old man" to Peer Gynt, Wilfrid, his beautiful trembling voice projecting every word throughout the entirety of the Auditorium, slowly and emphatically said "You ... can ... bloody well ... sod off". Then, still firmly holding on to the handle of his casting-ladle, he crashed backwards down onto the Stage oblivious to all and everything around him.

The two Spotlights were immediately 'killed' [switched off] thereby momentarily throwing the Stage into complete darkness. The Tabs were then very quickly opened sufficiently enough to allow Wilfrid to be grabbed and, still firmly holding on to the handle of his casting-ladle, pulled back behind the now fast-closing Tabs. With the Audience completely bewildered and with a semi-panic-stricken Leo McKern groping his way backstage, the unconscious Wilfrid lay on the floor behind the closed Tabs for a while before slowly coming-to whilst repeating "I am so sorry, so very sorry. I do not know what came over me. Nothing like this has ever happened to me before. Nothing like this has *ever* happened to me before".

By now the Auditorium lights had been brought fully back on and - as Wilfrid, now sitting up and being plied with black coffee, stayed on the floor immediately behind the closed Tabs - the FOH Manager, having hurried backstage to find out what was happening, went in front of the Tabs to announce to a still bewildered, and by now concerned Audience that "Mr Lawson is feeling none-too-well this evening". He then collected Wilfrid's Button Moulder's bag of tools and returned backstage to find out what on earth was going to happen next. Would the performance have to be abandoned or what ? He had to tell the Audience something.

After what seemed like an eternity, during which Wilfrid had downed a fair quantity of black coffee, Wilfrid, in true 'The Show must go on' fashion, then announced that he now felt fit enough to continue. Then, still firmly holding the handle of his casting-ladle, Wilfrid was helped back onto his feet and handed his bag of tools, and the FOH Manager went back on stage in front of the Tabs and announced to the, very quiet Audience, "Mr Lawson feels able to continue".

Greeted by a round of applause Leo McKern, as Peer Gynt, went back on stage and recommenced Scene Seven of Act Five. On cue, the Tabs were again opened, and Wilfrid, to a very loud round of applause, appeared and again slowly made his way back to the Apron where, as before, he plonked, one after the other, his feet firmly down, banged the base of the casting-ladle's long handle down hard, lowered his left arm down and this time placed his bag of tools on the Stage. Then again he slowly raised his left arm. This time however he slowly swept his arm in an arc from right to left whilst pointing his hand rigidly at the Audience and, as he did so, he, loudly and boldly, simply said to all and sundry "And … you … can … bloody … well … sod off … too !!" Then he again crashed down backwards onto the Stage; and this time everyone knew not only that he meant it but also that that was well and truly the end of that night's performance of Ibsen's *Peer Gynt* !!

Adrienne Corri was an Actress who seemed to take delight in entertaining us sometimes bored, sometimes very bored Scene Shifters as we, at times, stood around behind the Scenery with little or nothing to do whilst Actors and Actresses performed. It was, for instance, her practice, on having exited Stage Left in order to effect a complete costume-change, whilst crossing behind the Scenery before entering Stage Right, to strip off completely save for her panties, then dash behind the Scenery into a costume held for her to instantly put on by a Dresser. A talented Actress in many ways, as she made her dash behind the Scenery she would lift up her two frontward-projecting assets, point them in our direction, and, before reaching her Dresser, grinningly say something like "Milk anyone ?" Given Adrienne Corri's titillating activities at The Vic it came as no surprise that she subsequently went on to star, as a rape victim, in Stanley Kubrick's 1971 film *A Clockwork Orange* !!

Amongst the acting talent that graced the stage of The Old Vic during my time as one of that historic Theatre's Stagehands was that of Esmond Knight. A fine Actor before the Second world war, he was severely injured, and completely lost the sight in both his eyes, when, as a serving sailor aboard *HMS Prince of Wales* in 1941, his ship was attacked by the German Battleship *Bismarck,* the *Bismarck* having turned on the *Prince of Wales* after having sunk *HMS Hood*. After a couple of years or so later Esmond Knight regained partial sight in one of his eyes; and it was in that condition that he continued, with much success, his acting career. Theatres often abound with mechanical equipment - sometimes manually operated, sometimes machine operated - and as such can be dangerous, sometimes very dangerous, places. One piece of such mechanical equipment is a Trap Door the opening of which enables things and people to be elevated up to the Stage or lowered down from the Stage. Commonplace, 'Traps' are respected by those on stage, but they are sometimes forgotten about, or partially forgotten about, causing, when they are open, accidents to sometimes happen. Such was one of the accepted hazards of life on stage.

The Old Vic stage had a Trap beneath which was a lift elevation system which allowed things and people to be mechanically raised and lowered. Esmond Knight was well aware of its existence and, being substantially blind, always took perhaps greater care than most would have done whenever he was near it. However, it was not as a result of any negligence on stage that the incident occurred but as part of a performance wherein Esmond had to arrive on stage having been elevated there by the below-stage mechanism of the Trap. Everyone who accessed the Stage via a mechanical Trap mechanism received assistance. Because of his blindness Esmond not only had that assistance but had extra assistance when mounting the Trap's platform to ensure that he was properly positioned on the platform so that he would safely pass through the Trap's on-Stage opening. Unfortunately, as the platform travelled upwards towards the opening, Esmond, without himself or anyone else realising it, allowed one of his feet to slide slightly forward so that his toes were over one of the edges of the platform. The result was painfully agonising for Esmond and visually agonising for all, including members of the Audience, who saw his toes being squeezed between the platform and the edge of the opening as the platform neared the end of its upwards journey.

I was often 'partnered' in my time at The Vic by a slightly-older-than-I Australian lad for whom Stagehanding was something to do to earn money whilst in the UK for a year or so. To-gether we would run Scenery, lash, with sash cord, Scenery to-gether, and generally function as a 2-man team; and it was in this capacity that we regularly worked to fly a tree out of sight of the Audience. At the end of the Scene in which this well-made, and somewhat solid, tree had been a feature we had a twenty-second Scene-change blackout in which to manually haul the thing out of sight of the Audience. The theory of our operation was quite simple: Attached to the top of the tree, and out of Audience-sight, was a rope which went upwards, over a single pulley, and thence at an angle down to where the two of us were, in a 'silence at all times' void in near total darkness, waiting. Whilst the Scene was being performed our end of the rope was tied round a large metal cleat that was well secured to a wall. When, during the last moments of the Scene, our cue came one of us would, without effecting the stability of the rope to thus ensure that the tree did not wobble, take hold of the rope whilst the other one of us would take hold of the lose end of the rope in readiness of unwinding it from the cleat as soon as the blackout occurred : And as soon as the blackout occurred the one of us holding the rope would take the strain on the rope whilst the other of us furiously unwound the rope from the cleat. Then each of us would 'lurching', and not being able to speak to each other, pull like hell on the rope so as to elevate the tree as fast as was possible until it could go no further. Then the one of us who had unwound the rope off its cleat would then re-wind the rope on the cleat so as to secure the tree thereby enabling both of us to release the rope, relax, and, still in enforced silence, regain our strengths : And when the lights came back on the Audience could no longer see the tree due to the fact that its base was now parked out-of-sight behind a masking Drop Border that flew above the Stage from one side to the other. Unfortunately not all good ideas always go to plan; and on one occasion we had not managed to pull the tree the entire length of its upwards journey by the time that the lights came back on again. The results were that: For the audience, they had to spend the next Scene looking at about a foot [300mm] or so of tree hanging, in full view, below the bottom level of the Border; and for my silent Australian colleague and me, we had, because we had been unable to tie-off the rope onto its cleat in time, to spend the entirety of the next Scene using our full strengths hanging on to a rope at the end of which was a tree the weight of which, as time passed, seemed to get heavier and heavier and heavier and heavier. We had, of course, two other alternatives: Either we could have continued the process of 'lurchingly' pulling the tree out of sight and then tying it off, but to have done so would have probably engendered comedy into an otherwise very serious piece of entertainment or we could have let go of the rope, but to have done so would have caused the tree to have descended rapidly downwards onto, and perhaps partially through, the Stage. So, in continued silence, we just held on to it, and prayed. Fortunately after a while we devised a system of - whilst still keeping the rope, and thus the tree, motionless - one of us taking the entirety of the strain whilst the other of us relaxed his muscles a wee bit. But nonetheless it was an excruciating, and never to be repeated, experience !!

Many of those who, as Members of the Audience, attended such productions, at Theatres like The Vic, as Peer Gynt and The Merchant of Venice are, or consider themselves to be, experts or semi-experts. Rarely in my time at The Vic did I go front-of-house; but on one occasion when I did so just after a performance of The Merchant of Venice had ended I was in the foyer as the Audience was streaming out. Down the main stairs came a seemingly learned gentleman with his coterie of admirers; and I could not help but hear him saying, as he demonstratively flailed his arms in all directions, to his open-mouthed followers "Of course, what Shakespeare really meant was not what Shakespeare wrote. No, what Shakespeare really meant was to express his deep inner self, to express the deeper meaning of inner man"; and so the babble of his false expertise went on. "What utter nonsense," I thought as I watched him and his gaggle of naïve believers pass by through the foyer and into the cold outside world beyond the inviting warmth of the famous Old Vic Theatre's foyer.

Adjoining the Theatre itself was The Old Vic's own Scenery Workshops where Scenery was both made and painted not only for The Vic itself but also for The Old Vic in Bristol and for The Vic's then associate Theatre in London, Sadler's Wells to and from which we Stagehands sometimes travelled in order to convey items from the one Theatre to the other. One mid-morning I, with some fellow Stagehands, happened to be in the Workshops when a load of Scenery, including three painted backcloths [cloths], was returned to The Vic from The Old Vic in Bristol. Out of curiosity I asked what was going to happen to it and was informed that the flats and so forth would be put into stock for use in other productions and that I could have the three cloths for free if I wanted them as they were otherwise destined to be scrapped. Although no longer suitable for professional productions of the kind staged at The Old Vic the cloths were in not too bad a condition; and so some days later I transported them, one at a time in my Mother's A40 car, from The Old Vic to the workshop kindly made available to me in Kenilworth Court.

During my time at The Vic a longtime friend of my Parents, 'Aunt' Bessie, stayed for a few days at the flat in Putney. A very Jewish couple, neither she nor her late Husband, 'Uncle' Abe, was a blood relation but they clearly had a very close connection to my Father. Why I do not know and have never been able to find out, but I have little doubt that - possibly during, or in the years immediately before, the Second World War - my Father had rendered them or, if not them directly, a member of their Family a considerable service, a service which, I feel, had some connection with my Father's subsequent, but unsuccessful, determination to drive into that part of Germany beyond the East German Border Guards when my Parents and I had holidayed in Continental Europe after the Second World War. I knew Uncle Abe's and Aunt Bessie's surname as being 'Flowers' : But whether that was Uncle Abe's original surname or, if it was an Anglicised version of an original Jewish surname, what his birth surname was I do not know. Both Uncle Abe and Aunt Bessie had been my Father's guests when we had lived at Highlands but Uncle Abe had died prior to Aunt Bessie's visit to Kenilworth Court, at which time Aunt Bessie was living at 488 Street Lane, Moortown, Leeds, Yorkshire. Before that she, and Uncle Abe, had lived nearby in Harrogate Road, Leeds to which they had moved from Knowle Avenue in Blackpool. But the 'mystery' of Uncle Abe and Aunt Bessie is, for me at least, made more puzzling not by the fact that previous to living in Blackpool they had lived in Coolmore Park, North Circular Road, Belfast but by the fact that when they lived in Coolmore Park, Belfast they had, seemingly out of a deep respect for my Father, named their house "Loveday". Furthermore, Uncle Abe, a Tailor by Trade, had, whilst living in Belfast, donated to my Father three perfectly fitting suits that he had, over an extended week-end, handmade for my Father. By any stretch of the imagination the handmaking of three such suits over an extended week-end was an achievement, even for a skilled Tailor such as Uncle Abe was, but - when one takes into account that, being a devout Jew, Uncle Abe would not have undertaken any work on those suits during that week-end's Jewish Sabbath - the making, entirely by hand, of those three suits was, to my mind at least, a remarkable achievement and, with the naming of his house as "Loveday", evidences, I believe, that whatever it was that my Father had done, or had had done, was certainly something very special. [*see copy of the relevant part of the page of my Father's Address Book*]

I know that my Father had Theatrical friends and acquaintances in Germany prior to the outbreak of the Second World War and I know that, being within the Theatrical Profession, many of my Father's friends and acquaintances, in the UK and elsewhere, were Jewish. But to me 'Uncle' Abe and 'Aunt Bessie' remain a mystery.

My arrival back at Kenilworth Court from The Old Vic one Sunday afternoon whilst Aunt Bessie was staying with my Mother and me had followed an unexpected invitation that I had received some days previously from my Old Vic Australian colleague to go out to Perth in Western Australia to help set up a Television Studio during what were then the infant days of Australian Television. I was enjoying life, and the company of friends and acquaintances whom I had made, at The Old Vic but the hours were, even though I was fit physically, draining me of energy; and so I very much welcomed the invitation moreso as it would enable me to be 'in' in the early days of Australian TV. In those days the Australian Government was inviting UK adult citizens to, in exchange for a payment of only £10, go to live in Australia. The policy was called 'Assisted Passage' and was a scheme operated by the Australian Government from 1945 to 1972 with the deliberate intentions of increasing Australia's population and its skills' levels. Anyone interested had to apply to the Australian High Commission at Australia House in The Strand in London : And so, given that Australia House was just a short walk across Waterloo Bridge from The Old Vic, during one afternoon whilst having nothing else to do I walked over Waterloo Bridge to Australia House for a chat and was given the necessary forms to complete and return and told that - as I would have a job in Australia to go to, as I had a valid UK Passport, and as I also had the necessary £10 - my Application would undoubtedly be accepted. Because of the facts that, other than on Sundays, I left Kenilworth Court early each day and arrived back very early the next day, I did not raise the matter with my Mother until that Sunday afternoon; and Aunt Bessie - who, whilst staying at Putney, had a habit of 'shadowing' my Mother everywhere she went - was present when I mentioned it. "Oooh," said the, as always, excitable Aunt Bessie, "I've got friends in Sydney in Australia. After you get to Perth you must pop over one afternoon and have tea with them !!" I somehow think that the kindly soul had no idea that Perth is about 2,460 miles [3,960 kilometres] from Sydney. Later that evening, whilst Aunt Bessie was having a bath, my Mother called me from the Kitchen, where I had made my intention known to both her and Aunt Bessie, to the Lounge where, turning to me and with tears in her eyes, she said "How can you ? How can you ? How can you leave me, a Widow ?" So I never went to Australia; and years later, when I saw, on television, the splendour of Western Australia's superb City of Perth and realised how stupid I had been to have turned down such an opportunity, I said to myself "What a mug you were to have fallen for the stunt that your Mother pulled that day !!" - For subsequent experiences had by then caused me to realise that my Mother's real intention had nothing whatsoever to do with her being a Widow but was instead an attempt to block my returning to the world of Television.

I stayed at The Vic for a wee while longer and when I left it I did so with good memories, for instance, of Fred Hornsby - a London 'Black Cab' Taxi Driver who came in every evening to work as a part-time Scene Shifter/Stage Hand and whose description of the Brunskill and Loveday Scenery that he had, as a Scene Shifter in other London theatres, handled over the years as being "Bloody good solid well-built stuff but *bloody* heavy !!"; of my Australian rope-heaving Stagehand colleague who enthusiastically encouraged me to take up the Australian TV Offer "Rigadless of wot yer flaming Mother says"; of that fine and always considerate-to-us-Stagehands Australian Actor, Leo McKern (famous for his part of Horace Rumpole in the long running television series *Rumpole of the Bailey*) ; of The Vic's Stage-Door Keeper who, regardless of the hour, seemed always to be there and was always cheerful; of the wonderful, but no means always sober, character Actor, Wilfrid Lawson; and of many others - such as the excellent Actresses, Catherine Lacey and the titillating Adrienne Corri; and of the fine Actors, Fulton Mackay, Trevor Peacock, Esmond Knight, Vernon Dobtcheff, James Maxwell, Russell Hunter, and others - each of whom, I confess, we Stagehands sometimes took for granted as indeed did they us. However, I left The Vic having had a good physical training in the skills of running Scenery, flying Scenery, and so on. Also, I now knew not only how to design and build Scenery but also how it feels like to actually have to operate it.

One other thing that I missed on ceasing to work at The Vic was the delicious Ham and Tomato semi-crusty Rolls offered for sale at Waterloo Station. I never had time on my arrival in the mornings to purchase any and by the time that my zombie self arrived back at the Station to make the return journey to Putney the woman and her trolley from which the Rolls were sold had long since gone; and so most afternoons, and sometimes also during the mornings if work permitted, I would venture to the Station and onto its main Platform concourse area to purchase a couple of them, the like of which I have never since tasted. Hmmmm, delicious !!

So, having resigned from The Vic, it was back to Putney with nothing particular to do. A local Vehicle Repair business sited in a road adjoining Putney's Lower Richmond Road employed me for a short while on a part-time basis as a sort of 'Odd Job' person during which I worked both at the business's premises and in my Workshop in Kenilworth Court where I undertook specialised Joinerywork for the bosses of the business. It was totally boring : But things changed a short time after, in 1963, a new Supervisor for Kenilworth Court appeared on the scene. I had always got on well with the previous occupant of the job whose tied flat, No. 101A Kenilworth Court, backed onto a small yard across the other side of which was sited my Workshop. To get to my Workshop I would enter the yard via a gate sited adjoining the Bricklayer's Arms, a popular Public House sited in Waterman Street alongside Kenilworth Court and tenanted by a guy called Sullivan, and, if I saw the Supervisor either in the yard or in his flat, I would always chat to him. However, though very willing and pleasant to talk to, he was somewhat of a nervous, timid man whose conversation was not really that interesting to me. Douglas Henry Lindsay, the new Supervisor, was noticeably different. His Father had been an 'Army man' through and through who, on retiring from the Army proper, continued his Military life by becoming a Yeoman Warder [or, to give it its more casual name, 'Beefeater'] at the Tower of London, the principal building of which - the White Tower - had been constructed, with stone brought over from Normandy, in the 1070s by order of William the Conqueror with the intention of protecting himself and his Norman troops from the then hostile, to William and his invading Normans, citizenry of London. Born in 1917, Doug Lindsay's childhood had been enveloped entirely within the British Army and its culture and it was therefore not surprising that he himself would join the Army. Indeed, it had been expected of him. Aged 22 when the Second World War started, Doug subsequently had much experience both within Wartime and within Peacetime as a serving Soldier in the Royal Artillery [the British Army Regiment (or, more correctly, group of Regiments) which, in 1861, had taken over the Honourable East India Company's 48 Field Batteries of Artillery and 21 Horse Batteries of Artillery when the East India Company was wound-up by HM Government in the 1860s. Like many Service Personnel whose lives were totally committed to their profession Doug had, on leaving the Army, found it difficult to come to terms with life in 'civvy' street and thus, having left at the rank of WO1, he returned to it a short while later to retire again at the very slightly lower rank of WO2. After his second, and final, retirement from being an employee of Her Majesty this intelligent and upright-bearing man and his 3 years younger than he Wife, Joan, took over a Public House in Woolwich, just a short 'spit' from his colleagues in the Royal Artillery's Headquarters in nearby Woolwich Arsenal. But life as a Publican did not work out too well; and at this point an old Army friend, a Major Wright, came up with a solution as to what Doug might do next - For Major Wright was the self-same Major Wright who had gotten himself the job of Manager of Kenilworth Court : And it just so happened that Kenilworth Court's Supervisor was leaving thereby causing Kenilworth Court to have need of a new Supervisor.

The staircase and other common features, and the removal of rubbish and waste, within each block of flats within Kenilworth Court were daily attended to by elderly gentlemen, each of whom was allocated to one or two blocks, employed by the Management Company via Major Wright for the purpose. Sid was the name of the gentleman employed to look after the block in which our flat, No 28, was situated. Prior to Doug's arrival Sid, along with the other elderly gentleman who looked after the other blocks, would, early each weekday morning, arrive in the yard in which my Workshop was situated, collect their brooms and other cleaning items, and then go to their respective block of flats and start work. But the routine changed as soon as the former Warrant Officer, Royal Artillery arrived. Once in the yard they would each collect a broom. Then they would file in line and 'slope arms' as if in the Armed Forces. Then Doug would climb out of his groundfloor flat, Number 101A, via its kitchen window and enter the yard wherein he would go down the line and inspect his 'troops' to ensure that they had 'sloped arms' properly. Then he would order them to 'present arms'. Then he would again go down the line and this time inspect his 'troops' to ensure that they had 'presented arms' properly. Then he would 'dismiss' them; after which he would climb back into his flat via its kitchen window and make them each a mug of tea. Only after they had all drunk their teas would they then collect the rest of their cleaning items and go to their respective block of flats. After Doug had been at Kenilworth Court for a while I asked Sid whether he and his colleagues objected to this Gilbert and Sullivan-type activity. "Good God, no," replied Sid. "We think the world of him and thoroughly enjoy playing along with him. Besides, he makes a *bloody* good mug of tea !!"."

Doug Lindsay and his Wife, Joan, had two Children: A Son, Peter Henry, aged almost 18 when they arrived at Kenilworth Court and a Daughter, June Catherine. Although, when in the area of my Workshop, I often had occasion to chat with Doug I had never met either of his Children until one day in July 1963 someone knocked on my Workshop's open door and then, having taken one step down to come partially inside the Workshop, said "Dad says 'Would you like a cup of tea ?' " There, standing in the doorway, was a slim, very attractive-looking 16-years' old blonde. Not only am I an 'only child' but also my entire formal education had been within schools the environments of which in no way offered any 'training' as to how to 'cope' with girls : And so the best that I could do was stare at this delicious-looking creature and force the words "Yes, please" out of my mouth. She, seemingly as shy and as embarrassed as I was, then turned and went back to her Father. I, as fast as I could, put down what I was doing, left my Workshop, and went the short distance over to the window of Doug's kitchen. But only Doug was there, his delicious-looking messenger having absented herself completely.

"Who was that ?" I asked.

"Oh, that was June," Doug replied as he passed a cup of tea out to me.

I never saw June again that day but I did see her on many occasions over many years thereafter.

Doug and I, not because of Doug's Daughter but because of Doug's own personality, became very good friends, a friendship that lasted until his death in the late 1990s. To say that Kenilworth Court was fortunate to have obtained the services of such a man would be an understatement for, save for one short period when he left Kenilworth Court for employment selling Insurance for the Eagle Star Insurance Company, his commitment to Kenilworth Court and to the wellbeing of its Residents, all of them, was, until his retirement in the mid-1980s, total. Besides conscientiously doing his contracted job as Kenilworth Court's Supervisor he did many little jobs for many of the flats' residents. They only had to say to him such as "Oh, Mr Lindsay, do you think that you can do me a favour and …" and he would, if he could, readily oblige. His good nature was often taken advantage of.

Doug and I co-operated on various little projects due in part because I had lots of spare time and in part because my Workshop and my joinery skills enabled me to construct items which Doug, with his limited facilities, was unable to construct. Requests for Doug to 'assist' by making wooden pelmet boxes were not uncommon especially from owners of flats which had bay-windows in them. Doug would measure-up, I would construct them, and to-gether we would carry them in one completed piece from my Workshop to the flat concerned wherein we would climb step-ladders, fix them in place, and Doug would return at a later date and paint them. We were mugs enough to charge only for materials, and even then there were some seemingly wealthy people who seemed to have a reluctance to pay.

Joan, Doug's Wife, worked, throughout the period of Doug's employment at Kenilworth Court, in several of London's principal Department Stores - First in Peter Jones in Chelsea, then in the now-no-longer Bourne and Hollingsworth in Oxford Street, and finally in Harrods in Knightsbridge where, her speciality being Perfumery, she was in charge of much of the Perfumery 'floor' and as such supervised and co-ordinated the activities of the many international Perfumery firms granted franchises to sell their products within Harrods.

Not only was Doug's 'tied' flat at 101A inconvenient insofar as access to the Yard was concerned - for for many years it had no means of access to the Yard other than to climb out of either its kitchen window or a window sited in its hallway - but also, with two teenage Children each of a different sex, Doug had need of three bedrooms whereas 101A had only two bedrooms, a livingroom, a bathroom, and a kitchen. But - whereas nowadays most, if not all, persons employed as a Supervisor would, if 'tied' accommodation forms part of the employment contract, demand, and would more likely than not receive, 'tied' accommodation properly suited to their needs - attitudes in those days were more 'flexible'; and for Doug, with his military background and worldwide experience of Army accommodation, the lack of a bedroom could easily be overcome by adapting the layout of the livingroom within 101A so that it would also accommodate a bed. He was fortunate in that the livingroom was a large room of a size more than sufficient to accommodate not only living and dining areas but also a bed. Of the two bedrooms, Doug and Joan used one and Peter, being the older of their two Children, used the other. Thus the occupant of the bed in the living room was June who by then had left school and had got a job as a Receptionist in an upmarket Hairdresser's Salon in Chelsea's then increasingly famous King's Road, the once private royal road by which King Charles II used to travel, via Fulham and Putney, to Kew.

The major problem with June's sleeping in the livingroom was that, in order to provide her with the privacy which she required and to which she was entitled - and Doug and Joan were very respectful of her privacy - life within the flat had, sometimes somewhat inconveniently, to revolve around June's use of the livingroom as a bedroom. So, any visitors had to vacate 101A well in advance of June's wanting to go to bed. Another problem with 101A was that, given that it was centrally sited within the blocks of flats, many of Kenilworth Court's residents would disregard the Lindsay's out-of-hours entitlement to privacy and knock on their frontdoor at any hour that they wished in order to request Doug's, or even Joan's, attention to some or other, real or imaginary, problem which often could have waited to the next day or which often was of no concern of Doug, or certainly of Joan, whatsoever. Indeed the thoughtlessness of many of the residents in unnecessarily disturbing the privacy of Doug and/or

Joan - who although not an employee of Kenilworth Court nonetheless would voluntarily assist residents whenever she could - eventually, some years after I had moved out of Kenilworth Court, determined Doug to, on Joan's retirement from Harrods, terminate his employment at Kenilworth Court and retire to a pleasant little house that he and his Wife bought on the South Coast in Seaford, Sussex.

Joan came from Houghton-le-Spring in County Durham. How she met Doug I am not sure. I know that he was, during or just after, the War stationed at a Military Camp in Berwick-upon-Tweed, a Camp the site of which is nowadays occupied by a Golf Course and scores of static caravans many of which form part of a Holiday Camp Site. Joan, Doug, Peter, and June were a very 'close' family. Peter - whose middle name, like that of his Father, is Henry - because of Doug's nomadic Army lifestyle, had obtained much of his formal education within an English, part-Army funded, Boarding School but June, whose middle name is Catherine ......

Well, let's call that the end of ACT ONE and take an Interval shall we and thereafter move on to my departure to Gillingham in ?

ACT 2

I arrived in Gillingham, one of the Medway Towns in Kent, in late 1963. I knew very little about the retail Grocery and Greengrocery Trades and very little about the County of Kent. However, courtesy of my Father's having taught me how to run a business and of the limited experience that I had had flogging nylon stockings and so forth down the East End of London, I did at least know something about 'Business'.

Sited partway down a hill at the corner of Church Street and Forge Lane and opposite the interestingly-named Christmas Street, 67 Church Street was a small 'Corner Shop' with living accommodation comprising of, on the ground floor, a living-room, a kitchen beyond which was a bathroom and a toilet, and, on the first floor, a very large bedroom, a medium-sized bedroom, and a small bedroom. The very large bedroom sat above the Shop itself and below the Shop lay a cellar. Outside was a small garden at the end of which was a one-car garage whose walls consisted entirely of second-hand wooden doors and whose roof of corrugated tin. Between 67 Church Street and the next house in Church Street lay a derelict piece of garden ground owned by Gillingham Corporation. In return for my paying a small annual sum I had contracted to rent the land from 'the Council' as an extension to 67 Church Street's garden. Apparently a house had once stood upon the land but had been demolished courtesy of Adolf Hitler and his War.

A Mr and Mrs Bailey had been the previous owners and occupiers of 67 Church Street and they sold the freehold to me for £2,500. The business's Stock had been valued by an Independent Valuer; and this I paid extra for to the Bailey's. However I paid nothing to them for the advice which, they said, they would give me anytime that I wanted it. All that I had to do, they said, to get the advice would be to travel the 10 miles [16 km] or thereabouts to their retirement home near Sittingbourne and ask. I tried it once but, having arrived at their home and had the door opened to me by Mrs Bailey, all that I received before the door was closed in my face were the comments "Oh, hello, it's you. We're just about to go out".

My Mother accompanied me to Gillingham the Sunday that I moved the 40 miles [65km] there from 28 Kenilworth Court. The first thing that we did - after we had looked around and checked that all the Stock that I had paid Mr and Mrs Bailey for was in fact there - was to go to a Dog Breeder's Kennels near to Maidstone, the 'County Town' of Kent, to collect a dog. My preference had been for an Alsatian but, as my Mother always came out in a rash every time that she was near an Alsatian, I had decided upon a Scots Collie. 'Mischief' was her name. "Why 'Mischief' ?" I asked the Breeder. "Because she's the most mischievous of the bunch," the man replied - Although, given that Mischief seemed to wish to isolate herself from the rest of the litter, she certainly did not look mischievous at the time. She was to prove herself, right up until almost the hour that she died of a tumor in Edinburgh's 'Dick Vet' Hospital eleven years later, the most loyal of friends and the greatest of companions.

We had in fact been to the Kennels and seen and chosen Mischief a few days earlier. It had been a journey not entirely without incident for, after having been to the Kennels, we decided that, rather than drive back to Putney, we would first drive aimlessly around, look at the very pleasant sunlit countryside and some of its villages, and find ourselves a Pub in which to have a 'quiet' drink. Isolated deep within some woods somewhere vaguely near to Maidstone was, what we thought, exactly what we were looking for. Oddly, however, the Pub's big wooden front-door was uninvitingly both shut and seemingly bolted. Having banged on it a couple of times and then, having received no response, we started to retreat towards our car when suddenly we heard an upstairs window being opened. Looking up we saw a shotgun quickly being poked out through the open window.

"What d'you want ?" a loud voice demanded.

"A drink," I shouted back.

"Why ?" demanded the seemingly aged shotgun-holding female as she leant out the window and 'faced' us.

"Because we're thirsty," I replied.

Sticking her head back inside, but holding the gun pointing directly towards my Mother and me, the aged female shouted to someone else within the building "Let them in !!"

We then heard two bolts, one at the top of the front-door and one at the bottom of the front-door, being slid, presumably open, and then we saw the door being opened.

"Please come on in," another, younger sounding, female voice said.

With a great deal of hesitation my Mother and I ventured inside the dimly lit room. It was as if we were entering something out of Dickensian History for not only was the place dimly lit but the sources of the lights were not electric lamps but candles, the building having, apparently, neither electricity nor gas.

Sitting over to our left was a man who, as we entered, raised a tankard as if to greet us whilst at the same time making an attempt to reassure us by saying of the aged shotgun-holding female "Don't mind her. She's always like that with strangers".

The woman who had unbolted the door and let us in went behind the bar and, once there, in a very pleasant voice asked us what we would like to drink. She then apologised for the actions of the older woman, her mother, whom, she said, was distrusting of nearly everybody but was, in reality, harmless. The shotgun, apparently, was not loaded, never was. We had one drink each, paid for them, and then left.

My Mother had intended that, on that day that I moved into 67 Church Street, I drive her back to Putney earlyish that evening and then, courtesy of her largesse in lending me the car for a few weeks till I managed to get myself settled in in Gillingham, drive back to Gillingham. However, as we sat in the livingroom having a 'cup of tea', there was a knock on the front-door. It was a man calling himself the 'Honorary Secretary of the Ancient Order of Buffaloes'. I had never heard of the Ancient Order of Buffaloes but Mr Bailey was, so the Honorary Secretary informed me, a Member of this so-called 'Ancient Order' and had suggested to its Honorary Secretary that perhaps I, too, might be interested in becoming a Buffalo. Given that I knew, apart from the Baileys, absolutely no-one in Gillingham or anywhere near Gillingham, initially it seemed to me that becoming a Member might at least give me some form of social activity within my new environment. So, with our guest accompanying us, our 'cup of tea' extended itself an hour or so beyond, what had been intended to be, my Mother's time of departure back to Putney.

Our guest was, without doubt, very enthusiastic about the Ancient Order of Buffaloes. As he left I told him that I would think about becoming a Member and contact him within a few days to let him know my decision. "You should join," my Mother told me several times before she herself left. "It would give you something to do down here when the Shop is closed." However, going around calling myself a 'Buffalo', ancient or otherwise, did not engender much, if any, enthusiasm in me, in part because I was only twenty years of age and in part because what had been described to me seemed more suited not only to people much older than I but also to people whose outlook on Life was more limited than mine : And so, a couple of days later, I telephoned the Buffaloes' enthusiastic local Honorary Secretary and gave him the, to him, disappointing news that I was not interested.

Opening time next morning for the Shop was 9 o'clock but before then I had to cope with two deliveries, the first of which was 'fruit and veg' and the second of which was bread. Milk, the other delivery of the day, would arrive, I had been told by Mrs Bailey, at about 11 o'clock in the morning.

Bill, my 'fruit and veg' man arrived just after 7 o'clock, an agonising time for me for, despite the fact that for years Haileybury had tried to make me get up at around that time, rising in the mornings was not something that came, and still does not come, easily to me. The firm for which Bill worked, a Family Business by the name of SP Howland & Son, was sited just across the road from 67 Church Street at 25 Christmas Street [*Copy of an SP Howland & Son's Invoice follows*].

Being almost clueless insofar as the buying of fruit and veg was concerned, I had become very nervous by the time that I heard Bill knocking on the door : But I need not have been for Bill not only knew well the amount of business and types of fruit and veg sold at 67 Church Street but also was, and remained throughout my stay in Gillingham, the most helpful of people. Furthermore, my having told him, once we had introduced ourselves to each other, of my lack of enthusiasm to be up and about at, or before, 7 in the morning, we struck a deal: Long before he got to my Shop Bill had to load up his lorry and thereafter usually made two or three 'drops' before taking a break for coffee in his cab; and so the arrangement that we made was that he would arrive outside, not my Shop door but, the front-door to my 'living quarters'; then he would knock on the front-door to let me know that it was time for me to get up; then he would return to his cab, and then take his time having his coffee thereby giving me sufficient time to at least get up and get dressed. Bill taught me a lot about fruit and veg: What to buy; how to store what I bought; how to present it for display; how to prolong its 'shelf life' by, for instance, removing the outer, yellowing, leaves of cabbages so that they always, within reason, looked fresh regardless of the number of days that they awaited buyers; what were the best types of potatoes to buy for different usages [chips, boiled, jacketed, etc]; and how to carry, at one time, four 56-lbs [25.4 kilos] bags of potatoes, the latter being achieved by means of first placing, and carrying, a bag under each arm and then, by turning and backing-up to the platform of his lorry, receiving and balancing a bag on each shoulder. Not easy, but can, with practice, be done !!

The delivery of bread, from the Gillingham bakery of Betabake Limited, arrived at around 8 o'clock by which time Bill had gone and I had managed to wash and shave. Pete was the name of the cheerful lad, only a couple of years or so older than I, who delivered the stuff : But he, like Bill, could not have been either more helpful or more co-operative; and, like Bill, usually knew exactly what it was that I needed to buy - How many sliced loaves, how many unsliced loaves, how many rolls, how many cream buns, how many cakes, how many Danish pastries, and so on; and, if, for some reason, I took too many, he would always take them back next day. Although, as with Bill's educational instruction on to how to keep things looking fresh, they were, he taught me, ways and means of keeping bread looking fresh even when it was not by, for instance, giving a day-old sliced loaf a mild but sharp karate-type blow in its middle. There were no 'Sell By' dates printed on goods in those days : A considerable benefit, no doubt, to the woman who owned a 'wee sweetie' shop part way up Church Street between my Shop and Gillingham's nearby Old Town centre - For that dear lady, whenever she received a delivery of boxes of bars of chocolate and the like, just piled the boxes of the new stuff on top of the boxes of boxes of the old stuff some of which, because of her method of 'stock control', dated back, it was said, some twenty to thirty years and was as good as new when eaten.

My reasons for buying - with money initially lent to me by my Mother from money that she had obtained through selling her share of Brunskill and Loveday Limited - a shop and accompanying living accommodation were that [1] as much as I liked Kenilworth Court and Putney, the strained relations between my Mother and me caused me to feel that I must remove myself from her environment; [2] I had, by my Father, been taught to 'run a business'; [3] despite what had happened to my Father, my Mother was still my Mother and thus for me to go, as I could then so easily have done, back into Scenery Design and/or Set Building was something which would doubtless have caused a complete breakdown in our relationship, and that was something which I most certainly did not wish to happen; [4] I had, in my experiences down the East End of London, enjoyed selling things; and [5] I needed somewhere to live. I also felt that I had, due to my having spent many years living, and being academically educated, within one of England's 'great' Public Schools, a somewhat biased attitude to life, an attitude that could only be counterbalanced by my spending a year or so living amongst people who lived on a Council Estate [or, as Scots would say, a Housing Scheme].

Initially I was not fussy as to what type of shop I chose and I thus looked at various types, including, in Hertfordshire somewhere, a shop which sold knitting wool and so on. However, given that I am slightly colour-blind, as I talked with the woman who owned the knitting wool shop and as I handled the various wools that she had on offer as being for sale I realised that selling wool was not for me if only because I found it difficult to tell the difference in the shades of many of the colours. Besides, I could not knit, had never knitted, and really had no desire to knit. It was in fact during the journey back to Kenilworth Court from that Hertfordshire Wool Shop that it dawned on me that not only did I want a shop with living accommodation but also I, like everyone else, had to eat and therefore what better type of shop to buy than one which sold food !!

67 Church Street, Gillingham fitted all my requirements - It was a shop that sold food; it was a shop which had ample living accommodation attached; it was a shop which, although not exactly on a Council Estate, had a Council Estate next to it; and its purchase price seemed about right. Unfortunately, although I suspect that Mr and Mrs Bailey knew about it, at the time I knew absolutely nothing about Harold MacMillan's Conservative Government's just-coming-into-force Abolition of Resale Price Maintenance Act, an Act of the

United Kingdom Parliament which was to decimate the livelihoods of many thousands of 'small Traders' throughout the length and breadth of the United Kingdom.

I was soon to learn that trade on Mondays is such that it was hardly worth my financial while opening my Shop. Everyone roundabout had known of the Bailey's departure and many were therefore curious to meet their successor. Thus I was very busy the first hour or so of my opening Monday morning, but, although most who came in bought, or at least asked for, something, I did not really do all that much trade: A bag of sugar here, a loaf of bread there, a few potatoes, a half-pound [0.23kg] of carrots … That type of thing. The one thing that many people did want was milk : But, given that my supply of milk did not arrive until about 11am, I had to turn many Customers and so-called Customers away and watch them either go diagonally across the adjoining Forge Lane to a nearby competitor who did, so he said, have 'fresh' milk or go further down Church Street to a small parade of shops which contained a Confectioners, a Butchers, and a small General Store with Post Office which, likewise said, did have 'fresh milk'.. Given that both my competitor across the road and Mr Goodie in his Post Office received their milk from the same Delivery Person as I did, they, if they had any 'fresh milk', could only, that morning, sell as 'fresh milk' that which they had failed to sell the previous Saturday.

Harry Salthouse, a Milkman from Bourne and Hillier's Dairy in nearby Chatham, arrived at around 11am. He and his Wife, Hilda, owned and lived with their young daughter, Lynda, in a small house in Gillingham's nearby Gad's Hill. Natives of Manchester, Harry, Hilda, and Lynda had, just a few years earlier, moved to Gillingham from Manchester at the suggestion of one of Harry's Sisters, Anne, who had married Danny Bull, the son of the owner of the most successful retail, and semi-wholesale, Fruit, Veg, and Florist's business in nearby Chatham. The front room of the house that Harry and Hilda had bought was a smaller version of my Shop : But their shop's turnover was nowhere near sufficient to provide them with enough income to live off. So Harry reverted to the job that he had been doing before he left Manchester - Window Cleaning. However, even with the added income that he achieved as a self-employed Window Cleaner Harry and Hilda could barely 'make ends meet'. So, for a short while, he went, as an employee, to Startright's, a nearby Engineering firm; and then, hearing of a vacant job at Bourne and Hillier's Dairy, he applied and became a Milk Deliveryman whilst Hilda, burdened by increasing deafness, valiantly continued to struggle to keep their Shop going.

Harry's initial normal daily Mondays' to Saturdays' Milk Delivery procedure had been to arrive at 67 Church Street at around 11am, deliver whatever milk was requested, take back whatever milk was unsold from previous deliveries, and then settle up financially. However, we soon evolved a routine wherein Harry would arrive and shout "I'll leave this milk here and come back later". Thus just inside the doorway he deposited one metal milk-crate partially filled with glass bottles the shape of which I recognised from my many years of drinking milk and another metal milk-crate partially filled with bottles the like of which I had never seen before but which I was to very soon come to learn were 'Sterilised Milk'. Throughout my childhood and my time in Kenilworth Court we had always had a large electric refrigerator ['fridge] at home and therefore I had made the assumption that every household had a 'fridge. Indeed, my Shop had a large 'fridge, albeit a gas 'fridge, in which butter and some other items were kept; and so - until the arrival in my Shop of these, to me, bottles of unusual shape - I had no idea that for most households to have a 'fridge was a rarity. Hence Sterilised Milk, although it had a different taste to 'ordinary' milk, was a much bigger seller than 'ordinary' milk for, whereas 'ordinary' Pasteurised milk had a very limited lifespan, Sterilised Milk, due to the fact that it had passed through a process in which the milk was heated to increase its shelf life, had a much longer lifespan. I liked the taste of Sterilised Milk but the taste of Sterilised Milk was, however, not to everybody's liking : Hence I had also to stock 'ordinary' milk.

The fact that my shop had a gas 'fridge meant that there was mains gas into the building. And so I decided, once I had gotten myself organised, to have a gas fire in the livingroom and a gas cooker in the kitchen. So, up to the local showroom of the South Eastern Gas Board I went and ordered a Sahara gas fire, a gas cooker with a rotissomat, and the necessary lengths of copper piping, iron piping, fixtures and fittings, and a flue to enable the South Eastern Gas Board [SEGB] to plumb the whole lot in. The only thing that I did not order was a date whereby the SEGB would do the work; and so the result was that weeks went by with nothing happening other than my having to put up with yards/metres of piping lying here, there, and everywhere in the house [but not in the Shop] along with boxes containing my Sahara gas fire and gas cooker with its rotissomat. Time and again I contacted SEGB's showroom and time and again I was fobbed off with promises that the work would start soon. Eventually November arrived and the excuse this time from SEGB was "Sorry, Sir, but it's too cold and wet to do the job this time of year" to which I replied "Well, if you open the roof to insert the flue and rainwater gets in … Well, don't worry about that." SEGB's reply ? "It's not your roof we're worried about, Sir : It's our men getting wet whilst they're up there, Sir." In those days I did not know much about the Law nor about plumbing but the word 'storage' came to mind. So I sent a bill to SEGB for my having had to store the pipes and so forth : And whoosh, suddenly SEGB's workers arrived and installed the pipes, gas fire, gas cooker, etc..

Harry's Milk Round existed principally to serve retail customers thereby causing him to be in competition with me in that also !! As was Bourne and Hillier's routine he would deliver, usually on Customers' doorsteps, a bottle or bottles of milk in the morning and then go back in the afternoon to collect the moneys that the Customers owed - not always an achievable goal !! Harry and I therefore developed a routine wherein he would deliver milk to me in the morning and, instead of being paid there and then, return in the afternoon not only to be paid what I owed for the milk but also to have a chat. We became very good friends and remained so until his death, long after he retired, in Broadstairs many years later.

The afternoon that first Monday was 'dead' insofar as trade was concerned, a pattern that was to repeat itself throughout my time in Gillingham. Tuesday was, however, a much more encouraging day; and I began to develop 'regular' Customers who would over time loyally come to my Shop as their first 'port of call' only going elsewhere to purchase things that my Shop did not have. However at about 10:30 on that first Tuesday night, some hours after I had shut the Shop, I was mug enough to fall for a trick which - had I had more experience, been more savvy, and not felt a desperate need to cultivate Customers - I should have been wise enough not to fall for. There was a knock on the front-door of the house. I went downstairs and answered the door to be greeted by a woman saying "I bought this egg from you to-day. It's off. I want another". I apologised, went into the Shop, got another egg, returned to my front-door, and, still apologising, handed the replacement egg to her. I have a reasonably good memory for faces and it was only as I went back upstairs did I realise that I had never seen the woman before and that, in all likelihood, either she had bought the egg when the Baileys owned the Shop or, if she had bought it that day, she had certainly not bought it from my Shop.

The Wednesday had its moments, one of which resulted from a woman asking if she could buy the one and only large can of Fowler's black treacle that sat very noticeably upon one of my rows of grey metal shelves. I knew that it was there and was eager to sell it. Indeed, I was eager to sell anything. However, fortunately I had a wariness about this can of treacle and so, having explained to the woman that I had only just taken on the Shop and that the age of the can of treacle was unknown to me, I suggested that I first open it to check it. So, with my intending purchaser's agreement, I carefully began to prise the lid off the can and, as I did so, there was an almighty 'whoosh' sound as the lid flew off and black treacle exploded out of the can in almost all directions splattering me and everything roundabout in dozens of streaks and hundreds of droplets of black treacle. "I don't think I'll have it after all," said my would-have-been intending purchaser.

By the Thursday of that week I felt that I was beginning to settle into my new lifestyle and thus was becoming confident about meeting Ernie Watts - the Representative from Scholars, a long established Medway Towns' family firm which wholesaled Groceries and Provisions - who, Mrs Bailey had told me, called every Thursday to collect 'the Order' for delivery next day on the Friday.

Ernie was smartly dressed, polite, courteous, and a very helpful man who, like Bill of Howland's and Pete of Betabake, did much to assist me in my early days. Having introduced himself to me he then, offering me a booklet, said "This is this month's 'Shaw's List' ".

"This month's what ?" I asked.

"Have you not seen one before ?" he replied and then, realising that I had absolutely no idea what 'Shaw's List' was, went on to explain 'Shaw's List' to me.

The retail prices of most goods in the Grocery Trade were, Ernie told me, controlled, mainly by the manufacturers of the goods, and it was thus unlawful to sell at a higher or lower price than the controlled price. 'Shaw's List' was published each month and it contained the then current controlled prices for most items retailed within the Grocery Trade. Thus I would need 'Shaw's List' each month, Ernie explained, so that I would know exactly what the prices were that I should be charging. By Retailers relying on such as 'Shaw's List', Ernie went on, all prices remained the same throughout the land regardless of where the shops were.

"But what about Jack Cohen ? [Jack Cohen, the Founder of Tesco, and others were renowned in London, and elsewhere, for cutting prices.] What about the various cut-price Supermarkets that are springing up even in Gillingham High Street ?" I asked.

"What they're doing is illegal," replied Ernie. "But it won't be soon," he went on, "because the Government's getting rid of Price Controls."

"And what'll happen then ?" I asked.

"Heaven only knows. There'll be a free-for-all probably. Survival of the fittest. Big firms will get bigger and small firms will go under," he replied.

My having, with his assistance, given Ernie my Order to be delivered next day away Ernie Watts went leaving me to get on with it. What I [and probably Ernie also as well as most people who ran small Grocery businesses] was unaware of was that Harold Macmillan, the United Kingdom's Prime Minister at the time, had for many years been of the opinion that controlled, or fixed, prices worked against the interests of Consumers and believed that the removal of fixed prices would create competition which would cause prices to be reduced and Consumers to benefit. Born in 1894, and thus aged 70 by the time that I arrived in Gillingham, Macmillan, the grandson of a Scottish Crofter, a former Grenadier Guardsman, a member of the famous Macmillan publishing family, son-in-law of the Eleventh Duke of Devonshire, and future Earl of Stockton - had - in his pursuit of seeking to protect 'ordinary people' against, what he regarded as being, excessive prices due to their being fixed, principally, by manufacturers - overlooked, it seemed, the fact that the abolition of resale prices would cause to come into effect the policy of 'survival of the fittest' thereby resulting in the loss and destruction throughout Great Britain of many thousands of small independent retail businesses in favour, eventually, of just a few very large multiple businesses whose financial clout would be such that they could, and would, themselves control to devastating effect not only retail prices but also, to a considerable extent, those who produced the goods that the very large multiples chose to sell. Assisted by Britain's Liberal Party, Macmillan's Abolition of Resale Price Maintenance Act [RPM] of 1964, [an Act strongly opposed by the Leader of Britain's Labour Party, Harold Wilson, who described the abolition of RPM as being an Act that would keep the Consumers' Cost of Living higher that it would otherwise be] came into being just before the October 1964 General Election and was described by Ted

Heath, the Minister who steered it through the United Kingdom Parliament, in his autobiography *The Course of my Life* as having been "one of the most satisfying successes of [his] ministerial career". Had I known about the intended abolition of maintained resale prices and had I realised the damage that that abolition would eternally do to small retail grocery businesses I would not have bought a Grocery Business. However, I had bought it and thus was stuck with it until I managed to sell it in, I thought, a year or so's time. At least that was - as I had told June Lindsay, that attractive, then 16-years' old blonde girl who had knocked on my Kenilworth Court's Workshop's open door the previous year - my intention, an intention that was, however, not to go quite according to plan.

My Customers were just ordinary folk, some of them living in nearby privately-owned houses and some of them living on the adjoining Council Estate the houses of which started in Forge Lane bang next to my wooden-doored garage. The divide between my Customers who lived in Council houses and my Customers who lived in privately-owned houses was about equal. Socially there appeared to be no divide. However, I was not only an 'incomer' thereabouts but also with my English Public School background [which caused me to have a somewhat 'unusual', some might say 'stuck up', accent for that part of the world] coupled with the fact that, at 20 years of age, I was much younger than most, if not all, other owners of shops I was undoubtedly a person of some interest. Thus much curiosity abounded; and therefore, whenever I was asked what I had done before I had bought the Shop, I deliberately played down my many experiences within the Theatre and the BBC. However, 'Old' Mrs Lushey, a splendid and somewhat crafty character, soon extracted some information from me about my Theatrical background, although she was kind enough to keep much of it to herself. Born and brought up in Tottenham, in London, Mrs Lushey had married a Toffee Maker who subsequently became an employee of Sharpe and Company, then a very famous firm of Toffee Makers in Maidstone. By the time that I arrived in Gillingham she was a widow aged, I suspect, somewhere in the region of 75 to 80 years. 'Tottenham', as I called her, and I got on well right from the start and indeed as I did with others such as Mrs Simmons and Mrs Baker. Daily each would come into my Shop in part for a gossip and in part to buy their groceries and fruit and veg. I provided two wooden chairs within the Shop one of which was always regarded by my 'regulars' as being for 'Old' Mrs Baker who, upon her arrival, would, as she puffed and panted, always make straight for 'her' chair and plonked herself down on it whilst making a sighing comment such as "Haaaah … That's better". What a shock it was to those of us in the Shop one day when, having plonked herself down on 'her' chair, she sighingly slowly said to us all "Well, I'm fiftyfour, y'know". My Customers and I looked at each other in amazement for everyone of us had - from 'Old' Mrs Baker's daily routine of panting, and sighing - gained the opinion that 'Old' Mrs Baker was a darn sight older than fiftyfour.

Mrs Lushey's weekly purchases always included a packet or two of Granola Digestive biscuits and at least one box of candles. I mainly sold biscuits loose out of cube-shaped 4-lbs [1.8kilos] tins with detachable metal-framed glass lids through which intending Purchasers could view what was on offer. The intending Purchaser having decided which type of biscuit and how many, by weight, of biscuits were wanted, the biscuits would be taken, by hand, out of the tin(s), weighed, and then placed into a white or brown paper bag which, by holding an end of the open top of the bag in each hand, would be flipped over with a twisting motion so as to partially seal the bag before handing it to the Customer. Within the Grocery Trade pre-packaged biscuits were, however, replacing loose biscuits thereby causing Purchasers not only to be unable to see what they were about to buy but also to have to buy in quantities that they did not necessarily want. Mrs Lushey's need of candles was due to her house having no electricity, a not altogether unusual situation in those days even in a town such as Gillingham.

Mrs Simmons's daily purchases almost always included a pound [0.45 kilo] or a half-pound of onions and a pound or a half-pound of carrots each of which she herself would select. She had three strapping adult sons and a large, seemingly very fit husband and every week-day, and week-ends also, she fed them either mince or stew, neither of which I sold. A constant smoker of cigarettes that she usually bought from me, she, apparently, would, with cigarette in mouth, lean over a large cooking vessel and regularly, doubtless inadvertently, drop into whatever it was that she was stirring one ingredient not mentioned with Cookery books - Cigarette ash !! Much to my regret, for it decreased my sales of cigarettes, for a short period she determined to give up smoking; and in consequence ceased to drop cigarette ash into whatever it was that she was stirring. After a few days her sons and her husband protested about the deteriorating quality of her mince and stew with the result that she reverted to cigarette smoking if only, she said, to keep her sons and husband happy.

Some weeks after my arrival in Gillingham a smartly dressed woman, clad in a Tweed suit and carrying a briefcase, arrived in the entrance to my Shop. Fortunately it was devoid of Customers at the time.

"I'm from Lillywhite's," she loudly announced as she stepped inside. "Please tell your boss that I'm here."

"I'm the boss," I told her.

"Young man," she exclaimed, "do not be cheeky. Tell your boss that the Representative from Lillywhite's is here."

"I *am* the boss," I repeated as she, by now having stridden across the Shop, plonked her briefcase on one of my Shop's two chairs [not the one used by 'Old' Mrs Baker].

"Young man," she repeated in an exasperated voice," I have already told you to tell your boss that the Representative from Lillywhite's is here." "Now, kindly do so," she ordered.

"Madam," I replied," I have already told you that I am the boss. So, how can I help you?"

"Well," she said as she withdrew her briefcase from my chair and began to turn to face the door, " if you think that I am going to deal with you …"; and out she strode. I never saw her again.

Her firm's product, Dr White's Sanitary Towels, was something which, along with Mene Sanitary Belts, I had, until I arrived in Gillingham and discovered exactly what it was that I had bought by way of Stock, never heard of. However both Dr White's and, to a much lesser degree, Mene's Sanitary Belts were 'good sellers'. When I took over the Shop from the Baileys all the boxes of Dr White's were on the top shelf : And so I kept them there and, somewhat foolishly perhaps, did not pay any attention to what they contained. Thus, when I was first asked for a box of Dr White's, I climbed up a small set of steps, grabbed a box, climbed down the steps, and just handed them over.

"Er … wrap them, dear," said my intending Purchaser.

"Pardon ?" I asked bewilderedly.

"In newspaper will do," came the reply.

So I grabbed hold of a nearby copy of the local newspaper, the *Rochester, Gillingham, and Chatham News*, and did exactly what she asked. It was only after my Customer had gone and I had looked more closely at a box of Dr White's to find out what Dr White's were, did I realise why it was that she wanted no-one to be able to see what she had bought. Thus I now fully realised why when the arrogant and aloof Tweed-clad Representative from Lillywhite's called she would not speak with me - She was, unlike an Asian 'Salesman' who called at my Shop some weeks later, far too embarrassed.

The Asian 'Salesman' was in fact not a Salesman but an out-and-out con-man. Entering my Shop he strode quickly over to its main counter upon which he placed a leather suitcase and, seemingly almost at the speed of light, opened it.

"You buy ties for you," he said as he pulled a tie out of the suitcase and waved it in front of me.

"I not buy ties for me," I told him.

"Why not you buy ties for you ?" he demanded to know.

"Because I have ties," I replied.

"How many ties you have ?" he almost shouted at me.

For some reason or other my Father had, throughout his 78 years, seemed to have kept, stored in shoe boxes, every tie that he had ever owned; and on his death I thus acquired seventy ties which, perhaps for sentimental reasons, I had kept and taken to Gillingham with me. Thus straightaway I truthfully answered "Seventy".

"Seventy," he shouted. "You lie. You lie," he went on as he quickly put his tie back into the suitcase and slammed its lid shut. Then, walking backwards towards my Shop's door whilst constantly waving a menacing finger at me, he kept repeating "You are cursed. You are cursed. You are cursed …". Whether or not I was cursed I have no idea but his 'curse' might explain the incidents involving a small black van that I purchased soon after his visit.

Standing one day whilst chatting with a customer a teenage boy came zig-zagging down Church Street on a moped. "Look at that idiot," I said. "That's my Grandson," said the Customer. "Oops, sorry," I said. "Don't worry," she replied at which moment the lad fell off the moped and landed on the road whilst the moped carried on down the hill. I started to rush out to him. "Leave him," said his Grandmother, "and let him learn the hard way". So leave him we did and watched him pick himself up, recover his moped, and slink away whilst his Grandmother shouted at him "Serve you bloody well right".

Maidstone and District Motor Services was a 'bus company based in Maidstone which operated in Gillingham. One day, armed with impressive pieces of artwork featuring some Maidstone and District 'buses, a pleasant-looking character came into my Shop, introduced himself as a Salesman for Maidstone and District 'buses and suggested that I might like to have an advert featured on the rear of some 'buses. That way, he said, the name of my business would be 'broadcast' throughout Gillingham, Chatham, and Rochester. The price he quoted of £12 [£200 in 2021] seemed reasonable given the benefits from the publicity that I was likely to achieve. So, I signed up, got a receipt, and, just before he left my Shop, shook hands with the guy. Then I waited and waited and waited : And I am still waiting. I had, of course, been conned !!

Despite the fact that she had more or less given up driving my Mother's generosity in lending me her A40 car evaporated late one very cold Sunday night whilst I was visiting her in Putney for she told me that I could no longer have use of her car and that I must therefore find an alternative method of getting back to Gillingham that night. Even though it was financially not worth my while opening my Shop on Mondays I had to do so, if just for the mornings, for otherwise my increasingly loyal band of Customers would have thought that I did not really care about them and their custom and in consequence they would have taken their trade elsewhere. Thus, despite the fact that my Mother's decision caused me to now have no vehicular transport, it was crucial that I return to Gillingham so that I could, even if I could not get there in time for Bill's arrival with my fruit and veg, at least get there in time to open my Shop at 9 o'clock. My best bet, I felt, was to go to London Bridge Railway Station and catch a train that would take me to Gillingham Railway Station from whence I could walk the three-quarters of a mile or so to my Shop. The trouble was that there were no means of public transport that would, at that time of night, take me from Putney to London Bridge; and therefore - given that, because I had little money with me and my Mother would not lend me any, I could not afford a taxi - my only option was to walk the eight miles [13km] or so from Kenilworth Court to London Bridge Station. Nothing seemed to be in my favour that night for not only did it rain throughout much of my walk but also the only train going to Gillingham that was available to me when I arrived at London Bridge was an unheated Newspaper Train intended to carry not people but newspapers. Although I was welcome to travel on the Newspaper Train, I had to travel in the same fashion that the newspapers did: Stopping at every Station en route and in a carriage without any seats and without any form of heating. To say that the journey was slow and bl++dy cold would not be an inaccurate description. However, I arrived in Gillingham and managed to get to my Shop in time to take my somewhat concerned very loyal dog, Mischief, for a walk before greeting Bill and my delivery of fruit and veg.

Despite the discomfort that I had had to suffer throughout the early hours of that morning I remain grateful to that Newspaper Train not only for getting me to Gillingham but also for making me realise that it was essential to me that I own my own transport. Therefore that week - having scoured the advertisements in the *Rochester, Chatham, and Gillingham News* newspaper - I telephoned, and made an appointment to meet, a man in Chatham who advertised that he had a small van for sale.

Having, after I had closed my Shop for the night, walked, with Mischief, to the man's hillside terraced house I saw, what I took to be, the van parked outside. Other than knowing how to drive I did not really know that much about vehicles; but, under the light of a street lamp, the van looked okay to me : And so I walked up the several steep steps to the Seller's front-door; rang his front-door bell; introduced myself; received his assurances that it was "a good little van" the battery of which was, he said, "a bit flat because I haven't been out in the van for a while"; haggled and agreed a price; handed over the purchase money; received a receipt, some paperwork, and some keys; went back down the steps; enthusiastically unlocked the van; climbed, with Mischief, into the van; and, with pride, was now the owner of my very own means of transport.

Eager to try out my new purchase I quickly put the key in the ignition, turned it, and, discovering that the battery was too flat to start the van, then bump-started the van down the steep hill whilst at the same time turning on its side-lights : And off Mischief and I went back to my Shop. Having reached my Shop I parked my new acquisition outside in Church Street, turned its somewhat dim lights off, and then took Mischief inside the house. Having fed her, I went back to my new acquisition whereupon, having found that its battery was still too flat to start the vehicle, I bump-started it again, turned on its lights, and then headed off down Church Street, turned right at the bottom of Church Street, and went along Pier Road into Gads Hill and passed Harry Salthouse's little shop, and then headed towards the Isle of Sheppey, a distance of about ten miles [7 km] or so. There were no other vehicles on that back road to Sheppey that night and, apart from small hamlets such as Lower Halstow, there was little to be seen at all save, at times, for the River Medway to my left. Nonetheless it was exciting, very exciting. One thing however seemed a bit odd, namely that every time that I eased my right foot off the accelerator the vehicle's lights dimmed, something that I had never experienced with my Mother's A40 car even when I had driven it down to Gibraltar and back. By the time that I reached the main road of Sheppey Way I had reached the conclusion that the battery was probably faulty and not holding a charge and that therefore, were I to stop the van on anything but a reasonable hill, I would be unable to restart it : And so I gave up on the idea of driving to the Isle of Sheppey and instead turned the van round in one complete circular motion and headed back to the 'Lower Road' from whence I had just come. Having turned into the 'Lower Road' and driven along it for a couple of hundred yards [183metres] or so I noticed another vehicle turning off Sheppey Way and beginning to follow me. As it drew closer the beams from its headlights began to cause me to be unable to see sufficiently within the lights from my own vehicle to enable me to judge the road properly. I was getting a wee bit frightened and thus I eased back on the accelerator in the hope that the following vehicle would overtake, which, if the other vehicle was okay, would have given me the advantage of being able to follow it at a quicker speed than my vehicle's dimming headlights were enabling me to travel. Therefore, every time that the road widened I slowed down in the hope that the other vehicle would overtake. Not only did the other vehicle not overtake but also each time that I decelerated my vehicle's lights dimmed causing me ever greater difficulty in seeing exactly where I was going. Then suddenly my vehicle's engine cut out leaving me with no option but to stop causing my newly purchased van to have no functioning lights. The fact that the following vehicle had not taken any opportunity to overtake me caused me increased alarm for there was no other sign of any life whatsoever nearby and the isolation of the 'Lower Road' was the ideal place in which to be attacked. My apprehension increased when the vehicle that had been following me stopped some distance behind my vehicle and its two occupants got out. I wound-up my open driver's window and, finding the door locks' push-buttons, locked the doors and sat there waiting to be 'done over'.

"Evening, Sir," said one of the two men as he arrived alongside my door. "Having problems are we, ?" he asked.

Despite the fact that he was wearing a Police uniform I was very reluctant to open my window when he tapped on it and asked me to do so. However, open the window I did, to be greeted by his saying "Would you mind stepping out, sir".

So, with little option but to get out, I got out.

"We've been following you since you turned off at Sheppey Way," said his colleague," and it seems … Well, that you've got problems. Do you own this vehicle, sir ?"

"Yes," I told him, "I do," and then went on to explain that I had just bought it and was trying it out.

Meantime, armed with a torch, the first Policeman was inspecting the vehicle here, there, and everywhere.

"Do you have your documents ?" asked the second Policeman.

"Yes," I told him, "they're on the passenger seat".

After he had asked me if he could look at them I lent into the van, got hold of the purchase receipt and the other document that my Seller had given me, and handed them to him.

"And the Insurance document, sir ?" he asked me.

"What Insurance document ?" I asked naïvely.

"Well," said the Policeman," you need two documents to be allowed to drive a vehicle on the Public Highway. "A Registration document, which you seem to have, and an Insurance Certificate which, I take it, sir, you do not have".

"I think you'd better come back to Gillingham Police Station with us, sir," he went on. "I gather you can't get the vehicle started. So, you get in our car. My colleague and I will start your vehicle and then he'll drive it to the Station and you and I will follow him."

So, I got into the Police Car; using jump leads, they started my van; and then, with the Police Car in front, we all went to Gillingham Police Station.

After I had sat in the lobby of the Police Station for a while a Police Inspector came out of a doorway and invited me into a room 'for a chat'. Once in there I explained the entirety of what had happened; and when I had finished he informed me that, following our arrival at the Police Station, his Officers had inspected the vehicle and found it to be a very dangerous vehicle. Not only, apparently, was its battery useless but also, amongst other faults that he quoted, its brakes were faulty and its clutch was none-too-good either. I had been well and truly conned.

By now it was nearly 2 o'clock in the morning and I was tired and was, to say the least, none-too-happy and expecting to be charged and have to appear in Court. I was thus certainly not expecting the Inspector to suddenly say to me "Do you want your money back?" Of course I did : And so he and I went in the van from Gillingham Police Station to Chatham and after our arrival outside of Scumbag's house, with the two Policeman whom I had first met sitting in their car behind the van, the Inspector and I got out of the van, walked across the road, and went up the steps to the Seller's front-door. It was by now gone 3'oclock in the morning and, after the Inspector had rung the door-bell several times, Scumbag, clad in his pyjamas, opened the door.

"Did you sell that vehicle to this gentleman ?," asked the Inspector as he pointed towards the van with the Police Car parked behind it.

"Yes," answered Scumbag.

"And are you going to buy it back for the same price that you sold it for ?" continued the Inspector.

"No," was the very firm reply.

"Are you sure ?" asked the Inspector.

"Yes," came an equally firm reply. "I sold it to him. So it's his vehicle now, not mine."

"In which case," continued the Inspector," I shall charge you with…"

"I'll buy it back," came the instant reply.

I got my money back there and then and then was driven back in the Police Car to my home at 67 Church Street. As regards the - well-known to the Police, I understand - scumbag ? Well, I have no idea what happened to him : But I remain very grateful to that kindly Inspector whose application of commonsense was, in my opinion, an excellent course of action for him to have taken. I met him briefly on three more occasions: On the first two occasions, as he passed by my Shop on his way to The Strand [a small Pleasure Beach area at the bottom end of Church Street] he called in "Just to say 'Hello' " and on the third occasion he called in to say "Good-bye" as he was, I recall, having to leave the Force due, I think, to his suffering from gout. *I can not help, as I reflect back to that kindly soul, but be of the opinion that commonsense should be used more.*

Shortly after that incident my Mother appreciated/accepted that I and my business had a genuine need of her car and so she made her A40 available to me again : And with it I was able to undertake, every Friday night after my Shop closed, several pre-ordered deliveries [*See following photograph. The car is the same A40 that my Mother and I went to Gibraltar and back in.*]

I confess that after only a very short while of living the life of a self-employed Grocer/Greengrocer, I began to feel trapped in an existence that, whilst I enjoyed it at times, was not really to my liking. Thus when I received a totally unexpected telephone-call from Alan Mansey, one of my former colleagues in the Props Department in BBC Television Centre, I was very pleased. I was even more pleased to the extent of being overjoyed when he told me the purpose of his call: To re-join the Rugby Section of the BBC Club.

"But I can't. I no longer work for the BBC," I told him.

"We'll make you a Guest Member," he replied. I was, and still to this day remain, very honoured by Alan's request of me for it enabled me to rejoin not only the company of many whose friendships I had always much enjoyed but a world within which I had, since my very early days with the Corporation, always felt very much at home.

When I had taken over the Shop there were two circular signs each stuck on the inside of a window proclaiming to the world at large: On each's top - "Eat More Fruit", in each's middle - A selection of fruit, and on each base "The Retail Fruit Trade Federation".

"What on earth, "I asked myself," is 'The Retail Fruit Trade Federation' ?"

Its Head Office, I found out, was in Russell Chambers in London's very historic, and in those days very active, Covent Garden Fruit and Veg Market and its General Secretary was someone called Tommy Matkin. So I telephoned Tommy Matkin, spoke first with his Secretary [who happened to be also his wife] and asked him what exactly the Retail Fruit Trade Federation [RFTF] was. He explained to me that there were many thousands of retail Greengrocery businesses throughout Great Britain, that the RFTF was their 'trade' organisation which provided its Members with publicity, legal assistance, and, via Regional Associations and District Branches, social activities. As part of his response he suggested that I meet with a Mr Loosely, the Federation's Medway Towns Branch's Honorary Secretary who, with his wife, owned and ran a small Greengrocery Shop in Gillingham not too far from my Shop in Church Street.

"Do you," I asked Bill of Howlands when he next called on me," know someone called 'Loosely'?"

Yes, he knew, and delivered to, a Mr and Mrs Loosely but his comments about them were not all that encouraging for he painted a verbal picture of a miserly couple who were becoming 'past their sell-by date'. Bill knew little of the RFTF except that it issued to its Members colourful and eye-catching publicity material which was helpful in attracting people into shops to buy fruit and vegetables, something which, Bill felt, could be of use to me and my Shop. I thus telephoned Mr Loosely and arranged to meet with him 'after hours' in his shop, a somewhat dark establishment which, when I arrived, stuck me as being of an era then now almost past.

Enthusiastic about the RFTF, its Annual Conventions, what the RFTF did for its Members, and so on this relic of Grocers Past encouraged me to become a Member and to thereafter attend its Medway Towns Branch Meetings, the next one of which would take place in the Loosely's home - which was, like mine, within the same building as the Shop. The principal Item on the Agenda would be to discuss the forthcoming Annual Convention of the RFTF to be held, in May, in the Norbreck Hydro Hotel [subsequently the Norbreck Castle Hotel] in Blackpool in Lancashire, the town where, in 1952, I had appeared on stage with Jack Warner and others in *The Blue Lamp..*

I can not say that I was impressed by the turnout for the first Medway Towns Branch Meeting that I attended for present were only [1] the Branch's Honorary Chairman, namely Loosely himself, [2] the Branch's Honorary Secretary, namely Mrs Loosely, and [3] one other Member, namely me. Hospitality for the occasion consisted of one cupful of tea each, made by Mrs Loosely during an Adjournment called for solely to enable her to make the tea. Not that anyone had asked but I take a small amount of milk and a large amount of sugar in my tea and, whereas my tea was almost drowned in milk, sugar was only provided once I had asked two, if not three, times for it. The word 'skinflints' came to mind !!

Anyhow, the Federation's Annual Convention in Blackpool sounded interesting moreso given that I was informed that the Branch was permitted to send three Delegates and that each Delegate's expenses would be paid out of Federation's funds. It would be, I was told, "a sort of holiday. Indeed, for many Greengrocers this would be their annual holiday". Thus I agreed to accompany, as a nominated Branch Delegate [who, at the time, knew very little about fruit and veg], the Looselys to the Blackpool Convention : And my agreement was duly noted in the Minutes by Mrs Loosely.

As I was leaving the Loosely's that night after the Meeting Mr Loosely started chatting to me about the "Good old days when, if I ran out of bananas, I could always borrow a hand or two [of bananas] from a fellow Branch Member and, if he ran out of, say, cabbages, he could always borrow some cabbages from me". Then he went on to quietly tell me, as we stood in the street, that he and his wife could hardly make a living from the income that their shop was providing - something which I had already concluded from the sparsity of that evening's 'hospitality' - and that they were therefore seriously considering selling not only their business but also the 'profitable' Greengrocery Delivery Round that they had built-up over the years. He went on to tell me they would have sold up earlier had it not been for the facts that they had a loyal employee, a spinster of State Pension age by the name of Ivy Marsh, who had been with them for many years and whom, they felt, they could not, at her age, terminate her employment for such might cause her financial hardship.

Save for their concern for Ivy Marsh's wellbeing I was thoroughly unimpressed by the Loosleys; but his comments about the 'profitable Greengrocery Delivery Round' and about the loyal employee kept bugging me to the extent that I eventually concluded [1] that a 'profitable Greengrocery Delivery Round', which doubtless had a vehicle that went with it, could be of financial benefit to me and [2] that a loyal employee could, were I to employ Miss Marsh, enable me to have some spare time. So I returned to the Looselys at a later date to negotiate a deal: I would buy his round, its non-perishable stock, and its vehicle and would also take over the employment of the loyal Miss Marsh [about whom I had made some enquiries and received not only encouraging responses but also the knowledge that she lived only a few yards from my Shop at 146 Pier Road].

Ivy turned out to be an absolute treasure throughout the period when I employed her. Of the Looselys' vehicle for their 'Greengrocery Delivery Round' ... Well, that, the Loosleys told me, was not for sale because it was the only vehicle that they had and, as they could not afford to buy another vehicle, they needed the van to visit their daughter who ran a General Store-cum-Post Office in Weston Green near Kingston upon Thames. The non-perishable stock - which I did buy - consisted in part of a variety of sizes of cans of carrots, peas, and the like which, I suspect, they could not sell and in part of several cases of tins of grapefruit segments, which doubtless they had bought at a reduced price and which, I likewise suspect, they had also been unable to sell. Thus I committed myself to buying a Greengrocery Round, a multitude of canned fruit and veg, and no means of getting it anywhere : And so, before I actually took over the Greengrocery Round it was essential that I obtain a vehicle in which to put it.

My Mother was horrified at the idea of her beloved A40 being used for such an undertaking; and so I again found myself seeking a van locally. Fortunately this time I had heard of a couple of Butchers in Gillingham whose Corner Shop Butchery business had for sale a surplus Bedford CA van with long side-windows and long slatted bench seats. The two Butchers and I negotiated a price, a deal was struck, and, my having this time ensured that I first obtained Insurance cover, I happily drove my new dark blue van away from their Shop to mine.

As I had anticipated, the van's long bench seats were, with slight modification, ideal for displaying fruit and veg and the long side windows were ideal for permitting potential Customers to view what was on offer. Thus - with Ivy installed within my Shop and getting on very well with my Customers, many of whom she had known for years - off I went, accompanied by a list of Loosley's Greengrocery Round's Customers and their addresses, to meet my first Greengrocery Round Customer. With his many years' experience Mr Loosley had detailed to me not only the days that the various Customers should be called upon but also, what he considered to be, the best routes to take when calling upon them. Thus I started with the first Customer on his list. "You're late. It's 9:45. Mr Loosley's always here prompt at 9:30," was the first, somewhat humorless, greeting that I received. "Not a good start," I thought. However, I persevered and, anxious to get away from this miserable encounter and move on to my next Call, began to get back into my van as soon as the transaction - a sale of only two onions - was completed. "Well, you're a fine one. You've only just got 'ere and now you're gone," said the woman. "Mr Loosley was never away so sharp," she added.

"I'll stay a wee bit longer next time," I said as I mustered the best smile that my annoyed self could muster. Then off I went to my next Call.

"Oh, so you're the young lad Mr Loosley told us about," said my second piece of human inspiration. "Well, I darn't want nuffink this morning but I'll want somefink tomorra. I'll see ya tomorra then," she said. So, back into the van I climbed and off to the next hoped-for financial transaction I went.

"Blimey, you're early," said that morning's third apparition. "Mr Loosley darn't get 'ere for another ten minutes or so. Never mind. What ya got ?" she asked.

"It's in the back of the van. Have a look," I replied.

So, out of her front-doorway and across the pavement to my van she came. "I'll have a cauli and three of them carrots," she announced after ten seconds or so of viewing me, my van, and my van's contents.

One thing that was abundantly clear was that none of the women whom I had so far met had referred in any way to Loosley by his forename : It was always an unfriendly "Mr Loosley". Another thing that was abundantly clear was that Loosley's so-called 'profitable Greengrocery Delivery Round' was anything but profitable. I stuck it out until the end of the week by which time it was very clear that I had not even made enough profit to cover the cost of my van's fuel consumption which, given that many of those upon whom I had called lived in houses built on a steep hill, was considerable. "I'll give it one more week before I decide whether or not to continue with this farce," I decided. However, fate intervened and kindly made my decision for me.

The height from the ground of my van made it impossible for me to park it inside my garage; and so that Friday night of my Delivery Round's first week I, as I had done every night that week, drove the van, empty of its wares, down to a public Car Park in the nearby Strand Pleasure Beach area at the bottom end of Church Street and parked it there. On the Sunday I strolled, with Mischief, down to The Strand only to find that some 'kind' person, or persons, had hurled a sheet of corrugated iron through one of my van's side windows and had left it projecting out through the other side window. So, there endeth my one and only attempt at operating, what had been, Loosley's Greengrocery Round.

The vandalising of my dark blue Bedford van caused me to again be without my own means of transport, a situation resolved by my Mother's agreeing to finance, out of the moneys that she had obtained from selling her *Brunskill and Loveday* Shares, my purchasing an Estate Car. The condition of the Loan was that I had to repay her by means of weekly instalments until every penny loaned had been repaid. It was a deal that I was determined, and did, keep - for I in no way wished to remain obligated to her for longer than it was necessary for me to be so. Thus from 28 Kenilworth Court, where the deal had been struck, I walked up Putney Hill, alongside Wimbledon Common, to Old Wimbledon where, in the Wimbledon Motor Works, I purchased a Morris Oxford Estate Car, registration 6164 PG. It was brand-new save for the fact that it had been used by the Garage as a 'demonstration model', a fact which enabled me to achieve a noticeable price reduction.

My Morris Oxford was an absolute 'godsend' for it enabled me to do many things which I could otherwise not have done. For instance, every Saturday before one o'clock I departed Gillingham, confidently leaving Ivy in charge of the Shop, to go to wherever it was in London that the BBC Rugger Section was playing rugger and to return late that night or early next morning to take Mischief for a long walk before falling, exhausted from a combination of rugger and of socialising, into bed. It also enabled me to commit myself to, the following May, going to my first Retail Fruit Trade Federation Convention - at the Norbreck Hydro in Blackpool, the town in which, back in 1952, I had thoroughly enjoyed myself when I had - with Jack Warner, Gordon Harker, Bonar Colleano, and Susan Shaw - appeared, at The Grand Theatre, in *The Blue Lamp*. It was thus, for me, a town of happy memories. However, it was to be, with the Loosleys, an experience of mixed feelings.

Foolishly perhaps, I had agreed to take the Loosleys with me in my car and bring them back with me in my car, a gesture which, I thought, would at least engender some expression of gratitude from them. Nowadays technology within cars is such that they are more reliable than they were and thus a 560 mile [900km] or so drive to Blackpool and back to Gillingham is no great trial : But in 1964 such a journey was more akin to an expedition. Therefore, as a precaution, before we departed I had had the car fully serviced in Chatham by Gray's of Chatham. Then, with himself sitting on the front passenger seat and with Mrs sitting by herself on the back passenger seat, we, late one Saturday evening, set off for Blackpool. Traffic was nowhere near as 'heavy' as it is nowadays and, with most freight then going by rail not road, lorries were, thankfully, few and far between.

Having passed through London we went onto the M1 Motorway and, as we did so, Loosley spotted, way ahead in the distance, the tail lights of a lorry and, in so doing, said the word 'Lorry' to me in the most dull and boring voice imaginable. It was a routine that he was to repeat every time that he spotted a lorry ahead of us. Other than to say the word 'Lorry', both he and Mrs Loosley rarely spoke throughout the entirety of the journey. [To-day every car has at least a built-in radio if not also some other form of in-car entertainment : But that was not the case back in the early 1960s. However, I very soon, after we arrived back from Blackpool, got myself a portable radio and installed it in my car.]

The Loosleys and I arrived in the southern outskirts of Blackpool early on the Sunday morning just as a Gift Shop was opening up. Seeing the Shopkeeper hanging-up his 'seaside goodies' on the shop's canopy Mrs Loosley decided that we should stop so that she could buy a souvenir for her grandchild. So I stopped the car, and into the Gift Shop we went. The shop was overstuffed with all sorts of souvenir junk; and, having ceased driving, I now began to feel very tired. My tiredness increased due to the fact that my two passengers seemed to take an eternity deciding what it was that they were going to buy. Suddenly I inadvertently caught the corner of a large display of cheap china 'seaside' ornaments causing many of them to crash down onto the floor and shatter. Immediately a Shop Assistant shouted that I would have to pay for them. So pay for them I did, and it was only after we have driven away and I had fully re-awoken that I realised that I had been suckered for not only had the items and their display unit been an obstruction for which the Shopkeeper was probably at least part-liable but also it was likely that, as with my business back in Gillingham, the Shopkeeper was insured should such an event happen. So much for, in the guise of its local Branch Chairman and Secretary, the Retail Fruit Trade Federation's free legal advice to its Members. However, I was on holiday - So what the heck !!

The actual Convention, which ran for two and a half days, took place within Blackpool itself and was attended by well over one hundred Delegates many of whom, like the Loosleys and I, were staying in the Norbreck Hotel where we enjoyed not only the hospitality of the Norbreck itself but many side stalls and other means of hospitality provided to us by, for instance, the Fruit Trades Journal magazine; John and Leonard Van Geest of the Van Geest fruit and vegetable importing business; Elders and Fyffes Limited, Banana Importers; and the Israeli Jaffafruits organisation. It was a wondrous occasion, but I felt very isolated at first for not only did I not know anyone other than the Loosleys but also there I was, an almost complete novice insofar as fruit and veg were concerned, surrounded by scores of experts many of whom had spent years in the Trade.

The Medway Towns Branch of the RFTF was but one Branch within the Federation's South-eastern Region, a Region that encompassed Kent, Surrey, and Sussex; and soon the Delegates from Eastbourne, knowing Mr and Mrs Loosley, came up and introduced themselves to me. They were George Bridger and his wife, Beat; Den Hunt whose wife had recently died [of cancer, I recall]; and a lovely 'rolly-polly' of a man by the name of Billy Booth. George and Beat owned not only, what he and his colleagues described as being, "the finest Greengrocers in Eastbourne" but also a Market Garden on the outskirts of Eastbourne; Den had his own Greengrocery business in

Willingdon, then on the outskirts of Eastbourne; and Billy Booth had retired some years earlier having been the owner of "the finest Greengrocers in Eastbourne" before he sold it to George and Beat. Despite knowing that I was 'green' insofar as greengrocery was concerned, they straightaway made me feel that I was one of them; and, with George having deliberately distanced himself and his Eastbourne colleagues from the Loosleys, the five of us - George, Beat, Den, Billy, and I - spent much of the time to-gether, both in the Convention and in the social activities, as if we had known each other for years.

George and his friends had all travelled to Blackpool in George's car and clearly one of George's principal concerns was for the well-being of his friend, Den, who undoubtedly was feeling the loss of his wife : And so, once we had gotten to know each other, George suggested to me that, in an attempt to cheer up Den, we go around telling all and sundry, even those whom George had known for years, that George was Den's father and that Den was my father. Thus George set about introducing me to many of those present by saying "You haven't met my grandson before, have you ?" It left many people completely bewildered and was an 'act' that George, Den, and I kept going for several years.

The Convention that year, being in Blackpool, was hosted by the North-western Region of the RFTF some of whose Members, like many Greengrocers in those days, were quite, if not very, wealthy. I did not realise this until George, Den, Billy Booth, and I stopped for George to introduce me to one of his friends from the North-western Region. Having gone through the bewildering patter of my being George's grandson, etc., George then announced to me that the Greengrocer concerned was "a very wealthy man". Whether or not my expression perhaps indicated that I did not quite believe George I do not know but the portly Greengrocer concerned straightaway said "Yes. I never carry less than two grand on me". In those days two grand [£2,000] was a very large sum of money; and at that point I must have evidenced disbelief for the man, prising himself out of his seat, said "You don't believe me, do you Lad ?" Then he raised his sweater and untied a money belt that he had around his waist. "There," he said as he evidenced the belt's contents, "there's over two grand there." Given that a 'good' week's wage was then between £10 and £20, the fact that somebody was carrying over £2,000 with him in a belt around his waist seemed not only incredible but very, very foolish.

One goes to Conventions not only for the formal and informal business activities that take place but also for the social activities that take place; and, besides George and his Eastbourne colleagues, my social activities at Blackpool revolved round Jaffafruits or, to be more accurate, Miss Jaffa Oranges, a delightful and very attractive Israeli girl. She and I got on very well and in consequence spent quite a lot of time to-gether going into Blackpool itself and generally enjoying ourselves. The problem was, although we never saw them, it seemed that wherever Miss Jaffa Oranges and I went the Loosleys also went.

"What have you been doing to-day," the Loosleys would ask me at dinner each evening.

"Oh, Miss Jaffa Oranges and I went to [wherever it was that we went to]," I would reply.

"Yes, we know. We saw you there," Mrs Loosley would say. I just could not get rid of the wretched couple !! Had I not undertaken to take them back to Gillingham I would have followed George's oft repeated advice to "just dump them".

A week or so after the Loosleys and I returned to Gillingham a Medway Towns Branch Meeting was convened and on the Agenda was an Item entitled 'Convention Expenses'. As before, only three people attended the Meeting: Mr Loosley as Honorary Branch Chairman, Mrs Loosley as Honorary Branch Secretary, and I.

"We're very sorry," said Mrs Loosley when it came to discuss 'Convention Expenses', "but there are only sufficient funds out of which to re-pay the Expenses of two, not three, Delegates."

Needless to say, the two Delegates to whom the money went were Mr and Mrs Loosley, he as Chairman and she as Secretary. I did not receive even one penny towards the cost of the petrol consumed by my car in taking us up to Blackpool and back. To say that I was annoyed would be an understatement. Had it not been for a telephone-call that I subsequently received from George Bridger the Retail Fruit Trade Federation and I would have parted there and then.

The RFTF's two principal Branches in the Southeast Region were Eastbourne and Brighton each of which considered itself the better of the two. George Bridger was the Honorary Chairman of the Eastbourne Branch and Don Kimpton was the Honorary Chairman of the Brighton Branch. Given that each was a thriving Branch, the Medway Towns' Branch paled into insignificance by comparison, something which George - a very lively, entertaining, and progressive personality - blamed upon the Loosleys and their antiquated attitudes to Life. "Stick with it. Take over the Branch," said George despite the fact that he knew as well as I that I knew little or nothing about the Trade. "Go up to Russell Chambers. Have a chat with Tommy

Matkin. I've already told him about you. He knows you're coming". So, a few days later, up to Russell Chambers in London's Covent Garden I duly went and, amongst all the lorries that were unloading and loading-up with fruit and veg, I found a very convenient parking space for my car right outside the RFTF's front-door.

I had a long, very frank chat with Tommy, a chat which lasted a little under two hours. He told me about some of his background and I told him about some of mine; and eventually I agreed to do what I could to resurrect the once very active Medway Towns Branch despite the fact that, so Tommy informed me, the Loosleys intended staying on as Honorary Chairman and Honorary Secretary.

When I left Russell Chambers I found, against the kerb outside its front-door, several stacks of wooden crates of oranges each stack being (i) slowly reduced in height by two men standing on the stacks who threw the crates to 'Barra' Boys' on the pavement who loaded the crates onto their barrows and then carted them off to several of the many nearby Wholesale outlets and (ii) then immediately increased in height by more crates landing on the stacks. It was a continuous process the source of which was a large lorry parked immediately on the far side of my car over which, with a clearance of only about 6 inches [150mm], two men, standing on the lorry's platform, were hurling the crates. Wooden crates filled with oranges are heavy, and, as I stood there watching each crate as it flew over the top of my car, I was darn near terrified that any moment the trajectory of one of the crates would be such that it would destroy the roof of my car. Eventually one of the men who was hurling the crates shouted "Want into yer car, mate ?".

"Yes, please," I shouted back.

They all then suddenly stopped.

"Get in then," said the other of the two men on the lorry.

So in I got and waited in expectation that they would move their, still half-laden lorry, out of the way to enable me to drive away. But no … Once I was in the car and had shut my door the whole performance started up again : And so, having no choice in the matter, I just sat there until, eventually, all the crates had been offloaded.

"Thank God for that I thought." Wrong again : For another fully-laden-with-crates-of-oranges lorry drew up on the far side of the first lorry; and the whole ritual started up again. This time, however, two men on the second lorry threw its crates onto the first lorry where the two men on the first lorry picked them up and, as before, hurled them over the top of my car to the men standing on the stacks who, as before, threw the crates to 'Barra' Boys' on the pavement and so on.

Eventually all the crates on the second lorry, seemingly hundreds of them, were finally, via over the roof of my car, offloaded; and the second lorry pulled away. Then the driver of the first lorry, before he drove his lorry away, got out of his cab, came over to my car, and said to me "You ain't gonna park 'ere again are you mate ?" I had sat in that car, terrified, for well over an hour !!

During the months immediately prior to my going down to Gillingham June worked as a Receptionist in a Hairdressers in The Kings' Road in Chelsea, then, with Carnaby Street in Central London, London's most fashionable, and one of its most sought after, places. She seemed to enjoy her job a lot for many of those whom she met, or spoke with on the telephone, such as Samantha Eggar, were well-known personalities of the day. Eventually however, after I had moved to Gillingham, she left the Hairdressers in favour of a job as

Receptionist at the principal London premises of Sanderson's, a then very well-known and much respected Manufacturer and Supplier of 'upmarket' fabrics, furnishings, wallpapers, and so on. Going up to visit her at work one day I first had a call to make in Russell Chambers and, having had the very unpleasant and not-to-be-repeated experience of parking my car outside of Russell Chambers, I decided to park in The Aldwych. In those days Parking Meters were somewhat of a rarity but none-the-less I parked at a Parking Meter and walked the short distance to Covent Garden. It was my first experience of Parking Meters and, having discussed with Tommy Matkin whatever it was that I wanted to discuss, I left Russell Chambers and walked to Sanderson's to see June. I had completely forgotten about the Meter. Thus, when I eventually returned to my car my time 'on the Meter' had well and truly expired. I was, however, greatly relieved, when returning to my car, to find that I had not 'got a Ticket'. Eventually though I received a communication which informed me that, as I had not paid my Parking Fine, I was to be prosecuted in Wells Street Magistrates' Court. I was furious and decided to fight this injustice - For how dare they prosecute me when they had not even given me a Ticket ? So up to Wells Street Magistrates Court on the duly appointed Monday morning I went, determined to argue my Case before the Magistrate [District Judge - Criminal, to use the job's current title].

When I arrived it seemed that the only other persons outside the Court Room that day were Traffic Wardens. Eventually my Case was called, and into the Court I went. The Magistrate asked me to confirm my name, my address, that I was the owner of Morris Oxford 6164 PG, and that I had caused it to be parked in The Aldwych on a certain day at a certain time. My having so confirmed he then called a Traffic Warden into the Witness Box and asked him to have his say. The

Traffic Warden then stated that he had 'affixed' a Parking Ticket onto my vehicle on that certain day at that certain time. When the Traffic Warden had said all that he wanted to say the Magistrate invited me to ask questions of the Traffic Warden. I first stated that I had never received a Parking Ticket, and then I asked the Traffic Warden "How do you 'affix' your Tickets onto vehicles ?"

"With Sellotape [*a proprietary name of a make of adhesive tape*]," he replied in a tone of voice which indicated a degree of annoyance.

"And what happens if you run out of Sellotape ?" I asked.

"I *never* run out of Sellotape," he snapped back.

At that moment the Magistrate, clearly fed up by the days' events so far, suddenly intervened. "Mr Loveday," he said," I have full sympathy with you. These men in Westminster [by which he meant the United Kingdom Parliament] sit on their backsides making these rules and we have to try to implement them. I therefore *have* to fine you ten shillings [50p] with ten shillings Costs." [Trivial sums of money to-day but 'noticeable' sums of money in the early 1960s.] I duly paid the money at the Court's Office and left the building. Some weeks later a letter addressed to me arrived at 67 Church Street, Gillingham. It was from the Wells Street Magistrates Court and contained a ten shilling note, a Compliments slip, but, mysteriously, no explanation whatsoever.

Another incident involving parking occurred on London's Embankment under Waterloo Bridge. John Mannion, Haileybury's Lawrence House Servant, was much appreciated by most, if not all, who passed through Lawrence during his time there; and thus many Old Laurentians [as those who had been in Lawrence House and had left Haileybury are called] would, out of courtesy to and respect for him, call upon John in his tied cottage in Hailey Lane. During my time at Haileybury I, and many others, resented the fact that one could only purchase, within the College, food from one source, namely the 'Tucker' as we in Lawrence House called it [or 'Grubber' as those in other Houses called it]. Shortly after I had acquired my Morris Oxford Estate car a firm called 'Massmart' opened in Gravesend. Massmart was a 'Cash and Carry', a wholesale form of trading recently introduced as a means to enable Small Traders to attempt to compete with the bulk-buying power of the Supermarkets which were now rapidly coming onto the scene here, there, and everywhere courtesy of the Abolition of Resale Price Maintenance Act. Cash and Carry Wholesalers offered goods at prices noticeably more competitive than conventional Wholesalers. On my initiative, prompted by my resentment of boys at Haileybury being, in effect, held to ransom by the Tucker, John and I had, once Massmart had come on the scene, discussed the possibility of my 'flooding' Haileybury with canned and other foodstuffs at prices noticeably below those charged by the Tucker. My part would be as Supplier of the goods and John's part would be as Distributor via a network of College Servants and the like. Thus one night as I was driving my laden-with-goodies car from Gillingham to Hertford via London I approached the underside of Waterloo Bridge. As I did so I decided to pull in and check something. To my left directly under the Bridge was a generous parking space with an articulated lorry parked-up on each end of it; and so into the parking space I drove. After I had been sitting there for a few seconds someone tapped on my window. "You gonna move ?" he asked.

"No," I answered.

"You are gonna move," he said.

"No, I'm not," I replied.

"Oh, yes you bleedin' are," he shouted at me before turning towards the lorry in front of me and whistling loudly in its direction.

Suddenly the lorry in front started backing towards my car and then the lorry behind me, which was facing my car, started pulling forwards towards my car. Realising that my Morris Oxford was about to be physically squeezed by these two wagons, I started-up my car and got the hell out of there as quickly as I could.

"You know why they did that," John said when I told him.

"No," I replied.

"You'd parked in a Prostitutes' pick-up point and were interrupting business."

The selling of 'goodies' at Haileybury, although not really profitable insofar as I was concerned, seemed to go well not only with those boys to whom the goodies were sold but also with an increasing number of the Domestic Staff and, as the Dartford Tunnel [now part of the Dartford Crossing] beneath the River Thames had been opened in 1963, I decided that - whilst I enjoyed driving at night through the City of London, always very quiet and seemingly almost deserted once the daytime workers had left their offices and so on - I would go to Haileybury via the then not-that-much-used-at-night Tunnel and thereafter via Epping Forest.

The Government always requires businesses to evidence receipts if asked to do so and therefore I was somewhat surprised when, having arrived at the Tunnel's Toll Booth and paid the, then manually controlled, Toll, I was, having asked for a receipt, told by the Government's employee "We don't give no receipts".

"How am I going to evidence this expenditure to the Taxman if he asks," I enquired.

"That's your problem, mate, not mine," was his response.

So, having paid my Toll to the Government but with the Government's having refused to evidence that it had collected it, I drove on - my Estate car heavily laden with canned goodies and boxes of very popular cheese and onion-flavoured crisps made by Golden Wonder - towards Epping Forest, a sometimes eerie, frightening place in the dark of night. Part way through Epping Forest I caught up with the only vehicle that I had seen for quite a while. Given the very slow speed at which the other vehicle was travelling it seemed that the vehicle's driver was looking for a turning. Suddenly its driver slammed on the vehicle's brakes causing me to do likewise with my car which, as my car came to an abrupt halt, caused several of the boxes of cans of peas, soup, and baked beans that were piled up behind me to slide forward many of them onto me causing me to be pushed forward onto the steering-wheel and onto the circular horn 'push' contained within the circumference of the steering-wheel. As if all hell had been let loose the penetrating sound of my vehicle's horn burst into the eerie silence of Epping Forest. Some two or thereby minutes later, I managed to extricate myself from the weight of peas, soup, and baked beans that had landed on me and, with my car's horn now silenced, continue my way on through the Forest to Hertford Heath. The other vehicle had long since gone.

Sadly my sideline of competing with Haileybury's Tuck Shop came to an enforced end. Apparently the franchised operators of the College's Tuck Shop had - with, in my opinion, some cheek, given the prices that they were charging - complained to the School's Bursar [Haileybury's financial administrator] about the unfair competition that someone unknown to them was causing them to have to suffer. Various distributors, including John, within Haileybury of the food that I was supplying were instructed to attend upon the Bursar to have it stated to them that, unless they forthwith ceased selling, their jobs would be immediately terminated which - in the case of many of them, including John - meant that they would also lose their tied-to-Haileybury homes.

My re-involvement with the BBC Rugger Club had a 'spin-off' of bringing me back into contact with Stephen Bundy, the Senior Designer at Television Centre who back in 1962 had asked me to consider doing some designwork for the BBC, which gave me yet more opportunities to 'escape' from Gillingham and the added bonus of, when in London, being able to call at 101a Kenilworth Court on the off chance of seeing the delightfully attractive June Catherine Lindsay with whom one night I drove, at the request of my Mother, to the home of Rosie Doyle - a Lady Ratling whom I had known for many years and whose devotion to raising funds for the GOLR's 'Cup of Kindness' Charity Fund, usually by means of selling common or garden dolls which she had purchased and then converted into luxurious toilet-roll covers, was, within the Lady Ratlings, legendary. By then, I suspect, aged in her sixties, Rosie lived in a firstfloor flat off London's Tottenham Court Road access to which was first via an archway which seemed to afford shelter for several young 'ladies' seeking and entertaining 'customers'; then via a courtyard where other young 'ladies' were - in full view of June and me, and of anyone else passing through the courtyard - hard at it 'entertaining' 'customers' whom they had, in return for money, 'hooked'; and then via an outside staircase which led up to Rosie's and other flats [Rosie, I hasten to add, had, as far as I knew, no connection whatsoever with the 'trade' that was going on thereabouts] : And the object of our visit was to collect my Mother with whom Rosie had spent much of the day. Always pleased to see me, and keen to meet and know about June, Rosie - as June, my Mother, and I prepared to leave after June and I had been there for a half-hour or so - said to me "Be a dear, Edwin, and take these two lads home as well". So, having departed from Rosie's flat and made our way through the various degrees of frenzied activities that were going on round about, June, my Mother, and I, accompanied by the "two lads", made our way to my car and thence to where the "two lads", the gayest of men whom one could possibly meet, lived. To say that June and I were verbally entertained by them would be an understatement. They were outrageous !! Once back at Kenilworth Court I first dropped off my Mother outside the block of flats which contained No.28, then drove June to her flat, and then went to No.28 intending to say "Goodnight" before I set off back to Gillingham. All hell then let loose : "How dare you bring the Caretaker's Daughter with you" being only one of the volley of criticisms hurled at me for my having been with June.

A girl called Roni [Veronica] Germains was much more to my Mother's liking insofar as I was concerned. Roni, the daughter of a Lady Ratling, and whose Father was a Circus Ring Master, was a Cellist in Manchester's famed Hallé Orchestra, an Orchestra founded in Manchester in the 1850s by Charles Hallé. A pleasant enough girl, Roni invited me to Manchester to hear her and the Hallé play in the Hallé's famous 'home', Manchester's Free Trade Hall. So, from Gillingham up to the Free Trade Hall I drove arriving somewhat later than intended by which time Roni, the rest of the Hallé, and the Hallé's famous Conductor, Sir John Barbirolli, were well into that night's Performance. I entered the Free Trade Hall via its Stage Door and then - having had, over the years, many experiences of being backstage in Theatres - I went, as quietly as a mouse, into the offstage left area of this great Concert Hall's Stage intending to stand silently behind one of the downstage curtained Leg Drops, a position which would give me an excellent view both of the Orchestra and of Sir John Barbirolli. Unfortunately, as I arrived at my intended position and silently placed my right foot down so as to steady myself, the board beneath my foot quietly, but very audibly to Sir John, let out a squeak causing the great man, as he wielded his Conductor's baton, to immediately turn his face away from his beloved Orchestra and glare at me as if I were the most obnoxious character whom he had ever encountered : And time and again, as he led his Orchestra through the remainder of the 'piece' that he was conducting, he turned towards me and repeated his glare. When the Curtain had come down at the Interval I went on stage and met up with Roni whilst all the while expecting the great Sir John to come over to me and express to me in words that which his glare had already fully acquainted me with - But he never came. After the Concert Roni and I, and many of the Musicians, went to a nearby Public House; and never in my life had I before ever encountered so many seemingly gay men. It seemed as if at least fifty per cent of the male members of the Hallé was gay. Next day I had to drive back to Gillingham but before I did Roni and I went shopping. Well, Roni went shopping : I, it seemed, was there purely for the purpose of paying for whatever it was that caught her eye, including a pair of the most expensive 'Spanish' shoes that I had ever seen !! Not only did my experience of shopping with Roni cause me to discontinue any interest in her that I might have had but, sadly, I never did get to meet Sir John Barbirolli, one of the greatest of British Conductors.

However, my principal responsibility was to my Shop and its Customers; and journeying to Manchester was, in reality, a luxury that I could not afford. Neither, really, could I afford the regular trips that, in the early days of my owning my Shop, I made up to Whitechapel,

Stepney, and other areas of the East End of London that I had gotten to know well in my days, as a teenager whilst at Haileybury, of selling nylon stockings down Petticoat Lane - For, whilst most of what I sold, or attempted to sell, in my Shop was supplied to me by the Medway Towns firm of Scholar's I still retained my connection with the East End by purchasing such things as Sanilav [a toilet cleanser], toothpaste, bars of washing soap, and washing-powders from East End Wholesalers such as those whose goods were piled high in and outside their shops on such busy trading streets as the Mile End Road. Doubtless many of those with whom I dealt were, or had been, rogues to some degree or other but it was all good humoured and a contract concluded on a handshake was, at least in my experience, never broken. I would arrive on a Sunday morning and anything that I wanted that they had not got would, they said, be there for me "next Sunday".

"I can't come next Sunday. It'll have to be the following Sunday," I often had to say.

"Right, mate. It'll be here for you the following Sunday" :" And, having shaken hands but passed no money, it always was there for me "the following Sunday". Wonderful characters !!

However, the economics of travelling up to London and back to Gillingham were, in reality, just not on - A situation resolved for me by the opening, in Gravesend, of Massmart's 'Cash and Carry' Warehouse. I was there at Massmart's opening and was, I think, its third Customer; and I was impressed not only by its prices but also by its range of goods, including shirts which I purchased at 2/6d [12½p] each and retailed at 10/6 [52½p] if not more. They were well cut, well made but came only in mono-colours [yellow, blue, green, red, etc..]. However, given that it was the age of the 'swinging sixties', mono-colours were popular and, in consequence, the shirts were a good 'little earner'. June was attracted to them and so, as I passed through Putney late one night on my way back to Gillingham from BBC Television Centre, I dropped 6 shirts off outside the front-door of the flat in Kenilworth Court, close to 101a, in which she was now renting a bedroom. With the shirts I left a wee note. However, when I telephoned her next day she made no mention of the shirts. Unlike my experience with Roni Germains I had never known June to be demanding of anyone nor ungrateful to anyone; and so I was puzzled by her lack of any reference to the half-dozen shirts that I had left her.

"You idiot," she chucklingly said when I told her what I had done. "You didn't give them to me : You gave them to the bloke who cleans the stairs."

In my tiredness as I travelled back to Gillingham I had forgotten that early every weekday morning anything and everything left outside front-doors within Kenilworth Court was removed and taken to, and placed in, large 'Paladin' bins [large circular metal refuse bins on wheels] to await collection by the local authority's Refuse wagons. However, I still wonder whether the elderly gentleman who looked after the stairs of the block in which June then lived did, having gathered up the six brand new cellophane-wrapped shirts into his arms, ever allow the shirts to reach the Paladins let alone the local authority's Refuse wagon !!

Harry and Hilda Salthouse had, sadly for them, to - due to decreasing numbers of Customers caused mainly by the increasing number of, by to-day's standards, small Supermarkets in Gillingham High Street - close down their Shop which, being within their house, they converted into a 'front room'. I was fortunate in that I had by now gotten to know Harry quite well and he kindly, before closing down his Shop, directed his Customers to my Shop thereby increasing, but only slightly, my Shop's turnover. In the small parade of shops sited diagonally across Forge Lane from my Shop the General Stores there was, by its owner, converted into a small Supermarket but of a size somewhat smaller than those then now sited in Gillingham High Street. Thus competition that was unfair to Small Shops, insofar as the 'High Street' Supermarkets were concerned, was now growing apace; and so I decided that to attempt to combat it I should open another shop but one which sold primarily fruit and veg due to the fact that the profit mark-up on fruit and veg was noticeably, provided that one managed one's stock efficiently, higher than the profit mark-ups on other food items. So I found, not too far away in Pier Road, an empty shop premises available to rent; and into it, after I had converted it into a retail Greengrocery outlet, I plonked two of my 67 Church Street Customers each of whom not only had expressed an interest in working for me but also knew many of the people in the area of, what was to be, my second Shop.

Then, within a day or two of my having opened my second Shop, out of the blue I received a letter written by Sir John Clements on behalf of Michael Yates, the Head of Design at Associated-Rediffusion, then one of London's two television programme transmitting companies. The letter [*which is reproduced under*] invited me "to come along if you are free to and are interested" in becoming an Assistant Designer with Associated-Rediffusion.

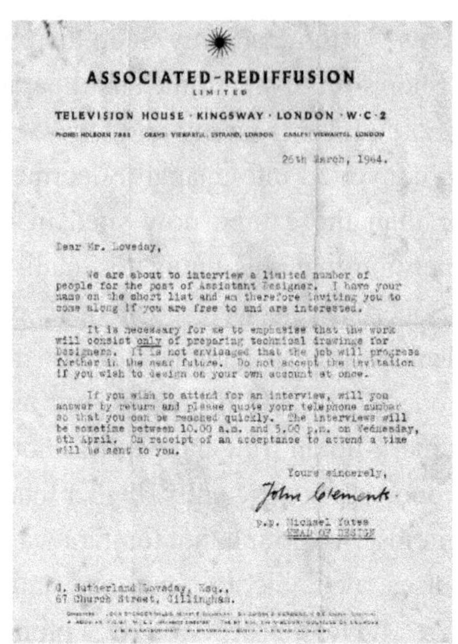

ASSOCIATED-REDIFFUSION
LIMITED

TELEVISION HOUSE · KINGSWAY · LONDON · W·C·2

26th March, 1964.

Dear Mr. Loveday,

We are about to interview a limited number of people for the post of Assistant Designer. I have your name on the short list and am therefore inviting you to come along if you are free to and are interested.

It is necessary for me to emphasise that the work will consist only of preparing technical drawings for Designers. It is not envisaged that the job will progress further in the near future. Do not accept the invitation if you wish to design on your own account at once.

If you wish to attend for an interview, will you answer by return and please quote your telephone number so that you can be reached quickly. The interviews will be sometime between 10.00 a.m. and 5.00 p.m. on Wednesday, 8th April. On receipt of an acceptance to attend a time will be sent to you.

Yours sincerely,

John Clements

p.p. Michael Yates
HEAD OF DESIGN

G. Sutherland Loveday, Esq.,
67 Church Street, Gillingham.

Dear Mr. Loveday

We are about to interview a limited number of people for the post of Assistant Designer. I have your name on the short list and am therefore inviting you to come along if you are free to and are interested.

It is necessary for me to emphasise that the work will consist <u>only</u> of preparing technical drawings for Designers. It is not envisaged that the job will progress further in the near future. Do not accept the invitation if you wish to design on your own attempt at once.

Yours sincerely

John Clements

pp Michael Yates

HEAD OF DESIGN

I had known the Actor/Producer/Director John Clements for years but had neither met nor had any contact with him since my Father had died. I did not know, nor to my knowledge had ever met, Michael Yates but I knew that he was a superb Designer of Theatre and Television Scenery who had become Head of Design at Associated-Rediffusion sometime in the mid-1950s. I was thus very flattered by the, wholly unexpected, content of Michael Yates's/John Clements' letter which, due not only to my commitments at 67 Church Street but also to my having only just opened my second Shop, arrived at a time when I just could not even consider the offer that was perhaps being gifted to me. Thus when I travelled to Associated-Rediffusion's Kingsway [London] Offices a few days later to meet with John Clements I did so out of courtesy to him and to Michael Yates, to thank these two great Theatricals for the kind offer so unexpectedly made to me, and to explain why it was that I was unable even to consider the offer. [What I did not know until some years after Eric Maschwitz's death in 1969 was that Eric Maschwitz had, in 1963, transferred from the BBC to Associated-Rediffusion and it was thus likely that the originator of Michael Yates's/John Clements' letter to me had perhaps been Eric Maschwitz !!]

My second Shop, sadly, did not last long for it seemed never to make even a penny's worth of profit. Indeed, contrary to all projection calculations, it seemed consistently to make losses. As to why I could not understand until one day I sent someone, who was completely unknown to my two employees, into the Shop as a Customer. She waited there for a while whilst my two employees ignored her and gossiped with, and 'served', a Customer who undoubtedly was a friend; and in the course of that wait my 'spy' witnessed my employees gifting a couple of apples, an orange, and a packet of Woodbine cigarettes. I very soon afterwards went down to the Shop, dismissed my two employees, closed the Shop, and transferred its stock to 67 Church Street.

I was by now very fond indeed of June but two events occurred which were to cause me to contain my emotions almost to that of a good brother/sister type of relationship. The first happened on a Saturday afternoon in the August of 1965. Two teenage lads were standing outside the Forge Lane window of my corner Shop chatting to two teenage girls each of whom was sitting on the window's outside ledge; and as they chatted away the backs of each of the two girls were, to my increasing annoyance and concern, innocently banging against the window's glass. I knew one of the lads by sight but had never, to my knowledge, seen any of the other three youths before. Intending to order the girls to get off my window's ledge I went outside; and that is when I first saw Patricia Mary Rubery, although, of course, at the time I had no idea who she was. Dark-haired, she looked absolutely gorgeous : And so, instead of ordering the two girls off my window's ledge, I asked them to move and then silently retreated back inside my Shop determined to find out who the gorgeous-looking one was. My enquiries eventually, in the February of 1966, led me to find out that she was the Daughter of one of Harry and Hilda Salthouse's Customers who, when Harry and Hilda had closed down their shop, had become a Customer of mine. I was just twentytwo years of age at the time and Mrs Rubery's Daughter was almost sixteen. Nowadays a six years' age gap seems almost irrelevant but back in the 1960s it seemed, to me and to many, to be considerable; and thus I could not just 'muscle in' and attempt to strike-up a relationship - Besides, I had the lovely and very attractive June Lindsay to consider, a 'problem' which June herself inadvertently substantially resolved, at least for me, for when in London I went as usual to see her at her Reception desk at the rear of Sanderson's. It was just before Christmas and she told me that she was going to spend Christmas and New Year with one of Sanderson's Designers at his parents' home in Switzerland. Despite my feelings for the girl in Gillingham whom I had yet to meet I was furious. However, when next I called at Kenilworth Court and met June very shortly after the Christmas/New Year period she and I went out for a drive in my car. Intending to go nowhere in particular we ended up in London's Heathrow Airport - then a much, much smaller place than it is nowadays - where, over a cup of coffee, in some distress she told me that things had not gone too well in Switzerland for, whereas June had apparently innocently gone to Switzerland, her Designer friend had more in mind than June had. The result, after June had resisted his intentions, was that she had, as 'punishment', apparently been, by the frustrated Designer, imprisoned in a cupboard. After June and I had had our coffees we drove around and sat in my car for some considerable period of time : And, given that I still had very strong feelings for June, I had not the heart to distress her further by even indicating to her that my affections now included a girl in Gillingham. Thus June and I continued as before but with the relationship now, at least insofar as I was concerned, somewhat more akin to that of brother and sister.

Having, by the February of 1966, gotten to know who the dark-haired mystery girl was I informed her Mother, who by now had become a 'Regular' Customer of mine, that I was thinking of employing someone for a few hours on Saturdays and asked her if she knew of anyone who might be interested. She suggested, as I had hoped, that her Daughter might be interested : And so I asked her if her Daughter had had any experience of shopwork. Her reply was "Well, she worked in Wooly's over Christmas". I, of course, knew that by 'Wooly's' Mrs Rubery meant the then very well known, but now no longer, 'chain store' firm of FW Woolworth and Company but nevertheless I could not resist responding with the well-worn corny comment "Why, was she cold ?"

A Pupil at Chatham Grammar School for Girls, Tricia [pronounced 'Trish'], as her Mother called her, started working for me every Saturday morning, and on some Sunday mornings, very shortly thereafter and was an immediate hit not only with me, not only with Ivy but also with my Customers many of whom already knew her and clearly respected and admired her. Always casually but smartly dressed, she was very efficient, very polite, and very trustworthy. As an employer one could not have asked for more. She was also an instant hit with my dog, Mischief.

My Mother, once she had realised that I had a 'soft spot' for June, had been in the habit, when speaking with me in June's absence, of referring to June, although she liked June and enjoyed speaking with her, as being "the Caretaker's Daughter", a 'put down' description no doubt intended to emphasise to me that a social 'gap' existed between me, an educational product of the English Public School system, and June. It thus did not take my Mother long - once she had been acquainted by me with the facts that not only was I employing a 16-years' old girl, albeit on a part-time basis, but also that I was very fond of her - to find a snide way of imparting to me the fact that a relationship, other than that of employer/employee, between me and Tricia also did not meet with her approval. Tricia's Father, a former professional Boxer, was a Welder in Chatham's famous Naval Dockyard : But this time my Mother steered clear of emphasising the Father's job and instead would, every now and then, interject into some of the conversations involving Tricia that she and I had that I was 'child-snatching'. I just learned to live with the comments.

Often, when out at night taking Mischief for a walk, I would call at Harry and Hilda Salthouse's house for a chat and to enjoy a corned beef sandwich which Hilda, bless her, always made for me. Because of dampness suffered by one of its random-rubble external walls due to the inclined outside ground level that abutted it the Shop area, although converted for residential use, was never used by the Salthouses. Instead what had once been the Shop's back room, accessed by an indoor passageway running alongside the former Shop from the frontdoor, was where we sat and chatted.

The Salthouses were kindness itself. Their Daughter, Lynda, was about the same age as Tricia and had, until the two of them sat the State School system's 11+ Exam [a selective, and often much criticised, examination taken during the last year at Primary School to determine which, in the Education Authority's opinion, type of school - Grammar, Secondary Modern or Technical - each student should progress to], attended the same school. Also, when Mrs Rubery had been a Customer of Harry and Hilda's Shop Tricia had occasionally called at their Shop. Thus Lynda and Tricia knew each other quite well : But the divisive nature of the 11+ Exam had caused friction, not too serious, to develop between the two of them. Thus by the time that I got to know both Lynda and Tricia the unnecessary hostility that had developed between them had adversely influenced Lynda's attitude towards Tricia and Tricia's attitude towards Lynda. Lynda's comments to me about Tricia were therefore occasionally none-too-favourable. However Harry and Hilda, although understanding of their Daughter's attitude, thought highly of Tricia, a fact often made noticeable when Harry made his regular Saturday Milk Round visits to my Shop. "Is he treating you okay ?" Harry would jovially ask as he bounded in. "Well, Mr Salthouse …" Tricia would, with a smile, begin to respond.

"I wouldn't put up with him if I were you," Harry would then say.

"I don't," Tricia would reply; and, encouraged, I confess, by me, there were times that she got, she thought, the better of me. For instance, on one occasion when the Shop was devoid of Customers she said to me "What do you want me to do now?"

"Clean out the freezer," I told her.

"Clean it out yourself," she replied. Then, as I stepped towards her and the freezer, with feigned reluctance she threw herself, heart and soul, into removing the freezer's contents, cleaning the inside of the freezer, and then neatly replacing the contents.

At least once in every Financial Year Stocktaking had to be undertaken; and Tricia and I got it down to a fine art. We undertook the job on a Sunday when the Shop was closed. Tricia would come in for an hour or so and, once the two of us had gotten ourselves organised, she would go round the shelves counting and calling out to me the numbers of cans of beans, packets of cigarettes, packets of butter, and everything else that my Shop had in it and I would write the numbers down on sheets of paper. Then, with the job done, back home she would go for lunch leaving me to look forward to her return the next Saturday.

In January 1967 I was involved in a serious car accident very early one Sunday morning after having played rugger and then gone on to - with Ray Jones, a BBC rugby Club colleague whose job at the BBC was to drive around the television Studio floors sitting on a machine that removed from the floors everything, such as carpets and camera positions, that had been painted on them - 'gate-crash' a Party known by Ray to be being held in a BBC employee's flat somewhat. Having left the Party at around midnight I was driving back to Gillingham via the then A2 road and had reached the area of the Black Prince Public House when I noticed, via its lights shining in my car's offside wing-mirror, a car attempting to overtake mine. The road at that point was wide enough for two vehicles but not for a third, and coming towards me in the opposite direction on the other side of the road was a stream of cars. In my opinion the overtaking car would not be able to successfully overtake my car, a view seemingly also arrived at by the overtaking car's driver for the car, much to my relief, dropped back and pulled in behind my car. Then, suddenly, the car behind me pulled out and again began to overtake. This time, coming at speed, it did not stop; and so I pulled my car as close to the kerb as I safely could so as to give the overtaking car as much space as I could. Suddenly, as I had already realised that it would, the overtaking car hit a car coming in the opposite direction causing the offending vehicle to turn, at speed, into my Morris Oxford car and project it off the road and into the air. The point of impact occurred at a position where the A2 road began to pass over another road; and in consequence my car and I found ourselves flying rapidly through the air and eventually landing on the road below, then bouncing three times before sliding sideways then coming to a stop. Seat belt legislation was not compulsory in those days but fortunately, although my car was damaged, I was not hurt other than that my glasses had projected themselves from my face thereby enabling a very small piece of glass from my car's by now shattered windscreen to end-up in my left eye. I groped around inside my car, found my glasses, put them on, forced open my car's driver's door, got out of my car, and climbed up the grassed embankment that led from the lower road up to the A2 where the sight that greeted me was one of considerable carnage. The offending vehicle had been split almost in half with its front half pointing in the direction of where my car had been, in effect, catapulted to, and with its back half lodged in the front of the car that had been travelling in the opposite direction. Four groaning-in-agony people were trapped in the offending vehicle and three, if not four, groaning-in-agony people were trapped in the other car. Various other cars had stopped here, there, and everywhere whilst other vehicles sought their ways around the carnage in order to continue their journeys. Several people, some from other cars that had stopped and some from nearby houses, were milling around the injured occupants of the two cars, and it seemed to me that what I needed to do was to try to control the flows of traffic - a thought that seemed also to occur to another man for, almost at the same time as I stood at the southern end of the scene of the accident and started to wave my arms around, he took up a position at the northern end of the carnage and started to wave his arms around; and to-gether the two of us managed to control the traffic until the first police car arrived, a half-minute or so after the first ambulance had arrived. There were only two Police Officers in the police car, one went straight to my arm-waving colleague and took over from him and the other came straight towards me : But instead of relieving me from my arm-waving activities he, as he got near to me, shouted "Can you carry on ? I've got to attend to the injured."

Enthusiastically - for I was enjoying my 'job' - I shouted "Yes"; and so I was left, until well past 3 o'clock, to carry on, in conjunction with his colleague, controlling the seemingly vast amount of vehicles that passed by the incident that night. Nothing, I learned that night, is more interesting to people than to see other people suffering - For rarely did a car pass by without its being slowed down almost to a halt by its driver so as to enable the driver and the vehicle's occupants to gawk at the mess and suffering that lay alongside them.

Just after 3 o'clock the several ambulances that had attended had gone, most of the police vehicles that had attended had gone, and the two badly damaged cars had been removed and taken away.

"Thanks very much for all your help. You can go home now," a Police Officer said to me.

Whilst I had been controlling the traffic I had noticed that some of his colleagues had been taking Statements, and so I asked him if he wished me to give a Statement.

"Why," he asked," did *you* witness the incident ?"

"I was in the third car," I replied.

"What third car ?"

"That *third car* down there," I said pointing down to my Morris Oxford.

"Well, we've taken Statements from several Witnesses and not one mentioned a *third car*," he, as he looked down at my battered vehicle, responded with amazement. So, I learned another lesson that night for, whereas each 'Witness' genuinely believed that he/she had witnessed the accident, what they had witnessed was what they had seen after they had heard the impact and turned towards the source of the sound, by which time my vehicle had been catapulted off the road into the darkness of the night.

The Police arranged for my car to be removed and for a taxi to take me home to Gillingham where, bless her, my dog, Mischief, was eagerly awaiting my return. However, before I took her for a walk I scribbled a note to Tricia on a piece of paper. The Shop was not usually open on Sundays during the Winter months but for some reason or other - perhaps for Stocktaking - Tricia was due to come to work in the Shop at 10 o'clock that Sunday morning; and so the note simply stated, without emphasising the severity of the incident, that I had been in a car accident and asked her if she could come in a few minutes early : And, as Mischief and I walked passed Tricia's home in nearby 48 Layfield Road, I very quietly pushed the note through her letterbox.

"I'd never known her to get up so fast on a Sunday," her Father told me a few days later. Apparently he had found the note on the floor behind the frontdoor, read it, and straightaway taken it up to Tricia who, as soon as she had read it, got up, got washed, got dressed, gobbled her breakfast down, and came to 67 Church Street as quickly as she could. I was, to say the least, very flattered by her concern; although I could have done without her persistent insistence that I should straightaway go to the local Hospital to get the piece of glass removed from my eye and my eye and myself thoroughly checked. Fortunately very shortly after one of my ritualistic replies that I would be okay the piece of glass resolved the problem by coming out and disappearing on the floor somewhere. I felt like giving Tricia a big kiss to evidence to her my appreciation of her : But instead all that this coward could do was muster the *macho* response: "There you are. Told you so". I would not have blamed her had she hit me ... But she never did !!

By now I was wearing several 'hats': I had my Corner Shop at 67 Church Street, Gillingham; at Stephen Bundy's request I was designing, on an unpaid freelance basis [in return for which - by arrangement with Alec Lee, the overall Secretary of the BBC Club - I was granted free access to many BBC Club facilities] bits and pieces of Scenery for BBC Television; I had become the Medway Towns'

Secretary of the Retail Fruit Trade Federation and then the Federation's Area Secretary for the South-east of England; and in early 1965 I had purchased a Printing Company, The Highfield Press Limited, in Thames Ditton, a delightful 'upmarket' village situated near to Hampton Court Palace.

I knew nothing about the 'technicalities' of printing but I was tempted when I saw the advertisement of its being for sale in, I think it was, *Dalton's Weekly*; and, knowing something about design and something about running a business, I assumed that running a print business would be none-too-difficult. I was, for once, assisted by my Mother for she considered my being the Managing Director of a printing company to be much more socially acceptable than my being the owner of a small Grocery/Greengrocery business. Thus she and I travelled into the heart of rural Surrey to meet with the Business Transfer Agent who had inserted the advertisement. I forget his surname, but Frank was his forename; and both he and his wife, Ella, greeted us with enthusiasm when, by appointment, we arrived at their bungalow.

All the Shares of The Highfield Press, which employed 11 staff, were owned by a Mr and Mrs Simpkins, an apparently moderately wealthy couple who lived in a secluded Private Estate in Surrey's so-called 'Stockbroker Belt'. Mr Simpkins, apart from being the Managing Director of The Highfield Press, worked for a firm of Law Publishers. Apparently, according to Frank, who with his wife traded as Frankella, although The Highfield Press was a good business financially Simpkins was finding it difficult to both run The Highfield Press and satisfactorily undertake his full-time job, apparently at management level within Sales, within the Publishers, the very same

Publishers whose Shaw's List I had relied upon at the commencement of my life as a Grocer/Greengrocer.

My Mother and I, as we sat in Frank's Office in his bungalow, were impressed not only by his, we thought at the time, apparent honesty but also by the fact that, as the three of us endeavoured to negotiate, time and again one or other of the two telephones on his desk would ring causing him to say "Excuse me whilst I deal with this call" and then involve himself, over the telephone, in negotiations which often lasted several minutes. In all my Mother and I were there for nearly three hours during which time the Master Telephone Negotiator received and dealt with in excess of a dozen calls.

My Mother and I left Frank and his wife having conditionally agreed a purchase price of £5,000 for all the Shares subject to my inspecting The Highfield Press's premises, its machinery and so on and to my having had the Accounts of The Highfield Press looked at by my late Father's private [non-Brunskill and Loveday Limited] Accountant, William Frank Reginald Gazzard of Bennett, Gazzard, Flynn and Company, Victoria Street, London, who also attended to my Grocery/Greengrocery business's Annual Accounts and liaising, on behalf of my Grocery/Greengrocery business [and thus me], with the Inland Revenue [as it then was]. Next day, after I had returned to Gillingham, I telephoned the Simpkinses, spoke with Mrs Simpkins, and arranged to meet her at her home so that she and I could, that night, go to Thames Ditton to enable me to look at The Highfield Press's assets and the leasehold premises that it occupied in the Yard of Furness and Company, Bakers of Thames Ditton. Unfortunately the heating system in my car had broken down some days before, and the Tweed-suited, high leather boots-wearing aloof Mrs Simpkins several times as we journeyed to and from The Highfield Press that night made known to me her displeasure at having to be driven in a cold car. Had it been I who was in the company of someone to whom I was hoping to rid myself of a business I would have kept my mouth shut and put up with the discomfort : But that was clearly not Mrs Simpkins's attitude. Thus by the time that she and I arrived at the Yard's locked double-gates the tension between us was … Well, a wee bit noticeable : And the facts that she seemed to know little or nothing about what lay beyond the gates nor appeared to have much, if any, interest in what lay beyond the gates did not improve matters. Nevertheless into The Highfield Press we went.

Insofar as print machinery was concerned, The Highfield Press owned, amongst other things, within its leased single-storey building three Heidelberg platten presses, one Mercedes rotary press, a lithographic print machine, and, in a room specially allocated for it, a largish Victory-Kidder guillotine machine which also, in part, seemed to act as principal support for holding up the room's corrugated iron roof. Adjacent to the Guillotine Room was a room which was pilled high with large and small sheets of paper and which had a door to the outside world via which deliveries of paper were received. In those pre-computer days type in small printing firms such as The Highfield Press was, in the main, handset on site by Compositors; and so a room existed within the 'main building' which, other than a duck-boarded area intended to accommodate a standing Compositor, was substantially full of galleys of type and self-standing wooden units each with several drawers full of type. Adjacent to the Comp(osit)ing Room, sited between it and the 'main building's' entrance door was another room. "That's Mrs Wensak's Office," said my somewhat uncommunicative guide.

"Whose Mrs Wensak ?" I asked.

"The Secretary," Mrs Simpkins replied.

"The Company's Secretary ?" I enquired.

"*I* am the Company's Secretary," retorted a horrified Mrs Simkins. "Mrs Wensak does the wages, looks after the books on a day-to-day basis. That type of thing."

"And how many Employees, including Mrs Wensak, are there ?" I asked.

"I'm told that there are eleven including George Swain," my, seemingly largely ignorant, guide replied.

"Who's George Swain ?" I asked.

"The General Manager. He runs the place," the guide responded.

I had known Frank Gazzard most, if not all, of my life. He lived with his wife and their only child, Peter, in Kenton, Harrow in what was then Middlesex but is now London. Peter at the time was a Student at, I think, Saint Andrew's University in Fife and he had my sympathy for, without doubt, his parents were … Well, cautious with money which perhaps was the reason for the fact that Frank did not drink alcohol only, even when socialising, water. In fairness, Frank had not had it easy after he had qualified as an Accountant for not only had he, armed with his new qualification and desperately seeking work, time and again been rejected but when he did find work his wage was pitiful. 'Old man' Bennett, who had been my Father's Accountant prior to Gazzard becoming his Accountant, was the man who ended Gazzard's depressing search for work. Having, by appointment, arrived in Bennett's Office after having received yet more rejections, each on the basis that he had no 'track-record' as an Accountant, Frank Gazzard, by no stretch of the imagination the boldest of men, made his pitch and yet again received the by now stock response: "I'm sorry, Mr Gazzard, but you've had no experience : And we are looking for an experienced Accountant".

"But how the hell am I to get experience if no-one'll give me a job ?" Frank suddenly snapped back.

"A very good point," 'old man' Bennett replied. "You've got the job. You start on Monday." Thereafter Frank Gazzard remained loyal to 'old man' Bennett until the day, some years later, when Bennett retired.

At 10 am a couple of days or so after I had seen over The Highfield Press's premises Frank and I met up outside the Simpkins's Solicitors' Office in Guildford High Street in Surrey. Our purpose? To enable Frank Gazzard, and me, to examine The Highfield Press's Accounts to ascertain whether the Shares - and thus the business, its goodwill, machinery, stock, and so forth - were worth the £5,000 that my Mother and I had conditionally agreed with Frank, the Business Transfer Agent. Given ample facility, including occasional cups of coffee, by the Simpkins's Solicitors Frank Gazzard and I pawed our ways through the various account books and were impressed by the names of some of The Highfield Press's Customers, Customers such as Trianco Boilers, the UK's principal manufacturer of solid fuel boilers whose Works and Offices were, relative to The Highfield Press, in nearby West Molesey; the Ophthalmic Division of the National Health Service; AC Cars, a manufacturer of specialist motorcars; Solatron, a manufacturer, based in Farnborough in Hampshire, of precision technical equipment; Rola Celestion, a major UK manufacturer, based in Thames Ditton, of speakers for hi-fi and other types of equipment; and Surrey County Council.

At just before 1pm we discontinued our labours in favour of going across the road for luncheon in a picturesque oak-beamed, seemingly very popular, restaurant. We each had cottage pie and, at the end of our meal, we went to-gether to the cash-point to pay for what we had eaten.

"I'll pay," I said to Frank.

"No, it's alright, Edwin, I'll pay," replied my friend of many years.

"No, I'll pay," I insisted.

However, Frank paid. The total sum ? One pound. [When I received his bill some weeks' later and saw, under the heading 'Hospitality', that he was charging me ten pounds for what I had seen him pay only one pound I was furious.]

Having paid, back across the road to the Solicitors' Frank Gazzard and I went and by mid-afternoon Frank had concluded that The Highfield Press was indeed worth £5,000. Thus some days' later back to Frankella the Business Transfer Agent my Mother and I went and duly signed the Contract whereby we agreed to purchase all the Shares of The Highfield Press Limited for £5,000. It was only after the deal had been concluded that I discovered that Frank was not as impressive as he had seemed when my Mother and I had first called upon him. Leaving him and my Mother chatting away I got up to go to the toilet and, as I did so one of Frank's telephones rang. By now I had gotten used to Frank being interrupted by 'business' calls : But, having gone out of his Office, as I passed his slightly open kitchen door on my way to the loo I noticed not only his wife sitting, more or less with her back to me, at the kitchen table but also, sited to her left on the table, a Second World War Army Field Telephone of a type then readily available, now that the War was long since over, from many 'Army Surplus' and other shops. She was holding the handset to her head. "Odd, very odd," I thought : And so, once I had completed the object of my visit to Frank's loo, after I had, very quietly, washed my hands I, as silently as I could, opened the door, crept out and over to a position adjacent to the kitchen door which enabled me to hear, without being seen, what his wife was saying. What I heard was sufficient to enable me to confirm to myself that the 'businessperson' to whom Frank was talking was none other than his sitting-in-his-own-kitchen wife. I thus crept back to the toilet, somewhat loudly closed its door, and walked back passed the kitchen to Frank's Office where I found him putting down his telephone's handset.

"Sorry about that," he was saying. "As you know, it happens all the time. I'm supposed to be semi-retired : But you can't turn business away, can you ?"

"You lying b*st**d," I thought.

Arthur Sidney Coldham, my Father's Solicitor who lived in Chingford, Essex, attended to the necessary legal work whereby ownership, using £5,000 from the money that my Mother had realised from the sale of her Shares in Brunskill and Loveday Limited, of The Highfield Press Limited passed to me with my Mother being named as a Director and I being named as Managing Director. Unfortunately neither Frank Gazzard nor Arthur Coldham, nor anyone else, had said anything about 'Working Capital' to me; and thus I, foolishly, assumed that I could run The Highfield Press in the same manner that I had been running my Grocery/Greengrocery business, namely, by paying bills out of income received. The fact that The Highfield Press had eleven full-time employees and the fact that the Print Industry was a totally different type of 'ball-game' to the

Grocery/Greengrocery Trades had not, in my mesmerised enthusiasm to buy The Highfield Press, crossed my mind.

Without the talents of, and full co-operation that I received from, George Swain, The Highfield Press's General Manager, the survival of The Highfield Press under my ownership would not have lasted very long. A 'Print Man' through and through he had come to The Highfield Press from 'Fleet Street', then a hotbed of, often very corrupt, Trades Union-controlled activity where calling men out on strike was more-or-less a regular Union activity, one which George had had enough of. His eventual decision to resign from a way of life which he found financially very rewarding but morally very repugnant came about in the early hours of one morning when he sought to do a favour for a work colleague. Arriving at the foot of an iron stairway George had found his colleague idly standing waiting for another person to come down the stairway to collect a galley of type that his colleague was carrying. As he was himself intending to go up the stairway, George as a favour took the galley of type and carried it up the stairway in order to pass it to a man who was waiting at the top of the stairway to receive it. As it was not George's job to carry the type up the stairway, the man at the top of the stairway refused to receive it; and in consequence of George's goodwill action the Union not only called that particular newspaper's staff out on strike but also called all the other London newspapers' staffs out on strike. Thus George subsequently answered an advertisement for a General Manager for The Highfield Press that my predecessors, when owners of The Highfield Press, had placed and not only, despite a considerable drop in earnings, became The Highfield Press's General Manager but also, using some of the considerable moneys that he had received through working in Fleet Street, bought a bungalow in nearby Hampton Court Way for himself and his wife in part to be near

The Highfield Press and in part to detach himself from, what he and others considered to be, the corruption that was 'Fleet Street', a corruption that involved many scams being perpetrated on newspaper Owners including the regular signing-on and signing-off by one man of many men each of whom got paid, often very handsomely, for undertaking work with which they had no involvement whatsoever.

Because of my feelings for Tricia I always ensured that I was in my Shop on Saturday mornings. Also, I had developed a two-, sometimes three-, Customer Friday-Night Delivery Service, which I enjoyed, and thus I also had to be in my Shop during the latter part of Fridays. My first call on Friday Nights was to the Dawkins Family in their Council house in nearby Knight Avenue. Ron Dawkins, a large jovial man, was a talented, much in demand, self-employed Builder who, during the time that I knew him, concentrated mainly on Tiling and internal and external Plastering. Married, he had two sons and two daughters. Colin, the elder of his sons, and the eldest of his four children, on leaving school got himself a job as a Rat Catcher in Chatham Dockyard. The youngest of his squad of Chatham Dockyard Rat Catchers, Colin's job often required him to stand, with a colleague, at the end of tunnels whilst their other, older and doubtless wiser, colleagues entered the tunnels at their other ends. Then, walking towards the two lads, the others would, by their noisy presence, drive the rats down the tunnel to where the two lads were standing and then, as the rats rushed towards the two of them, Colin and his mate would, with only their glove-covered hands, reach out and try to grab the rats as they sought to scurry passed them. Not a job that I would have liked - But apparently Ron's son enjoyed it !!

To-gether Strood, Rochester, Chatham, Gillingham, and Rainham formed the Medway Towns with the River Medway being the core feature of the area and the historic Rochester Cathedral forming the area's religious centre. The most active and productive area of the Medway Towns was, however, where Tricia's Father, a Dockyard Welder worked, namely Chatham's historic naval dockyard. Principally entered from the main road by Chatham Dockyard's Crimean Memorial Arch the place was a hive of military and naval activity. However, as a civilian I could only look in from outside; not go in. But on one occasion I did venture to have my haircut from a highly trained wielder of navy scissors who operated from a barber's shop just outside the bounds of Chatham Dockyard. Next day and for several days thereafter "Had your hair cut at Chatham Barracks I see" was the smirking comment of several of my customers who, instead of being greeted by my somewhat unkempt hair style, were greeted by a well known, to them but not previously by me, product of a very short back and sides, and top of head, naval hair cut. For a few hours it was very embarrassing but it soon became fun.

One of Ron Dawkin's tiling 'talents' was to disguise faults that had appeared in a newly-built private housing scheme on the outskirts of Maidstone, Kent's County Town. Built on a hill on, apparently, what had been a rubbish landfill site the stability of the foundations of some of the houses was somewhat suspect causing them to, until the foundations settled, slowly sink and slide down the hill and for cracks to appear here, there, and everywhere within the houses. To-day Consumer and Construction Laws within the United Kingdom would not enable a House Builder to 'get away with it' but such was not the situation in the 1960s. Thus the tiling talent of Ron Dawkins was brought in to cover the cracks with tiles the areas of which were then described to potential buyers by the House Builder by such phrases as "unusual artistic features".

Having delivered the Dawkins's 'weekly shop', been given a cup of coffee by Ron's wife and been entertained by a recital by Ron of some of the jokes - usually crude, if not very crude - that had been in circulation in the building site(s) that week, I would either then go on to Danny Bull's to deliver his 'weekly shop' or to Layfield Road and thence to Danny Bull's.

My Layfield Road call, sadly, had nothing whatsoever to do with Tricia. I went instead to deliver smallish bags of coal to her elderlyish next-door neighbour. Small bags of coal were, certainly during the winter period, a regular 'seller' : But everyone who bought them, save for Tricia's neighbour, always carried them away from my Shop themselves. He was the one and only exception; and he never, save for an occasional packet of cigarettes, bought anything else from my Shop. Whether or not I agreed to deliver them to him in the hope that I might somehow 'bump into' Tricia I can not now recall - Perhaps I did !!

I had gotten to know Danny Bull and his wife, Anne, as a result of my friendship with Harry Salthouse, Anne's brother. As a complete novice, insofar as Greengrocery was concerned, when I had arrived in Gillingham to assume ownership of my Shop I had at first been somewhat intimidated by the knowledge that Danny was perhaps - through being the son of the owner of the most successful retail, and semi-wholesale, Fruit, Veg, and Florist's business in Chatham - the most knowledgeable and experienced of Greengrocers for miles around. Indeed, although Danny's father still owned the business, it was Danny who, through his father's more or less total retirement from the business, now ran the business : And in those days Greengrocers such as Danny Bull really knew what Greengrocery was all about. However, not once did Danny ever make me feel inferior insofar as the Greengrocery Trade was concerned. He and his wife were, like Harry and Hilda, very kind to me; and my weekly delivery of Groceries to them was always to be looked forward to, was always very enjoyable, and always included a couple of glasses of Guinness, the last being downed by me just in time to enable me to leave so that I could be home by midnight to take Mischief for a walk. Of their three children - two teenage daughters and a teenage son - I have many memories including of their teenage son, a pleasant lad by the name of Robert, saying to me not only that Tricia was beautiful but also that he fancied her [a comment made to me by others such as [1] a lad who worked in a Sports Shop in Gillingham, a business that was owned by his professional football-playing brother and [2] an employee of a Shopfitter whose firm was contracted by me to undertake an upgrade and other works to my Shop]. Robert knew that Tricia worked for me but whether or not he knew that my feelings were similar to, and probably stronger than, his I do not know. [Many years later, out of earshot of Robert's nearby wife, he repeated the comments when we met up again on the very sad occasion of Harry Salthouse's funeral.]

By now I was travelling up and down the A2 Trunk road like a yo-yo either going from Gillingham to Thames Ditton and back, from Gillingham to Thames Ditton then to BBC Television Centre and back, or from Gillingham to wherever it was that I was playing rugger for the BBC and back. My car's petrol consumption was huge and, in reality, financially unsustainable. Ideally I should have sold, and did intend to sell, my Shop once I had gotten to grips with The Highfield Press : But the existence of my Saturday Morning Assistant kind of kept delaying and delaying that idea. As it was essential to me to keep this juggling act going, when my car was severely damaged in the accident that occurred on the A2 near to the Black Prince Public House I, next day after Tricia had gone back home, went to Harry and

Hilda, told them about the accident and the fact that my car had been removed to a Garage alongside the South Circular Road in Eltham in South London and asked if they would kindly (a) take me back to where the incident had occurred and (b) so as to enable me to retain my confidence insofar as driving was concerned, allow me to drive their former police-car back to Gillingham. They agreed without any hesitation : And so, in what had previously been a black, but now bell-less, Police Car, back with Harry, Hilda, and their daughter to the scene of the accident I went. It was only when we arrived and I was able, in daylight, to see not only where the accident had happened but also the distance that my car had travelled through the air did I realise how lucky I had been to survive virtually uninjured and how unwise I had perhaps been not to have followed Tricia's advice that I should have gone to hospital to get myself checked out. However, as I now felt perfectly okay I continued not to follow her advice - a decision which, fortunately, I subsequently had no cause to regret.

I had occasion, some weeks later, to repay Harry and Hilda's kind generosity in allowing me to drive their car. They and Lynda had, as part of an Audience Participation arrangement, gone to BBC Television Centre to watch a Show and, my being in Television Centre that night, I met them there after the Show, showed them around some areas of Television Centre that they would otherwise not have seen, and then took them back to Gillingham. As with many things in my life, all did not go quite according to plan. Harry - a short man whose Second World War experiences had included his having to crawl, with a radio, as close as he could to Japanese lines in order to report the activities of the Japanese - sat in my car's front passenger seat whilst Hilda and Lynda sat on the back passenger seat. We had just gone through a set of traffic-lights and into a slight righthand bend when suddenly a mini-car, travelling at speed, overtook us and, just before the road passed under a railway bridge, stopped. Two largish men, each with a lorry tyre-lever in hand, got out and came running back to us. "Get out and have a fight," one of them, by now alongside my door, shouted at me. So I got out and leant upon the top of my door in part so as to disguise my height of nearly six feet two inches [2M].

"Come on then. Have a fight," he went on.

"Okay then," I said raising myself up to my full height and, slightly standing on my toes, beyond my full height. Then I turned and shouted to Harry "Out you get, Sergeant."

Somewhat taken aback and, I suggest, now a wee bit frightened at perhaps having confronted a couple of Soldiers, the two men then turned, ran back to their mini, got back inside it, and drove away like a bat out of hell. Harry was startled, Hilda and Lynda were terrified, and I was left wondering what on earth it had all been about. A couple of thugs out looking for a punch-up I suppose.

Not that that was the only odd experience that I had in my drives back to Gillingham from London. One night, having left Television Centre at around midnight after having met with Stephen Bundy and then had something to eat in a BBC Canteen that stayed open to cater for Late Shift Staff, I travelled down Brixton Hill and then into the one-way system at the foot of Brixton Hill and then had to stop due to a set of traffic-lights being 'at red'. In front of my car, waiting adjacent to a traffic-light, was another car, seemingly a Police Car, with a blue light flashing on its top. Alongside that vehicle, to its left, was another waiting car and behind it, alongside my car, was another waiting vehicle. What struck me as being odd was that the Police Car in front of me, not only by its blue flashing light but also by the fact that every three seconds or so it kept edging forward a few inches, evidenced that it was seemingly on a call. "But why, given that its light was flashing and that there was no obstruction in front of it, did not the driver of the Police Car just 'put his foot down' and drive on," I kept wondering to myself.

One of the BBC Television Shows that I was involved with at the time was 'Z Cars', then and for many years afterwards a famous 'cutting edge' series about the Merseyside Police. That series involved two Police Cars, 'Z Victor 1' and 'Z Victor 2', which, of course, were, in reality, not Police Cars but television Props : And, as I sat there watching the car in front of me, I began to wonder if it too was not, in reality, a Police Car but, like the television Props, a car made up to look like a Police Car. Suddenly the traffic-lights changed and the car in front of my car shot off at speed and, as it did so, it, for no apparent reason whatsoever, slightly cut across the car in front of the adjacent row causing its driver, who by now had become to accelerate his car forwards, to have to slam on his car's brakes in order to avoid a collision. "That's it," I thought, "that car's not a Police Car at all" :" And so I gave chase which, with the car in front of me constantly gathering speed causing me and my car to drop further and further behind, was no easy task. It was, however, an exciting experience as, travelling at God knows what speeds, we went round the one-way system until, eventually and with considerable disappointment, I lost sight of my quarry. Then, suddenly, I saw him as he turned, at considerable speed and in opposition to a sign stating 'No Entry', into Denmark Hill in the direction of Herne Hill. So, into Denmark Hill some several seconds later I went; and there he was, stationary on the lefthand side of the road with a young woman getting out via the car's nearside rear door and a man in Police uniform getting out via the car's front passenger door.

As the woman and the uniformed man arrived at the front-door of a nearby house I drove my car to a stop behind the Police Car, got out, and went alongside the Police Car to speak with its driver, a man whose jacket's chevrons indicated the rank of Police Sergeant. His window was open, and so I bent down and said to him "Can I see your ID, please ?"

"This, Sunshine," he said as he twice tapped the chevrons on his jacket with the fingers of his left hand, "is all the ID you're gonna get."

He then wound-up his window and - the man in the Police uniform having run back to the car, climbed inside it, and slammed the front passenger's door - off, at speed, the car went.

Not only was I furious but by now I was convinced that the vehicle was not a Police Car but a fake : And so, there being no such things as mobile 'phones in those days, I drove to the nearest Telephone Kiosk, telephoned the Metropolitan Police at Scotland Yard, and asked if the Metropolitan Police had a car of the Registration Number of my quarry. Having been asked why I wanted to know, I explained what had happened; and, as communication by computers did not then exist, I was asked to wait whilst the car's Registration Number was checked out. After a while, the Police Operative and I having meantime chatted away to pass the time, I was informed that the Metropolitan Police did not have a car with that Registration Number but that Surrey Police did; that the car had been taken from Sutton Police Station without permission; and that the car had entered the Metropolitan Police Area without any knowledge of the Metropolitan Police. By now I should have been very tired but the adrenalin was flowing fast and so, when asked if I would go to Sutton Police Station - whose Inspector had by now been informed of the incident - and identify the Officers, I readily agreed. So, I drove the 11 miles [18km] to Sutton Police Station, had a brief chat with the Station Inspector, and agreed his request to sit down and await the arrival of the Officers. They were four of them in total - The uniformed Sergeant, the uniformed Officer who had escorted his girlfriend to her front-door in Denmark Hill, and two plain-clothed Officers who had been sitting in the back of the Police Car : And I had been sitting for only a few seconds when in came the four Officers concerned. "Are these the Officers?" the Inspector asked.

"Yes," I replied as the four of them each turned towards me with a look of horror on his face.

I gave a Statement, agreed to leave the matter in the hands of the Police, and arrived back in Gillingham a couple of hours or so later absolutely shattered.

Another incident involving a Police vehicle occurred sometime after one o'clock one weekday morning in November shortly after I had left the Canteen at the BBC's Broadcasting House [BH]. My arrangement with Stephen Bundy and Alex Lee, the BBC Club's Secretary, enabled me to use the splendid Canteen facilities at BH whenever I wanted (provided, of course, that it was open). BH, apart from being the BBC's 'Head Office' was the 'centre' of BBC Radio, a service which in those days transmitted more hours per day than Television did. Sited on the top floor with magnificent panoramic view over London the Canteen would, after midnight when it re-opened after a short shut-down during which cleaning and other operations were undertaken, be host to all sorts of interesting and fascinating people who, trays in hand, would queue up to buy and enjoy the excellent food on offer. It was a place of much humour which on one occasion briefly centred around a popular member, as most were, of the Canteen Staff who had just returned from a two-weeks' holiday.

"Where did you go ?" she was asked.

"Twyford," she replied.

Expecting her to have replied something like "Madeira" or "Spain" a surprised queuing diner shouted "Twyford !!"

"Yes," she replied, "Twyford".

"But that where the toilets come from," shouted another queuing diner as we all burst out chuckling at the unfortunate woman's expense. [Twyford was the name of a well-known manufacturer of bathroom suites.]

Leaving BH's Canteen my journey that morning took me from the Car Park outside of BH down past All Souls' Church in Langham Place, then left into Mortimer Street. It was as I was travelling along Mortimer Street that a Police Van overtook me and, as it did, its bell sounded briefly. Then the Van pulled in and stopped in front of me. Its sole occupant got out and came back to me.

"Yes, Officer ?" I asked as I leant out of my driver's window.

"Sorry to stop you, Sir, but you've got no lights on."

I looked at his vehicle and then said "Neither have you, Officer".

The two of us burst out laughing. He then said "Thank you, Sir. Sorry to have inconvenienced you".

"That's okay, Officer," I replied as I switched on my vehicle's lights.

He went back to his vehicle, climbed in, and switched on his vehicle's lights; and then each of us went on our way, he no doubt as amused as I at the incident.

One other meeting with the Metropolitan Police comes to mind. Throughout most of my childhood and teenage years I had known Brixton in London's Borough of Lambeth quite well but I had never seen its famous street Market and so one night whilst taking some curtains, blankets, and so forth from my home in Gillingham to the flat in Putney I decided to go via Brixton Market. It was about one o'clock in the morning when I got there. The Market was, as I knew that it would be, all closed up. Suddenly a Police car blocked my way giving me little choice but to stop my car. Two Officers got out of their car and ordered me to get out of mine, walk round my car, and spreadeagle myself on my front passenger door. Then they demanded to know what I had got in the car and why I was driving through Brixton Market in the early hours of the morning. So I told them: That I was transferring curtains, blankets, and so forth from my home in Gillingham to the flat in Putney. They then searched the inside of the car, each then punched me very hard in my ribs, then told me to get back in my car and to "Sod off". I was not a 'happy bunny' but clearly, given the dark environment that I was in and that I was on my own, I followed their 'advice' and got the hell out of there.

Without doubt the arrival on the UK's Statute Book of the 1964 Abolition of Resale Price Maintenance Act caused much trading hardship to many Traders including myself; and I well remember the occasion of my telling one of my Customer's how much I would sell her a 56lbs [25.4kg] bag of potatoes for.

"They're 6p [2½p] cheaper in the High Street," she said : And so to the High Street, armed with her shopping-bag-on-wheels, she went.

My Shop was sited just over half way down a steepish hill. Some time later Ivy and I stood in my Shop watching her as she struggled down Church Street desperately trying not to lose control of her bag of goodies as gravity insisted on pulling it faster and faster down the hill. When she reached the junction of Church Street, Forge Lane, and Christmas Street she and her goodies should have turned right : But at that moment she and her shopping-bag-on-wheels parted company for, as she began to make the turn, the by now almost out-of-control shopping-bag-on-wheels decided not only to continue its gravity-motivated downward path towards the bottom end of Church Street but also to jettison the bag of goodies thereby causing the bag to split wide open and 56lbs of potatoes to be discharged here, there, and everywhere all over the public highway.

"And all for 6d [2½p]," laughed Ivy to me in a very loud voice as each of us turned to go back into my Shop.

As the Abolition of Resale Price Maintenance Act began to make its presence felt it began to be clear that shops like mine were being increasingly 'used' by many solely as a place in which to purchase either small quantities or items that had been forgotten when shopping in Supermarkets. One increasingly felt as if one was being 'used'. Such was the feeling that I had one afternoon when a young lad - whose mother that morning had purchased one or two, but not many items, from my Shop - arrived with some carrots in one hand and a note in the other. He passed me the note. It read "Dear Mr Loveday. Please could you change these carrots to onions". I sent him back to his mother after I had returned her note to him having written on it "I can't but maybe God can !!"

Another feeling of being 'used' arose the day that a well-publicised-in-advance promotion for the washing-powder Omo was being undertaken in the area. A customer of mine whose 'big shop' was by now always undertaken in Gillingham High Street suddenly, as the Sales Promotion people were randomly knocking on nearby front-doors in order to give a £5-note to anyone who produced a box of Omo, realised that she had forgotten to buy Omo when in Gillingham High Street. She rushed down to my Shop and, saying "Excuse me" to everyone whom she barged aside, abruptly said to me "Lend me a packet of Omo, would you ?"

On the assumption that she would at least, regardless of whether or not she would be the lucky recipient of a fiver, come back and pay me for a box of Omo I lent her one. Out of the Shop she went as quickly as she had come. Ivy and I could see her front-door very clearly from within the Shop and were able to watch as, some minutes later, the Promotion People knocked on her door, she produced the borrowed box of Omo and received a £5-note. Later that day, much to my relief, she returned to my Shop.

"Thanks," she said as she handed the box of Omo back to me. Then she turned, went out of the Shop and back home having made a clear profit of £5 !!

The Rep [Representative] from Princes Foods called one day. Princes Foods, a major producer of canned food products, was running, he told me, a "Special Promotion' for Small Retailers to help them combat the growing influence of the Supermarkets. Buy a half-dozen cases of tins of Creamed Rice Pudding and receive a 10% discount off the normal Trade price". Not only were tins of Creamed Rice Pudding a 'steady seller' but also I liked Creamed Rice Pudding and thus my own consumption of the stuff would assist me to dispose of them. So I ordered a half-dozen cases of the stuff : But when the Invoice duly arrived from Princes Foods no 10% discount appeared on it. I thus queried this with Princes Foods whose blunt reaction was that they knew nothing whatsoever about any such promotion and that I therefore had to pay the full Trade price. I have never bought any Princes Foods product since that incident.

Injuries are part and parcel of playing the game of Rugger and thus, during the Rugby Season, I would occasionally arrive back in Gillingham late on a Saturday night or early on a Sunday morning in some pain if not agony. In those days the studs in boots were nailed onto the boot, usually by the wearer of the boot himself. I was fortunate in that I had, and always used, a Shoemaker's Last [a iron model of part of a foot which, when placed inside a boot or shoe when hammering-in such things as studs, turns over or blunts the pointed ends of nails so as to prevent the nails from penetrating the skin]. Nonetheless, on one occasion a nail in a stud in one of my boots, whilst I was playing, penetrated my left foot enabling the dye from my sock to enter my blood stream causing, in turn, the big toe on my left foot to swell up and become infected. I tried dealing with it myself but eventually, after the infection had decided to also attack the big toe of my right foot causing me to be in considerable pain when walking, I conceded defeat and sought assistance from the National Health Service Doctor in Gillingham with whom I had registered but whom I had never met before. His diagnosis was that I had in-growing toenails and that therefore I should first see a Chiropodist and then have minor surgery. So I made an appointment with a local qualified Chiropodist whom he recommended. She was a delightful woman whose husband had only very recently also qualified as a Chiropodist and gotten himself a job as a Schools' Chiropodist, an occupation which I considered to be unfair to children given that he had only very recently qualified and thus had had very little practical experience. She and I agreed a course of treatment lasting several weeks, the left toe to be attended to on Tuesdays and the right toe to be attended to on Thursdays, at a cost of half-a-crown [2/6d (12½p)] per toe per session. Eventually the poison in each toe was gotten rid of and I then made an Appointment at Saint Bartholomew's Hospital in Chatham to see a Surgeon, Mr Greenwood, to arrange for my in-growing toenails to be attended to, my having, during my treatment with the Chiropodist, been humorously told off one day by her after being asked "Which toe is it to-day?", I inadvertently said "It's my right-hand toe".

"Your toes are on your feet not your hand," was her theatrically stern rebuke.

Mr Greenwood was well over an hour keeping his side of the Appointment, which to anyone, let alone someone who is self-employed, is a major inconvenience. I thus, given that I had arrived in good time, expressed my displeasure to him.

"I'm afraid that this is something that happens every day," he dismissively replied.

"In which case," I replied, "as it happens every day you should adjust your Appointments accordingly".

"I take your point," he said.

His diagnosis was that only the big toe of my right foot needed to be operated on. Thus another Appointment was made; and this time, bar just over two minutes, he was there 'on the dot'.

He had decided that he would cut off a small sliver of nail on the right side of my toe and remove the 'roots' that lay directly underneath the sliver. To me, as a Designer, his intended treatment did not seem quite right but, given that he was the Expert, who was I to argue ?

Thus I lay on my back on a bed, local anaesthetic was applied, and, armed with a pair of scissors, he proceeded to cut off the sliver of nail. I was in agony and, turning to one of the two Nurses in attendance, I shouted "For Christ's sake say something !!"

"What do you want me to say ?" replied the pathetic piece of humanity standing alongside me.

"Anything," I shouted back : But, instead, she chose, supported by her colleague, to say absolutely nothing as Greenwood first cut off the sliver of nail with his scissors and then scraped away at the 'roots' with something which I, who could not bear to look at what was going on, assumed to be nothing more than a crude scrapper.

Throughout the many years that have passed since that very unpleasant experience I have been burdened not only with having to cope with in-growing nails in both my big toes but also with a sliver of nail which regularly grows virtually independently from the rest of the nail on my right big toe in almost any direction in which it, of its own accord, wishes to grow. However, rather than return to the Medical Profession, on each occasion I choose to cut, by means of clippers, as much of the offending sliver as I can and, by means of inserting the curved end of a metal nail-file and thereafter using a pair of scissors, removing those parts of my nails which persist in diverting themselves into my toes. They may be crude procedures but they are much less painful than the procedure adopted by Mr Greenwood.

Other colleagues within my Rugger team also, needless to say, suffered injuries; and always on hand was, with his Ambulance and its, somewhat by to-day's standards, very basic equipment nearby, a Member of Saint John's Ambulance Brigade. Ever loyal to, and supportive of, our team he was the most unathletic of individuals but, when it came to his being needed, he was the most efficient of people insofar as volunteer Medics were concerned. On the day that my heavyweight Welsh colleague Ray Jones was injured he was straight onto the field of play to diagnose the problem; and then, having diagnosed the problem, to his Ambulance he went and then, carrying, as best he could, a stretcher, back to Ray whereupon he placed his stretcher alongside Ray and, with the help of myself and others, carefully and swiftly lifted this stalwart of our team onto his stretcher. With the Saint John's man and another rugby colleague at the front of the stretcher and with myself and another rugby colleague at the back of the stretcher, everything was ready for Ray to be lifted and carried to the Ambulance. Unfortunately the stretcher was not only rarely used but also it was constructed solely of canvas with a wooden pole inserted along each side; and so, when the four of us lifted it, Ray and the canvas remained on the ground and we ended up having lifted only the two poles, the canvas having ripped and divorced itself from its poles.

"I'll get up and walk to the Ambulance," said the obliging Patient.

I went with Ray in the Ambulance, with the Saint John's lad driving, to Kingston Hospital. Ray and I got out and, whilst the Ambulance started its journey back to the BBC's Sports Ground at Motspur Park, Ray, with my support, limped into Casualty.

"What have we here ?" demanded Sister.

"He's been injured on the rugger field," I replied.

"Huh, a rugby injury. Put him over there where he can wait until we've sorted everyone else out," said a clearly unsympathetic-to-rugby-injuries Sister.

Another incident involving my rugby-playing colleague Ray Jones also involved The Old Haileyburian Rugby Club at its ground in Surrey. I knew some of the Old Haileyburian team and for me the result of OH 53 BBC 0 was embarrassing to say the least : But even more embarrassing was the attitude treatment that Ray Jones received. The BBC team was composed of Propmen, people from BBC Publications, Camera Operatives, Lighting Crew, Researchers, Producers, Directors, and so on - A whole host of professions and skills which to-gether helped create the Shows that the BBC transmitted to the Public, including those transmitted to my old Haileybury colleagues. Because of the, in those days, use of camera cables running across studio floors carpets were often painted on studio floors rather than actual carpets being used. Removing these painted carpets once a transmission had been completed was achieved by use of a special machine, and Ray Jones was the operative of one such machine. After the rugby match had ended an Old Haileyburian asked Ray "What do you do ?" "I clean the studio floors," replied himself. After that it was very obvious that some OHs considered Ray to be beneath them socially for they surreptitiously turned away seeking conversations elsewhere. Whilst I personally had found the scoreline embarrassing I found the attitude of those who shunned Ray .. Well, I say no more.

Some of my Gillingham Customers also suffered injuries - But not, as far as I am aware, on the rugby field. One, a Schoolteacher in the nearby Forge Lane Primary School, came into my Shop one day to buy his usual supply of cigarettes. His head was bandaged and his arm was in a sling. Apparently he had had a meeting in the school with a mother concerning the violence of her young son, a lad in his Class. She had not taken kindly to his criticisms of her beloved and, in consequence, had, assisted by other mothers, returned to the School and 'done him over' !!

Ivy and I also suffered at the violence of a child, this time a teenage child who was one of two sons of a 'good' Customer. Opposite, internally, my Shop's doorway was the Shop's principal counter on which stood, amongst other things, a glass display unit containing a selection of Provisions and a wooden display unit housing bars of chocolates and behind which were a gas refrigerator and other things including shelves holding fortysix different brands of cigarettes, shelves holding glass jars of lose sweets, shelves holding large jars full of pulses [split peas, lentils, and the like], and shelves holding bottles of orange and other squashes. Other than Ivy and I being behind the counter there was nobody in the shop when the lad came in and stopped, just inside the doorway, alongside a wooden crate containing oranges. Suddenly he bent down and, grabbing the oranges, started hurling, in machine-gun fashion, a tirade of oranges at us. As Ivy and I ducked down behind the counter, the oranges smashed into just about everything on top of, and beyond, the counter. Orange squash poured out of smashed bottles, loose sweets from broken sweet jars cascaded everywhere, dinted and damaged packets of cigarettes rained down upon us, bits of broken glass from broken bottles and jars flew everywhere. It was sheer hell. Then suddenly it stopped and the lad was gone. Fortunately Ivy and I were okay; and after we had closed the Shop and begun to tidy up I went across the road to Christmas Street to where the lad lived and spoke with his mother. "But what can I do ?" she said whimpishly. She and her husband had, it seemed, little or no control over either of their two teenage sons. Fortunately nothing like it ever happened again.

To say that Mrs Simmons, one of my most loyal 'regulars', had no control over her sons would be anything but the truth. She was a smallish woman who lived with her husband and their three 'strapping adult' sons in Forge Lane. Regularly, very regularly she would come into my Shop to buy many things always included within which were cigarettes, a commodity which, apart from her family, seemed to be the mainstay of her life. Things like stews and minces were what she regularly cooked for her family, and, because of her husband's and sons' not inconsiderable appetites, she always cooked whatever it was that she was cooking in large containers. As she cooked she smoked; and, rather than use an ashtray into which to discard her ash and cigarette ends, into whatever it was that she was cooking went, as ingredients, the ash and cigarette ends. On one occasion she did attempt to give up smoking. Her husband and sons, however, did not approve of the meals, for in their opinions, the meals no longer tasted as nice as they had done when ash and cigarette ends formed part of the ingredients. Thus Mrs Simmons reverted to smoking, and everyone in the Simmons household was happy !!

Having heard of the incident wherein Ivy and I had had to shelter behind the counter to avoid being hit by the oranges, flying glass, and whatever Mrs Simmons next day said to me that if ever I, or Ivy, felt threatened just let her know and she would send her sons to sort out whoever it was who threatened me : And she meant it too !!

Mrs Simmons was a wonderful character. One very hot Sunday afternoon she was sunbathing in her back garden whilst, unbeknown to her, her next-door neighbour and one of his friends were, accompanied by a wheelbarrow and a blanket, breaking into the back of a shop in Gillingham High Street. Having gotten in they went straight to the shop's safe not to break into it but to put it in the wheelbarrow, cover it with the blanket, and wheel it to the house next to Mrs Simmons's so that they could sit it down in the next-door neighbour's garden and then break into it. Having loaded it into the wheelbarrow and placed the blanket over it they then wheeled it out of the front-door of the shop; then along Gillingham High Street; then passed Gillingham Railway Station; then eventually, with great difficulty because of its weight, down Church Street, into Forge Lane, and thence into the garden of the house next to Mrs Simmons's whereupon they set to with a 4lb [1.8kg] Lump hammer and a Bolster chisel - neither of which is an ideal tool for breaking into a safe [not that I have had any experience of breaking into safes]. Time and again Mrs Simmons told the two would-be safe-crackers to keep the *bloody* noise down. Increasingly eager to break open their captured safe the two would-be safe-crackers ignored her; and so Mrs Simmons eventually got up and looked over the fence not only to find out what they were doing but also to repeat her demand that they keep the *bloody* noise down. However they continued to ignore her; and so eventually, unable to tolerate the noise any longer, Mrs Simmons went to the nearest telephone box, 'phoned the Police, and reported what was going on. "I couldn't care what they were doing," she told me next day. "It was the *bloody* noise I couldn't stand !!" Doubtless had her three sons been at home that afternoon she would have chosen them, not the Police, to restore peace and quiet to her sunbathing.

My old Haileybury friend, John Mannion, had an altogether different approach to dealing with people who annoyed him. I had driven up from Gillingham to call on him one night and, before I left to return home, he and I went, in my car, for a drink at The College Arms Public House on Hertford Heath. The bar was an elongated 'U' shape; and as John and I sat on barstools supping our drinks at one end of the 'U' a man, clearly somewhat the worse for drink, sat at the other end of the 'U'. I neither knew him nor, to my knowledge, had ever met him before, but every so often he waived a finger at me and said "You can f**king well sod off". Both John and I became increasingly annoyed but, despite John's telling him time and again to keep quiet, the man persisted. Eventually John and I had had enough and decided to go. So I first went to the toilet, and whilst I was there John went to my car. When I got to my car there was John sitting on the front passenger's seat waiting for me. It was almost pitch dark as I drove away from The College Arms; but I had not gone very far down the road when, via my car's headlights, I noticed a heap in the middle of it. "What the hell's that ?" I said.

"Remember the guy who kept swearing at you ?" John asked.

"Yup," I replied as I swerved the car to avoid running over whatever it was.

"Well, that's him."

Apparently, after I had gone into the toilet John had got hold of the bloke, marched him outside, knocked him unconscious, and dumped him in the middle of the road so that a passing vehicle might run over him !!

For me the rugby field was a wonderful place in which to release pent-up aggression. Mind you, we who played for the BBC were by no means as violent as some members of one of the teams, Battersea Ironsides, against whom we regularly played. Made up mainly of Stokers who shovelled coal into the furnaces which kept Battersea Power Station going, Battersea Ironsides seemed to be something akin to humanity's version of solid rock. I was playing in the Forwards one day when, as we were desperately trying to stop ourselves being pushed violently backwards in a Loose Scrum, a grinning face suddenly almost rammed itself into mine. "Trouble with you lot," said its voice," is that you're too bloody soft", a sentiment sometimes agreed with by our most loyal of Supporters, Miss Muriel Fox, whose dedication to supporting us through all types of weather over a period of many years resulted in the BBC Club building, especially for her, a wooden shelter to at least protect her, now that she was then approaching seventy years of age, from the wind and rain that sometimes assaulted the BBC's Motspur Park Sports Ground.

Muriel - who had joined the BBC, as a Secretary I believe, almost on the day that the BBC commenced its life as a Public Corporation back in 1927 - was by now retired but her loyalty to the BBC Club's Rugby Section never diminished. Like Mrs Simmons in Gillingham, Muriel was never short of a crude expletive as a means by which to express herself; and she would, by such means, make her views well known whenever any of us made a mistake or evidenced what she considered to be a weakness. Most of us just ignored her verbal tirades which included stock phrases as "Pull your fingers out, British". However, one colleague, immediately after having been shouted at by Muriel as to exactly what he could do with himself, marched off the field of play and went straight to her and, in as loud a voice as she had used when shouting at him, said "You come on and play the f**king game then". She, of course, never did but instead just carried on faithfully supporting us in her uniquely stalwart way.

Another loyal supporter of our Rugby Team was Charles [later Sir Charles] Curran. Born in Dublin in 1921 Charles had joined the BBC in 1945 but resigned shortly thereafter only to re-join the Corporation in 1951 where he rose to become Director of External Broadcasting and then, in 1969, the Corporation's Director General, a position that he held until he resigned in 1977 to become Managing Director of the

News Agency VisNews. He died, following a heart attack, in 1980 aged only 58. He was reckoned by some who worked within the BBC as having been one of the best, if not the best, of the Corporation's Directors General - although others feel that he perhaps stifled to some degree the innovative approach of his Director General predecessor, Sir Hugh Carleton Green. Charles often refereed our home Matches and in so doing did so without incurring from any of our opposing teams any criticism of bias. Of the memories that I have of Charles Curran during the days that I was subject to his Referee's whistle I well remember the occasion when, hardly able to breathe due to a heavy cold, I quickly ran off the field of play to take a slurp from a bottle of medication that I had positioned a couple of metres or so beyond the touch line. I was playing [or, to be more truthful, trying to play] on the left wing and, a Set Scrum having been ordered, I thought that my quick departure and return would not only not effect anyone but also be unnoticed by the Referee. However I was wrong for suddenly I heard Charles's voice shouting "What's up, Ted?"

"Just taking a swig of cough mixture," I shouted back.

"That's okay then." he replied, "We won't miss you !!"

[As Director-General of the BBC Charles Curran was always aware of my voluntary 'services' to BBC Television and, after I finally ceased doing voluntary bits and pieces for the BBC, I wrote a brief note to him. A copy of his reply to me on 21 December 1971 (along with a copy of a subsequent, handwritten letter that he wrote to me on 21 December 1972) appears under. He was a very nice man, and the fact that the following year he delayed for a half-hour or so a BBC Scotland Board Meeting in Edinburgh to meet again with me and my (by then) Wife, and will always be, and remain, very much appreciated.

01-580 4468
Broadcasts London PS4
Telex 22182

BROADCASTING HOUSE

LONDON W1A 1AA

21st December 1971

Dear Ted,

    I was most touched to think that you should have chosen to write to me on your departure for Edinburgh. What you say about me personally is very kind indeed, but what you say about your association with the BBC is reassuring and gives confidence to me that we have a good society in which to work.

    I shall remember if I am ever in Edinburgh that I should try to make touch with you through your wife whom I expect will still be working with us. The formalities of D.G. visits are difficult to escape but I think that something should be possible.

    My very best wishes to you for 1972 and beyond.

(Charles Curran)
Director-General

E. Sutherland Loveday, Esq.,
73 Falcon Road,
Morningside,
Edinburgh, EH10 4AE

01 580 4468
Broadcasts London PS4
Telex 22182

BROADCASTING HOUSE

LONDON W1A 1AA

21st December 70

Dear Ted,

Many thanks to you and Margaret for your Christmas good wishes. It was a real pleasure to see you in Edinburgh, and I hope we may have a chance to meet again — when I could hear news of your political progress — if any — in that cold climate!

All good wishes to you both!

Yours ever
Charles

21 December 1971

Dear Ted

I was most touched to think that you should have chosen to write to me on your departure for Edinburgh. What you say about me personally is very kind indeed, but what you say about your association with the BBC is reassuring and gives confidence to me that we have a good society in which to work.

I shall remember if I am ever in Edinburgh that I should try to make touch with you through your wife whom I expect will still be working with us. The formalities of D.G. visits are difficult to escape but I think that something should be possible.

My very best wishes to you for 1972 and beyond.

Charles Curran

Director-General

21 December 72

Dear Ted

It was a real pleasure to see you in Edinburgh, and I hope that we may have a chance to meet again - when I could hear news of your political progress. All good wishes to you both.

Yours ever

Charles   ]   ]

My January 1967 car accident caused me a major problem - It left me without my own means of transport; and my lifestyle was now such that it was essential to me that I get myself another vehicle. Having been informed by the Police as to where my damaged car had been taken I telephoned the Garage concerned and was informed that I had two options - either consider the car a write-off or wait some considerable period of time until all the damage had been repaired. "How long will that take ?" I asked.

"Three months or more," I was told; and I was mug enough to believe them.

However, I was very emotionally attached to my Morris Oxford Estate Car; and, besides, it was not my car's fault that it had had to suffer such damage. So I, with my Insurance Company's agreement, instructed that it be repaired. The options open to me meantime were, my Insurers told me, either to hire a vehicle or buy a replacement vehicle. I opted for the latter. The financial options put to me by the Insurers favoured the buying of a replacement vehicle for, once I had gotten my Morris Oxford back, I could sell the replacement vehicle and thus perhaps make a wee financial profit. Thus I travelled by 'bus to the Morris Car Dealership in Maidstone intending to buy another Morris Oxford Estate : But they did not have one. Instead I bought an Austin Cambridge Estate which, they rightly said, was identical all bar the colour and the fact that the Austin Cambridge had an automatic gearbox whereas my Morris Oxford had a manual gearbox. Having effected the transaction and been instructed in how to use the automatic gearbox I left the Garage and headed back to Gillingham, stopping on the way to get some petrol. Having got and paid for the petrol I climbed into the car and, having forgotten much of what I had been told about operating the automatic gear box, found that I was unable to drive away from the petrol pump. It was then that I discovered that I had no Instruction Manual : And as I sat there, in an increasing panic, trying to get the car to go forward a Police Car, with two Policemen in it, drew up alongside my car but on the other side of the petrol pump from which I had just been served with petrol. As I sat in my car struggling the two Policemen sat in their car looking. Then they got out of their car and came round to the open driver's window of my car.

"Is this your car, Sir ?" asked one of them.

"Yes," I replied. "I've just bought it."

"And what's its Registration Number, Sir ?" asked the other.

"I've no idea," I replied thinking that any second now they would accuse me of having stolen it.

"What's the problem, Sir ?" I was asked : And so I explained what had happened and that I had never driven a car with an automatic gearbox before.

"You get out, Sir, and I'll show you," he said : And so I got out and he got in and showed me.

After he got out, as I was getting in I asked him how he knew that I had not stolen the car.

"Simple," he said. "If you had stolen the car the first thing that you would have done would be to write the Registration Number down probably above you somewhere so that, if stopped, when asked you could look at it and then reel it off. However, when I asked you you clearly hadn't a clue and, as your eyes didn't search around looking for it … Well, we knew that you hadn't stolen it."

Thus, courtesy of the newly-acquired Austin Cambridge Estate, it was back to 'business as usual': The Shop in Gillingham, The Highfield Press in Thames Ditton, designing bits and pieces of Scenery for BBC Television, playing Rugger for the BBC, occasionally calling at 101a Kenilworth Court to chat with June, occasionally calling at 28 Kenilworth Court to pay my dutiful respects to my Mother as her Son, and, of course, there was Tricia who, the previous September, had declined my Invitation to take her to that year's Grand Order of Water Rats' Annual Ball at London's Grosvenor House Hotel. Why, I do not know but doubtless the, then sometimes seemingly unbridgeable, gap of six years between our ages played its part.

That previous year's Water Rats' Ball, held on 27 November, was - as Water Rats', and Lady Ratlings', functions usually are - very enjoyable save for one, very sad, occurrence. King Rat that year was Arthur Haynes [*see under, copy of 1966 GOWR Ball brochure*], then at the height of his very successful career as a performer on Television and Radio comedy. Indeed, he was at the time considered to be Britain's most popular Comedy Actor. The Grand Order of Water Rats, founded by Variety Artists for Variety Artists, has always been an exclusive organisation and to be voted, in secret ballot, King Rat by one's fellow Water Rats is a considerable honour; and the Annual Ball is the pinnacle of that honour. Thus 27 November 1966 was, for Arthur Haynes, to be a truly memorable occasion. However, eight days before his 'Great Night', on 19 November 1966, he died of a heart attack : And I well remember the sadness that all of us, including those such as I who had never met the man, present at the Grosvenor House Hotel that night felt - for Arthur Haynes was a true comic genius who gave pleasure to millions.

My visits to June continued and included one in which, just as I was leaving 101a Kenilworth Court, she offered to give up her job in favour of going down to Gillingham to, she said, help me in my Shop - for by now I was, as June well knew, totally fed-up with the place. I had never had the heart to tell June about Tricia's existence - a cowardly attitude perhaps but an attitude genuinely motivated by a desire not to hurt June's feelings. It was around midnight when she made her very tempting offer but I knew full well that, were she to turn up in Gillingham, all hell would be let loose with the highly likely result that neither June nor Tricia would ever speak to me again. Thus I meekly replied "It's okay. I'll cope" - an inexcusable response I know.

Driving on the A2 road from Gillingham to London had its interesting moments. For example, one dark rainy night, after I had set out in my car to meet with Stephen Bundy at Television Centre, as the right-hand curved one-way slip-road at the top of Strood Hill passed over a bridge that led down to the dual-carriageway that the A2 then was I saw the beams of some lights fast approaching in the opposite direction. Having made this journey many times before I had never experienced this phenomenon and thus thought it wise to slow down and pull over to my left. As I did so a car heading towards Gillingham, and travelling at considerable speed, shot past me on my right. Clearly not only had the maniac who was driving the speeding car been driving the wrong way along the A2 for several miles but also I and my car were darn lucky not be victims of his bat out of hell driving. On another occasion, as I drove to London during the day, I found myself sitting several vehicles behind an open lorry carrying 8ft x 4ft [2440mm x 1220mm] sheets of hardboard. Every so often some of the sheets of hardboard divorced themselves from their mates and rose high up into the sky where, for three or four seconds, they stayed horizontal and seemingly motionless before, turning onto one of their longer sides, they suddenly, like guillotine blades, descended groundwards and 'chopped' into anything and everything that they hit. With great hesitation, car after car overtook the lorry, their drivers frantically waving to the lorry's driver trying to get him to stop. As my car became the car immediately behind the lorry the lorry did stop, its driver seemingly clueless as to the chaos and destruction his unsecured load was causing : And as he climbed out of his lorry there were sheets of hardboard flying upwards, sheets of hardboard lying seemingly motionless in the sky, sheets of hardboard violently descending downwards, and sheets of hardboard lying on the road and in the fields on both sides of the road. The whole episode resembled a scene from a Silent Movie and would have been funny had it not been for the danger that the dozens of flying sheets of hardboard caused.

One place I always liked was Broadstairs, on the Isle of Thanet. Some Sunday evenings I would drive there to swim in Viking Bay; and sometimes at night I would, with Mischief, drive to Broadstairs just for something to do to relieve the boring monotony that I often experienced after I had shut my Shop and had something to eat. In those days there existed a roundabout just before one entered Thanet Way; and alongside the roundabout the Automobile Association [AA] had an Emergency Telephone Box from which Members of the AA could, using a special key which the AA loaned to Members as part of their Memberships, telephone to summon breakdown assistance via the AA's Area Office in Maidstone - For this was in the days long before mobile 'phones had come into being. On the dark night concerned my car was not functioning properly causing my car's lights to often become very dim with the result that, at times, I had difficulty seeing where I was going. I had no AA Membership of my own and thus relied entirely upon my Mother's Membership - then an acceptable, informal if not formal, procedure. Thus, when I reached the AA's Telephone Box, I stopped the car, and, using my Mother's Membership, telephoned the AA's Maidstone Office and explained the problem that I was experiencing to, seemingly, the one and only Member of AA Staff on duty. "A Patrol will be with you within the hour, Sir," said the efficient-sounding voice in Maidstone. After an hour had passed no-one had arrived, and so, cold and fed-up with waiting, I again went to the Telephone Box and again I telephoned the AA. "Glad you 'phoned, Sir," said the same voice. "I regret to have to say that I have been unable to find our Box on our map," he, now sounding less efficient, continued. "Could you please tell me exactly where you are ?" he asked. So I described where I, the roundabout, and the AA's 'phone-box were : And eventually a Patrolman, on a motorbike with sidecar, came out to me, diagnosed that my car had a faulty alternator, informed me that he could not repair the alternator, and arranged for my car, with me and Mischief in it, to be towed back to 67 Church Street by another Patrolman in an AA van. Boy, was I glad to get home that night !!

Driving from Gillingham to The Highfield Press and back again nearly every weekday and, during the Rugby Season, driving 60 miles or thereabouts from Gillingham to the BBC's Sports Ground at Motspur or to some other venue where the Rugger Club was playing and then, perhaps via a Party in London somewhere, back to Gillingham made my life 'tight' financially. Initially The Highfield Press had been intended not only to pay for itself but also to certainly make its contribution to my travelling costs. However, it soon became apparent that The Highfield Press, despite Frank Gazzard's good opinion of it, was not worth the £5,000 that, in effect, my late Father had paid for it. It is one thing to run a business, such as my Shop in Gillingham, wherein one instantly received cash for the goods that one sold : It was, as I very soon found out, quite another thing to run a business, such as The Highfield Press, wherein one handed over finished goods in the hope that one day one might be paid for them. Indeed, I soon released that small businesses such as The Highfield Press are, in reality, used by larger businesses as a means of obtaining Interest-free loans; and the larger the larger business the larger the Interest-free loan made available to it by the small business. I have no criticisms of Trianco, of Rola Celestion, and of others who, without fail, immediately paid up at the end of the 30-day credit cycle usually given by businesses to businesses. Of the Ophthalmic Division of the National Health Service I have nothing but praise for the swiftness with which it paid off its indebtedness to us, a swiftness countered by the fact that not only was our profit mark-up on NHS business minimal but also our agreement with the NHS was that within minutes of our receiving a telephone-call requiring, say, a multi print-run as a result of a Government announcement we had to put everything else on hold in order to swing into action and work flat out on satisfying the NHS requirement. However, of many other customers - ranging from the large who supplied computer equipment to the then being-developed Concorde supersonic aircraft to the small local organisations who portrayed to the world at large an image of existing for charitable purposes my feelings are somewhat different. The stunt was always the same but with the large organisation the issuing of settlement cheques were, it was often said, being delayed due to some 'technical' reason within 'the system' whereas with the small local organisations the issuing of settlement cheques were, it was usually said, being delayed due to the fact that they required the signatures of at least two Office Holders, such as Madam Chairman and the Treasurer, and either one or both was away on holiday or on business elsewhere. It was a financial nightmare, a nightmare made worse by the fact that I had no working capital whatsoever; and if The Highfield Press did not pay its bills around about the end of its 30-days' credit period The Highfield Press got no supplies and thus could not function. Thus I brought into being an 'intermediary', Goldberg Investments, whose name originated in my having, in my teenage years when trading with the Regent Warehouse Company in the East End of London, been 'Mr Goldberg'. Goldberg Investments was a means which enabled me, without any loss or profit whatsoever to Goldberg Investments, to transfer the meagre profits that I made in Gillingham into The Highfield Press. However, given the paucity of my Gillingham profit's the reality of the idea could not, and did not, last for long. Thus I turned to The Highfield Press's Bankers, Lloyds, for assistance. Peter Lockyer, the East Molesey Branch Manager not only was very helpful but also became a good friend. "Yes," he said after I had outlined my case, "you can have your loan but on one condition".

"What's that ?" I asked.

"I'm the Tory [Conservative] Candidate in the Local Government Election, and you must help me."

Lloyds Bank in East Molesey not only had, as its Manager, a interesting character in Peter Lockyer - who, with his wife, Monica, lived in a flat above the Bank - but also had, as its Chief Cashier, a somewhat dour character by the name of Cudmore whose entire banking career had, apparently, been driven by a desire to, having entered the banking system as a Junior Clerk, make his way 'along the counter' to eventually become the East Molesey branch's Chief Cashier.

Around about the time that I was 'negotiating' for funds in East Molesey I was asked by Harry and Hilda Salthouse if I could help their daughter, Lynda, get a job in banking. The Kismetical irony of the request did not escape me. My business in Gillingham banked with the Westminster Bank; and, being on good terms with my Gillingham Bank Manager, Mr Blackbourne, I telephoned him and made him aware of the request.

"Come out to lunch, and we'll talk about it," was his response.

So, out to lunch - an entirely liquid lunch - we went; and the result was that Lynda was offered a job, which she accepted, in the Westminster Bank's nearby Chatham Branch. I was particularly pleased with that result because the Salthouses had been wonderful friends and I felt that that was the least that I could do to evidence my gratitude to them.

Back at The Highfield Press things continued on a downward spiral. The efficient Mrs Wensak, having demanded a wage increase that I could not afford, left and was replaced by a late-middle-aged woman by the name of Miss Slaymaker whose telephone attitude turned out to be disastrous.

Miss Slaymaker's telephone rang. "It's Mr Lefevre here," said the Buyer of one of our larger customers.

"Mr Who ?" Miss Slaymaker semi-shouted in reply.

"Lefevre," came back the response.

"Mr Hay fever ?" Miss Slaymaker retorted.

"No. Lefevre," the annoyed voice at the other end of the telephone shouted.

By now I and my General Manager, George Swain, were listening in on an extension in my Office for we knew from Miss Slaymaker's attitude that things were going somewhat astray.

"Hay Fever ?" Miss Slaymaker repeated.

"No," the by now very irate voice shouted back. " Le… Fevre."

George and I stared at each other in disbelief as again Miss Slaymaker said "Hay Fever?"

"No. Lefevre, woman. Lefevre !! Why the bloody hell do you keep saying 'Hay Fever' ?"

"I thought it was funny," the disastrous Miss Slaymaker replied.

George Swain immediately interrupted, took over the conversation, and, with profuse and very genuine apologies, managed to retain Mr Lefevre and his firm as a customer.

I immediately summoned Miss Slaymaker into my Office and sacked her there and then. George Swain having finished his telephone conversation, a very tearful Miss Slaymaker went up to him. "Mr Loveday's told me to go," she said.

"What the hell are you hanging about here for then ?" snapped back George Swain, a man whom I had never ever heard swear before.

I have always tried to look after my vehicles but I have never been a person who has his car serviced regularly. However there were times when my car's considerable mileage caused it to require attention. Gray's of Chatham, a Garage in the centre of Chatham, had a Petrol Station near to a roundabout sited close to Chatham Dockyard's Brompton Barracks; and it was there, because it was convenient for me, that I often went to get petrol. Usually the person serving the petrol was a Mrs Campbell, a youngish woman who, apparently for 'domestic' reasons, had fled her native Glasgow. Often chatting to Mrs Campbell, seemingly because he 'fancied' her, was a pleasant lad of similar age to myself. He was the son of the owner of Gray's of Chatham and, due to my regularly meeting him at the Petrol Station, I decided to have my car attended to at his father's Garage. In return for my custom Mr Gray Senior always loaned me a car free of charge - That was part of the deal, otherwise he would not have got my custom. The car that he usually loaned me was a Ford Cortina. There were three main reasons why I had bought a Morris Oxford Estate, and subsequently the Austin Cambridge Estate: The first was its large carrying capacity, the second was its seemingly solidish construction, and the third was the fact that at each end it had bumpers sufficient in size and construction to protect the car from at least a moderate impact. The Cortina's carrying capacity was not large, its construction seemed to be anything but solid, and its bumpers would, had they had the chance, have run away from any impact coming their way. However, it had one, then revolutionary, feature that neither my

Morris Oxford nor my Austin Cambridge had - The ability of its driver to manually, by means of a handle attached to a wire, set its speed. So, once one had reached the speed of, say, 60 mph [96 kmph] one pulled on the handle which pulled out the wire which, in turn, presumably adjusted something under the bonnet so as to keep the vehicle's speed at a constant 60 mph. The only drawback that this, in my opinion, home-made by Mr Gray Senior's device had was that there was no way of disengaging it other than to put one's foot onto the clutch pedal, so as to disengage the gears, whilst trying to manoeuvre the handle and its attached piece of wire back from whence it had come. Thus, if, for instance, one had to suddenly brake to slow the car down to, say, 20 mph [32 kmph] one had to, whilst one foot was on the brake pedal, very quickly put one's other foot on the clutch pedal whilst at the same time desperately, with one hand whilst keeping the other hand on the steering-wheel, trying, via its handle, to push the wire back in whilst all the time listening to the roar of an engine that still wanted the car to be travelling at 60 mph. It was, at times, a nightmare, a nightmare compounded by the fact that the vehicle was so light that when travelling at more than a moderate speed on an open road, such as the A2 in Kent then was, it would, assisted by cross-winds, bounce all over the place.

Throughout many centuries Arabs and Jews have, to one degree or another, been at war with each other. Mr Gray's somewhat remote-from-the-Middle East Petrol Station did not escape : For around mid-day one day a large black very noticeable car drew-up alongside one of the petrol pumps. On his own in the back sat a largish man very noticeably clad in Arab costume, and in the front sat a very Arab-looking Chauffeur. The Petrol Attendant on duty that day was a young, very pleasant, totally non-political British Jewish lad. As the

Jewish lad approached the car the Arab Chauffeur was getting out and instantly realised that the lad was Jewish.

"You're a Jew !!" exclaimed the Chauffeur.

"Stay away from my car, Jew," shouted the largish Arab as he unwound a rear window.

"I'm not going to do anything to your car. I'm just going to put petrol in it," replied the lad, totally clueless as to the existence of hatred between many an Arab and Jew.

"Stay away from my car, Jew," the largish Arab again shouted, at which point his Chauffeur grabbed the lad round the throat, pushed him away from the car onto a petrol pump, and, taking one of his hands off the lad's throat, began to move as if to punch the lad hard in the stomach. At this point I and another man had reached the Chauffeur, grabbed him, and told him to lay off the boy. His boss then ordered him back into the car, and off away from the Petrol Station they went. It was an almost unbelievable situation - Not that a similar occurrence did not happen elsewhere in Gillingham : But this time with 'Gipsies' - not Arabs and Jews.

I was driving up Gillingham's Grange Road one Friday evening when, to my right, I heard people screaming. Looking through a gap in a hedge I saw a group of, seemingly very distressed, people in a semicircle watching two men as they wielded large Felling Axes at each other. Neither man was small, and each had a woman trying to drag him away from, what was clearly, a very bitter fight. With much bravado but great stupidity I slowed the car down, turned it towards the fight, and, with its horn blaring, drove through a larger gap in the hedge and up towards the two axe-wielding men. My not-thought-out intention was to drive between them thereby breaking-up the fight :

But I never reached the fight, for suddenly everybody - the screaming group, the two women who had been trying to pull the men away from each other, and the two axe-wielding men themselves - turned on me and told me exactly what I could do with, and where I could put, myself. I hastily put the car into reverse and drove backwards out through the hedge and back onto the road. Apparently, so I found out later, this was a weekly ritual between father and son to settle an argument, or arguments, that they had had during the week; and the two women trying to stop the fight were the father's wife and the son's wife. Weird, quite weird !! Mind you, that was not the only occasion that I had attempted to use my car to break-up a fight.

As I turned right, through traffic-lights, into Putney High Street from Wandsworth Bridge Road one night I could hear people shouting "Go on, smash his face in", "Kick him in the b**ls", and the like coming from the foyer of a Cinema to my right on the other side of Putney High Street. There, lying on the floor of the foyer, was a Policeman being kicked by some yobs whilst a group of youths, shouting 'encouragement, stood around them. Everybody, everybody who walked passed the Cinema just looked but did nothing thus leaving the unfortunate Policeman to have to suffer the kicking that he was being given. So, with bravado and stupidity similar to the occasion when I had determined to break-up the fight in Gillingham, I turned my car and, with the car's horn blaring, headed towards the steps that led up to the Cinema's foyer. Fortunately I never had to test my car's ability to be driven up steps for, just as my car was about to reach the kerb, all hell let loose - Police cars, with bells and sirens sounding, seemed to arrive from all directions. So I reversed my car back to the other side of the road and continued my journey.

I was to experience Police cars with sirens sounding on one other occasion whilst in Putney. One night whilst staying at 28 Kenilworth Court I took Mischief, my dog, for a long walk; and, as I did so, I passed, on the other side of Upper Richmond Road, a Churchyard sited on the corner of Gwendolen Avenue. To my left was a parade of shops just before Upper Richmond Road's junction with Charlwood Road. As I began to cross Charlwood Road Mischief stopped and looked to her right towards the Churchyard. There was hardly any light by which I could see anything in the Churchyard but I could just about see the outlines of bushes and what seemed to be three people amongst them in the Churchyard, one moving slowly on the Gwendolen Avenue side of the Churchyard and the other two more or less stationary just beyond the bounding wall on the Upper Richmond Road side of the Churchyard. It all looked very suspicious; and so I went to the nearby Putney Police Station to report what I had seen. I was asked to go back to the parade of shops where I would find, I was told, a largish advertising sign sited on the wide pavement between the shops and the road which I could 'hide' behind and keep an eye on things until the nearest police vehicle could arrive. So, with excitement mounting, and with Mischief faithfully by my side, I left the Police Station and went and 'hid' behind the sign. Nothing much in the Churchyard had changed, the three people were still there albeit that they had moved around a wee bit. Then suddenly all hell let loose as one police car, having come down Gwendolen Avenue at speed, screeched to a halt in Gwendolen Avenue outside the Churchyard and two other police cars, having come along Upper Richmond Road from the direction of Putney High Street, screeched to a halt in Upper Richmond Road outside the Churchyard. Even before, it seemed, the vehicles had stopped police officers rushed out, vaulted over the Churchyard's walls and piled on top of the three mysterious characters. It was a wonderful sight added to which Mischief was barking with loud enthusiastic excitement. The guy who was on his own in the Churchyard was duly arrested and marched-off to the nearby Police Station. The other two guys ? Well, they were none-too-happy for they were plain clothed police officers from out of the area who had been following the third guy and were just about to arrest him when the circus of police cars arrived and their occupants got out and flattened them. Not only had there been, apparently, a total lack of communication between the officers from outside the area and the Police in Putney but also …. Well, the whole thing looked like a sketch from Mack Sennett's early 20th century *Keystone Kops* films.

My January 1967 car crash introduced a year in which my life took a totally unexpected turn. As South-east Area Secretary for the Retail Fruit Trade Federation [the 'RFTF'] I had committed myself to going to that year's Annual Convention in Scarborough. Trade, and Political, Conventions are a combination of business and social activities, the latter often/occasionally involving extra-marital romance if not also sex. Because of my feelings for Tricia I was determined … Well, not to involve myself. Certainly no Miss Jaffa Oranges this year !!

The Convention formally got under way on Monday 15 May. Most delegates were staying either in Scarborough's Grand Hotel or in Scarborough's St Nicholas Hotel, both hotels being sited on St Nicholas Cliff, the one hotel being opposite the other. As a Yorkshireman might say "Each 'otel were then very grund".

The BBC Rugger Club's Annual Dinner was to be held that year at the BBC's Sports' Clubhouse in Motspur Park on the Friday night before Monday 15 May. Most RFTF Convention delegates would be arriving in Scarborough on the Saturday or Sunday. I intended leaving

Motspur on the Friday night some time after the Dinner and, in my Austin Cambridge car, driving the 280 miles or so to Scarborough. I had never been to, or anywhere near to, Scarborough before, knew little or nothing about the place, and was therefore looking forward to the journey and seeing it. I anticipated two problems, namely [1] the BBC's Clubhouse had a small swimming pool-sized plunge bath into which, on occasions such as Annual Dinners, it was tempting to throw, fully clothed, one's colleagues in and [2] as was usual before I embarked on long, longish journeys I had had my car serviced. Insofar as [1] was concerned, with driving up to Scarborough, I did not have the time to dry wet clothes neither did I have a spare 'back-up' change of clothes other than a dinner suit that I intended to use on formal occasions in Scarborough if such occasions arose. Fortunately those who threatened to throw me in the plunge bath heeded my requests not to do so and insofar as [2] was concerned ….

An advantage of Austin Cambridge Estate cars and Morris Oxford Estate cars was that they had decent-sized metal bumpers which were of some practical use in protecting the car from minor bump damage. Another advantage was that, with the back seat down, one could sleep reasonably comfortably in them; and, given that I was very tired when I left Motspur and started on my journey north, it was not long after I had gotten 50 or so miles north of London that I decided to pull into a lay-by and have a sleep. It was some hours later that I woke up and, attempting to pull my car back from a car that had been parked close to the front of my car, discovered to my horror that I could not get the car to go into reverse. The car would only go forwards. What the heck … I would just have to make sure that I did not get into a situation that required my car having to go backwards.

I arrived at the then prestigious St Nicholas Hotel shortly after 6pm that Saturday. My room, a single room, was on the ground floor. Nothing special but comfortable; and the evening meal was being served. However, although I was hungry, very hungry, I was also grubby, very grubby; and so I decided to have a bath and then, after having dressed, go suss out the layout of the Convention whilst at the same time seeking George Bridger and his cronies who, I more or less knew, had arrived earlier. It did not take me long to find him because he was hunting for me. So we met up and decided to decamp over to The Grand Hotel to where the Convention's social activities were based. Out of the St Nicholas we went and across the 'Square' that separated the two, then up the steps into The Grand Hotel's main entrance. To our right was an impressive 'grand' staircase with a splendid Bar and Cocktail Lounge sited nearby at its foot. Thus to the Bar and Cocktail Lounge we went; and lo and behold there were George's Wife, Beat, and his cronies Den Hunt and Billy Booth.

Next day was Sunday - Do nothing day. Day of rest except that I hit upon the idea of going for a drive in my car up from Scarborough to Whitby. So into my car George, Beat, Den, Billy, and I got and away up the East Coast we went. I have made the 20 miles' journey many times since but on that occasion I really did not know where we were going. "Just head north and we'll get there" was George's advice. Even years' later the Scarborough-Whitby Road, with its narrowness, its many hills, and its many sharp bends is a challenge; but on that occasion fog, increasingly thick almost impenetrable fog, eventually forced me to have to declare that we could go no further. So, given that I could not get my car's reverse gear to operate, I eventually found an area in which I could, whilst silently praying that no vehicles were coming the other way, swing the car round in one continuous manoeuvre and drive back to Scarborough.

That night we had a problem with the evening meal in that the Management of the St Nicholas seemed not to have taken into consideration that most, if not all, of the guests staying in its hotel were involved in the greengrocery trade and would not take kindly to being served canned vegetables. Much of the protest originated from our dining table, namely from George [never one to stay quiet], and ably supported by many other greengrocers; and indeed by the attractive mini-skirted waitress allocated to our table - who seemed enthusiastic to wish to display her assets every time that she reached over the table to serve the meals and collect the plates. I honestly can not recall how the hotel's faux pas was resolved, but resolved it was; and canned vegetables were never again offered to us.

I was by now the RFTF's Area Secretary for the South-east of England outside of London; and this involved my having to travel here, there, and everywhere to offer advice on fruit and vegetable matters. One such advice involved a Market Gardener in Kent whose neighbours had complained to the local Council about his crop spraying techniques affecting their gardens, etc. He was not an easy character to deal with but, after I emphasised to him that the Council had made it very plain that it would commence Court proceedings unless he ceased his activities, he did undertake to write to the Council to accept what it said. "Did you write to the Council ?" I asked him some weeks later. "Yes," he said, but then went on to say, "but I'm damned if I'm going to do what they say". Some time later he went out of business.

I really do not like Conferences. I find them boring, if not very boring. Had it not been for George Bridger and his Eastbourne colleagues and the nonsense activities that we used to get up to, such as George going around bewilderingly telling people that Den was his

Son and that I was his Grandson, I think that on the Monday after I arrived in Scarborough I would have escaped from the St Nicholas and Grand Hotels and spent my time exploring Scarborough. However, that evening of Monday 15 May 1967 changed my life.

George and I, with Den and Billy, had gravitated to where the laid-on entertainment action was. With drink in hand, standing on the right hand side of the room looking towards the stage I glanced over to my left and saw this very attractive girl standing on the other side of the room looking towards the stage. I have always been a person motivated by instinct. Completely forgetting my feelings for Tricia and June and my obligation to myself not to involve myself with anyone I nudged George and "Over there," I firmly announced to George, "is the girl I'm going to marry !!"." "Let's go over and meet her," was his reply. So, we made our way from our side of the room to where this attractive young lady, seemingly by herself, was standing.

Despite the image that I apparently give of being a confident person I am in fact quite shy : And for me, as I did, to say to a girl whom I had never met "Would you like a drink?" was very much out of character. But "Would you like a drink ?" is exactly what I said. "No," she replied, "I don't accept drinks from strangers". "I wouldn't either," said George with his usual mischievous attitude to Life. "He works for the BBC".

Well, we chatted. She agreed to have a drink. Told me that she had no connection with the Retail Fruit Trade Federation and its Conference, that she and her Mother were staying at Scarborough's Grand Hotel and that she had only wandered into the room to see what was going on. George, tactfully, disappeared leaving the two of us yattering to each other before she returned to her Mother and I returned to a very inquisitive George Bridger who wanted to know what I now knew about her. "Her name is Margaret Blackburne with an 'e'. She's from Barnsley in South Yorkshire, is 20 years old, is studying Domestic Science in Leeds, is staying in The Grand with her Mother whilst they are on a visit to friends from Barnsley who have a butcher's business in Barnsley and a bungalow a few miles down the coast from Scarborough in Filey. Her Father is a Dentist in Barnsley and her Mother is a Councillor in Barnsley".

I met Margaret the next evening and, as we wandered through the several promotional stalls displaying all sorts of fruit and vegetables then available in the United Kingdom, discovered that she has a liking for grapefruits and oranges. So to a display of grapefruits and oranges we went where Margaret was gifted several huge grapefruits and oranges the sizes of which we have never seen since. From there I was taken by Margaret to meet her Mother. Two ladies sat on a comfortable-looking settee. The more talkative one of the two, after Margaret had briefly introduced me to them, got up and shook hands whilst the other one remained seated and, as if she was royalty, put out her hand for me to, I think, hold it and kiss it. Instead I just shook it believing the first of the two women, the more friendly one, to be Margaret's Mother. I was wrong : The somewhat snobbish one was Margaret's Mother. It seemed that, by having been elected a Local Government Councillor, she was now a superior person. The other female was Mrs Hirst who with her Husband Albert, known throughout Barnsley and beyond as the King of Black Puddings, owned several butcher's shops.

From The Grand Margaret and I crossed back to the St Nicholas where we just chatted and chatted and decided that next day we would, in my car, drive up to Whitby where, I assumed, I would be able to drive the car round the streets so as to head back to Scarborough without my having to admit that its reverse gear was not working.

The further north that we went the thicker the fog became and the slower our progress towards Whitby. Clearly Margaret - who, like I, had never been to Whitby before - was getting concerned - moreso perhaps because she was in effect with an almost complete stranger, a stranger from London indeed - and so, my riving at a speed at which I could have overtaken my car had I been walking, she said "I think Mum'll be getting concerned" I had to confess that I could not turn the car round, moreso as I could not see where we were going and/or whether or not there were any other vehicles nearby. Did she panic ? No. Did she express annoyance ? No. With, as she told me many times since, complete faith in me she, seemingly calmly, sat there alongside me letting me continue in the knowledge that matters would be resolved. "I had," she has since said, "complete faith in you". What a wonderful girl !!

Next day, Wednesday, having the previous evening said 'Goodbye' to Margaret and arranged to visit her in Barnsley a couple of weeks later, I got up, put on a pair of trousers, a shirt, my slippers, and my dressing gown and went to see George, Beat, Den, and Billy to wish them well on their 300+ miles journey back to Eastbourne. I then went back to my room and shortly thereafter there was a knock at the door. Lo and behold, and very much to my surprise, there stood Margaret. "I've come to see you off," she said. Staying with Mrs Hirst, Mrs Hirst had clearly realised that Margaret was eager to see me again and encouraged her to go back to the St Nicholas to see me off.

So later that day off to London I went and thence down to the drudgery and boredom of my humble greengrocer's business in

Gillingham, Kent. One of the things that went through my mind was that clearly Margaret and I had gelled and so what was I to do about Tricia and about June neither of whose feelings I wanted to hurt ?

My relationship with June - to whom I had never mentioned Tricia - had sort of evolved into a brother/sister relationship and that, I felt, could continue. But my relationship with Tricia was another matter. The Saturday after I got back from Scarborough Tricia came to work for me in my shop as usual. Hitherto I had always looked forward to her arrival, and this Saturday was no exception but I was a bag of nerves trying to work out how I was going to tell her that I had met this girl, called Margaret, in Scarborough and that things between Margaret and me seemed serious. "Best way to tell her," I thought, "was to tell her". So tell her I did; and I received no comment other than a quick sarcastic "Good for you". Thereafter Ivy, Tricia, and I carried on serving customers as per usual until, at 1 o'clock, Tricia, after I had paid her, went home for lunch each of us saying "See you next week". "Phew," I thought, "That went okay".

Not the next Saturday but the one after that I drove from Gillingham up to Margaret's Parents' home, 40 Church Street, Barnsley. Leaving Gillingham on the then A2 road I passed through the City of London where I 'picked up' the A1 and stayed on it until after passing near to Doncaster I excitedly turned off left at a sign stating 'Barnsley' and onto the Doncaster-Barnsley Road.

I had arranged to be there at 9am but my enthusiasm caused me to be there at just after 6am. Now, until I arrived at Barnsley that day, my image of a Yorkshire town was of a picturesque town nestling amongst rolling hills. However, passing through the grubby mining town of Grimethorpe I began to realise that my image of Barnsley might not accord with that of a picturesque town nestling amongst rolling hills. When I arrived in Barnsley it seemed as if a wholesale digging of roads was being undertaken by the then Yorkshire Electricity Board and other diggers-of-holes. It was a mess. But there standing aloof in the town's centre was Barnsley Town Hall, built in the early 1930s and funded by monies which many people thought should have been more properly spent on improving appalling local housing and poor living conditions of the miners of Barnsley's then 70 coal mines. Next to the Town Hall was, as Margaret had told me, the Parish Church of Saint Mary : And next to the Parish Church was Margaret's home, 40 Church Street.

So, what to do with the spare nearly three hours. A quick drive round Barnsley and it was back on the Doncaster Road, this time two or three miles towards Manchester, until I found somewhere to park up and rest before smartening myself up to go back to 40 Church Street so as to arrive exactly at the agreed time of 9 o'clock.

Ever since I was about 15 and had had, after an accident when drinking out of a glass bottle, a couple of my front teeth levelled off by a grinding wheel without any anaesthetic Dentists, in their professional capacity, have never been my favourite type of humans. The fact therefore that Margaret's Father was a Dentist and the fact that his Surgeries and Waiting Room were in 40 Church Street must therefore have meant that Margaret was truly someone special. Nevertheless - when, after I had rung the front-door bell and explained who I was to the person who answered, I entered the building to be greeted by, to me at least, an overwhelming smell of dental surgery - I had to muster some extra courage to go in, especially as I was instructed by the person at the door to go into the Waiting Room and sit down with the rest of the Patients !!

After what seemed like an eternity Margaret arrived, apologised that she had kept me waiting, and extracted me out of the body of suffering appointees and took me into the adjoining, pleasant and comfortable, Dining Room. Given the fact that I had had to drive 200+ miles from Gillingham she and her Parents had not expected me to arrive anything like on time.

After mountains of chit-chat, introduction to her Father and a re-introduction to her Mother, she asked me if I would, in my car, take her to the nearby Halifax Building Society branch. I could not park directly outside the branch so I dropped her off and then began to drive a wee distance along the main road. As I was powering-up the car to cross over an empty zebra crossing, a traffic warden, left hand held high, suddenly stepped off the kerb to my left. As I was very near the crossing I could not stop the car before I reached the crossing; and so I stopped the car immediately after I had crossed over the crossing and wound down my driver's window to apologise to him and explain that he had not given me sufficient time to stop. But he was not interested. Instead he bent down almost to my face and started blurting out in an accent that I could not understand. Time and again I said "Sorry, but I can't understand you" and on each occasion he seemed to get more and more agitated. "Welcome to Barnsley" I thought. Suddenly he walked away to fetch a nearby policeman who, after a few seconds of listening to what the traffic warden was saying, came over to me. I explained what had happened and that I could not understand what the traffic warden was saying. Smiling he said "Up 'ere, lad, we talk slightly different. I'll have a word w'im and calm 'im down whilst meantime you get on your way". What a nice and sensible man !!

The Wedding between Margaret and me took place on 15 August 1968 at St Mary's Church, next to Margaret's then home, in Barnsley. Neither June nor Tricia would attend [I wonder why ?] but we were, on my side, graced by, amongst others, several Members of the Grand Order of Lady Ratlings representing both the Lady Ratlings and the Grand Order of Water Rats, a gaggle of my BBC Rugby Club colleagues, and a gaggle of friends from the Eastbourne Branch of the Retail Fruit Trade Federation as well as friends from Leicester and elsewhere. [Nowadays attending a wedding in far-off lands is not that unusual but in 1968 even travelling from London to Barnsley was a bit of a challenge for many.]

~~~~~~~~~~

ADDENDA

(a) I ceased doing 'bits and pieces' for the BBC in 1971 when Margaret and I moved to Edinburgh, she to take charge of Catering in the BBC's then Broadcasting House in Edinburgh's Queen Street and I, being half-Scottish, to involve myself in Scottish Politics. [See above letter dated 21 December 1971 from Sir Charles Curran, Director-General BBC.]

(b) On 14 August 1979 my Mother died when a patient in the South Western Hospital, an NHS [National Health Service] mental health facility in Stockwell in South London. During one of my visits to her prior to her death I asked her whether she had in fact deliberately killed my Father. With a little hesitation the answer was "Yes" !!"

(c) Whilst driving my Uncle Angus to the Railway Station following his stay in Putney for his Sister's [my Mother's] cremation, he discussed my Father's death with me. "I blame your Granny, not
~~~~~~~~~~

your Mother, for your Father's death for your Granny took in theatrical lodgers to help pay the bills. Not your type of theatricals, Edwin, but the lowest of the low; and night after night your Mother, as a child, was made to sleep on hard, cold bare floorboards. She hated it, hated it and in consequence she had a deep hatred of the Theatre, and vowed that one day she would get her revenge. And sadly your Father's death was that revenge !!"

Ted Loveday

www.theatrical-scenery.info